THE GATE TO CHINA

THE GATE TO CHINA

香港

A New History of the People's Republic
& Hong Kong

MICHAEL SHERIDAN

**WILLIAM
COLLINS**

William Collins
An imprint of HarperCollins*Publishers*
1 London Bridge Street
London SE1 9GF

WilliamCollinsBooks.com

HarperCollins*Publishers*
1st Floor, Watermarque Building, Ringsend Road
Dublin 4, Ireland

First published in Great Britain in 2021 by William Collins

1

A catalogue record for this book
is available from the British Library

ISBN 978-0-00-835622-4 (hardback)
ISBN 978-0-00-835623-1 (trade paperback)

Typeset in Minion Pro
Printed and bound in the UK using 100%
renewable electricity at CPI Group (UK) Ltd

MIX
Paper from
responsible sources
FSC
www.fsc.org **FSC™ C007454**

To Sophy

Contents

Maps   ix
List of Illustrations   xiii
Dramatis Personae   xv
Acknowledgements   xix
A Note on Names   xxiii

Introduction: Hong Kong, China   1

1   Merchants and Mandarins   11
2   Reform and Opening Up   40
3   A Long Farewell   70
4   The Iron Lady versus the Steel Factory   97
5   A Joint Declaration   122
6   The Eighties   136
7   The Change   172
8   Two Journeys   205
9   A Mandarin for All Seasons   233
10   Transitions   245
11   To Seek a Wider World   278
12   The Rivals   290
13   One Country, Two Cultures   308
14   Chaos under Heaven   349
15   Hunger Games   372

Afterword   401

Notes   407
Bibliography   429
Index   437

Maps

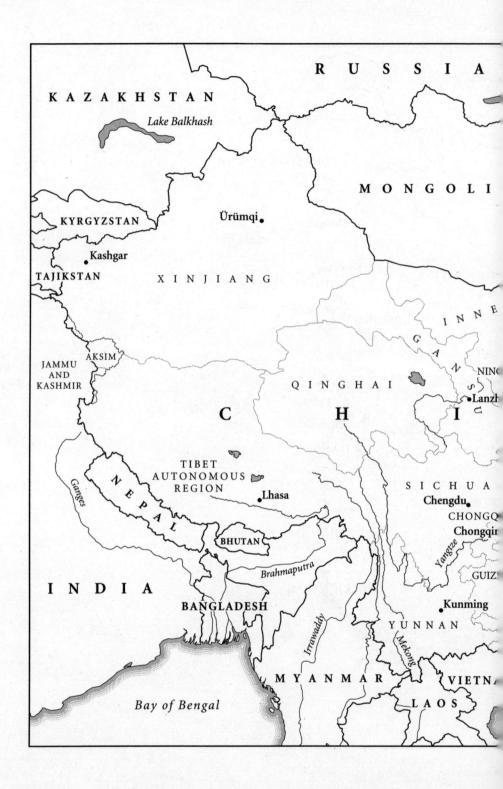

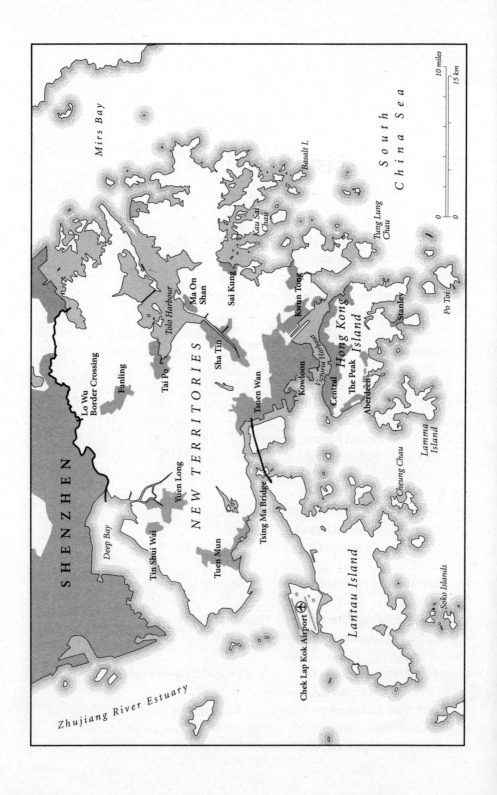

Mirs Bay

South China Sea

Basalt I.

Kau Sai Chau

Tung Lung Chau

Po Toi

Sai Kung

Ma On Shan

Kwun Tong

Stanley

Tolo Harbour

HONG KONG

Tai Po

Sha Tin

Kowloon

Victoria Harbour

The Peak

Island

SHENZHEN

Fanling

Lo Wu Border Crossing

Tsuen Wan

Central

Aberdeen

NEW TERRITORIES

Lamma Island

Yuen Long

Cheung Chau

Deep Bay

Tin Shui Wai

Tuen Mun

Tsing Ma Bridge

Lantau Island

Soko Islands

Chek Lap Kok Airport

Zhujiang River Estuary

10 miles

15 km

List of Illustrations

The signing of the Treaty of Nanjing (Engraving by John Burnet/ incamerastock/Alamy)

Hong Kong harbour in the late 19th century (Photo 12/Getty)

British Royal Navy 'Bluejackets' march through Hong Kong in 1927 (Underwood Archives/Getty)

Victoria Peak (Culture Club/Getty)

The British Royal Navy takes back Hong Kong after the surrender of Japan, 1945 (A 30517/IWM)

Hong Kong stock exchange in the 1980s (Serge Attal/Sygma/Getty)

Hong Kong port (Brian Harris)

Deng Xiaoping and Margaret Thatcher (Peter Jordan/Alamy)

Percy Cradock and his wife, Birthe, with guests at the British Embassy (Cradock Collection/photographer unknown)

Protester holding 'No more violence' banner (Brian Harris)

Policeman surrounded by crowds in Shanghai (Brian Harris)

Guards in Tiananmen Square (Brian Harris)

Christopher Patten (Gerhard Joren/Getty)

Christopher Patten speaking to the people of Hong Kong (Roger Hutchings/Getty)

The Handover in 1997 (Robert Ng/South China Morning Post/ Getty)

A group bidding Patten farewell (Richard Baker/Getty)

Children in the classroom during the SARS epidemic of 2003 (Reuters/ Alamy)

Medical staff mourning the deaths of their colleagues during SARS (Bobby Yip/Reuters/Alamy)

Occupy Central: mass protests in 2014 (tuimages.com/Alamy)

Joshua Wong rouses supporters of the 'Umbrella Movement' (Felix Wong/South China Morning Post/Getty)

'Lennon Walls' featuring poems, slogans and political demands (David Wong/South China Morning Post/Getty)
Huge rallies during Hong Kong's second wave of protest in 2019 (Paul Yeung/Bloomberg/Getty)
Insurgents fighting riot squads (Isaac Lawrence/AFP/Getty)
A protester hauled away by the police (Thomas Peter/Reuters/Alamy)
A barricade during the 2019 protests (Alamy)
Martin Lee at West Kowloon Magistrates Court (Vernon Yuen/ NurPhoto/Getty)

Dramatis Personae

CHINESE LEADERS

Mao Zedong (1893–1976) Poet, revolutionary and political philosopher, a key founder of the People's Republic of China in 1949. Mao said that Hong Kong was an issue for the 'next generation' to solve, bequeathing the task of its restoration to Deng Xiaoping.

Deng Xiaoping (1904–97) Marxist and statesman, China's paramount leader from 1977 until shortly before his death. Deng opened the economy to the world and struck a deal over Hong Kong but opposed political reform and crushed the democracy movement in 1989.

Jiang Zemin (1926–) The former Communist party boss in Shanghai, Jiang took over as leader of the party, the state and the army after the crisis of 1989, holding power into the early 2000s. He oversaw the handover of Hong Kong and led China into the WTO.

Hu Jintao (1942–) China's leader from 2002 to 2013, served as Communist Party chief in Tibet, presided over the 2008 Olympic Games and steered the country through a global financial crisis. Hu revived the role of the state and ruled as a low-key collective leader.

Xi Jinping (1953–) Supreme leader of China from 2013, restoring the party's dictatorship. A 'princeling', son of veteran Xi Zhongxun, served as governor of Fujian province, later vice president with responsibility for Hong Kong and Macau affairs.

KEY FIGURES IN THE HISTORY OF CHINA
AND HONG KONG

Li Qiang (1905–90) A spy, bomb-maker and lifelong militant, Li was China's foreign trade minister as the country began to open up. His visit to Hong Kong in 1978 paved the way for talks between China and Britain on the future of the colony.

Liao Chengzhi (1908–83) Born in Tokyo, a wily and sophisticated revolutionary who was trusted by Mao and Deng to forge policy on Japan, Taiwan and Hong Kong. He is said to have invented the concept of 'one country, two systems'.

Xi Zhongxun (1913–2002) Joined the Communist Party in 1928, guerrilla leader in the 'First Generation' of revolutionaries. Purged by Mao Zedong, he returned to head the party in Guangdong province, pioneered reforms and Special Economic Zones. Father of Xi Jinping.

Zhao Ziyang (1919–2005) Marxist-Leninist turned liberal reformer, served as Communist Party chief in Inner Mongolia and Sichuan, later premier. Became party leader 1987, purged 1989, died under house arrest in Beijing. His memoirs were smuggled to the West.

Zhou Nan (1927–) Ultra-patriot and ardent Marxist, China's main negotiator with Britain and Portugal over Hong Kong and Macau, later head of Xinhua in Hong Kong. An expert in English literature. Also served as ambassador to the United Nations 1980–1.

Zhu Rongji (1928–) As Mayor of Shanghai Zhu oversaw a peaceful end to 1989 protests. Later governor of the central bank and prime minister, he reformed financial sector, fought corruption, encouraged foreign investors, ran China's negotiations to join the WTO.

PERSONALITIES IN HONG KONG

Anson Chan (1940–) The first woman and the first Chinese civil servant to lead the Hong Kong administration under British rule, At one time the city's most respected public figure, Chan spoke up for democracy and was later denounced by China as a colonial lackey.

Carrie Lam (1957–) A Roman Catholic, Lam won promotion as an efficient administrator under the British and rose to become the fourth chief executive of Hong Kong. Her policies set off mass protests and in 2020 she embraced China's National Security Law.

Martin Lee (1938–) Jesuit-educated barrister, revered as the founder of Hong Kong's Democratic Party and for his fearless rhetoric. He lost out to a younger, more radical generation of activists before his arrest in 2020 under the National Security Law.

C.Y. Leung (1954–) Third chief executive of Hong Kong 2012–17, Leung was unfailingly loyal to Beijing and was alleged to be an underground member of the Communist Party. His tenure was marked by protests, middle-class discontent and dour inertia.

Donald Tsang (1944–) The son of a policeman, Tsang rose by merit to become financial secretary and later the second chief executive of Hong Kong 2005–12. A devout Catholic, he was later jailed for misconduct in public office: the charges were quashed on appeal.

Tung Chee-hwa (1937–) Shanghai-born shipping tycoon picked by China as the first chief executive of the HKSAR, 1997–2005. Driven from office after mass protests and economic upheaval. His family firm was later sold to a Chinese state entity for $6.3 billion.

Joshua Wong (1996–) The teenage face of Hong Kong's youth rebellion, an evangelical Christian whose gifted oratory and digital skills inspired opponents of authoritarian rule. Jailed for his activities, he later faced serious charges under the National Security Law.

THE BRITISH

Percy Cradock (1923–2010) British ambassador to China, later foreign policy adviser to Margaret Thatcher and head of the Joint Intelligence Committee. Cradock masterminded the deal to hand Hong Kong back to China and warned against radical democratic reforms.

Christopher Patten, Lord Patten of Barnes (1944–) British Conservative politician, 28th and last governor of Hong Kong. Patten defied the wrath of China to introduce wider democracy; his reforms did not survive. Later European Trade Commissioner and Chancellor of Oxford University.

Margaret Thatcher (1925–2013) Prime minister of the United Kingdom 1979–90, duelled with Deng over the fate of Hong Kong but conceded to his demands after winning guarantees that the territory's freedoms would endure for fifty years after the handover in 1997.

David Wilson, Lord Wilson of Tillyorn (1935–) Sinologist and diplomat, Wilson met Deng in 1979, negotiated the text of the Joint

Declaration and was 27th governor of Hong Kong, 1987–92. He carried out major reforms in politics, education and infrastructure.

Edward Youde (1924–1986) Served as a young diplomat in China, fluent in Mandarin, ambassador to the People's Republic of China 1974–1978. Appointed 26th governor of Hong Kong 1982, admired by many Chinese for his scholarship, died on a visit to Beijing.

Acknowledgements

Due acknowledgements to people in Hong Kong are necessarily limited at the time of writing. Many of those I would like to include do not appear here. In reconstructing the past, however, I am able to thank Anson Chan and Sir Donald Tsang for discussing the administrative, economic and financial questions which faced the first two governments of the Hong Kong Special Administrative Region.

I have drawn on my own contemporary notes and published articles between 1989 and 2019 for descriptions of events and for interviews with Tung Chee-hwa, Martin Lee and other politicians, business people, lawyers, journalists, police officers, academics, students and individuals from many walks of life in Hong Kong.

The librarians at the Hong Kong Central Library oversee a scrupulously managed collection of books and academic papers on their city's history; long may it continue to accumulate. I am obliged to the other libraries and institutions in Hong Kong whose resources contributed to my knowledge. Generations of journalists from afar are indebted to the staff of the Foreign Correspondents Club in Hong Kong, who handle news events and manage their turbulent tribe with calm efficiency in good times and bad.

History is not all about news, thankfully. One of the pleasures of writing this book has been the opportunity to return to Cambridge University to work in its libraries and archives. I am grateful to the Master and Fellows of Churchill College, and in particular to Allen Packwood, Andrew Riley and the team at the Churchill Archives Centre, for allowing me to consult the personal papers of Margaret Thatcher, a treasure trove that runs to handwritten notes, travel schedules and menu cards as well as documents on affairs of state. The Thatcher Foundation website, overseen by Chris Collins, remains the indispensable resource for students of her premiership. Material copyright Lady Thatcher is reproduced here by permission of the Thatcher Estate.

Material from the private papers of Sir Percy Cradock is cited by permission of the Master and Fellows of St John's College, Cambridge. I am indebted to the Special Collections Librarian, Dr Kathryn McKee, and to Dr Adam Crothers for their welcome at the Old Library, where this remarkable archive has come to rest in their care.

Two former governors of Hong Kong, Lord Wilson of Tillyorn and Lord Patten of Barnes, were generous with their time and their recollections during several recorded interviews and in subsequent written exchanges. I am additionally indebted to Lord Patten for our conversations and interviews in Hong Kong during his last year of office from 1996 to 1997. I drew on contemporary briefings and interviews with three British foreign secretaries, Lord Hurd of Westwell, Sir Malcolm Rifkind and the late Robin Cook, as well as talks with diplomats and officials who would not thank me for identifying them.

At HSBC I must thank Sir Sherard Cowper-Coles for introductions to two towering figures in the bank's history, Sir William Purves and Sir John Bond; and I am grateful to both of them for illuminating the financial landscape of Hong Kong and China over two extraordinary decades from 1980 to 2000. In reviewing the end of British rule, I am obliged to Hugh Llewellyn Davies, Senior Representative on the Sino-British Joint Liaison Group, for permission to use information from his privately published memoir *1997 Hong Kong, Handling the Handover*. I drew extensively on a pioneering insight on the use of cyberwarfare in the 2014 Umbrella Protests by Ian Williams in his MSc dissertation 'The use of cyberweapons against the Hong Kong democracy movement' (Royal Holloway, University of London, 2018), and I am grateful for permission to quote from it.

In a sense this book has been thirty years in the making, so my original debt is to Stephen Glover, then foreign editor of the *Independent*, who sent me to China in June 1989, and to the peerless photographer Brian Harris, who came on that journey. Two editors of the *Sunday Times*, John Witherow and Martin Ivens, employed me as their staff correspondent in Asia from 1996 to 2016 and generously funded reportage and travel across China, never failing to stand up for the right to report and publish on the country. Successive business editors at the *Sunday Times* allowed me to cover the Chinese economy without fear or favour, and forgave my occasional mistakes; I am thankful to John Jay, Rory Godson, Will Lewis, John Waples, Dominic O'Connell and Iain Dey for their commitment.

Fittingly for a book that deals with globalisation, people in many places lent a helping hand. In Budapest, the late Norman Stone gutted my original outline with the caustic charm he had brought to supervisions in Cambridge four decades earlier; Ildiko Moran of the Central European University shared her memories of Father László Ládányi, and, with astonishing generosity, Dale Martin lent me his precious bound collection of Fr Ládányi's life work, the *China News Analysis*. Keith Rockwell at the WTO in Geneva was an impartial guide to its history; the WTO's archives are a mine of facts and figures, and I was fortunate to get a unique Hong Kong perspective on China's accession from Stuart Harbinson.

Professor Ikuhiko Hata in Tokyo explained the importance of militarism in Sino-Japanese history and Henry Scott Stokes shed light on the philosophy of the author Yukio Mishima; thanks also to Shota Ushio, the perfect interpreter, and to Yuki Hasegawa of the *Yomiuri Shimbun*. In Paris, François Godement, doyen of French Sinologists, shared his views on his country's policy, and Lord Llewellyn of Steep, the British ambassador, gave shrewd pointers about the last colonial administration of Hong Kong. In Berlin, Annette von Broecker and Uli Schmetzer read the outline and helped to frame a Marxist perspective on China after the fall of European communism.

Roberto Peruzzi in Venice shared his scholarship on the finances of imperial China and conducted me around the palazzo housing the Università Ca'Foscari, built for a doge in 1453, where students labour over their Chinese texts a stone's throw from the house of Marco Polo. Research can rarely be so agreeable and I was also lucky to find writing retreats in Gstaad, thanks to the hospitality of Bill Scott, and as a guest of Liadain Sherrard at Katounia, on the Greek island of Evia, where greater talents than mine have polished their prose.

Sections of the text were read and commented on by Andrew Gowers, Tim Jepson, David Lague, Jane Macartney, Tom Miles and Alan Wheatley; naturally all errors remain my own. Thanks also to Annabelle Whitestone for her kind help in picture research.

I wish to thank the following for help, advice, discussion (and sometimes healthy disagreement) at various points over the last three decades: John Ashton, Bao Pu, Max Benitz, Nicholas Bequelin, Philip Bowring, Jean-Pierre Cabestan, Geoffrey Crothall, Frank Dikötter, David Eldon, Marc Faber, Jonathan Fenby, Angus Forbes, Edward Gargan, John Gerson, John Gittings, Peter Humphrey, Martin Jacques, Christina Lamb, Emily Lau, Kerry McGlynn, Richard Margolis, Jonathan Mirsky, Mark O'Neill, Charles Parton, Bob Peirce, James Pringle, Francesco Sisci, Greg Torode, Steve Vickers, Stephen Vines, Wang Xiangwei, David Webb and Jason

Wordie. All conclusions are mine alone and no endorsement is sought or implied.

In London, I am grateful to my agent, James Pullen, at the Wylie Agency, and to Arabella Pike at HarperCollins, who had faith in this project from the start.

Some of those I would have thanked are no longer with us. The late Frank Johnson, editor of *The Spectator*, published some of my original writing on the end of British rule and introduced me to David Tang, who lit up the place until his untimely death in 2017. Both of them are missed. The late Roderick MacFarquhar of Harvard University gave wise counsel and spent a whole afternoon in Hong Kong in conversation with the principal researcher on this book, an extraordinary encounter between the heights of Western academia and the world of the self-taught Chinese peasant intellectual. Among others lost, the legendary Sinologist Simon Leys (Pierre Ryckmans), the businessman Peter Sutch, *tai-pan* of the Swire Group, Robin Munro of the *China Labour Bulletin* and the academics Michael Williams and Gerald Segal were all generous interlocutors.

My greatest debt is to the researchers, translators, scholars, officials and journalists in the People's Republic of China who contributed to making this history. One day it may be possible to name them.

Geneva, June 2021

A Note on Names

This is a book for the general reader, therefore Chinese names of people and places are given in the most widely recognised form. The pinyin system of transliteration has been used in most cases, with a few historical exceptions, such as Chiang Kai-shek. In Hong Kong, individuals may take a Western name in addition to their Chinese one, for example Martin Lee Chu-ming; some adopt initials as a preferred form of address, for example C.Y. Leung. In all cases the form most commonly accepted in the Hong Kong media has been observed.

The Hongkong and Shanghai Banking Corporation was generally known as Hongkong Bank, especially in the colony, from its founding in 1865 until the bank instituted its global HSBC brand in the 1990s. In this book it is referred to by the terms appropriate to the period.

Introduction
Hong Kong, China

The skyline is a forest of towers that captures the eye from afar. The streets buzz, the hoardings blaze and the noise deafens. The harbour is a scene of perpetual motion uniting islands and peninsula. For hundreds of years only a few settlements stood in these waters to mark the boundary between China and the world beyond. But in the nineteenth century a band of piratical adventurers planted a flag and built their colony on a rock above a deep-water anchorage. Today it is one of the world's great cities.

Hong Kong was the gate to China when the country lived behind a wall of isolation. Until late in the twentieth century a pilot could spot it from hundreds of miles off as he flew under night skies across a vast darkness. Airliners followed a corridor of radio beacons through empty quadrants of sky reserved for military aviation. Rolling south beneath the wings, towns in the People's Republic unfolded as pinpricks of light in a carpet of gloom. There were no superhighways, no high-speed trains moving like glow-worms below. Long before the descent, at the point where the dim land gave way to the utter blackness of the sea, the crew saw a blaze of light that marked Hong Kong.

Now the gate stands open. A pilot navigates above a sea of brightness extending from central China down to the old treaty ports before dissolving in star-showers across the Pearl River Delta. In four decades the region has become the greatest industrial complex in human history. Hong Kong can only be picked out by its distinctive geography. By day, the approach is signalled by a dun-hued haze enveloping the cities, the islands and the waterways.

The city's politics and culture, too, are blending with those of mainland China, a slow saturation that seems as irresistible as the tides.

Sailing in from the South China Sea, the mariner crosses a line where the water turns from aquamarine to murk. Here the Pearl River spills into the deep, its turgid flow, laden with half the elements in the periodic table, leaching into the ocean. Ships bring raw materials from Africa, Australia or Brazil, oil and gas from the Middle East, technology from Japan or South Korea, parts from across Asia, meat, fish, grains and luxuries for Chinese consumers. They sail away with cargoes of manufactured goods for markets on every continent at prices to decimate the competition. The joint efficiency of container ships and Chinese factories has transformed the world economy.

For more than a century, Hong Kong's docks meant sweat and toil. Big ships moored at the quayside, tugs, lighters and small junks fussed around them, pilots guided vessels in and out of the crowded waterways. Stevedores swarmed into the holds, coolies heaved loads onto trucks and handcarts, gangmasters and brokers congregated around the godowns, or warehouses, each with its scarlet, smoke-wreathed shrine to Tin Hau, the goddess of the sea.

With computerised cranes and smaller crews, the volume of cargo has multiplied and only the fiercest typhoon interrupts the rhythm of commerce. The modern port of Hong Kong competes with rivals on the China coast. Hong Kong does, however, retain some advantages: its banks, finance houses and traders grease the wheels of business and invest its profits with unique freedom, its courts arbitrate commercial disputes impartially and its administrators, by and large, do not have their hand held out.

In colonial days, when the thwack of cricket balls could be heard on the green, a few stolid banks and trading houses stood above the Victorian settlement radiating out along the north shore of Hong Kong island to the Royal Yacht Club and the noonday gun immortalised in Noel Coward's song 'Mad Dogs and Englishmen'. Westwards stood a grand market hall in granite and brick surrounded by a hive of commerce – vendors of ivory, dried fish, abalone and sharks' fins, fragrant mushrooms and chests of aromatic tea; apothecaries perched amid glass cases of ginseng roots and cabinets of wizened herbs, each drawer labelled in benevolent calligraphy; all serenaded by a clamour of traffic, the calls of porters and yells and obscenities in Cantonese, the dominant tongue, and in a babel of dialects.

Trams still clatter by along metal lines laid at the dawn of the twentieth century, while above the old buildings tower the spires of finance and dozens of apartment blocks which appear to defy gravity, clinging to the slopes of the Peak. In the middle of Western District, imposing as a fortress, forbidding as a ziggurat, resembling a space rocket adorned by an odd sci-fi sphere at its apex, stands the Liaison Office of the Central People's Government.

Building-as-statement is part of the city's spirit. The British architect Norman Foster designed a hollow metallic leviathan for the Hongkong and Shanghai Banking Corporation, the bank branded around the world, with a distinct lack of romance, as HSBC. The new headquarters cost its shareholders almost a billion US dollars. Chinese-American wizard I.M. Pei, who grew up on the China coast, designed a glittering 1,205-foot pinnacle to house the Bank of China, HSBC's Communist rival, on the site of a Victorian-era barracks for British officers. Some said the tower's soaring, sharp-angled style broke the principles of *feng shui*, the traditional art of geomancy employed to site buildings auspiciously, and it passed into Cantonese slang as 'the knife'. By contrast, the staff at HSBC worked in a headquarters said to enjoy fine *feng shui* because its open atrium permitted dragons to pass to and fro between the sea and the mountain.

As for the third great tower in the area, the headquarters of Cheung Kong (Holdings), the tycoon Li Ka-shing's conglomerate, it was designed by the celebrated architect Cesar Pelli but its corporate rectangular lines were best described by the Greek consul, a man who knew his Doric from his Ionic, as 'merely the box which the Bank of China came in'.

More skyscrapers rise on the Kowloon peninsula, a tongue of land named after nine dragons that juts southwards into the harbour. Until 1998, the height of buildings in Kowloon, among the world's most densely populated districts, was restricted because airliners flew low overhead on their final approach to the old Kai Tak airport, a manoeuvre demanding icy skill as the pilot had to aim his plane at a chequerboard painted on the hillside, then veer sharp southeast to skim the rooftops and land on a single runway set in the waters of Kowloon Bay. Mistakes were rare. But the insurers sighed with relief when a new airport opened off Lantau Island and the property developers rushed in below the abandoned flightpath.

The richness of Kowloon endures; its markets and temples, its streets of sleaze, carpet emporia, mosques and small electronics stores, the plaintive tailors who waylay tourists, the industrious triad gangsters, the beckoning girls and the mama-sans of a dizzying selection of spas and massage joints, some of which may even be respectable.

Not for Hong Kong the hushed streets of Singapore or the mayhem of Bangkok. In normal times its citizens' behaviour – orderly but not regimented – is a rebuke to those who claim that only authoritarian rule can avoid chaos in a crowded Chinese society. Thousands of office workers troop across intersections obeying the pedestrian signals. In the gleaming underground railway system, the crowds keep a civilised pace, while schoolchildren and the elderly come and go without fear of being crushed. Everybody appears to pay the fare and crime on the network is all but unknown, even when revellers go home at night. Hong Kong has its share of rude, reckless cab drivers, and only the brave or those with no choice ride the green and cream-coloured light minibuses that ply up and down the spiralling roads of the Peak. In general, though, it is a safe and law-abiding place.

Religion and traditional morality play a surprising role in a society often known for brash acquisition, pitiless business practices and indulgence in gluttony and vice. Hong Kong ceded its reputation as the wickedest city in the Orient to other places a generation ago. The influence of Christianity is conspicuous. It may even have grown in the new era of dissent, whose rhetoric often borrows from scripture. An Anglican cathedral, ornate Roman Catholic churches, innumerable biblical prayer halls, schools, convents, hospitals, and church-run social centres and old people's homes all show the tenacity with which this imported western religion clung to its foothold on the south China coast through a century and a half of persecution, massacres and expulsions on the mainland.

Yet Hong Kong stands for plurality, not preaching. Tolerance is embedded in its cosmopolitan heritage. Its red-hued Taoist temples, fragrant with incense and glimmering with gold, attract legions of supplicants. Buddhism infuses Chinese traditional religion; thus many serene images of the Buddha appear on the altars of temples alongside glowering deities and coiled dragons to soothe the majority of worshippers who feel comfortable with a blend of Buddhism, Taoism, the philosophy of Confucius and a set of moral values resonant with a perceived Chinese identity. By himself, the Buddha is venerated among Hong Kong's Thai community in hundreds of household shrines draped in jasmine and lit by candles, presiding over rice traders, banks, restaurants and spas.

Flower-wreathed statues adorn Hindu shrines as elaborate as any in India or Nepal. On Fridays, Muslims crowd the mosques dotted around the territory, notable by their elegant green domes and modest minarets. A Jewish community of some 5,000 traces its roots to the early colonial days of Hong Kong; it boasts a fine principal synagogue dating to 1901 and its distinguished members include the Sephardic business dynasties of the Kadoories and Sassoons, while the 'golden mile' of shopping on one of

Kowloon's busiest roads bears the name of the Edwardian British governor and engineer who built it, Matthew Nathan.

It was not just trade but culture that flowed through the gate. Although a British colony, Hong Kong was key to the survival of Chinese art, music, opera, novel-writing, film-making, calligraphy, pamphleteering and journalism, all free from the censor. Its scholars preserved the intricate beauty of ancient classical ideograms after the Communist Party introduced a simpler character system in New China. For good or ill, a steady supply of antiques came out of the People's Republic, making their way to auction houses and dealers who asked few questions; it was caveat emptor for the buyer, and doubtless smugglers and fakers profited, but the alternative might have been destruction at the hands of the Maoist Red Guards in their crusade against the 'Four Olds' – customs, culture, habits and ideas. In that way Hong Kong, like Taiwan, became an ark of Chinese civilisation.

Alongside the Chinese tradition came western musical recitals, avant-garde theatres and daring art shows. Hong Kongers absorbed foreign influence unbothered by the claims of party propagandists who saw plots everywhere to subvert Chinese identity. In late colonial times, legions of serious schoolchildren in British-style uniforms sawed their way through quartets or sonatas, then immersed themselves in Chinese comics on the subway home. The next generation was glued to smartphones and social media. At liberty to read and watch what they liked, Hong Kongers showed no wish to abandon their beloved Cantonese language and culture. Hong Kong did not have complete democracy but it did have freedom – freedom that allowed almost everything to flourish that was constrained by the state in mainland China: profit-making, families, worship, love, knowledge, expression, experimentation and making mistakes. For a place rooted in uncertainty, Hong Kong grew a sense of self-confidence.

During the late nineteenth century Hong Kong was a breach in the wall; a haven for reformers and dissidents fleeing the executioners of the Qing dynasty. A stream of south Chinese literati, political activists and students flowed through the colony as they travelled to Japan to study how another ancient Asian power was reforming and opening up to the world. Hong Kong sheltered republicans, nationalists and revolutionaries through the violent political awakening in China that led to the abdication of its last emperor in 1912. All sides used its ports, its telegraph services, its hospitals, banks and printing presses.

In the 1920s the long Chinese civil war broke out between warlords and revolutionaries. A nationalist party led by military officers, the

Kuomintang, emerged from south China to become the most powerful force in the country. Then it was the turn of left-wing radicals to take refuge in Hong Kong, under the watch of the British colonial police.

Japan's invasion of China in the 1930s brought a fresh influx of spies from all sides, while fugitives sought safety in the colony and proxy wars were waged in its backstreets until the city fell to the Imperial Japanese Army in December 1941. At the end of the occupation four years later, British colonial rule was restored but Hong Kong had barely got back on its feet when the civil war resumed in China. The Communists won in 1949, pushing a horde of defeated nationalists and refugees into the colony. It became an outpost for diehard anti-Communists, who were opposed by a small but vigorous leftist movement. Its people lived in a competitive, frenetic and unrepentantly capitalist society. Work, accumulation and inheritance defined their way of life.

Hong Kong prospered while wars raged in Korea and Vietnam; and it grew rich as the rest of China stayed poor. Its colonial subjects were well-fed while famine stalked the mainland. It was a refuge for millions of poor Chinese, a safe haven for capitalists from Shanghai and a sanctuary for religion. Colonial rule was stable and did not threaten China, and as we shall see, the rulers of New China decided to leave well alone. In time this meant Hong Kong could be the gate through which China marched to greatness.

In 1967 the ultra-left fomented riots in sympathy with the Cultural Revolution raging in China, until the political wind from the north changed and the rioting burnt out. A period of tolerance ensued in which opponents and supporters of the Communist regime published, broadcast, rallied, ran their own social services and staged political events, despite the fact that there was no democracy in Hong Kong and thus no way to run for office. Free speech also enhanced the city's value to foreign powers as a vantage point from which to study the closed society of Maoist China.

When China began to open up, Hong Kong flowered. It prospered on trade, built factories, practically invented the supply chain and pioneered outsourced manufacturing. Yet in 1989 the people of Hong Kong, long deemed apolitical and wealth-obsessed by their complacent elite, rose up in protest against the Tiananmen Square massacre in Beijing. A new activism was born. Books, magazines, pamphlets, broadcasts and faxes flowed into China.

This defiance did not stop at the handover from Britain to China in 1997. At first Hong Kong reaped unique gains as a Special Administrative

Region with a 'high degree of autonomy'. Then China grew richer and its Marxist leaders began to focus on the 'contradictions' in their prize. A struggle broke out over political power, wealth, identity, data, freedom and conformity.

Successive local leaders installed by Beijing came and went, all failing to stem a tide of political activism that saw a broadly peaceful mass movement for democracy in 2014, then huge demonstrations and pitched battles against the police in 2019. The strife divided families, split the elite and brought warnings from Beijing that 'black hands' and hostile foreign forces were stoking a 'colour revolution' that aimed at regime change in China.

In 2020 the Chinese government imposed a National Security Law which led to the arrest of democratic activists, a new curriculum in schools, loyalty oaths for civil servants and a free hand for China's security agencies to spirit people away. Some fled before they could be caught. Chinese leaders hailed it as the restoration of order, while their opponents said it was the end of liberty.

The characters who populate the story of modern Hong Kong make up a vivid cast. Some are renowned: the captains and the kings, governors and tycoons, traders and money men, the dynasts who reared to the sky that forest of towers that glittered from afar and the shipping magnates whose vessels plied the sea lanes. The last governor, Christopher Patten, the billionaire Li Ka-shing, the casino king Stanley Ho, the Scottish banker William Purves, style arbiter David Tang; crusading, eloquent democrats, like the barrister Martin Lee and the young champion Joshua Wong – all have won international recognition.

The most influential actors, however, were rarely if ever seen publicly in Hong Kong. They were Chinese Communists steeped in revolutionary secrecy and party discipline, immune to the lure of fame, careless of public approval. This book will show that time and time again the critical decisions about Hong Kong were taken in conclave by men – and they were all men – with cruel experience of war, conspiracy, bereavement and sacrifice. They did not hesitate to kill or to imprison but they displayed an impressive ability to calculate for the long term. By the lights of Chinese statecraft, they did well between 1977 and 1997. They recovered Hong Kong from colonial rule, buried two treaties they had long declared unequal and defeated the strongest British prime minister of the post-war era, Margaret Thatcher, who had yearned to cling on to Britain's insular possession. They did it all without firing a shot, obeying the dictum of the ancient writer

Sun Tzu, who held that the finest victory was one achieved by guile alone.

Some of these men were world figures. Mao Zedong, the founder of the People's Republic, his lieutenant Zhou Enlai and their heir, Deng Xiaoping, are in all the history books. They entrusted the party's work on Hong Kong to veteran Marxist-Leninists whose names may come before many readers here for the first time. One such character was Liao Chengzhi, the Japanese-speaking Comintern agent, jailed at least seven times, purged and rehabilitated, who flitted between roles in the shadows and stepped forward in his late sixties to forge a policy that worked for China and for Hong Kong, dying on the threshold of the high office that would have been his reward. Another was Li Qiang, whose bland role as foreign trade minister in the 1970s belied a life story out of a spy novel, ranging from underground work in colonial Hong Kong to a fearless expedition to North Vietnam at the height of the American war, all due to his reputation inside the party as a technical and financial wizard. A third figure, Xi Zhongxun, deserved more attention than he has received: as the chief of Guangdong province, he talked the Communist Party leadership into the first reforms that opened up trade and investment between Guangdong and its neighbours, Hong Kong and Macau. He also merits a footnote in history as the father of Xi Jinping, a future ruler of China.

The stories of all these people, and many others, light the path that led China from the isolated socialism of the seventies to the heights of globalisation, a journey from digging ditches to managing capital flows that changed the planet.

There was a Faustian bond between the prosperity of Hong Kong and the oft-proclaimed perception that, since it had no ruling party, it therefore had no politics and business interests should govern it. This applied so long as Hong Kong stayed quiet and its grandees trooped up to Beijing, all smiles, to welcome the funds of the Communist Party's great families and their own opportunities to make money in the People's Republic. Neither side counted on the young, the clever, the indignant, the disadvantaged, the exploited and the smartphone-agitators of Hong Kong. They would write the next pages of its history.

For a nation as great as China, Hong Kong was a tiny enclave. Yet it had outsize psychological and political importance. It is sometimes forgotten that Russia and Japan took greater bites of the Qing Empire's territory than any western power. But it was the British seizure of Hong Kong in the drawn-out conflict in the 1840s known as the Opium Wars, and the later Anglo-French expedition which burnt down the Summer Palace in

Beijing, that inflicted greatest damage on the Chinese psyche. The foreign incursions of the nineteenth century shattered assumptions of cultural superiority. Their effects were traumatic upon monarchists and revolutionaries alike.

That is why today's battles over freedom, order and progress in Hong Kong revive ancient fears in the capital. There is always something reactive about the presence of tiny foreign vessels in a huge body. They can act as catalysts or as agents of decay. Karl Marx said that complete isolation was the prime condition for the preservation of the old China. 'That isolation having come to a violent end by the medium of England,' he said, 'dissolution must follow as surely as that of any mummy carefully preserved in a hermetic coffin, whenever it is brought into contact with the open air.'

Marx wrote those words about the last imperial dynasty, the Qing, but his dictum was taken to apply to any autocracy built on isolation and ritual. In recent years many have thought that foreign influence on the Chinese state after decades of righteous seclusion would prove Marx right again and that exposure to capitalism and liberty would hasten its decline. The men who governed China had no intention of allowing that. In less than half a century their nation became the second largest economy in the world after the United States. Its rise was the most disruptive global transformation since the Second World War. Its continued ascent depended, they believed, on firm rule and a burning national pride, requiring the constant reminder of past weakness and shame.

Xi Jinping, the Communist leader who took supreme power in China after 2012, put it like this: 'Only by knowing the nation's history of humiliation after the Opium War can one understand the Chinese people's strong yearning for national rejuvenation.'

Actually, it goes back an awful lot further than that.

1

Merchants and Mandarins

Traders from the West appeared off the coasts of China in late antiquity. Early records from the Tang dynasty tell of a cosmopolitan throng in the city of Panyu, now known as Guangzhou, and in the West until the late twentieth century as Canton. In far-off Beijing, rulers took a lofty and often benevolent view of barbarians on the fringes of their domains. The notion developed that those excluded from the celestial realm must perforce have come to it to perform rituals of tribute and obeisance.

It is worth looking into this distant past. Many aspects of it resonate across more than a thousand years of war and revolution down to modern times. It also demonstrates that the arrival of foreigners in nineteenth-century China was neither as strange nor as unprecedented as is sometimes depicted by historians.

In the Tang dynasty, between AD 618 and 907, Guangzhou was the most prosperous of the country's southern cities. It was a frontier town, set amid wilderness populated by savages and rife with plague. Around it, though, grew plentiful lychees, oranges, bananas and banyans. Within its triple walls lived 200,000 people. In the ninth century some 120,000 of them were foreign merchants, according to the Arab chronicler Abu Zayd al-Sirafi. He praised China for its rule by law and admired the simplicity of its state finances, which were based on a poll tax and on the ruler's monopoly of salt and tea, whose properties, he explained, were an antidote for many ills. Abu Zayd marvelled at the Chinese genius for manufacturing. In all of God's creation, he wrote, no people were more skilled at engraving and craftsmanship. They worked in ivory and metal, jade and stone, wood and precious minerals.

Not all was grace and refinement, however. Abu Zayd deplored the Chinese habit of wiping themselves after defecation instead of washing with water, while his fastidious nature recoiled at their failure to clean their hands and teeth before eating. As for the Chinese practice of having sex with their women during menstruation, their tolerance of organised prostitution and, indeed, their propensity for attractive boys provided for that purpose in the temple quarters; from these Abu Zayd averted his eyes in dismay.

Ninth-century Guangzhou throbbed with commerce. Marvellous sights awaited its visitors and its streets bustled with strangers speaking strange tongues. One account spoke of its port jammed with the argosies of Brahmans, Persians and Malays to a number beyond reckoning, laden with aromatics, drugs and precious items. They brought fragrant tropical woods and much-coveted medicines to swap for bolts of silk, crates of chinaware and slaves. China imported gum resins, sandalwood, aloeswood, camphor, patchouli, cloves, frankincense and myrrh. Chinese businessmen gave up the comforts of the north for the profits of the south, their revenues raising the governor to such high estate that he carried six yak tails and possessed majesty and dignity worthy of the son of Heaven. The administration was managed by eunuchs, one of whom was 'a gorgeous rascal', and graft was rife. As long as revenues flowed to the court, along with luxuries such as luminous pearls, kingfisher feathers and the occasional live rhino, the city was left to its own manners and customs.

There was a foreign quarter, where Arabs and Sinhalese mingled with 'white barbarians', Indian Buddhists (whose monasteries hid pools adorned with perfumed blue lotuses) and Shia Muslims from Khorasan, who had fled persecution and worshipped in their own mosque. All obeyed the summons of a drum to the great market at noon and dispersed to their own districts at the boom of the drum at sunset. The poet Chang Chi complained of 'the babble of barbarian voices in the night markets'. While the foreign traders awaited favourable winds to set sail for home, they were ruled by a chosen worthy. They enjoyed some extraterritorial privileges, but few details of these, which would become contentious in later centuries, are known.

Southern China was not a land of calm content. Rebellions broke out, thieves roamed the streets, murders were common. The captain of a Malay vessel murdered the governor, Lu Yüan-jui, who had extorted money from him. In 758 a band of Arab and Persian pirates raided the city, looted its stores, burnt houses and drove out the governor before escaping to a lair on the southern island of Hainan. For half a century afterwards, many foreign ships chose to sail to Hanoi instead of Guangzhou.

Neither was the Tang period always a time of easy cosmopolitanism. Lu Chün, the governor of Guangzhou from 836, was scandalised to find foreigners and Chinese living unsegregated and even intermarrying. He put a stop to that and banned foreigners from buying houses. An imperial edict forced Turkic Uighur Muslims, who were resented as moneylenders, to wear their distinctive costumes at all times. In the taxonomy of Chinese prejudice, Persians were rich, Malays were dark-skinned and thus ugly, southeast Asians went naked and were immoral. Young poets ogled Iranian waitresses in wine-shops, literati admired harpists and dancers from Central Asia, but the ninth century was also 'an age of suspicion and persecution of foreigners'.

Attitudes towards commerce and foreigners were ambiguous. Trade was sometimes blamed for rising prices and disorder. Some outsiders gained favour and could rise to office in the government; the new gentry class which emerged through the introduction of an examination system was more open-minded than the hereditary aristocracy. Some used their skills, poised between two worlds, to mediate contracts, duties and disputes among traders and their haughty, distrustful Chinese counter-parts. The privileged interlocutor was a position established more than a thousand years before the European colonial powers set foot on the shores of Hong Kong and Macau.

Even in the ninth century, the Chinese state took a commanding role in business. Aristocratic attitudes to commerce were ambiguous and trade 'was never free from political entanglements'. This was an age when the dynasty held monopolies on domestic goods such as salt, iron, currency and some basic commodities. Officials saw these as models for the control and taxation of luxuries pouring into Tang China from abroad. In the eighth century the emperor established a Commissioner for Commercial Argosies at Guangzhou, his duties being to buy up goods which the state wished to control and to organise their distribution. Foreigners were expected to offer some of their goods as gifts in tribute to the son of Heaven and to demonstrate submission to his universal power. The rest of their consignments had to be deposited in government warehouses and could only be sold in the markets under official supervision. It was a rash foreign trader who would dare to sell his wares directly to the public.

Then there was the vexed notion of exchange and barter. Commerce was hampered by regulations which could be imposed in the name of morals, revenue, sumptuary laws or national security. One edict of the eighth century banned the export or sale to foreigners of tapestries, damasks, fine silk, embroidery, yak tails, pearls, gold and iron. There was no fixed medium of exchange: Tang tombs have yielded up Byzantine gold coinage and Arab traders at Guangzhou were said to use gold Islamic dinars to settle accounts. From time to time officials decided that this or that foreign commodity might weaken, deprave or corrupt the Chinese consumer. Such regulations were capricious and often temporary, but they made it hard for merchants to fix prices or make contracts.

Finally, the Tang laws enshrined xenophobia. If a foreigner took a Chinese wife or concubine, a decree of AD 628 obliged him to remain in China: in no case might a Chinese woman accompany him home. If the foreign trader died in China his goods were sealed and confiscated by the state.

Like the Persian kings demanding soil and water from prostrate cities in classical Greece, the rulers of China expected symbolic acknowledgement of their supremacy from the tributary states around them. The emperors claimed that, far from threatening their august status, the arrival of foreigners not subject by birth to their graciousness tended to confirm it. This exalted attitude was to have consequences which reverberate down to modern times.

At the dawn of the Age of Discovery in the sixteenth century, China was still remote and mysterious to Europeans. Immured behind its barriers of desert and mountain, washed by the waters of seas yet to be charted, it was a realm made for medieval romancers. The accounts of early travellers, like Marco Polo, who went by land and returned by sea in the late thirteenth century, spoke of a Great Khan, of marvels and riches, of Tatar paladins and a summer palace called Xanadu, where wild beasts roamed amid woods and fountains. He told of a splendid port called Zaiton, 'for all the ships that arrive from India laden with costly wares and precious stones of great price and big pearls … a marvel to behold'.

Many of the travellers' tales were fantastical. They had little authentic news about wars and politics, and what they claimed to be insight into the economy of China was little more than a simple reaction to the taxes and tribute demanded of them. Their accounts depict the manners and customs of the Chinese as strange and sinful. These foreign storytellers were free to invent and exaggerate, safe in the knowledge that the Chinese court would never read their works and their readers were most unlikely to see China because it was so far away.

Yet China was not isolated. Caravans along the Silk Road had connected the Han dynasty with the Middle East during the empires of Rome and Parthia. Chinese trading ships plied the coasts of Asia and East Africa.

Under the Tang emperors, who reigned from the seventh century to the tenth, the port of Guangzhou was one of the busiest entrepôts of the world. Western religions were known in China from the same period, as a stele in a museum at Xi'an from AD 781 inscribed in Syriac and Chinese attests. As the empire expanded, Persians and Arabs held military and administrative posts. Chinese cultural and political influence expanded to Korea and Japan. If China withdrew into seclusion while Europe flowered in the Renaissance, it was still seen from afar as a land of silks and spices, a refined civilisation pursuing arts, literature and music under an almighty ruler and his caste of mandarins. By most measures of the time, the Chinese economy was the biggest in the world.

The balance of power and fortune changed in the sixteenth century. The kings and queens of western Europe grew mighty and ambitious; it was the era of Henry VIII and Elizabeth I of England, François I and Henri VI of France and Philip II of Spain. The Christian monarchies triumphed over the Ottoman Turks, who had carried the green banners of Islam to the heart of Europe. In 1529 Suleiman the Magnificent abandoned the siege of Vienna and in 1571 an alliance defeated the Turks at the sea battle of Lepanto. The tide had turned and the European nations began to look outwards. It was the start of four centuries of world domination by Europe in which China was eclipsed.

The growth of European power in Asia was not linear, and it was propelled by forces which no Chinese strategist of the time could have grasped. One key event was the collapse of Spanish power in continental Europe between 1640 and 1714 through foreign wars, inflation, bankruptcy and internal strife. 'Here was a country which had climbed to the heights and sunk to the depths; which had achieved everything and lost everything; which had conquered the world only to be vanquished itself,' wrote one historian of the Spanish Empire. Addicted to treasure from the Americas, prey to economic forces its devout monarchs did not understand, Spain still sent its galleons between Acapulco and Manila laden with silks and silver. But its part in the European adventure in Asia was at an end.

The second victim of economic change was the Venetian republic, which had grown rich on Mediterranean commerce and the overland trade with Cathay. Its decline was less steep than Spain's. But it never recovered from the voyage of the Portuguese navigator Vasco da Gama around the Cape of Good Hope in 1498. Da Gama opened a sea route to the East and destroyed the centuries-old Venetian grip on trade through the Levant. Venice, said the French philosopher Montesquieu, was 'thrown into a corner of the world'. Today Chinese tourists troop along the flag-stones of the Rialto to Marco Polo's house, past quays where argosies laden with the silks and spices of the east once moored, where moneychangers dealt in bills of lading from all the known world and a republican oligarchy built, in Shelley's words, palaces 'like fabrics of enchantment pil'd to heaven'. Venice has vanished as a world power.

Two enterprising maritime nations, England and Portugal, seized the opportunity they had long sought for an all-water trade route to the Indies. In 1557 the Portuguese opened a base in Macau with the wary consent of the Chinese authorities. Their British rivals, the East India Company, began to build an empire in India and turned their eyes to China. The French and the Dutch were not far behind. All the European powers fought one another from time to time, but even if China had possessed the political skill to divide and defeat them it was in no posi-tion to do so.

In 1600 the late Ming empire seemed to be at the peak of its splendour. The dynasty had ruled China since the fourteenth century. From his majestic capital in Beijing, the son of Heaven held sway over 120 million people, more than in all the nations of Europe. There was no empire like his on earth. Mughal India was breaking up. Spanish conquistadors and foreign diseases had laid waste the Aztec and Inca empires of Mexico and Peru. The Ottomans were in retreat. Russia was a geographical expression. Japan was in the last stages of civil war before a powerful shogun of the Tokugawa clan unified it and set up his capital at Edo, modern Tokyo. In China, the imperial government was hallowed by ritual and administered by officials chosen through rigorous examinations. The wealthy enjoyed the fruits of a rich cultural and economic life accompanied by a sense of peace and order. The late Ming period produced some of China's finest painting and some of its greatest works of literature: *The Peony Pavilion*, a play by the dramatist Tang Xianzu, which featured a poetic scholar-offi-cial, *The Journey to the West*, a picaresque tale of a monk and a monkey on the road to India, and *The Golden Lotus*, an erotic reverie.

But just as the European powers grew confident and powerful, China fell into a crisis from which, some of its intellectuals argue, it has never truly recovered. Corruption, intrigue and decadence weakened the Ming dynasty; floods, famines and a brief ice age ruined farmers, trouble in the borderlands forced tax rises to fund the military; in despair the peasants and artisans upon whom Ming prosperity rested rose up in rebellion.

Much later, some Marxists argued that Portuguese traders at Macau – that tiny foreign body in the great organism of China – were to blame because they bought up Chinese silk and traded it for silver, which was pouring out of the mines in Mexico and Peru; the resultant huge inflow of silver into China's agrarian economy led to inflation, wild speculative excess and a boom-and-bust cycle which the Confucian scholar-administrators of the time were incapable of managing. In this telling, like the Spanish Habsburgs, the imperial house of China fell to forces of modernity it did not comprehend. The causes and effects of the worldwide silver crisis in the sixteenth century are still debated by economic historians, but it left a legacy of suspicion of foreign speculators among all subsequent rulers of China.

In 1644, after a long decline, the Ming dynasty collapsed. Invading tribal armies from the northeast conquered the country and installed a dynasty of Manchu warriors. The last Ming emperor, Chongzhen, murdered his consorts, then slunk away to hang himself from a tree near the Forbidden City in Beijing. Generations of literati mourned the fall of the Ming as a cultural apocalypse. Some of the nobility scorned the Manchus. Their strange language was foreign to the dominant Han Chinese and their customs were thought vulgar. From time to time rebellions broke out and, tellingly, resistance lingered longest in the south. But the new dynasty, known as the Qing, won loyalty by adopting not just Han Chinese values and rituals, but the existing ruling elite. This new regime was to rule for more than two and a half centuries.

It was during the height of Qing magnificence that King George III of England sent envoys to the court of the emperor Qianlong. (Chinese emperors took regnal names, thus Qianlong was born Aisin Gioro Hongji and adopted his new name, which means 'Perfect Eminence', on acceding to the throne in 1736.)

Throughout his long reign Qianlong vacillated between opening and closing the borders of the realm. Relations with barbarians were regulated by the Imperial Household, the Office of Border Affairs and the Ministry of Rituals, the better to prescribe the degree of their submission. Under the Ming, the Jesuit missionary Matteo Ricci had been allowed to reside at the court in Beijing in 1601. The scholar-priests translated the principles of western mathematics, cartography and astronomy into Chinese and translated the works of Confucius into western languages. Jesuits were trusted by Qianlong's grandfather, the emperor Kangxi, to draft the Latin text of the Treaty of Nerchinsk, regulating borders and commerce between China and Russia, in 1689. Trust, however, was a commodity in the shortest supply at court.

By the late eighteenth century, foreigners were pushing at the doors of the Qing empire in the south. To repel them, officials clung to ritual and rules, with decreasing conviction or effect. They dropped the pretence that the visitors had come to offer tribute and conceded that they might trade with the celestial empire at selected ports. At one of these, Guangzhou, local merchants set up a guild, known to foreigners as the Cohong, in 1720 to monopolise contacts with the traders and to control prices, fees and rakeoffs. The combination of bowing to the inevitable while seeking to manage the foreigners and to profit from them became enduring Chinese policy.

In 1760 an exasperated emperor ordered that all trade must be restricted to Guangzhou. The foreigners were permitted to reside there only in the trading season, which was governed by the monsoons and ran from October to March. Moreover, they could deal only with the Cohong and might communicate only with its members in the event of disputes. Imperial officials remained in aloof seclusion, did not condescend to meet the barbarians, and often disdained to examine their petitions. To a certain cast of mind this was meant to inspire awe and to many Chinese it appeared magnificent. In an age when the Western powers were growing in military, economic and diplomatic might it was extremely unwise.

During the long reign of Qianlong the Chinese empire appeared to foreigners to exist in a state of political and bureaucratic inertia. In fact, Chinese histories record that government by its philosopher-officials was more flexible and responsive than it has been given credit for. But the ambitions of the East India Company, the pressure of Dutch seaborne commerce, the residual power of Spain, the resolute Portuguese foothold at Macau and the first appearance of ships from the newly independent United States off the south China coast did not allow the guardians to recline and contemplate.

In 1792 the British government of King George III dispatched one of its ablest diplomats, Lord Macartney, on the voyage to China. Macartney was an Irish nobleman who had toured Europe, met Voltaire, served with distinction as envoy to Catherine the Great of Russia and completed a term as governor of Madras without scandal. His mission was to prise open the gates of the Qing empire and to become Britain's first ambassador to the court at Beijing. The aim was to put trade on a sure footing and to compel China to enter the international state system then coming into existence. The Chinese throne had no intention of permitting any of these things to take place. The comedy of errors that ensued was recorded in Macartney's own journal and the accounts of others in his suite, becoming a feast for cartoonists back at home.

Macartney was greeted with exquisite courtesy, which turned to alarm as the mandarins in attendance realised that their guest did not intend to perform the 'kowtow', the requirement to fall to his knees before the emperor and to prostrate himself nine times. Travelling by canal towards the capital, his lordship became aware that the banners adorning the fleet of junks proclaimed him to be an ambassador bearing tribute to the throne.

The emperor was at his pleasure dome at Chengde, known in those days as Jehol, pursuing affairs of state far from the heat and noise of Beijing. He would receive the emissaries there. Meanwhile the English party was conducted to Beijing and given palatial quarters while they awaited word from the court and negotiated over the precise form of obeisance that would take place. Macartney adopted a principle of reciprocity that would bedevil encounters between China and the West for ever after, maintaining that he would pay the same respect to the emperor as he would to his own monarch. The negotiations became fraught.

Meanwhile presents from George III, including crystal chandeliers, Derbyshire porcelain, a globe, clocks, a barometer and an orrery, a clockwork model of the solar system, were arranged in the summer palace known as the Yuanming Yuan, the Gardens of Perfect Brightness, for Qianlong to inspect on his return. Many came to gape but some professed indifference; one courtier was at pains to emphasise that the items were not gifts, but tribute.

The awkward diplomatic interlude was resolved by a summons from Chengde announcing that the emperor, in his graciousness, would receive Lord Macartney and that the customary protocol would be eased in recognition of the great distance he had travelled and the presents he had brought. It appeared to be a victory for British prestige. It was also a foretaste of misunderstandings and disappointments to come.

Macartney and his suite traversed the Great Wall and reached Chengde in mid-September 1793. At the appointed time, mandarins led him to his place. He had donned his velvet robes of the Order of the Bath and fastened his diamond decorations. As the emperor swept by in his palanquin, Lord Macartney fell on one knee and bowed, as did all the British present, while the Chinese prostrated themselves in the dust. Qianlong ascended the throne and the peer knelt before him to present a bejewelled box containing a letter from King George III, receiving in return a jade sceptre. At the banquet which followed, the emperor, who was eighty-three, enquired after the English sovereign's age and health. It was becoming clear to the ambassador that neither Qianlong nor his ministers had a very clear idea of exactly where England was, or knew much about it. They had, however, heard with horror about the French Revolution and had no intention of allowing pernicious doctrines such as the Rights of Man to take root in the celestial kingdom.

While Macartney lingered at Chengde he met the most influential member of the imperial retinue, the principal minister named Heshen. As a young Manchu guards officer, Heshen had caught the ageing emperor's eye. He became Qianlong's favourite and had risen to high and lucrative rank through diligence, guile and charm. If Lord Macartney was aware of the scandalous rumours around Heshen's unparalleled ascent, he did not dignify them with comment, recalling his interlocutor as a handsome and fluent man. The two went riding around the imperial gardens and parkland, exchanging pleasantries which served to probe each other's true intentions, as practised diplomats do. In his journal, Macartney noted that Heshen's suspicions were aroused by the fact that the English were both infinitely curious about China and yet well-informed about its history. It was an encounter which foreshadowed others in the centuries ahead between intrusive foreign envoys and wary Chinese office-holders.

Both the Manchu court and its barbarian visitors maintained a veneer of courtesy to the end of the Macartney mission. The ambassador met Qianlong several times, the emperor deigned to inspect the gifts laid out in the palace of the Gardens of Perfect Brightness and for a while Lord Macartney was tempted to believe he might be permitted to remain in China. He was soon disabused of the notion. A date was fixed for his departure and in reply to the letter from King George III, the envoy received an edict from Qianlong which even at a distance of more than two centuries resounds with doomed magnificence.

The British had asked China to liberalise the trading system at Guangzhou, to open up more ports for commerce, to fix tariffs in line with international practice and to allow an ambassador to reside at Beijing. For Qianlong and his ministers these were impossible demands.

In his response the emperor acknowledged the 'tribute' proffered by George III but pointed out that China had 'never valued ingenious articles' and did not 'have the slightest need of your country's manufactures'. As for the request to station an ambassador at Beijing, 'apart from not being in harmony with the regulations of the Celestial Empire' this would be 'of no advantage to your country'. Therefore the 'tribute envoys' had been commanded to return home, while their monarch was enjoined simply to 'act in conformity with our wishes by strengthening your loyalty and swearing perpetual obedience so as to ensure your country may share the blessings of peace'.

The edict had been drawn up before Macartney's disembarkation at the Gulf of Bohai months earlier. His expedition cost the East India Company £78,000, for which it got nothing, although the peer himself cleared a handy £20,000 profit. It was a failure.

On his way home, Macartney wrote down a famous set of impressions which have influenced generations of Western diplomats until the present day. 'The Empire of China is an old, crazy first-rate man-of-war, which a fortunate succession of able and vigilant officers has contrived to keep afloat for these one hundred and fifty years, and to overawe their neighbours merely by her bulk and appearance,' he judged. But it would drift and be dashed to pieces on the shore when officered by less competent rulers. History was on the side of progress and the Qing, he believed, were conducting a vain attempt to arrest the progress of human knowledge. For China, resistance to modernity was futile.

In 1816 the British government dispatched a second embassy under Lord Amherst to seek a trade agreement. It, too, was repulsed after the British envoy declined to perform the kowtow to Qianlong's successor, the emperor Jiaqing. Serene and impassive, the Chinese ship of state sailed on. But things were changing fast inside and outside China. Among the first casualties of the new reign was the astute if over-covetous Heshen, who was brought down by his rivals for corruption and was graciously permitted to strangle himself with a silken cord presented on a cushion. The new emperor seized Heshen's palaces, his golden treasure and his cache of precious stones, fortifying his own authority by a relentless fixation on ceremonial and sumptuary rules. In this way the dynasty exchanged a perverse but effective ruling partnership between Qianlong and his principal minister for a hollow crown, one preoccupied by over-mighty vassals and deaf to counsel. There could not have been a less auspicious time for China to retreat into empty absolutism.

Beyond China's shores, trade and finance were making the modern world. The first American vessel to sail for Guangzhou, the *Empress of China*, left in 1784 laden with silver currency and thirty tons of ginseng root from the woods of New England, returning to New York the next year carrying teas and silks. In the following decades, traders from the United States crossed the Pacific with goods sought by the Chinese: sandalwood from Hawaii, furs from Alaska and bêche-de-mer, or sea slugs, which were dried and packed in Fiji. The port of Salem, Massachusetts, grew wealthy on trade funded by consortiums of investors who pooled their money to finance the early voyages to China. A man could get in on it for as little as $100; the average was $4,000. The biggest investor in one consignment of 1819 paid $100,000. The ships went out with barrels of silver Spanish dollars, raw cotton, pigs of lead and kegs of quicksilver in addition to ginseng and other commodities. They came back with porcelain, tea, silk, lacquer, tortoiseshell combs and toys. Wives, children and friends made detailed requests for goods to be bought on their behalf in Guangzhou. A sophisticated system evolved in Salem to run the business: shipbuilding, dock works, finance, accountancy and law, crewing, victualling and navigation. The United States was in the Pacific Trade and would never look back.

On the far side of the world, commerce between British India and the China coast grew rapidly as the British expanded their possessions and British merchants looked for opportunities and growth. The Napoleonic Wars distracted the attention of the government in London but after 1815 Britain's forward march resumed in Asia. France ceased to be a serious rival in the east after Waterloo. The Portuguese were reduced to their foothold at Macau. As for the Dutch, with whom Britain had fought wars and traded colonial possessions, their Golden Age was over. The Anglo-Dutch treaty of 1824 made the British dominant from India to the South China Sea and confined the Dutch to the East Indies. A small trading post named Singapore, founded in 1819 and ruled by Britain, marked the boundary between their spheres of influence.

So, by a combination of developments which were all but unknown to the rulers of China, a small island chain on the far side of the world had become their most powerful adversary, less than three decades after Lord Macartney had been sent on his way. All the European maritime powers dispatched cargo ships to China, but British naval power, military skill and financial resources made London the arbiter of events. A steadily increasing volume of trade flowed up and down the Pearl River Delta. Chinese exports of tea, silk and porcelain were carried to the new consumers of Europe, a continent at peace and poised on the threshold of prosperity.

Even in its high and palmy years the Qing dynasty's own ordinances unwittingly increased British influence. The value of Chinese exports through Guangzhou in the first decades of the nineteenth century was more than double that of China's imports. The balance was paid by the foreigners in silver currency. At first the East India Company had to ship silver to Guangzhou by the barrel. Then it turned out that merchants in Guangzhou were sitting on piles of silver because the Chinese government forbade them to export their cash profits. So they handed over their silver to the East India Company, whose financial wizards issued bills of exchange which could be redeemed in London or Calcutta. The company's buyers then used the silver at Guangzhou to buy shipments of tea for the thirsty British market, thus at a stroke removing the risk of shipping specie and increasing the growth of London as a global centre of finance. At the same time, the immense sums of money handed over in duties and fees threw off rich opportunities for official venality and generated a stream of revenue for the imperial coffers. This helped the Qing pay for the military expenditure needed to hold down a tide of rebellions and disorder across China. The money was addictive. The dynasty could not have stopped commerce even if it had wanted to.

Eventually this system succumbed to four fatal afflictions. The plague of official corruption became a drag on the functioning of Chinese government. In 1833, Parliament in London ended the East India Company's monopoly on trade, throwing open the marketplace and creating a free-for-all. The Anglo-Chinese monopolists – the East India Company and the Cohong merchants of Guangzhou – henceforth faced intense competition from new houses founded in Calcutta and Bombay, which offered lower interest rates and plunged into commodities through destabilising cycles of boom and bust. The final blow, however, came through the ceaseless and apparently unstoppable growth of investment and trade in what has been called the third great Indian export crop after indigo and cotton. This was opium.

The trade in opium and the connected Anglo-Chinese wars dominated relations between China and the West in the nineteenth century and inflicted a wound on the Chinese psyche that has yet to heal. To Marxists and to non-ideological Chinese patriots alike, they remain the epitome of imperialist crime. For economic historians, they provide a textbook study of the interplay between commerce and state power, set in a distant time when nations behaved towards each other in ways unrestrained by the corpus of modern international law and when most societies were organised in ways that would be unacceptable today.

* * *

Opium was not introduced to China by the British. It had been used in the empire since the Tang dynasty. The first opium-yielding poppies may have come to China with Arabs and Turkish traders. The drug's medicinal properties were listed in the Chinese pharmacopoeia perhaps as early as the fifth century, and its addictive character was understood. For around a millennium it was eaten unprocessed as a medicine.

But in the seventeenth century users on the island of Formosa, modern Taiwan, began to mix it with tobacco and smoke it. During this period Dutch and Spanish colonisers vied with Chinese armies for control of Taiwan; there was frequent intercourse with the mainland and the opium-smoking habit spread. China produced a small quantity of opium but most of its supply came from India, a low-grade variety named Malwa that was shipped by the Portuguese through Macau.

In 1729 the Qing rulers banned the import of opium. Mandarins fretted over its bad effects on society, although the drug continued to flow into China through greased palms. In 1773, the East India Company decided to compete against the Portuguese by paying farmers in Bengal to grow high-quality Patna opium. The company knew that its business was illicit: in 1796 it abandoned direct exports to China. Instead the drug was sold to private merchants at auction in Calcutta. The chests were still shipped in company vessels but the opium itself was peddled to the Chinese by others, saving face all round. Between 1800 and 1818 the trade was stable at an estimated total of about 4,000 chests weighing 140 lb each.

From 1819, however, prices fell due to intense competition between British and Portuguese traders and the opium trade boomed. The dynasty ordered a crackdown in Guangzhou. The foreign traders simply moved their contraband stocks to floating hulks off Lintin Island in the Pearl River Delta. Chinese wholesalers bought the opium, rugged Tanka rivermen carried it upstream in forty-oared boats known as 'fast crabs', imperial functionaries pocketed bribes, and Chinese gangsters and Triad secret societies distributed the drug inland. Between 1822 and 1830 the trade grew to an estimated 18,760 cases a year. The East India Company recorded that £4 million was sent back to England in 1830. Most of it was converted into opium to be sold in Guangzhou, the revenues being invested in teas for export to England, on which the British government reaped a further £3.3 million in tariffs. Investment in opium, private profits and government revenues from the trade became a central element of British policy in Asia.

China found its balance of payments going into reverse. In the first decades of the nineteenth century it had earned a surplus, but after 1820 it went into deficit. The historian Frederic Wakeman, writing in the 1970s, concluded that it was opium which shifted the balance and ended up financing much of the later colonisation of India. So compelling was the commercial logic that the East India Company took over shipments of Portuguese Malwa opium through Calcutta in 1831; five years later, opium imports into China were valued at 18 million silver dollars. In volume, the trade surged to 30,000 cases in 1835 and 40,000 in 1838. This was, Wakeman wrote, 'the world's most valuable single commodity trade of the nineteenth century.'

Inside China, the growth of addiction – and the little-understood effects of the outflow of silver currency – caused perplexity and anguish. The emperor Daoguang deplored the drug's impact on morality and urged the mandarinate to manifest virtue, but the lure of easy riches had corroded his administration. Huge swings in market forces began to disrupt the order of Qing society. Peasants earned their pittance in copper cash, but their land taxes were calculated and remitted to the government in silver. By 1838 the number of copper coins needed to buy one silver tael had risen from 1,000 to 1,650; by 1842 it had risen to more than 2,000. (The tael, an ingot of silver, varied in weight by region, but was usually about 37 grams or 1.3 ounces.) The real rate of taxation doubled, ruining many. The most populous and heavily taxed regions of China south of the Yangtze became turbulent. Poverty, discord and rural rebellions multiplied. In the Communist Party's historical view, misery begat addiction and both were fuelled by foreign poison. In the mid-nineteenth century there were about 450 million people in China; few reliable estimates exist of how many used opium but their number grew fast. A study by Professor Jonathan Spence of Yale University calculated that by the 1880s the number of smokers may have reached 10 per cent of the population.

In response, Daoguang initiated a debate between 'legalisers' and 'moralists' to determine how the government could manage the crisis. The 'legalisers' argued that prohibition was futile, enforcement merely led to corruption and it would be better for the dynasty to permit and regulate opium consumption, thereby earning revenues from it. The 'moralists' held that obedience to the law was the foundation of the Confucian order and that China might strengthen the throne and achieve moral rebirth by adhering to it.

The emperor's own instincts lay with austerity and control. Perhaps he did not know that officials in the south sent him false reports of natural disasters in order to secure tax remissions rather than admit or explain the

desperate straits to which small landowners were reduced by silver inflation and their fiscal burden. It would not be the last time that rulers in
Beijing were badly informed about their distant provinces. In any case, the
emperor was vexed by complications. It was plain to him that 'foreign
mud' was a curse, but it was not simple to eradicate it.

The economics were inconclusive and, given the standards of data
available in nineteenth-century China, its rulers can be forgiven for being
fuddled. Critics of imperialism, however, saw in the opium trade a classic
example of exploitation. Marx argued in the 1850s that the Western
powers depended on the drug traffic to offset their imports from China
and were addicted to its revenues for their own expenditure. It followed
that the huge outflow of silver currency from China was draining its economy and pushing up the domestic price of the silver tael, causing rural
misery in China while cushioning the rentiers of Europe.

It was not as simple as that. The silver price in China was also affected
by a worldwide shortage of the metal. Within the empire, silver soared in
value after Qing officials debased the copper currency by minting cheaper
coins in response to falling production at the copper mines in Yunnan
province. This amounted to devaluation and to a surge in the circulation
of copper cash. Gresham's law, which states that 'bad money drives out
good,' came into operation and silver became so sought-after that it grew
scarce. A final complication was that calculations of the flow of silver were
distorted by the fact that some of it never physically left China because
western brokers in opium and tea at Guangzhou settled their accounts by
bills exchanged in London.

Weighing the arguments on both sides of the debate, Daoguang decided
to back the moralists. Sweeping aside complexity, the emperor saw a
narcotic not only corrupting his subjects but also introducing uncontrollable financial volatility and insulting barbarian encroachment on the
celestial empire, which, he believed, could certainly be repulsed.

China and Britain almost came to blows in 1834, when Lord Napier,
appointed as the first superintendent of the China trade, tried to break
with precedent by announcing himself in a formal letter to the governor
of Guangzhou instead of abiding by the regulations, which forbade direct
contact between Chinese officials and foreigners. The governor ordered
Napier to leave and, when he refused, sent a fleet of war junks to block the
Royal Navy from coming to his aid. Trade halted. Broken by malaria and
let down by the merchants, who feared for their businesses, Napier
retreated to Macau, where he died.

The Chinese and the British drew diametrically opposed conclusions from the Napier fiasco. In Beijing, the emperor read the exultant memorials from his officials and felt the barbarians could be held hostage with ease to compel their obedience. In London, the government realised it was rash to challenge the Qing dynasty without having sufficient force at its disposal to fight a war. It was in the interests of both sides for trade to continue, but this tragicomic misunderstanding meant that the period of calm was only a truce.

Britain and China did not declare war. They drifted into it. In 1838, Daoguang appointed Lin Zexu, a stern scholar-administrator of incorruptible rectitude, to exterminate the opium trade in Guangzhou. Today Lin is a national hero, memorialised in statues, in which he invariably looks severe and dignified in his robes of office, in the cities of the south. Lin won the emperor over with a memorial grounded in Confucian philosophy, arguing for a campaign against traffickers that would be tempered by the enlightened treatment of addicts and the sparing use of executions. The outcome of his efforts, however, was a disaster for China.

Upon Lin's arrival in Guangzhou as imperial commissioner the tempo quickened. He ordered local officials and the gentry to act against smugglers and dealers, relying on traditional methods of surveillance and psychological coercion to persuade the smokers themselves to abstain. Investigations, arrests and seizures of opium began across the region. Lin wrote a Letter of Advice to Queen Victoria in stylised court language, informing her that the emperor was 'in a towering rage' and deploring the arrival of barbarians selling a 'poisonous drug' in China which – he had heard – 'is very strictly forbidden by your country'. This was an error. In fact opium was not prohibited in Victorian England, where it was 'the aspirin and benzodiazepine of its day', consumed by all classes as pills and taken as a liquid in the form of laudanum, a tincture laced with alcohol. Its literary adherents included the poet Samuel Taylor Coleridge, who wrote his celebrated verses on Kublai Khan in a trance, and Mary Shelley's character Victor Frankenstein, who used laudanum to numb himself asleep. Once again, Anglo-Chinese incomprehension was mutual and complete.

Lin told the Chinese merchants in Guangzhou that the foreigners must hand over their opium stocks without compensation and sign bonds promising never to deal in the drug again. The traders agreed to surrender a token quantity of 1,056 chests. Unconvinced, Commissioner Lin seized two Chinese hostages and ordered the arrest of Lancelot Dent, head of the second largest foreign firm and president of the British Chamber of Commerce. Thousands of Chinese troops surrounded the riverside enclave where the foreigners lived and had their 'factories', compounds which housed accommodation, offices and warehouses known as godowns. The alarm was sent to Captain Charles Elliott, the British superintendent of trade, who was at Macau.

Elliott, a former naval officer, had been appointed by Lord Palmerston, the foreign secretary, who wanted to pursue a more robust policy towards China. Palmerston was a member of the Whigs, a political party which combined reforming zeal and a belief in the supremacy of Parliament at home with dedication to free trade and the expansion of British power abroad. The principal opium merchants, partners William Jardine and James Matheson, had his ear. Palmerston had an acute sense of what the public expected of its ministers in upholding British prestige. He also understood that to the Chinese, 'protocol was the essence of the tribute system', and forbade Elliott to submit to it.

Palmerston was not alone in his view. During this time of imperial expansion, it was unthinkable that the subjects of Queen Victoria should be subject to arbitrary prosecution by a foreign power. An Englishman could expect the protection of his own government, whether or not he was an opium trader like Dent, and no minister could agree that Englishmen must sign bonds acknowledging the jurisdiction of the emperor of China and submitting to trial and decapitation if they broke those bonds. The principle became known as 'extraterritoriality', and it was to vex relations between foreign powers and China until the Communist Revolution of 1949 put an end to it. For Palmerston, as for Elliott, it was a principle which created the conditions for war. For the first time, the Chinese were dealing with a representative of the British crown, not an employee of the East India Company. If that distinction was lost on Commissioner Lin, it was clear to Elliott. He did not have absolute powers but he had authority to call on his old service, the Royal Navy, and on British forces stationed in India.

Elliott arrived in Guangzhou to find himself blockaded with his compatriots. Facing the same dilemma as Lord Napier, he capitulated. The traders agreed to hand over 20,000 chests of opium and almost all were allowed to leave for Macau. To the rage of Lord Palmerston, Elliott undertook that the British government would compensate them for the loss. Cynics noted that the traders, stuck with a surplus of opium due to Commissioner Lin's campaign, must have gratefully received the government's generosity and

had inflated their stocks. But that was a British problem. Commissioner
Lin wrote a triumphant memorial to the throne. He supervised the
destruction of almost three million pounds of raw opium by hundreds of
labourers, who mixed it with water, salt and lime in trenches, then flushed
it into the river and out to the ocean while the commissioner prayed to the
spirit of the Southern Seas to bless his purifying deed.

Having expelled the British from Guangzhou, Lin found that American
merchants were willing to sign his bonds and step profitably into the
breach as middlemen in the legal trade in tea and silks. Obedient to the
law of unintended consequences, the commissioner pursued his quarry to
Macau, intent on stamping out British impudence for good. Lin's resolve
hardened after a Chinese farmer named Lin Weixi was killed in a brawl
with British sailors. Elliott, while paying compensation, refused to hand
anyone over to imperial justice. It was the principle of 'extraterritoriality'
again. Lin ordered war junks to blockade the Portuguese enclave while his
soldiers mustered on its fringes. Portuguese morale crumbled swiftly and
the British were told to leave. On 24 August 1839, Captain Elliott and his
companions boarded their ships and sailed across the gulf to anchor near
the best deep-water bay on the southern coast at Hong Kong, the 'fragrant
harbour'.

In London, where William Jardine had returned in wrath, the government put its faith in gunboat diplomacy. Advised by Jardine and his fellow
lobbyists, Lord Palmerston drew up a list of formidable demands for
China. Britain prepared a fleet commanded by Captain Elliott's cousin,
Admiral George Elliott, of sixteen warships, four armoured steamers and
troop transports. They carried an army of 4,000 equipped with artillery
and rapid-firing guns.

Speaking in the House of Commons for the Whig cabinet in the debate
of 7 April 1840, Thomas Babington Macaulay said Britons on the China
coast 'belonged to a country unaccustomed to defeat, to submission or to
shame; to a country which has exacted such reparation for the wrongs to
her children as has made the ears of all who heard it to tingle'. In response,
the young William Gladstone, at that time a Tory, uttered words which are
known in China to this day. 'A war more unjust in its origin, a war more
calculated to cover this country in permanent disgrace, I do not know and
I have not read of,' he said, adding that the British flag was hoisted on the
coast of China 'to protect an infamous contraband traffic'.

The war, when it came, was drawn-out but decisive. Between 1840 and
1842 the British won a series of victories. The fleet forced its way up the

Pearl River, bombarded Guangzhou and imposed a blockade of the city. British ships sailed north to threaten the Zhoushan islands, off the port of Ningbo. A broadside from HMS *Wellesley* put the inhabitants of Zhoushan to flight. British soldiers landed and raised their flag. An early British visitor, Sir George Staunton, had compared the charms of Zhoushan's harbour to those of Venice. Whoever possessed the small archipelago commanded the approaches to the Yangtze, the mightiest river in China.

At first the British aggression created shock at the emperor's Grand Council. This turned to fear as the fleet sailed on northwards to the forts guarding the Hai River, the water route to Beijing itself. Daoguang did what Chinese rulers have often done when facing failure: he replaced the official on the spot. Commissioner Lin, who had prided himself on aweing the barbarians into submission, was dismissed and exiled to the wintry borderlands with Russia.

A rich and sophisticated Manchu governor, Qishan, took over. He began negotiations with Charles Elliott. The English warships sailed south again while the envoys talked. Britain was demanding the cession of Hong Kong, a huge indemnity, direct contact with the throne and trade on British terms: in short, a manifesto to force open the old China and shatter its value system. For all his political skills, Qishan found himself in a plight that would be replicated in centuries to come by Chinese negotiators with the West. Confronted by a powerful opponent, assailed by conservatives at court, suspected by his emperor of being an appeaser, he miscalculated. Qishan appreciated that the handover of Chinese territory was the worst outcome and felt the English might trade Hong Kong for more money and new ports. But time was not on his side; the British resumed military action and instructions from Beijing took weeks to arrive. On 20 January 1841 the two envoys agreed the Convention of Chuanbi, which conceded the British demands and fixed an indemnity of 6 million silver dollars. Six days later Elliott proclaimed British sovereignty over Hong Kong, although he had no authority to do so. In return, Britain was to hand back Zhoushan.

Few agreements have been so swiftly and unanimously disowned by their principals. The emperor, aghast, dismissed Qishan and ordered his execution, a sentence later commuted to the confiscation of his wealth. He left Guangzhou in chains. The ire in London, though less draconian in its consequences, was compounded by surprise. Lord Palmerston could not understand why Elliott had traded Zhoushan for the 'barren island' of Hong Kong. The twenty-two-year-old Queen Victoria called Elliott's conduct 'unaccountably strange' and said he 'completely disobeyed his instructions and tried to get the lowest terms he could'. For his part, Elliott was the first but not the last British negotiator with China to face similar accusations.

A new envoy, the Anglo-Irish soldier and diplomat Sir Henry Pottinger, was appointed and Britain went to war with China again. Pottinger arrived from India in August 1841 with a new spirit of initiative. He refused to treat with a minor Chinese envoy, stiffened the backbone of the merchants, inspected the new building works at Hong Kong, rallied his soldiers and ordered the naval commanders to make ready, disdaining two severe typhoons. His amphibious campaign was daring and swift. The British captured Xiamen and Ningbo, retook the island of Zhoushan and launched an offensive in May 1842 to cut China's inland waterways, aiming to force a rapid surrender.

The war was shocking and psychologically transformative. At Ningbo, the gates were opened after British naval guns destroyed its nearby fortress. Pottinger ordered his men to 'remove, carry away or destroy public property (in which I include whatever belonged to the Emperor or his officers) ... and the official residences of the authorities, the granaries, timber yards, war junks and boats. I would carry this work of destruction of whatever buildings may be public to the extremest point ... burning any furniture or other articles found in them that may not be worth, or be too heavy, or cumbersome, for removal.' It was, he said, an act of retribution for the ill-treatment of Britons that would serve as 'an example and warning to other places'. Pottinger had been outraged to hear that survivors of a shipwreck, including the master's widow and two boys, had been manacled, put into bamboo cages and paraded to Ningbo amid 'the hootings and howlings of the assembled savages'.

The Chinese squandered their counter-attack at Ningbo by sending tribal levies from Sichuan province, armed only with long knives, to charge into the teeth of British grapeshot and land mines, while panicky raw recruits piled in behind them and were cut down in hundreds until blood ran in the streets. The slaughter repelled even those inflicting it. Such scenes were repeated on battlefields along the coast.

Cruelty was the currency of war, but the British found that in China they had discovered refinements to it which began to harden the hearts of Pottinger and his commanders. The body of a British private was found mutilated with his own razor, which had been used to cut off his ears and nose and to cut out his eyes, prompting an officer to reflect of the perpetrators that it was 'great proof of their ferocity ... amidst the horrors of their own situation, expecting almost immediate death'. At Zhenjiang, the Manchu garrison of 1,600 bannermen killed themselves rather than surrender, first cutting the throats of their wives to spare them from rape and murdering their own children. Contemporary British accounts told of soldiers treading amid heaps of Chinese bodies swollen and blackened from poison while corpses hung from roof beams and floated in shallow wells. Pottinger's biographer noted that he stored up these things in his mind and 'realised that he was dealing with a callous culture of a kind not previously experienced.'

The shock was many-textured. On the Chinese side, the suicidal loyalty of the Manchu clansmen was offset by a creeping suspicion that the dynasty could not count on its own Han Chinese subjects in its fight to survive. Rogues from the Pearl River Delta followed the British army to plunder and burn Chinese homes. The opium trade had created a nexus between the Westerners and all those criminals, secret societies and small merchants in the southern coastal cities who chafed against the hand of authority. Rumours of treachery spread among Manchu commanders, who saw spies everywhere among river junk captains, salt smugglers and rural bandits. Before the self-slaughter at Zhenjiang, the Manchu soldiers had turned on the local people in a reign of terror, murdering any who were thought to be suspicious.

Political as well as military considerations, therefore, compelled Daoguang to come to terms with the invaders. The seizure of Hong Kong was a decisive loss, and defeat in the first Opium War marked the beginning of the end for imperial rule in China. Western technology had won against raw bravery and the well-drilled British military confounded traditional Chinese generalship. The war did not overthrow the Qing system, but ultimately it eroded the Manchu dynasty's faith in itself and destroyed its people's confidence in it. After 1842 the Chinese ruling order was in retreat until, according to Communist histories at least, Mao Zedong founded 'New China' in 1949.

China was unlucky, too, in the political timing. In the summer of 1842 Britain needed a feat of arms to restore confidence in its own ruling elite after a catastrophic defeat in Afghanistan. During the retreat from Kabul in the winter of 1841–2 an entire army was lost, one of Pottinger's own nephews was killed and another was wounded and taken hostage.

This was a period in British political life of reaction versus reform, of a contest between the aristocracy and the rising new classes, and of a bold new debate over whether the right to govern was due to merit or to birth – a tantalising comparison, for those who knew of it, with the meritocratic elite chosen by examinations to serve the Chinese state, even if the emperor's Manchu clansmen held its great offices and commands. In the latter stages of the war Britain entrusted its ambitions in the field to the hereditary aristocracy: Lord Elgin, a brace of knights and an admiral of distinguished lineage, all of whom did their duty well, and in some cases heroically; while its diplomats on the China coast served foreign secretaries who included a duke, a viscount and five earls. 'It is almost impossible to picture the deference, the adulation, the extraordinary privileges accorded to the nobility in the first half of the nineteenth century,' a British historian of the period wrote. In 1842 the Duke of Wellington himself returned as commander-in-chief for life of the British Army at the age of seventy-three, unflinching in his view that 'the army was not to be dictated to by the House of Commons.'

Yet Britain's adventure in China also advanced a new elite. It created entrepreneurs who made fortunes and it promoted administrators like John Bowring, a liberal polymath who was knighted only when he became the fourth governor of Hong Kong, and Harry Parkes, a brash linguist and diplomat, 'a typical example of the self-confident go-getter of modest background who seized the opportunities afforded by the empire.' Notably, many of the men who governed the empire in the east or who prospered in it were Scottish or Irish.

There was more at stake for British policy in China than a 'barren rock' and profits from opium. It was also about power and control. The British army in China was led by gentlemen who purchased their commissions, a system upheld by Wellington, who felt it kept a connection between the army and the higher classes of society, avoiding the emergence of the type of professionally officered armies which had led to military despotism in Europe. Military prowess safeguarded British commerce and extended Queen Victoria's realms; it was not to be interfered with by elected politicians. A successful punitive expedition in Afghanistan and victory over the Chinese empire vindicated this opinion.

The Treaty of Nanjing, which sealed the British victory, was signed on 29 August 1842 on board HMS *Cornwallis* by Pottinger and three Chinese representatives: Qiying, Yilibu and Niu Jian. The documents were bound in silk. Each of the Qing emissaries imprinted them with a great red rectangular seal and inscribed the required assent in fine calligraphy. Sir Henry scrawled his signature across the page. During the exchange of courtesies, Qiying fed Pottinger several sugar plums directly into his mouth, saying this was an old custom.

Plums aside, there was nothing to sweeten the bitterness of the Treaty of Nanjing for China. It has been called the most important treaty settlement in China's modern history. It handed the island of Hong Kong to Queen Victoria and her successors 'in perpetuity', opened five treaty ports to foreign merchants, abolished the Cohong merchant monopoly, imposed an indemnity of 21 million silver dollars on China to be paid in instalments, set unspecified 'moderate tariffs' on trade and formally buried the grandiose language of subservience with an agreement that henceforth the countries would address each other as equals.

The agreement was seen by patriots as the first unequal treaty between China and a foreign power. But all treaties are unequal, for if a perfect balance existed between states no diplomatic agreements would be needed to keep the peace between the weak and the strong. The first concessionary treaty of the Qing dynasty had been made on China's Muslim frontier in 1835 with the Khan of Kokand, a predatory neighbour who dominated the trade route to Central Asia. It conceded a swathe of demands to the Khan, even allowing his consular representatives in China's far west to try cases and levy taxes on foreigners, the principle of extraterritoriality which caused such conflict with the Western powers. The trade concessions were similar to those granted to Russia at its solitary permitted trading post in northeast China. Appeasement, therefore, had been a tool for the Qing empire in the past. Mandarins like Qiying argued that it would work against the barbarians. The trouble was that it did not.

China had been wrenched open by the British but other nations soon followed them. In 1843 President John Tyler sent a Massachusetts congressman, Caleb Cushing, to negotiate trading privileges with Qiying. The treaty they signed allowed Protestant missionaries access to China, abolished attempts to prevent foreigners learning the Chinese language and conceded extraterritorial powers to American consuls. The French came afterwards, with an even more exacting treaty which compelled the emperor to issue an edict of toleration for Roman Catholics, abolishing a ban on missionaries instituted by his ancestors. As for the British, they could afford to build up their new possession at Hong Kong while others increased pressure on the Qing, for under a 'most favoured nation' clause attached to their own treaty they would receive the same benefits as those won by any rival power. This remarkably inept diplomatic bargain by Qiying robbed the dynasty of any chance to play the barbarians off against each other.

Despite this raft of concessions, which many Chinese saw as the start of one hundred years of humiliation, the foreigners were not satisfied. Qiying had persuaded the throne that the devil was in the details and that China would wear down the intruders by patience, rules and formality. During the 1840s the dynasty recovered its poise and foreign traders grew disappointed with their lot, even as Jardine Matheson sent a fleet of eighty clippers to run the opium trade, which grew to 60,000 chests a year.

At court, the view that China possessed a superior civilisation had not yet been shattered. But at the end of the decade a millenarian revolt broke out in eastern Guangxi province, inland from Hong Kong. It was led by a charismatic rabble-rouser, Hong Xiuquan, who declared himself to be the younger brother of Jesus Christ and proclaimed a Heavenly Kingdom of Great Peace. The Taiping rebellion against the 'Manchu demons' consumed the reign of the emperor Xianfeng, who succeeded Daoguang in 1850; and while its Christian origins initially attracted Western sympathy, the foreign powers soon perceived it as a threat, helped to finance and organise the Qing armies that put it down, then gazed on while some 20 million Chinese lives were lost.

In 1854, the British took advantage of the chaos to press for renegotiation of the treaty of Nanjing, demanding commercial access to all of the Chinese interior and legalisation of the opium trade. The return of Lord Palmerston as prime minister licensed the boldest counsels, while the xenophobic Qing governor at Guangzhou, Ye Mingchen, was haughty, provocative and indifferent, inciting the public to hatred of the barbarians while apparently unaware of the change in British policy which would lead to his defeat and death in exile.

The governor of Hong Kong, the newly knighted Sir John Bowring, found the *casus belli* he sought in 1856 when Ye's bravos boarded the *Arrow*, a lorcha, or sailing vessel rigged Chinese-style, that was owned by a Chinese, Fong Ah-ming, had been registered in Hong Kong, and was nominally captained by Thomas Kennedy, from Belfast. Its registration papers had expired but Bowring and his consul, Harry Parkes, brushed that detail aside. Rear Admiral Sir Michael Seymour sailed his fleet up the Pearl River, seized the forts guarding the approaches to Guangzhou and bombarded the city. Ye remained immovable, trade halted and a row broke out in Parliament in London.

A year later the British returned in force, joined by the French, after a delay in the arrival of reinforcements due to the Indian mutiny. This time

Guangzhou fell. The allies installed a joint commission to rule the city, exiled Ye to India, and appointed a puppet Chinese governor in his place.

An expedition commanded by Lord Elgin then headed north to threaten the port of Tianjin and the capital itself. This set off a battle between diehards and appeasers at the court of the ineffective young emperor. Caution prevailed; the dynasty capitulated and signed the Treaty of Tianjin, whose provisions were the harshest yet. Opium was to be taxed and regulated, more cities were opened up to commerce, foreign trade was permitted deep in the interior, Christian missionaries could evangelise and ambassadors would reside at Beijing. As a final touch, the Chinese character for 'barbarian' was banned from documents.

All this was shame enough, but the bitterest fruit to swallow was that state-to-state relations between the celestial empire and the barbarians would be conducted on an equal basis. With Western armies at his gates, and the Russians pressing on his northeastern borders, the emperor Xianfeng temporised while he clung to protocol. Foreign envoys might only come as if bearing tribute, travelling along the imperial post roads under escort, they might not ride in sedan chairs or carry weapons, and they would be allowed in only every few years. Fed up with such ineffable intransigence, and enraged by the murder of a group of his negotiators, including a correspondent of *The Times* of London, Lord Elgin marched on Beijing. The emperor fled, sending his brother, Prince Gong, to parley. In October 1860 the Anglo-French force looted and burned to the ground the summer palace of the Yuanming Yuan, the Gardens of Perfect Brightness, where Lord Macartney had displayed his wares for a more sagacious ruler of China. In the Convention of Beijing, signed by China, Britain, France and Russia on 24 October 1860, Britain was awarded the Kowloon peninsula facing Hong Kong island in perpetuity. Dissipated and worn out, Xianfeng died at the age of thirty the next summer.

Britain had taken Hong Kong island and the tip of Kowloon through victory in war. The next step of British acquisition would not be formalised for another thirty-eight years, but in the intervening period China became weaker and weaker. Japan joined the predatory powers around it, the enfeebled Qing dynasty sank into decay, elite reformers failed to save the established order and Chinese society was convulsed by rebellions and social chaos, while domestic production of opium increased and imports of the drug became less important.

By the end of the nineteenth century the opium trade no longer played a critical part in the struggle between foreign powers and China, but it has been termed 'the most long-continued and systematic international crime of modern times'. In China, there are frequent calls for Britain to apologise. The closest that any British government has ever come to a semi-official apology was the valedictory speech by the last governor of Hong Kong, Chris Patten, delivered in the dark and the rain at Britain's farewell ceremony, which was not attended by any Chinese leader, on 30 June 1997. 'This chapter began with events that, from today's vantage point, at the end of the following century, none of us here would wish or seek to condone,' Patten said. 'But we might note that most of those who live in Hong Kong now do so because of events in our own century which would today have few defenders. All that is a reminder that sometimes we should remember the past the better to forget it.'

For China, the long nineteenth century wound to a close with a further humiliation. This time disaster unfolded through an ill-advised war against Japan for control of Korea. The newly organised Japanese army defeated the Qing forces in a masterful land campaign and Japan's navy mauled the Chinese fleet. The Qing court sent its leading statesman, Li Hongzhang, to negotiate the Treaty of Shimonoseki, signed on 17 April 1895, whose exactions included the loss of Taiwan and part of Manchuria to Japan, acknowledgement of Japanese primacy in Korea and huge financial indemnities. As the dynasty reeled, France, Germany and Russia compelled it to grant leases of up to ninety-nine years on ports, cities and railways.

The Qing dynasty had been a prudent borrower. It had largely used domestic capital to finance its expansion of military arsenals, steelmaking and shipbuilding. Its total foreign debts between 1861 and 1894 have been estimated at around £12 million sterling, principally a British loan syndicated by the Hongkong and Shanghai Banking Corporation at a rate of 5 per cent and a similar loan from a consortium of German banks. In 1895 the imperial finances buckled under the indemnity to Japan. The Qing government faced a payment that has been calculated, with interest, at £54.5 million.

It could not hope to pay such a sum from its own resources. Not the least of its problems was that the payment was fixed in British sterling on the gold standard used by the West, while China itself still computed its revenues on the silver standard. Hapless, the empire had to turn to foreign financiers, setting off a scramble among the powers to finance the indemnity. The City of London, a Franco-Russian syndicate and the German banks competed to capture the loans. The bankers summoned their diplomats in aid. Count Witte, the Russian foreign minister, believed that financing the Chinese imperial debt gave St Petersburg leverage to extract railway concessions in Manchuria, built up its prestige at court and weakened the traditional power of Britain over Chinese affairs. In practice, most of the foreign loans to China up to 1913 passed through the hands of the Hongkong and Shanghai Bank after the Foreign Office abandoned its Victorian laissez-faire approach and stepped in with diplomatic support. The Hongkong Bank, too, was a victor of 1895.

The winner twice over was Japan. Its military triumph financed the birth of the modern Japanese capitalist system. The indemnity amounted to more than three times the annual national budget. A sum so large, paid in sterling, then the world's leading currency, had 'incalculable' effects on Japanese capitalism, according to a scholar of the period. It made it possible for Japan to join the top rank of global powers by adopting the gold standard in 1897.

The rentiers of the West did comfortably out of the coupons on their loans as the Chinese laboured to pay back the debt. Encouraged by the precedent, foreign powers would later impose further punitive indemnities for the Boxer Rebellion in 1901. For China, the disaster was complete. In the name of the balance of power, the British government instructed its minister at Beijing, Sir Claude MacDonald, to press for a lease of ninety-nine years on the land between Boundary Street in Kowloon and the Shenzhen River, together with the surrounding islands. The 'New Territories' became part of the Crown Colony of Hong Kong by the Second Convention of Beijing of June 1898 under a rent-free lease expiring on 30 June 1997. At the time, it seems that nobody gave much thought to the expiry date. The name of Li Hongzhang became a byword for shame, and was invoked by Deng Xiaoping himself when China decided to reclaim its sovereignty.

Hong Kong grew in population and prosperity as China went through decades of upheaval in the early twentieth century. A succession of governors built roads, improved the port, set up schools and hospitals, watched over the courts, kept an eye on the police and maintained the European social order while refraining from interference with Chinese customs and practices. Peace, commerce and the chance of prosperity attracted a steady flow of settlers from southern China under the British flag.

In China, the Manchu dynasty fell. A republic was set up, only to fall into warlordism and chaos. Bold young officers at the Whampoa military academy near Guangzhou led a nationalist movement, the Kuomintang.

Inland, the Communist movement spread. In the late 1920s the two sides fought one another while the Kuomintang ran a short-lived republican administration from Nanjing amid a fractured mosaic of warlord fiefdoms. The Chinese civil war was interrupted when Japan invaded the northeast in 1931, launched a war of conquest across China in 1937, then joined the Second World War on the side of Germany. War with Japan marked the end of Western dominance along the China coast. Hong Kong clung to its fragile post as a centre of British naval and intelligence operations, but even Winston Churchill admitted the colony was doomed and it fell to the Japanese on 25 December 1941.

In 1945, after the surrender of Japan, a British fleet sailed back into Victoria Harbour to reclaim the colony, despite grumbling from the United States and the Chinese nationalists. The work of reconstruction began. But as Hong Kong stabilised, China fell into a new round of civil war. It ended with victory for the Communists in 1949, an exodus from mainland China of defeated troops and refugees, and the eviction of foreigners from everywhere else on China's seaboard. While China passed into three decades of isolation under Mao Zedong, the skills and energy of the Chinese people in Hong Kong drove its outwards expansion by exports and trade. Under British rule they built a society that was contradictory – bustling, unequal, tradition-minded, modern, proud of its mainly Cantonese culture and infused with a sense of its own fragility.

Hong Kong was an outpost of capitalism and a precious asset to the West, but to the Communist regime in Beijing it was 'a problem left over from history'. So when Mao died and the Maoist experiment waned in the late 1970s, it was inevitable that the new rulers of China would turn their gaze south across the Shenzhen River to the city by the sea.

2

Reform and Opening Up

In November 1977, Deng Xiaoping left the chill of Beijing for the milder climes of China's southern coast to visit Guangdong province. The local officials received him with the deference due to a new member of the supreme body which ruled China, the Politburo standing committee. Twice purged, a victim of Mao's Cultural Revolution, Deng was on the way back to power after years in the wilderness. He had been disgraced and his family humiliated, while his eldest son, Deng Pufang, was left a paraplegic when Red Guards tossed him out of a window. But he remained one of the best-known politicians in China.

The country was all but prostrate. Its industrial plant was fossilised and dirty. The rhythm of agriculture beat like a faltering heart. The population was growing faster than the economy. In isolation, China's scientists had missed advances in technology, basic computing and public health that were transforming rival nations. The Soviet Union still loomed as a threat, while there had been scant reward from reconciliation with the United States. China had a huge army and nuclear bombs; one was obsolete and ill-led, the other of no practical use. Years of purges had drained the Communist Party of intellectual vitality; the survivors of the Mao era had narrowly defeated his widow, Jiang Qing, and her trio of allies, Zhang Chunqiao, Wang Hongwen and Yao Wenyuan, in the ultra-left Gang of Four.

Not everything was quite as bad as Deng's propagandists later made it out to be. There was little foreign debt. The harvests came in and people mostly did not starve. China was largely self-sufficient in energy. Crime was hardly known, punishment was harsh, and people would later recall a bleak sense of solidarity. The elite transition after Mao had taken place, remarkably, without bloodshed. The machinery of government worked in a creaking fashion. Unlike some societies in Africa and the Middle East, China had never collapsed absolutely, even at the end of the civil war. But after almost thirty years of socialism, most ordinary citizens were still poor. While neighbours like South Korea, Thailand and the Philippines were getting richer, China had fallen behind almost every other country in Asia. Hundreds of millions of Chinese people existed in absolute poverty. For millions, the repository of their hope for better things was Deng Xiaoping.

Photos and news reports from the visit to Guangdong showed Deng, who was small in stature, surrounded by officials smiling awkwardly as they towered over him, while he fixed them with an owlish interrogatory look, unfiltered cigarette in hand. It was, to all appearances, a ritual which unfolded according to the script. The local worthies gave talks and led Deng to inspect farms and factories. He swept through the cordoned streets and sped along causeways through green-gleaming rice paddies in a cavalcade of cars. Few of the public saw him. In closed sessions, however, Deng shed his amiable mask and became brusque. He sat impatiently while Guangdong's provincial party leadership briefed him on a security problem. They told him that in Bao'an country, which bordered the British territory of Hong Kong, there had been several mass escapes across the barbed wire.

The British had closed the border in 1950 after some three million people from China headed for Hong Kong, seeking sanctuary from war and revolution. More than 100,000 had crossed the small bridge at Lo Wu every day at the peak of the exodus in 1949. For the governor, Sir Alexander Grantham, enough was enough. His decision ended the tradition of free movement into Hong Kong which had endured since the foundation of the colony. It was a tradition abandoned with some heartache, as it spoke to a blissful confidence in the attraction of British rule. But it was not abandoned completely. Natives of Guangdong province could still come and go. Immigration officers gave them a language test. If a person responded in Cantonese, they could pass. It was a typically Hong Kong solution.

For its part, the new government of the People's Republic of China at first let its people go, content to see capitalists and supporters of the Kuomintang leave the country. In 1950, this *laissez-aller* view changed. China began to adopt the restrictions on travel common to socialist countries like the Soviet Union. By the time of Deng's visit in 1977, a harsh yet inefficient regime operated along the border.

Most of China's borders were with socialist countries or were remote, inhospitable and scarcely populated. Guangdong was special. It had been a point of entry and exit for centuries, a constant woe to the mandarins of the Chinese empire. The Communist Party, remembering the flow of arms and goods into wartime China from Hong Kong, did not intend to go the same way as the mandarinate. A bamboo curtain soon descended across the flatlands separating south China, the British capitalists in Hong Kong, and the Portuguese in Macau.

In 1951, the People's Liberation Army had expelled thousands of people from the border region. Those who were not residents of Shenzhen or who were politically unreliable were packed off to the interior of Guangdong. Five years later, the PLA designated three defence lines across the zone. It declared the frontier a prohibited area. People needed permits to cross into Hong Kong.

None of it had worked. In their thousands, people waded across the Shenzhen river, climbed spiky grass hills and hid in the bushes to dodge patrols on both sides of the fence. Obsessed with security, the Chinese authorities sent army units to hunt escapers and to deter others from trying. The party secretary of Guangdong admitted to Deng that the troops could not stop the flow. 'This is because the problem is our policy,' Deng cut in, 'the problem can't be solved by the army.' Deng said little more, leaving the officials to ponder his enigmatic words as he went back to Beijing. To challenge long-held party policy was not a route to promotion. Wu Nansheng, the provincial party secretary, decided to adopt the safer role of diligent pupil. He went to Shenzhen and demanded data.

'The huge contrast between the income of local people and that of farmers just across the river in the New Territories was thought-provoking,' stated an official Communist Party history. Wu learned that the per capita annual income of villagers in Shenzhen was 134 yuan, while that of villagers in the New Territories was roughly equivalent to 13,000 yuan. The official historian concluded: 'The problem of which Deng Xiaoping spoke was clear. The "front line" was also a "poverty line".'

To govern China in 1977 was a task that would have daunted a titan. The economy was rudderless. The Communist Party had decimated itself in campaigns and purges. Political life resumed slowly after one-man rule under Mao, who had died on 9 September 1976. Broadly speaking, there was a liberal faction in the party and a core of rigorous Marxists. They shared Lenin's doctrine that the party reigned supreme but disagreed on how to run a modern country. Beyond that lay a thousand nuances in the power network of big personalities, rival clans, regional loyalties and a chequered revolutionary heritage. Foreign governments and the Chinese people, who were not consulted, spent much effort trying to understand who was up and who was down. Divining the true state of affairs inside a command economy run in strict secrecy was exceptionally difficult. Fortunately, the passage of time has eroded party discipline so that much that in 1977 was a state secret is now known.

Zhao Ziyang began rural reforms to dismantle Mao's people's communes when he was party secretary in Sichuan province in 1975. He would later take the top position as general secretary of the Communist Party and become premier of China, but he fell from power in 1989. Through long years of confinement in his home in Beijing, he prepared a memoir which, after his death in 2005, was smuggled out and published abroad. It remains a rare authentic testament as to how China's leaders thought and acted in the days after Mao.

'For more than two decades, farmers had not had enough to eat after handing over the grains they had produced to the state after every harvest,' he wrote of the period before 1975. 'For many years – before and during the Cultural Revolution – we had been lagging in many respects, including urban construction, agriculture and people's living standards. To shift to a healthier economic state we had to go through a process of "relearning". In this situation it was impossible to attain rapid economic development.' Zhao, who was then a vigorous sixty-year-old, became an alternate member of the Politburo in 1977. He took a leading role in rebuilding the economy. 'I believed strongly ... that there was huge potential in foreign trade for the coastal regions. Our system and policies had suffocated it,' he wrote.

Eventually Zhao and Deng would fall out over the pace and nature of reform, setting off a grave crisis in the party's rule, but in the late seventies both men spoke openly of the need to change. 'Relearning' was an acceptable maxim of party methodology. 'In agriculture learn from Dazhai!' enjoined a Mao-era slogan in praise of a pioneering commune, whose achievements turned out to be fraudulent. 'In industry learn from Daqing!' went another exhortation inviting all to study the heroic work of oil drillers in Heilongjiang, in the bleak northeast.

Learning from foreigners, however, was still politically sensitive. China dispatched high-ranking missions to the West and to Japan in a sincere effort to examine different economic models, but such visits were stilted by protocol and hampered by the constraints of language and culture. In addition, there was always a well-founded suspicion on the Chinese side that the foreigners, while rolling out the red carpet, were chiefly intent on selling them things which China did not need and could not afford.

Deng hit on an idea. The government would learn from its compatriots in Hong Kong and Macau, who practised capitalism with Chinese characteristics. It would then deftly adopt such aspects as it saw fit in order to establish socialism with Chinese characteristics. There was an ideological elegance to his solution.

Deng turned to a trusted subordinate, Duan Yun. The two men had worked together since the 1950s. Little known outside China, and a minor figure in mainstream Chinese accounts of the period, Duan was to play a critical part in opening up the country.

Duan was born in 1921 in Ningxia province, a sparsely inhabited region of deserts and nomads, where turbulent ethnic minorities and an ancient population of Muslims lived alongside the Han Chinese. He joined the Communist Party at an early age and became a revolutionary bureaucrat, learning to master the paper flow of directives and petitions through which the leadership exercised its authority. It was good practice for the administration of government. By the early 1950s, the party was in control of the state, Deng was running its southwest China military administrative committee and Duan was the director of his office. According to a memoir 'Recalling Comrade Duan Yun', by the party author Hu Bangding, the two men operated so well together that they seemed to function as a single unit. 'Whenever Deng Xiaoping had something to report to the central committee he would pace up and down the office dictating out loud to Duan Yun. As Deng finished speaking, Duan would finish what he was writing. Deng would read it just once, sign it without hesitation and send it off to Beijing immediately. From this we can tell that Duan's skills as a note-taker were extraordinary.'

Duan was also an accomplished calligrapher and painter, the memoir said. In 1980 he held an exhibition of his works at the Beijing Art Museum. Despite his classical aesthetic bent and his political association with Deng, Duan got through the Cultural Revolution. By the late 1970s he was deputy director of the National Planning Commission. Both survivors, both attuned to the dissonances in elite politics, Deng and Duan understood one another and grasped the intricacies of what must be done. Their next move was a masterpiece of bureaucratic subtlety.

Without much fuss, the party elders in the State Council, the Chinese cabinet, were persuaded to approve the formation of a Hong Kong and Macau economic and trade investigation team. It sounded innocuous enough. Its mandate was to explore how Hong Kong and Macau had achieved economic growth, establish how overseas Chinese skills and capital could be attracted, examine the role of foreign investment and look at the use of advanced technology. Its members were drawn from the state planning commission and the Ministry of Foreign Trade. It would be led by Duan. The group would write only an outline report of its findings; the real message would be delivered in an oral briefing to the central committee.

The group's arrival in Hong Kong on 10 April 1978 drew widespread coverage in the colony's media. Government officials laid on a formal welcome, ensuring a respectful and smooth reception by the public. There were no protests to disturb the equilibrium of the men from Beijing, who wore the customary drab attire of safe-hands party functionaries. Nor did they spend too much time with the official Chinese representatives in Hong Kong, perhaps aware in advance of the ideological line they were sure to hear from the denizens of the Communist press agency Xinhua, known in Hong Kong as the New China News Agency (NCNA). Instead they concentrated on seeing and hearing things that were new to them.

Delighted, if unsure of what it might all mean, the British colonial government organised a visit to the stock exchange, meetings with businesses, calls on the administration and tours of the outlying parts of Hong Kong – those that could be seen so alluringly across the Shenzhen River. In Macau, the team collected more evidence, met the Portuguese authorities and saw for itself how a tiny enclave had become prosperous. They chose to overlook its casinos, gambling being a hideous social blight in Communist teachings. Instead they talked about industry, trade and development.

Duan and his associates returned to Beijing on 6 May 1978. Even today, the official history of their trip and their subsequent report, which was delivered in draft on 30 May, conveys a sense of the amazement and envy aroused inside a society which had been closed to the outside world for so long.

On 3 June, the leaders gathered to hear the report. Although most Chinese people have long forgotten it, the party's own account acknowledges it to be 'a truly great historical document which took the first step in reform and opening up'. It amounted to a renunciation of central planning and a step back from the universal application of Marxist-Leninist economics throughout Chinese territory. In fact, it reverted to the concept, neuralgic to many elders, that there could be separate zones inside China run on different lines from the rest of the country. The very idea had echoes of treaty ports, foreign privileges and all the hateful baggage of an era of humiliation which the party said it had brought to an end. Yet so compelling was the evidence that even the orthodox Maoist Hua Guofeng, the chosen successor to the Great Helmsman, would give it his blessing.

Today the principles laid out by Duan and his team seem bland statements out of any economics textbook. In a closed party session in the Beijing of 1977 – one can imagine the heavy armchairs, the steaming cups of tea, the weary heads rested on antimacassars and Deng's spittoon set near the seat where he reposed, chainsmoking – they came with political risk.

Duan told his listeners that the group had been shocked by the boom they found in Hong Kong and Macau. The British colony alone, the official report said, did US$19.6 billion in trade in 1977, compared with US$14.8 billion for all of China. Hong Kong had limited resources of land. It relied on foreign capital and advanced technology to spur its economic growth. Hong Kong had no controls on foreign currency and thus enjoyed abundant flows of capital for investment. Its labour costs were low. Light regulation allowed companies to import raw materials and advanced technological equipment with a minimum of trouble. Compared to the labyrinth of Chinese socialist bureaucracy, all those listening knew, this was a strange new world. In addition, Hong Kong's products were targeted at export markets.

The investigation team summed up by saying that China could copy the methods of Hong Kong. It could use foreign capital and cheap local labour, import raw materials or semi-finished products, bring in the necessary equipment and then export the finished articles to the world. Special zones would be set up to conduct the experiment, retaining political control and the ability to shut down trade if the party felt it had gone too far.

This was, perhaps, the first manifesto for globalisation heard inside the councils of the Chinese Communist Party. It shrewdly paid deference to the Four Modernisations, of agriculture, industry, national defence and science and technology, goals officially embraced by the party since the 1960s which had been revived, sloganised and rebranded to signify the new policies of Deng Xiaoping. Adopting the stirring tones favoured for party exhortations, it said: 'Now is the time to emancipate the mind and to act.'

(Within the ruling order, it paid to recognise the limits of such emancipation. We now know that Deng himself had no intention of allowing the Chinese path to socialism to be diverted into a social democratic experiment with a mixed economy, competing political parties and free elections. A dissident, Wei Jingsheng, issued a famous call for a 'fifth modernisation' – democracy – by posting an essay later in 1978 on the capital's short-lived Democracy Wall, where intellectuals and workers were allowed to let off steam. Wei went to prison for a total of eighteen years, and the 'fifth modernisation' remained anathema when he was finally deported to the United States in 1997 after Deng's death and the return of Hong Kong to China.)

The reformers succeeded in 1978 precisely by keeping politics off the agenda. What they proposed was radical enough. They suggested that China set up its first two Special Economic Zones in Bao'an county – henceforth to be known generally as Shenzhen – and the coastal city of Zhuhai, across the Pearl River. The official account summed up their appeal like this: 'Shenzhen and Zhuhai have conditions for developing export zones that are unmatched anywhere else in the country. Let us learn from Hong Kong and Macau! Imagine that after three to five years hard work we have constructed the infrastructure, developed a production base for industrial and agricultural exports and won over the hearts of our Hong Kong and Macau compatriots. Why, even tourists will flock to see it. Let the two counties become our new frontier cities.'

Even via the leaden prose of the propaganda department, it is hard to escape the sense of excitement and opportunity that must have seized those drafting the document. They had worked on the detail, too. There would have to be a 'special management approach' with the best cadres sent in to strengthen the local leadership in a far-flung and often unruly part of the south. The import and export department of the Ministry of Foreign Trade would deal with the authorities in Hong Kong and Macau. The provincial authorities in Guangdong were to be responsible for raw materials and equipment. They were authorised to take out loans and to import whatever was necessary through Hong Kong and Macau. As a sweetener, some of the revenues from the new exports would be kept by the local government.

The omnipresent organs of state security, whose caution was to be expected, were told to simplify the procedures for admitting Hong Kong and Macau 'compatriots' who held the necessary documents, and their 'foreign guests'. Small scale cross-border trade, outlawed amid the chaos of the Cultural Revolution in 1967, was to be restored. Fishermen along the coast would be allowed to have foreign currency and to trade, a signal

that restrictions on their movement would be eased. It all pointed to liberalisation. 'Socialism does not exclude a market economy,' was Deng
Xiaoping's refrain. He was in favour of the experiments at Shenzhen and
Zhuhai and would later add the old treaty port of Xiamen, in Fujian province, to the list.

In time, keepers of the Soviet flame would react against the Special
Economic Zones. Chen Yun, the most influential party elder after Deng
Xiaoping, insisted that central planning must prevail. He complained that
the zones would erode socialist economics, drain resources and investment from poorer parts of China, act as a distraction from the country's
main tasks and, worst of all, create a two-class economic model all too
redolent of the bad old days. 'Chen Yun had always objected to the idea of
Special Economic Zones,' wrote Zhao Ziyang in his memoir. 'He never set
foot in any of them. I've heard that he sent envoys to the zones who at first
returned with negative reports, but later were more positive. But he always
had doubts and objections.'

In the heady summer of 1978, however, Deng Xiaoping and the reformers had momentum on their side. It was clear to all that China had to try
something new, even if the factions disagreed as to exactly what that
should be. The central committee and the State Council agreed to the
recommendations in Duan Yun's report. This meant that both the political
leadership and the government had given it their imprimatur. Hua
Guofeng, the uncharismatic Maoist who chaired the Politburo standing
committee, issued a statement of approval 'in principle'. It marked a
moment when Hua – nominated by Mao as his successor because, the
chairman said in his last days, 'with you in charge my heart is at ease' –
conceded political ground. He told the planning officials, 'Go ahead and
do what you say.'

The decision in Beijing came almost too late for party officials strug-
gling to restore order and confidence in southern China. The period from
the second half of 1978 to the middle of 1979 saw a peak in numbers
escaping across the border to Hong Kong, according to official histories.
'Not only farmers but also officials, workers and their children, even teenagers and primary and middle school students were escaping,' said one
account. The statistics were fluid but one speaks volumes: in a village
called Liantang almost all the population, some 1,200 people, had fled,
half the land lay untended and production targets had been abandoned.

One day in July 1978, the party secretary of Guangdong, Xi Zhongxun,
set out on an inspection tour of the border areas. The journey is recounted

in unusually vivid detail in his official biography, a matter of significance because Xi Zhongxun was not only a credible Communist veteran whose opinions were taken seriously by the Politburo. He was also the father of Xi Jinping, who would become leader of China in 2012.

Xi Zhongxun was born to a rural landowning family in central China's Shaanxi province on 15 October 1913. Despite this dubious class background, his revolutionary pedigree was immaculate. As a youth he joined student demonstrations and was arrested by the nationalist police. While in prison, he became a member of the Communist Party in 1928. On release, he entered the turbulent military politics of northwest China, where he ended up with Communist guerrillas operating north of the Wei river. A natural leader, he emerged as chairman of a Soviet that spanned Shaanxi and Gansu provinces, then became one of a collective leadership running a big Revolutionary Base Area in the bleak northwest.

His story now quickens: Xi fell victim to a party 'rectification campaign' in 1935. Murderous purges of this kind periodically swept the Communist areas. Some scholars believe permanent struggle was ingrained in the Stalinist methodology imported from the Bolsheviks as an undeclared means to centralise authority in one man. Clan and regional rivalries also played their part. The official version is that Xi was days from execution when Mao Zedong arrived with his troops, spared his life and integrated Xi and his comrades into the Yan'an Soviet. This became hallowed in party history as the redoubt in which Mao recovered from the Long March and built the foundations of New China. Once rehabilitated, Xi Zhongxun was enshrined in the Yan'an pantheon of the First Generation of Chinese revolutionary leaders.

Xi prospered as a soldier, an administrator and a Marxist. The biography notes that he organised the war economy in the Communist-held northwest, served on the military staff and held an influential post in the party's organisation department, which governed personnel and appointments. In all policies, it emphasises, he was seen as moderate and pragmatic, rejecting radical left-wing methods and arguing for political solutions. This is, of course, officially licensed biographical hindsight. In post-revolutionary China, however, the records show him pursuing an astute strategy of bargain and compromise to put down a rebellion in the ethnic Tibetan province of Qinghai. He defused the class struggle in Xinjiang, a vast area of the northwest where the radicals sought to impose land reform and class divisions among resistant and bewildered herders.

The young Dalai Lama met Xi in Beijing in the 1950s and decided that he was 'open minded and very nice'. He gave the Chinese cadre a gold Omega watch. Yet Xi was no liberal but a loyal Communist trusted by Mao as a veteran of bloodshed, repression and pitiless intra-party feuds. He rose to supervise propaganda, education and culture policies from a vantage point at the apex of the party. He was on the central committee and served as a vice premier, reporting to Zhou Enlai. Let it be noted that these were the years of Mao's Great Leap Forward, a rash bid for industrialisation, years of socialist policies which caused a great famine. The death toll through starvation and violence of these doomed experiments has been put at 15 million by official statistics, at some 36 million by the investigative journalist Yang Jisheng and as high as 45 million by the critical historian Frank Dikötter of Hong Kong University.

It all came crashing down for Xi in 1962 when Mao unleashed a purge that served in its methods as a precursor to the Cultural Revolution. In classic style, it featured a contentious book, a long-forgotten disgraced cadre and a coded effort to rehabilitate an old enemy of Mao. The details were irrelevant: what mattered was that Mao saw it all as an 'anti-party plot'. Downfall, self-criticism and exile to a tractor factory swiftly ensued. In that time Xi's family was scattered and his son, Xi Jinping, was banished to the countryside to labour on a commune in Shaanxi. The venom of rivalry flowed through the party's veins in the following years as the Cultural Revolution spread across China. The radicals imprisoned and tortured Xi Zhongxun, then put him under house arrest. It was not until the death of Mao and the waning of the utopian Chinese Marxist experiment that he emerged. By 1978 he had recovered his physical strength and his political authority. Deng dispatched him to Guangdong.

The province was ripe for change. Its people had witnessed scenes that stayed with them for the rest of their lives. Zhang Weihang, an entrepreneur, recalled going out as a child with his mother during the latter days of the Cultural Revolution along the pleasant riverside walk in Guangzhou by the Pearl River: 'I looked up and I saw people hanging from the trees. They were hanging on the end of ropes. They were wearing simple blue clothes like everybody did at that time. I noticed that their bodies were slowly turning round and round, swaying in the breeze and the branches of the trees bent as they moved. My mother told me not to look up, to look straight ahead and to walk on. We were never to say anything to anyone about it.'

Zhang's parents were a highly cultivated couple who had worked in the Cantonese opera. Their home had been full of music and splendid

costumes and colours until drab conformity and political control strangled the art form. Worse, they had come from a wealthy background.
Zhang's grandfather had owned a factory before Liberation. They had lost
everything. The family lived in a two-room apartment. Zhang's parents
and his aunt slept in the same room as the boy and his sister, their beds
separated by light curtains. They shared a toilet and bathroom at the end
of the corridor with five other families.

Wei Han, a soldier in the People's Liberation Army, had similar recollections. Wei came from less refined origins but had made himself into a
self-educated peasant intellectual. Army service taught him discipline in
learning and he seized every educational opportunity the PLA offered its
troops. He served in bandit country down in the subtropical forests of
Yunnan province until his unit was posted to Guangdong. It was a time
when the party leadership began to use the PLA to restore order and to
put an end to the violent anarchy that had gripped cities and countryside
alike in the Cultural Revolution. But the PLA was not always effective and
its political mandate was ambiguous and ever-shifting. One day Wei was
marching with his unit along a dyke through the rice paddies when the
soldiers heard and saw a commotion to their left:

'It looked like hundreds of people lined up in the field, about two
hundred metres away. They were being shot by the Red Guards. Executed.
We saw the gunsmoke and heard many shots. They fell over like ears of
corn or like animals when they are killed in the village. All of us soldiers
were shocked. How could this be? Killing Chinese people? We were young.
I had been a Red Guard, I had even led a march to Chairman Mao's birthplace in Shaoshan when I was a teenager. But it was still very shocking to
see this. My comrades and I said we must intervene. But our officers were
very strict. They said: "Men! This is nothing to do with us. We are PLA
men doing our duty. This is political work and not for us. Keep your eyes
on the road and keep marching ahead." We obeyed of course. But none of
us could ever forget what we saw.'

For decades ordinary Chinese had kept their eyes on the road ahead
and had not dared to look around them. That was why, one day in the hot,
humid season, Xi Zhongxun set out on a journey that opened his eyes. The
trip came shortly after the summer solstice, his biography says, a reminder
that even in Communist China, the passage of the heavens was associated
with harvests and plenty. Xi rode in a seven-seater minibus with Wang
Nanguo, a local party official, and Zhang Hanqing, deputy editor of the
Nanfang Daily, a regional newspaper, who left an account of their trip.

'July and August were harvest time,' Zhang recalled, 'but we did not see any busy farming in the fields to the south. Xi was visibly upset. Seeing this scene, a heavy shadow fell upon Xi Zhongxun's heart.'

On the way back to Shenzhen, the minibus stopped by the side of the road. Its occupants watched PLA soldiers seize two fugitives and handcuff them. 'Where will these men be held?' Xi asked officials at the scene.

'There's a temporary shelter in Liantang, where people who are caught crossing the river are taken first and held overnight. They are sent on elsewhere the next morning. It's like this every day,' came the reply.

It was dark when the minibus arrived back in Shenzhen along the narrow country roads. Xi ordered the driver to find his way to the temporary shelter. He was dismayed at what he found. The official biography provides an account that, while undoubtedly varnished for propaganda purposes, conveys the political message of the moment: 'Socialism is supposed to be so good because we are masters of our own destiny, so why do you go to Hong Kong to be slaves and to be exploited?' Xi asked the fugitives huddled in the shelter.

'We are poor and there's not enough to go around,' said one, 'and it's easy to find a job in Hong Kong.'

The party secretary of Bao'an County, Fang Bao, told his eminent visitor that people who made it to Hong Kong began to send money back shortly after they got a job. Their families would be able to build new houses within a year or two. That is why they took risks to cross what the party history defined as 'the poverty line'.

Desperation led to scenes that never appeared in the Chinese media. The detention centres for captured escapers in Shenzhen were horribly overcrowded. One was built for 400 people but held up to 3,000. In the summer heat, there was a constant stink from poor sanitation. Drinking water ran short. The sick and injured had to fend for themselves. Ominously for the party authorities, law and order teetered on the verge of breakdown. 'During repatriations some people jumped out of the vehicles, there were crowds lying in wait and stealing from them,' says the official biography of Xi, 'there were repeated cases where people set upon the escorts, beat them up and stole their weapons. For security reasons the escorts resorted to handcuffing the escapers and roping them together but this also caused a bad effect.'

Episodes of anarchy might stain the record of the most ardent party official and Xi was well aware that something must be done. It would be tempting to be sceptical of the official biography's rendition of his strategic oversight. The evidence, however, is that Xi resisted the instincts of the police to stage a merciless crackdown on escapers. There was another element in his decision-making. On their way back from Hong Kong, the investigation team led by Duan Yun had stopped in Guangzhou to call on him. They all agreed that it was time to learn from Hong Kong and Macau. All that was needed to restore security were prosperity and hope.

Xi called a meeting of party officials and heads of government departments. 'These fugitives are our fellow countrymen and can't be treated as our enemies,' he told them, 'how can we call them stowaways if their own living conditions aren't good enough to solve their problems? There are contradictions among the people, not between us and some enemy. We should not just catch people. We should build up our inland areas and lure them to our side.'

He proposed that the detainees should be set free and sent one of his deputies, Huang Jingbo, to Shenzhen with orders to let them go. The result was another outbreak of anarchy. Rumours spread like wildfire that the amnesty meant the border was open. More than 70,000 people from townships in the border region rushed to the frontier posts and tried to force their way through. 'Only after the Shenzhen municipal party committee and the border forces tried their best to dissuade them through education did the situation calm down,' the official biography states coyly. More than eight hundred people did succeed in escaping and there was the inevitable official inquest. 'On learning the facts, Xi Zhongxun felt that he had made a hasty decision to release all the detainees before taking preventive measures, a decision which was not in line with the reality along the border. Xi made a self-criticism and realised that these escapes would only stop when the mainland had reformed and its living standards had been raised up,' it said.

The two-volume biography from which this anecdote comes is itself a revelatory example of political construction. The first volume was published in 2008, four years before Xi Jinping, the subject's son, came to supreme power. The second volume appeared in 2013 after the tumultuous succession of 2012 and may thus be presumed to take a more cautious approach about such things as errors and self-criticism.

It was written by a trusted party historian, Jia Juchuan, who began work on his subject in 1996. He was a native of the dry, poor central province of Shaanxi, where the elder Xi spent part of his 'revolutionary journey' in the Communist Party base areas during the war against Japan. The biography was approved by party leaders, a sign of esteem which guaranteed the author access to his subject. 'Old Xi was still alive,' wrote Jia, recalling that he felt 'great responsibility but very lucky'. As the task progressed, up to eight other contributors joined an editorial committee but by a collective decision Jia was named lead author. The text is, naturally, a homily in hindsight but the lessons for Xi Zhongxun and his comrades in 1978 contain a historical truth: reform could not be delayed.

The Chinese minister who called on Sir Murray MacLehose, the British governor, in December 1978 was also a veteran of Hong Kong. Li Qiang had been sent by the Communist Party through nationalist-controlled China in 1929 to set up a secret radio station in Kowloon. He was only twenty-four at the time.

In a less crowded age Li would merit a biography of his own. Spy, scientist and ideologue, China's foreign trade minister had come late in life to the polished corridors of officialdom after a career at the hard end of revolution. He had no love for the British. At twenty, Li was a student leader in the May 30th Movement of 1925, a campaign launched against Western imperialism, named for the day when the Shanghai Municipal Police, under British officers, shot dead strikers and protesters in the city's international settlement. The incident drove many youths in Shanghai to join the revolutionary movement; to patriots, it evoked all the worst aspects of the foreign presence in China: extraterritoriality, exploitation, the arbitrary use of force and brutal repression. In its aftermath, protest strikes and boycotts spread down the coast to Hong Kong. While an array of Chinese and international legal luminaries held inquiries (the foreign-led inquiry cleared the police), the young Li and his comrades were fired up.

According to his official biography, Li became an expert bomb-maker during the workers' armed uprising. He moved rapidly to the core of the party and was noticed by its strategist, Zhou Enlai. The party would call upon him to don various masks – in the thickets of factional rivalries of the 1930s, in the Soviet Union, in organising a gigantic arms industry deep in the interior. Finally he would don the mask of diplomacy to meet foreign envoys and the colonial governor of Hong Kong. Li was recognised early on for his scientific prowess but he was no colourless academic. His career was steeped in political violence, formed by espionage and marked by a lifelong suspicion of traitors.

Zhou entrusted him with setting up the party's first underground radio station in Shanghai. He had to find and train a group of ardent young talents under the noses of the Kuomintang, their street-smart gangster allies, the colonial police Special Branch, Japanese military intelligence and a slew of other interested parties. Li made it a success. The radio station in Kowloon was a second link in the party's propaganda chain. This, too, succeeded without being noticed by the British. The stations were soon broadcasting messages from the central committee across the country.

Li evaded the treachery and massacres that decimated the Communist Party in Shanghai in 1927. It is said that his name was among those later betrayed to the nationalists by Gu Shunzhang, the party's most notorious traitor of the 1930s. The mild-mannered Zhou Enlai ordered Gu's family to be killed in reprisal; one lurid Nationalist version has it that the victims were strangled and buried in the concrete floors of houses. Li escaped to Harbin, a city in the northeast borderlands with Russia, then made it to Moscow. There he trained in telecommunications. He published research papers on radio transmissions that won official recognition from the Soviet scientific authorities; one theorem, the Chinese history says, was known as the Li Qiang formula.

As if this was not adventure enough, Li returned to northern China to join Mao and Zhou in the drab Loess Plateau around Yan'an. Fortified in their isolation after the Long March, the Communists decided to set up their own arms industry. The party history credits Li with masterminding the construction of weapons factories, munitions plants, steel mills, pharmaceutical laboratories and oil refineries. The first guns were ready in 1939 although the scale of production was modest. None the less, Li had established plants capable of turning out rifles, light artillery, grenade launchers, grenades and mortar shells, as well as repairing equipment that came in from the field. After the Communist victory in 1949, basking in praise from Mao himself, Li took charge of the development of the radio industry, presided over the Yan'an academy of natural sciences and devoted himself to training a generation of technicians and scientists for the 'New China'. Like many in that time of rapture, Li felt that he was in his element.

Once again, however, Mao had need of his talents and Li submitted to the party's will. With fluent Russian, scientific renown and managerial experience, he was chosen to be China's minister of foreign trade. In those days trade meant commerce with fraternal socialist countries. Li navigated the courtship with the Soviet Union, oversaw a period of co-operation and then managed the abrupt split between the two in the 1960s. The old spy's craft came in handy as China did its best to keep state secrets and technical data from the Soviet side.

Li's stature at the core of the party and the state served him well during the Cultural Revolution. So did his sheer enthusiasm for risk-taking. At the age of sixty-five, Li made a secret visit to Vietnam and travelled down the Ho Chi Minh trail to see for himself what China was getting for its billions of dollars in aid to the war against America. He was evidently unhesitating in his support: in 1995 the Vietnamese government would award him its medal of friendship.

In economics, he was a pragmatist. When Richard Nixon cut the link between the dollar and gold in 1971, Li saw an opportunity. The world's monetary system trembled after the American president unilaterally cancelled the convertibility of its leading currency into precious metal and imposed wage and price controls. Few in Beijing understood the ironic connectivity of the move: Nixon was fighting inflation unleashed by spending on the Vietnam War, in which China was among those financing the Communist side. As a good Marxist, Li went to his boss, Zhou Enlai, and persuaded him to take advantage of the chaos gripping capitalism. China expanded its foreign exchange operations in Hong Kong and took tighter commercial decisions in foreign trade, most of which flowed through the Pearl River ports. Within a year, Zhou praised his subordinate for reaping a gain of $3 billion.

During the turbulent period after the death of Mao, Li survived the vicious politics that accompanied the fall of the Gang of Four to emerge as a voice of renewal. 'After the Cultural Revolution the septuagenarian Li Qiang, with his profound knowledge, broad vision and keen thought, was the first to propose to the central government the use of foreign loans, he promoted opening up to the wider world and even brought the first Coca-Cola production line to China,' the official hagiography stated. Li served as minister of foreign trade for twenty-nine years. And when he died of liver cancer, at the age of ninety-one, in September 1996, there was just a small sum in his deposit account, a gratuity from the Chinese Academy of Sciences. This was the man who walked into Government House to meet the twenty-fifth governor of Hong Kong.

Crawford Murray MacLehose, Baron MacLehose of Beoch, KT, GBE, KCMG, KCVO, DL, was the longest serving governor of the colony. His four terms in office covered more than a decade between 1971 and 1982. Towering in his customary dark suit at more than six feet tall, he appeared to all intents and purposes to be a living epitome of the British establishment in the east.

Rugby School, Balliol College, Oxford, a 'good war', the Foreign Office; in hindsight his progress can appear effortless. But MacLehose applied a Scottish rigour to his work and had reserves of intellect that made him a scholar of the Chinese language at a time when that skill was scarce. His career, like many others, shaded into the byways of intelligence during the Second World War, when he had trained Chinese guerrillas to operate behind Japanese lines.

MacLehose was not a soft pair of hands. He was picked for hard postings; none harder, perhaps, than his period as private secretary to George Brown, the Labour foreign secretary, in the late 1960s. Brown was prone to flashes of brilliance – he claimed credit for the UN resolution 242 of 1967 that still defines the parameters of peace in the Middle East – but was more often erratic and emotional. MacLehose needed all his diplomatic talents to pacify his master and to navigate the cross-currents between the foreign secretary and his prime minister, Harold Wilson. Trusted by both, his reward was a job as ambassador to South Vietnam in 1967, the critical year when American policy buckled. Wilson was desperate to keep Britain out of Lyndon Johnson's war. It was a posting that called for the sharpest political skill, broad shoulders and a security clearance that let the ambassador see the whole chessboard, from the Mekong Delta to Beijing and Moscow. It was apt preparation for what came next.

The surprise, for most colonial residents, was that when MacLehose arrived as their new governor in 1971 he came not as a walking relic, all stuffed plumage and arch protocol, but as a reformer. Like many civil servants, he had absorbed the ideas of post-war Labour governments even if he despaired of their efficient implementation. Hong Kong provided a laboratory for moderate social progress and his autocratic powers swept away tiresome obstructions, although, naturally, committees there were in plenty. In short order, among other edicts, he extended compulsory education, set up a house-building programme, built the Mass Transit Railway, brought in labour protection, raised the paltry social security payments for which Hong Kong's old and sick were eligible, established the Independent Commission Against Corruption and made Chinese an official language.

He was, in short, the kind of social democratic reformer whom Marxists loathed. He had, however, one pragmatic conviction from which he did not deviate and which, if the Chinese guessed it, undoubtedly informed their decision to deal with him. As a veteran of Hong Kong and China, MacLehose was convinced that importing democracy to Hong Kong was a bad idea. It would alienate China, he argued in a stream of minutes and briefings, and China would inevitably take control of Hong Kong no matter what any British government could say or do about it. It was hard, then, to conceive of a better fit for diplomacy than the British and Chinese representatives who came face to face when Li Qiang visited the colony in 1978.

The highlight was luncheon at Government House. It was a moment to be savoured by the Chinese visitors. Guards snapped to attention as Li's car swept into its semicircular drive. Deferential, white-jacketed staff stood poised with refreshments. The governor greeted his guests with the formal yet easy charm honed on a host of minor royals and grandees. Inside, the grandeur of stucco and colonnade was tempered by the comfortable furniture installed by the British to create the atmosphere of a Norfolk country house wherever they governed, beneath palm or pine. The Chinese, one of the visitors recalled, looked around with great attention, perhaps unaware that politeness was a weapon deployed to considerable effect in the service of the Crown.

MacLehose had none of the hardened, conspiratorial experience of his guest but he was steeped in the administrative complexities of Hong Kong, grasped its commercial life with an understanding that eluded Marxist central planners and foresaw opportunities that would create winners on both sides. 'MacLehose did a lot of good things for the people of Hong Kong after he became governor in 1971,' an official Chinese history conceded. 'Hong Kong's remarkable economic performance in the 1970s is inseparable from Mr MacLehose's contribution.'

Over luncheon, the talk was cautious but cordial. The British side had endlessly rehearsed the agenda, staking out positions that the Chinese would eventually bat away. The Chinese had to do little more than state what Deng Xiaoping had ordained; that Hong Kong would revert to China in 1997 but that it would do so through negotiations, not by a revolutionary act. Afterwards, British officials expressed relief. Li had been formal but courteous. To the Chinese the significance of the moment was grand. 'Li Qiang was the first person holding the rank of minister to visit Hong Kong since the foundation of New China,' the *People's Daily* later recalled.

For the Chinese, the colonial administrators were the supplicants once again and a natural balance was restored. For the British, the opportunity to open a dialogue with Beijing was a boon. The politics were set fair. In due course an invitation arrived from China. The governor was to visit the capital and to meet Deng Xiaoping himself. Before that happened, however, the Chinese leader was to stage a political *coup de main* that would transform his country and shape the destiny of the world for the remainder of the twentieth century.

'From the 18th to the 22nd of December 1978 the Communist Party of China held the third plenary session of the 11th Central Committee in Beijing,' read the dry communiqué, which gave no hint in its preamble of the drama that had taken place. The session was called at the behest of Deng Xiaoping, whose popularity and political power were at a peak. Restored to an array of offices in 1977, his energy and drive commanded enthusiasm among administrators and people alike. Slowly, officials had begun to accept that the risks of compliance were low. Traumatised by decades of seesaw politics, in which the correct line one week might be heresy the next, many cadres had habitually opted for the time-honoured policy of inaction much as their imperial predecessors had done. Deng planned to use this plenary session to formalise his changes and to establish a party line that would give security to officials called upon to carry out the decisions of the government.

He had no fear of a genuine popular uprising. Forgotten in the images of chaos and confusion stereotypical of the period is the fact that China's internal security apparatus kept its Stalinist grip throughout the 1970s. The country was stable. A panopticon system of residence permits, internal travel authorisations and regulations tying every citizen to their *danwei*, or work unit, allowed the authorities to quench any spontaneous action and to orchestrate whatever the party decreed. It was not infallible; there were riots, outbreaks of lawlessness, crime waves and noisy protests all over the country. But the enveloping power of the state, perfected over decades of repression, eventually crushed all opposition and swallowed up opponents. Plus, Deng was genuinely popular. A sign of his enduring charisma came in the summer of 1977, when Deng made one of the dramatic gestures, replete with symbolism, that punctuated his public career.

The Hong Kong youth football team had come to Beijing to play China's own young footballers. The match, on the hot evening of 30 July 1977, was in the Workers Stadium, a squat arena surrounded by apartment blocks in a grid of streets north of the diplomatic quarter. One can imagine the noise, the sweat, the 80,000 crowd, almost all male, the thousands of bicycles left outside, the drab clothes, the peanut shells and cigarette stubs underfoot and the reek of collective humanity.

There was a burst of applause as the two teams trooped onto the pitch. Then a short, lean figure walked briskly up to the rostrum. A contemporary Chinese account gives a breathless, but most likely accurate, description of what came next:

'Deng Xiaoping has come to watch the football! As the news was broadcast by loudspeakers, the entire Workers Stadium became a sea of joy. Tens of thousands of hands were waving at the same time. The applause was thunderous and enduring. Deng, who had been silent in the political sphere for more than a year, was in lively spirits, waving to the spectators and the Hong Kong players. Many shed emotional tears.'

With one apparently innocuous appearance Deng had tested his own popularity, presented himself as a leader for all Chinese and sent a message that his compatriots in Hong Kong would play a part in his vision for the nation.

The same account explained: 'Hong Kong has become a living chess piece for the modernisation drive, international relations and the reunification of the motherland. In the context of Deng Xiaoping's vision, the issue of Hong Kong is a paramount one.' Such gestures won easy applause, but the Chinese leadership faced a raft of huge and fundamental policy decisions far exceeding the importance of a single coastal city under colonial rule. It was notable, however, that in a far-sighted way the Chinese leaders integrated policy on Hong Kong into the politics of reform and made it a talisman of patriotic integrity that also served as a signal that China would be more open to the world. It is difficult, today, to understand the profundity of that change to tens of millions of Chinese people.

To underline the commitment to Hong Kong, but equally to separate it from the other functions of government, the State Council, China's cabinet, agreed in secret in April 1978 to set up a Hong Kong and Macau Affairs Office (HKMAO). Although its existence was not officially disclosed, this body would be the interlocutor for British and Portuguese negotiators. Its first task, though, was 'to clarify certain erroneous far-left policies and to improve relations with the business communities of Hong Kong and Macau'.

The plenary session was one of those gatherings beloved by Communist regimes in need of a rubber stamp. The Soviet model, adopted in various forms from Budapest to Baghdad and Pyongyang, was meant to impart legitimacy to decisions already taken at the apex of power. It moved through a liturgical cycle of congresses, central committees and plenums, ordained to prove the party's fidelity to its origins and to remind party members that they belonged to an elect. Perhaps in the hope that the general public might grow bewildered and weary, the tone was generally

ponderous and the communiqués leaden to the point of satire. The
Chinese version, however, often included authentic backstage revolutionary drama and shrill speeches, which to this day can often come to an
operatic crescendo. In Beijing, politics was not suspended at all, merely
enacted behind a screen.

Officially, the meeting that opened on 18 December 1978 is called 'a
great turning point'. Recent Chinese and foreign scholarship has shown
that it was not quite that. Many of its policies were worked up in small
groups organised by Deng beforehand and its decisions were likely
ordained in advance by the sheer weight of his influence. But its political
significance was undoubted. It would be cited by leaders for a generation
to come as validation of reform and opening up. 'It ended two years of
wandering about since the crushing of the Gang of Four ... and broke
down the guiding dogmatism and the personality cult,' an authorised
history declared. Its conclusions shook the Communist Party to its core.

All known Chinese sources are clear on one point that seems to evade
foreign commentators. Deng Xiaoping and the leaders of the Communist
Party of China took these steps *because* they were Marxist-Leninists and
not because they were closet capitalists quietly subverting from within, or
geriatric ditherers who knew the game was up. They would not ultimately
roll back the frontier of the state or hand over the commanding heights of
the economy to multinational corporations; that was wishful thinking on
the part of foreigners. The leaders believed that there was a Marxist analysis that fitted China's conditions. It called for a flexible approach to the
economy to make people richer. They accepted that some would get rich
faster than others, verily a contradiction among the people, as Mao would
have said. But to read the memoir of Zhao Ziyang and the speeches of
other leaders at the time is to understand that they genuinely believed
there was a Chinese road to socialism and that it must lead through stages
that would have offended a purist. The goal was the thing.

The meeting that December threw out the 'two whatevers', a leftist
maxim that said whatever decisions Mao had made must be upheld and
whatever instructions Mao had given must be followed. This was a formula
for static authoritarian government. China needed dynamic change, not a
priesthood clinging to immutable doctrines. 'We must re-establish the
ideological line of emancipating the mind and seeking truth from facts.
We should stop using the slogan of "class struggle" and made a great decision to shift the work of the party and the country to economic
construction, reform and opening up,' the final statement said.

In this lay a claim that would later be contested by Maoists, the ultra-left and the discontented. Deng Xiaoping claimed to be restoring the party's ideological line of empirical Marxism, not abolishing it. 'Correcting the wrong ideas' was the first premise of the meeting. The second was to 'restore the party's tradition of democratic centralism'. Broadly, this hallowed Communist principle held that party members could debate a policy before it was passed but all must uphold it afterwards. It remains a keystone of what is known as 'the people's democratic dictatorship'. It was a step away from the fawning courtiers around Mao's poolside villa but a far cry from a full-throated political assembly. None the less, to politicians emerging from the twilight of an imperium to build a form of collective leadership, it was an insurance policy.

The plenum also paid due deference to the rule of law, civil rights and the protections enshrined in the constitution, none of which have meant very much in the decades since 1978. Ominously for the rule of law, it established the party's own inquisitorial wing, the Central Commission for Discipline Inspection, wielding powers over errant party members outside the legal system. A generation later, the commission would serve the interests of Xi Jinping by destroying his foes in a selective 'anti-corruption' campaign. At the time, though, the plenum's most effective decisions were to push forward agricultural reform, forging a path between the old guard and the new, and to give its approval to the principle that China should reform and open up.

The year 1978 in China changed the lives of most of humanity. It set in motion one of the great developments of the late twentieth century by making it possible for China to emerge as a giant manufacturing power, thus allowing the creation of a globalised economy. In July 1979, Deng Xiaoping climbed the Huang Shan mountain to symbolise his energy and stamina. The following year he secured the appointment of three supporters to the Politburo standing committee. They were Hu Yaobang, later general secretary of the party, Zhao Ziyang, an ardent reformer, and Wan Li. Under their guidance the Shenzhen experiment gathered momentum. In Hong Kong, bankers, lawyers, traders and developers all thirsted to join in. It was the start of the great proletarian commercial revolution.

Successful reform in the Communist Party depended upon winning bureaucratic legitimacy. After the Third Plenum, the architects of this new China had to transform political will into acts of government or risk everything. Orthodox Maoists and radicals stood ready to pounce if failure and chaos ensued. The archives of Guangdong province reveal the care Xi Zhongxun took to protect himself against political criticism and to allay the ever-present fear of regional secession. His game was, on the face of it, impeccably played.

On 3 April 1979, Xi travelled to Beijing. 'He went carrying the expectations of 50 million people in Guangdong,' the province's official account stated. Xi gave himself two days to prepare for a central work conference at the Jingxi hotel, a drab government-run place where great decisions could be taken undisturbed.

He took the floor on the morning of 5 April. In the chair was Hua Guofeng, the loyal Maoist who held the office of party chairman. Hua had served alongside the Gang of Four. But he engineered their downfall after Mao's death in 1976 and emerged as a political survivor to be hailed, for a while, as 'the wise leader'. All those gathered at the Jingxi hotel on that spring morning of 1979 knew, however, that Hua's power was on the wane. He is seen today as a transitional figure, doomed to lose office and to vanish into obscurity, unpersecuted but unsung, until his quiet death in 2008.

Xi, the rising man, spoke bluntly. Power and economic management in China were too centralised, he said. It was not enough to 'expose contradictions' in theory, it was time for practice. The relationship between the centre and the provinces had not been handled well. He said Guangdong was close to Hong Kong and Macau, it was full of overseas Chinese hungry to do business. Let Guangdong go first, he argued, and watch the results.

Hua interjected sharply. 'Comrade Zhongxun, what rights do you want?' he asked.

Power, Xi replied. Guangdong, he said, was like a sparrow, a bird which in Chinese culture symbolised spring and happiness. 'Though the sparrow is small, Guangdong is fully equipped, it is like a big sparrow, with 50 million people, the size of a country, even two countries.

'Right now, the province has too little power. Central government control is too rigid and it is too bound up together to allow the economy to develop. Our request is that – under the central leadership of course – just let go a little and liven things up a little. In this way it will make things better for both local and national interests.'

This promising region of China was being strangled by state planning, he argued. It was seriously short of electricity because oil supplies for power stations were not guaranteed and production could come to a halt. As a result Guangdong had to buy electricity from Hong Kong to keep its factories humming. It was ironic, he said, that the People's Republic was exporting the very oil to Hong Kong that generated power in the colony to be sold back to China! 'Calculate the amount,' Xi told his listeners, 'the capitalist in Hong Kong buys 100,000 tons of heavy oil which they use to generate electricity and then resells it to Guangdong. They can make a profit of three million yuan. For our country this is unreasonable and uneconomic.

'Guangdong can contribute more foreign exchange to the country as long as it is allowed more flexibility. These are all institutional issues which must be addressed.'

It was a high-risk political pitch. The momentum of the times, however, was on Xi's side.

About two weeks later the Politburo convened to discuss the plan. This time Xi faced a heavyweight lineup. There sat Hua Guofeng once again, along with his deputy, Li Xianian, a leaden-faced apostle of orthodoxy. But Deng Xiaoping was keen. He brought along Gu Mu, a vice premier he entrusted with key tasks in the drive to reform.

The idea, they heard, was to open up Shenzhen, the town of Zhuhai on the Pearl River Delta, and the port of Shantou as 'trade co-operation zones'. They were near Hong Kong and Macau, bustling with overseas Chinese and ripe for investment.

Deng was brisk. He had heard that Singapore won foreign investment and built new factories by offering special tax rates. Surely, he said, by attracting all that overseas Chinese money, China too could rise within a few years. The term 'trade co-operation zone' was not radical enough for Deng. Cutting through the haggling over ideologically correct terminology, he got brusquely to the point: 'It's better to call them special zones. The central government has no money to give you. But we can give you policies.'

In the early summer, Gu Mu went to Guangdong to finalise the all-important documents that would underpin the policy and anchor it to the party line. Deng also sent him to the coastal province of Fujian, where a similar experiment was to be conducted.

Over two months the drafters back in Beijing worried over their texts. For once the official language did not exaggerate when it called the documents from the two provinces 'of great historical significance'. Like the great imperial seals affixed to commands of old, the red stamps on the reports eventually issued by the central committee on 19 July 1979 were meant to inspire an awe of authority. The experiments were to go ahead.

Like bureaucrats anywhere, when in doubt Chinese officials like to convene a committee. In the Communist system, collective decision-making protected the individual. Meeting after meeting succeeded one another like a cycle of harvests. No one could measure the gallons of tea sipped, the unfiltered cigarettes smoked, the papers discarded as they ploughed on. This was slow, patient policy-building. The house of reform would rise brick by brick. It was not just aversion to political risk but a cautious incremental method that would have been familiar to the agrarian administrators of ancient Chinese dynasties. When you rule over a giant agricultural nation, you govern at the pace of crops and water.

The lesson for anyone looking at the Chinese way of government is that it operates on a time-tested belief that construction layer by layer builds resilience. The mandarins of imperial times had built dykes, canals and walls, calculating that some might fail but enough would hold firm. Floods, disasters and famine could be endured; these were, in any case, viewed as acts of heaven. The edifice of China was so large that, with resilience, the country could withstand repeated shocks. In this sense the conveners of late seventies China represented continuity, not change. The biography of Xi Zhongxun calls him 'a proletarian revolutionary'; if so, he was one who might have served an emperor with dexterity. As it turned out, the reformers would need keenly honed survival skills.

In late December, Xi rallied his loyalists in Guangdong. He acknowledged the leadership of Hua Guofeng in Beijing and did not bother to mention him again. He paid homage to the political campaigns of the time against Mao's disgraced successor, Lin Piao, and against the Gang of Four, then dismissed them. 'The whole province's mass movement against Lin Piao and the Gang of Four has basically come to an end. The focus of our work should be shifted to the Four Modernisations,' he said.

His agenda was ambitious. The special zones would bring in advanced technology and foreign capital. They would promote tourism. Industrial and agricultural production would increase. Higher exports of food and commodities to Hong Kong and Macau would bring in revenues. But it was Xi's peroration which foreshadowed the gigantic changes that would shake the economies of the rest of the world.

He set out a plan for China to dominate every sector of manufacturing on a scale that must have daunted the monochrome ranks of cadres, whose bicycles were stacked outside the conference hall. 'Our province has a long history of exporting ... light industrial products, so we have great potential, he said. He ticked off a checklist: textiles, light industrial processing, machinery, advanced precision engineering, electronics, chemicals, metallurgy and minerals. To spur exports, the party would allow innovation. Officials predicted a boom in assembling supplied parts. They saw low-cost labour as a boon for processing everything from fish to transistor radios. Factories would learn how to make samples, win customers and draw foreign firms into 'technical co-operation'. They would learn from foreign management experience. China would expand foreign trade, increasing the export of building materials and contracting projects with the objective of entering the international construction market; all this decades before Chinese infrastructure projects began to proliferate everywhere from Africa to Latin America.

In 1979, in an era before personal computers, mass migration or the internet, this was a manifesto so comprehensive that it must have seemed unimaginable to many of Xi's listeners. Since the Chinese revolution of 1949, the country had remained in defiant isolation from global capitalist markets. Few Chinese had any experience of foreign trade. No foreigners were in the hall.

The party had thought out how to make it happen, Xi explained. Foreign companies, overseas Chinese businessmen and 'compatriots' from Hong Kong and Macau would invest on their own or set up joint ventures in the special zones. China would sell its goods and services abroad and the profits would flow back into the country. The central bank would relax restrictions on the trade in foreign currencies. Foreigners could remit their share of the profits abroad through the Bank of China, a giant state-run institution. Left unsaid in this detailed exposition was any praise of free enterprise, market economics or the private sector that was about to emerge. This was a vision of a China renewed, powerful, prosperous and run by the government. Capitalism was for foreigners. China would trade through its state-owned enterprises and banks.

That was Xi's message. If foreign observers later interpreted reform and opening up as a move towards political liberalisation, that was their mistake. There was nothing in Xi's words or in the numerous party documents to support the idea. Chinese officials saw no harm in allowing foreigners to deceive themselves; in this China was blameless.

For Xi and his loyalists gathered in Guangzhou, the moment would never be more auspicious. His audience was ready. Proud southerners felt far from the cold, isolated cities of the north. They were ready to trade. 'Guangdong has been an important portal for China's economic and cultural exchanges with foreign countries since ancient times,' declared a local chronicle. 'The origins of the Silk Road are famous all over the world. During the Qin, Tang and Song dynasties Guangzhou was the country's foreign trade centre.

'In the Yuan, Ming and Qing dynasties it was one of the largest trading ports in China. Now with the Communist Party it is entering a new era.'

To the educated southerners listening to Xi Zhongxun, this harked back to a golden era deep in the past, so distinct from the northern cities in its richness, its cosmopolitanism and its intercourse with foreign lands that it represented a tradition which both gloried in worldliness and aroused deep suspicions among the authoritarian rulers of China. Once again, change would come from the south.

The reforms which began in 1978 were modest yet revolutionary. On paper, they were piecemeal administrative measures that imposed no blueprint on the whole country. The broad lines of policy were set and local authorities were allowed to experiment.

It was less contentious to let things happen through benign non-intervention than to tear down Maoist ideology. It also made it easier for Deng and his followers to make changes. The trick was to use banal, unexciting terms such as the household responsibility system, which in effect abolished the People's Communes. Its effect was to divide the collective land into plots worked by families. They could sell some of their produce on the open market for cash as long as they also sold a fixed amount to the state. Peasants would once more gain an incentive to work and save. The results were rapid: agricultural production rose by a quarter between 1975 and 1985.

Deng transplanted the agricultural model to industry. A dual price mechanism broke the monopoly of the Stalinist quota system. State enterprises escaped the rigid rules of Maoism and could sell any goods they produced in excess of the quota. Officials relaxed the rules to let commodities be sold at market prices as well as at rates fixed by the Five Year Plan. The management of companies changed, too. Under the industrial responsibility system, a team of managers or a local institution could contract to run a state-owned enterprise with the aim of generating profit. The days of absolute government control were waning. In time, Chinese managers would discover that more subtle and elusive methods kept the Communist Party's authority intact, but in the early days of reform it seemed to some as if opportunity was limitless.

The state took tentative steps to allow private businesses to operate for the first time since the suffocating hand of Maoist socialism had stifled China's traditionally vibrant commercial life. Price controls were eased and a small service sector emerged in a land that had forgotten what service and convenience were like.

Phrases like the household responsibility system did not resonate like the stirring slogans of Mao, which will endure as long as there are college dormitories and students to put up posters on their walls. But Deng's words were intended to change people's way of thinking in just the same way. In that, Deng was not new but very old. Two thousand five hundred years before Mao, Deng and the Chinese Communist Party, the teacher Confucius had written that if he was ever entrusted with the government of a territory his first task would be to 'rectify the names'. To most Westerners this is an enigma (although as Simon Leys, the modern translator of Confucius, pointed out: 'Orwell would have immediately understood and approved'), but in Chinese culture it was perfectly clear.

'If the names are not correct, if they do not match realities, language has no object,' Confucius said. 'If language is without an object, action becomes impossible – and therefore all human affairs disintegrate and their management becomes pointless and impossible. Hence, the very first task of a statesman is to rectify the names.'

Mao had used the same verb 'to rectify' time after time in ideological matters. Rectification became a standard party campaign tool. It was a word bland enough to deceive and sufficiently ominous to intimidate. The method suited Deng perfectly. By words alone, Maoist politics were drained of passion and converted into a kind of authoritarian managerialism.

It was a template for what happened in the decades to follow and one which would in time be copied by regimes in other places beyond China. In 1978 it was the linguistic innovation Deng needed for reform to survive and endure. The period marked a sea change in the way China interacted with the rest of the world. For Hong Kong, the opportunity was heaven sent.

There is often a political message in Chinese art. Down the ages, emperors commemorated their deeds, hallowed their ancestors or promoted their sons by way of intricate formal paintings. In 2018, the national art museum in Beijing staged an exhibition to mark the fortieth anniversary of reform and opening up. One of the exhibits was a painting called *Early Spring*.

The subject matter was artistically unpromising. It depicted a central work conference at which Communist Party leaders proposed the establishment of the Special Economic Zone bordering Hong Kong. In the centre of the painting, not coincidentally, stands Xi Zhongxun, the late father of the man who ruled China in 2018, Xi Jinping. Xi Zhongxun holds a document in one hand while in the other he grasps a red pen pointing at a map showing Shenzhen. He is surrounded by party luminaries, like the saviour encircled by his disciples in a Renaissance European work, all readily identifiable to the Chinese viewer. There was Deng Xiaoping, of course, and the vice premier Gu Mu, as well as, among others, Hu Yaobang and the veteran Yang Shangkun, later president.

The picture laid the final piece in a jigsaw of party hagiography. For Xi Zhongxun had died in 2002 after years suffering from dementia. His obituary occupied almost an entire page of the *People's Daily*. It praised him as 'an outstanding proletarian revolutionary'. The entire standing committee of the Politburo turned out for his funeral.

Absent from the frame was Hua Guofeng, Mao's nominated successor. His approval had been crucial to the success of the Shenzhen experiment but he died in obscurity in 2008. In new China, he had simply vanished from history.

3

A Long Farewell

The British departure from Hong Kong was made inevitable, like so much in modern China, by Mao Zedong, the mightiest figure in twentieth-century Asia. 'For a century, demons and monsters danced,' wrote Mao. He laid down the path for the return of the colony in policies followed by his successors. The goal was always first, the methods secondary. In reuniting China, the second generation of Chinese leaders saw negotiation and compromise as necessary tactics which made them legitimate heirs to Mao.

On its return Mao was resolute. Referring first to the Summer Palace in Beijing destroyed in 1860, he said in 1956, 'The forces of the imperialist powers burned down our Yuanming Yuan, and seized our Hong Kong and Taiwan. Hong Kong belongs to China. Why was it snatched away?' On how it would be done he was a realist. Mao and Zhou Enlai agreed early on, during the 'morning deluge' of their victory in 1949, that China would treat Hong Kong according to how useful it was to the revolution. By and large the Maoists kept to that.

There was no doubt of how Mao really felt. 'The Western world is considered good for everything, whereas we yellow people, black people and brown people are considered good for nothing,' he once told a group of African visitors. This did not prevent him from conducting the affairs of China well into his old age with the necessary courtliness towards Western politicians.

By the time he received Edward Heath, the former British prime minister, Mao was ageing fast. When his guest came in he rose, slightly hunched, wearing a grey jacket that hung off his frame. He extended his arm to shake hands with Heath, who was serving as leader of Britain's Conservative opposition. In the photos published by the Chinese state news agency, the chairman was wreathed in a rubicund smile. In a snapshot taken for one of the British group, however, his jaw was slack and his cheeks were pallid.

It was 25 May 1974. Heath had lost a general election to the Labour

Party and was in search of the world stage. Mao had no need of it. But he was always intrigued by Conservatives, preferring the clarity of disagreement to the fake solidarity of fellow-travellers. By this stage of his life the chairman rationed his time for good reason.

We now know from Li Zhisui, Mao's doctor, that Mao's body was ravaged by a multitude of diseases. In his memoir, the only independent account of life at Mao's court by a member of his circle, the doctor wrote that Mao had congestive heart failure and chronic lung disease. His life-long addiction to cigarettes had destroyed the lining of his lungs. He fought off bouts of pneumonia, emphysema and bronchitis. His survival had depended on an American-made respirator sent to China by Henry Kissinger. Like everything about Mao, his will to live was titanic. There was more. As Heath, in the pink of health, silver-haired and besuited with a neat white handkerchief in his pocket, greeted the chairman, Mao's gaze seemed to wander. The doctor had noted that, so bad was his eyesight, he could barely see a finger in front of his face. He could just tell light from dark. His speech was so poor that even his longtime collaborators struggled to make it out. A strange muscular atrophy weakened his right side.

Nobody in the room knew it, but Mao's symptoms had led his doctor to believe that the chairman was doomed. Two months after the meeting with Heath, Dr Li and a group of Chinese specialists would reach a diagnosis so terrifying that initially they feared to tell the Politburo. The chairman was suffering from an extremely rare form of amyotrophic lateral sclerosis, known in the West as Lou Gehrig's disease or motor neurone disease. As it progressed, the patient's critical nerve cells would die, resulting in paralysis, inability to swallow and respiratory failure. The man who had conquered China by force of his words would be silenced forever. He might even choke to death.

Such was the twilight atmosphere at Mao's court when the British delegation called. The chairman rallied his mental and physical energies, for he did nothing without purpose. The two statesmen exchanged banter. Mao wondered why Heath had not received a guard of honour. His premier, Zhou Enlai, explained that it might offend the current British prime minister, Harold Wilson of the Labour Party. One of Mao's female retinue, Wang Hairong, a member of his extended clan, asked if he was not afraid of offending Wilson. 'No,' said Mao, turning to Heath. 'I cast my vote for you!' he joked.

The remainder of the transcript of their conversation serves chiefly as a reminder that the mighty can be banal. Mao was grandiose and vague.

Heath lived up to the clichés about him, alternating between fawning agreement with the chairman and harping references to his own wisdom. When Mao enquired whether Heath could not help Richard Nixon weather the Watergate scandal, Heath replied: 'If he had asked me for my opinion at that time, I would have advised him to thoroughly crush that matter eighteen months ago. But he didn't ask me at that time.'

The small talk done, Mao and Heath went on to grand strategy, ranging from Japan to Europe, the Soviet Union and the United States. Most of their observations are worthless today except for the chairman's unprompted remarks which, by coincidence or not, are the last paragraph on the last page of his collected works *On Diplomacy*, the Chinese version of which was published in 1994: 'All this is now history. Only the question of Hong Kong remains. We won't discuss it at present. We shall consult together at the proper time about what we are going to do. This will be the business of the younger generation.' In the event, the chairman lived on as an invalid until a series of heart attacks ended his life on 9 September 1976.

It was generally agreed that by the 'younger generation' Mao meant Deng Xiaoping. The fate of Hong Kong was not high among Deng's priorities after Mao's death, however, because China was going through great travails. Deng had to deal with the Gang of Four, marginalise the radicals, placate the elders, rally his forces and undertake the huge political-bureaucratic task of reform. The die was none the less cast by Mao's words in 1974. Heath returned to London to brief the British government that China would inevitably seek a resolution of its status.

The mutual esteem between Heath and the Chinese Communist Party was long-enduring. The former premier went on to visit China twenty-five times after his first meeting with Mao and he was trusted by Deng to pass on important policy decisions to later British prime ministers. On his death in 2005, obituaries in the state media hailed him as 'an old friend' of China, while in 2014 the Chinese ambassador to Britain, Liu Xiaoming, paid a visit to Heath's home in the Cathedral Close at Salisbury in southern England to examine his grand piano, his hand-painted Chinese wallpaper and a collection of photographs showing Heath with Mao, Deng and other party leaders. The ambassador laid a wreath in tribute upon Heath's tombstone in the cathedral and reminded his retinue of an old Chinese saying: 'when drinking the water you should not forget those who dug the well.'

* * *

The chairman cast a long shadow over all who came after him. He reverberated down the decades through his writings and poetry, his utterances, asides, jokes, barbs, venomous rhetoric and flashes of insight. Even from his mausoleum, he made his successors seem like miniature figures in a Chinese landscape.

In 1949 Mao had laid out principles for dealing with the foreign imperialists that governed how all Chinese governments have behaved ever since. It sounded radical. In fact it was carefully phrased and pragmatic. In the plain words of a Hunan peasant, the Communist leader said China had to 'set up another kitchen' and 'clean up the house before inviting the guests'.

The first principle meant that New China refused to acknowledge the legal status of 'diplomatic personnel and journalists recognised by the Kuomintang'. The Communists equated news bureaux or 'imperialist propaganda agencies' with foreign embassies, an assumption that prevails to the present day. The people's government would refuse to recognise 'treasonable treaties of the Kuomintang period' (these did not, however, include the three nineteenth-century treaties establishing the status of Hong Kong). They would take immediate control of foreign trade.

The second principle of 'cleaning the house' sounded innocuous, but would lead in time to the purging of foreign influence from China. After the regime had dealt with diplomats and journalists, it would turn to 'the remaining imperialist economic and cultural establishments', said Mao. 'They can be allowed to exist for the time being, subject to our supervision and control,' he judged. In due course foreign companies, academic bodies, churches, religious orders and small entrepreneurs would leave the People's Republic and their influx would transform Hong Kong. At the end of the 1940s there was a changing of the guard as embassies and institutions of the socialist world began to establish themselves in China. So far as the masses were concerned, however, Mao had ended privileges for foreigners, fulfilling a propaganda vow that had eluded waves of revolutionaries since the waning years of the Qing dynasty. Even in victory, though, the words of Mao allowed for a pragmatic view of commerce after liberation: 'As for doing business with foreigners there is no question; wherever there is business to do, we shall do it and we have already started; the businessmen of several capitalist countries are already competing for such business.'

Mao and his comrades watched the defeated Nationalists streaming south across the Pearl River Delta and into Hong Kong, content to watch their foes quit the battlefield. It was indeed the 'morning deluge', in the phrase poetically chosen by the author Han Suyin for the title of her sympathetic history of the time. Modern Chinese historians, however, have reconstructed a shrewder and less tempestuous policy which Mao and Zhou Enlai agreed. It conformed both to revolutionary theory and practice, holding that Hong Kong was a chess piece in the contest between East and West. The British Empire was in decline, America was emerging as its rival and China could use the colony to 'exploit the contradictions' between them.

'Why did the People's Liberation Army not enter Hong Kong after it attacked and occupied Canton?' the writer Xu Bing asked in an officially approved history published one year before the handover in 1997. 'It was left to Edward Heath to solve the mystery of history: Mao Zedong and Zhou Enlai had already worked out the strategy of our long term use of Hong Kong.'

In 1949, Xu wrote, the British cabinet had met under Clement Attlee, the Labour prime minister, and decided to send reinforcements to the British army garrison, fearing that the loss of the colony would be felt throughout southeast Asia and would add to Britain's defence burdens there: 'Could Hong Kong remain a stable boat in the wind and rain?'

The Communist Party mouthpiece in Hong Kong, the daily newspaper *Wen Wei Po*, founded in Shanghai in 1938 as an organ of Communist propaganda, had already sent a signal through its columns to the governor, Sir Alexander Grantham, warning that 'it would be a historic mistake for Hong Kong not to actively adopt a friendly posture towards China.' Through secret channels, Zhou Enlai sent a message to Grantham outlining three 'red lines' that were to prove consistent over the decades. First, Hong Kong must not be used as a military base against the People's Republic of China. Second, its government must do nothing to 'destroy trust' with China. Third, personnel from the People's Republic in Hong Kong must be protected. The colonial government, Xu writes, acceded secretly to these conditions, aware that vengeance and vendetta by the losers in the Chinese civil war could bring violent chaos to the colony and might precipitate an invasion. In 1951, Zhou received the head of the Xinhua news agency in Hong Kong, Huang Zuomei, to explain the party's outlook. China's policy towards Hong Kong was part of its overall strategy in the struggle between East and West, he explained, adding that 'it could not be measured or determined by the narrow principle of territorial sovereignty.'

China had decided before Liberation that it would not take Hong Kong back, Zhou said. But this was neither a soft line nor a concession. It was instead to be 'an active attack and struggle' designed to fit into a long-term revolutionary global view. Britain, he said, had been swift to recognise the new government of China because Attlee wanted to preserve the interests of the British Empire: 'Hong Kong is a symbol of the political and economic power of the British Empire in the Far East, and in this framework there are big contradictions between the United States and Britain. The United States wants to eat away at British power in the Far East and Britain wants to preserve it.'

At the time Zhou spoke, China was fighting the United States, Britain and their allies in Korea. Hundreds of thousands of Chinese 'volunteers' crossed the Yalu River to join the Korean War, which raged from 1950 to 1953. Their losses were heavy, and included Mao's son, Mao Anying, who was killed in an air raid. In response the US imposed a total ban on trade, while the United Nations – where the defeated Nationalists sat in the seat representing China – had imposed sanctions. Therefore, said Zhou, it was better to keep Hong Kong in the hands of the British than to take it back or let it fall into the hands of the Americans. By doing so, China entangled Britain in complications and widened the 'contradiction' between Britain and the United States. The British, he argued, dared not follow American policy slavishly.

'Hong Kong is of great benefit to us,' Zhou said. 'In this case Hong Kong is our gateway to the world of southeast Asia, Africa and the west. It will be our observatory and our bridgehead. It will be the front line for us to break through the blockade imposed on us by the phalanx of western powers led by the Americans.' The Xinhua chief was sent away in no doubt of Chinese strategy, which was carefully obscured from the masses. From time to time, the organs of propaganda would tear into British colonialism for its racism, its violence and its exploitation. Mysteriously, none of the rhetoric translated into military operations. In 1967, when anti-British riots inspired by the Cultural Revolution shook the colony, Zhou personally intervened to forbid the PLA commander in Guangdong, Huang Yongsheng, from leading an invasion.

Even in the depths of the Cultural Revolution, while ministries seethed in political turmoil, Zhou kept an eye on the long term. In 1972 he ordered the Chinese ambassador to the United Nations, Huang Hua, to submit a memorandum to the UN removing Hong Kong and Macau from a list of territories recognised as colonies. Duly approved by the general assembly in November 1972, the resolution in effect accepted Chinese sovereignty, avoiding the possibility that foreign countries could once again interfere in Chinese affairs and making it inevitable that Britain and Portugal would have to negotiate one day.

By the late 1970s the Chinese leadership was focusing on economic development, not world revolution, and the importance of Hong Kong became even greater. The guidance laid down by Mao and Zhou was enduring. China's 'red lines' in the twenty-first century would not be radically different from the three points laid out by Zhou to the governor in 1949 and by the UN resolution of 1972. Chinese politics were steadfast, affirming that Hong Kong would come back to the motherland and rejecting its status as a colony. The propaganda was fiery, embittered, intermittent and selective. Tactical calculation was embedded in every decision.

From the end of the Mao era, Chinese governments kept to these principles with a remarkable degree of continuity. They would entrust Hong Kong affairs to a corps of officials who balanced ideology, patriotism and flexible calculation with sufficient skill to keep the policy on track throughout years of dramatic economic and social change in China. Some of these men had been steeped in the politics and society of the colony since the 1930s. A few of them came from the same families, guaranteeing to the regime a reliable political pedigree. All of them were highly trained as negotiators and drafters of documents. In general, it is fair to say that the Chinese government fielded its top team in the service of a cause which the leadership deemed to be of high national importance. Fortunately for historians, a handful of the Communist elite turned out to be corrupt, erratic, devious, lacking in finesse, amazingly flawed in their judgements and untruthful in their reporting to Beijing. It is on these that the drama depends.

To many of the British, the message from Beijing that Hong Kong would assuredly return to Chinese rule must have seemed like a small cloud appearing on a clear day above the South China Sea. The high and palmy state of colonial administration appeared unruffled in the late 1970s. The governor ruled with formal autocracy using a light touch. Hong Kong, with its history of riches, tragedy and rebirth, continued to prosper steadily after the Second World War while the United Kingdom entered a cycle of inflation, economic decline and political conflict.

'Entranced by Hong Kong, rising almost vertically across the water,' wrote a young British diplomat, Douglas Hurd, on his arrival by ocean liner in 1954 en route to a posting in Beijing; it was, he thought, a 'successful mix of traditional British order and Chinese energy'. For many, the Crown Colony was an exercise in living nostalgia. Hurd was lodged at the Harbour View Hotel, which reminded him of Bournemouth. The cooking was 'sternly British' and was consumed in silence by British families off plates decorated with pictures of Edinburgh Castle and Holyrood House.

Denis Bray, who retired in 1984 as Hong Kong's secretary for home affairs, recalled the atmosphere of his early post-war days thus:

> a place where bare feet are common in Central, where only the smartest offices and none of the homes have air conditioning, where there are practically no teenagers or old people, where primary schooling is a privilege, where tuberculosis is the biggest killer and lepers have to be isolated, where a large part of the population lives in flimsy wooden shacks that burn down leaving thousands homeless, where night soil ladies clean most of the lavatories ... this was Hong Kong as I found it when I came to work here at the beginning of the second half of the twentieth century.

Austin Coates, a young civil servant, found himself appointed as a special magistrate, or *li man fu*, administering justice in the rural New Territories in the early 1950s without having passed a law examination. Nor did he speak a word of Cantonese. Coates learned that an ordinance passed when the New Territories were leased from China permitted cases to be heard according either to common law or to Chinese law and custom. The latter seemed an insuperable barrier, since there was only one known textbook, written by a Jesuit in the eighteenth century. There were, he recounted, three disadvantages to this tome: 'Only one copy of this book was known to exist, owned by the University of Hong Kong. It could not be borrowed, and it was in French.' For David Ford, the last Briton to head the civil service as chief secretary for administration from 1986 to 1993, the world of the Hong Kong Chinese in those early days was a more robust and bracing place than (he implied) the social welfare states taking root in the gardens of the West. 'A stroll through the streets of San Po Kong or Sham Shui Po meant dodging the lorries, the baling trucks, the handcarts and the jostling, high-spirited labourers who knew what the word "labour" stood for and were not afraid of it,' he recalled.

Well into the 1990s, it was possible to hear similar stereotypes from well-heeled expatriates, dispensed over cocktails served by pinafored maids on balconies high above the harbour or over a tray of drinks on the polished afterdeck of the corporate yacht. One head of a great finance house held an audience of Western suburbanites enthralled by his account of how an old, wrinkled Chinese crone appeared every morning to sift through the rubbish bin outside his office, sorting out tin or aluminium, paper and card, all to be baled and re-sold. This was, to him, the epitome both of a perfectly operating economic order and a natural way to privatise the recycling of goods, which was then coming into fashion.

'In our society yesterday's hawker can be today's millionaire,' Ford wrote. It was, he judged, 'a society mercifully spared the divisions of class and caste that have bedevilled the efforts of so many other societies to achieve anything like the same unanimity of purpose.'

His views were still those of a remote and exalted few, expatriates and Chinese, whose perception of Hong Kong society would prove to be woefully under-sophisticated. To be fair, Ford conceded that 'old style paternalistic administration would be out of place in this new age of awakening expectations'. But government by the elite and for the elite was a concept shared by the departing British and the local grandees who took their place.

The British administration of Hong Kong was none the less a many-splendoured thing. It worked flawlessly right up to the end, even though it was one of the most esoteric constitutional mechanisms still functioning in the late twentieth century. To the Chinese experts studying it, the colonial government of Hong Kong was like a museum piece. It resembled the system which generations of mandarins had served. For propaganda purposes, of course, it was an illustration of British hypocrisy. Many Chinese officials secretly admired it.

To some extent this admiration may have been wistful. Government in China after 1949 was revolutionary, proletarian and politically volatile. It was subject to whims, slogans, purges and bewildering changes of policy direction. By contrast the civil service in Hong Kong evoked memories of a calm and lofty imperial administration. The scholar Simon Leys put it like this: 'For more than two thousand years, the empire was ruled by the intellectual elite; to gain access to political power one had to compete successfully in the civil service examinations, which were open to all. Until modern times, this was certainly the most open, flexible, fair, and sophisticated system of government known in history.' The governor sat in magnificent isolation at the summit of the colony. Appointed by the Queen, he flew the flag of Hong Kong, a blue ensign with the Union Jack in its upper left quarter. Apart from this emblem of an imperialist foreign power, it was adorned by a coat of arms which showed a lion and a dragon, a crown, a fortress and two trading junks in sail on a tranquil sea. Serene and proud it was.

Invited to dine at Government House by Sir Alexander Grantham in 1954, Douglas Hurd found it a more splendid occasion than any he had attended in London, Eton or Cambridge. 'We ate roast beef and Yorkshire pudding by candlelight, served by footmen in scarlet waistcoats, at tables flanked by banks of gladioli and gardenia.' Hurd sat next to the wife of the Korean consul-general. Over post-prandial whisky, Sir Alexander discoursed on the lessons of the French Revolution and upon the chaos and corruption of the defeated government of Chiang Kai-shek. Intelligent and well-read, Hurd knew the dark side of Britain's history with Hong Kong, the Opium Wars and the unequal treaties. But he also knew that the Chinese who lived in the shacks on those hillsides 'were not a subject race yearning to be free'. They had fled there within the last five years, escaping from upheaval and persecution in China, 'seeking order and the rule of law as administered by Sir Alexander'. The toast to the Queen at his table was more than an empty formality.

The administration placed great store on heraldry and ritual, much of it recently invented. On receiving his letter of appointment in 1949, Austin Coates was aghast to discover that he was required to arrive in Hong Kong with a ceremonial sword, a gold-braided white uniform and a pith helmet.

The governor's authority derived from the Letters Patent issued under the Great Seal of the United Kingdom. The Letters Patent and the Royal Instructions formed the constitution of Hong Kong. They granted great responsibility to one man, who could in principle take grave decisions on the spot. By convention, however, the governor rarely exercised the full extent of his powers. He was bound to obey instructions from the Queen or from the Secretary of State for Foreign and Commonwealth Affairs. Within those confines he operated with a degree of freedom which depended on an element of trust between London and its man on the spot. It is a tribute to tradition that most of the time this seemed to work.

The governor ruled through an Executive Council, usually known as 'Exco'. Some of its members were ex-officio, such as the chief secretary, the Commander of British Forces, the financial secretary and the attorney-general. In addition the governor appointed others, usually worthies

drawn from the ranks of commerce, finance and the law. The Executive
Council played a role similar to a cabinet, operated mainly by consensus
and met once a week in camera. Efficient it may have been, democratic it
was not.

Laws were passed by the Legislative Council, or 'Legco'. It had the functions and trappings of a parliament. In theory it had spending powers. In
the late colonial period there were fifty-seven members who met once a
week. Legislation went through three readings and a committee stage. Bills
passed by Legco were sent for the governor's assent, after which they
became 'ordinances' or laws. There was a Finance Committee to oversee
spending, conventionally of an austere disposition. A Public Accounts
Committee scrutinised government expenditure and conducted audits.

From its foundation in 1844 until 1985 all Legislative Council members
were appointed by the British. Only in October 1985 were the first twenty-four members elected indirectly by small group electorates in local
councils and the professions. It was not until 1991, under the governorship
of Sir David Wilson, that the council had its first eighteen directly elected
members. The Chinese language was not used in council proceedings until
1972.

Behind this tranquil façade lay one enormous lever of economic power.
All land in Hong Kong was owned by the Crown. The only exception was
the plot on which St John's Anglican cathedral stood above Victoria
Harbour. Since 1841, land had been sold on leases and would ultimately
revert to the government. This was one thing the British never changed in
their haste to modernise the governance of Hong Kong. It was simply too
powerful a tool to surrender. Apart from holding the magic key to low
taxes and balanced budgets, it conferred dizzying influence on the officials
who – in circumstances of the utmost probity, of course – deliberated on
how much land would be auctioned to the hungry property developers
every year. Many complained that rigging the land supply led to the roots
of Hong Kong's astronomical property prices, the exclusion of the poor
from home ownership, the perpetuation of inequality and the eventual
upsurge in social outrage which exploded on the streets after 2014. British
officials would simply have shaken their heads and maintained, straight-
faced, that land auctions with competitive bids were merely an example of
the capitalist free market in action.

Liberals and left-wingers suspected that real decisions emerged from
lunches at the Hong Kong Club and weekends sailing or on country
retreats. The ironies were not lost on the colonial civil servants themselves.

One recorded that in 1973 a group of visiting Chinese officials 'were intrigued and appreciative members of the audience at a public performance of a light opera which is rich in political satire, *The Mikado*'.

An iconoclastic observer might well have compared the cosy arrangements in Hong Kong to government by a Gilbert and Sullivan libretto, but at least satire was permitted.

Less light-hearted, a veteran British official recalled the days before Sir Murray MacLehose cleaned up the colonial government: 'We had a myth about ourselves. British Hong Kong was corrupt. The police were absolutely corrupt. There was bribery, even though we preached hypocritically about decency and values. There were government secretaries who went home to Britain with bags of cash.'

The British evolved a system of local government which extended some powers to the Chinese population. There were nineteen district boards. Urban councils ran municipal affairs. A regional council ran the New Territories, which was a complex mosaic of clan and rural power centres. None the less, this remained a centralised form of government. The administration, which was known as Public Service, controlled the police, the fire brigade and the civil service. The chief secretary enjoyed wider sway and greater powers of intervention than did the interior minister in many small countries.

If the structure of Hong Kong's administration echoed the post-Victorian order of British government, its legal system represented a transplant from the West into a society on the other side of the world which on the eve of the handover numbered 6.3 million and was 95 per cent ethnically Chinese. The law of Hong Kong 'generally followed that of England and Wales' according to the official guide. Some of its practices must have required a cultural sea change for aspiring lawyers. The Application of English Law Ordinance of 1966 required them to be familiar with such statutes as the Justices of the Peace Act of 1361 (in China, the waning years of the Mongol Yuan dynasty) and the Distress for Rent Act of 1689 (for Chinese, the early period of the Manchu Qing emperors). Compared to all that, dressing up in wigs and gowns and memorising Latin phrases must have seemed positively normal.

There were exceptions. In the rural New Territories, which were governed under the Second Convention of Peking of 1898, litigants could choose – as Austin Coates discovered – whether they would have a magistrate hear their suits according to the common law or according to Chinese law and custom. The cultural confusion which ensued was amusingly described by Coates, who had affection and respect for local traditions and the Chinese concept of legality. But adjudicating disputes over cows, concubines or paddyfields was not the same as judging cases involving huge sums of money or matters of life and death. For these the majesty of English law was inescapable.

The legal code, The Laws of Hong Kong, ran to thirty-two volumes. 'Hong Kong courts apply a doctrine similar to that of English courts,' the official handbook declared. The Court of Appeal was bound by its own previous decisions. Final appeal from the Court of Appeal was to the Privy Council in London. For all its flummery, the legal system became a bedrock for Hong Kong. In this case British administration was broadly benevolent and, paradoxically for a colony, it placed Hong Kong in the progressive vanguard of societies in Asia. It spoke volumes to the Victorian ideal of enlightened government that the first law passed by the Legislative Council in 1844 was the Slavery Ordinance forbidding human bondage, a legal necessity which illustrated the state of colonial society at the time.

The last execution in Hong Kong took place in Stanley Prison on 16 November 1966, when Wong Kai-Kei, twenty-six years old, was hanged. Thereafter the governor formally commuted all death sentences to life imprisonment under the royal prerogative of mercy. Following the abolition of capital punishment in Britain, the practice was formally abolished in 1993. Crime rates continued a steady decline through the final years of British rule and at the handover there was no question of going back to the old days.

In contrast, China remained the world's top executioner through the late twentieth century and into the twenty-first; this was in part due to the size of its population, but its citizens ran a high risk of execution for a swathe of offences including white-collar financial crimes and corruption. Even in democracies like Japan and Taiwan, the noose and the firing squad awaited the condemned. Indonesia, Thailand, Malaysia and Singapore continued to execute drug dealers, to the widespread approval of the public. Hong Kong, meanwhile, continued on its lonely liberal path. Successive governors, encouraged by the Foreign Office, quietly introduced laws which strengthened people's rights in Hong Kong. In 1976 the International Conventions on Civil and Political Rights and on Economic, Social and Cultural Rights were extended to Hong Kong. Their continuous application after 1997 was written into the Joint Declaration of 1984 by Britain and China and provided a foundation for the rights movements which gripped the city from 2014. Hong Kong's own Bill of Rights was introduced under Sir David Wilson in July 1990, just over a year after the slaughter of protesters in Beijing had awakened local people to the stark differences between their two systems.

All causes were not equal in the eyes of public opinion, however. Parliament in London decriminalised homosexuality in 1967 but it took the Legislative Council (by then partly elected) until 1991 to bring Hong Kong law into line with the United Kingdom. Faced with the question of homosexual law reform in the late 1970s the governor, Murray MacLehose, feared that it would offend the community and opted to do nothing.

British colonial civil servants were moreover proud, perhaps justly so, of their commitment to raise the level of education in the colonies, and while the opportunity for benevolent intervention vanished with independence for one place after another in the aftermath of the Second World War, administrators in Hong Kong went on with the task. Hong Kong University (HKU), the city's first, was established in 1911 along the lines of a British university. The Chinese University of Hong Kong was set up in 1963, the Hong Kong Polytechnic came into being in 1972 and the Hong Kong University of Science and Technology began taking students at a modern campus above Clear Water Bay in 1991.

Marxists, anti-colonialists and Communist Party analysts took a sour view of such institutions. They were seen by 'patriots' as a way to embed alien ways of thinking in their young students, who were mostly Cantonese. Radical leftists interpreted the creation of a highly educated workforce as a way to support the needs of capitalists instead of raising the basic standards of the entire proletariat. To the average Hong Kong family, however, higher education offered a staircase to advancement that was the traditional aspiration of Chinese people. The Confucian heritage of reverence for the intelligentsia, or at least the literati, remained intact in Hong Kong while Red Guards trashed the colleges of China and beat or killed their professors. This meant that Communist propaganda had little impact on the Hong Kong public, who knew very well what was going on next door.

Businesses flourished against this backdrop of an effective, if undemocratic administration, a solid rule of law and an increasingly well-educated and adaptable population. Taxation was low, the workforce was willing, pay was modest and bosses were not bothered by too many rules and regulations on hiring and firing. If it was anathema to the left and to a growing and vocal trade union movement, it was a paradise for the *tai-pans* and their shareholders. British businesses and the great trading houses still predominated, but international companies began to move into Hong Kong as economic reforms in China held out the promise of profit and demanded an efficient local base from which to do business. All of this convinced the Chinese government of the truth inherent in the saying that Hong Kong was like a precious porcelain vase which neither China nor Britain wished to shatter.

Deng Xiaoping once said that China did not practise personal diplomacy, but in 1978 he picked a man who was perfectly cast for the job of regaining Hong Kong. Liao Chengzhi was one of the most unusual figures that the Chinese Communist Party ever produced. Little known in the West, he was lionised by the party for his record of covert service in Europe and Asia. In Japan he is recognised as an architect of restored relations between the two wartime enemies.

Liao came of age in a period of conspiracies and loyalties that flowed like water and spent much of his life underground or in jail. He remained enigmatic until the day of his death. Even the place of his birth is uncertain. According to official obituaries, he was born in a suburb of Tokyo, Japan, on 25 September 1908; the foreign ministry website and other sources state that his birthplace was Huiyang County, in Guangdong province, adjoining Hong Kong. His father, Liao Zhongkai, was a well-known Kuomintang leader and financier. His grandfather, who had five wives and twenty-four children, had represented the Hongkong and Shanghai Bank in San Francisco.

A background combining foreign capitalism and the Kuomintang was not auspicious for a revolutionary. It would haunt Liao Chengzhi, but it was no more than a reflection of China's complex and swirling history in the twentieth century. His father had attended Queen's College in Hong Kong, the first public secondary school founded by the colonial government. In 1903 he moved to Japan, joining many idealistic young Chinese who flocked to see how an ancient nation was rapidly modernising itself. It was a time when Japan was engaged in 'reform and opening up' on a daring scale in the late Meiji period, creating industries, institutions and a modern army and navy. The Chinese exiles found that Meiji Japan was an incubator of radicalism. They had their first opportunity to study *Das Kapital* and other Marxist works in Japanese translation at a time when no Chinese language versions were available.

Liao's mother, He Xiangning, was an early feminist and revolutionary. She had been left behind in Hong Kong but the couple eventually reunited and settled down near Tokyo, which was already one of the fastest growing

metropolises in the world. The elite Chinese diaspora in Japan lived in a
tight social group united by a common language and by clan ties. Liao's
parents got to know Sun Yat-sen, the first leader of the Kuomintang, who
also hailed from Guangdong province. They mixed in circles where there
was heady talk of a new China emerging from the ashes of the Qing
empire. Liao's father joined the Sun Yat-sen movement. When it formed a
national government in Canton, he became finance chief. He was seen as
the most left-wing member of the government, favoured accommodation
with the emerging Communist Party and was entrusted with reorganising
the Kuomintang along Marxist-Leninist lines.

These efforts were cut short when gunmen assassinated him in
Guangzhou on 20 August 1925, as he stepped out of his car to go to a
central committee meeting. The killers were linked to the ultra-conserva-
tive faction in the Kuomintang. Inquiries and executions followed.
Rumours swirled in China that the British were responsible for his assas-
sination, but no evidence for the claim has come to light and a former
governor of Hong Kong called the idea 'totally unlikely'. Today's official
verdict hallows him as a martyr 'devoted to the cause of the liberation of
the Chinese people' who urged co-operation with the Communist Party.

Liao Chengzhi's mother took him back to safety in Japan. He too joined
the Kuomintang but broke with it in 1927 after Chiang Kai-shek unleashed
a massacre of Communists. Arrested twice by the Japanese police for
political agitation, he was then expelled for 'continuous participation in
patriotic activities'. The official account says he joined the Communist
Party in Shanghai in 1928.

Liao became a genuine international proletarian revolutionary. The
party sent him to Europe in 1929 to organise Chinese seamen in Germany,
Belgium and the Netherlands. He joined a 'progressive' organisation called
the China Anti-Imperialist League. The Dutch and German police arrested
and expelled him on separate occasions. In all, according to the authorised
version, Liao was jailed at least seven times in four countries and was
severely beaten by the Japanese police while in detention at the Akasaka
detention centre in Tokyo. Liao's adventures continued back in China,
where he was detained twice by the Kuomintang, was rescued by his
mother, then rejoined his comrades on the Long March, only to be put in
irons in a factional dispute. He was released thanks to Zhou Enlai and put
in charge of the broadcasting section of the Xinhua news agency.

How much of Liao Chengzhi's biography is distorted or fabricated
remains unclear. None the less, Xinhua was established as a front organi-

sation and from its foundation employed correspondents who doubled as intelligence officers. Liao was one of the few senior Communists to speak Japanese fluently. And he was trusted with sensitive political tasks. The party sent Liao to Hong Kong after Shanghai fell to the Imperial Japanese Army in 1937. His job was to organise supplies from the British colony for the Communist forces. At first the colonial authorities turned a blind eye. They allowed the mainland Chinese activists to set up a liaison office under cover as the Yue Hwa Company, notionally a wholesale tea merchant, at 18 Queens Road Central. The police Special Branch kept a quiet watch. Safe under the British Crown, Liao and his comrades organised funds, films, printing, leaflets, propaganda and resistance work for bands of guerrillas fighting the Japanese. But in 1939 there came a bolt from the blue. Under intense Japanese pressure, the police raided the Yue Hwa Company and ransacked its offices. Liao Chengzhi went underground.

The period between 1939 and 1941 was inglorious for colonial prestige. The British ambassador in Tokyo, Sir Robert Craigie, had persuaded Whitehall that it was worth placating the Japanese militarists if concessions might avert a war. The British made similar gestures of appeasement in Tientsin, modern Tianjin, in the forlorn hope that peace was worth preserving. The arguments were made on moral and realistic grounds: British military attachés knew that Japan possessed overwhelming force. To the Chinese resisting Japan, however, it was a blatant case of Western perfidy which left a legacy of distrust in many of those who negotiated in later years with Britain. It was, in any case, useless.

Liao escaped from Hong Kong in June 1941. He is said to have returned at great risk to help a group of prominent people escape in January 1942. Then he made his way to join Mao Zedong and the Red Army inside China. As the Second World War ended he became one of the party's key figures in its United Front Work Department, which handled relations with other parties and its foreign representation. The leadership trusted him to pioneer the restoration of relations between the People's Republic and Japan. Liao played a prominent role in defusing tensions with Taiwan; he may even have paved the way for the emergence of democracy on the island by reassuring its leader, Chiang Ching-kuo, that China was not about to invade it.

In a life of such adventures there was little to separate Chinese revolutionaries like Liao from their Western counterparts of the time, men like Murray MacLehose, who had carried out dangerous work alongside guerrillas in southern China during the Second World War. The era produced extraordinary achievers who in the course of their careers were soldiers, guerrillas, spies, politicians, administrators and diplomats. Liao Chengzhi was one of them. His life story tends to support speculation in the overseas media that he was a long-serving intelligence operative. One author specialising in espionage labelled him a Comintern agent and suggested that he may have recruited one of China's best spies inside the CIA, Larry Wu-Tai Chin, in Okinawa, Japan, in 1952, although there is nothing in Liao's published curriculum vitae to place him there at the time.

Like many of the old guard, Liao was purged during the Cultural Revolution but was rehabilitated before Mao's death and promoted to the party Central Committee. He was named to a 'leading small group' created to examine Chinese policy options on Hong Kong in keeping with party practice to retain sensitive decision-making within a tight circle. When Deng Xiaoping was looking for a reliable, cosmopolitan and wily veteran to take charge of the Hong Kong dossier, Liao was his choice.

Britain was alert to any opportunity for influence or contact with Chinese officials, who were trained to be elusive and noncommittal. The demand for information was constant in Whitehall and in Government House. As the political wind changed in China, British officials sought any clues about what was coming. So, when an alert intelligence officer in Hong Kong spotted that Liao Chengzhi had passed through immigration at Kai Tak airport on his return from medical treatment in the United States and was staying somewhere on the island, the news was relayed promptly to Government House.

Governor MacLehose conferred with his political adviser, Dr David Wilson, a Sinologist from the Foreign Office. MacLehose's instinct was, as usual, to act. The two men quickly established that Liao had been spirited to a house on the Peak owned by China Resources, a state-owned conglomerate that handled the Beijing government's commercial operations in the colony. Wilson contacted the offices of the New China News Agency, which fulfilled a similar political and diplomatic role. A dusty formulaic answer came back to the effect that Comrade Chengzhi did not think it would be very appropriate for him to visit the residence of the British governor. However it seemed Liao would be ready to meet him somewhere else. MacLehose summoned an unmarked car and set off up the Peak with Wilson, relishing the cloak-and-dagger atmosphere as the pair swept past policemen and passers-by. They found that Liao was 'extremely well informed about Hong Kong', Wilson recalled, and he confirmed the political signals from the new Chinese leadership.

The British did not know it precisely, but they had got the right man. Liao had revolutionised Chinese thinking about Hong Kong. He saw that ultra-radical policies, such as those which led to riots in 1967, had disastrous results. Trade between China and Hong Kong had fallen by almost one-fifth and took three years to recover. The party's own internal figures showed a sharp fall in membership of the pro-Beijing trade unions. Circulation of five newspapers deemed to be 'patriotic' had slumped: barely 10 per cent of Chinese language newspaper readers bothered to pick them up.

Trusting in the party's methodology, Liao started with propaganda. In December 1977 he instructed media cadres to 'cleanse your minds of the Gang of Four and deal with the actual situation in Hong Kong and Macau'. On 31 January 1978 he told a forum on the Hong Kong film industry that 'production can be more extensive … anything conducive to the patriotic united front can be shot'. Broadly, his mandate was to bury extreme left-wing policies, which left the party in purist isolation, and to expand Chinese political influence across a spectrum of Hong Kong's political, cultural and social life – the 'united front' tactic which had served the Communists well in taking control of the mainland. It was, perhaps, too early to reach out to capitalist businessmen, as the Communists had few incentives or threats to brandish at the time.

Throughout 1978 Liao's influence grew, while China evolved a pragmatic and more effective policy towards Hong Kong. In January, a special conference abolished the slogan that put 'anti-British activity' first and 'recovery of Hong Kong' second. In May 1978, when the party secretly established the Hong Kong and Macau Affairs Office under the State Council, Liao was appointed its first director. One of his early acts was to convene a meeting at which he told his officials that 'all our work must proceed from the real local situation, not copying the practices on the mainland'. The government, he said, 'had to clear up the interference and damage caused by the far-left route to Hong Kong and Macau'.

On 20 July, a new director was named to the Hong Kong office of Xinhua, the New China News Agency. The NCNA was staffed by officials of the Ministry of Foreign Affairs, intelligence officers and a few journalists. Their tasks included routine news agency reporting, the publication of newspapers, magazines and books, and sending back secret (and often misleading) reports on Hong Kong, which were known as *neibu wenjian* or internal documents, restricted to party leaders. The Communist Party itself remained an underground organisation and had no public presence.

The man named to the NCNA job was Wang Kuang, a veteran of the Guangdong party committee who had been engaged in its work on Hong Kong and Macau since the 1950s and 'specialised in cultural propaganda'. For the first time, Beijing quietly transferred two officials specialising in economic analysis to the office.

The NCNA began to emerge from its ideological fortress. On 3 August it sent two staff, Li Jusheng and Luo Keming, to a financial industry event. At the end of September, the governor was invited to its annual reception for China's National Day. In return MacLehose invited Wang Kuang, the NCNA director, to a banquet. It was this social exchange which paved the way for Li Qiang's history-making visit to Government House.

The self-imposed isolation of China at the time, when travellers from Hong Kong had to walk across a bridge connecting the border town of Lo Wu to the village of Shenzhen, made the change momentous to all who witnessed it. 'One thinks back to how astonishing it was that there was no physical connection between Hong Kong and mainland China until roughly that time and then you get the first aircraft coming in with Shanghai crabs,' said Wilson, referring to the seasonal delicacy flown in to please well-heeled diners in Hong Kong. 'Then you get the first through train [from Hong Kong to Guangzhou] and then you get the ferry boats going directly up the river to Guangzhou. And up to that point you had to walk across the bridge. It was a huge change. The tectonic plates were beginning to change. Had they not been changing we could never have got involved in the negotiations on the future.'

Once the Chinese foreign trade minister had come and gone, leaving his invitation for the governor to visit Beijing, the die was cast. On 29 March 1979 MacLehose and Wilson flew to the capital, where they conferred at the British embassy with the ambassador, Percy Cradock. Their mission was complicated by something that did not trouble the Chinese side: a general election. On the very eve of MacLehose's arrival, the minority Labour government of James Callaghan had lost a vote of confidence in the House of Commons and the prime minister had called an election for 3 May.

As MacLehose and Wilson sat down to breakfast they were joined by Cradock. He brought the news that Callaghan's ambitious and energetic foreign secretary, Dr David Owen, could not fly to China to join them because of the events at home. 'There will be no medical inspection,' said Cradock in a solemn tone. When the others looked puzzled, he said: 'Dr Owen is not coming.' To MacLehose, who regarded Dr Owen's enthusiasm for a breakthrough in Chinese diplomacy with suspicion, this was welcome news. But it posed an immediate challenge.

The absence of the foreign secretary was an important tactical factor. The governor of Hong Kong would have to go in to negotiate with the leader of China without political authority for anything he might have to say, and so no deal could be agreed on the spot. On the other hand, that provided an escape clause if the two sides needed more time. With the future of 5.5 million people in Hong Kong in their hands, a small group of unelected British officials had to make tactical decisions that might affect generations to come.

They huddled at the embassy, debating the options as the clock ticked down to their appointment with Deng Xiaoping. It was the first official visit by a governor of Hong Kong since 1949 and both MacLehose and Wilson knew that there was no guarantee of another audience with China's supreme leader. Cradock, who spent much of his time in Beijing harrying the Chinese for appointments, agreed. Their main question was whether to raise the future of Hong Kong at all. In hindsight the dilemma appears absurd. If the British governor was to meet Deng and *not* raise the future of Hong Kong, then why was he there? The diplomats debated whether a token mention of the treaties would do as a prelude to a gradual, considered negotiation.

Wilson, the political adviser, thought the difficulty was tactical. 'The normal way of dealing with a big issue in China was to take it up the line of command and give a warning of what you are going to do because it then goes up to the top leadership,' he recalled. From the Chinese perspective, normal tactics were to start negotiating at lower levels, with a final seal of approval given in a high-level meeting. However in this case China had chosen to reverse its normal diplomatic practice by inviting MacLehose to meet Deng first, a rare instance of top-down negotiation.

Wilson felt that they had no choice but to put the future of Hong Kong on the table. It was now or, maybe, never. 'It was the key issue and you were being asked to see Deng Xiaoping. How could you *not* raise it? So, a difficult decision but in the greater scheme of things I don't see that it made a difference.'

The trio headed off to the Great Hall of the People, where MacLehose arranged his tall, angular frame in a ceremonial armchair next to Deng. The Chinese leader chainsmoked, grasping his cigarette in his left hand, and spat at intervals into a white ceramic spittoon set on the floor between the two. Usually Deng chose to indulge this habit just as the governor was starting to make a point, which Wilson, who was well used to Chinese customs, found 'slightly sort of off-putting, even for somebody like Murray'. Deng, a vigorous seventy-four, spoke energetically and gesticulated at MacLehose while three translators and note-takers scribbled away. Percy Cradock sat, sphinx-like, observing them.

The Chinese leader opened by taking the initiative and at an early point said that sovereignty over Hong Kong belonged to the People's Republic of China. It would undoubtedly return to the motherland, but Hong Kong could practise capitalism 'for a long time' into the next century while the rest of the country continued to practise socialism. These words foreshadowed his theory of 'one country, two systems', but Deng did not call it that at the time. 'What Deng Xiaoping laid out was that whatever happens in 1997, these things will follow: Hong Kong will remain different, Hong Kong will be a free port, and please tell the people of Hong Kong "*fang xin*" – put your hearts at ease,' Wilson recalled.

In hindsight, it was obvious to Wilson that the Chinese had not yet decided what to do about Hong Kong. His impression was that Deng spoke in terms of 'whatever happens in 1997', but it was unclear what that might be. Later, some Chinese accounts of the meeting painted Deng as sternly resolute that China would take control of Hong Kong. It seems likely that these accounts are a party-approved smoothing out of history. Wilson again: 'My impression, for what it's worth, is that … China had not made its mind up at that time about what to do and it is not until early the next year that China internally comes to decisions that they will resume sovereignty and they will resume control. But not at the time of Murray's visit.'

MacLehose was later criticised for trying out a suggestion that China would resume formal sovereignty while British administration of Hong Kong continued for an agreed period. The idea had been considered by David Owen, who recalled in his memoirs the concept that Britain might even give back sovereignty before 1997 if there was a legally binding framework in place for continued control by its seasoned administrators. The solution was much in vogue among businessmen and officials who felt that China did not know how to run Hong Kong, was likely to make a mess of it and would prefer to outsource it under a management contract to the experienced British. From the point of view of unelected colonial civil servants and the clubby circle of business people in Hong Kong this was, no doubt, an ideal proposal. Wilson himself felt it was probably naïve.

The idea that Britain might continue administering the city was not as deserving of scorn as its critics thought. Although the British did not know it at the time, the option was discussed seriously among the Chinese leadership. Zhao Ziyang, the reformist who became premier in 1980, told his political secretary, Bao Tong, that he had no objection to the idea of the British staying on as administrators so long as China took back sovereignty. In addition, Zhao did not even think it necessary for China to station troops in Hong Kong if an agreement was arrived at. Inside the foreign ministry, legal experts and the Western European department argued for keeping arrangements as they were. So did the Foreign Trade Ministry, which liked to keep things predictable. Even within the Xinhua news agency, a propaganda organ, some officials felt it would be best to keep the status quo. These were, however, internal discussions among the upper echelons in China which the British could only guess at in early 1979. They would not be settled until Deng Xiaoping himself made a firm decision two years later.

For MacLehose the immediate issue was a practical one. Leases in the New Territories were running down because the Crown could not grant tenure beyond 30 June 1997, meaning that businesses feared to invest and banks would be unwilling to grant mortgages, which were usually for a duration of fifteen years. The uncertainty was a drag on economic growth. It had broader psychological effects on confidence in Hong Kong's real estate and its stock market. These were the colony's engines of prosperity at the time because China had not yet opened up and the profits from its markets were small.

So, after more than a century of dramatic events involving the prestige and power of two great nations, it had come down to this: the leader of China and the governor of Hong Kong sparring over bundles of documents tied with ribbon in lawyers' offices setting out titles to parcels of land on which stood farms, villages and suburban plots.

There followed an interlude of comedy. As MacLehose mentioned the need to deal with the leases, meaning the individual leases held by tenants in the New Territories, the Chinese interpreter made a mistake, suggesting that he was referring to the main lease held by Britain over the whole territory. The expression on Deng's face must have been a study as he heard this. Breaching protocol, Wilson intervened to put him right. 'I did the thing you're not meant to do and said in Chinese, "that's not the correct translation,"' Wilson recalled, 'it could have been an awful mistake.'

Mistakes were avoided and face was saved – just about. Deng did not respond in detail to MacLehose's point about the leases but emphasised that investors in Hong Kong should rest at ease. The meeting ended cordially.

That night, the governor and Wilson headed off for another unpublicised rendezvous with Liao Chengzhi somewhere in Beijing. This time it did not go well. The Chinese were angry because MacLehose had discussed the future of Hong Kong with Deng in detail by raising the complex question of the leases and the idea of continued British administration. 'Liao Chengzhi said "Look, you shouldn't have raised this with Deng Xiaoping because it would have been better if we'd all been warned," which was of course true,' Wilson conceded. 'The counter was that if you were going to see Deng Xiaoping it was terribly important that if possible you should get a nod from Deng Xiaoping to say "Yes, we'll look into what to do." And we didn't get a complete negative. We only got the complete negative later.'

The British would make their way back to Hong Kong in a leisurely progress that did not suggest there was anything urgent afoot. After a few days in the ancient capital of Xi'an, MacLehose and Wilson arrived in Guangzhou. 'We saw Xi Zhongxun, Xi Jinping's father. I thought he was splendid. Murray was asking him about what life had been like while he was under house arrest for so long during the Cultural Revolution and Xi Zhongxun said "Well, it gave me an opportunity to read a lot of stuff. I read all of Winston Churchill's histories of the war. I read Adam Smith, I read all these things" – he produced a whole list of the books he'd read, in Chinese.'

The governor and his party returned to Hong Kong on the first train from Guangzhou to the station at Kowloon. In Hong Kong, an enthralled audience was hanging on every word said in public. MacLehose was highly selective in what he told them. His use of Deng's phrase 'put your hearts at ease' made every headline. Wilson, who was a great admirer of his boss, admitted: 'That produced a sort of artificial euphoria in Hong Kong without perhaps sufficient realisation that this was not the end of the story. It didn't mean that British administration was going to go on, not at all, nothing like that.'

Denied full knowledge of the talks, and unaware of the ambiguity of their outcome, Hong Kong investors went on a spree. Real estate and stock prices soared over the next year. Meanwhile the Chinese began to work out what they meant to do. Back in Britain, the voters had elected Margaret Thatcher to head a new Conservative government with a majority of forty-three seats. The British, having had their best shot, could do little but wait while the Conservatives found their feet.

The Chinese political-bureaucratic machine began to work in its practised way to fix a line and to ensure conformity. This was a textbook example of its methods.

First, like any Western government, it worked out its talking points. Then it repeated them ad nauseam. For example, in May 1979 the assistant foreign minister, Song Zhiguang, who had been the first Chinese ambassador to London, told a French delegation that 'Hong Kong is Chinese territory and its future will be resolved between Beijing and London.' On 7 October, Hua Guofeng, who was still chairman of the party and premier, told a press conference that China 'will consider the interests of Hong Kong investors'. The second Chinese move was to stop Britain doing anything that might interfere with Chinese sovereignty after 1997. It indicated the evolution of a hard line.

MacLehose had suggested that in order to get around the 1997 problem, the Hong Kong government could issue leases in the New Territories with no expiration date. He wanted to announce the plan in his autumn policy address. In Beijing, Cradock took the proposal to assistant foreign minister Song. After a long delay, a reply came back. China found the idea inappropriate and unnecessary, urged Britain to desist from it and warned of adverse consequences if it went ahead. Cradock, disconcerted by the blunt response, urged London to keep the rejection secret.

In November 1979, Hua went to London and met Mrs Thatcher at 10 Downing Street. The British record of their talks shows that the Thatcher government was keen to sell arms and technology to China, including Harrier jump jets and Rolls-Royce aero engines. Both sides were preoccupied by the Soviet Union. They sought common ground in world affairs. It was only late in the afternoon that Mrs Thatcher and Hua turned to the future of Hong Kong. She invited her foreign secretary, Lord Carrington, to speak. He could hardly have been more emollient. The governor had made proposals about leases which the Chinese government found unacceptable; very well, the British government 'would not pursue these' but would be 'very grateful' if Premier Hua could give some thought as to how confidence in Hong Kong could be maintained. Mrs Thatcher interjected that, of course, she 'did not expect an answer on the spot'.

Hua said his government had given the matter serious thought but 'they had to be very careful what was said about Chinese territory'. As to *what* they had thought, the premier was vague. Fortunately for him, the party line provided an easy answer. He said that they would keep in touch with the British government and, meanwhile, 'would take account of the anxieties of investors'.

In 1980, Hua and Deng Xiaoping received the former Labour prime minister, James Callaghan, who found them unhurried but ready to repeat the mantra that investors in Hong Kong had nothing to worry about. When Lord Carrington met Deng on a visit to China in 1981, Deng told him that the Chinese reassurances 'can be trusted' but gave no details of what was in his mind.

Behind the scenes, Deng ordered Liao Chengzhi to develop a policy. On 17 February 1981 he gave Liao authority to convene ministries and agencies as he saw fit. Two choices presented themselves. One was to let Hong Kong go on in the same way that China had allowed Portugal to continue governing Macau and to 'wait until the time is ripe.' The other was 'to respect history and reality' and take Hong Kong back. There was no doubt of Deng's personal view that the second course was the only one which could be justified by history, ideology and patriotism. In the light of that, there was no way that British administration could continue. The idea was dead and buried.

Liao came up with a simple, striking recommendation. China should borrow the policy it had already worked out for Taiwan in the event of the island's peaceful reunification with the mainland. It was 'one country, two systems' – one China, practising socialism on the mainland and capitalism in Taiwan. 'One country, two systems is not just the correct policy for solving the Taiwan question but also the only correct policy for solving the Hong Kong question,' said his report.

There was no mention of democracy in the 'one country, two systems' theory, for the simple reason that there was no need for it: in 1981 Taiwan was still a one-party military dictatorship under the Kuomintang and would remain so until political reforms in 1987. The Chinese Communist Party did not evolve the 'two systems' concept with democracy in mind at all. This basic fact has often eluded observers, and it has bedevilled China's relationship with Hong Kong from the first negotiations until the present day. 'The fact is that our original idea of "one country two systems" was intended to solve the Taiwan question but the Hong Kong question came up first,' recalled Zhou Nan, the leading Chinese negotiator.

The party's central committee met twice, in April and December, to consider Liao's proposals. By December Liao had readied a document. It established its ideological credentials by basing its thesis on 'nine articles' for reunification with Taiwan laid down earlier in the year by Marshal Ye Jianying, one of Mao's founding marshals of the PLA; these included the promise of 'a high degree of autonomy' and proposed that Taiwan's 'socio-economic' system could stay unchanged. Votes, elections and liberty did not appear on his list.

Liao was wise enough to know that this would not do for Hong Kong. He increased the number of articles to twelve and expanded the provisions for freedom of speech, religion and assembly, enshrining the concept that Hong Kong would be governed by local people and that its leaders might be chosen by the central government, appointed through consultations or elected locally. The December 1981 meeting of the central committee approved the broad outlines and relayed a deadline from Deng: the leader wanted a final package within three months. A United Front Work Conference heard the basic outlines at a meeting which concluded on 6 January 1982. Liao revised his paper and put it in. On 21 March, Deng agreed in principle to the plan. In the words of a Chinese historian: 'China was ready to go head to head with Britain.'

4

The Iron Lady versus
the Steel Factory

At the start of 1982, the Chinese government was ready. It had decided on a policy to take back Hong Kong from which it would not deviate over the next four decades. The way it was carried out was to serve as a model for China's next generation of leaders and bureaucrats. It was systematic, impressively well-timed and implacable.

The first British official to hear of it formally was a junior foreign office minister, Humphrey Atkins, who was visiting Beijing. He was received by Zhao Ziyang, who had replaced Hua Guofeng as premier. They met on the same day, 6 January, that the party conference formally wrapped up its deliberations on Hong Kong. Zhao told Atkins that China was ready to negotiate on the basis that Hong Kong would retain its different status, operating as a capitalist financial and commercial centre with a free port. It was agreed that Mrs Thatcher would visit China later in the year.

The Chinese soon realised that Atkins was not viewed in London or Hong Kong as a heavyweight and that although he had accurately relayed their position, the message must be reinforced. In April, the ever-attentive Edward Heath arrived once again to pay a visit to Deng. At their meeting Deng laid out the reassuring concept of 'one country, two systems', committed China to negotiate and made it clear he wished this information to be passed on to Mrs Thatcher. So, too, was a warning from Deng: 'If China does not take back Hong Kong, none of us will be able to explain it to the people.'

Deng was more precise when he met the North Korean dictator, Kim Il-Sung, at the end of the month. Now, he said, China's policy was to reclaim Hong Kong island, the Kowloon Peninsula and the whole of the New Territories by 1997. Kim heartily approved.

In Beijing, London and Hong Kong, officials and diplomats rustled through sheaves of long-forgotten telegrams and pored over the clauses of treaties drawn up by their ancestors. For Britain, the first half of 1982 brought a great distraction. On 2 April, Argentina invaded the Falkland Islands, a British dependent territory in the South Atlantic. Mrs Thatcher went to war to win them back, achieving victory in June. On the other side of the world in Asia there was an uneasy, deceptive interlude of calm.

The Chinese bureaucracy had rehearsed its script on Hong Kong for years before its political masters decided what to do. In Margaret Thatcher they encountered a mistress of detail whose capacity for work defined the style of her government. In the summer of 1982, after defeating Argentina, she turned her attention to Hong Kong, confident as never before of her political strength, renowned around the world for her willingness to use force and firm in her belief that dictatorships were detestable, brittle and, ultimately, doomed. Fortified by her victory in the South Atlantic, she did not like the idea of surrender.

A Chinese perspective on the prime minister came from Zhou Nan, the fluent English-speaking cadre whose fondness for Shakespeare belied a fierce negotiating style, a deep suspicion of foreigners and a strength of ideological conviction which led one future leader of Hong Kong under Chinese rule to call him 'a dyed in the wool Marxist'. 'This so-called iron lady had just won the Falklands War and taken the Malvinas [i.e. the Falkland Islands] from Argentina,' Zhou recalled in his oral memoir. 'She didn't want to return Hong Kong to us at first. She considered international co-ownership, a referendum, a second Singapore, even a military confrontation with China.'

There is no evidence that Mrs Thatcher gave prolonged consideration to any of these ideas. But China had also resolved that it was prepared to fight if necessary. In a meeting with members of the Politburo, Deng Xiaoping had said that if all else failed, the People's Liberation Army would be sent in to take possession of Hong Kong. Lu Ping, who later headed the Chinese negotiators, confirmed in his retirement that Deng was 'ready to resort to requisition by force'. In his memoir, Zhou Nan also related how China was prepared to consider 'non-peaceful means'.

For her part Mrs Thatcher knew that this was not Argentina and the Falklands, where swift military action had reversed aggression and restored the status quo. There was no prospect of that. With typical thoroughness, the prime minister asked her chiefs of staff for their professional opinion. The soldiers told her that Hong Kong could not be defended for very long against the PLA.

The risk of Chinese military intervention was never to abate until the evening of 1 July 1997, yet Mrs Thatcher was firm in her own mind about three things. First, she believed that Britain held Hong Kong, Kowloon and the New Territories under three valid international treaties. Second, as a lawyer, and as a politician brought up in the 1930s, she felt that treaties were sacrosanct: as David Wilson put it, the legal principle of *pacta sunt servanda* – agreements must be kept. Third, she thought that Britain could hold on to Hong Kong island and the tip of Kowloon because both had been ceded in perpetuity, even if it had to hand back the New Territories in 1997.

China did not accept any of these premises. Each of them contradicted Deng's commitment to take back all of Hong Kong in 1997. The dangers went far beyond the scope of the Anglo-Chinese dispute. It was the height of the Cold War, when both the Western allies and the Soviet Union put their trust in a skein of international agreements – from a divided Berlin to a divided Korea – to reduce the chance of a nuclear war. If treaties were casually broken and tossed aside, the law of the jungle would return as it had in Mrs Thatcher's childhood before the Second World War. China herself had been a principal victim of lawless militarism in that conflict. The stakes, therefore, were higher than the fate of Hong Kong. They were limitless. Only a few people could see this at the time. Fortunately, one of them was Her Majesty's recently knighted ambassador to China, Sir Percy Cradock, a professional dispeller of illusions.

Mrs Thatcher always demanded a stream of briefings from both government and unofficial sources. Some of them were accurate. She received a prescient warning from Lord Shepherd, a businessman with interests in Hong Kong, who reported that 'Chinese friends' had found Deng and Zhao intransigent at recent meetings. 'There is therefore no possibility for the lease to be extended; and Hong Kong island, which is ceded territory, according to the former treaty will <u>not</u> be exempt from the sovereignty reversion,' he wrote. Mrs Thatcher underlined 'not' in her own hand. 'Like you, I doubt whether their objective to leave Hong Kong <u>in practice</u> as it is and their formula are compatible. It is going to be a very difficult visit,' she wrote back to him.

A sunnier view came from the former Conservative Chancellor of the Exchequer, or finance minister, Anthony Barber, who chaired the Standard Chartered Bank, the second most influential British bank in Hong Kong. Barber and his group managing director, Peter Graham, told Mrs Thatcher's private secretary Ian Gow that 'they took the view that if we were to surrender sovereignty over the island in return for continuing administration … that would be entirely acceptable.' The bankers were not entirely sanguine. They warned that if there was no agreement, British administration might have to be withdrawn to the area within Boundary Street on the Kowloon peninsula. Graham also delivered a widely held view among business people. Democracy was not on. In his view the optimum outcome would be that the role of governor or chief administrator 'should also continue to be in British hands and should not be elective'.

A private research group report passed to Mrs Thatcher by her political guru, Sir Alfred Sherman, contained some remarkably frank appraisals by prominent members of the Hong Kong colonial elite. Like Barber, they betrayed not the slightest awareness of the realities as seen from the Chinese side. The head of HSBC, Michael Sandberg, told its author that 'British sovereignty must be maintained' and any cession of it could only be 'purely symbolic'. The report also quoted Sandberg as saying: 'the idea of the Chinese administering Hong Kong is like a disaster scenario … the realm of fantasy.' The head of the Hong Kong General Chamber of Commerce, James McGregor, was emphatic that 'the people of Hong Kong need not be consulted'. As for Sir John Bremridge, a successful businessman who had become financial secretary, he had 'no confidence in the FO [Foreign & Commonwealth Office] lawyers' and saw a huge contrast between Hong Kong and China. 'Hong Kong is awash with money. It has lots of clever people and no trade unions,' he maintained, whereas China 'is like fifteenth century Europe with its barons, its feudalism as well as its living style and standards'.

Bremridge's views might have come as a surprise to the Hong Kong Federation of Trade Unions, a leftist, pro-Beijing group which had existed since 1948 and commanded the allegiance of hundreds of thousands of workers. Its well-educated supporters would go on to play a significant part in the political movements allied with China which dominated local government after 1997. It was, moreover, one of a spectrum of organised labour groups active in Hong Kong, where there were plenty of trade unions in the early 1980s but not much in the way of labour rights.

Sherman added his own words to stiffen Mrs Thatcher's ideological backbone: 'It is widely argued among groups sympathetic to the present regime (e.g. the FCO and its echoes in the quality press) that Deng and his colleagues in power are "pragmatic". It is worth asking what is meant by pragmatic and what is meant by power.'

The Foreign Office was justly nervous, something that did not deter Mrs Thatcher in the least. She distrusted its diplomats, feeling they were too prone to compromise with foreigners. She had lost one foreign secretary when Lord Carrington resigned after Argentina invaded the Falklands and she was in the process of breaking another, the sceptical 'wet' conservative Francis Pym. Mrs Thatcher scathingly dismissed Pym's suggestion that Britain should resign itself to handing over Hong Kong and its people to the Communists. Among the foreign secretary's urbane turns of phrase, one stood out: 'we must not allow our consideration for "the wishes of the people" to develop into acceptance of the paramountcy of the will of the population, that would not be realistic.' Mrs Thatcher was not impressed. 'This paper is pathetic and it is a recipe for a sell-out,' she wrote in blue ink on his memo. She herself would take charge of the policy.

No British prime minister had visited China while in office, a confidential briefing note from the head of the Foreign Office informed her. This was therefore a consequential, pioneering trip. The diplomats reminded Mrs Thatcher that Britain carried weight because it was a key Western power in the Cold War. Deng Xiaoping's big strategic worry was the Soviet Union and he looked to Britain to help what was known as 'Soviet expansionism'.

It is worthwhile to recall how deep was the conviction among Chinese leaders that a war with the Soviet Union might be inevitable. Their preparations and deployments implied a nuclear exchange with the Soviets, not with the West. After the Sino-Soviet split of the 1960s, Mao Zedong saw himself as the heir to Stalin and the party talked of itself as the guardian of Marxism-Leninism against those it dubbed 'revisionists'. China boasted of its role as a beacon of Third World liberation from imperialism but in the socialist world it was isolated. It built labyrinths of bunkers in its cities, relocated entire heavy industries deep in its interior and prepared its military for a war of defence, presumably to be waged in the desolate aftermath of a first nuclear strike.

In strategic terms, China felt encircled. To the north it faced Soviet divisions along a disputed border enclosing territories which the Chinese considered had been stolen from the Qing empire by the Tsars, a theft formalised by yet more unequal treaties. In the west, China had subdued Tibet and incorporated the deserts of Chinese Turkestan, known today as Xinjiang, securing a barrier between central Asia and the Han heartland. But in 1979 the Soviet invasion of Afghanistan had brought the Kremlin's troops to China's doorstep. In the southwest China had gone to war with

India to dominate the Himalayas, but that victory had strengthened India's drive to become a nuclear-armed state.

Even the triumphant wars of liberation in Indochina created strategic problems for China because Soviet intervention had turned them into proxy conflicts: Moscow backed North Vietnam, the Chinese propped up the ultra-Maoists of the Cambodian Khmer Rouge, and both sides vied for influence over Laos. In 1979 Deng Xiaoping launched a short war against Vietnam from which the PLA retired with a bloody nose. The rest of southeast Asia was held by staunchly anti-Communist monarchies, military governments or capitalist semi-democracies. Then there was Taiwan, the unsinkable aircraft carrier; the Korean peninsula, packed with American forces; and the ancient enemy, Japan, sheltering under the American nuclear umbrella.

China was at a difficult stage in its relations with the United States. The two countries had agreed in the Shanghai communiqué of 1972 that 'all Chinese on both sides of the Taiwan strait maintain there is but one China', a study in ambiguity that let both sides claim that their principles had been upheld. On 1 January 1979 the Carter administration signed a second communiqué recognising the Beijing government, establishing full diplomatic relations with it and ending formal ties with Taiwan. These were political gains for China. But the election of President Ronald Reagan in 1980 brought to power a staunch anti-Communist whose Republican Party was resolute in defence of Taiwan. China and the United States were locked in negotiations over a third communiqué, which was eventually signed in August 1982, and it was clear that Reagan would continue to sell arms to Taiwan. Deng realised there was little chance of achieving reunification with the island. That made the recovery of Hong Kong all the more significant.

For these reasons, the conventional wisdom that Britain had 'no cards to play', often expressed by Mrs Thatcher's next foreign secretary, Geoffrey Howe, among others, was not completely true. Mrs Thatcher herself would play the global card by warning Deng face to face of the international consequences for China if it invaded Hong Kong.

On a practical level, Britain was on weak ground if it came to a confrontation. It held only 8 per cent of the territory by perpetual treaty and it could count on no allied support because most Western countries were eager to court the emerging new China. In private, the United States excused itself by saying its troubles with China over Taiwan meant that it could not play a helpful diplomatic role. The Western allies shared intelligence, but there was no appetite in Washington for a military showdown over a colony of just five million inhabitants left over from the empire on which the sun never set. The impression among British ministers and officials was plain. If it came to the crunch, Britain was on its own.

The moral case for Hong Kong burdened Mrs Thatcher. Her government had passed the British Nationality Act of 1981, which reduced Hong Kong people to British Dependent Territories Citizens (BTDC) who enjoyed the right to live in Hong Kong but not in the United Kingdom. At a stroke it had removed the political risk of mass immigration from Hong Kong but left its people with nowhere to go in a crisis. Many were scrambling for foreign passports or for green cards to reside in the United States. While Mrs Thatcher always rejected opening the gates to a flood of people, she was powerfully aware that China's own laws did not recognise dual nationality. Britain could not protect its BDTC passport holders in Hong Kong under Chinese rule except by offering them an exit. This would weigh on her throughout the negotiations.

There was also self-interest. Britain needed to boost exports to China as the country's economy began a long period of expansion. Marconi, Rolls-Royce and British Aerospace were all keen to sell military equipment. Mrs Thatcher was reminded that a bid by Vosper Thorneycroft to refit two Chinese destroyers would benefit a shipyard 'with the largest number of government-held marginal seats in its hinterland'.

Apart from studying grand strategy, politics and trade, Mrs Thatcher did not spare the organisers of her trip to China and Japan her attention to detail. To start with, she said she would 'prefer to go to China first – Communist countries are always the most stressful and I prefer to do them first'. This was not possible, however, so the trip opened with a tiring but less important visit to Japan. In China, she wanted two rounds of talks with Deng. Cradock 'promised to keep up maximum pressure but I cannot pretend the chances of a second call on Deng are particularly good'. In the event only one meeting took place.

The British ambassador in Beijing found himself not only managing expectations in high matters of state but negotiating with the caterers at the Great Hall of the People. It was customary for the Chinese side to offer a welcome banquet and for the guest to reciprocate. Cradock struggled to reconcile Mrs Thatcher's well-known insistence on economy with the requirements of prestige. 'The 50 yuan per head meal lacks e.g. Sharks Fin and sea slugs, both delicacies to a Chinese palate, which would be conspicuous by their absence on an occasion like this ... nor should we attempt to skimp on the drinks,' he advised mournfully.

A compromise was made on the menu, but the wine was a headache. An official noted that there was a local option of 'Dynasty' white wine from Tianjin 'which resembles a medium Hock, its only drawback is that it is the product of a Sino-French joint venture'. The issue was resolved by packing eight cases of English Beaulieu wine (1979) and three cases of Pommery champagne (1973), along with silver candelabras, flower bowls, a cigar box and cutlery, into the hold of the Royal Air Force VC10 jet which was to fly the party to China.

On the long flight itself Mrs Thatcher approved a seating plan and cast a vigilant eye over the menu proposed by the RAF. She selected a proper breakfast of orange juice, coffee, toast, marmalade and scrambled or poached eggs. A main dish named 'Supreme of Chicken Stanley', presumably after the capital of the Falklands, received a prime ministerial tick but next to a canape of caviar she put an 'X' – 'no – far too expensive!' The VC-10 touched down at Beijing on 22 September 1982, 'one of those glorious still and sunny afternoons which are the mark of the Peking [Beijing] autumn', as Cradock recalled it. Mrs Thatcher inspected a guard of honour in Tiananmen Square while the band of the People's Liberation Army played 'God Save the Queen'.

Mrs Thatcher's first meetings were with the premier, Zhao Ziyang, whom her diplomats had hopefully tagged as a moderniser. Among her party were Cradock, the new governor of Hong Kong, Sir Edward Youde, and two future ambassadors to China. Her private secretary, John Coles, recorded the conversations.

Since his private flirtation with liberal ideas on Hong Kong, which was known only to his close collaborators, Zhao, obedient to party discipline, had fallen into line. He said 'that the Chinese government was not bound by treaties signed between the British government and the Ching [Qing] dynasty. The Chinese people had never recognised those treaties'. By 1997, Zhao said, the legal basis on which Britain occupied the New Territories would no longer exist. 'Hong Kong island and Kowloon were similarly inseparable from the territory of China. So the only wise and practical course was that the entire area ... should be returned to China'. There was 'no alternative', said Zhao, using one of Mrs Thatcher's own catchphrases.

Zhao laid out the plan for Hong Kong to become a special administrative zone administered by 'local people', with a capitalist economy, a free port and its own currency, the Hong Kong dollar. British civil servants

The 'unequal' Treaty of Nanjing, ceding Hong Kong to Britain after the first Opium War, is signed on board *HMS Cornwallis*, August 1842.

By the late 19th century the harbour of Hong Kong was a thriving centre of trade between Asia and the West.

Colonial power: Royal Navy 'Bluejackets' march through
Hong Kong in a show of force after unrest, April 1927.

Privilege on the Peak: a law passed in 1904 after a plague banned most
Chinese people from these cool green slopes. It was repealed in 1930.

The Royal Navy takes back Hong Kong after the surrender of Japan, 1945.

Trade and finance turned Hong Kong into a global player:
its stock exchange was one of the world's largest by the 1980s.

Opposite: The port grew fast as China opened up; new tower
blocks rose to give Hong Kong's workforce better homes.

No meeting of minds: Deng Xiaoping, with spittoon, and Margaret Thatcher, with handbag, in Beijing, September 1982.

Sir Percy Cradock and his wife, Birthe, with guests at the British Embassy, 1980. *Left to right, seated*: Foreign Trade Minister Li Qiang, Wang Guangmei, widow of President Liu Shaoqi, and Vice Foreign Minister Han Kehua.

THE CHANGE: JUNE, 1989

The massacre of protesters in Beijing was a turning point. It marked the defeat of political reform in China and shocked people across the nation: in Hong Kong they marched peacefully in the streets to mourn the dead. The city's future turned bleak and confidence fell. Many of the inhabitants decided to emigrate.

Shanghai: a solitary policeman is enveloped by demonstrators as mass protests continue in China's second city for a week after the massacre in the capital.

Silence in Tiananmen Square: a handful of guards watch the Great Hall of the People while all traces of the democracy movement are erased from Beijing.

could remain in their posts. The city would be stable and prosperous. But China must be the governing power.

Mrs Thatcher argued this point. She said Hong Kong flourished due to British administration 'and without a British administration there would be no confidence'. She warned him of the consequences if it appeared that Britain and China had no 'meeting of minds' on this. 'I have to say that if the changes envisaged in Mr Deng's remarks to Mr Heath ... were to be introduced or even announced as a decision of your government the effect on confidence in Hong Kong would be disastrous ... there would certainly be a wholesale flight of capital.'

Zhao left her in no doubt. 'If it came to a choice between the two, China would put sovereignty above prosperity and stability.' It was time, he said, for the British government to show 'a spirit of co-operation' – not, perhaps, the best way to appeal to Mrs Thatcher.

She replied that the British government honoured its agreements and accepted that the lease on the New Territories would end in 1997. By the same token, British possession of Hong Kong and Kowloon would continue as a matter of international law. She knew that China wished to abrogate the nineteenth-century treaties, but it had to recognise that this could only happen if the British Parliament passed a law doing so. 'To settle the future of Hong Kong by abrogating the treaties alone would be unthinkable. It would produce immediate panic in Hong Kong. It would be a dereliction of British responsibility and would be rejected by the British Government and Parliament and by the people of Hong Kong.'

Mrs Thatcher said she realised that some of these points might be unwelcome:

but I must be candid.

The point was ... if the Chinese government abrogated one agreement valid at international law, what assurance could there be that they would keep any other agreement?

Mrs Thatcher said it was possible that the two sides could agree. Holding out the prospect of concession, she said that if the two sides reached agreements about administration and control of Hong Kong and if she was satisfied these would 'command confidence' and be acceptable to people in Hong Kong and to Parliament in London, then a new situation would arise in which she might consider the question of sovereignty. She understood that China had a principle about sovereignty, but the British government also had a principle, 'which ran strongly through the British character, about duty to those who for 140 years had put their faith, their future and their investments in Hong Kong under British administration'.

On that discordant note the proceedings ended and Mrs Thatcher, with her retinue, prepared to meet Deng himself.

The Chinese bureaucracy had prepared Deng thoroughly for his meeting with the British at 10.30 on the morning of Friday 24 September. The ritual setting was arranged for his convenience, with plush armchairs, antimacassars, teacups painted in classical designs poised on plain modern tables and the inevitable spittoon placed within range of the chairman. This time Deng would not be caught out. He had read the minutes of Mrs Thatcher's talk with Zhao Ziyang. She was now aware of the position of the Chinese government. He would like to hear her comments.

Mrs Thatcher repeated her line. She understood how important the principle of sovereignty was to China but sovereignty was also a difficult issue for her. She would have to convince Parliament and Deng had to convince the Chinese people. Without an agreement on administration and control of Hong Kong, she could not recommend its handover.

Deng interjected to ask 'what the prime minister meant by control'. She talked about Hong Kong existing under a different political order, with an 'assured legal system' and an independent currency. Deng was having no distractions. What, he persisted, with his training in dialectic, did 'control' mean? Was it control by a nation?

The prime minister explained that Britain foresaw a long period when it would continue to administer Hong Kong. If people did not believe that, it would damage confidence. Deng's plan would not work. Financial markets in Hong Kong had fallen sharply over the summer of 1982 amid uncertainty about the future. Pointedly, she said that 'people would make their present judgements against the background of recent Chinese history'. Those with money and skill would leave and there would be an 'economic collapse'.

Deng was unmoved. There was no leeway for China because sovereignty 'was not a matter which could be discussed'. Let it be clear today, he said, that China would certainly recover sovereignty over Hong Kong in 1997. This was a 'pre-condition' for talks. In a kind of peroration, he stated that the recovery of Hong Kong was an existential question for his government. He may have done so for the benefit of his senior party comrades, knowing that the talks were secret and that his words would not be broadcast to the public. (When cameras were let in at the end of the meeting, Deng turned to them and merely said he had told Mrs Thatcher that China stood firm on sovereignty.)

Deng told Mrs Thatcher that if China did not take back Hong Kong in 1997 its leaders and its government 'would not be able to account for it to the Chinese people or the people of the world'. It would mean that the new China was no better than the China of the Qing dynasty. Its leaders, like himself, would be like Li Hongzhang, the Qing dignitary who had signed the unequal treaties and was a figure of shame. The People's Republic had waited thirty-three years for the recovery of Hong Kong and in 1982 it was ready to wait another fifteen. But if it had not recovered Hong Kong by 1997 'the people would have every reason no longer to put their faith in their leaders and the Chinese government ought to retire voluntarily from the political arena.' This was an extraordinary statement by a Chinese Communist leader to the head of a foreign government about Hong Kong and it remains a text which should not be forgotten, because it is assuredly remembered in China.

Deng and Mrs Thatcher agreed on one thing. None of this could be disclosed for fear of panic in Hong Kong. China and Britain would have to talk in secret until they settled their differences. The two went on to speak about those differences in a way that highlighted the depth of their misunderstanding. Deng appeared to think that handing back Hong Kong would benefit Britain because it meant that the era of colonialism was over: 'this would redound to British credit.' Mrs Thatcher was uninterested by that prospect. She said that Britain had ushered many of its former possessions to independence but pointed out that Hong Kong was unique because it was going back to China. 'Britain simply wanted to carry out her moral duty,' she said.

For her part, Mrs Thatcher decided she had no choice but to state things clearly. She had been granted only one audience with Deng and, like Governor MacLehose in 1979, she might not get another chance. Once again, it was now or never. She told Deng that Britain was not asking for an extension of the lease over the New Territories. But Hong Kong island and Kowloon were different because they were held by treaties in perpetuity. China did not recognise those treaties but she believed they were valid in international law. Her aim was that 'if those treaties were to be changed they should be changed by agreement and not abrogated by one side or another.' She went on at length to explain that 'the atmosphere for investment was very bad', and that therefore Britain and China shared an interest in reaching an agreement to keep Hong Kong stable and prosperous. Finally and woundingly, she said, 'every survey showed that the people of Hong Kong wished the British system of administration to be maintained.'

At this point, it appears from the record that the atmosphere darkened. Deng replied that he was very sorry but Britain must understand that China would recover all of Hong Kong in 1997, 'that was certain.' There was no need for British administration to preserve prosperity. Hong Kong would remain capitalist. The Chinese government had thought through the consequences of its resolve and it would call Britain's bluff. 'Many people said that if the prosperity of Hong Kong could not be maintained this would affect China's modernisation drive,' he said, but this was untrue, for 'if the modernisation programme was based on the maintenance or decline of prosperity in Hong Kong then the modernisation decision was not a sound one.'

Deng next turned to a preoccupation which took the British aback but which, in the light of later events, was both ominous and deadly serious. 'There was one point upon which he did not wish to dwell but which he wished to make,' the British side recorded. 'If there were very large and serious disturbances in the next fifteen years, the Chinese government would be forced to consider the time and formula relating to the recovery of its sovereignty of Hong Kong.' Mrs Thatcher was so struck by this threat that she underlined it heavily in blue when she came to review the record for her memoirs.

The official account did not adequately convey the air of menace which filled the room. In fact the Downing Street record could be considered misleading in its dispassionate tone. It omitted a dramatic exchange which Mrs Thatcher herself later recounted in various settings. The two leaders had a verbal clash which, had it become known, would indeed have shaken confidence in Hong Kong.

Deng, who had punctuated his remarks by hawking vigorously into the spittoon, turned to her and said: 'You know, I could walk in and take the whole lot this afternoon.'

Mrs Thatcher was shaken but recovered her poise. She fell back on her lawyer's training and her impromptu skills honed at the dispatch box in the House of Commons. Yes, she said, 'there is nothing I could do to stop you.' But in the eyes of the world, she continued, it would be clear what China was really like. It would gain Hong Kong but it would lose everything. The diplomat taking the record, Bob Peirce, did not recall hearing words 'quite on those lines', but the exchange left a stark impression on Mrs Thatcher even if her later account of it was dramatised for effect. Peirce, who spoke Chinese, felt that Deng and his colleagues 'knew she was no pushover'.

Deng persisted in his worry about 'disturbances'. It was not clear who he feared might start them. He promised that China would consult to find acceptable policies for Hong Kong. From the heights of statesmanship Deng descended swiftly into the realms of conspiracy theories as he warmed to his theme. He seemed to believe that businesses would be involved. 'Take for instance the Hong Kong and Shanghai Bank,' Deng said. 'No-one knew how many banknotes it had issued.' The governor, Sir Edward Youde, intervened to say that the Hong Kong government knew. Undeterred, Deng warned that both sides 'should also prevent businessmen from doing things which were detrimental to the prosperity and stability of Hong Kong'.

Mrs Thatcher said Deng's attitude 'really worried her'. She was not contemplating disturbances but financial collapse. Privately, she was appalled by Deng's ignorance of how a capitalist economy worked and shaken by how quickly his veneer dissolved to reveal an implacable Marxist-Leninist.

At this stage both sides seemed to grasp that it was a question of salvaging the future of Hong Kong. They agreed a statement which opened with the lie that their talks had been held in a 'friendly atmosphere'. It went on to say that they would continue diplomatic negotiations. Accompanied by Sir Percy Cradock and trailed by her retinue, Mrs Thatcher stalked out of the Great Hall of the People and promptly fell down the steps in front of the television cameras.

Mrs Thatcher was asked twenty-five years later by a Hong Kong television interviewer if it was an omen. 'I had very high heels on and those steps were rather more narrow than the ones I was used to having and the heel caught on the edge of the step and my ankle went ... that's all it was,' she said, 'just bad luck.'

The Chinese did make one gesture. 'We were polite to her,' Zhou Nan recalled, 'the shot of her falling down the steps was not shown on our television news.' It was however, replayed on television around the world.

For Zhou Nan, the result was obvious. 'The "iron lady" could not defeat the Chinese "steel factory",' he said, using the nickname given to Deng by Mao Zedong. This was not the whole truth. She had made a strong impression by her steadiness and by her riposte to Deng's blunt threats. In later years, Chinese officials and diplomats were to confirm in numerous conversations that she had sowed enough doubt in Deng's mind to persuade him that China would be best to commit to a negotiated settlement.

He knew that this was the woman who had sent a naval task force to the South Atlantic after one of her commanders told her that if she did not act, the British people would wake up to find they were living in a different country, one whose word did not count. China's leaders could not be sure what Mrs Thatcher would do if it came to a showdown along Boundary Street and around Hong Kong island. They did not want Hong Kong to turn into a divided city like Berlin. In that sense Mrs Thatcher succeeded by force of personality, legal training and debating skill. She bought time for Hong Kong and made the Chinese government and Communist Party leadership think hard about their methods.

The cabled report of the talks to London from the British embassy in Beijing indicated how sensitive were the politics inside Mrs Thatcher's own party and government. 'The prime minister wished the content of this report to be very closely guarded. It should therefore be given very restricted circulation,' it said.

In the afternoon, Deng had an unpublicised meeting with Sir Yue-Kong Pao (known as Sir Y.K. Pao), a Hong Kong shipping magnate and Conservative Party donor, who cultivated Mrs Thatcher and had, indeed, persuaded her to launch one of his ships during this visit to China (the champagne bottle failed to break). Deng used the tycoon as a back channel to drive home his message, knowing that it would be passed on to the British. He repeated that sovereignty and the lease were non-negotiable. But he sought to reassure Pao by saying it was not Beijing's intention to send anyone to rule Hong Kong; instead 'the Chinese Government intended to appoint a Hong Kong Chinese to the top post.' They also intended to put 'low level' Hong Kong Chinese into the future government. There would be no change in the economy, finance and currency. The only change to the legal system would be that final appeal to the United Kingdom would cease. But these things would not even be announced for another one or two years.

Deng dismissed Mrs Thatcher's warnings of economic disaster. 'The Chinese had already made their preparations for the possibility of financial turmoil. They would buy up investments cheaply. They believed that the money which left Hong Kong would come back.' His remarks were duly conveyed by Pao to Mrs Thatcher, who continued to believe that Hong Kong would be 'unworkable' without British administration and that Deng was courting 'international disgrace.'

That night the British hosted the banquet to which Mrs Thatcher and Cradock had devoted so much attention. Deng did not show up. He preferred to clink *mao tai* glasses with his North Korean ally, Kim Il-Sung, who was also in town. A Chinese diplomat later confided that they had 'drunk many toasts' to Mrs Thatcher's discomfiture. Nor did Mrs Thatcher get to meet Hu Yaobang, a reformer, who headed the Communist Party as general secretary. He too was busy squiring Kim around China. The most senior Chinese leader to attend her banquet was Zhao Ziyang, the premier. Her remarks were uncharacteristically subdued.

In later years Mrs Thatcher drew her own defiant conclusion. 'I ... wish to goodness that our forebears had not signed a lease but had held the territory in freehold in perpetuity in which case Hong Kong would have been a free and independent nation long before now. She could be still if China would let her.'

Mrs Thatcher's officials warned her that the visit to Hong Kong would be just as challenging as her talks in China. The colony was hanging on every word from Beijing. The stock market fell by more than 7 per cent in the immediate aftermath of her meeting with Deng and it would lose a quarter of its value in the next few weeks.

The prime minister was unable to provide reassurance when she arrived in the colony. Her performance at a press conference was ebullient but short on detail, because she could say nothing of substance. In private, the contemporaneous record reveals her unguarded remarks which showed the shock of her encounter with Deng, the implacable Communist, and her bleak realisation that the Chinese regime had a completely different world view.

A confidential summary of her conversation with prominent Hong Kong businessmen encapsulated the dilemma Britain now faced. Mrs Thatcher also met 'unofficial' members of the Legislative Council and Executive Council, appointed by the governor to serve as a bridge between the community and the administration. Almost all drawn from the corporate or social elite, they formed a body known as UMELCO, which had its own office and acted as an interlocutor and a sounding board. Leftists and democrats found the notion that they were at all representative of popular opinion to be laughable. These were, however, the people to whom Mrs

Thatcher unburdened herself on Monday 27 September, three days after meeting Deng.

The prime minister told them she had found that Chinese leaders 'had a very limited understanding of what a free society was. They could grasp intellectually such concepts as the rule of law but they did not understand or accept that there could be fundamental rights which did not derive from the state. They thought that they could run a capitalist society but they did not know what it meant.' She 'had been told many times that Deng Xiaoping was "pragmatic" but his pragmatism counted for little compared with his Marxist-Leninism'. Mrs Thatcher – no doubt eyeing her well-connected grandees – said that Chinese leaders had not heard the truth about Hong Kong from the local worthies who were summoned up to Beijing from time to time. She had told the leaders the truth, so she was not surprised that the Chinese could not accept it. She explained the different views of sovereignty, administration and the treaties, reiterating that agreement would be very difficult because 'the Chinese leaders did not begin to understand the nature of a free society.'

Victor Fung, one of two brothers who ran the family trading business Li & Fung, which was expanding in China, said 'his personal opinion was that the ideal solution would be the continuation of the status quo indefinitely.' According to Fung, business people could use their contacts in Beijing 'to get across the message of how much Hong Kong depended on the free enterprise system'.

Gordon Wu, a tycoon who later became a cheerleader for the efficiencies of authoritarian rule, said Chinese leaders might say they wanted confidence and stability in Hong Kong. 'But how good was their word? Their track record was terrible,' he asked. He felt British administration 'would be essential' after 1997 because 'laws could change overnight in China.' Philip Kwok, the Harvard-educated scion of the dynasty which owned Wing On, a popular chain of department stores, asked Mrs Thatcher how the Chinese 'could be brought to understand what made Hong Kong tick'.

The prime minister had little comfort for them. There was a fundamental dilemma because of the wish to retain confidence and the need to keep the talks confidential. Lydia Dunn, a successful banker and business executive, told Mrs Thatcher that it was important politically for Hong Kong that the governor, Edward Youde, should be seen to play his part in the negotiations. While all this unfolded, the governor and Cradock looked on unhappily.

Charles Yeung, a real estate developer, who would later unhesitatingly embrace the Communist Party line and serve on the Chinese People's Political Consultative Conference, asked what weight China attached to international law and human rights, which – he emphasised – were widely supported in Hong Kong. Mrs Thatcher said all Communist countries were concerned about their international image and China would not want to be seen as a nation that broke its agreements and took no account of the wishes of the people of Hong Kong. Therefore, she said, contradicting the approved diplomatic thinking, 'not all the cards were on the Chinese side'.

She now entrusted her diplomats with the job of proving her right. Cradock bent himself to the task of cajoling, persuading and wooing the Chinese side to start the promised talks. For months they prevaricated. Personnel moves, party meetings, festivals – any and all excuses were produced for delay. During the autumn of 1982 Cradock languished awaiting the attention of a junior minister. He recognised that this was a tactic to put pressure on the British and told London as much. It was, however, a successful tactic. Cradock and Youde warned Mrs Thatcher that it meant the Chinese were holding out for a concession on sovereignty before they would talk. The problem was that business confidence and public morale in Hong Kong were founded on the belief that Britain and China were already negotiating. On 21 December Cradock confided in a telegram to London: 'we could not continue for long to tell the Hong Kong people that talks were proceeding about their future when they were not.'

The Chinese used the time skilfully to leak their own position in order to maximise among their opponents and their supporters alike the impression that China was implacably determined to take back control. In a speech to Hong Kong business delegates, Liao Chengzhi came close to spelling out 'one country, two systems' by telling them that after 1997 Hong Kong people would rule Hong Kong. All of this broke the agreement between Deng and Mrs Thatcher to keep things confidential, causing breast-beating and anguish among British officials who seemed torn between bewilderment at China's lack of scruple and horror at the prospect that the people of Hong Kong might discover the truth. Meanwhile nobody could miss the development of Special Economic Zones in the south, signifying China's vision of a prosperous future on its own terms, after the National People's Congress approved their creation in late 1982.

Disagreements on the British side intensified as the slow pressure from China worked its effect. Mrs Thatcher was at odds with her foreign secretary, Francis Pym, who clung to the idea of a dual administration by which Britain would govern Hong Kong island and Kowloon while China ruled the New Territories. Legally impeccable, politically dead on arrival, the suggestion never made it beyond Whitehall paperwork.

The deepening psychological realism, some might say defeatism, must have irritated the prime minister. A historian can only imagine the delight in the Politburo if its members had seen a 'Top Secret UK eyes only' paper on military contingency planning submitted to Mrs Thatcher by her defence secretary, Michael Heseltine, on 16 February 1983, in which Heseltine referred in quotation marks to 'the military effort which might be required to "defend" the colony'.

The crucial meeting took place at 10 Downing Street on 7 March. The governor of Hong Kong and the ambassador to Beijing flew back to sit down with a small group including Mrs Thatcher, her foreign and defence secretaries, her foreign policy adviser and her private secretary. It was time for a decision.

To Mrs Thatcher's enduring credit, she insisted on exploring every avenue open to Britain to fulfil its responsibilities to Hong Kong's people. She was genuinely attentive to the governor's report of worry and concern among the members of his Executive Council, the selected elite body which sat in secret. She wondered whether all of the people should be given a say in their future, perhaps within five years.

Youde voiced the traditional paternalistic view. He pointed out that Britain did listen to the people; a governor had not acted against the advice of Exco for more than twenty years. 'But if full democratic elections were introduced, then there would be political parties. If some of those parties were anti-Communist, the Chinese might decide to disrupt the system.' The governor advocated a 'collegiate' approach to representative government. In any case, this could not be done quickly and five years was too short.

To Mrs Thatcher, these may have seemed old and tired themes, trotted out too late in the day. She questioned whether 'we could not move Hong Kong fairly rapidly down the path towards independence, though stopping short of that final point'.

This must have alarmed the diplomats in the room. One of them, Alan Donald, asked whether she had it in mind that Hong Kong would become independent. This was not her intention, Mrs Thatcher replied; she envisaged a status like Bermuda, a self-governing overseas territory over which Britain retained responsibility for foreign and defence affairs. A genteel shudder and raised eyebrows among her listeners may have accompanied this remark, for the others present soon pressed her to move on.

The British government had learned from secret sources that China was preparing a statement to be released in June stating its vow to recover sovereignty over all of Hong Kong in 1997 and revealing its solution of 'one country, two systems'. They were anxious to avoid that, fearful of the effect in Hong Kong and the damage to their own negotiating position.

The defence secretary Michael Heseltine, a political rival of Mrs Thatcher's, decided to soften her up. He agreed that Britain should not concede sovereignty now but 'the fact was that we were going to have to do so in the end'. This was the cue for Sir Percy Cradock to remind Mrs Thatcher of her words to Deng Xiaoping that if satisfactory arrangements were made she would 'consider' making recommendations to Parliament about sovereignty. 'We should try to find ways of finessing the sovereignty issue,' he advised. Confrontation must be avoided. Cradock suggested sending a letter to Premier Zhao Ziyang worded in such a way that it would be passed on to Deng himself. He proposed writing in more definite terms to say that if a deal was agreed she 'would' recommend to Parliament that Britain give up its sovereignty. The vital thing was to get China to start talks. This concession might do it.

Having exhausted almost every available alternative and tested out every idea on her ministers and advisers, Mrs Thatcher was worn down. The meeting agreed to Cradock's proposal. A letter was drafted swiftly in the Foreign Office and prepared for her to sign. The key sentence read, in part, that if an agreement acceptable to Hong Kong, London and Beijing was reached, 'I would be prepared to recommend to Parliament that sovereignty over the whole of Hong Kong should revert to China.'

The British government did not risk transmitting the text even over its most secure communications. Cradock flew back to Beijing with the letter in his briefcase. He had to wait for more than a week before he could hand it over to Vice Foreign Minister Yao Guang. The two men discussed the precise Chinese translation of the key sentence to make sure the Chinese side had got the message. They had.

This was the fateful decision, and it was the crucial concession after more than one hundred and forty years of British rule. It allowed Deng Xiaoping to claim success where patriotic Chinese of imperial, nationalist or Communist stripe had failed. The Communist Party, aided by the counsels of seasoned experts like Liao Chengzhi, could now afford to be patient and, to some extent, forbearing.

It did not mean that the diplomacy would be easy, and China did not mean it to be. A flavour of the times can be found in the recollections of George Walden, who trained in the Chinese language in Hong Kong, was posted to the British embassy in Beijing, served as private secretary to two foreign secretaries and later became a Conservative Member of Parliament and a writer. 'Apart from iciness and abuse the main form of pressure can be boredom,' he wrote of his years dealing with Chinese officials, 'formal statements of surreal tedium are read out, normally in an eerily expressionless voice.

'So things can continue hour after hour, punctuated by the endless lighting of cigarettes and the occasional splat of phlegm in a white china cuspidor.'

Walden laughed off the notion that diplomats could engage with Chinese officials by the customary methods of making a joke or asking about their families. 'The idea was that, underneath, Chinese communists are just like you and me. They are not. They are the unappetising product of an alien doctrine and of historical circumstances harsher than anything we have remotely experienced.' Walden reflected the attitudes of those, like Cradock, who had served in China during the Cultural Revolution. Cradock himself recalled observing the absence of any 'human contact' between the Chinese leader Hua Guofeng and his entourage on a visit to Britain.

Despite the fact that it had formally recognised the People's Republic of China in 1950, Britain was short of experience in dealing with the Chinese government at high level. Mao had never visited Britain and, before Thatcher, no British prime minister had gone to China while in office. All foreign diplomats were isolated in their compounds in Beijing, spectators to convulsions they often did not understand. Their exchanges with the host government were confined to low-level, ritualised sessions of the kind evoked by George Walden. Meanwhile, Britain's influence had waned in Asia after it drew down its forces from bases east of the Suez Canal after 1967. It had little strategic business to conduct with China. The United States was the dominant power.

Britain's corps of Sinologists had watched with chagrin as the Americans revolutionised their own diplomacy, negotiated directly with Mao and with Zhou Enlai, built up access at the highest levels in Beijing and accumulated a wealth of experience. It was time for Britain to subdue its pride after centuries of diplomatic intercourse with China and to call on its closest ally for advice. The United States was the only government that it had confided in about Hong Kong. Even the Australians, vital partners in electronic eavesdropping and intelligence gathering in the colony, were cut out of the information loop, such was Mrs Thatcher's preoccupation with secrecy. It was therefore a reciprocal payoff for the 'special relationship' when British officials in Washington were given a privileged insight into negotiating with the Chinese, gleaned during more than a decade of talks between the US and China, from the early rapprochement conducted by Henry Kissinger to President Richard Nixon's visit in 1972 and later agreements on diplomatic relations, Taiwan and international security. The Americans felt that Chinese officials had advanced in sophistication and had moved on from the recitation of slogans to mastery of the agenda.

The secret US State Department document entitled 'China's negotiating style' was handed over at a meeting between British officials and John Holdridge, the US Assistant Secretary of State for Asian affairs, and his successor, Paul Wolfowitz. The assessment was treated by Britain as a valuable guide, based on facts and experience of high-level bilateral talks. Many of its observations remain valid today and could be profitably studied by any business executive or diplomat preparing to negotiate with China, whether in a boardroom or a conference chamber at the World Trade Organisation (WTO). The British may well have read it with rueful recognition at how well they had already been played over Hong Kong.

The document conceded that negotiating with China 'can be an exasperating ordeal' but noted that 'tenacity often pays off'. It said that although Beijing's original positions often were extreme, its ultimate objectives were seldom unrealistic. 'To the Chinese much of the bargaining process is not a search for compromise, but an opportunity to assess the resolve of the opposite side and to search for weak points,' it noted. Their method was to hold firm to an opening position while finding ways 'to draw out, soften up and extract concessions from the other side'.

Chinese negotiators usually laid down a 'principled position' while relegating to secondary importance the practical steps by which these 'principles' were to be implemented. 'Their objective is to project an image of uncompromising resolve and place the onus on the opposite side to come forward with concessions that will break the impasse.' However, such 'principles' might be little more than initial bargaining positions, according to case studies, and should not be seen as non-negotiable. The Chinese liked to remind foreigners that they were patient people, the document said, a characteristic meant to lend credibility to the firmness of their position. It warned that sometimes Chinese negotiators would camouflage their own rigidity and probe their opponent's flexibility by 'intermittent cordiality and hints of concession', but these should not be taken at face value. They would seize on events or remarks that could be interpreted to call into question the good faith of the other side 'often in abusive language', and liked to pose as the aggrieved party in order to get their opponents to make concessions as a way to show their good intentions. Officials sent to the conference table seldom had any significant authority of their own, and ideas put forward as 'personal' were authorised at high level. Negotiators should beware of bargaining, because any concession to China would be belittled as minor, while there was no guarantee that verbal or written concessions by China 'will not be partially retracted or encumbered by new difficulties at a later point'.

If all this sounded unpromising, the document did have some comfort and useful tactical advice to offer. Typically, the Chinese side only began to make significant concessions late in the talks, the document argued. 'The Chinese view the 11th hour as critical, final Chinese concessions often come at this point … sometimes only hours before the scheduled departure of the other side.' Negotiators could expect a last-ditch effort by the Chinese side to exact concessions, but in practice it was at the end of the day that Chinese officials had the political authority to settle for the best deal on the table. There was reassurance, too, for the secrecy-obsessed British government, in that 'the Chinese have also frequently shown a willingness to go along with secret side agreements as a means of circumventing differences', although it cautioned that such declarations were sometimes only oral.

In the case of Hong Kong, one paragraph in the US assessment would prove invaluable. 'If the Chinese see a strong enough political imperative to reach final agreement … they are often willing to accept ambiguous language that can be interpreted with different nuances as in the Shanghai communiqué.'

Finally, the document reminded its readers that the bottom line for China was set by its supreme leaders in line with their view of China's interests, the costs of failure and the political effects at home. 'Last minute interventions by Deng Xiaoping in negotiations with both Japan and the US have salvaged agreements,' it said.

Almost every one of these observations was to be vindicated in the talks between China and Britain over Hong Kong. They would remain valid in later years during China's bid to join the WTO, its trade talks with the United States and its battle against dissent in Hong Kong.

On a philosophical level, Mrs Thatcher sought the advice of Henry Kissinger, who came to dinner at 10 Downing Street. He believed that the Chinese sometimes sent subtle signals which were too refined for the crude occidental mind. Kissinger felt that everything said to him by any Chinese of any rank during any visit 'was part of an intricate design'. Armed with these troubling insights, Britain's diplomats headed for the negotiating chamber in Beijing.

On the Chinese side, Deng began to move his chess pieces. At the spring festival in 1983 he met a promising official named Xu Jiatun. The party chief in Jiangsu, the coastal province north of Shanghai, Xu was an economic liberal who had pushed ahead with market reforms and knew about international trade. He had succeeded in doubling the provincial GNP of Jiangsu. The province was a leader in agricultural and industrial production. The head of the Communist Party, general secretary Hu Yaobang, was also impressed with Xu. China needed somebody smart and open-minded who could assess public opinion and help to shape it. They decided to send him to Hong Kong.

Just as Xu began a round of meetings in Beijing to prepare for his new assignment, a blow fell. In the early hours of 10 June 1983, Liao Chengzhi died of a heart attack at the age of seventy-four in a hospital in the capital. A lifetime smoker who had enjoyed his share of greasy pork belly and hotpots seething with fat-laden juices, Liao had undergone a coronary bypass three years earlier at Stanford University Medical Centre in the United States. His death came just as he was about to become a vice president of China, a role that would have put him in an eminent position to provide wisdom and counsel on Hong Kong.

The loss of Liao Chengzhi remains one of the unquantifiable questions about Chinese policy in the years that followed. While he was a dedicated Communist, a long-time covert operative and a patriot, he was skilled in the subtlety of southern Chinese politics and had acquired an encyclopaedic knowledge of Hong Kong over many decades. David Wilson, the political adviser and later governor, called him 'an astonishing man'. Now his experience was gone for ever.

Deng swiftly moved to put Zhao Ziyang, the premier, and Li Xiannian, a relatively conservative party elder, in overall control of Hong Kong affairs. Xu was dispatched to the colony and a former foreign minister, Ji

Pengfei, who had dealt with the British, took day-to-day charge in Beijing. There was no time to lose.

On his arrival in Hong Kong, Xu discovered that the local party organisation was tired, ideologically lazy and prone to empty sloganising. It had been easy for the cadres to criticise British colonialism on cue and to collect the appropriate subsidies, safe in the knowledge that they would never have to put Marxist theory into practice. At the same time, the diet of optimistic and misleading reports they had fed to the central government painted a picture of an ardent people, restless under the yoke of colonialism and yearning to reunite with the motherland. This impression was reinforced by a coterie of businessmen who assured the party leadership that the population was loyal to them, when in fact many people in Hong Kong had fled from Communist China and many of its business dynasties remembered the false promises of 1949 before the new regime confiscated their assets. As the turncoat tycoon Gordon Wu had told Mrs Thatcher in private, its track record was 'terrible'.

The Communists faced the reality that they must prepare for government; no easy task for a party that operated underground, had no legal presence and hid behind the façade of the New China News Agency. A gregarious politician, Xu stepped out from behind the bamboo curtain. He went to schools, businesses, public housing estates, sports meetings and social centres for the elderly, spreading benign reassurance and listening to local people. In Xu's power base, Jiangsu province, the common language differed from the Cantonese spoken in Hong Kong, but he made sure to recruit more local people to the NCNA bureau, which quadrupled in size.

The change in tone was reinforced by a new deputy, Li Chuwen, whose background was unusual for a party cadre. Born in Zhejiang province and educated in cosmopolitan pre-war Shanghai, Li later worked in Geneva and did a postgraduate degree in theology at Yale University, returning to serve as a pastor at a Protestant church in Shanghai. He was entrusted with 'united front work' among Christians, played a quiet role in reaching out to the Vatican and held secret meetings in Hong Kong with Israeli officials at a time when the two states did not have diplomatic relations. Between them, Xu Jiatun and Li Chuwen changed the agenda for Chinese operations in the city.

For the first time, Xu promoted the interests of 'patriotic' businessmen to Beijing and laid the foundations of the alliance between tycoons and Communists that would shape the post-colonial order. His truth-telling and opportunistic realism did not go down well with traditionalists in the Politburo and did not make Deng change his plans. Li Xiannian thought the solution was more propaganda and 'united front' work, while many disapproved of making alliances with capitalists. But in practice, the Chinese political machine adjusted its tactics to win over local opinion and to train people to move into business and administration ahead of the handover. By Maoist standards it was a dinner party revolution.

5

A Joint Declaration

The Sino-British negotiations began on 12 July 1983 in Beijing with the first of twenty-two rounds of talks. At first the Hong Kong public took an intense interest, but as the same scenes of middle-aged men facing each other across a green baize table were replayed time after time, the novelty waned. The initial exchanges were sterile. China presented its 'twelve principles to resolve the issue of Hong Kong' which spelt out the concept of one country, two systems. Britain held to its view that British administration must continue. The impasse could not last because Deng Xiaoping had imposed a deadline of 1 October 1984 to reach agreement. If no deal was struck, China would impose its own solution. Once again, Edward Heath materialised to hear a declaration from Deng on 10 September that the British had to give in: their administration could not continue under the Chinese flag because he would not permit it.

In the absence of public information, rumours blossomed and the financial markets turned volatile. Over the hot typhoon months of the summer, the Hong Kong dollar weakened as capital flowed out of the colony. Thousands of families bought properties in Vancouver, Sydney and other places around the world where the Chinese diaspora congregated. As Mrs Thatcher had warned, money was voting against China even if its owners could not. In September there was a full-scale currency crisis. Finally, on 17 October the Hong Kong dollar was 'pegged' to the US dollar at a rate of HK$7.80 to the greenback.

According to the memoirs of Zhou Nan and other senior Chinese officials, the economic turbulence persuaded Deng and the elders that the British were conspiring to undermine China. Uninformed about the workings of a capitalist economy, they genuinely believed that the British government could manipulate the foreign exchange market. 'It was called the September storm,' a party history observed, 'people in all walks of life and all circles of public opinion in Hong Kong strongly criticised the

British attempt to play the "economic card" and it ended in failure.' Some Chinese leaders were also convinced that Britain planned to make off with the stacks of gold bullion which, so party lore had it, were stored in vaults beneath Government House. A deep suspicion that Britain would plunder Hong Kong before it left would persist in high party circles until the hand-over. In the autumn of 1983 it strengthened Deng and his cohorts in their determination to end what the Chinese side called 'a problem left over from history'.

As fruitless talk succeeded sterile exchange, there was a second significant concession on the British side. Cloaked in the necessary diplomatic obfuscation, Britain would give up any claim to administer or exercise authority in Hong Kong after 1997. It was surrender; and it began, as irony would have it, with a call on Deng Xiaoping by the president of the European Commission, Gaston Thorn of Luxembourg, in early November.

Deng 'repeatedly and insistently' raised the problem of Hong Kong and tore into Mrs Thatcher, while the European envoy wrung his hands, pleading that the UK was just one of many member states. Deng said the British premier was clinging to 'unequal treaties', that there was no way British administration could go on because 'this amounted to continuation of their colonial rule, which of course would not do'. Deng thought the most they could hope for was to keep on a few police officers and civil servants. He suggested that the newly liberated Zimbabwe, where China's friend Robert Mugabe had taken power, was a suitable example.

Thorn hastily passed on the tirade to the British embassy, where an alarmed Cradock telegraphed a summary to London along with his interpretation that the time had come to cave in at the sixth round of talks. He advised ministers to concede that there would be 'no link of authority between post-1997 Hong Kong and the UK', adding that the time for ambiguity had run out and the British surrender of authority 'needs to be made explicit'. To the surprise and dismay of officials in London this set off a dispute between Her Majesty's ambassador to China, Cradock, and her Governor of Hong Kong, Sir Edward Youde.

Youde countered with a message saying that his Executive Council in Hong Kong would be demoralised by such a capitulation, arguing that 'it would give away too much too soon'. The governor foresaw British authority ebbing away before 1997 as its elite supporters abandoned their posts and the Chinese pressed their advantage. 'We should no doubt be invited to renounce other British links before the game has started,' he said. 'I do not think we should let the Chinese push us into further concessions.' Cradock drily responded a day later that 'if we do not accept this, the course we are pursuing is doomed from the start.'

Behind the scenes, the pressure for appeasement was growing. The foreign secretary, Geoffrey Howe, asked the Royal Navy to call off a visit to Hong Kong by HMS *Invincible*, an aircraft carrier that had sailed in the Falklands fleet, and to 'reduce the visibility' of port calls by other warships.

After a lengthy exchange of telegrams, Cradock conveyed the new line to the vice foreign minister, Yao Guang. He had dedicated all his effort to building up a relationship with Yao. On one evening the two men had talked over dinner for four and a half hours. The best he could get out of Yao in response to the British concession was classic Ministry of Foreign Affairs language to the effect that Yao appreciated British 'efforts', as if his interlocutor was a pupil doing their best to comply. None the less the deed was done. The two sides moved ahead to discuss detail and the tension was defused.

At the end of 1983 Sir Percy Cradock left his job as ambassador to China to become principal foreign policy adviser at Mrs Thatcher's side in Downing Street. He was succeeded by Sir Richard Evans, a dutiful Foreign Office Sinologist who had done two tours in Beijing during the Mao era. From his new vantage point Cradock lost no time in casting Hong Kong as a mere chess piece in the great power politics between the West, the Soviet bloc and China. 'Hong Kong apart, China does not threaten our interests,' he wrote in a 'first thoughts' memo on foreign policy for the prime minister on 27 January, 'in fact, given the state of Sino-Soviet relations, she confers great strategic benefits on the UK and western Europe.'

The talks began again with renewed intensity to iron out the myriad details of how Britain would hand over power.

None of this, of course, was known to the people of Hong Kong, where anxiety continued to mount. In January 1984 the colony was shaken by its most serious riots for almost seventeen years after a two-day taxi strike in protest against a proposal by the transport secretary, Alan Scott, a British expatriate, to raise vehicle tax drastically. A blockade by cab drivers in Kowloon degenerated into running clashes with the police, Triad gangsters swooped on the opportunity to break into shops, and looting and arson continued into the early hours. Thirty-four people were injured and 150 were arrested. According to the media, some rioters were heard speaking in the accents of mainland China. But the NCNA issued a statement distancing itself from the dispute and calling for calm. The colonial authorities hastily backed down.

It was in this febrile atmosphere, rife with talk of suspicion and betrayal, that Jardine Matheson, one of the oldest British trading firms in Hong Kong, announced on 28 March that it was to reorganise itself as a holding company registered in the British-ruled tax haven of Bermuda. The pro-Communist press observed, correctly, that Jardine's roots lay in the opium trade. By the 1980s its interests sprawled across finance, construction, property, shipping, retailing and energy. The move to Bermuda was a blow to Hong Kong's position as a commercial centre.

Its chairman, Simon Keswick, insisted it was a 'prudent' decision which did not diminish Jardine's commitment to Hong Kong or reduce its plans to expand into China. However one of his directors, Raymond Moore, told the media that 'Hong Kong is an uncertain legal jurisdiction and uncertainty is the enemy of business.' The announcement stunned financial markets and there was a sell-off of local stocks. In bars and clubs across Hong Kong, conspiracy theorists had a field day. Some linked the Bermuda move to a recent boardroom struggle, others detected the hand of the Foreign Office. In Beijing it was widely believed to be a political move designed to put pressure on China by demonstrating the truth of Mrs Thatcher's claim that confidence depended on British administration. Whatever the truth of that, it made no difference in the end.

In April, the 'unofficial' members of Exco went to London to speak directly to Mrs Thatcher, Cradock and senior ministers about their growing trepidation. Their leader, the businessman-politician Sir Sze-yuen Chung (known as Sir S.Y. Chung), told her they were 'increasingly worried by HMG's tendency to retreat swiftly in negotiation and by the wrong assessments which had been made of the Chinese position'. Michael Sandberg, chairman of HSBC, said they had originally agreed with the British government that 'a bad agreement was worse than no agreement' but that this concept 'had been rapidly abandoned by the British advisers'. There were unhappy exchanges between the 'unofficials', Cradock, Howe and the prime minister herself as the realisation of their predicament and the absence of a solution sank in.

Geoffrey Howe flew to Beijing to hear about China's resolve from Deng himself. Although 'friendly and ebullient', the Chinese leader spoke of his own fears that Britain might drain capital and assets from Hong Kong before it left. He was scathing about Jardine Matheson, saying that some people 'were trying to leave things in a mess'. Deng proposed to set up a

Joint Liaison Group to keep an eye on developments in the years up to 1997, an innocuous suggestion that proved to be a source of bitter dispute. According to Zhou Nan, 'Deng Xiaoping was afraid of chaos during this period and thought it necessary to have a Sino-British joint organisation in Hong Kong.' Deng reassured the British envoy that Hong Kong would stay unchanged for fifty years after the handover. He was certain a deal could be made. It would be turned into a Basic Law to serve as a mini-constitution for Hong Kong.

Deng's most troubling remark, as far as the British foreign secretary was concerned, was that China would definitely send the People's Liberation Army into Hong Kong in 1997. Almost incredibly, the British appear to have regarded this as a remote and extreme possibility. A few months earlier, the ultra-realist Cradock had told vice foreign minister Yao that 'a decision to station troops in Hong Kong would be seen as fatally impairing the autonomy of the territory.' Britain thought a small internal security force would do. Since that exchange, Chinese figures including Zhao Ziyang, the premier, and Zhou Nan, the chief negotiator, had insisted that the PLA must deploy as a symbol of sovereignty. It should not have come as a surprise to the foreign secretary when Deng brought it up in the last few minutes of their talk. He said 'China would send a small armed force to Hong Kong ... its nature would be the same as the present British garrison.' Howe 'expressed his dismay', but in the words of the telegram from the British ambassador, Richard Evans, recounting the conversation, Deng 'tried to choke off any discussion' and said there was no time to go into it. The decision had long been taken and, coming from Deng, was irrevocable.

It seems that the trip to Beijing and his one-hour encounter with Deng converted Howe to a bleak realism of his own. He arrived in Hong Kong to give the bad news to the 'unofficial' members of the Executive Council and Legislative Council. These were the people who had put their trust in British diplomacy, and it was a bitter moment when they heard that Britain had failed in its bid to keep either partial control or administration over Hong Kong. The governor had the unhappy task of reporting to London their 'deep mistrust' of China and their 'great deal of anxiety' about the fate of Hong Kong people who held second-class British passports.

At a press conference watched by millions of Hong Kong people whose future he held in his hands, Howe backed into his dramatic announcement with the understated manner he had absorbed in the medieval courts of Trinity Hall, Cambridge, while studying law. 'It is right for me to tell you now that it would not be realistic to think in terms of an agreement that provides for continued British administration in Hong Kong after 1997,' he told a stunned audience. Peppered with questions by reporters, Howe delivered reassurance in the tones of a solicitor reading out a client's will. It was the embodiment of gentlemanly virtue in his mind to refrain from public emotion. The closest he came was in response to a barbed question from John Dickie, the correspondent of the *Daily Mail*, a conservative newspaper which adored Mrs Thatcher. 'The concept of a sell out, the idea of a sell out, is quite untrue,' he said.

Over the succeeding months the negotiators wrangled over principles, detail and wording. While much of the work dealt with obscure and long-forgotten aspects of public administration, some of it was crucial to the life of Hong Kong under Chinese rule. Here Cradock, who like Howe had trained in law at Cambridge University, proved himself a master of the sub-clause. For all the criticism directed at the prime minister's adviser, his watchful eye in Downing Street provided a guarantee that Sir Richard Evans and his negotiators would not be outflanked.

In some cases Cradock's foresight was eerie. On 28 May he was required to answer a query from Mrs Thatcher, who was anxious about reprisals against people in Hong Kong who had fled the People's Republic. Cradock pointed out that an annex to the draft agreement provided that the system of law would continue. 'This means no political arrests in the territory and attempts to remove anyone from the territory to mainland China would require reference as now to a magistrate and the governor/head function-ary,' he wrote. Cradock thought it unlikely the Chinese government would or could act against those who had left China, since they made up about half the population. Some said the safeguards in the agreement were worth little; he did not agree, but pointed out that if they were to prove valueless then 'assurances about no reprisals would be no more dependable'. It summed up the dilemma of negotiations between a democracy and a dictatorship. 'This is not to say that people in Hong Kong who are "patri-ots" in Peking's eyes will not do better after 1997 than others. But preferment is different from persecution,' he concluded.

Deng Xiaoping illustrated this point when he received Sir S.Y. Chung and the 'unofficials' on 23 June in Beijing. It did not go well. In front of the cameras, Deng greeted them in a 'cold and abrupt tone', lectured them on the duties of patriotic Chinese and warned them against holding a 'colo-nial mentality'. Sir S.Y. Chung told the British that in private Deng had been 'reasonably friendly but stern and inflexible'. A note from the Foreign

Office said Deng's conduct had created a bad impression in Hong Kong, where he was seen as 'a cantankerous old man impatient of other people's opinion'.

Deng cut off his visitors before they could make any substantial points but the group got a kinder reception from lesser Chinese officials, who listened with sympathy to their argument that Hong Kong people should participate in drafting the Basic Law. In his memoir, Zhou Nan made it clear how little such representations meant to the Chinese side. 'I told [the British] your so-called "public opinion" is actually the "official will," the "official will of the UK" not the "public opinion" of Hong Kong. What role do "public opinion" or "confidence" or "the economy" play? They are all futile!'

It became clear to Evans and Cradock that the British team in China needed refreshment as it worked into the muggy heat of the Beijing summer. They turned to David Wilson, who had returned from Hong Kong to become a senior official dealing with Asia in the Foreign Office. He was sent out to lead the negotiations.

'The senior level negotiations had gone on for a very long time, they had established sort of basic principles but it was becoming very apparent indeed that time was running out,' Wilson recalled. 'China had laid down a deadline of the first of October that year for reaching an agreement; if not, they would take unilateral decisions. There were obviously disputes on the British side – did that mean anything or did it not? Percy [Cradock] very much took the view that China did mean what it said and there was an urgent need to get on with writing down in detail what had been agreed.'

Wilson found 'a basic fundamental difference' between the two sides. 'The Chinese side just wanted the absolute minimum written down – just the broad principles of us handing over sovereignty and one country two systems.' This did not satisfy the Hong Kong government, which reflected the deep mistrust felt in the colony and sought legally binding assurances. 'The Hong Kong government side said it was absolutely essential that all the things that matter in Hong Kong should be written down in detail in a form slightly equivalent to the *Encyclopaedia Britannica*,' said Wilson.

The ever-vigilant eye of Mrs Thatcher also fell upon the British negotiators, who had to reconcile the mutual distrust of a Conservative prime minister and a Communist government. Wilson found that the Chinese would slice apart every sentence. 'We get back to suspicions. They would read into wording that we had put forward very subtle ways in which we were trying to twist the whole thing for our advantage which had not even occurred to us.'

His opponent, Zhao Nan, remembered the mood differently. 'The two sides were at loggerheads. This was reflected in the communiqué issued after each round of meetings,' he said. 'The first called the talks "friendly and constructive," the second dropped the word "constructive" in favour of "useful" and the third spoke only of "further talks."'

There were even wrangles over the venue, although Wilson, whose quest to understand the Chinese way of thinking bordered on philosophical inquiry, found this a useful lesson in sifting the rice from the husk. The Chinese hosts had set up the talks at the Beijing International Club, which was in the diplomatic district. It meant that Wilson and his team had to run the gauntlet of the Hong Kong press corps every time they came in and out. After a month or so, the Chinese came to Wilson full of apologies to say that they should all move to the Diaoyutai state guesthouse in the west of the capital. They murmured about better food, tighter security, quieter arrangements.

Wilson demurred. The club, for all its disadvantages, was near the British embassy, which made it easy to send and read telegrams. A gifted Sinologist, Robin McLaren, like Cradock a product of St John's College, Cambridge, dashed back and forth managing the exceptional flow of cable traffic. But the Diaoyutai was far away on the other side of the Forbidden City. Wilson politely said thanks, but no thanks. Embarrassment ensued. It turned out that the Ministry of Foreign Affairs had failed to co-ordinate with the relevant organs in charge of the club and the lease on the conference room could not be renewed. Once this truth became apparent, the British knew better than to make their hosts lose face.

All negotiators seek to discover their opponent's bottom line. But in Wilson's mind, the key was to discover what the Chinese really thought the issue was. 'Let's say, the judiciary. The Chinese would say "No, no, no, no, absolutely not, go away and think again." They wouldn't say what was the problem. So we would go away and think again and try to work out what the problem was. And when you could get to what the problem was it was usually possible to find a way of dealing with it.'

Technically, the talks were a marvel of the age. The text of the agreement was negotiated both in Chinese and English. The British had high-grade communications capable of transmitting a Chinese text in cipher back to London for overnight consideration. The next day they could produce a printout version in Chinese characters while Zhou Nan and his officials were still working off handwritten drafts. Some curiosity and envy was excited by this, but it was an important insurance policy. Both the English and Chinese texts were equally valid, but it was the Chinese text that would be read in Hong Kong. There could be no mistake.

Day by day, Wilson and his opponents fought over the wording. They forged agreement on a draft declaration by both governments, honed down to eight paragraphs plus three annexes and two memoranda. The final text won China its main objectives of sovereignty and administration. In exchange for these great prizes, Deng granted a list of concessions allowing Hong Kong to have its rights and freedoms for fifty years after 1997 as a Special Administrative Region of China. The devil would be in the details. But by late July it was clear that a deal was in sight.

In London, Sir Percy Cradock for once shook off his professional pessimism. 'I think we should just be able to reach a tolerable agreement. If we do, I am sure that history will judge we were right to persevere in this course and once the initial shock is over Hong Kong reaction may prove better and more resilient than seems the case at present.'

Two big arguments remained. The first concerned the Joint Liaison Group. The second was over how the leader of Hong Kong would be chosen under Chinese rule. It is one of the ironies of history that the first was thought so important that it almost wrecked the entire agreement and has now been forgotten, while the second entailed just one word of text but has influenced the politics of Hong Kong ever since.

That word was 'elections'. Towards the end of the negotiations, at exactly the stage identified by the Americans as most likely to see big demands or concessions, the two sides were arguing about representative government. The Chinese side considered that it was no business of the British to determine how the leader of the Special Administrative Region was chosen, but Wilson persisted: 'We were pressing for greater elections and the Chinese were resisting them.' Zhou Nan did not want the word to be mentioned at all. The final sentence read: 'The chief executive will be appointed by the Central People's Government on the basis of the results of elections or consultations to be held locally.'

The meaning of this sentence would be argued over for decades. But it seems indisputable that today's young campaigners for democracy in Hong Kong owe a debt to David Wilson and his group of self-effacing Cambridge Sinologists for their skill and persistence. It handed them a lifeline before many of them were even born.

By contrast, the sound and fury over the Joint Liaison Group might have wrecked everything. Great alarm had been aroused in Hong Kong by Deng's proposal that a group of British and Chinese officials should guide it through the handover. The governor and his Executive Council warned that it would be a Trojan Horse, that China would make it a bridgehead, people would see it as an alternative government, authority would ebb away from the British and the colony might become ungovernable. Mrs Thatcher, Howe and Cradock listened carefully to their arguments but decided they would not allow the talks to break down over it.

Wilson and Zhou succeeded in narrowing their differences to the point where both sides had to refer it to their national leaders for a decision. Closing the deal required Britain and China to concede and for their leaders to take a political risk. The similarities and differences in how they did so offered a fascinating example of two systems at work.

We now know from Zhou Nan's memoirs that the Chinese had reached the eleventh hour. He was summoned to see Zhao Ziyang at the premier's home in the leadership compound and found him a worried man. 'I spoke out and said it was time to give the British some "face" and let time take care of the problem by keeping the Joint Liaison Group out of Hong Kong for a year or two.' The premier considered the answer, then called his private secretary to order a special plane to fly Zhou and foreign minister Wu Xueqian to the seaside resort of Beidahe, where Deng Xiaoping was enjoying a break from the heat and dust of the capital. 'You're directly responsible, you're going to report to Xiaoping,' the premier said.

The duo landed at Beidahe early the next day and were escorted to the villa where Deng, in shirtsleeves, was dividing his time between playing bridge and chatting to his circle. 'Comrade Xiaoping thought about it a bit and then said "of course we have to move [the group] in to Hong Kong but we don't have to do it straight away. We can wait. Two years earlier or later doesn't matter. You work it out."' Armed with Deng's authority, the two flew back to Beijing to await the British.

Once again Geoffrey Howe flew to Beijing. He was accompanied by Cradock, who lunched with Zhou Nan. Over the lunch table, Zhou revealed that the Chinese were ready to deal and the two men began to bargain. In essence, the compromise they struck was that the Joint Liaison Group would be based in Hong Kong but would not go there at once; its meetings would rotate between Hong Kong, Beijing and London. And it would busy itself with economic and administrative matters, staying out of politics. It sounded reasonable, but there was a catch. If Howe did not agree to the proposal during this visit to Beijing, the deal was off 'and the negotiations as a whole would fail'.

Cradock sprinted back from his lunch to the guesthouse where his foreign secretary was staying. To avoid eavesdropping, the British went out into the garden and huddled under a tree. Once more a disagreement broke out. Cradock was sure that the moment had come to deal but Youde, as governor of Hong Kong, argued in favour of resisting Chinese pressure. The foreign secretary hedged his bets. He called on Zhao Ziyang and talked to the foreign minister. All delivered the same unbending message: no more delays, this was it. Howe was also in possession of 'secret material' forecasting that the Chinese leadership had scheduled a meeting to take final decisions. He sent a holding telegram to Mrs Thatcher warning her that 'we are therefore facing a difficult choice ... we have always taken the view that we should fight on as hard as we can to resist Chinese pressure on location of the joint group ... but this is not an issue on which we should allow the talks to break down.' His own view was that they could live with Zhou Nan's proposals. 'This is not an agreeable decision to have to take but I see it as the preferable course,' he concluded.

In London, Mrs Thatcher authorised him to continue talking. Their exchange of telegrams shows her pushing her negotiator to the utmost, mindful of her moral responsibility in handing over millions of British subjects to a Communist government. Though couched in the cold prose of statesmanship, it is none the less moving.

On the morning of Sunday 30 July, Mrs Thatcher was woken up early at Downing Street to be told that an urgent message had come in overnight from Beijing requiring an answer by 9 a.m. It was sent up to her in a brown paper envelope with a red tag marked 'immediate'.

The message was from Howe. The Chinese, he said, had compromised by delaying the arrival of the Joint Liaison Group in Hong Kong, by issuing assurances and bringing forward to 1989 the date on which a Basic Law would guarantee Hong Kong's status. There were more details, but the foreign secretary had come down to his own bottom line. 'In fact I believe that the new Chinese proposal meets the requirements set out in your telegram. I should be grateful therefore for your authority to settle on this basis, if at all possible by 0800Z (0900 UK time) ... agreement on these lines is likely to be key to a meeting with Deng tomorrow which will be important for substance and presentation purposes.'

It was the final chapter, and both Mrs Thatcher and Deng understood that. She agreed, comforted by Howe's verdict that 'I am clear that we have pushed the Chinese to the limit.'

In Beidahe, Deng Xiaoping was jubilant. He ordered a special train to take him back to Beijing. There he complimented Zhou Nan on his achievement, saying 'you have solved the big problems, now I can invite the Queen of England!'

Later that day Geoffrey Howe was admitted to his presence for ninety minutes. Deng spoke of his confidence that 'one country, two systems' would work and said both countries had an interest in stability in Hong Kong up to 1997. Even in his hour of victory he did not deviate from harsh truths. 'China did not want trouble but China was not afraid of it,' he told Howe. The new Hong Kong must be run by 'patriots', not necessarily left-ists, but 'those who loved Hong Kong and the motherland'. Deng waxed indignant once more about big business, saying that he had heard the Hongkong and Shanghai Bank was to follow Jardines out of the colony. Howe reassured him that this was not so, then an uneasy bonhomie resumed. According to Zhou Nan's memoir, which may be self-serving, Deng paid tribute to Zhou and to the ambassador, Richard Evans, prompt-ing Howe to joke that negotiations without this pair 'would be like a banquet in China without *mao tai*'. Deng laughed and invited the Queen to visit China. On that note, Howe left for the airport to break the news to Hong Kong.

The Hong Kong stock market enjoyed its biggest gain for two years when the agreement was announced. Public and political opinion in the colony reacted in a daze to the guarantees of a 'high degree of autonomy' and freedoms guaranteed for half a century after the handover. The Chinese-language press was circumspect. Most independent papers were 'positive but uneuphoric'. In an editorial, the leading daily, *Ming Pao*, said the agree-ment was likely to be the best that could be obtained, while the Communist newspapers were enthusiastic.

It did not mean that the negotiations got easier. In late August Cradock grumpily minuted that 'Zhou Nan has remained characteristically unhelp-ful although not totally intransigent ... we have been ploughing slowly forward through a mass of detail.' The next month Howe told his diplo-mats that he was 'increasingly concerned about difficulties which have arisen'. From Hong Kong, the governor reported that 'the end game has ... become vitally important.'

Most vexatious was the fate of British passport holders, an issue of confidence for millions in the colony because China did not recognise dual nationality and would treat them all as citizens of the People's Republic. It came as a shock for them to learn that they would not be allowed to pass on their British nationality to their children, not even for one generation and not even if they left Hong Kong permanently. In short, the British Hong Kong Chinese would die out. The 'unofficials' made a last plea to Mrs Thatcher, who underlined in blue ink the cold verdict of her advisers: 'the answer is that there is nothing to be done for those of Chinese race.'

With what must have been an intake of breath, the prime minister marched on despite her own reservations. Four days after accepting the fate of the British passport holders she wrote to President Ronald Reagan asking for his support and saying, 'I do not pretend that the agreement is ideal in every respect, but I am convinced it is a good one.'

The second day of the ninth moon, 26 September, had been deemed inauspicious for signing contracts by fortune tellers in Hong Hong. It was a day more suitable for cleansing oneself and making offerings to the gods. That morning, Zhou Nan, who as a Marxist did not believe in omens, marched into the Great Hall of the People to sit down next to Sir Richard Evans, the British ambassador. They initialled the agreement and shook hands. It was endorsed by the National People's Congress, the Chinese parliament, on 14 November and approved by the House of Commons in London on 5 December.

The debate in Parliament brought out deep unhappiness and ventilated suspicions that Hong Kong had been betrayed. However, a majority of the house accepted that the government had made the best of a bad hand. Paddy Ashdown, a Liberal Member of Parliament who had served in the Secret Intelligence Service (MI6), quoted a Chinese saying in the original Mandarin for the benefit of radio listeners in the Far East: 'There is nothing under heaven which is completely perfect.'

Mrs Thatcher flew to Beijing, where she signed the formal document on 19 December. With Deng looking on, Premier Zhao Ziyang signed for China. On her briefing cards, Mrs Thatcher wrote a reminder to herself to emphasise China's commitments. David Wilson felt that in her heart the prime minister still yearned to keep Hong Kong island as an outpost of freedom and enterprise under the British flag. 'She would have loved it,' he judged, 'it mattered a great deal to her. She deeply distrusted the Communists. But it was of no practical use.'

Her encounter with Deng was courteous but there was no meeting of minds. Mrs Thatcher paid tribute to his 'stroke of genius' in conceiving the 'deceptively simple' solution of one country, two systems. The Chinese leader responded that the credit should go to Marxist dialectics. She told him, tactfully, that people in Hong Kong had asked her to pass on their wish that Deng should live to see the city return to China in 1997. He said that he cherished the hope of visiting Hong Kong if he was still alive.

For Cradock it was the consummation of his life's work so far. In his memoir, the dry civil servant recalled that on the plane home, he and Mrs Thatcher found themselves reciting the lines learned in childhood from Alfred Lord Tennyson's poem *Ulysses*:

Tho' much is taken, much abides; and tho'
We are not now that strength which in old days
Moved earth and heaven, that which we are, we are;
One equal temper of heroic hearts,
Made weak by time and fate, but strong in will
To strive, to seek, to find, and not to yield.

6

The Eighties

While Mrs Thatcher bargained with Deng Xiaoping a new era was dawning. In China it was the age of experiment, but in Hong Kong it was the roaring eighties. The colony bounced back from the oil shocks of 1973 and 1979. There was a stock market boom and a surge in property prices, fuelled by a government which kept taxes on incomes and profits low, auctioned parcels of land to developers while restricting the overall supply, imposed no rent controls on commercial leases and allowed only basic protection for private tenants. Hong Kong was a landlord's playground in a way that to Chinese Marxists recalled the bad old days on the mainland. Its conspicuous consumption and devil-may-care deal-making shocked and fascinated visitors from the People's Republic. 'Fly-by-night companies blossomed, boutiques and high fashion names flourished, cognac sales boomed and Hong Kong set a record for ownership of Rolls-Royces (one of them being painted blancmange-pink),' wrote an observer of the period.

There was a surge in office developments and luxury hotels. Finance houses, advertising, public relations, graphic designers, film-makers and the media made up a new set of players in business life. The digital economy lay on a distant horizon, but Hong Kong was so sharp, so instant and so adaptable that it started to behave as a precursor to the modern age. The new entrepreneurs demanded showiness and trophies, so builders indulged in revolving restaurants and vast atriums for their clients while an army of nimble construction workers plied up and down bamboo scaffolding erected to the sky. The shortage of land pushed Hong Kong to build ever upwards, so that thin perpendicular towers clung to the slopes of the Peak and were packed into every authorised plot. In the heat of the boom, Hongkong Land, a British-dominated firm set up in 1889, became by some calculations the biggest property developer in the world.

The traditions of free speech and a strong legal system allowed the colony to flourish as an entrepôt of knowledge and information. Its stable of Chinese newspapers and magazines provided a cacophony of stories, opinions and cultural criticism. As Asia grew wealthier and Hong Kong looked outward, the international business media found a profitable niche. The *Far Eastern Economic Review*, published from 1949 to 2009, dominated the scene. It competed with *Asiaweek*, a regional magazine. The *Asian Wall Street Journal* spoke for liberal American capitalism on the city's news stands and the *International Herald Tribune* combined articles from the *New York Times* and the *Washington Post* with its own distinctive voice. Such magazines and newspapers were piled high in the executive lounges which began to adorn the region's busy airports. Young professionals in the world's fastest-growing region were hungry for real news and carried international titles as a badge of prestige. Advertisers loved them.

'Things really began to take off in the seventies with more money around and things happening in Singapore, Malaysia and Hong Kong,' recalled Philip Bowring, who edited the *Review* from 1988 to 1992, 'the number of educated readers was growing rapidly.' The magazine declined to write down to its readers, who were not put off by long, dense articles about diplomacy, commodities or institutions. It scored notable scoops about financial scandals and took a sceptical view of the colonial establishment. Eventually the *Review* fell into the hands of the Dow Jones company, which failed to grasp its eclectic ethos and lacked the vision to transform it to compete in a new media landscape. None of the titles survived the internet and smartphones. But in their prime they recorded the vigour of the age.

As incomes rose, the first generation of Hong Kongers to enjoy mass prosperity began to travel for leisure around the South China Sea, which so many of their compatriots had crossed in harsh conditions to seek their fortunes in the 'southern lands'. At home, developers planned villa-style property complexes on the south side of Hong Kong island and on the island of Lantau, facing south to soak up the sun. Progress from the cramped apartment blocks of Kowloon or Western to the neat town houses and American-themed apartments by the beaches did not seem a distant aspiration but a goal attainable by thousands of families. In the early 1980s the contrast with the plain, hard way of life of most people in southern China became stark.

The colonial government, which prided itself on fiscal prudence, dug into its coffers to keep up with the pace of change. Architects laid the early plans for a giant new international airport to be built on reclaimed land off the north shore of Lantau Island. They sketched the outlines of great bridges that would span the waterway between Lantau and the port. Less happily, they wrenched out the heart of the old Mid-Levels, a residential district which took its humdrum name from its location halfway up the Peak, and replaced avenues and trees with an ugly tangle of elevated highways. In the New Territories, block after block of public housing arose without sentiment in rural villages, linked by new roads. The Mass Transit Railway began to knit together the different parts of the Hong Kong machine. New lines connected the industrial zones of Kowloon with the financial district. The planners foresaw a route that would speed commuters along the north shore of Hong Kong island. In official circles, the answer to political uncertainty was held to be concrete optimism.

An independent view of what the Cantonese-speaking majority of people actually thought came from a poll conducted in 1982 by the Hong Kong Observers. This was the kind of pressure group which late colonial society excelled at producing. It drew together younger Chinese professionals educated overseas and some expatriates, all concerned for the future of their home. Among its members were a future chief executive under Chinese rule, Leung Chun-ying, and an ardent campaigner for democracy, Christine Loh. The group commissioned a survey of 1,000 people between fifteen and sixty years of age chosen at random from census data across districts and social strata. Field researchers interviewed all the subjects. The entire exercise was in Chinese. It was, for those who wanted to know, an eye-opener.

The Observers admitted in the preamble to their findings that the community in Hong Kong was stereotyped as rude, noisy, lacking in civic-mindedness, obsessed with money, anxious to emigrate to the West and short-sighted in their outlook. A more balanced society emerged from the data. While 79 per cent of those interviewed thought money important, more than 80 per cent of them considered freedom of speech, a decent environment and freedom of choice to be important as well. It was, perhaps, in keeping with one unobjectionable stereotype of the Cantonese that good food was the most valued material comfort. There was a high degree of contentment. Only 13 per cent considered crime a problem and less than a fifth of interviewees worried about housing. Yet people also criticised the authorities. Almost half felt they did not explain policies adequately to the public. Less than a third knew that they could contact the administration through district boards and offices.

In the absence of democracy, the poll was an authentic gauge of politics and identity. It found little support for independence. Only 33 per cent identified themselves as 'Hongkongers' while 61 per cent affirmed that they were 'Chinese'. However a resounding 95 per cent believed it would be 'acceptable' for Hong Kong to stay under British rule after 1997. Only a quarter wanted to see the return of the territory to China. And more than half said they would emigrate if they could.

These were complex and to some extent reassuring findings, but it appeared that independent inquiry into public opinion did not suit the British colonial administration. In 1980, a campaigning journalist in Britain, Duncan Campbell, revealed the existence of a government committee set up to conduct surveillance of pressure groups and to undermine, coerce or co-opt any of them that were not to the taste of the authorities. Its targets included the Hong Kong Observers. Campbell's article in the *New Statesman* had a bold headline: 'Colonialism: A Secret Plan for Dictatorship'. It alleged that the police Special Branch had been ordered to infiltrate pressure groups and to report to the committee on any subversive activities, a practice that would not have disgraced the Ministry of Public Security in China itself.

The government later admitted that a Standing Committee on Pressure Groups had been set up in 1977 to 'report to and advise the government on social and political trends and developments'. Following a public outcry, it was disbanded in 1982 and all its files containing assessments and reports were destroyed. Much later, legislators extracted an assurance in 1995 from the secretary for security, Peter Lai, that 'no such group or committee now exists'.

In that 1995 Legislative Council debate, it emerged that British security officials had monitored the activities of organisations which might be subject to Communist infiltration. The targets included the Hong Kong Federation of Students and the Hong Kong Professional Teachers Union. Members of the council claimed that officials had sought to influence any organisation which received government funds. It was, they said, an attempt to control opinion. One legislator, Anna Wu, quoted a leaked report from the committee which sounded like a masterpiece of paternalism, couched in the forbidding language of a schoolmaster chiding errant pupils:

Special Branch confirmed that while some pressure groups may be motivated more by self-interest than altruism, their activities have not generally been subversive and they do not seem to have had the effect of subverting the population so far.

But [the committee] has been tasked with examining the pressure groups more critically and does not feel able to see the groups in such a favourable light. It is the potential of pressure groups which is disturbing, the possibility of their developing into something more sinister or unleashing forces damaging to the whole community.

The activities of pressure groups can encourage a widespread critical and argumentative attitude when knocking the Government is fashionable. In itself not a phenomenon to be afraid of, it nonetheless provides an ideal breeding ground for discontent and trouble-makers while there is always the danger that any group, no matter how innocent and well meaning initially, can be taken over by more unscrupulous elements.

The committee gloomily concluded that while 'pressure groups are generally not subversive, the potential for subversion always exists'. However its members accepted that there was no evidence that any groups had been taken over by 'undesirable political factions from either outside or inside Hong Kong'.

The secretary for security refused to confirm or deny any of the claims made in the chamber. They remain unchallenged on the record of British rule.

In 1982, the economic bubble burst amid a global recession that began in the United States, where the Federal Reserve hiked interest rates to curb inflation. In Hong Kong a wave of bankruptcies rippled across property and finance companies. The collapse in property prices threatened the territory's deposit-taking companies, in effect small banks, and these had to be steadied by assurances of support from the Hongkong Bank, which took the unofficial role of de facto central banker. Companies hesitated to invest and banks pulled back from risky mortgage lending. At the same time, uncertainty over Britain's negotiations with China – which were conducted in secret – began to sap business confidence. It was in this climate that the colonial government began to grow nervous about social unrest.

In the event, the people of Hong Kong demonstrated the calm and law-abiding resilience which characterised their response to tough times.

There was no unrest. It was, instead, the financial markets which turned volatile. Many people in Hong Kong had decided to get their money out of the city because they feared the future. The generation of business families who had fled post-revolutionary Shanghai did not trust the Communists. The opaque diplomacy conducted between London and Beijing did not reassure them. Yet they could not simply export their assets. The way out was to sell properties or businesses, then to sell the proceeds in Hong Kong dollars on the foreign exchange market and use dollars, pounds or yen to buy safe haven assets out of reach of the Chinese Communist Party abroad. In a small, open economy with no capital controls and a freely floating exchange rate, the effects were inevitable. Steady, continuous sales drove down the value of the Hong Kong currency and began to cause inflation in the city as the price of imports rose in adjustment. The currency, which was bought and sold instantly, became a proxy for sentiment about the colony's future. Undermined by the first public statements from China that it would take back control in 1997, it began to sink.

For the first half of 1982, one American dollar could be bought for approximately HK$5.80. Over the summer the Hong Kong currency began to slide, reaching HK$6.10 in mid-August before staging a brief rally. But after Mrs Thatcher's first visit to Beijing in September 1982, the local dollar had a further rapid slide until, on 26 October, it hit HK$6.90 to the greenback. Its weakness continued through the first nine months of 1983, and by mid-September it took HK$7.78 to buy one American dollar. The colonial government, companies and households could see the value of their reserves, assets and savings suffering an inexorable decline. In Beijing, the Communist Party negotiators accused Britain of 'playing the economic card' by deliberately engineering a collapse of confidence. No evidence has ever surfaced of such a plan, which would have offended Mrs Thatcher's doctrine that 'you can't buck the market'. In any case, it would have been well-nigh impossible to conceal intervention by a sovereign state on the scale required.

But in late September 1983 the political atmosphere was so toxic that it threatened the conduct of diplomacy and there were signs of panic among investors. People began hoarding rice and groceries. Supermarkets could not restock their empty shelves. Some shops began refusing to accept local banknotes and would only take American dollars. Fears mounted of a run on the local banks. On Friday 23 September, the Hong Kong currency fell to HK$8.65 to the US dollar. The next day became known as 'Black

Saturday' as panic selling overwhelmed the government's defences against speculators and the rate fell to an all-time low of $9.60. The local price of gold, which was traded in US dollars and measured in traditional taels, equal to about 1⅓ ounces or 37 grams, soared above the international bullion price. To the relief of the authorities, the local foreign exchange market closed at 12.30 p.m.

On Sunday the *South China Morning Post*, the colony's leading English-language daily, blamed the collapse on 'yet another non-statement' at the end of the latest Sino-British talks, which it said 'can leave absolutely no doubt as to the political nature of the Colony's fast-dwindling exchange rate'. It reported 'almost panic buying of taels at gold shops throughout the territory' which drove up the demand for US dollars, while holders of the American currency were increasingly unwilling to sell. The paper described a 'decline and fall' of the Hong Kong dollar. Amid the chaos, banks quoted spreads between bid and offer prices 'at banana republic levels'. In the words of the man who was to save the currency, John Greenwood, the unit of value trusted by more than five million people under British rule was in an 'uncontrollable tailspin'. Their savings and assets, which represented more than three decades of hard work in post-war Hong Kong, were evaporating. The moment of crisis had arrived.

Hong Kong had no central bank. Its absence was a tribute to the laissez-faire doctrine that impressed libertarians like the economist Milton Friedman. Nor did the government control the money supply. Instead the authorities held an exchange fund which issued certificates of indebtedness to the two banks allowed to issue banknotes, the Hongkong and Shanghai Banking Corporation, at that time still colloquially known as Hongkong Bank, and the Standard Chartered Bank. All the local banks operated a cartel which set interest rates, thereby entrusting a key policy lever to the private sector. This was known as 'the interest rate weapon'. Elegant in classical economic terms, it proved inadequate to manage the politically inspired panic of 1983. The banks raised their prime interest rate to 13 per cent in early September, but that failed to turn the tide and over the next fortnight they threw in the towel. The interest rate weapon was a dud.

To Greenwood, a private sector economist with GT Management plc and editor of a specialist publication, *Asian Monetary Monitor*, the authorities had committed 'the classic error of confusing the price of money with the price of credit'. He argued that the real price of money was what had

to be given up for it in goods or services, whereas interest rates were just
the price of credit, or what must be paid to rent money for a fixed period.
In Hong Kong, the political risk was driving residents to export their capital at almost any cost, so that 'the currency could theoretically have been
driven to the point where Hong Kong dollars were virtually valueless.' The
rush to gold showed that local investors were desperate for security. He
believed the solution was a sound, credible link between the Hong Kong
dollar and a unit of value that would command widespread trust. At a time
when the gold standard was seen by most (though not all) as a barbarous
relic, there was only one choice, the US dollar. And the mechanism had to
be simple for people to understand in one word that stood for something
fixed and reliable. A peg.

Fortunately, Greenwood found listeners among the increasingly rattled
upper echelons of the administration. At 11 a.m. on Sunday 25 September,
while expatriate readers of the *South China Morning Post* were digesting
their bacon and eggs – if they could – the government convened an emergency meeting. The acting financial secretary, Douglas Blye, asked
Greenwood to join government economists, officials from the Monetary
Affairs Branch, the Commissioner of Banking, and representatives of the
Hongkong Bank and Standard Chartered. They assembled in a conference
room of the Monetary Affairs Branch on the twenty-fourth floor of the
Admiralty Tower, near the waterfront.

As it happened, officials had already considered a proposal for a fixed
exchange rate prepared by Tony Latter, the deputy secretary for monetary
affairs. From 1935 to 1972, when fixed exchange rates were the norm for
a great deal of the time, the Hong Kong dollar had been tied to sterling.
Between 1972 and 1974 it had been pegged to the US dollar before moving
to a floating rate, in common with many other currencies. The idea of a
fixed rate was nothing new to Hong Kong. But according to Joseph Yam,
later chief of the Hong Kong Monetary Authority, officials were not sure it
would work as smoothly in practice as it did on paper. They thought it
'prudent' to hear an independent view.

Over sandwiches and soft drinks, the men heard Greenwood outline
with impeccable academic logic the principles and application of his plan
for a peg. It is testimony to the cerebral character of those in the room that
the refreshments only appeared after Yam realised that his secretary, who
was due to serve them, was half an hour overdue. She was found passed
out from exhaustion in a lift. After Greenwood spoke, the officials met
privately and decided to adopt his plan.

The statement that Blye put out after the meeting spoke only of the exchange fund taking a 'more significant role' in the foreign exchange mechanism. It gave no details, nor, crucially, did it mention a target exchange rate. To dealers coming in to their desks on Monday it signalled insouciance and confusion, consistent with a colonial administration which many traders in Hong Kong felt was complacent, snobbish and out of date. The bankers felt that Blye, a career civil servant, was a weak character. It did not add up to a recipe for confidence.

None the less, the weekend meeting marked a crucial point. The frantic sell-off abated. The financial secretary, Sir John Bremridge, flew back from a finance ministers' conference in Trinidad. In the bankers' eyes he was made of sterner stuff than Blye. He had served in the British Army in the Second World War, read law at Oxford and made a successful career in business with John Swire and Sons, one of the great trading houses of Hong Kong, rising to become its chairman and the boss of Cathay Pacific Airways. Once he was back, decisions could be taken.

On Monday 26 September the Hong Kong banks raised their prime lending rate by three percentage points to 16 per cent and the government joined the two note-issuing banks to intervene. At the end of the day, the Hong Kong dollar settled around HK$8.32. Over the next few days the market vacillated in uncertainty while two unexpected events, which did nothing to help Hong Kong's reputation, took eyes away from the exchange rate.

While Yam and his colleagues were fighting the financial markets they were also working on the rescue of Hang Lung Bank, a local lender with twenty-eight branches. Hang Lung had suffered a bank run in September 1982, the first since the 1960s, in part due to uncertainty over talks between Britain and China. It was now unable to meet its obligations because it had run out of liquidity. In the days of laissez-faire, the authorities would have refused to act and left it to the financiers to sort out a lender of last resort, usually the Hongkong Bank or Standard Chartered. In the case of Hang Lung, it was Standard Chartered on the hook for HK$50 million on its clearing account. This time there would be no private sector solution. Standard Chartered did not want to take the initiative and the authorities could not countenance a bank failure in the middle of an existential currency crisis. On Tuesday 27 September the government rushed through legislation to take over Hang Lung in a specially convened session of the Legislative Council. Blye was dispatched to become its chairman. For free-market purists, Hong Kong had broken with its traditions.

At the weekend there came another reminder of the unedifying side of the city's casino capitalism when police arrested George Tan, the boss of a buccaneering property company, the Carrian Group, which owed around a billion US dollars to its creditors. The group collapsed in Hong Kong's largest corporate bankruptcy, a scandal that unfolded for more than a decade involving fraud, conspiracy, corruption, murder and suicide. The affair brought in Wardley, HSBC's merchant bank, which had advised and backed Carrian. It cost the bank an estimated HK$600 million. At the time it was a punctuation mark in a bigger drama.

While officials laboured over the technicalities of Greenwood's scheme, Sir Edward Youde gave his annual policy address to the Legislative Council. With breathtaking panache, Youde chose not to mention anything about the crisis. That night he flew to London with a number of local worthies to confer with the prime minister, the chancellor of the exchequer and the Bank of England. They decided that Hong Kong must stand on its own and ruled out any idea that its currency could be linked to sterling.

The Hong Kong delegation worked the corridors of Whitehall and the City. Charles Goodhart from the Bank of England and David Peretz from the Treasury, the UK finance ministry, flew out to Hong Kong to pore over the papers outlining the theory of a currency board. They gave it their assent.

The original plan was to fix the Hong Kong dollar at HK$8.0 to the US dollar, perhaps because eight was a lucky number in Chinese culture. But Michael Sandberg, the chairman of HSBC, advised against the suggestion on the grounds that it would be hard to justify a round number which 'sounded a bit artificial. I suggested pegging it at HK$7.80 or HK$7.90 to make it look as if we had carefully worked it out!'

According to Greenwood's account the decision was more scientific than that. The arguments against devaluation were persuasive and it was important to settle on a rate that did not concede to what Bremridge termed the 'unstable and irrational' depreciation of the currency. Whatever the ultimate reasoning, it was decided to fix the rate at HK$7.80.

On Saturday 15 October, Bremridge announced that from Monday morning the government would stand behind the new stabilised rate. 'Hong Kong has substantial foreign currency reserves, a generally liquid banking system and virtually no Government debt,' he said. To encourage savers to stay put, tax on interest paid to depositors would be abolished. It would be 'business as usual'. The financial secretary concluded on a resounding note. 'These measures are designed to stabilise the exchange value of the Hong Kong dollar and thus to provide a climate for growing prosperity with restrained inflation. The Government has confidence in the stabilised exchange rate. So can the people of Hong Kong. Let us now get on with our business.'

At Hongkong Bank, the colony's largest financial institution and its traditional lender of last resort, the managers were expected to play their part by intervening to support the currency alongside the government's exchange fund. They soon discovered that official confidence was shakier than the administration was letting on. William Purves, later chairman of HSBC, then an executive director, recalled the tension inside the conference room when the markets opened that week. The Hong Kong government had come close to surrendering, he said, leaving the bank to fight alone. 'It was announced at HK$7.80 and of course the government stood ready to make sure it didn't slip below HK$7.80. Well, international pressure continued and that day they held it but spent a lot of money,' he said.

Frantic dealing continued overnight in London and New York as a tug of war went on between buyers and sellers betting on the government's resolve. The markets did not know that in Hong Kong, the officials in charge of intervention were losing their nerve. In effect, under Greenwood's plan, the Hong Kong monetary base became simply a different denomination of the US dollar because the government guaranteed convertibility into US dollars at the fixed price. This was assured – but only as long as the authorities had sufficient foreign currency reserves to cover the entire issue of Hong Kong dollar notes. According to Purves, the Secretary for Monetary Affairs had come near to the end of his tether: 'The following day the pressure continued – a little less but nevertheless worryingly – and Douglas Blye said "I can't put any more Hong Kong reserves in" and we said "Well you must. What's going to happen? Because if it slips through HK$7.80 your credibility's gone."'

Had currency dealers known of these conversations, history would be different. Purves and his fellow executives realised that the future of their institution was at risk. The bank had survived the Second World War and Japanese occupation. They did not want it to go down to a currency crisis on their watch. 'The bank [HSBC] continued when the Hong Kong monetary authorities didn't,' Purves recalled. Watching hour by hour, its executives convened to take stock as their money went out. They included the general manager, John Gray, a Scotsman born in Hong Kong, who had

served as chief accountant and whose father had worked for the bank, and
Peter Hammond, the deputy chairman, an executive renowned for keeping a cool head. 'John Gray was in charge of the balance sheet and we
became concerned we were putting too much of the bank's capital and
reserves into supporting the Hong Kong dollar,' Purves said. The atmosphere in the room was low key but everybody knew that the stakes were
high.

'Hammond then said, "It's going to turn. It will turn. I can't tell you
when it'll turn but it'll definitely turn. This will not go on." We all thought,
where's he getting his messages from? Well, by Friday morning, it turned.'

The historical foreign exchange graphs show that despite the day-to-day
drama the Hong Kong dollar had been steadily gaining strength over that
week. Backed by the firepower of the biggest bank in the territory, it settled
just where the authorities had intended, in a narrow band around HK$7.80.

Decades later, Purves, who had won the Distinguished Service Order
for his bravery serving in the King's Own Scottish Borderers during the
Korean War, remembered the battle of the Hong Kong dollar as a near-run
thing. 'The Hong Kong dollar strengthened and the peg not only held but
has done [since then], and of course we were able to recover our reserves
et cetera and within a year or so things were going rather well again. So
that is the peg. But it came very, very close to not working.'

The contrast between the lightly regulated way of life in Hong Kong and
the bureaucratic order in China was known to both societies. It is worth
examining the difference in the 1980s, however, because it illustrated the
profound psychological division between the two.

From mainland China, the speculative cycle of boom and bust in Hong
Kong looked like a warning. The Communist Party seldom ceased to
evoke the financial chaos endured in the last days of Kuomintang rule as
proof that socialist economics were superior to capitalism. Debates raged
between its factions about how much reform was too little and how much
was too much. Hardliners feared the effects of free markets. Some younger
economists and cadres found the prospect exciting. Both realised, however,
the scale of the risk.

In 1982 the population of the People's Republic reached more than one
billion, the census of that year recording 1,008,175,511 citizens. The
number of people had doubled since the 1949 revolution. Birth control
had none the less reduced population growth after the Mao era, when
families of five to six children were common. Fertility per woman fell from

4.2 in 1974 to 2.2 in 1980, while a revised marriage law raised the legal age of wedlock for men from twenty to twenty-two and for women from eighteen to twenty. Social and economic progress were doing their work.

Although they felt they had performed moderately well since 1949 – life expectancy for men in the cities rose from sixty-three in 1957 to sixty-nine in 1982, although women could expect to live the same span of seventy-two years – Communist Party leaders feared that the slowing birth rate was not enough. China covered about the same national territory as the United States but it had only about half as much cultivated land, while the huge difference in population meant that per capita an American had eight times more cultivated land than a Chinese citizen. Generations of flood and famine were ingrained in the political psyche of China's rulers.

In September 1980 the party veteran Hua Guofeng (who had four children) announced that there must be a limit to births. As a means of coercion the new land contracts available under reforms were linked to child-bearing. The government ordered that women must submit to the fitting of intra-uterine devices after the birth of their first child. If a second child was born, compulsory sterilisation was ordained. The number of abortions multiplied, some forced. A harsh apparatus of state grew up to interfere in people's family lives.

In China, citizens were members of a *danwei*, the work unit which regulated their choices about education, jobs, marriage and where to live. Collective life and responsibilities were ordained by the *baojia* registration system inherited from the emperors and the Kuomintang. Every one hundred households were grouped in a *jia*; ten of these equalled one *bao*. At the next level the village unit, or *cun*, took the place of work brigades. The administrative township or *Xiang* replaced the commune. Larger units became municipalities or *shi*. The breakup of the Maoist communes signalled reorganisation, not more civil liberty.

China had a top-down system of governance which had prevailed over utopian ideas of mass politics based on the democratic decisions of workers and peasants. The state leadership reached down to local level through a tripartite structure in each province. A Communist Party secretary was in charge of the party's local apparatus, while a governor ran the civil administration. The senior military officer in place reported to the People's Liberation Army. The powers of these individuals varied according to personality, lineage and influence; it was too simple to assume that the party secretary was always the senior operative figure, although that was often the case.

Formally, there were three reporting channels from the provinces to the capital, where three centres of power constituted the core of the socialist state. The provincial government dealt with about thirty-five ministries in Beijing in the early 1980s, which were overseen by vice premiers and a premier sitting as the State Council, or cabinet. Above them the president served formally as the head of state.

Communist Party officials sent a flow of paperwork to the party secretariat, where the Central Organisation Department co-ordinated reports and implemented decisions. The department indexed and ran the Chinese *nomenklatura*: the central committee of some 250 people, a twenty-five-person Politburo drawn from its ranks and the standing committee of the Politburo, usually numbering seven or nine men, the supreme ruling body of China. The general secretary of the Communist Party sat at the apex of this pyramid. The army maintained its own lines of communication up to the general staff and the political department of the PLA, which reported in turn to the Central Military Commission.

All three top offices – president of the state, general secretary of the Communist Party and chairman of the Central Military Commission – were powerful. When combined in one man, as they were in Xi Jinping after 2013, they conferred supreme authority. Outside and around these structures flowed currents and cross-currents of power which were hard to identify, both for Chinese people themselves and for foreign observers. The leading families of the revolution operated within a web of kinship and political loyalties which only an insider might fathom. The organs of state security jealously guarded their own confidential networks of data and people. As we shall see, factions and competing agencies heightened strife within the system, although their conflicts did not weaken it when crisis came in 1989.

The scale of the task of governing China awed politicians and officials from lesser nations. In the mid-1980s one province alone, Sichuan, in the southwest, had 100 million people. Two, Henan and Shandong, counted more than 75 million each. Jiangsu, around Shanghai, and Guangdong, bordering Hong Kong and Macau, each had about 60 million people. The size and nature of the Chinese state were overwhelming and alien to the inhabitants of Hong Kong. Among them, though, were businessmen, bankers and administrators who began to grasp the scale of the opportunities created by Deng Xiaoping's embryonic reforms.

After the Red victory of 1949 and the abortive Cultural Revolution of 1966 to 1976, a third revolution was under way inside China. It did not entail political reform but it changed the way millions of people lived. Now the people's communes had been wound down, life in rural China was adjusting to the household responsibility system, which had replaced collective farming, and to a new language of economy which replaced the slogans of old. In fields golden with grain across the southern agricultural belt, peasants could choose among three ways to reap the gains of their work.

First, a labour contract system permitted them to accumulate work points, tradeable for goods and food, by farm work which met a fixed level of quantity, quality and cost. Second, an output-contract system allowed more risk-taking. Households were committed to produce a fixed quota of crops and could keep the surplus, but they had to make up any shortfall. Third, a net-output scheme rewarded families with freedom over how they cultivated their land and gave them ownership of tools and animals in return for an undertaking to meet a quota of production for the state and a surplus for the collective.

Under a primary reform document, contracts could be fixed for fifteen years, plots could be bought or sold, and different wages could be paid according to task and performance. All were steps away from equality, which offended cadres who believed in the ideals of communism. But they contributed to a huge surge in production and better lives for millions. Agricultural output grew by about 8 per cent a year, food prices fell, farmers diversified from rice and grains into cash crops, people ate more meat and rural incomes rose. 'No one had foreseen how good the results would be or that the changes would be so dramatic,' wrote the premier, Zhao Ziyang, in his memoir.

The joy of modest riches was to be seen on a visit to a collective farm in Guangdong province in 1985. It was a showpiece tour organised by the government-run travel service for the first wave of Western tourists entering the People's Republic. Even allowing for that, the stirrings of prosperity and individual freedom could be seen everywhere.

In Guangzhou, the modern White Swan Hotel stood in solitary distinction on Shamian Island, surrounded by grand colonial-era buildings now occupied by government offices or split up into collective apartments. Incense sticks clasped between their fingers, worshippers bowed in prayer before shrines inside the reopened temples, freshly painted in crimson. The shops were drab yet full of food and basic consumer goods. A tide of cyclists engulfed the avenues and backstreets while overcrowded buses wheezed through the throng. The group from the White Swan climbed into a Japanese-made minibus and set off past lines of apartment blocks, through suburbs to the open countryside. Outside the city, the broad thoroughfares soon turned to one-track country roads winding through gleaming paddyfields, where oxen still nodded at the plough while the occasional tractor carved its path through the mud. The tarmac roads ran along dykes connecting villages and outlying houses where television aerials sprouted on the red-tiled rooftops. One of the guides confided that they were tuned to commercial television channels from Hong Kong and that the peasants enjoyed soap operas and game shows.

The guides were pleased to show off progress and were sparing with political rhetoric. They were content, it seemed, to let visitors see for themselves the aspects of Chinese reform that had delivered results. If the tour was formulaic, the evidence was plain. The group arrived at a collective farm at noon, lunchtime. This was, they were told, one of the proud Communist collectives that had enthusiastically embraced the party's reforms while upholding the communal ethos which had liberated the Chinese peasant from millennia of serfdom and feudal exploitation. It may have been so; there was nobody on hand to dissent. There was, however, a large mess hall where dozens of men and women in from the fields were tucking into big portions of plain food – rice, green stir-fried vegetables and cubes of fat-streaked pork, all tasty and hot. It was too routine to be staged. The visitors, too, were fed, and the headman sat down to say a few words of welcome, avoiding anything political. An American couple shook their heads in wonder and declared that Communism was not what they had thought it to be. The foreigners drank Tsingtao beer and chatted about the spectacle they had seen as they sat on a fast modern train which clattered through the deepening dusk until the bright towers of Hong Kong appeared through the windows. It was a typical, unexceptional visit to China of a kind shared by hundreds of thousands of tourists and business people as the country opened up. To most visitors, greeted with the energy and cautious warmth of their hosts, it was impossible not to feel optimistic about China.

In industry, the challenges were greater but the transformation would be just as extraordinary. The Communist Party had turned away from Stalinist doctrines of central planning and control. It introduced incentives for state-owned enterprises, which still paid 55 per cent tax to the government but were allowed to keep half of their net profits. By decrees of the State Council, managers assumed greater authority over collective leadership in each workplace; they gained limited power to appoint factory heads and for the first time they might dismiss workers for incompetence. Prices were partially set free, at first through a cumbersome dual-price mechanism that let enterprises sell production in excess of state quotas at market rates. For the first time since Liberation, officials allowed private businesses to open up.

In 1984, encouraged by the results so far, the Central Committee authorised a total of fourteen Special Economic Zones and created three 'development triangles' around the Yangtze Delta, the Min River in Fujian Province and the Pearl River Delta south of Guangzhou. By then, foreign direct investment into China was running at almost one billion US dollars every year. China was rejoining the world: it entered the International Monetary Fund and the World Bank, ejecting Taiwan from both institutions. To the distress of some Maoists, the People's Republic was borrowing from foreigners again, raising US$1.05 billion on international loan markets. The economy surged so fast that it overheated, forcing the planners to retrench.

Not everyone was happy. In Beijing, party elders at odds with the reforms coalesced around the ideologue Chen Yun, the leading economic planner of Maoist China after 1949. Now in his seventies, Chen still wielded influence. A Shanghai printing worker who had risen through the party to a great national role, he was thus seen as a living symbol of the triumph of the proletariat and a guardian of the flame. He had endured abuse during the Cultural Revolution but survived to become the figurehead of orthodox resistance to Deng's reforms. In the mid-1980s he was a formidable roadblock.

The party stalwarts harboured two concerns. They disagreed with the march back from pure socialism, considering the introduction of commerce and management to be a betrayal of the working class. Their broader care – which was shared by Deng and his economic reformers – was of chaos and a loss of control. Zhao Ziyang's memoirs stress that China was a big country with diverse regional conditions alongside a huge and growing population. Disaster could arrive on the same scale as success.

In hindsight, Western economists and governments took more notice of the attractive, transformational economic aspects of reform than they did of its negative effects on a traumatised society with a fossilised political superstructure. By overestimating the gains to the world of Chinese economic reform, and underestimating the political risk within China itself, they operated half blind. The results for all sides were to be complex, bitter and enduring.

The first Chinese accounts that the worm might be turning came from within the party itself. Leftists openly 'raised the red flag' in opposition to change. Disillusioned youths who had been 'sent down' to the countryside under Mao watched as the social and political order changed in ways they had not been educated to understand. Those peasants who had fiercely believed in the people's communes felt bereaved. Zhao Ziyang recalled the party boss of Heilongjiang province, the land of the Black Dragon River along the border with the Soviet Union, saying that the rural reformers elsewhere might walk on their broad highways but he would stay on his single-plank bridge. Mid-ranking party opponents flooded official news-papers with critical articles. The 'conservatives', if that is the word for radical Marxists, seized on evidence that crime and corruption had reap-peared after decades in which these 'negative phenomena' had vanished from Chinese public life, either suppressed or concealed. To the guardians of order, these things were frightening because they emerged so quickly from reform and came on such a scale that they threatened to cause chaos, perhaps even to undermine the party's revolutionary legitimacy.

From May 1984, all citizens older than sixteen had to carry identity cards. People were on the move and officials began to realise that mass migration would break the bonds of workplace and commune, ending an era of enforced stability. There were reasonable fears among party econo-mists that a shift in economic momentum to the coastal cities and the south would strip the interior of workers and leave inland China poor and isolated. The state directed investment and projects to central and western China to redress the balance, reinforcing its role as chief economic actor rather than reducing it. In the age of experiment, though, shocks to the system were inevitable.

One of the most illuminating documents on the social ferment in southern China is also one of the earliest. On 13 March 1982, barely four years into the reforms, the standing committee of the Guangdong Provincial Congress admitted that there had been an explosion of crime and resolved that it was time to assess 'the danger of a great evil' unleashed by economic reform. 'Significant achievements have been made but at the same time smuggling, foreign exchange arbitrage, profiteering, specula-tion, theft of public property, pilfering and selling precious cultural relics, demanding bribes and other criminal activities have reached a shocking and intolerable degree', it said.

The committee heard that 'major cases have caused economic and political damage to the socialist cause and the interests of the people'. It prescribed heavier sentences for economic criminals, reserving the death penalty and life imprisonment for the worst offenders. In language that recalled the edicts of Lin Zexu against opium more than a century before, it chastised officials and vowed better detection and stricter punishment for state functionaries. It reverted to traditional methods of social control, psychological pressure and mercy for lesser fry, vowing to carry out a policy of 'leniency for confession and stern resolve for punishment'. The concluding exhortation is worth reading in detail for its insight into the unchanging mind of the Chinese scholar-official:

> People who turn themselves in to the police for their past crimes by 1 May shall be dealt with according to the relevant laws and regulations of the past; otherwise their crimes shall be regarded as continuing. This shows that our policy is still one of leniency and strictness which leaves room for repentance.
> Those who wish to be dealt with leniently, be aware! Turn yourselves in quickly. It is the only way out. Don't hang your heads! If you delay, you will be treated severely and it will be too late for regrets. All relatives, friends and superiors must seize this opportunity to exhort and to press such criminals to turn themselves in and to quickly and truthfully explain their crimes.

The Guangdong document followed a directive from the Central Committee to 'strike hard against serious economic crimes'. It was inspired by Chen Yun, who wanted 'a hard and resolute strike like a thunderbolt'. Where reformers saw human nature, Chen detected class enemies bent on 'sabotage and erosion of our system' and warned his comrades that 'bourgeois lifestyles have been on the rise'.

It was not just a change of economics but of mentality that vexed officials. One early ambition of the reformers had been to build an export processing zone and port at Shekou in the Pearl River estuary, directly across the bay of Shenzhen from Hong Kong. The potential was obvious but motivating the workforce was hard, despite slogans thought to be inspiring, such as 'time is money, efficiency is life!' The project faced delays because dredging in the murky waters around Hong Kong was taking longer than expected. The task was monotonous and hard. Workers had to haul carts of cut stone and rubble in muddy, wet conditions. It was slow work. Ruan Xiangfa, the party official responsible for the project, explained that managers had introduced a bonus system to speed up work on the

harbour frontage, and after the bonus was brought in, the rate of production more than doubled. 'The workers started to get up early in order to
increase production, they would get ready for work and prepare their carts
and machinery before daylight and still be cleaning them after nightfall.
Everyone was highly motivated,' Ruan recalled.

Then officials realised that some of the men were working so hard that
their bonuses exceeded their wages. This broke a regulation that nobody
in China could receive an annual bonus which came to more than two
months' salary. To put it in perspective, an average monthly wage on the
project was about Y100, equal at the time to about US$41. The officials
ordered an end to the scheme. 'The sky fell in,' said Ruan, 'we received
orders from our superiors: stop the bonuses! The workers weren't lazy but
from then on they just finished on time and that was that.' Production
slumped.

At that point a reporter for Xinhua filed a report on the project through
the agency's parallel channel, known as *neibu wenjian* or 'internal documents'. These were not written for the general reader but for official eyes
only. The report explained the rise and fall of the bonus system at Shekou.
When it reached the desk of Hu Yaobang, the general secretary of the
Communist Party, he was furious. 'Some of our departments are just
unreal!' he wrote on the report. 'When we discussed bonuses not one
comrade agreed with such restrictions. How can we be modern and make
positive reforms while still living by making rules and giving orders?'

Hu sent the report on to vice premier and economic reformer Gu Mu,
who was close to Deng Xiaoping. Within days, the bonuses were rein-
stated. Production soared once again and the project was completed a
month ahead of schedule.

Such, at least, was the authorised version. The picture of a wise and
benevolent central leadership intervening to correct the errors of local
officials serves the party's narrative and the Shekou case should, perhaps,
be taken as exemplary rather than typical. None the less, it illustrated a
general truth about Chinese reform. It was top-down, step by step and
constantly subject to reverses. Despite such fits and starts, by the middle
of the 1980s a great wave of change was rolling across southern China.

The first businessmen from Hong Kong ventured back into China in the
early stages of reform. They were not pampered guests. One of them, Yip
Kwok-wah, recalled queueing at four o'clock in the morning for the necessary permits at the old railway station on the waterfront at Tsim Sha Tsui,

then riding a train to the border at Lo Wu, where travellers walked across a girdered bridge and into a shed. Here soldiers checked their papers, after which they waited for their numbers to be called for customs inspection. Then they boarded a diesel-drawn train which rattled up to Guangzhou. 'When we got there it was already midnight,' he remembered. 'I had to spend the whole day to travel to Guangzhou at the time.'

The pioneers invested in ports and roads, built factories and trained workers who earned a fraction of the wages paid in Hong Kong. Entrepreneurs found a thicket of regulations to negotiate in the socialist system. Many dealt with uncertainty and risk by falling back on the bonds of clan, investing in their ancestral homelands, where friends and members of the extended family could be found. Their common Cantonese spoken language made dealings more comfortable and there was 'a sense of contributing to the development of the ancestral hometown'.

China was still groping its way towards a modern judicial system. Under Maoism, the legal tradition had been destroyed. Law schools only reopened in 1979. The ministry of justice and the court system were in their infancy. The country wanted foreign investment but its officials had little grasp of investor protection, the settlement of business disputes or cross-border transactions. Between 1965 and 1978 not a single specialist article on international law had been published in China. Now, in the first years of reform, new laws were passed on contracts, trademarks, patents, inheritance and bankruptcy. The government reorganised taxes on income, commercial profits, real estate, vehicles and agriculture. It set customs duties, tariffs and rules with the mentality of a protectionist state before realising that trade was the route to growth. Property rights, labour codes and rules on land use were in constant flux. Commerce equalled confusion.

By contrast, Hong Kong companies were used to a legal environment of impartial courts, case law and clear statutes; they paid low taxes and operated under light regulation. To venture up the Pearl River Delta was daunting. None the less, Hong Kong became by far the largest outside investor in China. Between 1985 and 2014 it accounted for almost half of all the foreign direct investment into the country, some US$744.8 billion.

For multinationals, China beckoned like an Eldorado. The bottling plant in Beijing opened by Coca-Cola in the early eighties with the encouragement of Li Qiang was followed by a car factory built by Volkswagen with the Shanghai Automotive Industry Corporation. General Motors stepped into a joint venture in Chongqing and BP drilled for oil in the South China Sea. Most companies still thought in nineteenth-century terms of selling goods to Chinese consumers – there were, after all, so many of them. The car giants were among the first through the open door. Toyota and Nissan multiplied their sales to China, while Citroën, Peugeot and Fiat elbowed their way into the market. Chinese photographers were soon shooting luminous colours on Kodak and Agfa film. Affluent smokers puffed on Rothmans cigarettes, while urbanites munched crackers from Nabisco and whizzed up and down on board Otis elevators. Corporations built their strategies on exporting finished goods to China or, in a daring minority of cases, forming joint ventures to manufacture locally for the Chinese market. One result was that China's import bill soared and it stumbled into trade deficits in 1980, 1984 and 1985.

The Hong Kong experience was completely different. From the start, the colony had practically nothing to sell to China which the mass of Chinese consumers could afford. Instead its companies focused on projects in construction and development which needed management, engineering skill and capital, offering a return, a completion date and an exit. But then some of its entrepreneurs had the idea of making things inside China to sell to customers overseas. The attractions for light industry of low-cost land and labour with preferential tax and tariff treatment were too strong to resist. They soon moved on to develop production systems and invented the supply chain. Hong Kong firms were already competitive in overseas markets, possessing sophisticated sales and distribution networks which could now be married to low-cost sourcing in China to escape rising labour costs in the colony itself. Even though many of the first entrants were small and medium-sized ventures, the theory applied to all. Employment statistics tell the tale. In 1981 local manufacturers employed around 870,000 workers in Hong Kong: twenty years later the number had fallen to about a quarter of that number. During the same period, Hong Kong companies went from a few local hires to employing an estimated 11 million people in the Pearl River Delta.

The risks and rewards of change were hotly debated in China. Sometimes the divisions have been simplified to the point of caricature as a binary conflict between an imagined 'left' and 'right', but the fears were real. Had the opponents of change prevailed, we would now be living in a different world.

Classical Marxists believed in making the Chinese people wealthier, but they argued that the country should take a different route. Chen Yun, for example, told his comrades that his reaction to the arrival of foreign finance was to re-read Lenin's work *On Imperialism*, which he found eminently valid for the times. The premier, Zhao Ziyang, later recorded the arguments with a certain amount of compassion towards people who clung to the integrity of the revolution. 'Chen Yun believed that foreign direct investments were not the solution for China's development. He often said that foreign capitalists were not just looking for normal profits, but "surplus profits" … he was also critical of joint ventures.'

Chen had gone so far as to hold up the joint venture between Volkswagen and Shanghai, keeping the file in his office for a long time before he eventually gave his consent. Zhao found such resistance irrational: 'Some people were fearful of being exploited. China had closed its doors for many years in the name of independence and self-reliance but in fact it was a self-imposed isolation. The purpose of implementing an open-door policy was to conduct foreign trade, to trade for what we needed. Some people felt ashamed about the idea of importing. What was there to feel ashamed about? It wasn't begging! It was a mutual exchange, which was also a form of self-reliance.'

Zhao pointed out that when foreigners invested in China they feared that China's policies might change. He argued that China itself had nothing to fear. He had heard some Maoists warning that the Special Economic Zones would turn into colonies; they claimed that Macau had originally been leased to the Portuguese to dry their fishing nets but had turned into a colonial foothold. That was in the days of a corrupt and impotent dynasty, Zhao said, but the People's Republic was nothing like that. The only fear that counted was the fear among foreigners that Chinese policy would change one day and the government would renounce its agreements and confiscate their assets.

Modern Chinese scholarship tends to take a strategic view of the decision to open up the economy, acknowledging the critical role of Hong Kong as 'an important window and bridge' but emphasising that the Communist Party always had a clear-eyed utilitarian view of the city. The party's own economists argued that China had to adopt the export development model because there was no other way to create demand in its vast domestic economy. Even a worker on a high-priority project, such as the new port at Shekou, was only earning the equivalent of US$47 a month. If people had no spare money they could not invest or spend it. Once they had cash to hand they could buy better food, new clothes, a motorcycle or a domestic appliance. China would once again discover the velocity of money and appreciate its usefulness. Without such a spur to the economy the population would remain forever trapped in survival socialism, and China would never recover its greatness.

Looking back, a researcher at the State Council's Hong Kong and Macau Research Institute named Cai Chimeng explained it like this:

> In the early stage of opening up, China needed a window to the world and Hong Kong was the best choice. By the late 1970s Hong Kong had completed the industrialization stage and was an international centre for light manufacturing. It was one of the 'four tigers' of Asia and a link in the global capitalist production system. Since the founding of the People's Republic of China the central government had adopted a strategy of 'long term planning and full utilisation' for Hong Kong. So it became the main window for connecting with the international market, a buffer zone for financial opening up and a testbed for internationalisation of the renminbi [i.e. the yuan] currency.

The Communist Party leadership accepted radical policy changes to promote exports. They authorised subsidies, cheap credit from state banks (there were no others), tax incentives, preferential land prices for factories, swift approvals for building projects and cheap rates for water and electricity. The focus was to be on labour-intensive industries where China held an unbeatable comparative advantage because its wages were so low. In exchange, China would earn foreign currency, allowing it to import foreign machinery and technology, thus raising productivity and starting the long climb up the manufacturing ladder. Cai Chimeng was explicit about how the party saw this as necessary, short term and pragmatic, a means to advance its long-term ambition to conquer world markets:

> During this period, China's economic development was highly dependent on foreign capital. So the strategy was to advance openness to the outside world in a progressive manner. The mainland's economy was short of capital, while its levels of technology and management were backward. Attracting foreign investors was a driving force and Hong Kong was the most important source of direct investment ... Hong Kong and overseas Chinese businessmen were the first to take advantage of the mild climate, geography and human capital; then foreign firms came in, bringing us much-needed funds, new technologies, concepts

of a market economy, management experience and a network of international contacts.

In two decades from 1980 to 2000 the global economic order turned inside out. China was not content to become the biggest customer on the planet; it aimed to become the biggest supplier, with Hong Kong as its gateway and its intermediary. Coastal China was the place where globalisation began on a grand scale. There were many forces at work around the world: lower trade tariffs, new technologies, financial deregulation, floating exchange rates, market liberalisation in the industrialised democracies and the collapse of command economies in the Soviet bloc. None of the results would have come about on the same scale without China's emergence as the workshop of a new world. 'Never before have so many people – or so large a proportion of the world population – enjoyed such large rises in their standards of living,' wrote the economics commentator Martin Wolf in 2004.

In the decade from 1980 to 1990 Chinese exports grew at 13 per cent a year; over the next ten years they still grew at 11 per cent. According to the World Bank, average real incomes in China rose 440 per cent in the last twenty years of the twentieth century. The statisticians also recorded a trend that would become politically potent in the new century. Incomes were growing much faster in developing countries than in rich ones. Globally, inequality was being reduced. But within many societies it was rising. In the heady phase of globalisation, few in the mileage-earning technocratic and managerial elite took much notice of that.

The changes in China inspired optimism and healthy greed in Hong Kong. Capitalists, long ostracised by the mainland, were summoned for banquets and toasts. Manufacturers reaped profits as they shut factories in the colony and moved production to the Pearl River Delta. Some tycoons saw limitless expansion in the People's Republic, which would need airports, hotels and shopping malls to serve a billion consumers. At home, the Hong Kong workforce had become better educated under British rule. Access to tertiary education prepared more young people for new jobs. Access to Guangdong province created new opportunities in the growing industrial zones. In the Chinese-language newspapers and magazines of the time, melancholy and doubt did not figure greatly.

Inside China, however, the era of reform brought anger about corruption and high prices, uncertainty about the state's 'iron rice bowl' and currents of nostalgia, self-questioning, even a philosophical debate about what it meant to be Chinese. Undetected by many foreign observers, these grew into a social and political movement. The intellectual ferment did not dismay the two politicians identified with reform, the party general secretary Hu Yaobang and the prime minister Zhao Ziyang. Fortified by his role in securing the return of Hong Kong, Zhao pressed ahead with the formation of a study group for the reform of the political system. It included one of the party's eight elders, Bo Yibo.

The British government invested heavily in Zhao Ziyang and Hu Yaobang futures. They saw reformers' continuation in power as an insurance policy for the future of Hong Kong and a guarantee of privileged relations with the emerging Chinese economy. Great care was taken to welcome both men to Britain. On 3 June 1985, Mrs Thatcher hosted Zhao at a dinner in 10 Downing Street. The seating plan, which she kept in her private papers, illustrates the confidence of both sides. The Chinese premier sat between Mrs Thatcher and her husband, Denis. His principal aide and confidant, Bao Tong, was placed next to Lord King, the boss of British Airways, facing the Duke of Buccleuch and Queensberry (a great Tory landowner who was confined to a wheelchair after a riding accident), the British ambassador to China, Sir Richard Evans, and Sir S.Y. Chung, the head of the Hong Kong 'unofficials' who had riled Deng Xiaoping. The conversation may have been livelier a few seats away, where the acerbic Zhou Nan, who spoke fluent English, was flanked by Mrs Thatcher's equally caustic minister Nicholas Ridley, by the former prime minister James Callaghan and the inevitable Sir Percy Cradock. On a lonely perch among the tycoons and grandees down-table sat Joseph Needham, the left-wing Cambridge polymath whose great work *Science and Civilisation in China* posed what is known as the 'Needham Question': a matter of great interest to Zhao Ziyang and his group because it asked why modern science, 'the mathematisation of hypotheses about nature', had enjoyed a meteoric rise in Europe but not in China or India. Near the top of the table was the governor of Hong Kong, Sir Edward Youde; in the very lowest place was the man who would succeed him after his early death, the foreign office Sinologist David Wilson. An evening of candelabras and crystal that may have been the high-water mark of friendship between Britain and China, it is one that now seems shadowed by irony.

Undeterred by the formal prickliness of all such encounters, even those with Chinese politicians supposedly as open-minded as Zhao Ziyang, the Foreign Office applied its finest minds to the visit of Hu Yaobang, the leader of the Communist Party, in June the following year. Robert Culshaw, a young star in the diplomatic service, sent a memo to the prime minister's office recalling a Chinese proverb that much courtesy displeases nobody, and listing a series of 'special touches' for the septuagenarian general secretary. These, it was argued, 'should help UK interests by making it harder for the Chinese to believe that we are not acting in good faith or are insensitive to Chinese values when we make proposals which cause them difficulty'.

Among the quintessentially English methods deployed to woo this hardened Marxist were a flower arrangement combining English roses with blooms characteristic of Sichuan province, a ceremonial band playing Chinese folk tunes and a gift set of playing cards ('Mr Hu is a keen bridge player') commemorating the appearance of Halley's comet, of which the first written mention was believed to be found in the Confucian 'Spring and Autumn Annals' of 651 BC. To show off British technology, Hu was also provided with an electronic bridge companion compatible with Chinese television sets. British Telecom engineers placed in the rooms of both Hu and the ever-suspicious Zhou Nan Prestel sets, an early video text service, programmed with a welcome message. 'The access code is made up only of auspicious digits (eg 8 = prosperity: and not 4 = death)', the memo noted. It is doubtful whether the guests, prepared for British deviousness by the ministry of state security, ever touched the devices.

A final touch to the general secretary's visit to Oxford was an after-dinner programme of madrigals and poetry readings at Balliol College, the nurturing ground for four British prime ministers. It included works by the Chinese poets Li Bai and Ai Qing. The planners seemed undaunted by the recollection that Zhao Ziyang had dozed off during a similar effort on his own visit.

In the end it was all in vain. In January 1987 Hu Yaobang vanished from public view, and on the sixteenth of the month the Chinese public were told that he had made a confession of his errors and resigned. His offence in the eyes of Deng Xiaoping and other elders was not to have opposed 'bourgeois liberalisation' with sufficient zeal. Zhao Ziyang took his place as general secretary, and fell into line with a show of wooden conformity that many found unconvincing. It was the first severe blow to the reformers, and it heralded worse to come.

For the moment, momentum was with them. In October 1987, Zhao declared at the Thirteenth Party Congress that China was at an early stage of socialism which called for market reforms as a means to the ultimate end. He also put forward a significant package of political reforms. But the storm clouds were gathering over China's economy and its society.

In 1988 Chinese national television broadcast a six-episode series called *River Elegy*. Viewers had seen nothing like it before. *River Elegy* opened with a sequence of three groups of believers, Taoists, Muslims and Buddhists, bowing in prayer. Its title shot unfolded in classical calligraphy, superimposed on a view of the winding, darkened Yellow River, while a plangent traditional song evoked the toil of the boatmen. The narrator, Zhang Jiasheng, spoke of young heroes who perished trying to run the rapids. He praised the spirit of China's youth, who refused to forget the shame of a time when Western gunboats controlled the coastline. 'Is it our history of passive defeat over the last century that has conditioned us psychologically or decades of poverty and backwardness?' he asked. China was a civilisation in decline. With that, the audience was taken straight back to 1840 and shown scenes of foreign atrocities against the Chinese people.

The documentary claimed that the roots of Chinese civilisation lay in the Yellow River, saying it had shaped the national destiny and character. Citing Marx and Engels, it linked the prevalence of oriental despotism with the need for mass labour under a central regime to carry out large-scale irrigation and agriculture. The 'Asiatic production model' required a society of countless insignificant individuals subservient to a supreme ruler. Democracy, freedom and equality could never flourish in such a state. A haunting song included these lyrics:

In the ancient East there was a dragon
China was its name
In the ancient East there was a people
They were all descendants of the dragon
I grew up under the feet of the dragon and became a descendant of
  the dragon
Dark eyes, dark hair, yellow skin, forever I am a descendant of the
  dragon

According to the programme, China's old civilisation had become silted up like the Yellow River itself. This became a metaphor throughout the series. For millennia the Chinese had clung to the yellow soil and bent their backs to the blue sky as they grafted for food. It was part of their souls. Few people, the programme said, had a more profound sense of history than the Chinese, but few were as fatalistic. Encircled by the Great

Wall, their agricultural civilisation felt secure, but the Great Wall was not a cause for pride. Rather than being a monument to power and prosperity it spoke only of isolation, conservatism and incompetent defence. It had 'embedded self-glorification, arrogance and self-deception into our national character'. And why did the glow of civilisation dim after the seventeenth century? The Chinese people had forgotten how to trade and compete. Paper and printing had been invented in China but only in Europe had they been used to destroy feudalism. In China, where 'reams of history were written', there had been no 'knowledge explosion' for a thousand years. This was indeed the 'Needham Question'. Intellectuals were only just venturing out of the 'stinking ninth category' to which they had been consigned by the Cultural Revolution. In a land which once revered Confucius, the status of teachers had sunk.

River Elegy lauded the Third Plenum of December 1978 as an 'irresistible historic tide' towards renewal. It warned the audience, however, that reform meant struggle, not just 'changing from sweet potatoes to steamed buns' or buying cars and refrigerators. In later years *River Elegy* was reclaimed as a manifesto for reform, but progressive Chinese in the twenty-first century would be uncomfortable with some of its ideas. It certainly did not fit into Western preconceptions about the rights of man and liberal humanitarianism. Apart from its sweeping generalisations about a perceived 'national character', the programme identified population growth as China's biggest problem, saying it produced a 'bitter fruit' in the form of 'low-grade people' – a script line delivered over film of poor, wrinkled, gap-toothed villagers. It said only markets could remedy a state where specialist doctors in a cancer hospital earned the same as an old woman selling potatoes at the gate. 'The death knell for capitalism sounded by Marx has been late in arriving ...' the script said sardonically. Capitalism renewed itself, and while some socialist countries were making reforms it was time for China to embrace a radical new form of market socialism with Chinese characteristics. In essence, this was a strident variation on the theme of Zhao and the surviving reformers.

A great flood was needed to cleanse and renew China, the series said. It had arrived from the Pacific Ocean. In the nineteenth century an expanding 'sky blue civilisation' engaged in international maritime trade had clashed with a 'yellow civilisation' wedded to agriculture and bureaucratic government, 'a clash like mixing ice with hot coals'. Ultimately the series offered a clarion call for national rallying and rebirth, concluding that the Yellow River was destined to flow into the azure sea. The foundation of Shenzhen in 1980 across the bay from Hong Kong had finally brought the yellow civilisation to the shore, 'turning its face from the land to the ocean'.

River Elegy provoked a backlash among the Communist Party leadership. The writers, Su Xiaokang and Wang Luxiang, had taken aim at ancient traditions which the party itself had long labelled 'feudal'. A deeper meaning, however, was clear to Chinese intellectuals, who saw in the script a coded critique of authoritarian rule. Neither was that lost on the party's ideologues. It reinforced their will to resist dangerous changes. Time was running out for political reform in China.

In October 1987 the capitalist system went through one of its periodic crises when stock markets crashed around the world. The shock reached Hong Kong, but the territory was well prepared after its near-death experience during the currency crisis four years earlier. The Hongkong Bank played a key role in supporting the financial authorities. It pumped more than a billion Hong Kong dollars into supporting local share prices, incidentally leading to a record profit for its investment banking arm.

Looking out from Beijing, the global business cycle seemed threatening and unpredictable. After a period of overheating and of surging trade deficits, the economic reformers had regained confidence. They lifted some price controls, allowed more incentive schemes for workers, granted more rights to peasants, encouraged open markets and reopened the stock exchange in Shanghai, where stock prices were chalked on a blackboard. Property reform allowed people to buy and sell the right to use land for up to thirty years. By the time of the stock market crash in late 1987, the Chinese economy was expanding again.

The problem for Zhao Ziyang and his acolytes was that prices were rising too fast. In his memoir, Zhou admitted that the government had bungled price reforms as it tried to tinker with a centrally planned system by raising workers' wages to offset the surge in prices. In 1987, inflation rose to 7 per cent. By the spring of 1988 public alarm was growing. People pulled their savings out of banks and rushed to buy commodities. By the time of the spring festival, some cities were considering a return to rationing to deal with shortages of meat and eggs. The government responded by guaranteeing savings rates to keep money in the banks. The turmoil shook confidence and undermined political stability. 'The bank runs and hoarding of commodities led to an overall panic which arrived with the force of a tidal wave,' wrote Zhao in rueful hindsight.

Zhao had planned great advances for 1988, expanding the Special Economic Zones to include the island of Hainan, broadening the scale of liberal market enterprises and examining how a shareholding system worked. He had met the economist Milton Friedman and was convinced that introducing shares was the way to 'deepen reform' in state businesses. With an eye on Hong Kong, he wanted to turn the whole of Guangdong province into a gigantic experiment in market reforms.

Hong Kong newspapers were the first to report that Zhao's ambitions had run into trouble. The hardliners Li Peng, the premier, and Yao Yilin, a vice premier, took back command of the economy through a series of rules, laws and regulations issued by the State Council, all meant to reverse reform and restore the old ways. Within the party councils, Zhao argued for Deng's ear. But, as he recalled, the old man's hearing was poor. Power slipped away from Zhao. When the Hong Kong press began saying that he had been stripped of real authority and would lose his post as general secretary at the head of the Communist Party, even Deng asked him why the papers were full of such rumours. Soon he faced open criticism in the Politburo standing committee, the supreme leadership body, where feuds and hatreds broke into the open. Battles between reformers and reactionaries multiplied across the government and party apparatus. The dawn of 1989 proved to be the moment when the seeds of crisis, long-planted, burst into bloom. The year marked the 200th anniversary of the French Revolution, the seventieth anniversary of the May Fourth movement of 1919, which had awakened China's youth to colonial injustice, and the fortieth of the founding of the People's Republic. It should have been a blissful dawn in which to be alive.

On 15 April 1989, the ousted party leader, Hu Yaobang, died in Beijing at the age of seventy-four. Seven days earlier he had suffered a heart attack at a Politburo meeting. He turned ashen, rose to leave and collapsed in his chair. His comrades jumped to their feet, laid him on the floor and pressed nitroglycerine tablets under his tongue. An elite medical team took him to hospital but he did not recover. He was duly commemorated by the party as a loyal Communist fighter and granted a memorial service at the Great Hall of the People. His ashes were interred at the Babaoshan cemetery in Beijing, a favoured place of rest for the privileged. Hu's widow, Li Zhao, did not hesitate to blame Deng and the elders for their treatment of him. She later pressed for the ashes to be removed to his hometown.

Few ordinary Chinese knew anything of these machinations. But as news of Hu's demise spread around university campuses in the capital, it set off a wave of public mourning unseen since the death of Zhou Enlai on 5 April 1976.

According to internal reports later published abroad, the party was slow to react when students began to mourn the lost leader on their campuses by traditional forms of respect: laying wreaths, carrying commemorative banners and reciting poetry. On the afternoon of 17 April, they marched into the centre of Beijing and laid wreaths at the foot of the Monument to the People's Heroes in Tiananmen Square. Some chanted slogans calling for democracy, freedom and the rule of law. From then on, events would cascade in a terrible stream to their denouement, a story told countless times in books and films but one which needs to be summarised again in order to understand its consequences.

The party staged its memorial service for Hu at the Great Hall on 22 April, with Deng and the elders in attendance, only to find students kneeling on the steps in supplication while their classmates staged a mock funeral. Two days later, students called for a boycott of classes and a group of student unions emerged to challenge the Communist Party's monopoly on organisations. Tiananmen Square became a permanent protest camp. Posters, speeches and music drew thousands. Hundreds of elegiac couplets, known as *wanlian*, were composed to eulogise Hu Yaobang. Soon the tone changed to savage rhetoric and satire against arbitrary power and corruption. The students voiced seven political demands in 'reactionary language', according to a report by the Beijing Municipal Party Committee, which listed them as follows:

Freedom and democracy.
Completely repudiate efforts to 'eliminate spiritual pollution'.
Lift all bans on newspapers and implement freedom of the press.
Require officials to resign for serious mistakes.
Make the Central Government subject to popular votes of
    confidence.
Publicise the incomes of leaders and their children.
Release political prisoners unconditionally.

From all over China, reports flowed into the party centre of mass protests, strikes and disruption. On 26 April, the hardliners took advantage of the absence of Zhao Ziyang, who was on a state visit to North Korea, to organise an editorial in the *People's Daily* reflecting the words of Deng, who had told the elders that the party faced a well-planned plot to throw China into chaos. Headlined 'The necessity for a clear stand against turmoil', the editorial outraged students and other protesters. Instead of rallying opinion, it created a fresh demand – for its repudiation – which energised the movement. On 4 May the student groups staged their biggest demonstration yet. Two days later, some protesters began a hunger strike. In mid-May, the Soviet Communist Party leader, Mikhail Gorbachev, having landed for an official visit, found himself lionised by the demonstrators to the embarrassment of his grim-faced hosts, who faced a diplomatic humiliation. A million people were said to have thronged the streets of Beijing on 17 May. Behind the scenes, the elders convened at Deng's home, where, with his casting vote, the old man decided to fight back. Martial law was proclaimed on 20 May. The next day, a meeting of party elders convened at Deng Xiaoping's home and decided to dismiss Zhao Ziyang from all his positions. The die was cast.

In Hong Kong, the upheaval in mainland China during the spring of 1989 was followed with astonishment, trepidation and hope. The demonstrations against martial law on 21 May were the largest the colony had seen in decades. An estimated six hundred thousand people from all walks of life marched against the Chinese government. Their ranks included students, teachers, workers, the elderly and religious groups. There was even a contingent from the NCNA, Beijing's unofficial representative office in the city. On 22 May, the leadership in Beijing learned that thirty-five delegates from Hong Kong to the National People's Congress and its associated body, the Chinese People's Political Consultative Conference, had voiced their opposition to martial law. This was an ominous sign for the Communist Party.

Capitalists, too, felt the strain. The local stock market fell sharply on news of martial law and the eclipse of Zhao Ziyang. Business travel and tourism declined. A steady flow of foreigners and Hong Kong residents bought air tickets out of China to find safety in the colony, where freedom, law and order remained intact. Two hundred thousand people joined a rally in Victoria Park on 26 May and a marathon concert for the protesters was staged the next day.

The colony was not a mere spectator, though. A secret report from the Ministry of State Security submitted to the party leadership on 1 June identified Hong Kong as a centre of American and Taiwanese espionage and detailed examples of local groups in the city which were raising funds and organising subversion to 'exploit' the protests and 'sabotage' the socialist system. Lost in the great sweep of the drama that convulsed China in 1989, these conceptions were not forgotten by the guardians of state security. They were to assume great relevance in the way the successors to Deng Xiaoping viewed Hong Kong thirty years later when the city's own mass political protests erupted.

Deng himself knew how useful Hong Kong was to his government. As late as 31 May, he reminded his colleagues that he had called for the creation of 'a few more Hong Kongs', because China could not develop if it did not open up. Lacking capital, it could only increase employment and tax revenue by growing industries. 'Look at Hong Kong; look at the benefits we get from it. Without Hong Kong we'd have no good information and that's just for starters,' he said. To the Ministry of State Security, however, such considerations counted for little when weighed against the perceived threat from the colony to the edifice of Communist power. Its report of 1 June said President George Bush had 'personally ordered' the US consulate general in Hong Kong to monitor events on the mainland closely and had dispatched a team of experts to boost its capacity to gather information on China's internal affairs. It informed the party leadership that 'reactionary forces in Taiwan and Hong Kong have run wild during this turmoil'. Certain people in Hong Kong had raised HK$51 million to support the student hunger strike, the money being carried into China in small batches of banknotes. They had already sent a support group to Beijing with one million Hong Kong dollars. As well as cash, they had sent 'various kinds of modern equipment such as high-power binoculars, walkie-talkies and tents – all for the purpose of preparing the protesters sitting in on the Square for "protracted warfare"'.

The state security report identified journalists from the *Hong Kong Express News*, the *Economic Daily*, the *South China Morning Post* and the *Hong Kong Standard* as troublemakers behind 'many distorted and inflammatory reports'. The media had reacted to attacks on its journalists by the security forces with a letter to Xu Jiatun, the head of Xinhua in Hong Kong, demanding an explanation; this, concluded the report, was meant to fan the flames of public sentiment in Hong Kong and China. The text closed with a profession of faith that is worth quoting in full since it illustrates the world view from within the citadel of the Chinese security state, as authentic today as the day it was written in 1989:

Many facts demonstrate that the international monopoly capitalists
and hostile reactionary forces have not abandoned for a moment
their intent to destroy us. It is now clear that murderous intent has
always lurked behind their protestations of peace and friendship.
When the opportunity arises they will remove the façade and
reveal their true colours. They have only one goal: to annihilate
socialism.

The rest of the tragedy is etched on the collective memory of anyone in
Hong Kong and China above a certain age. Between 29 May and 3 June,
Deng and his comrades made plans to clear the protesters out of central
Beijing. They ordered army units to move into the capital. The commander
of the Thirty-Eighth Army, Xu Qinxian, refused to dispatch his troops
from their base in the city of Baoding and was stripped of his command,
then sent to hospital. The party's internal documents recount a strong
campaign of ideological 'thought work' which hardened the resolve of the
junior officer corps and the rank and file. Troops began to take up positions at strategic points in Beijing. Meanwhile the students and their
supporters fell into a cycle of fear, doubt and defiance; many fled the
square, though others stayed at their posts while dissension and rivalries
split the movement as it disintegrated under extreme pressure.

In the final days, foreign governments became aware through their
intelligence services of intense military activity. According to Western
diplomats, analysts tracked communications between Deng's group of
elders, principally Yang Shangkun, the former president of the People's
Republic, and the commanders of key regiments. The exchanges showed
that the regime was making sure of their loyalty and cementing support
for a military solution. Deng personally spoke to generals and rallied the
old marshals of the PLA, who needed little convincing when it came to
putting down dissenters by force. 'We had several days warning when it
was absolutely clear what was going to happen,' said a diplomat privy to
the material.

The Western powers found themselves in a moral dilemma. There is no
evidence that they either tried to dissuade the regime from violence
through diplomatic channels – to be fair, Deng and the elite were in even
tighter seclusion than normal – or took steps to protect their own citizens
in China. The intelligence was not disclosed in order to protect its collection methods. We now know that most of it derived from intercepts of
Chinese military traffic by a British listening station, originally codenamed

Demos-1, at Chum Hom Kok, on the south side of Hong Kong island, where huge dishes perched on a shelf of rock overlooked the South China Sea, fenced off by barbed wire and patrolled by armed guards. From there the codebreakers scooped up the PLA's signals intelligence, civilian traffic, satellite communications and telemetry from missile tests thousands of miles away in the deserts of western China. The station was controlled by the British Government Communications Headquarters (GCHQ) but its 'take' far exceeded the needs of the United Kingdom. Its value to Britain lay in its value to the United States. The data was shared with the US National Security Agency, which had heavily invested in the facilities at Chum Hom Kok. As the pre-eminent historian of the subject, Richard J. Aldrich, wrote: 'Hong Kong was the single most valuable British collection station to NSA, providing offset in an otherwise unbalanced Anglo-American intelligence relationship.'

On the morning of 2 June, Deng, the elders and the Standing Committee of the Politburo voted to clear Tiananmen Square by force. Some voiced their hope that it could be done without casualties, although one, Wang Zhen, called the protesters 'bastards ... anybody who tries to overthrow the Communist Party deserves death and no burial.' Deng himself recalled the Opium Wars to claim that it was Western countries who had robbed the Chinese people of their human rights.

The next day, 3 June, violence broke out across Beijing as martial law troops entering the city encountered fierce resistance from citizens. At 6.30 p.m. the state media broadcast an ultimatum to everyone to leave the square and to stay indoors. A pitched battle erupted at the Muxidi Bridge, three miles west of Tiananmen. Around midnight, the first armoured vehicles crashed into the square, to be met with a hail of stones and petrol bombs. Thousands of troops went into action against demonstrators who had no firearms. The killing went on through the early hours of Sunday morning, a date that would live in Chinese history alongside so many other infamous anniversaries: June Fourth.

7

The Change

On the morning of 4 June, the twenty-seventh governor of Hong Kong, Sir David Wilson, awoke in his white stucco residence to a possession that had changed utterly. From the verandahs of Government House, the muted stir of the metropolis below sounded typical of a Sunday, but the city was in a state of shock.

All night long, local radio stations and television channels had carried live broadcasts from mainland China. Images from press photographers and video camera crews framed the public perception of events. This was an age before widespread use of the internet or social media. After dawn, people grabbed the first editions of the Chinese-language newspapers to read the accounts from reporters in Beijing.

For Martin Lee, an austere, Jesuit-educated barrister, the morning of June Fourth was a political milestone. He was the leading figure in Hong Kong's democratic politics. 'We knew about the nature of the Chinese Communist government but this was clear proof of what they were capable of,' he recalled. Like the rest of the city's democratic politicians, Lee's instinct was to mobilise public opinion. The people would have to fight for their future. The first demonstrators soon appeared on the streets.

Deng's decision to use force shook the colonial government and the foreign policy establishment back in London. Since 1984 they had placed their faith in the Joint Declaration and believed that China would honour its promises. But Wilson had watched from afar the tumult in Beijing and was convinced that it would end badly. 'There was a growing worry about what was going on in Beijing because I could not believe that the Chinese government would tolerate the taking over of the centre of their capital for any length of time,' he recalled of the spring of 1989, 'my own sense was that it just could not go on.'

With a sense of foreboding, Wilson had turned to his old contacts for information. The Chinese ambassador to London, Ji Chaozhu, was passing through Hong Kong on leave. Educated at Harvard, Ji was a sophisticated insider who had interpreted for Mao Zedong himself. Wilson sought him out: 'I invited him to come and have supper privately and said, "Look, I'm seriously worried because if this ends as it looks to me as though it's going to, well, it's going to have very serious repercussions on Hong Kong".

'He said, "Absolutely don't worry. There's no question of the Chinese government using force to deal with this".'

Wilson remained sceptical.

On the morning of June Fourth such hindsight became academic. The governor was expected to rise to the occasion. In retirement, he remembered how quickly he realised that everything would be different between Hong Kong and China from then on. 'I can tell you it was within about half an hour in Government House. I don't know about Whitehall. I had to make a decision – what do I do? – instantly.'

Wilson felt that he had to speak to the public, relying on his own knowledge of local Chinese culture and judging local expectations about how the government should react to the massacre. 'So I did. I went out on Radio Television Hong Kong with statements on it. I had to do that. I didn't consult London. It was clearly important to say something straight away – of great distress about what had happened – *but* also that we must keep ourselves calm in Hong Kong.' It was, he felt, 'absolutely central to express deep concern about what had happened'.

The governor soon heard that massive, peaceful demonstrations were unfolding in the city. He felt they were 'very, very impressive'. The solemn marches wound through the shuttered commercial districts without the slightest trouble. Wilson wanted to see for himself what was going on but did not wish to attract attention: 'I took an unmarked car without my flag and went to watch what was happening.' By the evening of June Fourth, hundreds of thousands of Hong Kongers had joined mournful processions through the city. Their display of political awareness confounded elite opinion, which held that 'livelihood issues' were the population's main, if not solitary, concern.

Monday morning dawned hot, dripping with humidity and in an atmosphere of tension. The stock market opened for trading as normal. Shares promptly crashed. The Hang Seng Index fell by 22 per cent that day, eroding the gains made in a climate of optimism about Chinese economic reform. During the afternoon, a thousands-strong march made its way from the central financial district, toiling up the steep path behind the Hongkong Bank building, passing under a canopy of semitropical trees past the Victorian-era buildings and along to the central government offices. Within its ranks walked dozens of Western expatriates in summer office clothes alongside a host of Chinese middle-class clerks, tellers, dealers, brokers and traders, cleaners, service staff and caterers. If ever the different communities in the city came together, it was in the days after June Fourth. Those days forged a model of street politics that would become customary over the next three decades in Hong Kong: plangent, cadenced chanting of slogans in a high-pitched tone, placards bearing outlandish cartoons of Chinese leaders dripping blood from their fangs, banners adorned with slogans in black characters, a stream of young and old, sweating in the heat, swigging water and sports drinks, patiently plodding along the tarmac. If the mood was angry it was also restrained, perhaps because a sense of foreboding gripped the population.

'The market was berserk today,' said a trader walking with his colleagues, 'for sure this is the end of Hong Kong.' Like most of those participating, he had joined a political demonstration for the first time in his life. It was a token of the difference between Hong Kong and the People's Republic that only a few police constables in light uniforms were needed to nod the crowd along. The march, like every other protest in the territory, unfolded in dignified grief.

Some small-scale trouble broke out in Kowloon, where suspected Triad gangsters took advantage of the moment to smash into shops and loot goods. The police quickly intervened. Wilson got David Ford, the chief secretary, to contact local activists to make sure that the combination of crime and mass demonstrations did not lead to a collapse in public order, and in characteristically law-abiding manner, the protesters agreed to put off their marches until the streets were under control. 'The organisers were very keen that demonstrations should be peaceful and to co-operate with the government. It was possible for David Ford to call the organisers and say "call off your demo for today" and they did so.' At times the classic colonial method of the quiet word behind the scenes still worked.

In Government House, there was relief at the civilised and responsible way in which the colony's people had responded to the state violence in Beijing. As fears of trouble in the city abated, Wilson's thoughts turned to what he could do to stop a bad situation getting worse. 'A lot of people didn't quite realise what was likely to happen. What did happen had an absolutely dramatic effect in Hong Kong. There was wall-to-wall TV coverage for days. It played to all the underlying fears of Hong Kong about what might happen in 1997 so it was really a very, very serious issue for us. There were a good many Hong Kong people involved in Tiananmen Square – not very clever to be involved. A good deal of money as well as tents and suchlike were going in from Hong Kong.'

The colonial government pulled the few strings it had to extract a group of Hong Kong political activists from China, where the security forces were beginning a mass roundup of opponents. It was a rare instance of co-operation between Wilson's officials and the Chinese bureaucrats at the New China News Agency. 'There were some political figures from Hong Kong – with help from the NCNA in Hong Kong and the British embassy in Beijing we got them out,' Wilson recalled. The June Fourth massacre had enraged many of the NCNA's own staff. Workers and journalists from the pro-Communist media joined the demonstrations winding through the streets. The political struggle in mainland China could not be isolated, and throughout the spring discord had grown between party cadres in Hong Kong. Well before the massacre, on 21 May, the faithful local newspaper *Wen Wei Po* broke ranks by replacing its editorial column with a blank space containing four Chinese characters – 'deep grief, bitter hatred' – in response to the declaration of martial law in Beijing. Theoretically under the control of the NCNA, the newspaper could not be held to account during the turmoil; punishment came later.

June Fourth led to the gravest internal crisis of the Communist Party in Hong Kong since 1949, although that was not clear at the time. Across the country shock and confusion reigned in the party's ranks. That allowed many dissidents to flee China before the net closed on them.

In Hong Kong, senior local officials in the civil service called in their contacts among the tycoons. Via sympathetic businessmen, they made the case to the central government's Hong Kong and Macau Affairs Office in the capital that it would be simpler to turn a blind eye while the troublesome Hong Kongers left than to get involved in the political complications of arrests, charges and trials. In most cases, the 'nuisance value' tactic worked. Groups of stunned but relieved passengers were allowed to board Cathay Pacific flights from the old stone-built terminal at Beijing airport.

Greater adventures awaited the fugitives who slipped away from the capital and other turbulent cities to make their way to the Pearl River Delta. Never disclosed publicly, personal contacts took place between native Cantonese-speaking officials in the Hong Kong government and the police with their counterparts in the Ministry of Public Security in Guangdong. The aim was to avoid unnecessary 'trouble', that all-encompassing concept known in Mandarin Chinese as *mafan*.

'Bribery worked as well,' said a Western intelligence official serving at the time, 'and in southern China there is always the village, the family and the clan. Local relationships are there for ever while the government in Beijing has always been far away. Plus you already had a network of smugglers and cross-border traders who were used to making their arrangements with the customs and the border guards. The police and the Gurkha units on our side were ordered to let it happen and to let the right people in.'

In the months after June Fourth, activists in Hong Kong set up an underground railroad, Operation Yellow Bird, to smuggle dissidents out of China, many ending up scattered from Canada to France. But in the first few days, a trickle of escapees were able to make their way by fishing boat, truck and train out of Guangdong and onto British territory.

For Sir David Wilson, the challenge lay in working out what the upheaval shaking China meant for the future. He had come unexpectedly to the governorship. Essentially a scholar-administrator in the Confucian style, possessing a love of Chinese culture and a mastery of the Chinese language rivalled by few, he had been on the inside of British policy-making since the early negotiations. He studied Chinese in Hong Kong, served as a young diplomat in Beijing, then left government service to edit the *China Quarterly*, a prestigious academic journal. He was lured back to the Foreign Office by Percy Cradock, for whom he formed a lifelong admiration, and found himself sent to Hong Kong as political adviser to the governor, Sir Murray MacLehose. It was these three men who had met Deng Xiaoping in 1979; Cradock and Wilson went on to conduct the talks which were crowned by the Joint Declaration in 1984, after which Wilson vanished into the wings at the Foreign Office. When Zhao Ziyang came to dine at 10 Downing Street with Mrs Thatcher in 1985, he was seated at the very bottom of the table.

Then, on the morning of 5 December 1986, the governor of Hong Kong, Sir Edward Youde, was found dead in his room at the residence of the British ambassador in Beijing. Youde had been on a working visit to the capital. The governor had worn out his energies and fought countless unsung Whitehall battles on behalf of the people of Hong Kong; he spoke Cantonese well and enjoyed considerable local esteem. But his health was weak, he had undergone cardiac surgery some years earlier, and his friends attributed his sudden death to the strain of ceaseless work and travel. His demise prompted a flustered search for a candidate to replace him, until the eye of the civil service fell upon Wilson. He would prove to be a good governor, one who has not received the recognition he deserved. In his five years in office, Wilson methodically laid the foundations of Hong Kong's constitutional development, its infrastructure and its higher education, paving the way for more than a decade of prosperous stability after the handover. He was a Scot of irreproachable character and quiet religious convictions; looking back after decades of bitter controversy, his successor as governor, Chris Patten, said he could not imagine Wilson doing anything dishonourable. It was a view which summed up most people's view of the governor. He was, in civil service code, a safe pair of hands.

'We didn't have any discussions about overall strategy, like would we go back on the Joint Declaration or anything like that,' Wilson recalled. 'Absolutely not. There was no question of anything like that. It was all practical, like how do you deal with getting Hong Kong people out of China.'

The governor was not a politician, but he found the political demands on him intensifying. At first, with a civil servant's detachment, he regarded the reaction in London and around the world – 'absolutely unacceptable, must break off with China' – as something that created administrative problems. 'Whitehall decided to suspend meetings. Understandable but not very helpful to us in Hong Kong.' Wilson saw it as his duty to navigate the storm and then take decisions to safeguard the future of Hong Kong. 'What were we going to do? The airport is the classic. My very strong view is we go ahead, we demonstrate we have confidence in the future of Hong Kong with the airport and a massive expansion of tertiary education.

'I think it's probably fair to say that as I looked toward the future in 1997 what I hoped to be able to contribute towards achieving was a Hong Kong which in all its key aspects survived through the transfer of sovereignty, to the extent you could try to make sure that the institutions are strengthened. Try to make sure that Hong Kong's infrastructure enables it to go on,' he said with a laugh. 'I intend to say "with a high degree of autonomy", with the greatest degree of independence possible, i.e. do not become dependent on the mainland for your key transportation. That leads on to the airport.'

The new airport at Chek Lap Kok off Lantau Island was a huge undertaking that would take years to complete. The administration did not have years to prevent an exodus of excellence from the city. Wilson recalled the challenge: 'We were losing quite a lot of talented people, and particularly after the Tiananmen incident some of the talented people in Hong Kong [were] moving out because of their worries about the future.' Therefore, he said, there was a need to strengthen as much as possible the educational institutions and increase the number of university places available. In this he succeeded: the Hong Kong University of Science and Technology, set in a verdant campus by the sea at Clear Water Bay, opened its doors to the first group of 700 students in October 1991.

It was no secret among the elite that some of the traditionally dominant Chinese business dynasties preferred the idea of a workforce educated only to the level required for them to perform mundane tasks. Wilson laughed off the idea that certain billionaires might blame him for the emergence of a politically literate, active citizenry. 'They may well, but you need more, not fewer, educated people … there was, deliberately, a huge increase in the people who were from families who weren't traditionally going into tertiary education.'

Both infrastructure decisions were pregnant with consequences. At first it was the expensive new airport that led to years of argument. Chinese negotiators at intervals declared it unnecessary, suspected a plot to squander the reserves, accused the planners of scheming to award contracts to British firms and challenged every technical, geological and aeronautical calculation. The project consumed executive time and exhausted political capital on both sides before it finally went ahead, with grudging Chinese consent. The rewards would be material and manifest once the airport was completed to general acclaim. But it was the governor's decision, taken long before they were born, to expand access to university and polytechnic tuition which created a new, assertive and freedom-loving generation of Hong Kongers who would write a fresh page in the city's history.

The massacre in Beijing and the ensuing purge across China awoke deep fear in many people on whom the British depended to keep Hong Kong running until 1997. Civil servants, policemen, business people and academics; anyone associated with the colonial ruling structure might face retribution if a righteous and vengeful China took back sovereignty. The fact was that many of them had nowhere to go. Some of their ancestors had fled cosmopolitan Shanghai after the revolution, many of their parents had trekked and sailed out of China to escape the civil war. Many more had crossed the border fleeing Chairman Mao's experiment with socialism, accompanied as it was by the midnight knock on the door, a web of local eavesdroppers, the extinction of free speech and religion – all the accoutrements of a secret police state. Hong Kong had been a haven. Now many saw it as a trap.

The origins of their fear lay equally with the immigration policies of successive British governments. Even the most patriotic British administrators conceded that this was not a field on which the United Kingdom had crowned itself with laurels. The story was long and complicated, but in its stark essentials it came down to this:

Under the British Empire, its subjects had come and gone unfettered within the sovereign's realms. At the waning of the imperial age, the British Nationality Act of 1948 established the status of Citizen of the United Kingdom and Colonies, which included the people of Hong Kong. From the early 1960s, however, the British government began to restrict immigration as its colonies gained independence, chiefly through the Commonwealth Immigration Act of 1962, which marked a turning point in policy and removed the right of Hong Kong citizens to settle in the United Kingdom.

The Immigration Act of 1971 further limited the right of abode in Britain to those with a parent or grandparent born there. The passing, ten years later, of the British Nationality Act, which came into force in 1983. made Hong Kong people British Dependent Territories Citizens with no automatic right to live in the United Kingdom. The distinction was reinforced by the Joint Declaration with China, whose rulers, in any case, saw all Chinese people in Hong Kong as their compatriots.

In 1985, the British government created the unique category of British National (Overseas) citizens for residents of the colony, holding passports which entitled them to live only in Hong Kong; this category, as we have seen, was supposed to die out with British rule in 1997. It was a slender thread on which to hang hopes for a family, a career or a lifetime of savings and property. A strong proponent of immigration controls, Mrs Thatcher was unrepentant about her refusal to allow an exception for the people of Hong Kong, however much she professed to admire their diligence, frugality and family values. In June 1989, that left 3.4 million people in Hong Kong, who were holding British passports or were entitled to them, without a safe haven.

Wilson had already watched the brain drain as bright and motivated people took their money out of Hong Kong and found residence rights or citizenship overseas. The United States, Canada and Australia, all of which had strong Cantonese-speaking communities, were among the favourite destinations. After June Fourth officials realised that anxiety was becoming acute. The police Crime (A1) Department and the Special Branch employed officers whose work entailed surveillance and detection of individuals connected to the underground Communist Party in Hong Kong and of powerful organised crime groups with political connections on the mainland. The customs and immigration departments also furnished the British with important classified information. The temptation for officers to turn a blind eye or to change loyalties was obvious. In addition, the most junior Hong Kong police officer knew what it meant to be a servant of the Public Security Bureau across the border. A specialist in the history of policing in Hong Kong, Kam C. Wong, put it like this: 'The party leadership considers "professional" police an instrument of the state to serve revolutionary ends ... with the Party in the lead neither "bureaucracy" nor "law" nor "profession" is allowed to stand above the Party and the masses ... a "professional" officer is above all a revolutionary cadre.'

The great and the good on Wilson's Executive Council were adamant that something must be done. The council's senior member, Lydia Dunn, flew to London to confront Mrs Thatcher in 10 Downing Street with a passionate call for all Hong Kong people who were eligible for British passports to be granted full citizenship and the right to live in Britain. She found the prime minister appalled by the massacre and clutching a copy of the photograph of a single man standing in the path of a line of tanks on Chang'an avenue in Beijing. Although her heart was rent in twain by the plight of Hong Kong, Mrs Thatcher retained a hard head, and she was to disillusion some of her most fervent admirers in the colony.

Shortly after June Fourth, Wilson went to London to meet the prime minister, to confer with officials and to speak to the Hong Kong Association. The governor believed that giving the right of abode in the United Kingdom to Hong Kong's British passport holders – only about 1.25 million actually held the documents – would be a helpful insurance policy which would greatly boost confidence. He felt that in fact, not many people would use their right to settle permanently in Britain. Wilson found himself in a predicament. He accepted the moral duty to speak up for the people he governed, but he was also a realist. It was obvious that there would be stiff political resistance to giving the right to live in Britain to millions of Hong Kong Chinese. Conversations with Mrs Thatcher were apt to be sticky at the best of times.

There was a brave effort to salvage some honour from the predicament. From retirement, the former governor Murray MacLehose spoke out in a debate in the House of Lords on 21 June to tell his peers that he had changed his mind about British obligations to those it had governed since 1841: 'The decisive solution would be to amend the British Nationality Act to provide Hong Kong British nationals with British citizenship. The object of doing that would be an insurance to encourage them to stay at their work in Hong Kong, as most wish to do. In the past I have asked for a home of last resort. Others have asked for the right of entry or the right of abode. It all comes down to the same thing in the end – citizenship.'

The government response from a foreign office minister, Lord Glenarthur, was bleak: 'We are all well aware of the very real difficulties which would be posed by a massive new immigration commitment for this country. Granting automatic right of abode here to all people from Hong Kong cannot be a realistic option.'

A pragmatic solution was eventually found. In the autumn of 1989 the government agreed to issue full British passports to fifty thousand people in key professions, and their families, under the British Nationality Selection Scheme, a decision formalised by an Act of Parliament in 1990. Applicants had to master a 32-page form and a complicated system of points to qualify. Education, family ties and career were all taken into account. There were complaints that the process was designed to be so daunting that it acted as a deterrent. But Wilson defended it as 'a remarkably well thought out' scheme: 'Fifty thousand families is a lot of people. It was important that people who might be at risk should be included in that.' Some public servants, like officers in the security services, he said, were obvious candidates who fell in to the 'got to be done' category. Then there were entrepreneurs, business people, academics, lawyers and other professionals. 'We needed to devise a scheme whereby people who were important for the future of Hong Kong should have an insurance policy so that they wouldn't leave Hong Kong. That was the guiding principle for selection.'

The Chinese government objected to the scheme, claiming that it breached the Joint Declaration and that, no matter what Britain might say, anyone of Chinese descent in Hong Kong was a citizen of the People's Republic. As Wilson put it, they did not object very strongly and the plan went ahead. But it was not a glorious outcome, and it was a lost opportunity to create a permanent link between the United Kingdom and millions of people at the heart of the East Asian economic renaissance.

The policy of denying most Hong Kong people the right to settle in Britain would remain in place for almost three decades. At the time, Mrs Thatcher had acted first and foremost as a domestic politician preoccupied by popular fears of mass immigration. But the governor was proved right in one regard. Take-up was slow, leading local commentators to conclude that many in Hong Kong did not, in fact, wish to move to a wet and cold island far away off the northwest coast of Europe, where taxes were high. The passport scheme solved the immediate crisis. As Wilson recalled: 'As far as I know the number who actually moved was very small. To my mind it is an enormous credit to Margaret Thatcher that although she didn't like the idea initially she was the person who said "we've got to do it" and did it.'

By good fortune, Hong Kong already had an insurance policy, in the form of the Basic Law proposed in 1984 by Deng. This was, in effect, a constitution hammered out on the template of the Joint Declaration and its annexes. It put in a legal document the commitments made by China to guarantee Hong Kong's rights and freedoms for fifty years after 1997 under 'one country, two systems'.

The Basic Law was the fruit of a period of comparative flexibility in China. On the instructions of Zhao Ziyang, the Chinese government had set up a drafting committee in 1985 and invited twenty-three representatives from Hong Kong to join its thirty-six mainland members. The committee was chaired by Ji Pengfei, a battle-scarred negotiator from the skirmishes with the British and an effective diplomat. The Chinese even invited the Hong Kong democrats Martin Lee and Szeto Wah to join the discussions. Naturally these were fraught. The Hong Kong delegates sought to maximise 'two systems', to embed democracy and to protect freedom. The Chinese government aimed to cement 'one country' in place, to minimise democracy and to focus on eliminating 'subversion'. The outcome was a compromise heavily weighted in favour of the central government. None the less, in the context of the twenty-first century it seems remarkable to reflect that the Communist Party did indeed consult, negotiate and debate with its opponents in the process of formulating the way that Hong Kong was to be governed by its own people.

The talks went on in China and in Hong Kong for almost four years. The text was argued over inside the Chinese system just as strongly as it was debated by lawyers and constitutional experts in Hong Kong. By late 1988 a first draft was published for public consultation. The second draft was approved at a meeting in Shenzhen in February 1989, just as the Chinese political system was poised on the brink of chaos. It was disliked by the democrats but, given the impending defeat of what passed for liberalism in China, it was a prize worth seizing. Within four months the reformers were driven from power. The Basic Law – its official text in Chinese running to seventy-three pages – was approved by the National People's Congress on 4 April 1990.

The key points were vital to the future of Hong Kong. China took back sovereignty, controlled foreign affairs and would station a military garrison in the city at its own expense. Hong Kong would enjoy 'a high degree of autonomy' as a Special Administrative Region. Its executive and legislature were to be drawn from permanent residents. The socialist system and policies were not to be practised 'and the capitalist system and way of life shall remain unchanged for fifty years'. Private property, the common law and an independent judiciary, with the power of final adjudication, were guaranteed. All land belonged to the state, as it had under the British Crown, and was leased to individuals or firms. No part of the central government, nor any province, might interfere in Hong Kong affairs. All residents 'shall have freedom of speech, of the press and of publication; freedom of association, of assembly, of procession and of demonstration; and the right and freedom to join trade unions and to strike'. These were rights not available to the 1.2 billion citizens of the People's Republic.

In addition, the Basic Law protected Hong Kong people against arbitrary arrest, detention, searches, torture and 'unlawful deprivation of life'. Their homes could not be searched without legal sanction, freedom and privacy of communications were protected subject to 'the needs of public security' or criminal investigation. They were free to travel, to engage in academic research, to practise religion, to marry and raise a family freely, to receive social welfare and even to take the government to court.

If all that sounded too good to be true, there were important caveats. In the event that the National People's Congress in Beijing declared a state of war, or if 'turmoil' in Hong Kong endangered national unity or security, the central government could impose a state of emergency and its own laws. The Hong Kong authorities could call on the PLA garrison 'when necessary' to maintain public order. Laws passed in Hong Kong were subject to the ultimate authority of a standing committee of the NPC and could be revoked. The Court of Final Appeal in Hong Kong was not the ultimate arbiter of laws concerning 'affairs which are the responsibility of the Central People's Government' or the relations between Hong Kong and the mainland: on these matters, Article 158 obliged the judges to 'seek an interpretation' from the standing committee of the NPC, a rule destined to set off political controversy.

All these seemed remote possibilities in 1990. But one provision, Article 23, laid down a task which no Hong Kong government was able to fulfil in the first decades after 1997. Article 23 required Hong Kong to 'enact laws on its own to prohibit any act of treason, secession, sedition, subversion against the Central People's Government or theft of state secrets'. Such legislation must also ban 'foreign political organisations or bodies' from conducting activities and should forbid local political organisations from establishing ties with foreign counterparts. This formidable demand would, in essence, submit Hong Kong to the security state prevailing in China. In the face of fierce local opposition it remained unmet until 2020.

The political system outlined in the Basic Law was reasonable-sounding but vague. The chief executive, who must be a Chinese citizen aged over forty, 'shall be selected by election or through consultations held locally', but the exact method would be determined 'in the light of the actual situation' on the principle of 'gradual and orderly progress'. Initially the leader would be chosen by an Election Committee of 800 people appointed by Beijing; less than a quarter of its members could be local elected politicians. However, 'the ultimate aim is the selection of the chief executive by universal suffrage' after their nomination. The chief executive enjoyed wide powers but was no autocrat; he or she could be obliged to resign if they failed to pass laws through the Legislative Council.

The chief executive would inherit the dual governing structure used by the colonial administration. There would be an appointed Executive Council to 'assist ... in policy-making'. The Legislative Council would make laws. It would sit for two years from 1997 and thereafter for four-year terms. With deliberate ambiguity, the Basic Law said this council 'shall be constituted by election', subject, as ever, to the elusive 'principle of gradual and orderly progress' with the 'ultimate aim' that all of its members would be chosen by universal suffrage.

Before June Fourth this sounded like plain sailing, allowing the British government thankfully to relinquish its responsibility and creep away with some tattered honour. After June Fourth it was no longer tenable. In December 1989 Sir Percy Cradock once again flew to Beijing in secret. He was accompanied by the Foreign Office Sinologist Robin McLaren, whom he viewed as 'an old friend and great expert, on whose judgement I could place complete reliance'. The duo presented the new Chinese leaders with a message from Mrs Thatcher. The British wanted to double the number of directly elected seats in the Legislative Council elections of 1991 from ten to twenty and to increase their number in later elections. They sought an agreement that legislators elected in the polls of 1995 would be able to serve a full four-year term. This was known as the 'through train', a comparison with the non-stop rail link between Hong Kong and Guangzhou inaugurated in 1979.

In his memoir, Cradock presented these negotiations on democracy with the 'tough and unyielding' Chinese leaders as a doughty battle against the odds. He conceded straight away that the British would not allow Hong Kong to be used 'as a base to subvert the authority of the Chinese government', although he had no authority to extend the laws which the independent courts and judges of the colony might use to suppress such unspecified activities. With somewhat more credibility he agreed that Britain would not 'internationalise' the question of Hong Kong by involving the United States or other powers. These concessions dispensed, Cradock found the Chinese side unmoved by his other arguments, which a less subtle intellect might have taken as a lesson in how not to conduct negotiations.

Cradock believed that behind the haggling 'lay a profound suspicion on the Chinese side of Western-style democracy as a force for political change, even chaos'. To China's new leader Jiang Zemin and his colleagues, 'it was associated with the threat to their rule in the past months and with interference from Hong Kong.' The edifice of Chinese power was fragile; it was not until the Fourteenth Party Congress of October 1992 that Jiang and his new Politburo would feel confident of their authority with the seal of public approval from Deng himself. The Chinese would refer 'apropos of nothing' to the European revolutions and hasten to make China's case that the collapsed regimes had been set up by the Red Army; whereas Chinese Communism was home-grown and firmly rooted. Cradock admitted that there was something to this, although the constant need to mention it 'argued a certain lack of confidence'.

In his own memoir, the Chinese foreign minister Qian Qichen said Cradock was 'a faithful emissary of Thatcher's policies' on this occasion, even though he disagreed with them. Qian sat through a fraught two hours with Cradock and Jiang Zemin while the two sparred over the future of Hong Kong. 'It was then that Cradock came clean about the true meaning of Mrs Thatcher's message; that it was all or nothing for Anglo-Chinese relations and that difficulties on one issue meant difficulty in making progress as a whole ... an understanding on Hong Kong was a precondition to restoring good relations,' Qian wrote. 'General Secretary Jiang immediately rejected this sort of pressure from the British side.' According to Qian, the British ambassador, Alan Donald, 'went out of his way to explain to our staff that these remarks were only made on instructions from London', an overture which can hardly have conveyed to the Chinese unanimity and resolve on the British side.

On his last day in Beijing a downcast Cradock confessed his disappointment to Qian that no breakthrough had been made and asked what
message he should take back to Mrs Thatcher. Qian responded that the
two sides must abide by the 'principles' of the Joint Declaration and should
not try to change their agreements. According to Qian, it was at this meeting that Cradock handed him a letter from the new British foreign
secretary, Douglas Hurd, the first of seven diplomatic documents on
future arrangements in Hong Kong that were exchanged in secret between
Britain and China. The letter, Qian felt, raised 'fresh disagreements ...
raising the asking price significantly'.

When the existence of these letters later became public a furore erupted,
but in Qian's account they were routine instruments of diplomacy. He
described them as 'unsigned written messages delivered by the ambassador in Beijing' between 18 January and 12 February 1990. The two
ministers reached an understanding, helped along by the indefatigable
governor of Hong Kong, who went to the Chinese capital for talks.

The deal provided for eighteen seats out of sixty to be chosen by direct
elections in the 1991 polls, rising to twenty in 1997. That was as far as
China would go until the handover. After that the number of directly
chosen members would rise to twenty-four in 1999 and thirty in 2003,
when half of those making laws in Hong Kong would be chosen by its
electors. Cradock felt that 'we had clear understandings ... the assurance
of a steady increase ... there was not going to be full and instant
Westminster-type democracy in Hong Kong but there would be steady
progress in that direction which, and this was the crucial point, the
Chinese had been brought to endorse.' To insist on more, he argued, would
have endangered the whole understanding.

Qian summed up what was at stake – and what he defined as the nature
of China's victory – in the following words: 'When people read the diplomatic documents in future they will wonder why the two sides got so
exercised about a number of directly elected seats ... in fact, what they
were fighting over was the dominant political system after the handover of
Hong Kong.' By this he meant that China had ensured that Hong Kong
would continue to be governed by an executive-led system rather than one
dominated by a democratic legislature; although the executive would take
public opinion into account, it was not to be in thrall to it. In his own
memoir Hurd had little to say on the exchange, noting only that the correspondence embodied the agreement on how to stage elections in 1991.
This was a truthful statement in that it acknowledged that a great deal was

left vague in 'understandings' with China, in particular over what might happen between 1990 and the handover.

The secret Anglo-Chinese talks concluded in time for the National People's Congress to rubber-stamp the Basic Law in April 1990. Hong Kong greeted the final draft with resignation. The first Legislative Council of the Special Autonomous Region in 1997 would have sixty members but only twenty would be returned by direct elections in constituencies. Ten would be picked by a committee and thirty would be chosen by 'functional constituencies', an archaic formula bequeathed by the British which allocated seats to representatives of commerce, the professions and assorted interest groups, some chosen by a handful of electors. In most democracies, functional constituencies belonged on the ash heap of history, but in Hong Kong they were to be perpetuated.

As for the 'through train', the Basic Law warned that the Legislative Council at the handover in 1997 might only continue sitting if it was 'in conformity with the relevant provisions of this Decision'. Only those of its members who 'upheld' the law, pledged allegiance and were approved by a committee to be chosen by China could expect to continue in office. Such were the battlefields which lay ahead for democrats and authoritarians in the coming century.

Approval of the law, more than seven years before it came into force, was just a prelude to ceaseless controversies over what it meant and how it was applied. But it was a bulwark against absolute arbitrary power and a restraint upon any Chinese government which required international acceptance. In the decades after the handover, arguments over the law would fuel strife, sow legal uncertainty and rally dissidents to the forlorn cause of Hong Kong independence. In the years between 1990 and 1997 it served the city well merely by its existence.

Assurances from China were enough to satisfy neither the people of Hong Kong nor foreign governments after June Fourth. The United States had made it clear that Britain was on its own in public diplomacy, but President George Bush told Mrs Thatcher that he sympathised with the fears for Hong Kong. As a veteran of China and a former head of the CIA, Bush was not easily shocked. But after June Fourth, China's behaviour made even staunch advocates of engagement question its usefulness in a crisis. When Bush tried to put a phone call through to Deng Xiaoping, the Chinese foreign ministry said they were not clear where he was and could not connect the American president. Bush then dispatched his national security adviser, Brent Scowcroft, on a covert mission to meet Deng.

Chinese military air traffic controllers were not told by their superiors that his C-141 Starlifter jet was coming and asked if they ought to shoot it down. The request went all the way to President Yang Shangkun, who cleared the plane for landing. On the morning of 2 July a safely delivered Scowcroft met Deng, who dismissed Bush's avowals of friendship as insufficient and without much more ado handed him over to Li Peng and the hardliners for further, profitless talks.

The declassified text of Deng's encounter with Scowcroft laid bare the reality of negotiating with China at its most intransigent and defensive, exactly as Cradock and Wilson had found it at moments of stress. It did not help that a vote in the US Congress by 418 to 0 for comprehensive sanctions had infuriated the Chinese leadership, while the US media coverage intensified Deng's own suspicions of a plot to overthrow his government. 'To be frank, this could even lead to war,' Deng said. 'The United States has impugned Chinese interests, has hurt Chinese dignity. That is the crux of the matter.'

The US ambassador to China, CIA veteran James Lilley, warned that the two sides had to find a way to step back. Lilley did not deal in illusions. Back in the 1970s, one of Henry Kissinger's aides, Richard Solomon, had confided to him that Kissinger, deep down, believed that 'America had to deal with the Chinese now, because if they ever got strong, they would be impossible to deal with.' This was also the Nixon view, and Lilley, who died in 2009, grew to share it.

While China was distracted by challenges on a strategic scale, Hong Kong sought its own path to reinsurance. This meant that 1990 became a whirlwind of unexpected change, making it the most significant period between the agreement to hand back the colony to China and the deed itself in 1997. It was, in hindsight, a tribute to Wilson as an administrator that he led the way to reshape a policy towards China of which he had been one of the principal authors, one founded on unspoken assumptions and well-crafted ambiguity.

The shock of the massacre destroyed any lingering hopes which some of the colony's administrators and business dynasties had entertained of perpetuating a system of low taxation, limited representation and deference to authority. Such hopes were founded on a patriarchal, outdated view of the mass of the population which held that a refugee mentality, gratitude for the chance to earn a living and fear of disorder would offset any desire to have a say in how the city was governed or taxes were spent. The theory had long been stretched beyond credibility. In 1987, there had been a last attempt to persuade the world that Chinese people in Hong Kong were not really interested in representative government when the public were invited to comment on a consultation paper devoted to that subject. The survey office established to collect the findings concluded that the majority did not want direct elections. This was a masterpiece of bureaucratic distortion, engineered by according more weight to collective submissions from groups sympathetic to the Chinese Communist Party than to individual citizens. It was rightly dismissed by Hong Kong's democrats as a cynical exercise, and even within the colonial administration the 'consultation' was later buried as an embarrassment. The last governor thought it verged on the dishonourable but blamed the exercise on Sir Percy Cradock and his acolytes. It took June Fourth to end once and for all the condescending orthodoxy that the people of Hong Kong were only interested in making money and not in politics.

In late 1989, the Hong Kong government's legal experts drafted a Bill of Rights, which was published in the official gazette on 16 March 1990. It incorporated freedoms enshrined in the International Covenant on Civil and Political Rights. Politically, this was a shrewd move. China had agreed under Article 39 of the Basic Law that the Covenant would remain in force after 1997. It also accepted in the same article that the International Covenant on Economic, Social and Cultural Rights, as well as international labour conventions, would continue to apply and 'shall be implemented through the laws' of the new region.

These were formidable bulwarks, and the new leaders in Beijing chafed in retrospect at the granting to Hong Kong of such concessions in the dying days of liberalism. The governor flew to Beijing to meet Li Peng, in itself something of a diplomatic concession by Britain. He found the Chinese premier, a man of grim resolve, unmoved by criticism but not overtly threatening to reverse the Bill of Rights. In March 1990 the chief secretary, Sir David Ford, announced plans for 'a more directly representative system of government' in the Legislative Council elections of 1991. In accordance with the deal reached with China, this raised the number of directly elected members to eighteen out of sixty. In April, the government sought to boost morale by unveiling the British nationality scheme. Later in the year, the age of majority was lowered from twenty-one to eighteen.

Wilson justified the cautious policy by asserting the need for Chinese consent to make sure that Hong Kong's political reforms would endure: 'There was during my time a very marked increase in the shape of the graph going upwards towards a more representative system, reducing the number of [appointed] official members of the Legislative Council, increasing the number of elected members ... and then trying to make sure that we had an agreement with China that this process would not just last through 1997 but would continue beyond that.' These moves were reinforced by pragmatic signals which certainly did not annoy Beijing. The Hong Kong government lobbied the United States to renew China's trading status as a Most Favoured Nation (MFN) partner and welcomed President Bush's controversial decision to do so in May. Talks on the new airport, though fractious, held out the prospect of a political and economic rapprochement with China. The chief secretary, Sir David Ford, went to the World Economic Forum in Davos to promote Hong Kong as a gateway to the mainland, a sign that elites in Hong Kong were ready to look beyond the slump in trade caused by the Tiananmen Square crisis and foreign sanctions.

These were tricky currents to navigate. The territory's biggest bank, HSBC, had developed a plan to take over Britain's Midland Bank and to move its global headquarters to London, where a holding company would be registered. There were sound business reasons for the move. But the timing was awful. The governor warned the bank's chairman, Sir William Purves, that he must tell the Chinese in advance. The Korean War veteran had the unenviable job of flying to Beijing to break the news to Premier Li Peng, who was still a pariah for most foreign dignitaries after the bloodshed at Tiananmen. 'We were ushered in to one of the bigger rooms in the Great Hall of the People,' Purves recalled, 'and in came Lu Ping who was in charge of the Hong Kong Office, followed by Li Peng.' The premier did not bring an interpreter, so a young woman employed by Purves had the daunting task of interpreting for both sides.

'The meeting did not start well since as I tried to explain our plan, the Premier interjected "Oh it is easy for you – all you do is to print more notes when you need more money".' It was not the first time a Chinese leader had misunderstood HSBC's role as a note-issuing bank in Hong Kong. 'He had limited experience of financial matters,' Purves observed.

'So I said, "Well, Prime Minister, I'm sorry but that is not correct," and went on to try to explain. He turned to Lu Ping – so my rather shaken interpreter told me later – and said "Is this foreigner telling the truth?" I could see Lu Ping shifting in his chair before saying "Yes, he is telling the truth." Li Peng became rather flushed and I decided I had better back pedal a bit and soften my approach, otherwise I might not be leaving Beijing that evening.'

The Chinese leader had little grasp of or interest in the technicalities of holding company structures. 'All he really wanted to hear was that the Hongkong and Shanghai Banking Corporation was not leaving Hong Kong and that its board and chairman would remain in Hong Kong,' said Purves.

The meeting ended after less than half an hour and the two men went out to face a crowd of photographers. Li told them that he had been assured that the Hongkong Bank was not leaving the city. On his safe return to Hong Kong, Purves had a call from his deputy chairman, Li Ka-shing, who was complimentary. 'Li Peng wanted a helpful message and that is what he heard,' the tycoon told him. According to Purves, the Chinese government still feared that the British were going to remove assets from Hong Kong and 'seemed to think that there were pots of gold in the Bank's basement, which was baseless'. The Hong Kong government did have a vault there, Purves said, but it did not hold a secret hoard. The banker only saw Li Peng once more, at an audience for insurance executives. The premier ignored him.

In 1991, the last full year of Wilson's governorship, the pace of change quickened. The Bill of Rights was enshrined by ordinance and became law. On 28 February the British passports scheme closed after more than 65,000 applications were received. Hong Kongers showed a slow but growing interest in ruling themselves: on 3 March more than 424,000 people voted in elections for the District Boards, a turnout of 32 per cent. The day afterwards, the head of the Beijing government's Hong Kong and Macau Affairs Office, Lu Ping, graced the colony with a visit to assess the mood. He got on cordially with the governor and the two agreed to meet again in Shenzhen, a symbol of the growing links with the mainland.

In May, 393,000 people voted in Municipal Council polls, a turnout of only 23 per cent. But in September, when Hong Kong people voted in the first ever direct elections to the Legislative Council, 750,000 people turned out to cast ballots in the eighteen constituency seats, a participation rate of 39 per cent. There were other signs of quiet progress. The Hong Kong authorities started the demolition of the Walled City of Kowloon, a gigantic warren of tenements and alleyways that stood as a reminder of old China in the heart of the modern metropolis. In November, the government issued its first infrastructure bonds to finance the web of public transportation that would make the Special Administrative Region one of the most efficient cities in the world. These were substantial achievements.

* * *

It was impossible to divorce the question of Hong Kong from the political threat that faced the Chinese Communist Party between the first demonstrations in Beijing in the spring of 1989 and the collapse of the Soviet Union on 26 December 1991. At first, Chinese leaders followed reform in the socialist bloc with interest, concern and fidelity to their own principle of non-interference. Bleak theorists, they had no sentimental attachment to comradeship between nations. Mao had studied Stalin but the Sino-Soviet split in the 1950s ushered in a period of mutual loathing tinged with racial stereotypes. In 1963 the Soviet Union and the United States even considered joint action to stop the Chinese nuclear bomb.

Six years later, the Soviet leadership weighed up detailed plans for a nuclear strike against China as the two Communist powers skirmished along their disputed border. Moscow sought an understanding with the United States to stay neutral in exchange for Soviet help in ending the Vietnam War. An official Chinese history published decades later credited President Richard Nixon with rejecting the deal, deterring the Soviets from military action and opting instead to accelerate his historic opening to China.

By 1989 the giants of the Marxist-Leninist world had edged back from conflict. It was one of the many ironies of the student protests that young Chinese were praising Mikhail Gorbachev for his reforms while old Chinese leaders prepared to welcome him for a state visit that should have marked a historic rapprochement between the Soviet and Chinese parties. That has been long forgotten, while Gorbachev's visit to Beijing is commemorated as a landmark on the road to June Fourth. To the students, Gorbachev stood for the question 'why not?' To their elders, the answer was self-evident.

China's state media tracked the ideological disasters that followed with an assiduous if bewildered chronology. Reform in Poland was followed by the fall of the Berlin Wall and the collapse of the East German state. The Warsaw Pact disintegrated while Gorbachev fought to hold the Union of Soviet Socialist Republics together. To the Chinese elders, the most salutary episode was the fall of the Romanian dictator, Nicolae Ceauşescu, who was overthrown and shot by a firing squad alongside his wife after a crude show trial at the hands of junior army officers. Brief Xinhua news agency dispatches telling of his arrest and execution were printed on the front page of the People's Daily without comment, none being necessary. Among the party elite and the army, videos circulated of the gruesome scenes in Romania, where secret policemen were lynched as the regime divided between rival groups. The demise of a leader viewed as a friend and ally of China, the chaos which followed his downfall and the spectre of Ceauşescu's failed personality cult taught clear lessons to the next generation of Chinese leaders. Party unity, collective leadership and a relentless grip on the security state were their watchwords.

Hong Kong was a sideshow, but the split in the Communist Party made it the stage for a sensational and mysterious operetta. In 1989 the top Chinese figure in Hong Kong was Xu Jiatun from Jiangsu province, a trusted Communist despite his reputation as a liberal. Xu had joined the party as a young man and served as political commissar in a guerrilla unit fighting the Japanese. He survived the purges of Maoist China to be appointed as party secretary and later as governor of his home province. In 1983, when Xu was already sixty-seven, the party picked him to go to Hong Kong as director of the New China News Agency, becoming the senior representative of Beijing in the colony.

Xu cut a reassuring figure in Hong Kong between 1983 and 1989. He cultivated sympathisers and opponents of the party. He built relationships with tycoons, persuading his comrades that an alliance between Marxists and the super-rich would serve China's interests. These were classic 'United Front' tactics of impeccable ideological lineage. His connections in Beijing crossed the spectrum to include reformers like Zhao Ziyang and diehards like the president Yang Shangkun, so his opinions on Hong Kong commanded respect. He was interested in literature and journalism, making friends with editors and commentators across the spectrum of the media. He cultivated the movie producer Sir Run Run Shaw and enjoyed his 'decadent' cinematic fare. Once Xu even appeared on a catwalk at a fashion show like a mature male model, sporting a well-cut Mao suit.

None of this should have deceived Hong Kong about his mission. Xu oversaw the flow of mainland money through compliant tycoons to local pro-Beijing politicians. He offered Martin Lee, the barrister and activist, money to found a party but Lee turned him down. Xu hinted that the party's cash was supporting Szeto Wah, a trade union organiser who later turned his back on it to become, with Lee, a founding father of the democracy movement.

Xu was adept at combining soft diplomacy with understated menace. He suggested that China had quietly brought 50,000 people into Hong Kong, where they were working their way into positions of influence in the civil service and the professions. If the British pulled out before 1997 these people would take over. The implication was clear: no opponent of Beijing could hope for preferment or advantage in the new Hong Kong.

Commissar, administrator and diplomat, Xu appeared to be a sound choice to handle his main task, running the underground Communist Party in Hong Kong. The party had never become public or contested an election. It remained usefully deniable, cloaked in discipline and secrecy. Its undeclared members were assets to place in positions of influence. Xu boasted later that he could arrange for a large number of Communists to join and thus to control a pro-Beijing party, the Democratic Alliance for the Betterment of Hong Kong.

Yet there were clouds over his political judgement. Xu confounded the purists by relaying to Deng Xiaoping a proposal by a group of super-rich Hong Kong figures to pay HK$10 billion to China in exchange for which the city could govern itself for ten years after 1997, a period these worthies clearly meant to be profitable for themselves. Suspicions grew in Beijing that the director of the NCNA had succumbed to the temptations of capitalism.

In the spring of 1989, Xu had advised the leadership that a peaceful solution to the mass protests was in the best interests of both China and Hong Kong, but he and his patrons among the reformers were swept aside by events. In the aftermath of June Fourth he had turned a blind eye when his staff joined the protests and did not punish anyone for attending memorials to the dead. By the autumn, Xu was on borrowed time. The party appointed the dour and implacable Zhou Nan, its veteran of the Sino-British talks, to replace him. Then it faced a dilemma because Xu refused to leave, arguing that the Hong Kong stock market would fall if he did.

The party ordered Zhou Nan to fly to Hong Kong. The two cadres had an awkward meeting at which Xu declined blandishments to live in a grand house in Nanjing with a chauffeured car at his disposal. He said he wanted to live in Shenzhen to be near Hong Kong affairs. Zhou grudgingly agreed and the duo appeared, faces fixed in waxen smiles, at a farewell drinks reception. Among their guests was the British governor. It was evident to those present that something was wrong because the two hosts were clearly not on speaking terms with one another. Xu went off to Shenzhen. Before departing, he handed back his official passport and told the Ministry of Foreign Affairs visa office in Hong Kong to issue him with an ordinary passport, saying he had a 'special mission' to fulfil.

On 30 April 1990, Xu left the Xinhua building in Shenzhen for his usual evening walk. He was joined by a member of his family. The pair headed for the Lo Wu border point and crossed into Hong Kong unchallenged. Xu did not carry a suitcase. He wore a golf cap pulled down over his face so that travellers might not spot one of the most recognisable faces in the territory. Then he boarded a local train. Xu rode only one stop to the station at Sheng Shui in the rural New Territories and walked about a hundred metres along the tracks. Kam Kin-yat, the son of a pro-Communist editor in Hong Kong who was one of Xu's old friends, was waiting there for him in a car. Kam later told the *New York Times* that he helped to plan the escape.

In escapes, timing is all. Xu did not flee a minute too soon. That night an order came from Beijing to the Xinhua office in Shenzhen to confiscate his passport. By then Xu was in hiding somewhere in the British colony. He wrote a letter to Deng Xiaoping vowing that he would not reveal any party secrets and asked that in exchange his family should be spared punishment. Kam posted the letter to the NCNA office in Hong Kong. In short order the United States Consulate issued him a visa. Not long afterwards, a sharp-eyed immigration officer at Kai Tak airport spotted Xu boarding a flight to the US and reported his departure to the Hong Kong government security branch. The news caused a mixture of astonishment and satisfaction at the blow to Chinese prestige. One high-ranking British official compared it to a Western ambassador defecting to the Russians.

It was left to the reliable Zhou Nan to condemn Xu in his own memoirs, which painted a less flattering picture of the exile as a womanising, corrupt dilettante. According to Zhou, his predecessor had 'succumbed to the worship of material gain' soon after his arrival in Hong Kong. He had persuaded the Chinese premier, Zhao Ziyang, to provide US$100 million to set up a trading company which Xu packed with cronies and relatives to share in the plunder. It duly went bankrupt, alleged Zhou Nan, who said that Xu's masters in Beijing had called him in for a 'self-criticism' meeting but took no further action.

As for the political flexibility Xu saw as a virtue, to hardline Communists like Zhou Nan it was mere dithering and weakness. In the 1980s a controversy had broken out over plans to build a nuclear power plant at Daya Bay on the coast of Guangdong, provoking a petition against it by anxious Hong Kongers. Xu relayed their protests to Beijing, only to be slapped down by Deng Xiaoping himself, who brusquely demanded to know what Xu would recommend if he got a petition against the return of Hong Kong or Macau. When the 1989 protests broke out, Zhou and his comrades felt the NCNA director had sown confusion among his own cadres instead of following the party line. Li Hou, deputy director of the Hong Kong and Macau Affairs Office, damned him for 'arbitrary personal decisions, talking to foreigners, acting without authorisation, stoking emotions in the ranks, promoting cronies and punishing loyal cadres'.

Thus the story from the Chinese side was that Xu had been removed from Hong Kong for corruption, had dallied with dissidence in order to blur the boundaries of his crimes and was on the point of being arrested by a special investigative team when he fled. Zhou Nan – no mean womaniser himself – sneeringly dismissed Xu's flight from Shenzhen as a way to dump his wife and run away with his mistress, claiming that he had put his wife on a train to Nanjing with their luggage and assured her he would be back in a day or two. 'But after that,' Zhou concluded resoundingly, 'he ran away with his concubine that very night, he was paid by Western anti-China forces to go to Los Angeles, where he sold state secrets and betrayed the party and the people.' Whatever the truth of these scandalous allegations, Xu was expelled from the party on the orders of the Politburo in 1991 and Hong Kong affairs were left in the hands of the incorruptible Zhou Nan.

In exile, Xu wrote his memoirs, which were informative but not revelatory, and lived in Los Angeles, where he died in hospital at the age of 100 in 2016 after suffering kidney failure and cardiac problems. In his own eyes he remained a patriot and a Communist, defending the party's dictatorship and warning that democracy was not the answer for China. He may have kept his vow to Deng, for none of his secrets ever crossed the desk of the British governor of Hong Kong.

It was time for the colonial administration to pull off a morale-raising show of confidence, the kind of feat its predecessors had accomplished in equally unpromising circumstances after the Second World War. The result would be a success which transformed Hong Kong into one of the most efficient Asian cities early in the twenty-first century.

The glory of Hong Kong and the reason for its foundation was the harbour. For a century or more the British had congratulated themselves on the superiority of their deep-water port and their liberal free trade regime over the Portuguese possession at Macau, where the anchorage was poorer and the bureaucracy was 'Continental'. 'The harbour is the chief physical asset of the territory and the prosperity of the territory and its standing in the world will depend in the future, as now and in the past, on how shrewdly and far-sightedly this asset is exploited,' said the official government report on the year of 1991. With a touch of bureaucratic poetry the anonymous writer recalled that the promontory at Castle Peak, in the western New Territories, looked out over an ancient harbour, long silted up, where until about a thousand years before foreign vessels had gathered to trade overlooked by a great Buddhist monastery.

The planners compared Hong Kong to Constantinople, noting that modern Istanbul had been founded originally as a small colony 2,500 years earlier, held 'a remarkably similar' position in the east Mediterranean to Hong Kong's place in the western Pacific and flourished in its most glorious era for half a millennium before entering a slow but still wealthy decline. 'The greatest harbour cities, especially those so placed as to be gateways to vast continental hinterlands, can enjoy very long runs indeed,' the report observed hopefully. Government officials, housed in their waterfront skyscrapers, were reminded that early governors of Hong Kong, enjoying in those days an uninterrupted view from Government House, could gauge the state of the economy by counting the vessels in the harbour.

By 1991 the arguments for bold transformation were compelling. The speed and scale of global trade argued for huge increases in shipping capacity. The old port depended on stevedores and anchorage served by buoys and lighters. The new one was a forest of cranes, stacks of containers and computer-controlled transfers. The city's airport at Kai Tak, renowned for that thrilling approach to its single runway, was at its limits, handling 24 million passengers a year. It could not meet the expected demand for air cargo.

At first the Chinese government had raised no objection when the idea of a new airport was raised. But in late 1989 it had become a political issue. Deng Xiaoping clung to the notion that the British meant to impoverish the new Hong Kong by stripping its treasury bare to fatten the profits of British companies engaged in infrastructure contracts. It also dawned on Chinese policy-makers that the project gave them leverage over Hong Kong. Almost half the investment was expected to come from the private sector and since the project straddled the handover, investors needed an assurance that China approved of it. The Chinese also reached for a greater strategic prize. In 1990 Margaret Thatcher fell from power and was succeeded as prime minister by John Major. The new premier was preoccupied by the Gulf War of 1990–1 and by battles over Britain's place in Europe, but it was inevitable that he should turn to broader foreign policy concerns – and the Chinese government yearned to secure an official visit from a Western leader to end its isolation since Tiananmen Square. The British wanted the airport project, the Chinese wanted a political reward; the airport became an unlikely means of forging a pact based on mutual interests.

Three rounds of talks between October 1990 and February 1991 failed to move the Chinese side from its insistence that large reserves be set aside for the airport and that China should have a veto on other big projects. This was raising the game with some skill. A visit by the foreign secretary, Douglas Hurd, to Beijing in April 1991 had no result, even if his counterpart, Qian Qichen, recorded that Hurd, as 'a man who knew Chinese affairs well and had met Chairman Mao', was accorded the highest courtesies.

It was time for the ineffable figure of Sir Percy Cradock to step forward from the wings. The architect of the Joint Declaration had remained in Downing Street as foreign policy adviser to John Major. He had passed the official retirement age of sixty and was not, perhaps, quite on top of the detail as in the past, for he recalled some confusion over his plan to go to Beijing on a discreet flight with the Scandinavian Airlines System, which was transformed in the telling into a plan for the SAS to fly him in. The envoy arrived 'by orthodox means' on 27 June to be met by his old friend Robin McLaren, now installed as British ambassador. Once more the duo made their rounds of the Chinese leaders. To Cradock's credit, he left them in no doubt that if agreement was not reached the British would shelve the whole project, which would be bad for the future of Hong Kong. The outlines of a cold bargain soon became clear. The premier, Li Peng, said he would reach an agreement if John Major would fly to Beijing in person to sign it. Major, consulted while he was at a hectic European summit in Luxembourg, swiftly concurred.

The rest was mere detail for a pair of master draftsmen like Cradock and McLaren. In return for financial assurances and consultation on the project, the Chinese side agreed to support the airport, to take part in building it and to recognise the rights of investors after 1997. The two sides would liaise on contracts and franchises. A ceiling was set on how much the Hong Kong government could borrow without reference to China. The fiscal reserves to be left to the successor government in 1997 were guaranteed.

Once again, Cradock had pulled off a deal by intricate negotiations in Beijing. From Hong Kong the governor wrote to thank him, recalling that they had both thought the chances of success no more than fifty-fifty. Wilson felt that the Chinese had finally been made to understand that the British were serious about shelving the project without a deal. It was a rare success for assertive diplomacy.

The price was exacted in September when Prime Minister Major visited Beijing, reviewed a guard of honour in Tiananmen Square and shook hands with Li Peng. The two men signed the airport agreement. The British briefed journalists that Major had vociferously raised human rights in their closed-doors meeting, but at least one senior figure present did not recall hearing him do so. When the coverage turned sceptical, Downing Street put it about that Major was irate at being manoeuvred by the old China hands into a public kowtow to Beijing. The reality that he was not, in fact, the first G7 leader to go to Beijing passed unnoticed. (That honour belonged to the Japanese prime minister Toshiki Kaifu, who had gone in August.)

In October, the governor was able to tell the legislative council that his administration had decided on a bold strategy. There would be an entirely new airport at Chek Lap Kok off the north coast of Lantau Island. Its runways would be laid on reclaimed land. The builders were to shave off the tops of hills and dump them in the sea to make the foundations. It was estimated that 250 million tonnes of earth, rock and seabed sand must be moved. The airfield would be equipped with technology to guide pilots on an approach which required inbound planes on the eastern track to pivot over the heart of Hong Kong and then descend safely past mountain peaks and a military firing range.

Wilson did not stop there. The new airport was just part of a master plan to shift the development of industry in Hong Kong towards the less crowded, more geographically favoured west. There would be a new port, bridges, highways, a high-speed train and a ferry dock to link Chek Lap Kok into a seamless matrix of trade and travel between Hong Kong, China and the world beyond. The bridge to Lantau, spanning some 1,400 metres, would be built to withstand the fiercest typhoon. All this would come at a gigantic price tag, which the governor put at HK$127 billion or US$1.53 billion expressed in 1989 prices.

The memorandum negotiated by Cradock and signed off by Li Peng did not settle all the disputes; instead it became proof of the dictum that in China the signature of an agreement is only the beginning of real negotiations. Chinese and British officials would spar in bad-tempered sessions over plans, budgets and contracts right up to the handover, a set of negotiations which left the participants visibly embittered and seemed to suggest that 'struggle diplomacy' had become for the Chinese side an end in itself.

It was not really about the money. The arguments which swung the day for such expenditure were forecasts of the phenomenon – not yet known as globalisation – which was transforming the economies of China and most of the rest of the world at the outset of the 1990s. The collapse of the Soviet bloc, victory over Iraq in the Gulf War of 1991 and the belief that a global economy was emerging based on liberal trade under agreed rules: all lent confidence to optimists who thought that a new world order was at hand, one built on free markets, the advance of democracies and the retreat of dictatorships. For a while, they were right.

For Hong Kong the opportunity was obvious. The city had been established as an entrepôt. It had lived by trade with China until the UN embargo at the start of the Korean War in 1950. Then its own industry had grown up thanks to investments by Chinese industrialists who fled Shanghai. The long isolation of Hong Kong from China from 1949 to 1976 was an exception, not the rule, a period when the city 'might almost have been a Pacific island miles from China' and it was said that 'nothing went out of the People's Republic except food and agricultural products and nothing went in except money'.

The planners believed that the reopening of China under Deng Xiaoping offered Hong Kong the chance of reinvention in its traditional role of entrepôt. The new economy meant a mass transfer of manufacturing to the Pearl River Delta; the wealth that came would not be 'the wealth of traders hoping to sell oil for the lamps of Canton' but wealth created by making things that people in other countries would want to buy.

These were world-changing predictions and they were bolstered by hard data. Next door to Hong Kong, the province of Guangdong was poised for takeoff. It had a population of 65 million people; its gross domestic product had grown by 12 per cent a year, on average, between 1979 and 1990. It exported US$10.6 billion worth of goods in 1990, around a fifth of all Chinese exports. By then Hong Kong companies employed three million workers in Guangdong, four times the number employed in manufacturing in Hong Kong itself. Companies based in Hong Kong accounted for 70 per cent of foreign investment in the province.

Typically, a Hong Kong company signed a 'co-operative production agreement' with the Guangdong entity. The Hong Kong firm shipped raw materials or half-made products to south China, the Chinese counterpart sent back finished goods and Hong Kong then re-exported them to the world. The system was so successful that, in 1990, 75 per cent of Hong Kong manufacturers had set up factories on the mainland. Sixty-two per cent of Hong Kong's nominal exports were actually made in China. More than three-quarters of the goods were traditional low-end items such as toys, shoes, travel goods and handbags. In reality, the industrial economy of Hong Kong had come to incorporate a swathe of industries in the Pearl River Delta.

China was in the early phase of sophisticated manufacturing but the proof of its ambitions – those outlined years earlier by Xi Zhongxun – was there for all to see. Between 1988 and 1990 the electronics industry in Guangdong grew by 31 per cent a year. Other sectors which began to take off were communications equipment, textiles, garments and processed food.

Links between Hong Kong and Guangdong grew by the year. In 1978 only 24,800 residents of the People's Republic entered Hong Kong and 1.3 million Hong Kong residents crossed into China. By 1990 the numbers were 370,000 and 16 million respectively. Trade between the two in 1990 was estimated to be worth HK$400 billion, fifty times higher than twelve years earlier. While Hong Kong's old industries declined and its workforce learned to move into services, small businesses in the Pearl River Delta grew by 20 per cent a year between 1985 and 1990, and the rate doubled in the five years after that. For a Chinese company, Hong Kong offered capital, infrastructure, skilled management and access to the world market. Its currency peg to the US dollar guaranteed price stability, a peerless gift to traders. The benefits to Hong Kong, in the eyes of classical economists, were the flow of profits to the city's enterprises and the development of its local economy and labour market. Labour unions and leftists warned that this transformation accelerated inequality, drove down wages and put many out of work. Yet according to the official statistics the labour supply remained tight with an unemployment rate of 2.1 per cent. In reality, workers in Hong Kong were powerless to stem the wave of disruption and workers in China were poised to reap gains from it.

China began to drive great changes in the global economy in 1991 through its opening up of the south and its embrace of capital and management from Hong Kong. The Pearl River Delta became a locomotive for export-led growth. It pulled in investment and pumped out manufactured goods. In the next few years this phenomenal expansion would attract more of the world's biggest companies and banks, making Hong Kong much richer as they set up offices, used services and paid local taxes. At the time, however, many people in the colony worried about 1997, sought to insure against uncertainty and focused excessively on what they thought were the twists and turns of political risk in Beijing. Predictions of the downfall of the Communist Party were a staple around Chinese family dinner tables, in bars where journalists and diplomats exchanged gossip, and at expatriate country club lunches. In fact the People's Republic was about to embark on an era of stability that would endure for the next two decades.

The political considerations also weighed in London. Mrs Thatcher had believed it would be best to have a heavyweight political figure as governor for the last stage of British rule. She came to understand that handing over millions of people to a Communist state was a deed fraught with uncertainty, however strongly it was underwritten by an international treaty. The pressure on her successor, John Major, had grown after June Fourth along with the realisation, fostered by his encounters with Chinese leaders like Li Peng, that mistakes could be deadly. For his part, the incumbent, David Wilson, also believed that the last phase required a change of style, although he had hoped that the last governor might step back while local politicians stepped forward. Political tensions between China and the democrats in Hong Kong after June Fourth made that a risky course, and it was arguable that the city's democratic politicians might be better insulated by a governor whose broad shoulders could take the blows which were likely to fall.

For all those reasons, the government in London decided that at the end of Wilson's five-year term he should be replaced. It was known that John Major had not enjoyed his visit to China and felt that he had been bounced into it by his adviser, Sir Percy Cradock. 'There was a lot of political gossip around how much he disliked it,' Wilson conceded. But in his memoir, Douglas Hurd, the foreign secretary, said he had decided by June 1991, before the Beijing visit, that the next and last governor of Hong Kong should be a British politician. The announcement was made at the end of December 1990, when the government said Wilson would receive a peerage and retire within twelve months. The choice of his successor was put off until after the British general election of 1992. There was no criticism of Wilson, Hurd wrote: 'A dedicated and experienced Scot, David Wilson and his wife Natasha were popular in Hong Kong. They represented one of the last flowerings of that tradition of wise British students of China, who enormously respected the Chinese people without deceiving themselves about the difficulties of dealing with its Government.'

Wilson was depicted by his critics in Hong Kong and London as too soft in his diplomatic dealings with China. But that was not the impression among the Chinese themselves. From the other side of the negotiating table, the governor's impeccable language skills and polite persistence were seen as dangerous assets. 'In every negotiation, we fought with Wilson,' said one of his opponents, Zhang Junsheng, a long-serving figure at the New China News Agency in Hong Kong. 'Wilson spoke Chinese so well that you could talk to him in Chinese instead of English but although he was a relatively sensible man, he was carrying out his government's policies. He had many arguments and conflicts with us over such things as the Bill of Rights.'

However, the Chinese trusted Wilson enough as an impartial observer to invite him on a private visit to the cities of the Pearl River Delta after June Fourth to see for himself that reform and opening up would continue. 'At that time not only the Hong Kong media but all sectors of society, including many patriots, were suspicious of China's policies,' admitted Zhang. It was bizarre but true that the colonial governor was deemed the most reliable witness to reassure Hong Kong. Permission was granted by the central government. Wilson spent about a week in China. His fluent Chinese allowed him to have frank conversations with senior officials, one of whom confided in ripe slang that the government had made a total mess of its own backyard.

Zhang, who was an important witness from a Chinese perspective on these turbulent years, recalled that the news of Wilson's exit came as a shock. On the evening in question Zhang got a call from the editor-in-chief of the pro-Communist daily *Wen Wei Po*, Zeng Decheng. The rumour had leaked out in London, Zeng said, how should the newspaper handle it? There had been no instructions from Beijing. If it was true and they did not report it, they would look like fools. If it was false it would look like a deliberate attempt to drive the governor out. The dilemma was vexing; so the item was published as inconspicuously as possible in the bottom corner of the front page and given the toxic label of 'foreign news'. Fortunately for the two dithering cadres, the leak was confirmed in London later that night.

The Chinese view was that this showed the 'dysfunctional' nature of Western government. Zhang saw it like this: 'How could he operate in his last months? The world is hot and cold, you have announced his transfer while he is still there to carry out his duties, so he will have no prestige.'

Coming from a system in which political decisions were never reached in public, Zhang may have misunderstood the workings of parliamentary democracies. But he had a perceptive analysis of how most decision-makers in the West got China wrong: 'The June Fourth incident was followed by the dramatic changes in eastern Europe in 1990 and the collapse of the Soviet Union in 1991. But the British misjudged the situation, thinking that the socialist countries, including China, would fall like dominoes. Their internal assessment was that it was unwise to think that Communist Party rule in China would last until 1997.' It was this error, said Zhang, that made them think they could change their tune on Hong Kong.

The Chinese government would have no tender concern for the prestige of the next governor. The world was about to embark on a great experiment in international trade which would benefit China enormously, and Hong Kong was about to exploit its privileged role in that process to try an experiment of its own in democracy. The experiments were intertwined, and in their unravelling there emerged a different city in the years up to 2020.

8

Two Journeys

On the morning of 22 January 1992, readers of *Ta Kung Pao*, a pro-Communist daily newspaper in Hong Kong, were treated over their breakfast congee to a news item which stood out from its usually lifeless pages. The paper reported that Deng Xiaoping was on a visit to Shenzhen, where the patriarch had inspected development and praised reform. It was his first conspicuous appearance for more than a year. During that time opponents in the party had blocked change, the new leadership had lacked the confidence to advance and the economy was in limbo. So Deng set off on a 'southern tour' at the age of eighty-eight to retake the political initiative. The trip was his legacy to China and the world.

Not a word appeared in the Chinese state media. Within days, however, the newspapers in Hong Kong were full of the news. A second pro-Beijing daily, *Wen Wei Po*, echoed the first reports from Shenzhen and the rest of the city's media breathlessly followed suit. Once again Hong Kong had become the window through which the world craned to get a look at what was happening in the most populous nation on earth. The papers chronicled Deng's progress as he moved on to the Pearl River Delta city of Zhuhai, then to the industrialising zones of Zhongshan and Shunde.

A cloak of deception shielded the tour from the moment Deng boarded a private train at Beijing station on 17 January, accompanied by sixteen members of his extended clan. Their journey was arranged by the People's Liberation Army and it was put about that the elder statesman was to enjoy a family holiday before the Lunar New Year. Members of the Politburo, including Jiang Zemin, the general secretary, were kept in the dark about its purpose.

The olive green-painted carriages went south overnight to the city of Wuhan in central China, where the local party leader and the governor awaited Deng on the station platform. Undaunted by the journey, Deng treated them to a sharp dressing down about too much red tape, too many meetings and too little action. There were, he said with the ripeness of a Sichuan peasant, more documents in the Chinese bureaucracy than there were hairs on a cow. The train rolled on to Changsha, capital of Mao Zedong's home province of Hunan. There Deng delivered a similar message to the dignitaries attending him on the platform, who had hastened to give him news of a good harvest and stood wreathed in smiles. He told them to get on with opening up the farming economy so that people could be prosperous.

By the time Deng's train pulled into Shenzhen on 19 January, word of his gambit had reached the leaders in Beijing. It was clear that, far from a restful family break, the former leader had embarked on a pilgrimage to the Special Economic Zones to evangelise on their behalf and to rebuke the leftists who, in his eyes, would deny China the means to regain its status as a great power.

In early 1992 the traditional Marxists had control of the message, suppressing news and commentary that was not to their liking in the state media. For most of the previous year, the paramount leader had been written about as a historical figure. It was only towards the end of 1991 that his partisans were powerful enough to change the tone so that he was once again seen as a man capable of issuing directives. Deng's southern tour was meant to be a symbolic gesture that could not be ignored. On that level alone it was like Mao's famous swim in the Yangtze in July 1966, a feat which showed that the chairman was alive, vigorous and inspirational; it heralded the onset of his Cultural Revolution. 'The southern tour was a risk,' wrote the author Yang Jisheng of Deng's trip, 'he had no formal position. He was just an ordinary member of the Communist Party. He was eighty-eight years old and his days were numbered. Some of his talk was critical. He knew the risks but he said to those around him "if you don't take a chance you can do nothing".'

Deng did not have the energy of Mao, who had been fifteen years younger when he plunged into the Yangtze. He rationed his energy by going out with officials during the morning, lunching with his entourage and taking an afternoon nap. Whenever he spoke, however, he fizzled with vim. His arrival in Guangdong was the psychological boost its leadership cadres needed to pursue their plans.

Deng went to factories, walked through malls, peered up at construction sites and beamed benignly upon hard-hatted workers toiling on bridges and roads. He was cheered and clapped by people who recognised him as 'Uncle Deng' and even 'Grandpa Deng'. Word spread of his presence, despite the silence in the local media. Hong Kong radio and television stations had a mass audience in the Pearl River Delta, so millions followed their news bulletins in Cantonese. His grand gesture done, Deng headed off to Shanghai to see in the Year of the Monkey, a sign associated in the Chinese zodiac with perseverance, guile and agility. He left behind a region in ferment.

Disputes in the party were to be kept from the general public. The battle over policy was also a battle over propaganda. But the reform faction, if it may be called that, was quick to use the message laid down by Deng's unchallengeable authority for their internal party arguments. Since 1979 Deng had spoken of his aspiration for China to become a society of *Xiaokang* or 'small prosperity' which gave its people a higher standard of living through consumption and trade. Jiang Zemin and his allies began to seed speeches, editorials and statements with the Deng line.

At first the skirmishes were conducted in code. In late February the state media carried an article praising 'the uses of capitalism' by an economics professor, Fang Sheng, which argued that 'so-called capitalist measures and ways do not belong to any class and can be used by either capitalism or socialism'. In private, party officials were studying a document from the Central Committee which talked about 'socialism with Chinese character-istics'. The key regional newspaper, the *Shenzhen Special Zone Daily*, ran a sequence of editorials from 20 February to 6 March expressing the key lines of Deng's speeches and even borrowing his words without attributing them to their author. For its part, the *People's Daily* picked up the banner with a call for bolder reform and the paper began to reprint provincial editorials on the same theme, a time-honoured tactic to introduce political changes to the audience in Beijing. A communiqué from the Politburo on 12 March formalised the new emphasis on building the economy and crit-icised the Left; it, too, refrained from mentioning Deng by name.

The Left pushed back. The deputy editor of the party's theoretical jour-nal, *Seeking Truth*, Wu Jiangguo, attacked those favouring 'privatisation ... which is incompatible with ownership by the people'. Chen Yun, the veteran economic overlord and guardian of revolutionary values, reminded his comrades that 'a foreign capitalist is still a capitalist.' Later, he elegantly borrowed a quotation from the Tang dynasty poet Li Shangyin, a favourite of Mao's, to the effect that 'the sound of the young phoenix is clearer than that of the old one.'

But the old phoenix had flown and it was too late for the Maoists. On 26 March, the *Shenzhen Special Zone Daily* published a reportage of

Deng's journey, complete with photographs. Four days later the *People's Daily* unblushingly reprinted it as 'news'. Even by the standards of that title, reporting an important event two months after it had taken place marked something of a professional record. On the same day, 31 March, the Chinese people finally saw their paramount leader on television in a long documentary broadcast by state television. The cat was out of the bag.

It would take years for a fuller account of Deng's journey to emerge and for an authorised version of his speeches and remarks to be published. There was, therefore, no immediate effect on Chinese domestic opinion. His influence on policy, however, was direct and profound.

There is some evidence that Deng sought reinsurance while he was in the south. The Hong Kong magazine *Chengming* reported rumours that Deng had convened a meeting of the Central Military Commission, which controlled the armed forces, in Zhuhai. The rumours turned out to be accurate. The meeting was packed with high-level commissars and staff officers. It was graced by the presence of Qiao Shi, the Politburo standing committee member in charge of security, who enjoyed a reputation as a tentative reformer. Deng's faithful allies, President Yang Shangkun and his half-brother, General Yang Baibing, were there to guarantee the loyalty of the army. They were the old men who had stood by him in the decision to storm Tiananmen Square. The message to Jiang Zemin and his cohorts was emphatic. In case the Politburo was in any doubt, an editorial in the *Liberation Army Daily* on 14 March threw its weight behind the flag of Deng Xiaoping's thought. For an accomplished bridge player, this must have been a satisfying round.

For none of these men was Chinese patriotism put in question by 'reform and opening up'. In retrospect, not all of Deng's words were as comforting as foreign investors hastened to assume. For example, he had rebutted Chen Yun's criticism by saying that China had complete political authority over foreign-owned companies and would make sure they served its interests. On a boat trip, later lavishly covered in accounts of the tour, Deng mused on the ruins of an imperial government building, saying that China would never again be backward if it seized science and technology and would never again be humiliated by imperialists. Deng never lost sight of his nation's agenda; it was just that his foreign admirers chose to pick and choose what aspects of his policy sounded most reassuring.

For the Chinese, Yang Jisheng's verdict was that Deng had prevented the reversal of economic reform but had abandoned the promises of political change made in 1980 and 1986. Outside China, the consensus as knowledge of the tour spread was that China was open to foreign invest-ment and that multinational companies would reap virtually limitless profits by entering the country, both to manufacture and to sell. But Deng did not see it that way. The full text of his standard stump speech was published after a decent interval. It laid out the line that was to be followed faithfully by his heirs.

'Reform and opening up must be more daring, you need to experiment, not be like women with bound feet,' Deng said in Shenzhen, 'the impor-tant experience of Shenzhen is to dare to rush forward.' Such phrases sounded as music to the ears of the ardent reformers who wanted to push China towards a market economy. Deng, by contrast, saw the market as a tool, not an end. The criteria, he said, were whether it 'developed the productive forces of a socialist society, enhanced the overall national strength of a socialist society and raised the living standards of the people', He pointed out that the Chinese term for the Special Economic Zone was prefixed by the term 'socialist' not 'capitalist'.

China's aim in attracting foreign capital was hard-headed, he said. 'Some people believe more foreign capital means more capitalism ... and yes, foreign businessmen always want to make money. But the state gets its taxes back, the workers get their wages back, we can learn about tech-nology and management, we get information and we can open markets. Foreign-funded enterprises are restricted by China's political and economic conditions, they are serving the interests of the socialist econ-omy and in the final analysis are beneficial to socialism.'

This was not the sort of quotation highlighted in presentations to share-holders in Western boardrooms. It was assumed by some that because a few Chinese businessmen were becoming fathomlessly rich while mass poverty still existed, the country's elite had cynically jettisoned Marxism and could not wait to become another India or Brazil. The leadership did not see it like that. In fact Deng and his successors, Jiang Zemin and Hu Jintao, all put inequality in a Marxist framework: that it was a necessary phase on the pathway to Communism via 'socialism with Chinese charac-teristics'. Deng himself admitted that China could never conform to pure Marxist theory, for the reason that it had never developed a big industrial proletariat and remained a mainly agrarian country. Peasants and workers ranked equally in the party's propaganda and Mao had conceived of the Chinese revolution as a rural Third World phenomenon, hence its early appeal to the colonised, the downtrodden and the peasant masses.

By the time of Deng's southern tour, the party line had matured. In his speech, Deng admitted that there would be inequalities on the path to socialism. Some regions would develop faster than others, but if the rich got richer and the poor poorer the socialist system should intervene. China's deep-rooted problems came from the Left, but the party would also be vigilant against the Right.

Deng exulted in the success of the regions bordering Hong Kong. Within the next twenty years, he said, Guangdong alone could become the fifth Asian tiger after Hong Kong, Singapore, South Korea and Taiwan. 'Looking back, one of my biggest mistakes was not adding Shanghai to the list of Special Economic Zones,' he admitted. China's industrial output had increased by almost 22 per cent a year at the end of the 1980s, he continued, and the homes of ordinary farmers had the 'four big items' – bicycles, sewing machines, radios and watches – while some could buy more expensive consumer goods. It was time to put the brakes on inflation, debt issuance and speculative building, he said, but this was what the state was for, 'to rectify the situation'. He saw nothing contradictory in this. 'For a big developing country like ours, it is impossible for the economy to grow at a faster pace and always be calm and steady.'

So much for the economics. Deng turned in his peroration to politics and national strategy, laying out a roadmap that would only become clear to China's economic rivals in decades to come. China, he said, should take advantage of the open international environment to exploit the strengths of its socialist system: its ability to mobilise resources, to drive for modernisation and take on large-scale projects. Gradually the government would transfer the surplus rural workforce to industry and China would climb the development ladder. He saw early on that it must capture science and technology to achieve its ends. 'Each line has a clear strategic objective and we must win in the field of high technology for China to take its place in the world ... intellectuals are part of the working class and I hope all the people studying abroad will return, especially the older scientists. Whatever their past political attitudes they can come back and make the appropriate arrangements.'

Deng held out no prospect of political change. He said the party should oppose 'bourgeois liberalisation' for at least twenty years, well into the new millennium: 'The basic line must be adhered to for a hundred years with no vacillation.' China was still in the 'primary stage of socialism' and to consolidate the socialist system required a long historical period. It would take 'the unremitting efforts of several, more than a dozen, even dozens of generations of our people'.

Deng held an unapologetically Marxist view of the Chinese dictatorship. He told his listeners that the Communist Party had wiped out 'decadent' things like 'drug taking, prostitution and economic crimes' within three years of the 1949 revolution. Capitalism could not do that, 'but the Communist Party can get rid of all that is ugly'. Its first leaders were old men; now it would train a third, fourth and fifth generation. It was telling that Deng ranked those who must be educated in this order: the army, the organs of dictatorship, Communist Party members, the people, and young people.

Deng tended to finish his talks by challenging the traditional Chinese reverence for age. 'Old people have strengths but also great weaknesses. Old people tend to be stubborn. On the other hand, the older you get the less mistakes you make in the end. The older you get, the more humble you become. We must select and train younger comrades.' Then he said this:

'Marx said that his real invention was not the class struggle, it was the dictatorship of the proletariat. Historical experience has proved that the newly emerging classes who have just seized power are in general always weaker than the forces of the rival classes and therefore they must consolidate their power by means of dictatorship. This is the people's democratic dictatorship.'

In other words, dictatorship was not a transitory thing to be sloughed off as China grew richer, its new classes multiplied and its society became more complex. Dictatorship was to strengthen the emerging classes and the newly prosperous Chinese groups created by globalisation. It was the key to national renewal. It was for ever.

With that, the old man left the centre stage of Chinese politics. Nobody in China could say his message was unclear. Nobody abroad could say they were not told, had they bothered to listen.

The United Kingdom held a general election on Thursday, 9 April 1992. To widespread surprise, the Conservatives won with a reduced majority of twenty-one parliamentary seats and John Major was returned as prime minister. Among the casualties, however, was Chris Patten, the party chairman, a friend of Major's and an architect of the Tory victory, who lost his seat in the prosperous spa town of Bath. On election night, Patten shed tears as his defeat was announced. Yet few believed this was the end of his career.

Aged only forty-seven, Patten was a moderate conservative, a gifted communicator with cosmopolitan tastes. He had a network of global connections which he had cultivated since studying at Balliol College, the ancient foundation of Oxford University that in addition to four British prime ministers had educated a president of Germany and an empress of Japan. In 1965 he had worked on John Lindsay's Republican campaign to be mayor of New York, an experience which left him 'smitten, head over heels infatuated' with politics. Had Patten kept his seat, the prime minister planned to make him chancellor of the exchequer, in charge of the nation's finances. In defeat it was evident that he still had a political future.

A week before the poll, Patten called on the prime minister with research that predicted the Conservatives would win the election. He also showed Major a list of constituencies which the party would lose, including his own seat in Bath. Major looked through it and raised his eyebrows. 'I've thought that for eighteen months,' said Patten, 'I've told you but you just think I'm a doomster.'

Now that his fears had come true, Patten was offered several establishment fixes. An obliging Member of Parliament might be persuaded to retire from a safe seat. Under Britain's constitutional arrangements, the government could make him a peer with a seat in the House of Lords which would open a back door to a minister's job. Patten did not like any of the ideas put forward. So, just one day after the election, Major asked his downcast friend if he would like to be the last governor of Hong Kong, exchanging a seat in cabinet for a place in the history books.

Major had already decided that David Wilson must be replaced as governor of Hong Kong. All sides were keen to say that this was no reflection upon his skills, and there was admiration for his scholarly command of the Chinese language and his overall decency. Both Major and Patten, however, felt Wilson was 'played out'. They believed that the prime minister and the governor had been humiliated by the Chinese over the airport deal and that the job needed a big political figure. Both men had come to distrust the doctrines practised by the Foreign Office's corps of Sinologists. Even people on the Chinese side had told the prime minister that Britain needed a political heavyweight who could take hard decisions. So would Patten take the job?

'I said "Like a shot",' Patten remembered. First, though, he had to talk to his wife, Lavender, who was his partner, friend and counsellor. They slipped away to their French country house in the Tarn to think it over. Inevitably, in a corner of southwest France colonised by the British middle classes, they bumped into a clutch of holidaying politicians. Among them was David Owen, whose career as a Labour foreign secretary had been cut short before his own ambitious plans for China policy could get off the ground. Patten was left in no doubt what they thought. 'They all said, "You don't want to go to Hong Kong, there's nothing to do there, it's all been decided and you'll be bored out of your mind", he laughed. 'Little did they know.'

Patten appreciated that the move would be tough on his wife, who had just embarked on a successful career as a family barrister. The couple had three daughters, Alice, Laura and Kate, whose education and welfare had to be considered. On the other hand there was the prospect of life at Government House with its fifty-six attentive staff, the governor's rural retreat at Fanling in the New Territories, his chauffeured Rolls-Royce and his gleaming white 27-metre official motor vessel, the *Lady Maurine*. The salary of US$273,000 was larger than that of the British prime minister, and it was tax free. The Pattens were middle-class comfortable but not rich. Their decision did not take long.

There was some harrumphing in clubland about a carpetbagging politician treading on the hallowed turf of administrators drawn in the past from the ranks of scholars and soldiers immersed in the manners and customs of China. The new governor was sent like a student to read and absorb the accumulated wisdom of generations. The course was in the hands of the head of the diplomatic service, or permanent under secretary, David Gilmore. Patten described him as 'immensely supportive', as perhaps might have been expected when a bureaucrat is ordered to prepare a close friend of the prime minister for a job.

'I was given a little office on the ground floor of the Foreign Office … and piles of files and the head of the Hong Kong department, Peter Ricketts, wheeling in file after file,' Patten recalled. 'It was all very well written. Good briefing, cleverly done, huge amounts of it and the underlying argument all the time was, "You have to avoid having an argument with China but at the same time you have to stand up for what we asserted in the Joint Declaration". There was a sort of pre-emptive cringe about it all.'

A 'succession of grandees' came to brief the student as he progressed in his labours. 'David Gilmore and Peter Ricketts organised a succession of people who allegedly knew what they were talking about to come in and see me. Hardly anyone from Hong Kong apart from one or two members of the Executive Council like Lydia Dunn.'

Among the callers was Sir Percy Cradock. Patten's first impression was that the foreign policy adviser and head of the Joint Intelligence Committee, in effect the keeper of the nation's secrets, was a 'clever' and 'arrogant' man. 'I was given a very dry lecture by Percy Cradock who said it had all been decided, there was nothing left to decide, you just had to implement it properly. I think his dislike of me had more to do with the fact that I was a sort of intellectual challenge to his idea of how you dealt with China, which was basically to surrender as slowly as possible at every point.'

The new governor personified the nightmare of every specialist who has laboured in a field for decades and is sure that a little knowledge is a dangerous thing. Patten and Major had come to believe that too much knowledge could also be a burden when dealing with a foreign power whose history, culture, bureaucracy and rulers exemplified the intricate. The adage that advisers advise but politicians must decide weighed upon them; particularly when the behaviour of your opponent suggested that inaction was always the safest policy.

In fact Patten was no neophyte in the Far East. In 1979 he had visited Hong Kong as a young parliamentarian with a delegation investigating the conditions of Vietnamese boat people who had sailed in leaky, crowded boats along the southern Chinese coast, braving storms and pirates to fetch up in makeshift camps in the British colony. In the process they got a look at how colonial government was failing to match the aspirations of a young, better-educated and more prosperous local population. The young Patten joined an old hand, the Labour politician Ted Rowlands, to press the governor, Sir Murray MacLehose, to introduce democracy at a local level in the territory. It was a brisk conversation in which the governor put his visitors right about matters in the distant East. The politicians were duly conducted to Kai Tak airport and ushered onto their plane home, no doubt to sighs of relief in Government House that yet another group of ill-informed outsiders had been sent on their way.

As Britain's minister for overseas development from 1986 to 1989, Patten had applied his curiosity and intelligence to the Chinese growth model. He was serving as vice chairman of the Asian Development Bank in May 1989 when the bank held its annual meeting in Beijing. The delegation of development ministers found themselves in a capital seething with political demonstrations while the security forces stood back. It felt to some of them like a carnival, and there was optimism in the air.

Patten and his colleagues came face to face with Zhao Ziyang, unaware, like most outsiders, that the leader of the Communist Party was about to lose his struggle for power. 'We were asked to go and see Zhao Ziyang, and we'd been spectators at these extraordinary events around us. It was like being in the middle of the French Revolution. It was extraordinary, extraordinary, so exciting. We're sitting around there and everybody's talking to him about rural electrification schemes and primary health care and female mortality rates; and I said after a bit, everything we've been talking to you about, Party Secretary, is very important but you won't mind if I ask you a question about the things we can see around us.

'At which point he produced a card from his pocket,' Patten recalled. The Communist Party leader read out his talking points: the leadership and the party shared the students' concerns about corruption, there was a way to resolve their demands legally, he hoped the demands would be heard, that other leaders would listen and that the hunger strikes would end. It was a preview of Zhao's valedictory remarks which he later made through a megaphone to the protesters in Tiananmen Square itself.

'He was a charming man and I remember he was wearing a Western suit, a very cheap looking light grey Western suit, and he was wearing long johns which you could see below his trouser leg.'

At the British embassy, Patten heard the views of Sir Alan Donald, a Sinologist who had trodden the classic career path – a junior posting in Beijing, political adviser to the governor of Hong Kong, a high-level job in London and a clutch of ambassadorships before the prize posting as ambassador to China. 'Alan Donald's view ... was that this was all part of a great Sun Tzu game that the Chinese were playing and that there wouldn't be any violence and this would be managed as the Chinese always managed these things with great sophistication,' he recalled. It was the same line that David Wilson, the governor of Hong Kong at the time, had heard from his distinguished Chinese visitor. Patten recalled that a group of 'hard-bitten' journalists at the dinner table, like Jonathan Mirsky, the correspondent of *The Observer*, were not convinced. 'They said, "You're joking. They're going to send the tanks in".'

The ambassador delivered a put-down with the accumulated wisdom he had absorbed watching China since the 1950s: 'Alan said, I remember, you don't know what you're talking about, if you look at the police they're wearing brown plimsolls and if you're going to grind the protesters you don't wear plimsolls.' Patten did not forget this example of British diplomatic expertise. By the time he set off for Hong Kong in 1992, authoritarians

in Asia had rewritten the script to interpret Deng's decision to send in the
tanks as wise, brave, even compassionate: a move that sacrificed a few to
gain stability and a prosperous future for the many.

On his way Patten stopped over in Singapore to hear the counsel of Lee
Kuan Yew, who had led the city-state after its independence from Britain.
The two sparred over politics and 'always argued' but got on well. From
very different perspectives, they shared a fascination for politics. Lee's
solution for the Tiananmen protests was simple, he told Patten; the
Chinese 'should just have introduced a bit of smallpox in the square'.

Patten enquired about the less drastic policies available to the governor
of Hong Kong. Lee's advice was that he should treat the governorship as a
political office and as if he had just won a resounding election. 'You should
set out what you're going to do over the next five years, make your priorities and then stick to it,' Patten recalled him as saying. 'And, he said, don't
break the treaties. Don't break the Joint Declaration but just fill in the gaps.
I thought it was extremely good advice and, by and large, it was what I
tried to do.'

The new governor arrived in Hong Kong on 9 July 1992, a sweltering
day, and was sworn in by the first Chinese chief justice, Sir Ti-liang Yang.
The *Lady Maurine* conveyed Patten, his family and his entourage across
Victoria Harbour to the ceremony. The governor wore a grey suit, white
shirt and patterned tie. Gone were the ostrich plumes, medals and white
dress uniform of the colonial era. Some expatriates were outraged. The
Chinese population watched their latest ruler with curiosity and a certain
wariness.

The job was in effect to be mayor of a big, prosperous city, running a
well-paid civil service and overseeing ambitious projects. Governors of
Hong Kong combined this role with the duties normally carried out by a
head of government; in this case one governing in the name of a distant
sovereign who was head of state. It was a curious hybrid. In his understated way, Sir David Wilson had grown into a distinct representative of
Hong Kong, travelling for diplomatic talks to Beijing, Shenzhen and
London, negotiating with the United Nations and Vietnam over the boat
people, intervening to nudge trade talks forward and speaking up for the
colony in policy debates. From the outset, however, Patten was trapped by
politics.

To Chinese officials the change from dealing with an administrator
like Wilson to handling a politician of Patten's calibre was unwelcome,
despite the Communist Party's own ideological precept that politics must

always take command. The reaction of Zhang Junsheng, the influential official stationed in Hong Kong, was typical: 'Patten was a typical Western politician. In the West, the words politician and statesman do not differ very much but in Chinese there is a big difference. A statesman has good character, excellent ability to serve and to achieve things for the country and society. A politician, on the other hand, is a fickle, double-dealing, dishonest person who acts for personal gain. Patten was just a politician.'

Zhang cited the words of an earlier governor, Sir Alexander Grantham, who said that while colonial officials did their best for the places they governed, in the end their interests were those of the motherland, not the colony. 'This was the truth,' he said. 'Patten did not tell the truth. He always talked about Hong Kong's interests. In fact he was full of old colonialist ideas and did not know the diversity of cultures in the world. He was stubborn and full of prejudice about China. His impressions of China were drawn from books by Wei Jingsheng and others and he even described some of the made-up books full of slander against Mao Zedong as "explosive".' In these words Zhang analysed the new governor's approach in the same terms as his critics in the Foreign Office and the business establishment, who argued that while claiming to put Hong Kong first he was putting it in jeopardy by confronting China.

Needless to say, Patten did not see it that way. He believed the best way to strengthen Hong Kong before 1997 was to build political institutions that would withstand the inevitable pressure of reunification. The way to do that was to expand the role of 'Hong Kong people ruling Hong Kong', a slogan that was formally shared by the Communist Party. The difference was that Patten wanted to do it by free elections, a prospect which the party found abhorrent. In his memoir of the governorship, he quoted a former Hong Kong civil servant as saying: 'Patten has got them completely wrong. They don't want to rig the elections as he fears. They just want to know the results in advance.'

Any plan to give Hong Kong more democracy was constrained by mathematics and diplomacy. The colony's electoral system was absurdly complicated, so it is worth keeping a simplified scheme in mind. In 1995 there would be a new Legislative Council of sixty members. Twenty were to be chosen by direct elections in 'geographical' constituencies. Thirty would be drawn from 'functional' constituencies representing trades and professions. The remaining ten were to be picked by an Election Committee. Beyond that outline, much was vague.

The geographical constituencies were simple. They used a first-past-the-post system in which the winner took all. The functional constituencies, as we have seen, were relics of a colonial-era effort to broaden representation without surrendering executive power, a method some thought suitable for Asian concepts of harmony and consensus. Patten's views were those of a democratic Western politician; he thought functional constituencies an abomination. 'Whoever had devised them must have had a good working knowledge of the worst abuses of British eighteenth-century parliamentary history, and had presumably concluded that such a system would appeal to the business barons of Hong Kong as it had to those of Britain two centuries before.'

It also appealed to the Chinese Communist Party. The number of voters was restricted. In one seat fewer than fifty people cast a vote. Well-regimented groups such as the Chinese Chamber of Commerce could be counted on to toe the party line. In many constituencies it was even simpler because only one candidate ever stood, so the vote was uncontested. Opaque, patronage-driven and prone to corruption, the system might as well have been designed for the party's United Front department, which had been adept at infiltrating such institutions in China since the 1930s.

The third pillar of non-democracy in Hong Kong was the Election Committee, which had ten seats in its gift. Chinese officials and colonial administrators alike envisaged a committee of handpicked worthies who might be trusted to deliver the right results. Here, too, the party was at its most skilful as an influencer and liked the idea of it.

It was a puzzle in multiple dimensions. Patten assembled a team that worked over his first sweltering summer to solve the conundrum. He brought two special advisers to Hong Kong: Martin Dinham, who had been his private secretary when he was overseas development minister, and a smart political operator called Edward Llewellyn, who had come from the Conservative Party and was, the governor realised, ubiquitously well-connected. But it was the brains and expertise of the Hong Kong civil service that created the city's first credible experiment in mass democracy. The mastermind was Michael Sze, the Secretary for Constitutional Affairs, who led a group of local officials distinguished by their drafting skills. The best and the brightest of the Hong Kong administration were summoned to the task.

'We straight away agreed that we couldn't change the number of directly elected seats, that was written in stone,' Patten recalled. This had been the crux of negotiations between the British and the Chinese two years earlier, and so concentrated was the focus on directly elected seats that perhaps both sides had forgotten to look at the room thus left for manoeuvre in other parts of the electoral landscape. The Patten team began to look for the gaps, to 'fill the interstices with rule of law and democratic possibilities wherever one could'. Their proposals were radical and, to the official Chinese mind, deliberately subversive. In short, the last colonial Hong Kong government proposed to overturn decades of incremental change and to throw its weight behind mass democratic politics in a city that had barely known the phenomenon.

The voting age was cut to eighteen from twenty-one. Full democracy was established in elections to the lower tiers of government, district boards and municipal councils, by abolishing all appointed seats. Elections from geographical constituencies to the Legislative Council would be conducted by one vote for a single member, replacing the old way of each elector having two votes and two members serving for each constituency.

The radical stroke came in an assault on the privileges of the twenty-one functional constituencies. Instead of trying to abolish the system, Patten diluted it by creating nine new constituencies. Corporate voting was abolished in favour of individual votes within each sector, making it harder for bosses to deliver bloc votes for China. More than a million new voters joined the electorate by this move, yielding a total of 2,572,124 people registered for the 1995 elections.

The problem of the undemocratic Election Committee, with its ten seats to allocate, was solved by choosing its members from elected councillors of the district boards. Just to complicate matters further, they would use a single transferable vote to pick legislators. As a gesture to Beijing, restrictions on delegates from Hong Kong to the National People's Congress standing in elections were removed.

The governor would keep his Executive Council of advisers, comprising official members drawn from the administration and unofficial members from the ranks of the local establishment. No elected politicians were to serve on it, thus separating the legislature from the executive. Patten had thought of appointing Martin Lee to the group, but the idea was provocative to China and it was dropped. Although Exco was formally powerless, it was influential. Patten himself regarded the system as 'a messy constitutional consequence of sunset colonialism', but it was the one he was stuck with. The plan was intricate and audacious but it was also a compromise.

'It was attacked from two sides,' Patten said. 'It was attacked in Hong Kong by the Democrats who said it didn't go far enough. Secondly it was attacked by China because we hadn't agreed with them first and we'd publicly said we had to talk in Hong Kong before we talked to them. This of course contravened one of their basic principles – if principle it is – that the future of Hong Kong had nothing to do with the people of Hong Kong.'

On one side, there was recrimination and regret that Britain had done so little to promote democracy in Hong Kong after the Second World War. In 1946, the governor, Sir Mark Young, had returned from captivity, having surrendered the colony to the Japanese in December 1941. He was conscious that the defeat had shattered British prestige, felt it was time for a new outlook and believed that 'the inhabitants of the Territory can be given a fuller and more responsible share in the management of their own affairs'. Young envisaged 'handing over certain functions of internal administration, hitherto exercised by the Government, to a Municipal Council constituted on a fully representative basis'. He felt that transferring part of government to such a council might be 'an appropriate and acceptable means of affording to all communities in Hong Kong an opportunity of more active participation, through their responsible representatives, in the administration of the Territory'.

These proposed reforms were far-reaching for the period. The 'Young Plan' sent to London after the inevitable local lobbying and procrastination envisaged a council in which two-thirds of the seats would be chosen by direct elections, the remaining one-third being appointed by institutions. All adults would have a vote, a radical extension of the franchise never contemplated before in the history of Hong Kong. The Legislative Council would be reformed to make it more representative, although voting for its members was reserved for British subjects. Young also called for the promotion of talented Chinese civil servants to senior positions.

But Young's health had been undermined by ill-treatment at the hands of the Japanese, who had shipped him to Taiwan, Japan and eventually to a camp in Manchuria. In 1947 he handed over to Sir Alexander Grantham, a product of Sandhurst and Cambridge whose view of Hong Kong was coloured by his pre-war military service in the colony. Grantham favoured benevolent autocracy and disliked fancy ideas about giving votes to the Chinese. The Young Plan was duly smothered in process, while the Labour government in London dragged its heels until the Communist victory in 1949 brought a million refugees pouring into the colony from China. With the outbreak of the Korean War in 1950 and the start of the Cold War,

Hong Kong became an isolated outpost of the West. Political reforms were shelved in 1952 as 'inopportune'. They would remain 'inopportune' for decades.

To many Hong Kong people, whether they loathed the British as colonialists or respected them as administrators, the sudden advent of the Patten reforms smacked of a retrospective attack of conscience or a hasty attempt to escape censure in the years to come. For Martin Lee, the most prominent Democratic politician, the reforms were too little, too late. 'The damage has been done throughout the years by the British government adopting a policy of appeasement, of course starting with Percy Cradock, appeasement by deliberately turning a blind eye. Appeasement was adopted all the way to Patten. He pushed for moderately democratic reforms. He got them. His most important achievement therefore was to allow the Hong Kong people to have a taste of partial democracy, thereby igniting, if you like, the flame of democracy.'

On this last point, if no other, the Chinese government agreed with Martin Lee.

Driven by an energetic politician, things now moved at a different pace from the stately rhythm of formal and secret diplomacy to which both Chinese and British officials had become accustomed. From the late summer of 1992 things were on a collision course. In the process, Patten became a popular success in Hong Kong. His detractors said it was a cruel illusion. From whatever perspective, the sequence of events was critical to everything that has happened since in Hong Kong, which is why both sides are keen to put their best gloss on it.

The governor himself deployed his considerable social skill in preparing the ground, or so he thought. He invited the Chinese ambassador to London, Ma Yuzhen, who had never visited Hong Kong, to pass through the colony on his way home for annual leave. 'Ambassador Ma was a good and silky and sophisticated fellow,' Patten recalled. The governor took him on a helicopter tour of the territory at night, landing on the outlying island of Cheung Chau. There they boarded the *Lady Maurine* for a buffet dinner at sea. 'I set out for him in terms what I was going to do,' said Patten. He felt the message had got through.

On 14 September, Patten flew back to Britain to brief the cabinet on his proposals. He won their approval. He also took the precaution of briefing two former prime ministers, Edward Heath and Margaret Thatcher, a former foreign secretary, Geoffrey Howe, and the two living former governors, Lord MacLehose and the newly ennobled Lord Wilson. None, he claimed, offered any criticism, although MacLehose viewed democracy with reserve and thought Hong Kong's democrats a noisy minority.

He returned two days later to the dubious pleasure of a dinner with Zhou Nan, the Chinese negotiator who had now been appointed as Beijing's proconsul in the colony. The observant Zhang Junsheng, his subordinate, has left a pen picture of the occasion from a Chinese point of view. It took place at Zhou's official villa at Stanley, on the quiet, leafy south side of Hong Kong island.

'The plane was late that day and we waited for a long time. There was just one table set for a family dinner so it would be us with Patten, his wife and two daughters. It was so hot in Hong Kong that I stood at the front door while Zhou Nan and his wife waited in the reception room. Eventually he arrived and we had a welcome talk with him. What would he say about political restructuring, we asked? His policy address was due on 7 October.

'If this was Governor Wilson, we could have had a friendly exchange of views. But Patten was very un-cooperative. He sat there with one foot up and his attitude was arrogant. As Zhou Nan asked him questions, he stroked his chin, rolled his eyes to the ceiling and said he hadn't considered the matter. At this, Zhou Nan gave me a wink, indicating that this person will not co-operate well with us – there's only half a month to go but he's saying he hasn't considered it. He wouldn't breathe a word to us and we didn't have much else to say. So we went in to dinner.'

The hosts fell back on the traditional gambit of plying their guest with *mao tai*, the fiery liquor quaffed in toasts at banquets. 'Patten loved to drink even though westerners cannot handle alcohol,' wrote Zhang, who was perhaps unaware of the convivial customs of the British Parliament. 'Give him a glass, he drank it. Pour another one, he quickly finished it. As he drank, one of his daughters shot him an anxious look as if to say he should not be drinking so much.' Neither the *mao tai* nor the conversational charms of Zhou Nan, who spoke fluent English and could quote Shakespeare, succeeded in loosening the governor's tongue that sultry night in the villa above Stanley.

The ball passed to the Chinese foreign minister, Qian Qichen, who headed to New York for the United Nations General Assembly. On the afternoon of 25 September he met Douglas Hurd, his British counterpart, who unveiled point by point the plan thus far kept secret. The talk with Qian lasted more than two hours, according to Hurd's memoirs. 'Always a cautious and disciplined interlocutor, he made no comment of substance,' Hurd recalled. That was not surprising, given the complexity of the plan.

But Qian said nothing about procedure, either. 'He did not complain that afternoon that we had no right to go ahead with announcing constitutional plans without Chinese approval.'

Qian covered his own back in Politburo diplomatese, which wreathed the noncommittal in highly indicative recitals of previous positions, adorned by such slogans as were thought appropriate. 'I made a statement on the spot stressing that the arrangements for the 1995 elections should be agreed upon by both sides and should be in line with the Basic Law,' he wrote in his own memoir. Qian added that he would pass on what had been said to Beijing.

If this was a Chinese rejection, it got past the Eton and Oxford reflexes of Douglas Hurd unnoticed. Most likely it was another example of cultural incomprehension, where one side thought it had made a point but the other failed to grasp it. The shades of Lord Macartney and Heshen, the Qing courtier, might have danced in the wings of the United Nations building that day.

In Beijing, the British embassy handed over a note outlining the plans. They were now inside the Chinese system, but the short timetable before Patten's policy address on 7 October put a strain on the bureaucratic and inter-departmental processes in Beijing. It is arguable that the deadline worked against creative thinking and forced Chinese decision-makers to take safe and inflexible positions. Equally, it could be argued that without deadline pressure the Chinese side would have adopted its customary tactic of wearing down its opponent and waging 'struggle diplomacy' over every minor clause.

It did not take Qian Qichen long to come up with a pithy formulation. He correctly saw through the blandness to grasp that this was an attempt 'to change the political system dramatically from one that was executive-led ... and to rapidly increase the power of the legislature'. Patten's plans, he wrote, broke the Joint Declaration, broke the principles of the Basic Law and broke confidential agreements and understandings between China and Britain that no constitutional changes in Hong Kong would be made without consultation. Qian labelled these the 'three violations' and when his words were amplified by Lu Ping, the head of the Hong Kong and Macau Affairs Office, the governor became known through a quirk of translation as 'the triple violator'.

The epithet brought ribald laughter in expatriate bars but the Chinese reaction was deadly serious. It is clear in hindsight that China viewed the package as a threat to the authority of the new sovereign power. Qian's verdict in his memoirs echoed the propaganda, yet it is an informed guide to China's attitudes to the politics of Hong Kong. 'The British side apparently decided to stir up trouble completely ignoring China's opposition,' he proclaimed. It was, he said, a deliberate attempt 'to provoke public debate' and to use public opinion to put pressure on China. Patten wanted to 'blackmail the Chinese side with a fait accompli and to get us to make counter-proposals based on his scheme.'

'We pointed out that the future political systems in Hong Kong before and after the handover could not therefore be reconciled.' So China demanded that Patten first 'change his attitude' and then publicly withdraw his political reform plan.

This was an interlude of deceptive calm. Behind the scenes, Chinese factions were coalescing around a rigid line. Zhang Junsheng described how the heads of the rival power centres – the New China News Agency in Hong Kong, the Ministry of Foreign Affairs in Beijing and the Hong Kong and Macau Affairs Office – buried their differences to draft a joint response rejecting the reforms.

The granite figure of Zhou Nan could be counted on for an unyielding stance. The foreign minister, Qian, had already decided that 'China did not want this to happen.' As for the Hong Kong and Macau Affairs Office, Lu Ping felt personally affronted. There was no place for his supposedly milder views in a matter of national sovereignty. Sometimes painted as a closet liberal, Lu held opinions favouring elite rule in Hong Kong which some might have thought uncharacteristic for a Communist; he felt, for example, that it was a bad idea to give votes to workers in the business constituencies because 'councillors elected in this way are likely to be ordinary employees who do not represent the interests of the business community since there are naturally more of them than there are bosses. That's not reasonable.' Lu was ordered by the central committee to take charge of handling the troublesome governor. 'Patten overthrew everything,' he recalled, 'so Deng Xiaoping said "That's it! Start all over again".'

Between the Qian–Hurd meeting on 25 September and the governor's address on 7 October, China thus raced into an adamantine position from which it would not resile for the next three decades, condemning Hong Kong to a cycle of rebellion and reaction that could not be resolved. We now know from the memoirs of Qian Qichen, Lu Ping, Zhou Nan and Zhang Junsheng that the Chinese government felt it would lose face if it accepted the reforms; not just because they were democratic but because

they were drawn up and unveiled in Hong Kong without public and deferential consultation with the capital in advance. In addition, the Chinese
system simply could not cope with the kind of rapid and flexible policy-making which statesmen can use to respond to changing circumstances.
It was locked into a set of ritual and long-ordained formulae which had
emerged through years of evolutionary discussion between 1978 and
1984. Carved in stone, its principles were not to be chiselled away. Deng
himself had said the Chinese people would not forgive or understand.

The question is whether the British side, enjoying the advantage of
possession while it still governed Hong Kong – with its alliances, its stock
of Sinologist knowledge, its undoubted diplomatic dexterity and its smart,
adaptable and occasionally unscrupulous politicians – could have risen to
the challenge with more understanding and guile. That is a hard point to
sustain. Douglas Hurd, who had served as a diplomat in China, believed
the proposals should have been seen as just that – proposals to be discussed
with the Chinese side and if necessary amended. He claimed the British
were open to consultation. What the Chinese really wanted, he said, was
secret discussions in advance of publication and a veto on the result. That
was the old way of conducting business, however, and times had changed.
Speaking more than a quarter of a century later, Patten remained convinced
that he had done the right thing in 1992: 'The idea that it would have been
better for us to have done Beijing's work and have five years arguing with
the democrats in Hong Kong – as it was, despite the rows with China,
Hong Kong was amazingly stable, and economically the period from 1992
to 1997 couldn't have been better. I was turned by Chinese propaganda
into much more of a democratic hero than I deserved because when you
look at what we were doing it doesn't amount to very much.'

On 7 October Patten took the rostrum at the Legislative Council to
reveal his proposals. He found the reaction from politicians, business
people and most of the media in Hong Kong 'very positive'. This was not
so at the New China News Agency, where Zhang Junsheng was already
fuming because a copy of the speech had not been provided to him in
advance, an omission he saw as 'intentional trickery'.

The public in Hong Kong were able for the first time to question the
governor on a radio phone-in about his proposals. There was a vigorous
question and answer session in the Legislative Council. The media debated
the pros and cons with verve. Public meetings took place to discuss the
complex details, which did not daunt potential voters. It was all unthinkable in the People's Republic, where the process was not seen as an example

but as a warning. In late October the Chinese wrath turned into a campaign of vitriol in the media which recalled the Cultural Revolution and began to worry the business elite in Hong Kong, whose tremors reached the political establishment in London.

Patten prepared to go to China while official denunciations of him mounted. He knew that the visit would be difficult, but he was not prepared for the discovery of what he later called 'a fuck-up'. It concerned the exchange of secret letters in 1990 between Douglas Hurd and Qian Qichen, which the Chinese saw as a confidential agreement that the governor had broken. 'I was saying before I made that ill-starred trip to Beijing, "Is there anything I don't know? Have they got something up their sleeve?" Because they hadn't been able to point to anything that we had broken in the Joint Declaration.'

The diligent Edward Llewellyn was dispatched to scour the archives at Government House. 'He came back ashen-faced,' Patten recalled, 'and said, well, there are seven letters between Douglas and Qian Qichen. Now we looked through the letters – there were copies of them in Hong Kong. Nobody had mentioned them. Nobody had seen fit to refer to them.'

Patten's view was that the letters were not a serious matter because they dealt with the dispute over the number of directly elected seats in Hong Kong, not his reforms. 'The embarrassment wasn't what they said, the embarrassment was that I didn't know about them. But it sort of helped sustain the narrative that here [in Hong Kong] I was a neophyte.' It was, to the governor, inexplicable that some of the diplomats who had drafted the letters were supposedly working on his own team but had said nothing about the correspondence. Over it all loomed the shadow of Sir Percy Cradock, who had retired to fulminate in the riverside London suburb of Twickenham.

In his memoirs, Hurd said that when he examined Patten's proposals in the foreign office in September 1992, none of his advisers drew his attention to the letters. Nor, he confirmed, had anyone shown them to the governor before he left for Hong Kong. As for the Chinese interpretation of them, Hurd claimed he had agreed to consultations but not to secrecy or to a veto. Eventually the letters were released and the row abated. But on the eve of Patten's 'ill-starred' trip to Beijing the discovery was unsettling.

A week before he went, the governor breakfasted with George Shultz, the former US Secretary of State, who warned him to expect a calculated snub, discussions worthy of Kafka, and a tide of abusive propaganda when they were over. Shultz's assessment was accurate.

Lu Ping sent the governor a private message asking him to behave 'properly' and to save Lu's face when he arrived in the capital. Then he sent his deputy to meet Patten at the airport to underline the coolness of his welcome. When they met, Lu brandished the letters as if they were both trophy and indictment. 'I said, Mr Patten, there are seven letters exchanged between the foreign ministers of China and the UK. Do you know that? He listened and asked the person next to him: are there? And the man said "Yes." He really didn't know. This guy was just toughing it out.' According to Lu, the governor 'tried to sell his plan, saying how good it was'. But Lu told him 'it would never work.'

Patten's memory of the occasion was different. He recalled a day 'locked in fruitless exchanges' in which Lu had little substantive to say beyond the infamous letters, 'which he produced with a flourish, towards the end of our meeting, only to discover to his surprise that I had read them'.

Shultz was right to predict that the talks could have been scripted by Kafka. Across the green baize table, or from the depths of their ceremonial armchairs, Chinese officials would accuse Patten of breaking agreements; when asked what exactly he had done the response was that 'you know what you have done', accompanied by the suggestion that he should admit his errors. These sterile exchanges were reminiscent of a secret policeman extracting a confession. While they served to reinforce the indignation of the Chinese, they reminded the governor and his entourage of the kind of psychology which reigned on the mainland and might soon apply to the people of Hong Kong. The foreign minister, Qian Qichen, bluntly told Patten that if he did not back down the Chinese government would simply ignore him and deal directly with London.

Both sides used a publicity blitz to promote their causes. When Patten landed in Beijing, Chinese officials displayed an unsuspected zeal for press freedom, allowing reporters and camera crews from Hong Kong to mob him and to crowd into the conference chamber itself, presumably the better to show off the humiliation of the barbarian. As a practised media manipulator, Patten was equal to the challenge, and once back on his home turf he turned his fluency and sarcasm onto the Chinese side. It was entertainment, but it was not diplomacy.

The Chinese state media and its supporters in Hong Kong heaped abuse upon the governor on his return from Beijing. Among the more colourful score-settlers was Lu Ping, who termed him 'a sinner for a thousand years', while officials and columnists dug into their Cultural Revolution vocabulary to call him 'a serpent', 'the whore of the east' and 'a tango dancer', the last of these a bemused response to Patten's statement that in talks with China it took two to tango.

Pressure mounted on the governor. Within his Executive Council there was dismay and dissent from those like Sir William Purves, the head of HSBC, who had advised against confronting China. 'They [the Chinese] were never happy,' said Purves in an interview in 2019. 'You turned it round as much as you could turn it round but … the Foreign Office wasn't helping and relations were not very good, and then arrives a new governor and things went pretty badly pear-shaped after his visit to Beijing. It was a very unsatisfactory visit which was entirely his own fault. He never got back to Beijing. And for the last governor, for that to happen, I think made the build-up to the handover more difficult.'

Purves expressed a forthright view which was widely held, if rarely voiced in public, among the rich and powerful – both expatriates and Chinese – in Hong Kong: 'If things were going to change they should have started twenty years previously. Who really were influencing Hong Kong? The businessmen, the property developers. Everything was going quite well, why make a change? Hong Kong was running very nicely, it had become a very successful trading centre, financial centre. Why change? He, Patten, wanted to make changes – too late! Far too late.'

Patten did, however, receive what he called 'wise and steadfast support' from Charles Powell, the former private secretary to Mrs Thatcher, who was on the board of Jardine Matheson. The Foreign Office seethed with diplomatic discontent but was kept in check by Douglas Hurd. Patten admitted to feeling debilitated and there were days, he wrote later, when the black dog of despair crept into his office.

Behind the scenes, however, the governor was getting reassuring advice from Britain's Secret Intelligence Service, MI6. The spooks, as he called them, predicted almost to the exact date when the propaganda onslaught would cease. Patten felt that these Cold Warriors were always more realistic about the Chinese than their diplomatic colleagues. He summed up the spies' advice: 'They're not going to pull the ceiling down. They're not going to pull the roof down. They can't afford to. They'll shout at you, they'll try to undermine you, they'll try to get the business community on side … they'll try to suggest London is going to recall you, but they're not going to do anything more than that.'

Almost on cue, the barrage stopped in late December 1992. China shifted to a patient, relentless strategy from which it did not deviate until the handover. Early in the new year, Qian Qichen recorded in his memoir the receipt of a letter from Hurd offering to negotiate. The Chinese were suspicious. Li Peng, the prime minister, warned delegates from Hong Kong to the National People's Congress that Patten was 'talking like a Buddha but thinking like a snake'.

After routine skirmishing over conditions, talks opened in Beijing on 22 April 1993. They were led by Jiang Enzhu, a deputy foreign minister, and a dutiful Robin McLaren, the British ambassador, whose health deteriorated as the negotiations dragged on for a cause in which McLaren did not have great confidence. There were seventeen wearying rounds. In September, so as to underline its resolve, China published the text of Deng Xiaoping's admonitory remarks about Hong Kong to Mrs Thatcher in 1982. Another meeting between Qian Qichen and Douglas Hurd at the United Nations failed to break the deadlock. Qian said he warned the British that China would not give in and that any Legislative Council elected in 1995 would be thrown out on 1 July 1997. 'Both sides understood that everybody was preparing for a breakdown,' he recalled.

In Hong Kong, events in 1993 took public attention away from the talks. On New Year's Day twenty-one revellers died in a stampede in the Lan Kwai Fong bar district, which was packed with expatriates as well as young Hong Kongers. Later in January the governor felt chest pains while he was playing tennis and was taken to hospital, where he underwent angioplasty, a procedure to improve the flow of blood to his coronary arteries. Those around him felt that diet, not stress, was to blame. There was a reminder in June of the darker side of Hong Kong's rapid growth when twelve men were killed on a building site at North Point.

But there was also steady progress towards making Hong Kong a financial centre that could stand on its own feet. It was agreed that the Bank of China would join HSBC and Standard Chartered as a note-issuing bank for the local dollar. In April, the territory got its first de facto central bank via the merger of the Exchange Fund and the Commissioner for Banking, which created the Hong Kong Monetary Authority (HKMA). The government launched a programme to help the growing number of middle-income families to buy their own homes. It announced that the city was now the first in the world to have an all-digital telephone network. The financial secretary, Hamish Macleod, raised spending on welfare, health and education by 7 per cent in an upbeat budget.

The British withdrawal gathered pace. In July, the Ministry of Defence revealed plans to draw down the garrison. The Government Flying Service replaced the Royal Hong Kong Auxiliary Air Force. Despite their political disputes, the British and Chinese governments reached agreement after seven years of wrangling on the future of land occupied by military bases in Hong Kong. The People's Liberation Army received a prime piece of harbourfront real estate crowned by the Prince of Wales Building, a 28-storey tower built like a fortress, which would become its headquarters in 1997 after the Royal Navy departed. In May, Mrs Thatcher, who may have cast a jaundiced eye on such recessional arrangements, paid a two-day visit to the Pattens to check on how Hong Kong was doing. There was a clear indication of the future when Patten nominated Anson Chan to take the job of chief secretary for administration. She was the first Hong Kong Chinese civil servant to hold the office, and Patten considered hers one of the best appointments he ever made.

But none of this could remove the shadow of uncertainty from the life of the city. 'I was really angry at that time,' Lu Ping recalled. 'How could Patten, as the governor of Hong Kong, break an agreement reached between the foreign ministers of the two countries?' This was the insurmountable obstacle; for China chose to argue that understandings were broken while the British denied it. The argument came close to theological dispute over the letter and spirit of the documents. In practice the Chinese government had already made up its mind to move on.

An article in Shanghai's *Liberation Daily*, which had recently published Deng Xiaoping's views and was therefore thought authoritative, tore into the 'colonialist' attitude of the British government and demanded Patten's removal from office. Its message to all the factions that made Chinese policy on Hong Kong was clear: the only safe option was the hard line. 'The route had been laid out after Deng Xiaoping's instruction to start again,' said Lu Ping. 'Since there was no "through train" any more we would have to start from scratch and set up a preliminary working committee, then a preparatory committee and a provisional Legislative Council.'

Lu called it 'a separate kitchen', insisting that the legislature must be dissolved in 1997 because 'Mr Patten's kitchen could not be used'. If he thought the homely metaphor might appeal to the average Hong Konger, he was mistaken. Inside Lu's office, workers hung a sign on the wall marking the countdown to Hong Kong's return to the motherland. Outside, there was far from unanimous acclaim for it. 'At the time many things were not understood by the people of Hong Kong,' Lu complained in an interview in 2009. 'Public opinion was not with us. Every day when I had lunch I used to put last night's leftovers in a lunch box, heat it up and eat them in my office. That was when I got to read the Hong Kong newspapers. As I sat eating and reading the newspapers, the more I read the angrier they seemed, always scolding us, it made my stomach ache.'

Lu was consoled by his mistress, a well-connected Hong Kong businesswoman, but his troubles were just beginning. He now had to set up a shadow government and would soon discover that backroom southern Chinese politics were similar on both sides of the border, replete with personal feuds, hot tempers, long-buried clan rivalries, avarice and the zealous preservation of 'face'. People clamoured to get on board Lu's new 'through train' on the Preliminary Working Committee (a term only a Communist could love), but he learned that they were far from comradely. Patten scathingly termed them 'old-time Communist coelacanths, tycoons on the make, ambitious third-raters, Knights and Commanders of the Most Distinguished Order of the British Empire who had found another empire to serve, the earnestly ill-advised'.

On 27 November the British unilaterally ended their negotiations with China. 'The talks fell apart,' recalled Qian Qichen, the Chinese foreign minister. Douglas Hurd told him by letter that the United Kingdom would put the reform plan to Hong Kong's Legislative Council in December. 'The battle about constitutional development in Hong Kong was over,' said Qian. 'The future of Hong Kong would be decided by the National People's Congress under the Basic Law. For China this was a matter of principle. We had gone our separate ways. This was now a showdown between the UK and China.'

On 10 December Patten published his reform bill. It was passed by just one vote in the Legislative Council on 24 February 1994 after a marathon session of lobbying and arm-twisting, both by the governor's side and by Lu Ping and his cohorts. 'I never knew really until we'd got it that we were going to win,' Patten recalled. 'I remember I'd been playing singles with Lavender on a friend's court in the New Territories … it was a lovely evening, sitting sweatily on a grass bank just afterwards and saying to her, "You realise we may have to leave this time next week," because if I'd lost that would have been it. Some people would have regarded it as running away from a mess, but I don't think I could have stayed.'

The last governor would stay on for three more years until the handover. He owed his success to tenacity, guile, political skill and keeping one's nerve, all supposedly traditional gifts of British statesmanship. But success came only after one of the most extraordinary episodes in the country's diplomacy, in which its intelligence services found themselves spying on their former master, whose inner turmoil led a brilliant career into twilight.

9

A Mandarin for All Seasons

On the morning of Monday, 17 August 1993, Sir Percy Cradock called at the imposing Chinese embassy in Portland Place. This smart address had been occupied by envoys of the Middle Kingdom since the late Qing dynasty.

He was ushered in to see the ambassador, Ma Yuzhen. The ostensible reason for the call was to seek clearance for the use of official photographs in Cradock's memoir of his experiences in China and to ask if anyone might help to identity a Chinese official in one of the pictures. It was a humble mission for a man who had guided British foreign policy and had been the custodian of its secrets as chairman of the Joint Intelligence Committee until a year earlier. On his departure the Director of the Central Intelligence Agency, Robert Gates, had written him a private card saying 'You have served your country (and mine) with great distinction.' It was therefore an opportunity which the Chinese ambassador was not about to pass up. He invited Cradock to stay for lunch.

The two men chatted in a desultory way at the table about political affairs, interrupted by members of the embassy staff coming in to try to put a name to the mysterious official, while the ambassador expounded on the merits of physical exercise. They spoke almost entirely in English. Ma was an expert in trading valueless gossip. He said Deng Xiaoping was very old but had no real troubles and was mentally alert. Li Peng saw foreign visitors occasionally but needed more rest. The key figure was Zhu Rongji, the former mayor of Shanghai, who was on the way up. The economy was important, of course.

The ambassador then quizzed his guest about the Hong Kong talks. Britain and China were still arguing about Patten's democratic reforms. Were they near breaking point?

Cradock said he had no special information but he believed the talks had a good way to go. The Chinese were keen to know if there was a deadline. Well, said Cradock, the governor might put his package to a vote in the Legislative Council, or he might finesse it and give an equivocal speech keeping his options open. Ma was intrigued by the word 'equivocal', so Cradock helpfully compared it to the Chinese expression *shuang guan de*, meaning vague or wishy-washy. The last word was a novelty to the ambassador and obviously appealed.

Pressing his theme, Ma enquired whether there was not, in fact, a deadline because the Hong Kong government would have to prepare for elections. Cradock said he was for negotiations, not confrontation. He was sure both governments wanted a solution, he felt Hong Kong people wanted to go on talking, although – he was careful to add – they supported the governor at the same time. It was not, Cradock said, in the Chinese tradition to humiliate their opponents; there would have to be concessions on both sides and although the Chinese had their principles they would have to bend them. The ambassador interjected that they would not bend them. Cradock replied that his host knew very well that they had been bent in the past.

The duo moved on to talk about visits to China. Cradock mentioned that he planned to be in Beijing on 25 November for a board meeting of the China Investment Fund, one of the business interests he had developed in retirement.

With that the lunch drew to a close and Cradock went on his way. He may have thought no more about it until he was invited to see Sir John Coles, the deputy under-secretary, at the Foreign Office on 27 September. The two were old colleagues, but it was not a pleasant encounter. Coles showed his visitor a report that had come into his possession, one which Cradock found 'so disturbing and inaccurate that I feel I must provide you with a written commentary'.

The report contained the details of a telegram from Ambassador Ma to Beijing giving an account of his table talk with Cradock. The British government had learned of it with displeasure. There is no clue in the publicly available papers how they had obtained its contents, but two possibilities are that they had done so either by intercepting secret communications or through a spy at high level in Beijing. It seemed, from Cradock's anguished and indignant letter in his own defence, that the Chinese envoy had gilded the lily to present the conversation as a back channel which undermined Patten and proved he lacked support inside the British government.

Returning home to Twickenham, Cradock put down his thoughts the next day and sent them to Coles. He said he had not reported the lunchtime talk because 'it was routine and generalised' and contained nothing not already in the press or the public domain. 'I think you can see from it how the Ambassador could construct parts of his telegram,' he wrote. 'For the rest, I can only assume that he misunderstood, or fed in extraneous material in order to make a juicy piece of political reporting.' He admitted talking about the negotiations – which were at a sensitive stage in late August – though he claimed it was 'in a much less dramatic and precise way' than the ambassador related.

He denied telling Ma that the British and Hong Kong governments would put the package to a vote if they could not get what they wanted by December. 'I had, and have, no knowledge of government intentions; so that I had nothing to impart even assuming I wanted to.' It was, Cradock argued, 'inconceivable that I would try to pass off my views as being those of the British government'. It was well known to the Chinese that in retirement he was an independent observer; he had just written a book critical of British policy 'which has been cleared only with difficulty'. He had taken care while on a visit to Beijing in May to avoid any 'misconstruction' of his role and it was 'totally implausible for me to pose as a government spokesman'. He ended with a pledge not to represent to the Chinese 'or anyone else' that his views were government views.

It was no secret that Cradock was a critic, sometimes a harsh one, but to be confronted with a suggestion that he had connived with a foreign power was a humiliating moment for a man who had been at the heart of British policy-making. His reputation in the secret world never recovered. Yet his legacy was undeniable, flawed though it was by an embittered retirement. Along with Deng Xiaoping he had played a continuous part in deciding the fate of Hong Kong from the first talks in 1979 to the Joint Declaration of 1984 and the aftermath of the Tiananmen Square massacre five years later. His strategy of playing for time was not glorious, but it bought decades in which a young generation of Hong Kongers flourished in freedom. Cradock's cold genius and his stark moral realism made him a less appealing character than, say, the last governor. But his influence was greater and lasted longer; it is no exaggeration to say that this self-effacing man shaped the lives of millions.

Percy Cradock was a pessimist. 'I take a bleak view of the international scene,' he had written in his 'First Thoughts' for Mrs Thatcher on becoming her foreign policy adviser in 1984, 'it is a world where as Thucydides put it "the strong do what they can and the weak suffer what they must".'

Cradock had seen that at first hand. He had been serving in the British embassy in Beijing when Mao Zedong turned the masses on the party in the violent chaos soon to be known as the Cultural Revolution. At first the foreign diplomatic corps followed its twists and turns with professional detachment. Fascination turned to fear, however, when it became clear, in Cradock's words, that they were trapped in 'a demented environment, an Alice-in-Wonderland world, governed only by its own mad logic'.

On 22 August 1967, after several ominous days, a mob of Red Guards stormed the British embassy, incensed by the detention of 'patriotic' Chinese journalists in Hong Kong and the closure of three pro-Communist newspapers during riots in the colony. Accompanied by the chargé, Donald Hopson, and their staff, Cradock retreated to the registry, while the attackers battered at its steel door amid shouts of '*Sha! Sha!*' (Kill! Kill!) The building was set ablaze, forcing them to stagger out into the hands of the crowd. Cradock was beaten, punched in the stomach and dragged up on a soapbox, his head forced down in humiliation, expecting a fatal blow at any moment and all the time feeling a 'strange sensation' that surrender had brought a sense of relief, like stepping over the side of a sinking ship. As the British men and women were flung one by one into a gatehouse, he remembered some lines of Virgil 'floating back over the years in the way the Classics masters assure us they do': *forsan et haec olim meminisse iubavit*, 'perhaps even these things it will one day be a joy to recall.'

They were rescued by soldiers sent to restore order and succoured by the courageous Dutch chargé d'affaires, Douwe Fokkema, and by their French colleagues. The chargé's office had been burnt out and the residence sacked. Then the diplomats were, in effect, held hostage until London and Beijing negotiated the safe exit of each other's personnel. It was theatre, Cradock realised, but the performance left its mark. Several of those who worked with him, and interviewed for this book, felt that it was a lesson in calculated cruelty which he was never able to forget.

Ironically, perhaps, Cradock had been on the Left in his youth. He came from a modest background in County Durham, where his father, Alfred, was a colliery auditor. His intellect shone early at grammar school and he won a place at St John's College, Cambridge, to study law and English language. He defeated a future Tory minister, Norman St John-Stevas, to become president of the prestigious debating society, the Cambridge Union, where a future Tory foreign secretary, Douglas Hurd, watched as Cradock 'paraded his left-wing views with outstanding panache and wit'.

At school, Cradock discovered Arthur Waley's translations of Chinese verse, which 'sang their siren songs' to him suggesting an inexhaustible treasury of culture to be found – a romance on the translator's part, he later realised, unmoderated by any rude contact with the country itself. Cradock joined the Foreign Office and was 'rash enough' to live and work in China, learning, in his own words, that it was an acquired taste, much of it bitter. The prizes fell into his lap: ambassador to Beijing and East Berlin, foreign policy adviser to the prime minister, spymaster in chief as chair of the Joint Intelligence Committee. Though world affairs consumed his time he always came back to the taste of bitterness, of which he was the supreme connoisseur.

Sometimes the bitterness was sweetened by Chinese manners and refinement. In a photograph from 1980, Cradock is taking tea in the gardens of his residence with official guests to mark the Queen's Birthday. Seated on a wicker sofa, he is engaged in animated conversation with Wang Guangmei, the widow of President Liu Shaoqi, who died in the Cultural Revolution, while his wife, Birthe, chats to the vice foreign minister, Han Kehua. When Cradock left China, Wang sent him a handwritten farewell note hoping that Sino-British friendship 'will be ever green' and asking him to pass on her regards to the Queen and 'my friend HE Margaret Thatcher'.

Cradock's long involvement with Hong Kong and China has been charted through these pages. Perhaps it has been fully illuminated for the first time. He was the paramount Sinologist of his era and, like others of that caste, he has sometimes received an unsympathetic press. Cradock himself appealed to the verdict of historians. Therefore it is worth examining the mind of the policy-maker, to give credit where it is due and to subtract the flaws which cracked his reputation. One of his loyal admirers admitted that there were two Cradocks. One was the masterful calculator who achieved what many thought impossible in the Joint Declaration. The other was the spiteful egotist who could not bear to see his work tampered with by lesser minds. The reader has seen the first of these fairly treated in these pages. It is time to examine the second, to understand what he thought and what he did.

Cradock was moulded by the Cold War and by his experiences in China, which he applied to the machinery of government. Far from being a one-dimensional bureaucrat, he believed that the beginning of wisdom was the confession of ignorance. His private commonplace book, which is kept in the library of his old college, St John's, reveals a magpie intellect, widely read, poetic and keen, endlessly studying the lessons of statecraft from antiquity to the Renaissance and the nineteenth century. When he found an aphorism or a maxim he thought useful, down it went in his crabbed, angular handwriting in blue ink. So Plato and Heidegger rubbed shoulders with Fouquet on Voltaire ('a chaos of clear ideas'), the Florentine historian Francesco Guicciardini and the dry prose of Lord Salisbury. He scribbled down advice by Richard Pipes on autocrats and the despairing poem by Cavafy, 'The God Abandons Antony'. He noted the Greek Stoic concept of *ataraxia*, meaning a state of undisturbed calmness. A phrase by Tacitus on the merits of imperial rule also caught his attention.

Cradock answered to ministers who answered to Parliament, but he did not idealise that process. He wrote down a warning from Benjamin Disraeli: 'If you establish a democracy you must in due course reap the fruits of democracy.' As for the public's right to know, he treated it as a plague upon foreign policy. He cited with approval Sir Eyre Crowe, an austere head of the Foreign Office who had warned against appeasing the Kaiser and who 'deplored all public speeches on foreign affairs'. On the other hand he appreciated that modern public opinion was politically important and 'no foreign secretary can act in eighteenth century disregard of it.'

Cradock believed in Lord Palmerston's dictum, faithfully transcribed, that 'we have no eternal allies and no permanent enemies. Our interests are eternal and those interests it is our duty to follow.' Scruple and morality could play a part, he felt, but the burden they placed on policy-makers reminded him of a saying by Cardinal Richelieu in seventeenth-century France: 'in matters of state, he who has the power often has the right and he who is weak can only with difficulty keep from doing wrong in the opinion of the majority of the world.' After this, he recorded the words of Pope Urban VIII on hearing of Richelieu's death: 'if there is a God then Richelieu has much to answer for. If not, then he was a great man.'

In the light of what happened to Hong Kong under Cradock's stewardship, these private notes illuminate our understanding of his philosophy. It was, as he said in his 'First Notes', a bleak one. His 'First Thoughts' of 1984 also set out the West's interests succinctly: 'Hong Kong apart, China does not threaten our interests,' he wrote, 'in fact, given the state of Sino-Soviet relations, she confers great strategic benefits on the UK and Western Europe.'

Britain indulged with his approval in one act devoid of scruple. It backed China's diplomatic protection of her clients in Cambodia, the

Khmer Rouge, who clung on to their seat at the United Nations after their genocide was well known. Vietnam invaded Cambodia in 1979 and put a stop to it. But Vietnam was backed by the Soviet Union. This made Cambodia's fate a matter of Cold War rivalry. British ministers presumably thought that supporting the Chinese position might help with the talks on Hong Kong; to be fair, they were also following a general Western line. The references are buried in British documents of 1979 to 1984, almost shame-facedly added as afterthoughts in talks with the Chinese.

Cradock argued at the time that the Soviet Union posed the principal threat to the West, not through invasion but by weakening European resolve so that nations conformed to its wishes: 'the game would be lost without a soldier moved.' This foreshadowed the debate about China in the next century. Cradock illustrated it with the maxim that 'the most success-ful conqueror is one who takes the city without firing a shot.'

The Soviet Union had gone by the time Cradock left office. Its collapse unanchored a set of principles which had guided people like him. In the early 1990s it was far from clear which power might take its place, if any. China seemed too weak, as well as disinclined, to do so. For those like Cradock, who had experienced its cruelties and its leaders at close quar-ters, China's power to intimidate was none the less real. That may explain his pain as he watched John Major and Chris Patten deviate from the intricate balance he had established.

Cradock left 10 Downing Street with a valedictory from Major, who said that 'without his skill in diplomacy Hong Kong would inevitably have fared worse.' As they parted, Major told Cradock that if he thought Hong Kong was going wrong he should let him know. By late 1992, Patten had unveiled his reforms and made his 'ill-starred' visit to Beijing, leaving Cradock so appalled that he went to see the prime minister and subse-quently wrote a six-page 'personal and confidential' letter to Major setting out his concern. It would be easy to caricature Cradock as a discarded mandarin writing a memorial of remonstrance to the throne. In the light of events, however, his arguments bear examination because he forecast almost exactly what was going to happen.

He warned the prime minister that Britain was on a course 'calculated to produce the most unconstructive and hostile response from the Chinese side'. It had led to the kind of crisis in which neither side could easily back down, something avoided in the tensest periods of 1982 to 1984. Cradock was not suggesting that Britain did not want more democracy in Hong Kong, 'but we surely want democracy that will survive beyond 1997 and that does not provoke a Chinese backlash and in consequence a more repressive regime after the handover.

'I do not dispute that the Chinese are being unreasonable and intolerable. Of course they are; they have never been anything else.'

Cradock did not try to argue that a quiet approach would have worked, but he pointed out that the Chinese 'are there and we have to work with them'. Then he told the prime minister what he thought would happen if Patten pressed on against Chinese opposition: 'They will not give way. They have a profound suspicion of democracy in Hong Kong as a British device for trying to detach the territory from the mainland and as a source of infection to the neighbouring provinces of southern China.'

Chinese leaders would be happy to have an excuse for dismantling the legislature when they took over in 1997; meanwhile they would pressurise local politicians and the community, threaten those who co-operated with the British, withdraw their own co-operation over important issues and ultimately 'there will certainly be a new legislature arranged to the Chinese liking.' This is precisely what took place. Cradock singled out Deng's words about 'a fresh start' to make his point, adding that the Chinese might seek to dismantle the judiciary and other institutions.

In perhaps his most prescient sentence, Cradock foresaw that allowing the Chinese to claim that Britain was in breach of the Joint Declaration and the Basic Law would allow them to weaken those parts of their own commitments to uphold freedoms and rights which they did not like: 'I cannot emphasise too much the importance to Hong Kong of the Joint Declaration: it is the territory's sheet anchor; without it Hong Kong people would be in Chinese hands with no protection at all.' He warned against courting 'short term praise' in Britain or counting on the majority in Hong Kong to support the governor once the costs became known. Many local people would seek to make their accommodation with the Communist Party and even if Patten won 100 per cent support it would not change China's mind: 'Indeed, the greater the level of popular support for what the Peking leaders will see as an act of subversion, the tougher their reaction will be.'

Meanwhile, Cradock warned the prime minister, he must expect attacks for mishandling Hong Kong and casting away one of the biggest achievements of the Thatcher government. With pessimistic foresight, he said, 'the issue of refugees from Hong Kong could again become acute.' The choice in his view was between more democracy in the short term followed by repression after 1997, and less democracy up to 1997 with a better chance of avoiding a repressive system afterwards. In the first case he thought there would be 'a high degree of Sino-British hostility' which Beijing would use to write off parts of the Joint Declaration. He admitted that it was 'a choice of evils', but he said there was only one answer: to take the second choice. Losing Patten's expanded democracy would be 'painful' but was a worthwhile price to pay for 'avoiding a repressive system of indefinite duration thereafter'. He urged the prime minister to think again, to modify the plan and to re-engage the Chinese in secret talks.

Cradock's advice was considered but the policy was not changed. From then on his tone sharpened. He began to attack Patten in the media. This was an unequal contest; as one of his admirers said sadly, 'there was Chris Patten the smooth televisual performer and then Percy would pop up on the screen looking like an angry owl.'

In December 1993 he took his concerns to the House of Commons Foreign Affairs Committee, appearing to his critics as if he was a spokesman for the Chinese government: 'They feel they have been cheated. They feel extremely strongly about it. I am not saying they are right or they are politically justified or legally justified. What I am saying is that this is their position,' he said.

Cradock left the committee in no doubt how difficult it had been to get the Chinese to commit to 'elections' in Hong Kong and how fragile was its limited democracy. 'The Chinese were adamant against it and we only managed to get that very generalised phrase in at the very last minute and with the personal help of Geoffrey Howe in a message to Wu Xueqian, the Chinese foreign minister. They made it plain to us that any move towards democracy in the Westminster style in Hong Kong would be regarded by them as moves towards independence.'

He warned them not to expect the United States or anyone else to come to the aid of Hong Kong. 'Back in 1982 to 1984 the UK used to have the happy illusion that friends and partners especially the US would pull our chestnuts out of the fire. But they made it perfectly plain that they had an agenda of their own with China and they were not going to use their capital on fighting our battles. So in the end we were on our own.' The last governor talked a good deal about the rule of law, 'but he seems to forget that the rule of law depends absolutely on the sanctity of the Joint Declaration. We have greatly accelerated political intrusion from the mainland into Hong Kong.'

Having failed to win support for his dire prophecies, Cradock seems to have gone behind the scenes to intrigue against Patten. He got in touch with Murray MacLehose, now elevated to the House of Lords. MacLehose was not about to join a conspiracy against the governor, but he made his opinions clear: 'From one side or another we really pulled it off, which makes it all the more bitter now to see the politicians pulling apart a structure which may have been rather shaky but stood a good chance of surviving to the great benefit of Hong Kong people, British trade and Britain's reputation for still being able to get things right.

'The lines of criticism are obvious but how to get out of the mess we have got ourselves into no-one seems to know. I don't think the removal of Chris Patten would solve the situation in itself because of the reaction in Hong Kong and the counter-reaction from Peking, from the very articulate Hong Kong politicians and their media supporters who have misled the British Government into this mire.'

Cradock despaired of Mrs Thatcher, who openly regretted that Hong Kong could not be given independence and spoke out in support of Patten. Their relations were not close; in fact he later complained in a private letter to Lee Kuan Yew, the elder statesman of Singapore, that 'her autobiography was very ungenerous.' He got a more sympathetic hearing from Lord Callaghan, the former Labour prime minister, who had privately warned Patten that he was wasting his time. 'I entirely support your belief that it is courting failure to treat a great and proud people with a culture other than our own as though you are engaged in a knockabout with the opposition across the floor of the House of Commons,' Callaghan wrote to him. 'As to the 21st century I have a strong feeling that China will grow in strength, will retain her unity (although with much decentralisation) and will become a real force in world events. How important that we should be on good terms, as we shall have no important interests to divide us except human rights which we share with others.'

But there is nothing so 'former' as a former prime minister and all Cradock's lobbying was for nought. With the ruthlessness that the establishment reserves for those who transgress its codes, he found himself excluded from its inner circles and he slowly receded from view. He did not get the seat in the House of Lords which might have been his due; and although he remained a member of the Privy Council, which advises the sovereign, there were no more honours. He used the time to write books on China, on intelligence and on grand strategy, deploying the dry elegance he had once been obliged to confine to secret communications. He corresponded with Lee Kuan Yew, their letters interspersing old men's health worries with gloomy strategic prognostications; both thought

China and Russia would always be at odds over China's lost northern territories, both agreed that the West was stuck in a war it could never win in
Afghanistan, and both deplored the inconstancy of America. From time
to time they dined quietly – the Japanese restaurant Nobu in London was
a favourite – but their meetings dwindled. Lee was an admirer. He called
the Joint Declaration 'a tour de force because it covered concepts and
systems that did not exist in China' and he saw Cradock as the Englishman
who knew China better than any other.

When Cradock published his book on the Joint Intelligence Committee,
after heavy redactions by Whitehall, Mrs Thatcher wrote him a personal
note which expressed her own characteristic view of intelligence: 'I cannot
help thinking that the requisite decision also depends enormously on the
personality of the person in charge and those around him. Otherwise it
would merely be a kind of mathematical calculation modified by experience. There is always a bit of a mystery about the precise factors that tipped
the balance – but then, life is about more than reason.'

Cradock was not an idle man; he and Birthe played tennis in Marbella
and on the Venice Lido and, having no children, they were free to travel.
But his health went into serious decline due to diabetes. One leg was
amputated in 2001, the other two years later. He bore it all with steadfast-
ness, receiving a stream of sympathetic letters from old colleagues. One
came from Len Appleyard, another China hand who had served as ambassador to Beijing, after a social call on the Cradocks for tea and cakes:

> We are clearly in the same circle of hell in Chris Patten's mind,
> not ever to be forgiven … Reflecting after our conversation I
> was struck once more about how difficult it was to deal with a
> spin-doctor politician. I went down regularly to Hong Kong for
> consultations, each time bringing up the issues I knew he was
> criticising me for. Each time he refused to address them and then
> briefed against me after I left. Happily, I think opinion has moved
> in our direction over the years but in Chris Patten's mind, I believe
> we committed the ultimate sin of standing in the way of his future
> political career.

Cradock's last years were cruel. As a double amputee he was housebound.
From corresponding with the mighty, his later letters included those
addressed to the local council complaining about noise from a rock
concert and haggling with a pension company. There were, however,

moments of *ataraxia*, stoic calm. The veteran China correspondent Jonathan Mirsky, an adversary of the Cradock line who had witnessed the massacre in Tiananmen Square, wrote to express his sympathy, and a warm correspondence between the two followed. Both men had almost lost their lives on the streets of Beijing, even if they drew diametrically opposed conclusions from the experience.

Sir Percy Cradock died on 22 January 2010. Mrs Thatcher sent a letter of condolence to his widow. This time she was generous:

> Percy was a most remarkable man. His brilliance and sharpness of mind shone out. His ability to reach a clear and vigorous intellectual position might sometimes be a little unnerving but it was none the less welcome.
>
> Perhaps Percy's greatest strength was that more than anyone else he understood the Chinese and their way of thinking. This was invaluable during the negotiations on the future of Hong Kong and gave me the confidence to push for a better outcome than perhaps our underlying diplomatic position might otherwise have achieved.

The obituaries were measured, fairly judging his achievement but somehow failing to capture the essence of a man who both loved and rued China. That was left to the historian Hugh Thomas, who wrote to *The Times* to fill in the gaps:

> I recall myself travelling in China with Percy, an incomparable companion on those bleak trains, with his splendid wife Birthe, and him reciting, in a restaurant hung over a river in Loyang, the lines of Auden:
>
> The Emperor's favourite concubine
> Was in the Eunuch's pay,
> The Wardens of the Marches turned
> Their spears the other way;
> The vases crack, the ladies die,
> The oracles are wrong:
> We suck our thumbs or sleep; the show
> Is gamey and too long

10

Transitions

The people of Hong Kong voted to elect the last Legislative Council under British rule on Sunday 17 September 1995. It was 653 days before China resumed sovereignty. The polls were free and fair. They were the most democratic in the history of the colony, but the turnout was low.

Just over 920,000 people, about 35 per cent of registered voters, cast votes in the geographical constituencies. After all the hard-fought battles for broader enfranchisement in the functional constituencies, 460,000 people, or just over 40 per cent of those eligible, voted in them. The Chinese-language press suggested that many people felt the exercise was pointless. Yet, far from boycotting the contest, pro-Beijing parties and their media supporters had waged a vigorous campaign for 'patriotic candidates who love Hong Kong and love the Motherland'. Their efforts were in vain.

The single biggest victor was the Democratic Party led by Martin Lee, which won nineteen seats. The democratic camp beat the pro-Beijing parties in both the geographical and the functional constituencies. They won a majority in the legislature. The Legislative Council, however, was on borrowed time. It would only hold office for twenty-one months. 'It showed that you cannot drop democracy if you want the rule of law and individual freedoms,' said Lee. 'Hong Kong people got used to that, so are no longer frightened and that is something which any chief executive will find it very difficult to follow.'

The evidence suggested that Hong Kong people were steadily discovering a wish to govern themselves. Two other fully democratic elections had already been staged. In September 1994, a record 693,223 voters participated in elections to the District Boards, a turnout of more than 33 per cent. And in March 1995, 561,943 voters turned out in elections to the Municipal Councils, representing about a quarter of those eligible. That was the prelude to the democratic triumph in September.

While the democrats basked in a daze of euphoria, the pro-Beijing forces conducted a rapid audit of their defeat. They were certain of ultimate victory in 1997 because China had said the legislature would be thrown out and it would appoint a chief executive, but they did not sit idly waiting for the rewards to fall into their lap.

The Communist Party itself operated underground in Hong Kong, but it had a well-oiled set of techniques to deploy through its United Front Work Department. It put these to good use. More funds flowed to overtly pro-Communist parties and individual legislators, accompanied by strict if stereotypical injunctions to 'get closer to the people' and 'better understand people's livelihoods'. Chinese officials worked hard to deepen their ties to the business elite. At the same time they intensified their efforts to reach out to unaffiliated members of the legislature and to influence businesses and social organisations.

Western intelligence agencies thought there was a split on the Chinese side between nationalistic 'hardliners' around the abrasive Zhou Nan and more flexible opportunists around Lu Ping. The latter was a smooth Shanghainese, capable of vituperation when required but the epitome of courtly reason on other occasions. In hindsight this was an attempt to stereotype Chinese diplomacy, which was certainly beset by factions but remained resolute and was not to be divided or played off. Much spooky effort was expended in monitoring Zhou Nan's amorous exploits, one senior Western intelligence official recalling the envoy as 'a great shagger'. In his file was a report that as a young diplomat in New York, Zhou had been infatuated with a woman at the British Mission to the United Nations. Experienced minds tried to puzzle out whether there was any advantage to be gained from Zhou's energetic personal life but it was decided to leave well alone. His womanising remained undisclosed.

To Hong Kong people, the difference between Zhou Nan and Lu Ping seemed to be one of style, which gave them an early lesson in the necessity of understanding their future masters. Lu cut a more reassuring figure, while Zhou epitomised the hatchet-faced ideologue. The head of the Hongkong and Shanghai Bank, Sir William Purves, got on well with Lu and dealt with him on sensitive political questions. Where there was room for manoeuvre, Lu would find it. Lu had waged his share of 'struggle diplomacy'; one diplomat recalled hearing Lu and Sir Percy Cradock shouting at each other and banging the table as they sat à deux in a conference room. One of the top civil servants in Hong Kong put it like this: China was a huge country with different regional characters, and Zhou was the incarnation of a mandarin from the inland capital while Lu was a native of a city on the sea, Shanghai, which had a cosmopolitan history of trade and cultural intercourse. He had a heritage in common with many of the Hong Kong elite.

There was a secret which may have weakened Lu's influence at this critical juncture. He was gravely ill. In 1994 his doctor had advised him to have a gastroscopy for his stomach pains. Lu put him off but the next year the doctor insisted. 'He showed me there was a large shadow and said they would wait for the tests but there was a ninety percent chance I would have to go under the knife.' Lu went ahead with a visit to Hong Kong, but on his return to Beijing in May 1995 he checked in under an assumed name to a hospital in Beijing where he underwent a gastric resection for stomach cancer. It was followed by a gruelling round of chemotherapy. Rumours spread. 'Many journalists came from Hong Kong to inquire but the hospital said there was no such patient,' he recalled.

'The chemotherapy was so rough that I lost all my hair. The specialists said I should rest for two months and come back for a second round. But how could I? How could I carry on my work? So I refused a second round. When I came out everyone could see I was weak and haggard. But I held on.'

Lu reappeared on the scene as the Chinese cadres marshalled their forces to drive ahead their planned political transformation of the territory. They were content, however, to allow the capitalist engine of Hong Kong's prosperity to tick over. In his 1995 budget the financial secretary, Hamish Macleod, reaffirmed a top tax rate of 15 per cent, even though the government would run a small deficit. 'We have a clear philosophy, consistently applied, which is based on a commitment to market forces, free enterprise and free trade,' said Macleod, 'we believe in creating an environment with minimum government regulation and interference, plus maximum government support in terms both of infrastructure and of protection for the needy, leaving business free to flourish.'

He wrote those words as Hong Kong became the world's busiest container port for the third successive year and the city was named the world's freest economy by the Heritage Foundation, a conservative think tank in the United States. The government also aimed to spread prosperity. Legislation was passed to set up a mandatory provident fund, borrowing some of the principles of social insurance successfully applied in Singapore.

In 1996, the last full year of British rule, the pace of change accelerated, while economic success gave a patina of confidence to the city's progress

towards its destiny. Envoys from Hong Kong turned up in Brussels and at
the World Economic Forum in Davos to talk up its role in the global trading system. It was a sign of the city's status when the Hong Kong Monetary
Authority became a member of the Bank for International Settlements. In
November, the Hang Seng Index rose above 13,000 points for the first
time.

These were heady times for advocates of globalisation. In May, Chris
Patten himself went to Washington, where he met President Bill Clinton
and argued for the continuation of China's Most Favoured Nation status,
which gave the mainland's exports equal access to the United States
market. The leaders of Hong Kong believed it would prosper as China
entered a rules-based world economy.

Across the administration, faces changed to reflect reality. Alongside
Anson Chan, more local people rose into the elite ranks of the civil service.
By the end of 1996, official figures showed it was 99 per cent localised.
Donald Tsang, the Jesuit-educated son of a policeman, became the first
financial secretary of Chinese birth in 150 years. Denise Yu, the Secretary
for Trade and Industry, represented Hong Kong at talks on the future
World Trade Organisation. An official language agency was set up to
promote the use of Chinese in the civil service. On 14 March a criminal
case was conducted in Cantonese in a district court for the first time.
There were other signs of a sea change. The Chief Justice, Sir Ti-liang Yang,
who had been in office since 1988, resigned his position, renounced his
British citizenship and gave up his knighthood in order to run for the
position of chief executive. The governor hastily installed an Australian
lawyer, Noel Power, to serve as interim Chief Justice until the handover.

The legal system was an asset to Hong Kong as commercially important
as the harbour. Cases were heard under common law before impartial
judges, a vital safeguard against corruption and influence. From 1840 until
1 July 1997 the power of final judgement lay with the Judicial Committee
of the Privy Council in London. It was agreed by Britain and China that
after 1997 this would, rightly, cease and a Court of Final Appeal would be
established in Hong Kong. That proved to be the simple part.

The court agreement had been negotiated in secret. When it was
revealed in 1991, there was uproar in Hong Kong. It was like the dispute
over elections: the Democrats sought to maximise judicial independence
and the Chinese government tried to maximise political control. Once
again it came back to the Basic Law, which said that 'judges from other
common law jurisdictions' might be invited to sit on the court. The law did

not say how many, but Britain had accepted China's demand that only one foreign judge would sit on the panel of five, including the Chief Justice, which heard appeals. All courts in China obeyed the Communist Party and this was, therefore, an area in which the party meant to expand its power, while maintaining with a straight face that Hong Kong would enjoy 'a high degree of autonomy'. It could always expect to count on the loyalty of four out of five judges.

The Democrat politicians Martin Lee, a barrister, and Margaret Ng, a fellow lawyer, led the chorus of complaint. 'They had already sold us down the river,' said Lee. In the furore, legislators voted against the proposal on 4 December 1991, leaving the colonial government with a problem. It was bequeathed to Patten, who found that his efforts to reach agreement with China on a new bill to set up the court foundered amid the general political recriminations. To the Chinese side this was an opportunity to pursue 'struggle diplomacy', which they did with glee. They were determined that the court should not be able to rule on 'acts of state', a convenient catch-all phrase. They had also decreed that the ultimate power to interpret laws lay with the Standing Committee of the National People's Congress in Beijing.

By 1995 the decision could be postponed no longer. China had created its own insurance; now its officials sat back to enjoy the infighting between the Democrats, an unhappy governor, ministers in London who were keen on trade, and the Foreign Office, in particular its Hong Kong Department. Inevitably the arguments turned on fine legal intricacies. But bigger principles were at stake. The British cabinet itself was divided on the wisdom of annoying China. Its 'big beast', Michael Heseltine, the President of the Board of Trade, was leading a delegation of more than 200 businesses to China. He felt the governor's stance was quixotic and unhelpful. The prime minister and the foreign secretary backed Patten, but they were becoming uneasy.

The Foreign Office specialists were aghast when Patten implied that he might go it alone to set up the court without agreement from the Chinese. They feared it would be a replay of the electoral reform battle which would produce an institution doomed to abolition at the handover. None the less, a bill was prepared for presentation to legislators, which did not satisfy the Democrats and incensed the governor's critics, who felt he was reckless. 'It all got rather nasty,' said one of Patten's aides.

Then at the end of May, as the arguments on the British side were in the balance, the Chinese negotiator, Chen Zuo'er, threw his opponents a lifeline. The two sides struck a deal in which Britain conceded on every substantial point. It was a bad-tempered exchange to the end, but a text was finalised near midnight on 8 June and signed the next day. Martin Lee defiantly argued that the bill served Beijing's interests, damaged the rule of law and undermined the independence of the judiciary. Most legislators, however, were convinced by Patten's argument – an ironic echo of pleas made by others negotiating with China – that this was the best agreement that could be achieved. It passed by thirty-eight votes to seventeen on 26 July 1995.

The governor felt that Michael Heseltine was his greatest critic for 'screwing up British business' during the dispute, but the promotional visit to China went ahead and Heseltine did not criticise him in public. In private, when he came to Hong Kong for the weekend, Heseltine took the governor aside for a word. 'He says to me suddenly, "I don't want to say something which is going to ruin our friendship, but there's something personal I'd like to say to you before I leave", recalled Patten. The two men stepped out onto the terrace at Government House, where Heseltine, a renowned gardener, ran his eye over the manicured gardens in the early morning light. '"Look," he said, "it's quite difficult saying this to you. But you're not pruning the bonsais properly".

Patten had avoided a cabinet crisis. Hong Kong got its Court of Final Appeal and Britain got its trade with China. 'The truth is that people would say these things about business and politics, but when you look at the figures from 1992 to 1997 when we were having all these blazing rows with the Chinese our share of trade as a proportion of OECD trade [with China] went up,' said Patten. He had learned the limits of negotiating with a resolute opponent who held most of the cards. The decisions taken in early 1995 were not glorious, but as Patten put it in 2019, the Court of Final Appeal 'is one of the things which still stands between Hong Kong and just being like mainland China'. As 1995 turned into 1996 and the handover drew near, people took comfort from such reassurances.

British influence was fast ebbing away, but John Major's government in London was determined to exercise authority until its last day. In March 1996 the prime minister visited Hong Kong and announced that holders of the new blue-and-gold passports of the Hong Kong Special Administrative Region would have visa-free access to the United Kingdom. A series of late-in-the-day agreements between Britain and China broke the deadlock on issues as diverse as a building a second runway at the new airport, air navigation over China, arrangements for the handover ceremony and the transfer of the Exchange Fund, which held Hong Kong's reserves, to the new authorities.

The Chinese government did not waste its time. At the start of 1996 it set up a Preparatory Committee of 150 suitable individuals from Hong Kong and China, chaired by Qian Qichen, who was flanked by the inevitable figures of the convalescent Lu Ping and Zhou Nan. The vice-chairmen from Hong Kong included the shipping heir Tung Chee-hwa, the man destined to be the first chief executive; one of his successors, Leung Chun-ying; Henry Fok, a business tycoon rooted in Guangdong; and the distinguished judge Simon Li, who told foreign visitors that the Tiananmen Square massacre had been caused by the aggression of the students.

This heralded the orchestrated transfer of power which China had long said it would carry out, and the script unfolded accordingly. In June, Tung resigned from the governor's Executive Council, where he was regarded as an affable, reassuring presence. Two months later nominations opened for a 400-member Selection Committee which would choose the new leader and the members of the Provisional Legislative Council. A total of 5,791 people put themselves forward. The 400 successful candidates convened at a hall in Shenzhen. Their first task was to pick a leader. There was a semblance of a contest as eight candidates stood for the top job. Three made it to the final round: Tung, Sir Ti-liang Yang and Peter Woo, an acerbic Shanghai-born billionaire. The most popular candidate among Hong Kong people, the chief secretary for administration, Anson Chan, decided not to stand, although she promised to stay on to serve 'without fear or favour'.

On 11 December Tung was elected by 320 out of 400 votes in a smoothly organised ceremony in the new Convention and Exhibition Centre on the harbourfront in Wanchai. Sir Ti-liang Yang gained forty-nine votes and Peter Woo thirty-six. The ritual was complete and Tung became chief executive designate. The election was hailed by President Jiang Zemin and Premier Li Peng as a democratic breakthrough because it was 'the first time in Hong Kong history that a Chinese had been appointed chief executive by the Hong Kong people.' Outside the Convention Centre, the police took away twenty-nine pro-democracy protesters who breached a cordon, including the legislator Emily Lau and the trade unionist Lee Cheuk-yan.

The next day the Preparatory Committee convened in Shenzhen to nominate 130 candidates for the Provisional Legislature. The democratic parties in Hong Kong did not put anyone forward. Once again the process moved smoothly to its second stage. On 21 December, the 400 individuals on the Selection Committee picked sixty men and women who would sit in the legislature to govern six million people in Hong Kong after the handover. They included thirty-three members of the existing legislature and ten people who had stood for election in 1995 and lost. Among the new members was Timothy Fok, son of the pro-Communist tycoon Henry Fok, who was close to Tung.

Qian Qichen called the process 'just, fair and open'. Patten described it as 'stomach-turning ... a bizarre farce'. The Democratic Party said it was 'a great leap backwards'. It was, however, the outcome China had promised, ordained and carried out. Rhetoric was fruitless. On 28 December Tung summoned Anson Chan to a two-hour meeting at which she agreed to go on working under him. The two knew each other well. She felt that he was still behaving like the head of an old-style Chinese family firm, not the leader-in-waiting of a sophisticated city state.

While public attention was on the politics, China quietly went about securing its military and security presence in the new Hong Kong. The People's Liberation Army began to assemble elite air, land and sea units in Shenzhen to form a garrison to be stationed in the city from 1 July 1997. The task was considered so important that its commander, Major-General Liu Zhenwu, reported directly to the Central Military Commission in Beijing, not to the Guangzhou Military Region. Liu was a seasoned officer in his fifties from Hunan province and a graduate of the National Defence University. His political commissar was Major-General Xiong Ziren, from Hubei, who had trained at the PLA Political Academy and fought in the 1979 border war against Vietnam. One of the vice-commanders, Colonel Zhou Borong, later promoted to major-general, was a graduate of the Beijing Foreign Languages Institute and a fluent English speaker.

The entry of the PLA into Hong Kong became a subject of bitter dispute. There was no goodwill between the Chinese and British negotiators; there was also a perpetual struggle to balance factions on the Chinese side between Zhou Nan at the NCNA, Lu Ping at the Hong Kong and Macau Affairs Office and a sequence of rote-trained envoys at the Joint Liaison Group, which existed to forge an agreement on how the handover would work.

The British representative on the Joint Liaison Group, Hugh Davies, kept a diary which he later turned into a privately published memoir. Davies saw Zhou Nan as a 'mixture of brash cockiness and bullying manner' and classified Lu Ping's deputy, Chen Zuo'er, who was engaged in the PLA talks, as 'a tough Fujianese with long experience as a party journalist ... one of the most stubborn and unyielding officials that we ever encountered'. In general, Davies felt he was dealing with a leadership that was 'nationalistic, vengeful and short-sighted'.

For his part, Chen loathed the British. When he arrived in Hong Kong in 1994, Davies' colleague, Alan Paul, took him out to lunch in a skyscraper restaurant, a gesture which merely confirmed Chen in his belief that the colonialists were not to be trusted. Chen later described how he learned that the telephones at the Chinese Foreign Ministry staff dormitory in Kennedy Town were tapped. He used three different cellphones, never spoke on the phone indoors and reverted to Shanghainese dialect in conversations with his boss Lu Ping in the hope, likely vain, that the eavesdroppers would be confounded. After each round of talks Chen retreated to a windowless office room with the PLA's representative, General Wang Jin, to draft their reporting telegram to the Central Military Commission in Beijing and prepare their brief for the morning. They dared not risk using computers, so the general wrote out a text in pencil, handed each sheet over for approval, then took the documents over to the New China News Agency for printing in a secure room.

The soldiers themselves got on tolerably well. The British commander, Major-General Brian Dutton, took the newly promoted Zhou Borong for a hard-drinking dinner on Po Toi, a fishing island, and went to visit the PLA in Guangdong. The Chinese officers made an impression of sincerity upon him. 'They've said to me specifically that the image the world has of the PLA is that of Tiananmen Square and "we wish to change that"', said Dutton. The officers wanted Hong Kong to be a window on the world; a showcase for the PLA as 'modern, mature and sophisticated armed forces'.

Dutton felt the PLA ought to get the benefit of the doubt, although he noted their 'robotic training', their entanglement with commerce and their political conditioning. There were, Dutton felt, a generation of senior officers in their mid-forties and fifties who aspired to serve in a respected professional army. They were particularly pleased with their shiny new Audi staff cars. 'They are all very much still children of their own society just as I am the child of my own society and they have not had the same exposure to alliances, to international affairs or to coalitions,' Dutton felt. The PLA would need to tread lightly and learn to be subtle in Hong Kong. 'Here we're returning sovereignty to a power which many would have considered alien until recently – still a Communist power and one from which many of the population in Hong Kong fled. It's a delicate situation.'

At the outset, China's negotiators had struggled to understand that Crown Land in Hong Kong meant land owned by the Hong Kong government, not by the British government or the United Kingdom. If it came as a surprise to them to learn that it would all be handed over without demur, they did not give anything away. The transfer of administrative and defence property was correspondingly smooth.

Dutton's headquarters in the Prince of Wales Building on the harbour-front, where smart young aides in white shorts poured tea and served biscuits to his visitors until the final days, were about to be taken over by the PLA. (Its walls were rumoured to have been seeded with eavesdropping devices by the departing British.) For the first time Chinese soldiers would stand guard at Stanley Fort, commanding the southern approaches to Hong Kong island. The single-runway air base at Sekhong, in the New Territories, passed to the PLA's air units. The Chinese navy would be occupying a shiny new base at Stonecutter's Island, the site of Britain's first station for intercepting communications in the 1930s, and whose facilities included repair workshops and a karaoke room. There was no publicity about the quiet removal of modern intelligence-gathering equipment from bases around Hong Kong; a phased withdrawal had been carried out over the years. Long-range interception and satellite surveillance were concentrated in a facility at Pine Gap in northern Australia jointly operated by the United States. All over Hong Kong, barracks were spruced up, flags folded and kit packed away.

Handing over real estate was one thing: the psychological reality of PLA troops marching in was another. The first unit of forty men, wearing a smart new uniform, drove across from Shenzhen in April 1997, followed by more in May. It was assumed that both sides would orchestrate a changeover with a small Chinese advance party and the departure of all British personnel by midnight on 30 June before the main PLA force arrived. Then came a 'bombshell'. A Chinese vice minister in Beijing told the British ambassador that the leadership wanted all their troops to march into Hong Kong with their weapons and vehicles before the British had left. Chinese negotiators in Hong Kong amplified the demand. The PLA staff envisaged up to three thousand troops marching in on 30 June, backed by twenty-one armoured personnel carriers, six helicopters and ten naval vessels. The order came from President Jiang Zemin himself.

Britain had a new Labour government led by Tony Blair. It was keen to turn a page in relations with China but its attention to Hong Kong had been light on detail. The new foreign secretary, Robin Cook, and his minister for Asia, Derek Fatchett, were not sensitive to the negotiating psychology which had built up on both sides; it was so confrontational that a dispute raged about the precise second at which the Chinese national anthem might be played at the handover. Symbols mattered; but Blair and Cook saw no reason to stage a fight with the Chinese over the deployment. The governor, in contrast, did not want the 'goose-stepping' PLA marching in a minute before they had to. Yet another three-sided squabble broke out.

In his privately published memoir, Hugh Davies offered a last glimpse of the Chinese negotiating style. China had long agreed that its forces would come in after midnight on 30 June; as soon as Jiang Zemin's 'autocratic wish' was known, the Chinese negotiator Zhao Jihua merely switched his line and uttered the new demand as if nothing had changed. It took weeks before agreement was hammered out on 21 June. The PLA would send about five hundred troops in advance, there would be no armoured personnel carriers and no weapons would be displayed before midnight. A formal handover would take place at the Prince of Wales Barracks. The last few hundred British ceremonial troops and naval crews were to leave before dawn. The main Chinese force of some 4,000 would cross the border at 6 a.m. It was, Davies said, a climbdown by the new ministers, who were hopeful of striking up a better relationship with China. It did not prevent secret suspense about China's military plans until the very last moment.

The bitterness and malevolence of these confidential exchanges, long after all major details had been settled, may puzzle those who take a Western view – particularly since, being secret, they served no public purpose. The memoirs of Chris Patten and his contemporaries reflect a sense of themselves as reasonable men confronted by the hectoring functionaries of a one-party state. A tone of mystification pervades their accounts – why can't these cadres just drop the propaganda and get down to process so we can make a deal? That is to underestimate the pride and rage which gripped their Chinese opponents, nationalistic and vengeful as they may have seemed.

Reading the recollections of Chinese officials involved in the handover provides a fresh perspective. To the Chinese side this was the end of a national humiliation. They were determined to make it drawn-out and bitter for the departing colonialists. That was not a diversion – it was the whole point. About one thousand Chinese officials were directly engaged in the handover and many of them swelled with patriotic pride as the foreigners inevitably submitted to their demands. To some it was vengeance for the poverty and suffering inflicted on past generations. 'The child stolen from its mother's breast had been returned,' is how one author put it.

Memoirs, articles and films dwelt on their hard work and sacrifice for the motherland. Zhou Nan himself delayed treatment for cancer until ten days after the handover. Lu Ping, as we have seen, refused a second round of chemotherapy so that he could return to duty for the final stages (in the event, Lu lived until the age of eighty-seven, dying in 2015). Many of the Chinese officials had forged strong bonds on the long road to Hong Kong's return. Lu, for example, could recall his years alongside the legendary Liao Chengzhi. He had accompanied Liao to the United States for his heart surgery, even staying in his hospital room. Back in China, adopting the role of a faithful amanuensis, he noted down Liao's deathbed injunctions as the old man struggled for breath to give his final advice about Hong Kong.

This was a degree of personal continuity which few political systems could match. It was in the nature of democracies and their administrations that faces changed from time to time, but on the Chinese side the same faces seemed to remain until death or disgrace intervened. Professional politicians and officials on one side were up against highly committed lifetime party comrades on the other. There was a psychological chasm between the two sides.

The people who trusted least in promises from Beijing were those who had already fled China once. All through the 1980s a steady trickle of Hong Kongers had secured foreign passports, bought real estate abroad and sent their children to be educated there. Some kept a foothold in Hong Kong with a bolthole overseas, others emigrated and brought extended families to their new homes, enriching the fabric of every society that welcomed them.

Many officials and policemen who had served the colonial government were protected by holding British passports first issued during David Wilson's governorship. For most of the disciplined services there seemed little to fret about. But former members of the Special Branch and anyone connected with the security services needed reassurance. A quiet exodus took place to friendly countries such as the USA, Australia and Canada.

A long-serving official, Simon Vickers, was tasked with combing the files for sensitive information. Anything which might put an individual at risk was sent to the archives in London or destroyed. A former history teacher at Bedales, a progressive boarding school in southern England, Vickers later joined the colonial civil service and was a fluent Cantonese speaker. Something of an idealist, he became disturbed and depressed by what he found as he went about his work. In 1997 he decided to talk to the press.

Over tea and dumplings in the quiet back room of a dim sum restaurant, Vickers explained that details of confidential applications for British passports by Hong Kongers had been passed to the Chinese government. This was, he said, just the tip of the iceberg. Infiltration, fuelled by graft, had been so successful that the British were covering up its extent to avoid embarrassment and a loss of public confidence. He said the former head of Hong Kong's immigration department, Laurence Leung, was 'rotten to the core' – he was corrupt and had been suborned by the Chinese security services to provide secret information. Although the British kept intelligence compartmentalised as far as possible, Leung's access to data meant 'the loss was extensive'. It exposed to Communist pressure local civil servants and police who were doing their best to be loyal to Hong Kong. Leung had stepped down in 1996, pursued by the whiff of scandal, although the Patten administration had kept to a straight-faced line that he had retired early for personal reasons. Vickers was now turning whistleblower.

His story was true. In 2019, declassified files from a Legislative Council inquiry would confirm that Leung was entangled with organised crime figures in the Triads, was a member of a racehorse owning syndicate, had made undeclared investments in mainland China and received HK$750,000 (US$96,000) from a company owned by an adjudicator in immigration cases. That firm's registered address had been linked to a drugs syndicate. In 1992, Leung's daughter, aged twenty-three, had been murdered in Canada by a shot from a crossbow. Many took it to be a Triad warning. It added up to a picture of a hopelessly compromised public servant.

Leung was allowed to enjoy a peaceful retirement despite failing an integrity check by the Independent Committee Against Corruption. In officially approved Chinese accounts he is described as 'honest and hard-working'. He died in 2008 at the age of sixty-seven. There was no such reward for Vickers. British officials suspected him of being the leaker and he was ostracised. He had always planned to leave Hong Kong with his family after the handover and he retired early with a generous pension, but he did not find his feet once away from the Hong Kong he had loved. He moved to Thailand, then returned to Britain, where his physical and mental health declined. Eventually he took his own life.

All over Hong Kong were people who feared the Communist Party for one reason or another. Some were recent political fugitives. A few were criminals. Others were accused of 'economic crimes' and had fled the mainland. Many old men who had fought for the Kuomintang or had worked for the defeated Nationalist administration were still alive in 1997. They had resided in Hong Kong under the British flag since the late 1940s while their comrades dispersed to Taiwan or into the diaspora. But the most fearful of all were those who knew the party's secrets.

Towards the end of colonial rule, the correspondent of *The Times* of London, Jonathan Mirsky, received a tipoff from Jin Zhong, the editor of *Kaifang* (Open), a political magazine. Mirsky, a scholar of Chinese who had received an award for his coverage of the Tiananmen Square massacre, was a busy man, but the bait dangled before him was hard to resist. It was not every day that a journalist was invited to lunch with one of Chairman Mao's mistresses.

Their rendezvous was at one of the smartest hotels in Hong Kong. Ms Chen, as he named her, was a plump woman in her fifties clad in a traditional *qipao* slit to the waist. She spoke in the strong dialect of Anhui province and talked constantly about herself, pausing only to slurp down oysters. Mirsky brought a female Chinese friend to help decipher her story. It was, as they say, a scoop.

His lunch companion told him of clawing her way up from the provinces to Beijing, of dancing from an early age and of making it into a troupe that performed for Mao Zedong himself in 1962. Mao was ever youthful when among pretty peasant girls in uniforms and caps; some were singled out for personal attention. She had danced with Mao as his partner and then he had invited her into his bedroom 'for tea'. She was fourteen years old the first time they had sex. The chairman, she said, was full of vitality.

It is hard to grasp at this distance how potent was the charisma of a man who was treated by hundreds of millions of people as a living god, and how intoxicating the experience was for a young country girl. But the court of Mao was ruled by caprice and few of the chairman's conquests were permitted to linger. One day she was summoned to his presence. Mao told her that his wife Jiang Qing had found out about them and was furious. She would be sent away from Beijing. While Mao explained this to her, she sat on his knee and he wept.

The chairman's aides found her a comfortable job in Inner Mongolia and in due course she was allowed to return home, where a marriage had been arranged. She had a son and settled down. Then her father – a life-long party member who had heard rumours about Mao but disbelieved them – found out about her tryst with the Great Helmsman. Aghast, he wrote a letter to Mao denouncing him. Fortunately, the local postmaster brought the letter back undelivered and advised him not to send it.

Somehow, Mao's dancer, now divorced, made her way to Hong Kong with her son. She was desperate to get away before the handover. And the reason she had sought out a famous journalist was that she wanted to tell her story. She had heard that Mao's doctor, Li Zhisui, had got a million dollars for his best-selling memoir *The Private Life of Chairman Mao* and wanted to emulate his success. Naturally, she needed a ghost writer.

Mirsky found that publishers were keen. But something about the task repelled him. For one thing, Li Zhisui's book was a historical testament which had been compared to the works of Tacitus. For another, Mirsky disliked the prospect of spending a year or more with the would-be author and her story, which promised to major on lascivious detail. He turned her down and after a second meeting at the hotel he never saw her again.

He did, however, go to see the American consul-general on her behalf. The Americans had a thick file on Ms Chen but really did not want her to come to the United States. They, along with the British, had investigated her story and the allies had reached a deal. With weeks to go before the PLA arrived, Mao's teenage dancer flew from Hong Kong to a new home in the United Kingdom.

China's prize on 1 July 1997 was one of the world's great cities; a port and finance centre poised on the edge of a giant expanding economy, laced by top-grade roads and railways, thriving with highbrow and lowbrow culture, home to a healthy and increasingly well-educated people and graced with natural beauty. It was also crowded, heavily polluted and profoundly unequal, a place where many laboured for little and the price of property put homes out of reach. It was a free port, its doctrine was free trade and its citizens enjoyed free speech, protected by a respected legal system with no fewer than 3,876 solicitors and 626 barristers. Its civil service was efficient even if its system of government was in dispute. In the thrill of transition, many were ready to accentuate the positive and to postpone the inevitable moment of truth.

On the eve of the handover the territory had a population of 6.3 million. Only a fifth of them lived on Hong Kong island. Kowloon, where the population density reached 53,610 human beings per square kilometre, was home to just over 2 million, making it one of the most crowded places on earth. Surprisingly, 46 per cent of Hong Kongers lived in the New Territories, the result of a drive to build that had put almost half the people in public housing. A handful, less than 0.5 per cent, inhabited the verdant outlying islands where the early fishermen had settled.

It was a young city. The median age was thirty-four and more than 18 per cent of its people were under fifteen years old. The birth rate was double the death rate. The ratio between the sexes was almost in balance, a sharp contrast to the prevalence of males in the People's Republic after decades of state-enforced birth control. A man in Hong Kong could expect to live to seventy-six and a woman to eighty-one.

Ninety-five per cent of the population were Chinese by origin, but they spoke in many dialects. Almost all understood Cantonese but a quarter also spoke Putonghua, or Mandarin, the common language of China; while there were small but influential groups whose mother tongues were the Chiu Chow, Hakka, Fujian and Shanghainese dialects.

Among them dwelled the foreigners. The largest group came from the Philippines, numbering 128,300 people. There were more Americans and Canadians than there were British; only 26,700 citizens of the colonial power were still official residents as the flag came down. They were almost matched in numbers by groups from Indonesia, Thailand and Japan, while contingents from India, Australia and Malaysia were growing. They made Hong Kong a colourful, mixed-up kind of city.

A free media resounded across the metropolis. The internet was in its infancy but consumers heard a cacophony of voices from radio stations and television broadcasters in Cantonese, Mandarin and English. The government-owned Radio Television Hong Kong (RTHK) observed the conventions of the BBC or National Public Radio. It was editorially independent. Lively commercial cable television channels kept up a din of speculation and controversy as 24-hour coverage was becoming the norm. No taxi ride was complete without the chatter of a talk radio show, bubbly Canto-pop or the wailing strains of Chinese opera. The news stands were a riot of headlines and contending opinions. The reader was free to buy the establishment daily *Ming Pao*, Jimmy Lai's noisy tabloid *Apple Daily*, the pro-Communist titles *Ta Kung Pao* and *Wen Wei Po* or a slew of lurid magazines promising scandal about Canto-pop stars or the secret lives of Chinese leaders. Two dailies, the *South China Morning Post* and the *Hong Kong Standard*, served Anglophone readers. All the international press was available. Bookstores were stacked with titles from mainland China, Taiwan and Japan in addition to literature in English. Nobody feared to sell books on Mao's famine, memoirs of the Cultural Revolution or histories of Tibet. In cinemas, audiences could choose between a documentary on the Tiananmen Square massacre and *The Opium War*, a patriotic epic that was showing in more than three hundred cinemas in China. Its director, Xie Jin, felt his film depicted a tragedy, not a black-and-white tale of good and evil, for it showed corruption at the imperial court and Britons who opposed the war. Perhaps its subtleties were lost in the scenes of battles and drug addiction which attracted audiences indifferent to its political message.

Hong Kong was also a city of diverse faiths. As the official handbook put it, all major religions were practised with complete freedom. The majority followed traditional Chinese beliefs but there was a powerful community of almost half a million Christians, alongside much smaller contingents of Muslims, Hindus and Jews. Many people joked that Hong Kong's true god was money.

There was plenty of that. The property and stock markets reached record highs in 1997, the economy was growing by almost 5 per cent a year and unemployment was just 2.6 per cent. Inflation was running at 6 per cent annually. The rich were fabulously so, but not all shared in the lucre: the average wage was HK$9,772 (US$1,256) a month. The wealthy could feel secure: the city was one of the safest in the world. Crime fell by 14 per cent in the year before the handover.

The wealth of Hong Kong came from trade; the colony was so prosperous that in 1997 it accounted for 18.6 per cent of China's gross domestic product, and by some estimates almost half of Chinese trade flowed through the city. Commerce between Hong Kong and the motherland grew by an average of 29 per cent per year between 1978 and 1997; investors from the colony had ploughed more than US$100 billion into the mainland, 40 per cent of which went to Guangdong. It was with pride that commentators in the People's Republic began to refer to 'China's Hong Kong'.

One titan would not be there to witness the triumph. Deng Xiaoping had often said he would go to Hong Kong on 1 June 1997 to see the colony return to the motherland. But over the winter his health declined. He died in Beijing at 9.08 p.m on 19 February at the age of ninety-two, of complications, according to the official communiqué, from a lung infection after years of suffering Parkinson's disease. It was 132 days before the handover.

Deng died during a cold, rainy week in Beijing. The mourning was as muted as the sky. The *People's Daily* had prepared the ground, for those alert enough to spot it, with a poem published on 13 February by Qiang Xiaochu, a party veteran who had joined Deng on a trip to the White Mountain: its opening line read, 'the mountain is high and the road spirals afar'.

The old man was an unsentimental atheist and a Marxist-Leninist. He disdained all personality cults. The state media broadcast images of his relatives and comrades paying tribute as he lay on a bier at the hospital. In a letter to the highest party authorities his family said Deng wanted his corneas to be donated to an eye bank, his body to be dissected for research and his ashes to be cast into the sea.

Ten thousand people attended a funeral service in the Great Hall of the People. No foreign dignitaries were invited. The eulogy was pronounced by Jiang Zemin, who appeared on the verge of tears as he read out its leaden script. There was little emotion on the street in Beijing that week. Eleven days after his death Deng's ashes were scattered in the East China Sea from an air force plane. 'Maybe the foam of the breaking waves will carry his ashes towards the shores of the motherland,' said the Xinhua news agency in a special dispatch, 'maybe towards Hong Kong and Macau, maybe towards Taiwan ... Deng Xiaoping glancing back should smile in peace.'

The colony awoke on its last day, 30 June 1997, to a gentle hiss of rain. On the border up at Lo Wu and at other crossing points, an orchestrated military ceremonial began. It was, said the *People's Daily*, a moment the Chinese nation had waited generations to witness. Soldiers of the People's Liberation Army checked their dark green lorries and polished their staff cars. By agreement, forged in the long and tortuous negotiations which had laid out the timetable of the day, there were no armoured vehicles. The reunification of Hong Kong with the motherland demanded orderly traffic control, not a blitzkrieg.

At the appointed hour, gates would open and salutes would be exchanged. There was to be nothing frightening about it. The convoys were to roll at a stately pace through villages and towns across the New Territories. The Royal Hong Kong Police, in the final hours of their colonial mandate, stood impassive guard. Most of the faces under the dark blue caps were Cantonese. 'We will carry on doing our duty to Hong Kong,' a commander told the curious television crews from around the world.

The PLA columns were destined for the waterfront at Victoria Harbour, where the British armed forces had cleared their headquarters at the Prince of Wales Building. Their route passed hilltops and crossroads where Britons, Canadians, Indians and local Hong Kong volunteers had fought and died to bar the Imperial Japanese Army in 1941, each bequeathing a name to the memorials which dotted the colony. The PLA staff maps, said one British liason officer, were pinpoint accurate. 'Thank goodness they weren't ranging artillery,' he said, 'that wouldn't have been an awful lot of fun.'

The maps traced the hopeless picket of dugouts and posts set up in 1941 across the hills and valleys, dubbed the 'gin drinkers' line' by the light-hearted colonials down in the clubs of the wartime city. In modern times, both the Chinese and British had drawn up staff plans envisaging an assault on Hong Kong and a defensive retreat. This was not mere contingency, as officials would blandly maintain, for China had more than once considered military action.

In 1967, a radical faction of the PLA had been ready to invade Hong Kong during pro-Communist riots, when the British authorities almost lost control of the colony to violent crowds inspired by the Cultural Revolution. This was no figment of expatriate imagination after a jolly good lunch; the story came years later from Lu Ping, the urbane head of the Hong Kong and Macau Affairs office. The PLA commander in southern Guangdong had suggested military intervention and occupation 'to put an end to the chaos', Lu recalled.

British naval and military forces were too small to offer more than a token defence. Hong Kong came within a hair's breadth of disaster; a Chinese takeover at the height of the Vietnam War would have been a graver test of Western credibility and prestige than the Soviet blockade of Berlin.

The invasion was only called off by a late-night order from Zhou Enlai, the premier, to the local army commander, Huang Yongsheng. Once more, Hong Kong had been a chess piece; for Huang was a prominent member

of a group loyal to Lin Piao, at the time Mao's designated successor. He was
a well-known womaniser and is said to have become the lover of Lin's wife.

Luckily for Hong Kong, Lin Piao was indecisive, sleepless and dependent on drugs to numb the nightmares of his civil war campaigns. His cabal
purported to believe in the violent export of revolution and were ready to
seize any opportunity for a military strike that would have intoxicated
patriots and confounded moderate rivals. They were, however, badly led;
and the premier retained enough authority to order the PLA to stand
down, saving Britain from almost certain defeat and the loss of its colony.

In time Lin Piao fled China on board a British-built Trident airliner and
died in a fiery crash in Mongolia. Huang was purged, given a show trial
and died in April 1983. But the lure of a swift, exalting conquest of the
colony did not die. According to Lu, Deng Xiaoping had become so exasperated by Margaret Thatcher during their talks in Beijing in 1982 that he
told his subordinates China 'was ready to resort to requisition by force' if
there was trouble in the colony. Deng feared that announcing the date for
the 1997 handover could provoke serious unrest in Hong Kong, forcing
China to march in. This confirmed – if in less dramatic terms – Thatcher's
recollection of Deng's threat at those 1982 talks to 'walk in and take the
whole lot this afternoon'.

There is no reason to doubt Lu's evidence. He spoke in 2007 in an interview with Dragon TV, a Chinese broadcaster. Zhou Nan, the senior
Chinese official who headed the mainland's representative office in Hong
Kong, said in his own memoir that Beijing had considered 'non-peaceful
means' to achieve reunification. And the threat had never gone away. In
fact, until the hour of midnight on 30 June 1997, intelligence officials were
prepared for it all to go dreadfully wrong. Throughout the final months of
negotiation, analysts in London, Washington and Tokyo had pondered the
Chinese insistence on a last-minute increase in the size of the PLA contingent to be deployed into Hong Kong.

According to intelligence sources in several alliance countries, two
pieces of information emerged which raised the level of alarm. One said
that Jiang Zemin had expressed his personal fear to the Politburo standing
committee that 'anti-China' forces would stage demonstrations and cause
chaos, sabotaging the great day and turning it into a 'spectacle of resistance'. The other came from signals intelligence. It showed that China had
reinforced army units and detachments of the People's Armed Police in
Guangdong province, bolstered the number of plainclothes security agents
in the province, and set up a command centre to run an operation to flood

Hong Kong with troops and police to crush resistance by force if the Politburo deemed it necessary. There was also a contingency plan for elite special forces units to rescue the Chinese leaders if they became trapped. Political control of the operation was left in the hands of Vice Premier Zhu Rongji; the nominal head of security, Qiao Shi, was already fading from power. Western intelligence officials could scarcely credit the information, but it could not be ignored.

For all his calm exterior, Jiang Zemin was an emotional man given to risk-taking. The military intelligence was incontrovertible. This was the nightmare scenario for which no war game had found a solution that was not catastrophic. A low-key operation to reassure the Chinese side through intelligence, diplomatic and military contacts was launched. But it was not until shortly before the ceremony itself that the head of British intelligence in the colony was able to put on his jacket and tie, leave his desk and hurry to the Convention Centre.

By good fortune the handover had not turned into a catastrophe, although only when the Chinese archives are open will we know if it was a near-run thing. And as the Chinese army columns prepared to rumble south, all over Hong Kong, the great and the good on both sides awaited the final, peaceful act.

They had come from far and wide. Inside the cabin of a British Airways airliner, Nigel Sheinwald, a Foreign Office official, had looked around at the slumbering grandees as the plane flew through the night from London. Sir Edward Heath appeared strangely androgynous in his old age. Others were up and about, networking in the aisles. The leaders of Britain's new Labour government were taking their first tentative steps on the world stage. A youthful Tony Blair would take the podium at the handover ceremony, accompanied by his foreign secretary, Robin Cook. There was nothing to worry about, though, for every step had been scripted in those long, exhausting talks with the Chinese. All they had to do was perform their part.

At the quayside, *Britannia*, the royal yacht, lay moored. It was a miracle of spit and polish; below decks every surface gleamed and crisp-uniformed crew came and went. In its salons the carpets were thick and there was a faint smell of furniture polish. The interiors of *Britannia*, like those of the governor's residence, transported the English country house to the most exotic climes. *Britannia* was to take the governor and his family away, like their long-departed predecessors, across the South China Sea. Kurt

Schork, a renowned war reporter, had been sent by Reuters to cover the turmoil that never happened. Instead he found himself, a day or two before the handover, conducted from salon to deck. 'This is pretty cool but not exactly what I came for,' said Schork, a soft-spoken New Yorker. The yacht bumped up and down idly at the quay, for there was already a slight swell. It was the typhoon season.

At the Hong Kong Observatory, whose bulletins, read out on the radio and television, governed the working day, there were worried faces. The forecast was for rain, lots of it. The low-pressure bands over the coast of Guangdong were unrelenting. Thick, scudding grey clouds crowned the Peak. A fine veil of humidity, mingled nicely with pollutants, hung across the harbour and wreathed the towers of finance spiking up along the shore.

President Jiang Zemin, whose owlish demeanour behind large tortoise-shell glasses concealed his inner fears, flew in on an Air China Boeing 747 from Shenzhen. He was soon installed on the Kowloon waterfront at the Harbour Plaza Hotel, which was owned by the patriotic billionaire Li Ka-shing. With Jiang were some of the men who had sent in the tanks to Tiananmen Square, including the funereal Li Peng, the premier, whose presence, it was feared, would draw protests. The Royal Hong Kong Police ringed the hotel; Chinese security agents, their faces set in permanent scowls, patrolled the foyer and guarded the lifts. In his suite, Jiang received the homage of lifelong local Communists (the party remained underground and undeclared in Hong Kong) and those who formed the United Front, a coalition of pro-Beijing groups marching under the flags of social work, municipal politics and patriotic propaganda. There also came millionaires aplenty, for who did not wish to make their number with the new rulers?

Prince Charles, the heir to the British throne, prepared for a duty which his family had perfected to a routine, usually around midnight, when the flag would come down in some far-flung possession to a skirl of pipes and a soft breath of jasmine-scented air. It was the last glad, confident performance of its kind for the Prince of Wales; his divorced wife, Diana, would die in a car crash in Paris almost exactly two months later. Before their separation, officials in Whitehall had considered Charles as a potential governor of Hong Kong with Diana as his consort, an arrangement that Princess Grace of Monaco might have envied for sheer style. In the event it was the middle-class Christopher Patten, the son of Roman Catholic immigrants from Ireland, who had come to perform the empire's last rites. 'It wasn't just the end of empire for Britain, it was the end of a period which people recognised,' said Patten. 'People saw it as the end of empire.'

Prince Charles contented himself with sketches and a private journal that later became public. The Chinese leaders, wrote the heir to the throne, were a 'group of appalling old waxworks'. The prince later sued the *Mail on Sunday* newspaper after it published these observations. From Beijing, reaction came there none; mindful of the waxed and polished Mao in his mausoleum the Chinese may not have taken it entirely as an insult.

All this was prelude. Diplomacy and protocol had dictated a round of final engagements for the governor and his visitors which the British had deftly exploited to set up the biggest exercise in networking outside the United Nations general assembly; much of it, no doubt, wired for sound recording. It was an accomplished feat of good manners and firm handling. Motorcades criss-crossed town and swept through the harbour tunnel. This was the early days of the internet age, so most Hong Kongers got their news from live television broadcasts and a cacophony of Cantonese radio stations. All, surely, watched the moment when an emotional governor received the folded flag from his aide-de-camp, bade farewell to his staff at Government House and left in a limousine to board *Britannia* in the late afternoon. There was a palpable air of disappointment among the war-hardened media veterans who had flocked to Hong Kong for a moment that had been etched in news diaries for more than a decade. Bar sales at the Foreign Correspondents Club climbed as the sweaty, calm afternoon dragged on.

'I remember the emotion of leaving Government House and with my favourite pipe tune "Highland Cathedral" being played by the police band,' Patten recalled. 'I remember at the beginning of the [British] ceremony with the rain lashing down, the Hong Kong official who'd been responsible for putting it all together coming up to me and saying, "It's raining so hard people think we should abandon the ceremony," and I said, "You must be joking! This goes on whatever happens".'

The British had chosen as the scene for their sunset recessional a parade ground set in the confines of a waterfront naval base called HMS *Tamar*. Long planned, it brooked no improvisation. Each service was represented. The bands, the music, the barked commands were all prescribed. It was billed as a farewell ceremony for the forces and no stout heartstring was left unplucked, from the swirl of banners to the strains of Elgar. The governor, the Prince of Wales and the dignitaries stood arrayed in one long line.

The parading troops faced them; they, too, were strung out in long lines that were hard to keep straight.

The rain, which had been building all day, began to fall heavily. Dense black clouds unloaded their torrents on the marching bands, the high and mighty and those occupying coveted seats in the stands. Rain dripped and trickled into every crevice, great sheets of it swirling in the lamplight as though the inhospitable climate of the south China coast was sending the barbarians off with a reminder of how little they had ever belonged there. Patten spoke. It was an elegy and a plea, crafted over days and months through drafts that had gone through assorted hands.

As a passage of prose straitjacketed by diplomacy, it wasn't bad. It was the governor's own wish, perhaps honed in those quiet moments shaving in the morning which he kept for reflection, to address the historic grievances of China. Nobody, he declared, would seek to condone today the customs and practices with which the story of Hong Kong had opened. He was, it seemed, referring to the opium trade and to how British imperialists had prised China open by force.

It was not an apology, just a statement of fact. He praised the ordinary people of Hong Kong, recalled their endurance and maintained that Britain had done its best for them. The governor's lip quivered and a tear – or was it a raindrop? – trickled down his cheek. The Chinese media were unmoved. The bands played again, the troops wheeled about and were dismissed. With some relief, all those in attendance scuttled off down the quayside to a giant modern convention centre where the act of consummation was to take place at midnight.

Once inside, cocktails flowed at a reception hosted by the outgoing Hong Kong government. Blair was ushered away for his first meeting with Jiang Zemin, who, he seems to have decided on the spot, was a fellow reformer. On the border the gates were flung open, engines revved and the first PLA units began to roll into Hong Kong. Down at the Legislative Council, a building in classical municipal style on the Victoria waterfront, a demonstration by the ousted democratic politicians on the council was already in progress, the participants holding bright yellow banners and bullhorns, and with umbrellas raised against the deluge.

Within the convention centre, all was quiet, timetabled order. What an artificial, stilted and soulless moment it was. It showed how brittle, lacking in warmth and devoid of trust was the relationship between Britain and China. For the Chinese leadership, it marked the reversal of a national shame and it was not an occasion for cordiality. Inside a grey-hued hall, the two parties took the stage. Every detail had been haggled over with ferocious precision, every standpoint and walking distance measured. The British, apart from their weary Sinologists, persisted mistakenly to the end of the night in expecting some gesture of friendship, some sign of relaxation. Instead the men from the Politburo stared blankly ahead like robots, or, indeed, waxworks.

'There had been endless negotiations with the Chinese about the precise sort of balletic formula for the last meetings, who had to come into a room first and who would come second,' said Patten. 'Eventually it was agreed that we'd take a firm line that the Chinese leaders and Prince of Wales would come into the room at the same time and we'd all file in after them.

'So we did all this and we sit down and the Prince of Wales makes some good remarks without notes and Jiang Zemin responds by saying the Chinese will follow the Joint Declaration and the Basic Law. Nothing happens – they've spoken for about twenty, thirty seconds, then the Prince of Wales tries to engage them in a discussion and very politely they make clear that's the end of that. So off we go. Completely absurd.'

The public ceremony was weirdly artificial, a display fit for a parade ground carried out in an air-conditioned bubble. It began with the Prince of Wales, who read a gracious farewell on behalf of Queen Elizabeth II. He stepped back to his place and, seconds before midnight struck, the British Union Flag and the Hong Kong Blue Ensign were lowered as the band played 'God Save the Queen'.

At the stroke of midnight, Chinese soldiers stepped smartly forward. The flag of the People's Republic, adorned by stars and a hammer and sickle, was raised alongside the new red flag of the Hong Kong Special Administrative Region, bearing its insignia, the five-petalled Bauhinia flower. The flags rose slowly and jerkily up the flagstaffs. Fans were needed to create a stiff breeze so that they looked as if they were billowing in a natural wind. The shrill notes of China's national anthem, the 'March of the Volunteers', rang out.

Standing on the stage, Anson Chan, the woman leading the Hong Kong civil service through the change of rulers, had mixed feelings. She felt a degree of trepidation because the two sovereign powers were so different. One was a parliamentary democracy with bottom-line values from which, she believed, it would not depart. She had in mind the rule of law, fundamental freedom, tolerance and a pluralistic society. The other was a totalitarian, one-party system. Yet Chan also felt 'a hope that things would work out' and that the new sovereign would 'exercise its considerable powers ... with considerable restraint'.

Jiang Zemin went to the podium and droned through his speech, replete with slogans and apt citations. His message to the Hong Kong compatriots was that he believed 'one country, two systems' would work. It was reassurance, of a kind. 'Watching the five starred red flag of the motherland rising, thinking of the foreign occupation of the motherland's territory and of how this story ended, one couldn't help feeling up and down as it was all condensed in this historic moment,' wrote Qian Qichen, the foreign minister, 'all over the world Chinese people felt the rain washing down, washing away China's century of humiliation and ushering in a new future for Hong Kong.'

In Beijing, fireworks exploded over Tiananmen Square and lit up the Forbidden City, within whose walls the emperor Daoguang and his counsellors had conceded the transfer of Chinese territory to the barbarians. A huge crowd celebrated, watched by a myriad of uniformed and plain-clothes security men. The scene was televised across China and intercut with images from Hong Kong, where the British were quitting the scene.

Chris Emmett, a British expatriate police officer, was in the police control room, where everyone gathered around the television. A champagne cork popped. There was a catch in his throat as he took off his Royal Hong Kong Police tags; all over Hong Kong officers were changing their tunics and badges. There was little for them to do. There was no trouble in the bars. A voice crackled over the radio to say that Chinese troops were streaming across the border. For years, Emmett recalled in a memoir, people had asked themselves what would happen after the handover. 'Now I knew the answer: nothing,' he wrote. As he drove home a young Chinese man roared up behind him on a motorbike, trailing from a pole attached to the pillion a huge red banner that bore the five stars of the People's Republic. He drew level, flashed the policeman an eye-catching smile and gave the thumbs-up sign.

Inside the convention centre, there was a subtle shift to Chinese protocol. The new chief executive, the amiable shipping magnate Tung Chee-hwa and the senior officials of his administration, many of them civil servants who had been trained by the British, were sworn in. Tung gave a waffling speech written to offend nobody. The Chinese-approved provisional legislature convened to pass its first laws. Glasses clinked once more as the Politburo sealed their approval of what was, by any measure, a victory.

Prince Charles, Patten and their entourages had left the hall and were driven down to *Britannia*. The rains had eased. The crowds, a mixture of Hong Kongers and expatriates, cheered and waved. A few hundred yards away at the Legislative Council, the Democrat leader Martin Lee and his allies, evicted from office, were shouting defiance from the balcony and proclaiming that democracy would never die. Now everybody was tired and wet, however, and there was almost a will for the night to end. Workmen were already taking down emblems of the crown on government buildings and removing portraits of the Queen.

The British politicians and their civil servants drove to Kai Tak airport, crowded onto a British Airways Boeing 777 and took off for London. Inside the Captain's Bar of the Mandarin Hotel, some of Patten's lieutenants, who were staying on, commiserated with friends over drinks. The governor had sent his last telegram to London. It read: 'I have relinquished the administration of this government. God save the Queen. Patten.'

Britannia's gangway rattled up and the yacht, with its distinguished passengers, turned into a murky and turbulent harbour, swollen with the typhoon's currents. The British had gone.

For the first time in this history, the people of Hong Kong themselves now stepped to the fore. There was a certain pragmatic reality behind the Chinese Communist Party slogan of 'Hong Kong people ruling Hong Kong'. The new chief executive, Tung Chee-hwa, was born in Shanghai. So was the head of the civil service, Anson Chan. Their families were among the late-arriving clans in Hong Kong who had fled Shanghai after the revolution. Many still spoke its melodious dialect, ate its soothing, sweet food and had replicated their old life, served by drivers, nannies and cooks on the circuit from office to country club, banquets, the racecourse and the beach. The Tung and Chan families were utterly different but shared a common heritage. The partnership between the two, uneasy though it was, would steer the Special Administrative Region through the first years of the new era.

Tung Chee-hwa was also Britain's choice to be chief executive. The heir to a shipping line, he crossed cultures and was at home among fellow tycoons. In person he was avuncular, courteous and steady. He was known as 'C.H.' among the establishment, which preserved the custom of calling some Chinese people by the initials of their given names. When he emerged as the preferred candidate to run Hong Kong, Chris Patten invited him to sit on the governor's Executive Council, where he did not rock the boat. He had the air of a patriarch and the comfortable manners of a gentleman, quite unlike some of the coarse cadres from the north. His family life was a model of rectitude. In 1997 he was in his sixtieth year and seemed the epitome of reassurance.

Tung did not like the vulgar press but he sat down with a group of foreign correspondents before the handover to muse on his world view. He spoke of 'Chinese values' such as a reverence for education, respect for elders, dedication to work, loyalty to family, diligence and frugality. When a Jewish correspondent present interjected that these could also be said to be Jewish values, or indeed universal values, he did not dissent. At one point, appearing bemused, he smiled and said the session was 'more like a philosophical debate than an interview'. The chief executive-designate had not lost the instinct for avoiding trouble which enabled him to straddle contending worlds. When the subject turned to his birthplace of Shanghai, it was natural to ask how his wealthy family had referred to the revolution of 1949. Had they spoken of 'the fall of Shanghai' or of 'the liberation of Shanghai'? The word for liberation, *jiefang*, is freighted with political import in China and is applied liberally to streets, parks, newspapers and anything thought worthy of the epithet. The chief executive-designate's brow furrowed. 'I really can't remember,' he said.

The Tung dynasty had lived out the vicissitudes of twentieth-century Shanghai; invasion by the Japanese, flight from the conquerors, a brief peacetime flourish of prosperity followed by the revolution of 1949 and escape with the defeated Kuomintang. Through it all their commercial acumen was intact. Tung's father, Tung Chao-yung ('C.Y.'), was a friend of Chiang Kai-shek and built up a shipping fleet in the years after the Second World War. He was not a man for illusions and diversified to Hong Kong and Taiwan before the collapse of Nationalist China. It was, on balance, unlikely that the family would speak of the 'liberation' of Shanghai.

Their fleet of ships, the Orient Overseas Line, had become a virtual flag carrier for the island of Taiwan. Its logo incorporated the plum blossom, the national flower of the Republic of China. The company thrived as east Asian nations became export-driven powerhouses while the Chinese mainland remained in righteous isolation. Tung senior built the biggest tanker in the world and bought the ocean liner *Queen Elizabeth*, a trophy purchase for the ages until it caught fire and sank at anchor in 1971.

The family did not lack political shrewdness. The young Tung Chee-hwa was sent to the Chung Wah Middle School, a left-wing institution set in the comfortable mid-Levels district of Hong Kong island. It seemed an odd choice for the son of a shipping magnate associated with the martial law regime in Taiwan, but in terms of credentials with the Communist Party it was a far-sighted investment. Tung went on to Liverpool University in the UK, where he gained a degree in marine engineering and became a fan of Liverpool Football Club. Then he went to work for General Electric in the United States before returning to take up a role in the family firm in Hong Kong. It was a trajectory followed by many sons of wealthy clans, whose patriarchs lived with one eye on the succession.

In 1982 C.Y. Tung died. His sons took over just as their fleet of big vessels was sailing into trouble. Worldwide demand was suffering from the aftermath of the oil shocks of the 1970s and a recession in the West. As a financial crisis threatened, Tung Chee-hwa scoured the banks and wealthy families of the Chinese diaspora but funds were not forthcoming. He turned to the pro-Chinese businessman Henry Fok. Born Fok Ying-tung in 1923 to a Tanka family in Hong Kong, Fok had made a fortune supplying goods to China during the Korean War in breach of a United Nations embargo. The Communist Party never forgot Fok's deeds and duly rewarded him with favours and preferment. With its blessing he had risen to lead the Chinese Chamber of Commerce in Hong Kong, built a business empire and became a philanthropist. In the early 1980s he was the man to go to when the big international banks had let Tung down.

Fok put together a syndicate to invest US$120 million in Orient Overseas, bailing out the company in 1986. The investment saved the Tung shipping empire. The tycoon himself was always engagingly vague about who had put up the money, referring only to 'Chinese friends'. The *Far Eastern Economic Review* later published an article which said the Bank of China had invested US$50 million, adding that it was joined by China Merchants, a state-controlled trading conglomerate.

After that, Tung's business expanded inside China. He returned to his birthplace, where he met Jiang Zemin, who served as mayor and party leader of Shanghai, in 1989. It was the consummation of a very Shanghainese affair.

The intermediary was Li Chuwen, the enigmatic and sophisticated functionary who had studied at St John's University in Shanghai in the 1930s, had gone to Yale and had become a Christian pastor before openly embracing Communism. (He may always have been an underground agent of the Chinese Communist Party instructed to infiltrate overseas communities.) Li served as the deputy director of the New China News Agency in Hong Kong from 1983 to 1988, retaining his ties to power brokers in Shanghai. He enjoyed a reputation as Jiang's confidant on society and politics in the colony, where he had mastered the files on anyone of importance. In the early 1990s he advised the Chinese leadership that Tung was perhaps a suitable figurehead for the new Hong Kong. Six years after their meeting in Shanghai, Jiang, by then the undisputed leader of China, publicly shook Tung's hand, anointing him for the job.

Tung had won the confidence of the Communist Party leadership and of the Hong Kong billionaires' club. It was a considerable accomplishment in a world of rivals. Henry Fok, the colony's richest tycoon Li Ka-shing, and the Kwok property family, among others, felt he was the right man. Both Tung and the Communist leaders kept any understandings to themselves, but the party liked to honour its long-term debts of gratitude. In 2018 a Chinese state-controlled shipping line, COSCO, paid the Tungs US$4.3 billion for their 68.7 per cent stake in the firm.

Tung may have embodied the wealthy Shanghainese exile who still served the motherland, but his chief secretary for administration, Anson Chan, outclassed him in patriotic pedigree. She was the granddaughter of a national hero, General Fang Zhenwu, who had joined the revolution which overthrew the Qing dynasty and later held office in the Kuomintang government. Fang fell out with Chiang Kai-shek and was assassinated by his agents as he left Hong Kong before the advancing Japanese army in 1941. 'Chiang Kai-shek wanted to fight the Communists and my grandfather wanted to fight the Japanese. So he was revered enough by the Beijing authorities that after his death the Communist Party erected a monument in his honour in his home town, which is in Anhui,' Chan recalled.

The Chan family were well-off, cultivated people who saw themselves as 'modern'. Chan's father was educated at the universities of Shanghai, Manchester and Columbia before his career in business began. Her mother was 'a staunch patriot ... also very much a renaissance woman' who became a leading Chinese contemporary ink artist well known for delicate landscapes. The family left Shanghai in 1948 and moved to Hong Kong, where Chan's grandmother owned properties and businesses.

'Like many of the other families we thought as soon as the civil turmoil dies down on the mainland we'll go back to Shanghai. But of course that was never to be,' she said. The clan was large. Chan had a twin sister, six brothers and an extended family numbering over a hundred. In 1950 her father died suddenly but the family wealth provided for them. Chan and her twin attended an Italian convent school, where she converted to Roman Catholicism and was baptised. She went to Hong Kong University, then joined the colonial civil service at a time when women cadets were paid less than men. She rose through its ranks by dint of icy professionalism and a reputation for astute judgement given in private. She was less successful in public relations. A media furore over the treatment of a child while she was in charge of the welfare department left her reticent and publicity shy. That did not harm her prospects inside an instinctively secretive colonial administration, and in 1987 she was promoted to the important post of secretary of economic services. Both the British and the Chinese kept an eye on her progress before Chris Patten picked her in 1993 to become the first woman and the first ethnic Chinese official to lead the civil service as its chief secretary through the handover. She was, he said later, one of the best people he ever worked with.

Chan's links with the mainland did not wither away. Her uncle, Professor Harry Fang, was an eminent Hong Kong surgeon who helped Deng Pufang, the son of Deng Xiaoping, and left confined to a wheelchair after the 1968 attack by Red Guards, to improve the rights of disabled people in China. This was a cause the paramount leader valued. It reinforced the sense among some Chinese officials that the hearts of the Chan family remained in the right place.

From time to time Chan received approaches from a family friend who was trusted by the Communist authorities, allowing her to maintain back channels of communication. In June 1995 the British authorised her to pay a secret visit to Beijing, where she met Qian Qichen, the foreign minister, and her fellow Shanghainese, Lu Ping, the head of the Hong Kong and Macau Affairs Office. She found Qian an urbane interlocutor and discovered that she had a lot of time for Lu Ping. But the talks confirmed her view that the chain of command in China was deliberately opaque and it was impossible to know who was taking the real decisions. It was not a good sign for managing relationships within 'one country, two systems'.

None the less, this was the card dealt to Tung and Chan, as he led Hong Kong into the new era and she made its government work. 'We just got on with what we had to do. What was uppermost in our minds was to make sure that in practice – other than, as Deng Xiaoping said, the change of flag and the change of sovereign power – nothing else would change.

'We got on with the day-to-day running of the civil service and the formation of policies and tried to settle minds so that those who bolted because they wanted an insurance policy would soon see that things were going well ... and would start coming back, which in the event actually happened. And in the early years there was considerable confidence in Beijing.

'We really didn't have any clue as to how our new masters would regard civil servants. We knew that the pro-establishment and the staunch loyalists in Hong Kong felt that the whole lot of us should have been thrown out and replaced by party loyalists. They gave us a particularly bad name in Chinese which if I translate it into English is "the bastard remnants of the colonial regime". That's how they termed us in the civil service. It's a very derogatory term. So we knew there were certain people who would be only too glad if we made mistakes.'

At first there was an eerie political calm. Chinese officials kept their distance and were often not even invited to official functions. It helped that localisation, in Chan's view, had gone smoothly. None of the expatriates who stayed on held sensitive security positions.

Chan felt that 'one country, two systems' was an experiment, one that required Hong Kong to stretch the framework as far as it could even if it met resistance from China. The practice of government meant a constant testing of boundaries; that was what day-to-day politics were all about. Tung, in contrast, was averse to confrontation, sought harmony and meant above all to avoid troubling the Chinese government. For a while, the balancing act worked. 'In the early years, certainly the four years I remained as chief secretary … they never attempted, not in word, not in deed, to interfere with a "high degree of autonomy" and "Hong Kong people ruling Hong Kong", she recalled.

There were good reasons for that. In 1997 China was on the threshold of the most profitable disruption of the world economy since the end of the Second World War, perhaps the most radical reordering of wealth and power since the nineteenth century. Its expansion was so fast and so far-reaching that it was changing the way that entire industries worked. It was creating whole new markets for exporters of commodities, from oil to minerals. Its own exports were flowing into markets where domestic producers had no hope of competing on price.

Thanks to the far-sighted rulers of Guangdong province, the industry of its people and the skills and finance provided by Hong Kong, southern China had started a world revolution in trade. The invention of the supply chain meant that its products could satisfy customers anywhere. The phenomenon of globalisation was in full swing. Seeking order, the major industrial nations wanted to bind China into a set of rules that sought to secure its own progress and to guarantee that all sides would win. The next step was for Beijing to join the World Trade Organisation, the group set up in Geneva in 1995 as the successor to the General Agreement on Tariffs and Trade. The Chinese leadership saw negotiations on membership as the route to a great prize. It would be crowned by a second accolade if the Olympic Games for 2008 were awarded to China, a decision that would come, like that on the WTO, in 2001. Nothing could be allowed to go wrong.

11

To Seek a Wider World

Hong Kong had made its fortune as a trading port on the China coast. Typhoons, plagues, wars and revolutions did not daunt its people, whose gifts for endurance and risk-taking were proverbial. But at the end of the twentieth century the city faced a new world. The colonial era was over, the rise of China was gathering pace and Hong Kong was no longer an Oriental curiosity but a centre in Asia of global finance and trade. If the opportunities were new, so were the risks.

The new Special Administrative Region swiftly found itself facing two threats. Its first challenge was an outbreak of lethal avian influenza which started across the border in southern China and spread to Hong Kong. Then came a financial crisis which began in Thailand, tore across Asia and almost destroyed Hong Kong's economic success. Both were defeated by determined and effective intervention. But they were tests for which nothing had prepared Tung Chee-hwa, who left the details to his subordinates. In their common theme of cross-border contagion they were omens of things to come.

Avian influenza, commonly known as bird flu, is a virus that has adapted itself to birds. It can be spread between animals and from animals to humans. It may be carried by wild birds but is more often found in domestic poultry. Livestock viruses were common in China, their spread exacerbated by the density of population, close contact between people and flocks, and crude practices of rearing and slaughtering. Across China, birds were reared on enclosed commercial farms or in backyards. They were sold alive in markets, then were killed on the spot or by the buyer at home. Hygiene was bad, for China, as its leaders insisted, was a developing country. Humans might be contaminated by handling dead infected birds, picking up avian fluids or touching surfaces soiled by droppings, blood or dirty feathers. The virus was highly pathogenic, which meant it could sicken the host. Whole flocks of birds could die within days of infection.

The virus also killed people, who died after suffering fever, aches, breathing difficulties and pneumonia. One early calculation indicated that 60 per cent of those who caught the virus died.

In 1996, the World Health Organisation recorded the outbreak of a type A bird flu variety in China which was christened H5N1. It was first isolated in a farmed goose in Guangdong province. Every year traders brought millions of live poultry into Hong Kong to meet local demand, which far outstripped supply from the territory's small-scale farms. The conditions of transport and storage were grim. Birds were crowded into stacks of cages, defecated on one another and squabbled in confinement until they were yanked out to have their throats cut. Cantonese cuisine valued the freshness of ingredients such as fish and poultry. The taste came at a high price.

The virus spread rapidly from Guangdong to Hong Kong, where for the first time it was transmitted to humans. Eighteen people were infected and six of them died. According to the WHO's later findings, none of them had worked with poultry. The potential impact on a closely packed community was frightening. Hong Kong had a high-grade cadre of scientists and experts in contagious diseases, and their remedy was drastic and effective. Cross-border shipments were stopped, after which the health authorities ordered a mass cull of every chicken in Hong Kong. Gruesome scenes of masked workers and heaps of dead poultry filled the television screens. The city's bustling live markets felt a little less lively. But the threat was contained. It was a success for the administration, which faced down vested commercial interests and ignored the political sensitivities involved in stopping a busy trade with the new motherland. It was to Tung's credit that he authorised these steps, but the decisions to react and intervene came from his civil service. It was an uneasy moment for a chief executive accustomed to corporate flattery and deference.

As bird flu faded from the headlines a financial typhoon swept across Asia. It started in Thailand, whose frivolous ruling elite had squandered the fruits of growth on cronyism, graft and conspicuous consumption. The Thai economy was in the hands of a clique, while many of its business dynasties were Sino-Thai clans. They had grown comfortable with corruption, cartels, rigged markets and smiling protectionism to shut out competitors. The good times were rolling in Bangkok. The Thai economy was growing at about 9 per cent a year, inflation was low, real estate and construction boomed, credit expanded and the wealthy snapped up assets abroad. The tycoons took out loans in American dollars, which were cheap because the central bank kept the Thai currency, the baht, pegged to the dollar at a fixed rate. In a royalist society it was natural that the bank should be governed by suave technocrats who hobnobbed with the plutocracy and moved in court circles, where all concerned were doing nicely out of the arrangement. It seemed a safe bet, even though most of the borrowers' revenues remained in baht while their liabilities were in dollars.

The mismatch caught the eye of international currency traders in the spring of 1997. In May the markets saw heavy selling of the baht. The Thai authorities defended the currency but their reserves were not up to the task. Nor was the prime minister, a venal, lizard-like military man, Chavalit Yongchaiyudh, who declared on 30 June that he would not devalue the baht. The government watched powerless as its economic miracle evaporated.

On 2 July, while all eyes in Hong Kong were still on the handover, Thailand gave in to the speculators. The baht lost half its value, the biggest finance company collapsed, the stock market imploded, building sites fell silent, millions lost their jobs and migrant workers trekked back to their villages. Bankruptcies spread as firms that had borrowed in dollars defaulted on their loans. The International Monetary Fund stepped in with a rescue package of some US$20 billion, contingent on reforms to financial regulation. The resilience of the Thai people, their Buddhist philosophy and an ingrained respect for the monarchy helped to preserve social order, but the stoic values exhibited by ordinary Thais did not extend to the elite. According to foreign investment bankers in Bangkok, some of the wealthiest and most powerful people in the country profited from inside information to speculate against their own currency as it went down. The 'Tom Yam Gung' crisis, so named after a favourite spicy soup, sowed the seeds of decades of political strife from which Thailand has yet to emerge.

By contrast, the impact in Indonesia was revolutionary. The vast archipelago, home to an energetic and economically dominant minority of ethnic Chinese, was a fast-growing nation. It ran a big trade surplus, kept inflation low and held substantial foreign currency reserves. But Indonesian companies had also borrowed heavily in dollars. Once again it seemed a safe bet. Their interest payments fell and their external debts depreciated as the Indonesian rupiah rose. Inevitably the central bank, the business oligarchy and the corrupt ruling circle around Indonesia's dictator, Suharto, were intertwined.

Between the summer of 1997 and the late spring of the following year, this house of cards collapsed. Speculative attacks on the rupiah forced the authorities into repeated devaluations. These led to a downward spiral as corporations raced to buy more dollars to fund their debts. The economy began to break apart. The stock market crumbled, the cost of imports soared, Indonesian government bonds were downgraded to junk status and firms shut their doors. Riots broke out in Jakarta and other cities. The rioters targeted ethnic Chinese traders, burnt out their homes and businesses, raped women and murdered whole families.

These atrocities awoke memories of the anti-Chinese pogroms of 1965 which had brought Suharto to power amid mass killings of alleged Communists. The security forces did little to stop them. Some of the violence was incited by people close to Suharto himself who sought to exploit the chaos. Frightened Chinese families sought sanctuary in Jakarta's five-star hotels, while smoke billowed from the city around them and gunfire sounded across the tennis courts. As they hid away, Indonesians arose en masse to demand *reformasi*, a slogan that came to mean regime change. Millions of protesters thronged the streets day after day, defying bullets and tear gas. Some in the elite wanted a Chinese-style crackdown.

Indonesia was on the brink of civil war when the head of the army, General Wiranto, went to Suharto and told him it was all over. 'I explained to him that we had to settle this in a spirit of harmony, that he and his family would be protected and this way the nation could be saved,' Wiranto said later. 'It was a difficult conversation but he was a wise man and he did not want to be remembered for shedding the blood of his own people.' The dictator stepped down on 21 May 1998. Democracy – messy, turbulent and imperfect – came to the world's most populous Muslim nation, where it has endured. There was no Tiananmen Square solution in Jakarta.

At first, the upheavals in southeast Asia were seen in Hong Kong as a matter of investment risk and potential losses. It soon became clear that the crisis was gathering pace. In Malaysia, it halved the value of the stock market. The central bank was unable to defend its currency, the ringgit, which fell by almost 50 per cent against the dollar. Bucking the trend, Malaysia's autocratic prime minister, Mahathir Mohamad, imposed capital controls, fixed the ringgit to the greenback and rejected aid from the IMF. His decisions averted a meltdown but destroyed the consensus within his ruling coalition. His deputy, Anwar Ibrahim, lost a power struggle with

Mahathir and was jailed on false charges of sex crimes. Their feud split Malaysian politics and set off two decades of turbulence. Rich in potential, Malaysia has neither achieved reform nor outgrown its ethnic and religious divisions between its Malay majority and the Chinese, Indian and Tamil communities.

Viewed from Hong Kong or Beijing, even the Malaysian crisis could seem petty. So were the slow-motion travails of the Philippines, where the currency halved and the stock market lost two-thirds of its value over the next few years. It was when the contagion came to South Korea, a mighty trading powerhouse, that alarm bells sounded in Hong Kong.

The 'miracle on the Han', named after the river which ran through Seoul, depended on gigantic conglomerates known as *chaebols*, brands like Samsung, Hyundai and Daewoo, whose tentacles extended from shipbuilding to cars, supermarkets, television networks and real estate. Controlled by low-profile dynasties, they had plunged into debt to fund expansion. They were vulnerable when the markets turned. The South Korean currency, the won, fell by more than half against the dollar and the stock market slumped. The Bank of Korea spent almost its entire foreign currency reserves to keep the banks afloat. Facing bankruptcy, the government was forced to accept a bailout of US$58 billion from the IMF, which imposed harsh conditions and compelled South Korea to abolish limits on foreign investment in local companies. The lesson was not lost on leaders in China, who had no intention of ever allowing such a thing to happen. As an open, capitalist trading economy, Hong Kong was used to 'manias, panics and crashes', but the damage inflicted on South Korea gave a warning that this was the worst financial crisis in Asia since the Second World War.

The impact of the financial crisis on Hong Kong was dramatic. Property and share values fell by about half. Unemployment rose and gross domestic product contracted by 4 per cent during the eighteen months after the handover from Britain. Yet the Hong Kong dollar was the only freely convertible currency in Asia that did not suffer devaluation. Its link to the US dollar in a band around HK$7.80 stood as a bulwark. It was also a temptation for speculators. They included the astute George Soros, although he loomed larger in demonology than fact. How Hong Kong defeated the hedge funds, saw off their strategy of attack, and returned the profits of intervention to the public through the stock market remains a textbook study of luck, skill and nerve in a financial crisis. And it was down to two men, the financial secretary, Donald Tsang, and the head of the Hong Kong Monetary Authority, the territory's de facto central bank, Joseph Yam.

Tsang, the son of a policeman, had worked his way up through the civil service. He was sharp, mercurial and bursting with confidence. He invariably wore a trademark bow tie. Yam, a more cerebral character, was a statistician, economist and administrator who had been involved in fixing the Hong Kong dollar peg in 1983. The pair answered to the chief executive, Tung Chee-hwa, but in their recollections it is noticeable how small a part Tung played in the day-to-day management of the crisis. In their own decision-making they showed that the ability to bend like bamboo, a willingness to abandon ideology and the capacity to change one's mind are often keys to success. As Tsang recalled: 'This is the sort of event you can't forget no matter how hard you may try. I went through some of the most traumatic internal struggles. As you know I was trained as a Chicago-oriented economist, believing devoutly in the open market and minimum government intervention.'

In a classically operating market like Hong Kong traders are free to take 'long' or 'short' positions. A long position is a bet that the price of an asset will rise; a short is a bet that it will fall. Traders take short positions by borrowing shares or sums of currency for a fee, selling them on the open market and buying them back at a lower price. The difference represents their profit. They may also make a 'contract for difference' representing a pure paper bet on the price. The common principle, though, is that the short seller must be able to cover their obligations. Shorting is rarer and more complicated than holding a long position and short sellers are not always popular. In mainland China they are sometimes labelled as 'unpatriotic'. But they play a crucial role in making a market work.

According to Yam, late in 1997 currency speculators began taking large short positions against the Hong Kong dollar with the aim of breaking the linked exchange rate. The authorities had little room to manoeuvre. 'Exchange controls are out of the question for Hong Kong,' Yam maintained, 'any attempt to introduce them, and to turn inwards on ourselves, would spell the end of our prosperity.' He believed that Hong Kong became a target because of the transparency of its financial system. 'We were singled out for our efficiency and predictability rather than for any fundamental flaws,' he said.

The peg to the US dollar worked through a system known as a currency board. Any change in the Hong Kong dollar's monetary base was matched by a corresponding change in the amount of foreign reserves held by the board.* It operated, Yam said, on 'autopilot'. A contraction in the monetary base caused interest rates to rise, an expansion caused them to fall. The mechanism ran smoothly and Hong Kong had ample reserves, but the interbank interest rate took all the strain; it was, Yam admitted, 'highly sensitive to speculative attack'.

The first attacks led to extreme volatility. On 23 October 1997, the overnight interest rate shot up to 300 per cent and the stock market tanked. The hedge funds, however, were caught in a trap. They had to borrow in the interbank market to fund their short Hong Kong dollar positions. The sky-high rates drove them to give up, unwinding their positions with heavy losses. The speculators retreated but Yam and the Hong Kong Monetary Authority came under sharp criticism for exposing the economy to interest rate shocks. Round one was over.

For Donald Tsang, the signs of a second round of market turmoil came in the spring of 1998. The financial secretary had watched as one country after another caved in, and was shocked when South Korea lost almost all its foreign exchange reserves in a couple of weeks. He felt that the future of Hong Kong depended on the link with the US dollar: 'We are conservative sovereign custodians of the Hong Kong treasury. I never believed that with a relatively small currency like Hong Kong's we could stand on our own without our dollar being buffeted.' Caught between much larger market and geopolitical forces, the Hong Kong dollar was vulnerable. 'In this world of ours, however well you behave you find yourself slaughtered.'

Tsang knew that the hedge funds were regrouping. He anticipated with dread another assault on the fixed exchange rate. 'Defending our dollar means the interest rate would go up … right through the roof. This could go on until we croak, probably in weeks, then we die, surrender, and break the link.' He did not know that the funds were accumulating Hong Kong dollars for a much more sophisticated play. They waited until the monsoon days of August, when trading was light, the latest GDP figures were poor and rumours that China might devalue its own currency were unsettling the markets. Then they struck.

* In Hong Kong the monetary base comprises certificates of indebtedness issued via the HKMA to back banknotes issued by commercial banks; notes and coins issued by the government; commercial bank balances kept at the HKMA; and Exchange Fund bills and notes issued on behalf of the government by the HKMA. Source: Hong Kong Monetary Authority.

Joseph Yam later explained the plan in simple terms. First, to avoid being squeezed by high overnight interest rates the funds built up stocks of Hong Kong dollars in the long-term debt market (Tsang called this 'their armoury'). At the same time they accumulated large short positions in the stock index futures market. 'They then sought to engineer extreme conditions in the money market by dumping huge amounts of Hong Kong dollars. This sell-off was meant to cause a sharp interest rate hike, which in turn would have sent the stock market plummeting. The collapse of the stock market would have enabled them to reap a handsome profit from the futures contacts they had taken out,' Yam explained.

The sums in Hong Kong dollars, according to Yam, were staggering. The HKMA reckoned speculators had borrowed more than HK$30 billion, costing them around HK$4 million a day in interest payments. They simultaneously held some 80,000 short contracts, which translated into a calculation that for every fall of one thousand points in the Hang Seng Index they stood to make HK$4 billion. If they could engineer such a fall within a thousand days they would break even. If they did it within a hundred days they would make HK$3.6 billion – almost half a billion US dollars. The crisis was at the door.

Donald Tsang was on a trip to Turkey to promote trade and investment when he got an urgent phone call from the secretary for financial services, Raphael Hui, who urged him to come home. The same message came from Yam at the HKMA. Tsang flew straight back to Hong Kong and went into a huddle with the two men, accompanied by the deputy chief of the HKMA, Norman Chan. The four officials and a handful of subordinates were the only ones who knew what was coming next.

'It was quite clear there was a congregation of hedge funds working together with some local newspapers, first speculating on the de-linking of the Hong Kong dollar and then massive shorting of our currency and securities market,' recalled Tsang. 'We spoke to stockbrokers and banks – said "Why are you shorting?" They replied: "Not us! We are acting largely on client instructions." Who were their clients? The clients, we believe, are Soros and company. And others. There's a lot of nominal accounts going through various places, the Virgin Islands, and all the rest of it. You were never able to trace exactly who these guys are. But we felt the heat.'

Quickly, if unwillingly, Tsang accepted that his Chicago free market principles would have to be jettisoned if Hong Kong was not to face the fate of its Asian neighbours. Norman Chan warned him that if they did not act interest rates would hit 50 per cent and stay there for weeks, 'and we will die, of course'.

The weight of responsibility felt awesome. 'That's why I had sleepless nights – the thought of losing all the savings Hong Kong had made through our colonial days right up to that point,' Tsang recalled. He and his colleagues felt outrage at the cold injustice of the situation. 'We asked ourselves – we've got no debt, zero debt. We never borrowed. Unlike Thailand and many others in Asia we had no foreign debt. And we had over US$100 billion in foreign exchange reserves. We struggled. And eventually I decided we had to move.'

In Franklin Roosevelt's phrase, there was nothing to fear except fear itself, even though fear and greed were driving the markets. Put simply, the huge reserves – the third largest in the world – meant that the authorities held enough foreign currency to cover all Hong Kong dollars in circulation seven times over and could always guarantee to buy or sell US dollars at a rate around HK$7.80. The peg could not be broken if they kept their nerve.

That gave Tsang and Yam the confidence to strike back. The Hong Kong team devised a plan. Instead of fighting in the trenches of the currency markets they would outflank the hedge funds by taking the offensive to the stock exchange. The Hong Kong government would buy billions of dollars' worth of shares in the leading companies on the Hang Seng Index. It would thwart the speculators, turn the tide and restore confidence. The move was a break with the laissez-faire doctrine of non-intervention which had been Hong Kong's guiding philosophy throughout the colonial era. For that reason, Tsang was set on an exit strategy. In a stroke of populist inspiration, he decided that the government shares would be sold back to the public through an index-linked instrument called the Tracker Fund.

Success was not guaranteed. On 12 August, Tsang went to see his boss, Tung Chee-hwa. He felt that the chief executive did not know the ins and outs of the operation in great detail but understood that it must be done. The law stipulated that the financial secretary, not the chief executive, was the ultimate custodian of the foreign exchange fund. So the buck really stopped where Tsang sat. This may have explained why the leader of Hong Kong remained calm: he knew it was his financial secretary's problem.

On Friday 14 August the Hong Kong government went into the market at 10 a.m. It was a cloak-and-dagger intervention. The need for secrecy until the last minute was paramount. But there was a technical obstacle. Hong Kong did not have a government broker to act in the stock market.

And Tsang did not trust the big international houses. As he put it, they had their own clients, namely the hedge funds. As for the major banks like HSBC, he felt they had their own agendas.

So Tsang and his team turned to medium-sized Chinese stockbrokers, the unsung footsoldiers of the marketplace. They placed a flurry of phone instructions – it doubtless helped that Cantonese is a language rich in slang for money. At first the calls with government orders brought surprise, then the brokers got into their stride. 'The local Chinese brokers we dealt with were very efficient,' said Tsang. 'They knew how the market worked and they moved quickly. We found also that women were very good traders in crisis situations. Most of the major stockbrokers we dealt with in that battle were women. And so was the person fronting for HKMA, giving out buying orders. Interesting but frightening as well!'

The financial secretary arranged reinsurance by calling up the finance minister in China, Xiang Huaicheng, to tell him of the move. That afternoon the premier, Zhu Rongji, issued a statement backing the Hong Kong authorities.

The flow of government money into blue-chip shares turned the tide. More importantly, it changed the psychology of the market. But it was a test of nerves on all sides. 'It was very frightening at one stage because we seemed to be the only buyer in the market. At the peak of the battle we were spending a hundred million dollars every five minutes,' recalled Tsang.

The hedge funds battled it out until the end of August. 'They brought in a few currency traders, gunslingers from New York, to Hong Kong to deal with us but they discovered (a) we had deep pockets and (b) we were fearless at that stage,' said Tsang. 'That was it. There was no turning back.' By the end of the month the Hong Kong government owned US$15 billion worth of shares in leading companies.

Then it had a stroke of luck. In early September, attention on Wall Street turned to the collapse of a top hedge fund, Long Term Capital Management, whose derivatives operations were the inverse of its brand name. Fourteen global financial institutions were exposed to losses of more than US$4 billion. The Federal Reserve Bank of New York corralled them to organise a bailout. In the same month the Russian government defaulted on its domestic bonds, sending shocks through the fixed-income markets. The action had moved on from Asia.

The Hong Kong government celebrated its success, but the intervention was controversial. Among the most trenchant critics was David Webb, a widely respected private investor and shareholder activist. 'By directly intervening, the government is like a referee running with the ball – things will never be the same again,' he said. 'When does "trading" become a "speculative attack"? When does "intervention" become "interference"?' He believed that Hong Kong had abandoned a free market philosophy that had served it well. It was a view held by many in the financial elite who, lacking Webb's guts and independence, did not voice it in public.

The counter-argument was put by Joseph Yam at the end of that turbulent year. 'Our actions in August were not the end of non-interventionism, nor an abandonment of our free market principles but a measure taken to ensure that those principles prevailed. Free markets cannot mean markets that can be freely manipulated, particularly by big players operating in small markets. Not to have acted would have been the very height of irresponsibility.' The government's shares were sold off at a profit to the public through the Tracker Fund, which remains a popular and heavily traded index investment.

Two lasting reforms were put in place in Hong Kong. On 5 September 1998 the HKMA announced seven technical measures to make the linked exchange rate 'less susceptible to manipulation by speculators to produce extreme conditions in the interbank market and interest rates'. In early 1999 the stock exchange, the futures exchange and the clearing houses were merged into a single holding company, Hong Kong Exchanges and Clearing Limited. Like the intervention, the reform caused controversy. Donald Tsang recalled the outrage, with brokers complaining that it amounted to confiscation and state control: 'We literally told the stockbrokers: "if you don't do as we propose, we shall follow Plan B, i.e. nationalise the exchange by law, and then float it off later."' Grudgingly, they complied.

'They are all laughing all the way to the bank now,' Tsang observed, 'as the HKEx share is now trading nearly one hundred times its original listed price. That is why we are now on par with New York and London in soaking in funds from all over the world.'

The financial secretary took away one big thought from the drama of 1998. He dreamed of a single Asian reserve currency that would be one of three major blocs alongside the dollar and the euro, trading around the clock for eight hours each. But his exploratory talks with the Japanese and the Singaporeans went nowhere. In 1998, when the rise of China and its yuan currency were not yet fully appreciated, it was an idea before its time.

Hong Kong, China and the rest of the world were however on the cusp of enormous changes that would transform through globalisation the way people traded, worked and thought in the new century. Decisions taken by a small circle of economic and financial policymakers would alter the lives of millions who knew little and understood less about the process. There was little political debate about it, and when voters later realised what had been done, their reaction stunned the elite that had brought the new order into being.

12

The Rivals

Far to the south of Hong Kong, on the Straits of Malacca, stood another monument to the colonial past. Sprinklers hissed on the lawns, while Gurkha guards stood silent and an aide waited in the shade of the rain trees that lined the avenue to the Istana, a white Palladian building where the Sage of Singapore, Lee Kuan Yew, had his office.

No figure like Lee existed in Hong Kong. In 1996, he was the senior minister of the former British colony he had led from independence until his retirement from the premiership in 1990. Singapore was an independent city-state. A multiracial republic, it had separated from the Malaysian Federation in 1965, prospering thereafter through trade, finance and investment under a party that held regular elections but was always returned to power. Hong Kong and Singapore eyed one another with a mixture of rivalry and curiosity.

In his later years the senior minister dispensed advice to world leaders, who saw him as a statesman larger than the stage on which he had conducted his political life. Henry Kissinger, who called him 'extraordinary', is said to have expressed relief that Lee was born to apply his formidable talent to ruling tiny Singapore, not China. Lee's preferred tone was the austere warning. It was founded on a hard view of human nature and the balance of power. In the mid-1990s he warned the industrialised democracies that they must take China into the world trading system or risk a conflict.

Lee believed that as long as a country was allowed to trade then it could avoid aggression. The rise of Japan from the late nineteenth century was his favourite example, perhaps because he had lived through the capture of Singapore by the Imperial Japanese Army during the Second World War. In the first half of the twentieth century Japanese militarists and financiers had pushed to conquer possessions and markets in the quest to sustain a population of 100 million crammed into their island chain. They felt the big powers were choking them.

'World War Two was caused because of empires and protectionism,' Lee said. 'Arising out of the depression of the 1930s every empire put up its barriers and fences around itself.' The Japanese built up their own tariff walls and then decided to include China in their empire, Lee argued, 'and the Americans thought that enough was enough, before you had a colossus to deal with.' In his view the United States decision to embargo oil to imperial Japan set off a world war.

Modern China was different but the principle was the same, Lee held. Admit a nation to the international exchange of goods and services and 'they can stay within their boundaries and their excess energy and skills and drive are used in producing goods and services or making investments and improving their people's lot.' Denied this opportunity, the temptation to grow by force was strong. 'If the West tries to isolate China economically it must be prepared for a military conflict at some stage,' said Lee. The Chinese response 'must be' to build up a sphere of influence dominated by their own goods and services – 'and that is bound to lead to conflict.'

By the mid-1990s the rise of China defied adjectives. The Pearl River Delta had become the world's largest industrial processing zone. The area including Hong Kong and Macau had developed into one of the biggest metropolitan regions on the planet as rice fields, temples and ancestral graves vanished from a bulldozed landscape and the sky grew murky with industrial pollution. Only numbers could tell the story and they were hard to grasp. Between 1979 and 1995 Hong Kong investors signed 23,605 'co-operative production' contracts with entities in Guangdong and invested some US$14 billion. The investments underwrote a transformation dubbed 'out-processing'. At first it turned the local manufacturing system on its head. Then it changed the relationship between China and the global economy inside out.

In the vanguard was the Hong Kong family firm Li & Fung, founded in Guangzhou in 1906 by Fung Pak-liu, an English teacher, and Li To-ming, a merchant. Among the first companies financed entirely by Chinese capital to export to the West, it grew rapidly from its beginnings trading in porcelain, silk, bamboo, rattan ware and jade until the Japanese invasion of south China forced it to move to Hong Kong in 1937. Li & Fung prospered in the era of cheap manufacturing in Hong Kong, but it was among the first companies to realise that the formula for profit lay in moving manufacturing back to China while keeping its base in the territory. It was a prime example of the historic and cultural links which bound many Hong Kong businesses to Guangdong. By the mid-nineties it was run by two brothers, William and Victor Fung, who divided corporate management and the firm's external diplomacy between them.

The initial line of business was re-exports. Raw materials or half-finished products were shipped from Hong Kong into China for processing. The Chinese factories returned the finished goods to Hong Kong, from where they were re-exported to world markets, benefiting from the colony's tariff agreements with its partners. It was a profitable formula, but Li & Fung did not sit complacently astride a stream of revenue. As Chinese factories grew more sophisticated and a slew of rival ports opened up at Yantian, Huizhou, Zhuhai and Shekou, and at Guangzhou itself, they perfected the management of a 'supply chain' weaving together raw materials, labour, manufacturing, transport and accounting into a seamless offer to overseas buyers, who were often bewildered and helpless when confronted by the reality of business in China.

This was the second great migration of Chinese industry in half a century. Between 1949 and 1951, according to a paper co-authored by Victor Fung, the industrial development of Hong Kong had surged due to the movement of capital, equipment and skilled workers from the Shanghai and Wuxi areas of China: 'It was almost a wholesale transfer of industrialisation from the long established and second largest Asian manufacturing base of 1920 to 1940.' Hong Kong itself had now experienced a 'transferred industrialisation'. Three decades on, the Fung clan were prime movers in a successive wave of development that spread back across the border and flowed up the Pearl River Delta. By the early 1990s three-quarters of Hong Kong manufacturers were operating on the mainland, more than 60 per cent of Hong Kong's exports were made in China and the manufacture of 80 per cent of its traditional goods such as toys, shoes, travel goods and handbags had shifted. In essence, after the reforms of 1978 the Hong Kong industrial economy incorporated the cities of the Delta.

The results inside China were extraordinary. Deng Xiaoping had called for Guangdong to attain a target he dubbed the *xiaokang*, or 'a little well-off' level. According to the *People's Daily*, in terms of income per head this was achieved eight years ahead of plan in 1992, although other criteria such as education, technology and a market economy were yet to be fulfilled. In 1993, the Special Economic Zone of Shenzhen witnessed gross domestic product growth of 30 per cent. With only 0.25 per cent of the Chinese population, the zone generated 1.35 per cent of national GDP.

The Statistical Yearbook of Guangdong for 1996 gave a snapshot of the long-run change from 1985 to 1995. Over the decade the output valued in yuan of electronics industries in the Pearl River Delta (excluding Hong Kong) multiplied more than twenty-fold, that of textiles grew by a factor of ten, food processing grew fifteen times and plastics by twenty times.

What excited the Fungs – and began to capture the eyes of executives around the world – was that the pace of growth was accelerating. In the five years after 1990, the *annual* rate of growth in electronics was more than 40 per cent, that of food processing was 58 per cent, plastics was 41 per cent and textiles were 30 per cent. Across key industries, Guangdong was witnessing expansion of more than 40 per cent every twelve months. The result was that a trail pioneered by small manufacturers from Hong Kong and Macau began to draw in capital and management from further afield. In the next phase, Taiwanese firms began to relocate computer manufacturing to the mainland. Encouraged by facilitators like Li & Fung, companies began to trust their Chinese operations with research and development as well as with making the products. Before most Western competitors had woken up to it, China had already embarked on a second transformation from primary to advanced manufacturing, with 'added value' increasing constantly. The multinationals began to step gingerly into the fray. The world was taking notice.

One of the earliest and most daring reformers was Zhu Rongji, the forceful mayor of Shanghai. In 1990, when the shroud of Tiananmen Square hung over business with China, Zhu led a delegation to Hong Kong, where he addressed financiers and industrialists with verve and self-deprecating humour. 'When it comes to cleverness, Shanghainese are no match for the Cantonese and even less so for Hong Kong people because they lack business sense,' he declared. After decades of a planned economy, Zhu said, people in Shanghai had 'rather poor market concepts' and a limited understanding of what it meant to open up to the world. The audience sat enthralled as Zhu laid out a vision of a modern, competitive and flexible Shanghai integrated once again into the global trading system. The Hong Kong speech was the first time some outsiders had heard of it.

John Bond, later group chairman of HSBC Holdings, recalled experiencing a 'lightbulb moment' after listening to Zhu outlining his ambitious plans for reform. In Bond's view, the challenge facing the Chinese government was to create demand. The nation's vast economy was inert after decades of Maoist socialism. Zhu and the reformers wanted to spark life by exporting goods and earning money that would flow into cities and the Special Economic Zones. The velocity of money would increase, spending would rise and a consumer society would be born.

Bond was conscious that he and his bank, with its long history in China, could not ignore what was happening. The Hongkong and Shanghai Bank had been in business before the Suez Canal opened and before Hong Kong was connected to the international telegraph network. Its institutional memory of turbulence and change in China was ingrained, as was the sense of opportunity with which the bank responded to this latest stage of its long revolution. 'It would have been unthinkable for HSBC not to be in the first wave of people going into China as it opened up,' said Bond. 'HSBC was founded in 1865, it opened simultaneously in Shanghai and Hong Kong. It had the explicit purpose of financing trade, which was mainly conducted between mainland Chinese and overseas Chinese.' Trade finance was still a core business of HSBC, Bond knew, as the overseas Chinese communities prospered in southeast Asia. 'Successful banks have successful customers,' he maintained. Bond liked to recall that as late as 1820, China's economy had been substantially larger than America's. Speaking in a 2003 interview quoted in a history of the bank, he posed a modern version of the 'Needham Question': 'how can 22 per cent of the world's population account for less than four per cent of the world's GNP?'

The Chinese masses voted with their feet. They streamed into the coastal zones from provinces and regions deep in the interior, eager to seize the opportunity to earn and save in a cash economy. There were no free and fair elections in China, but the people showed their approval of the new policies by the simplest possible method – participation. The influx grew so large that the authorities struggled to enforce permits and regulations to control the flow of migrants.

Conditions in the Special Economic Zones were harsh. Foreign activists later became involved in campaigning but the credit for the first realistic reporting on workers' lives belonged to the Chinese media itself. In May 1993 the *People's Daily* published photographs of the dormitories for factory girls in Baoan, a district of Shenzhen, depicting bored girls squatting on bunks, queueing in the canteen and crowding around communal water taps. It commented that this was a hard, lonely life. On 19 November 1993, eighty workers were burnt alive in a craftware factory in Shenzhen because the emergency exits were locked. The tragedy was widely covered in China and caused a storm of comment as people began to realise that the new economy was not an easy route to riches. It was a sign of the times that in the same year the ministry of labour held its first press conference since the foundation of the People's Republic in 1949.

China was in theory a workers' state. But divisions in the working class emerged as the economy developed. There were two million workers in Shenzhen alone. Many of them had no medical or accident insurance, nor any pension schemes. These were privileges reserved for employees of state enterprises and residents of big cities. The local press exposed companies that failed to pay wages, withheld some pay as an unexplained 'deposit', sacked workers if they suffered an accident, did not allow holidays and dismissed staff without compensation.

In September 1993 the *Workers Daily* published a bold article stating that China had been studying a labour law for fifteen years but had failed to enact one. A labour code, a social security net and better protection were needed. The paper singled out the new foreign-funded and private enterprises for criticism. It said their employees were 'recklessly' hired on illegal contracts. They had no job security or insurance. In Zhuhai, a booming port, only one in ten workers had a valid contract. Workers could be laid off at will. In addition, the paper said foreign firms broke the law by not paying the state labour insurance fees; more than half the companies in one district of Shenzhen were guilty of this.

At foreign-funded firms the average working day lasted ten to fourteen hours, the paper reported. Some employees were at their job for twenty-eight hours continuously. Certain firms made overtime compulsory but did not pay extra for it. In Zhuhai, workers were left penniless at one plant when the owners vanished, having embezzled their wages.

Life in the workplace was Dickensian. Workers spent their shifts crammed into 'extremely hot, noisy and polluted workshops'. A survey of seven joint ventures in Zhuhai found levels of toxicity eight to ten times the national standard. In Xiamen, almost one worker in ten at a factory had lost all or part of a finger. It was common for managers to forbid talking. Bosses beat up anyone who complained. Dormitories were searched. The worst conditions, the paper said, were in factories making plastics, toys, textiles, shoes and other labour-intensive items. These were, of course, the very sectors where Hong Kong investors predominated.

Not surprisingly, Chinese workers fought back. They were not the docile robots of occidental cliché. Strikes and disputes proliferated. Often these were unofficial because the trade unions, obedient to the interests of the state, sided with factory owners. When clashes and rioting broke out, the security forces moved in with a heavy hand. The government edged towards legislation, unemployment insurance and compensation schemes. In Guangdong, where officials foresaw damage to production and profits, the local government of Foshan, a particularly grim industrial zone, pioneered a compulsory social insurance scheme funded by a 20 per cent levy on wages to pay benefits to those 'deprived of the ability to work' such as pregnant women, the sick, the handicapped, the old and the unemployed. Universal coverage remained an aspiration. Most investors took little notice of the turbulence rocking Chinese society and relied on authoritarian rule to keep it in check. At this stage Chinese factories had not perfected the efficiency which later made their offer compelling. There was, however, one criterion on which they were unbeatable: price.

To the dismay of Leftists, there was no doubt that China was committed to 'opening up' to the world economy. The *People's Daily* sang the approved chorus line: in 1978 foreign trade was worth US$20 billion, but this figure had soared to more than US$195 billion in 1993. From ranking thirty-second in the world as a trading nation China was heading for the top ten.

In the advanced industrial democracies, the economic rebirth of China attracted intense interest in the top ranks of business and government but commanded little public attention. The Cold War was over; a war coalition had expelled Iraq from Kuwait, restoring the international order; the European Union was set to expand; and in the United States a new administration under Bill Clinton promised prosperity and growth. The thinker Francis Fukuyama, formerly head of policy planning at the State Department, suggested that the success of the liberal capitalist order meant the 'end of history'. In an era spared ideological conflict, so ran the consensus, nations could establish a set of pragmatic rules to trade with one another in the most efficient way.

As early as 1986, China had applied for membership of the General Agreement on Tariffs and Trade, known as GATT. Established in 1948, the organisation was set up to cut tariffs and to reduce barriers to trade. Its original preamble desired 'reciprocal and mutually advantageous agreements' and committed its members to 'the elimination of discriminatory treatment in international commerce'. At its lakeside headquarters in Geneva, trade diplomats and ministers haggled over arcane matters that tended to baffle and bore the uninitiated. The wife of one British envoy to the organisation greeted her guests to a dinner table set with silver, crystal and linen with the piercing injunction that 'nobody is to spoil the evening by mentioning the GATT.'

No one at the Chinese mission took a similar attitude. The *People's Daily* declared that admission to GATT would complete China's entry to the United Nations, which the People's Republic had joined in 1971. It would make China a great commercial power. About 85 per cent of its trade was with GATT nations, so membership would help it grow, while adopting agreed standards would raise the quality of Chinese products. There was another motive. The cost of modernisation was a rise in imports. In 1993, China ran a trade deficit of more than US$12 billion.

The major trading powers had agreed to transform the GATT into a new body, the World Trade Organisation, which would come into being on 1 January 1995. A myth has grown up that China was ushered into the WTO with little fuss by vested interests pushing for globalisation and a liberal free trade agenda. In this telling, Wall Street, the Fortune 500 and sundry conspirators manipulated policymakers to suit their aims. The reality traced in the documents is different. The road to accession for China in 2001 was long, painstaking and hard-fought.

One participant with a ringside seat was Stuart Harbinson, a Hong Kong civil servant who from 1994 to 2002 was the territory's representative to the Geneva trade bodies and later served as chief of staff to one WTO director-general, Supachai Panichpakdi, and special adviser to another, Pascal Lamy. He described the transformation this way: 'The GATT was a bit of a gentleman's club. Nobody knew what it was. It was completely off the radar.' The GATT dealt only with trade in goods but the new WTO would deal with services and intellectual property, using a strengthened mechanism to settle disputes. 'It was a step change,' said Harbinson.

The countdown to the birth of the WTO was fraught. China argued that as a developing country it should be allowed to keep its tariffs at 30 per cent. Its trading partners wanted to cut that to 15.5 per cent, on a par with Mexico. Their more challenging demands included the opening of the Chinese market, respect for intellectual property rights and enforcement of patent and trademark laws. Beijing had made some concessions, cutting tariffs to 7.5 per cent on 3,500 products.

Negotiations were subject to shocks. On 1 January 1994, the government abolished its fixed exchange rate of 5.8 yuan to the US dollar, acknowledging the gap between the official rate and the 'black market' rate at which most offshore business was done. The authorities set a new rate of 8.28 yuan under a tightly managed floating exchange rate system. On paper it amounted to a huge devaluation of about 30 per cent. There was outrage among China's rivals. Critics saw the country as a giant emerging predator. The devalued yuan became a totem for those who later argued that China had set out to destroy industries and to conquer markets with products that nobody could compete against on price. In its extreme form this version of history postulated a conspiracy hatched in Beijing to achieve global economic domination by ruining other nations. The dispute is arcane but politically toxic and hard to resolve, not least because a currency's exchange rate is just one among several factors which influence a nation's competitiveness. In practice, as *The Economist* pointed out, the offshore rate at which four-fifths of China's trade was done barely varied at all.

From a Chinese perspective, the move redressed a long period of overvaluation and amounted to 'integration' of the dual rate. Chinese economists argued that it was a laudable move to a more market-based system which corresponded to reality. 'The real devaluation of the currency was 6.7 per cent given the fact that eighty per cent of forex transactions then were done in the swap market,' said an official commentary. 'The rate integration changed the long-standing situation of renminbi overvaluation ... the renminbi strengthened by 4.8 per cent against the US dollar from 1994 to the end of 1997.' Taking into account high domestic inflation in China, it argued, the real appreciation of the yuan against the US dollar was 39 per cent over the period.

In the crucial year of 1994, however, the devaluation complicated the task of the Chinese negotiators at Geneva, who faced an increasingly hostile atmosphere. As autumn faded to a grey Swiss winter it became clear that China could not join the WTO at its launch. On 19 December the nineteenth round of GATT negotiations failed to break the deadlock, despite what the official media termed the 'extreme sincerity and flexibility' of the Chinese delegation. John Bond, the HSBC banker, grasped China's strategic objective through his extensive private conversations with its leaders. 'This was by far their best way to secure the future of their manufacturing – and ultimately it meant employment,' he recalled in 2019.

'China needs the WTO, the WTO needs China,' said Gu Yongliang, the chief delegate. But commentators in Beijing claimed that the USA and others were determined to use 'power politics' to put the brakes on their nation's rise.

Among hawkish nationalists, the mood grew dark. Three authors, Song Qiang, Zhang Zangzang and Qiao Bian, penned a best-selling polemic with the title *China Can Say No*. It claimed that foreign enterprises, not China, had a bad record on human rights. The foreigners inflicted humiliations on their employees. One Korean boss forced workers to kneel, it claimed, while many Chinese felt that 'if a pretty young lady takes a job in a foreign firm ... it is to become the sweetheart of the foreign boss.' The foreign presence was 'unwholesome', it argued, a threat to the moral values of China and the integrity of its national economy. Language like this evoked disastrous episodes in China's history, but it may unintentionally have strengthened the hand of its negotiators. Henceforth Chinese envoys in Geneva could justify hard bargaining by pointing to recalcitrant opponents at home. Their foreign interlocutors could warn their capitals of the risks posed by an isolated and aggrieved China.

The process of accession was complex and the record shows that every step was difficult for China. It was put through a tough negotiation with each major trading partner. The United States held the key. It was the biggest economy in the world and the most powerful player in the WTO. The US and China recognised that a deal could be in their interests, but political pressures in Washington and Beijing did not make it easy.

Under President Bill Clinton, American policy had evolved from punishing the 'butchers of Beijing' to negotiating with the new leaders of China, Jiang Zemin and Zhu Rongji. In 1992 Clinton linked the annual renewal of China's 'most favoured nation' status to its human rights record. The policy was soon dropped. In 1996 Clinton chose a sharp lawyer, Charlene Barshefsky, as the US trade representative. She led the negotiations with China for the rest of his administration.

For the next four years the political commitment to integrating China into the world economy proved durable. Talks between the US and China survived the Asian financial crisis of 1997–8 and a deep freeze after the American bombing of the Chinese embassy in Belgrade during the Kosovo war of 1999, which Clinton called an accident and apologised for. Hard bargaining between the Americans and the Chinese captured the headlines; there were twists and turns, last-minute dramas and photogenic dashes to and from capitals. Internal WTO documents show that the rest of the world also engaged in a protracted, assiduous and successful effort to extract heavy concessions from China. The original 'restricted' report of the working party on accession provides an invaluable companion to the battle. It also illustrates how the Chinese government saw its objectives, which were not the same as those imagined by some of its counterparts.

As their chief negotiator, the Chinese side settled on a formidable and experienced trade expert, Long Yongtu. His mandate was one of the most

complex that had ever faced a Chinese envoy on the world stage. Long had
to balance compromises struck in Geneva with political reaction at home,
constantly gauging the mood in Beijing, referring back to his masters on
details while always keeping his eyes on the prize. China had committed
itself to establishing a 'socialist market economy', Long Yongtu told the
nations gathered in Geneva. A reform package in 1994 had brought change
to banking, finance, taxation, investment, foreign exchange and foreign
trade. State-owned enterprises, he said, had been reformed. The Chinese
currency was convertible on the current account, which meant it was
freely exchanged for goods and services. It was stable in value.

If all this sounded as music to the ears of the trade diplomats, it came
with a blunt message. China, said Long, was a huge nation of 9.6 million
square kilometres (3.7 million square miles) with a population of 1.25
billion at the end of 1998. It was still a developing country 'and therefore
should have the right to enjoy all the differential and more favourable
treatment accorded to a developing country'.

Here lay the origins of much dispute. China's rivals knew it was industrialising at a fast pace, moving up the technology ladder and deploying
its arsenal of state controls to spur development; all this behind a protective screen of tariffs and regulatory barriers.

The working party met behind closed doors twenty-one times between
March 1996 and 17 September 2001. Its labours paused in the summer of
1998 and there were no meetings at all during the year of tension between
the US and China in 1999. But in early 2000 the trade diplomats got back
to bargaining.

The Hong Kong delegation in Geneva had a privileged view of the
process. Hong Kong had joined the GATT in 1986, ending a paradox by
which the colony's interests were represented by Britain; sometimes this
had required a member of the British delegation to stand up and present
Hong Kong's position on, say, textile quotas, which may have opposed the
United Kingdom's own stance. The colony won respect for its principles
and fair administration. It was natural for Hong Kong to move seamlessly
into the WTO in 1995 and at the time of writing, in 2020, it had never had
a trade complaint lodged against it.

The Chinese delegation in Geneva seemed fascinated by Hong Kong's
success in a tough multilateral forum. They were adamant that nothing
should spoil it during the handover to China in 1997. This was a case
where 'one country, two systems' served Chinese interests. Therefore it was
scrupulously observed.

A few months before the handover in 1997, the Chinese ambassador, Wu Jianmin, invited Stuart Harbinson to tea. 'He wanted to talk to me about my future and said that he thought that I'd been doing a very good job to represent Hong Kong in the GATT and he wanted to let me know that as far as China was concerned they'd be extremely happy if I were simply to continue in the role.'

China had sent one of its best and brightest to Geneva; Wu Jianmin was a linguist who had interpreted in French for Mao Zedong and Zhou Enlai, served as spokesman for the foreign ministry and held a string of postings abroad. The ambassador was well-informed. He knew that as an expatriate member of the Hong Kong government, Harbison could retire in 1997 with his pension. Wu said that the Chinese delegation would understand if he did that, but they hoped he would stay on. 'He said he could give me an assurance that China would not in any way suggest that Hong Kong should behave in a certain fashion or should say certain things – it would be totally hands off. Such was the atmosphere of the time,' said Harbinson.

After the handover, the Hong Kong delegation was under instructions to follow every step towards China's accession but not to say anything in the meetings or in public. Many other trade representatives, who had assumed the Hong Kong team would simply vanish into the folds of the Chinese delegation, were surprised to see them there. It was, of course, a subtle way for the Beijing government to show that it kept its pacts.

China needed every means of persuasion it could get. The documents show that it was challenged about its statistics, pressured to open its markets and told to dismantle its apparatus of discrimination against foreign businesses. As the record stated: 'The representative of China … confirmed that China would provide the same treatment to Chinese enterprises, including foreign-funded enterprises, and foreign enterprises in China. China would eliminate dual pricing practices as well as differences in treatment accorded to goods produced for sale in China in comparison with those produced for export.'

These were big promises. China also undertook to abandon its bureaucratic barriers to imports – methods such as 'product registration and certification, internal taxation, price and profit controls … licensing for imports and distribution or sale'. Its opponents dissected its taxes, business licences, product testing and inspections. They focused on detail down to profit margins on pharmaceuticals, the inspection regime for boilers and the intricate rules governing duty on spirits. 'The nature of WTO accession negotiations is that they're very tough, because you want to get in,' Harbinson observed. 'China got squeezed a lot.'

At the time public health was not a top priority in trade relations. It is none the less shocking to read that China, a country with a high mortality rate from respiratory diseases, was compelled to agree that 'immediately upon accession ... the number of retail outlets selling imported cigarettes would be substantially increased throughout the territory'.

Back in Beijing, Long Yongtu and his negotiators faced fierce criticism that they were giving too much away. Time and again he had to rely for political cover on Zhu Rongji, who became premier in March 1998. It was a bruising, and for some Chinese reformers, a disillusioning experience. The standard response was to indulge in 'struggle diplomacy'. The Chinese delegation was forced onto the defensive time after time as its interlocutors went into forensic detail, demanding commitments on intellectual property, copyright protection, patents, trademarks, test data, trade secrets, government procurement, minority shareholder rights and judicial remedies, among a host of other subjects listed in the working party's final report, which ran to almost two hundred pages.

While China conceded point by point in Geneva, it was also losing ground in its parallel talks with the American trade team. The end point would come when the WTO could orchestrate the agreements into one package.

The United States meant to be tough. American negotiators believed that they had let Japan into the GATT and the WTO too easily, for Cold War political reasons. One American told Harbinson, 'The Japanese were just waved through and we've regretted it ever since. We are not going to make the same mistake with China.' The dealings were run from the top. Clinton spoke directly to his Chinese counterpart, Jiang Zemin, at key moments. The Chinese ran high risks to pursue their ends. In the spring of 1999, premier Zhu was in the United States when a deal seemed in the bag until a vacillating Clinton took it off the table, fearing it would not pass Congress. Zhu swallowed the loss of face and flew home.

In May 1999 came the US air strike on China's embassy in Belgrade during the Kosovo war, killing three Chinese citizens and fourteen Serbs. The mood in China turned ugly, crowds massed outside the American embassy in Beijing and the state media whipped up popular ire. The Chinese public did not know it, but the response had been carefully calibrated. A magazine in Hong Kong, *Qianshao* (Outpost), later published what it claimed was a private memoir written in retirement by Jiang

Zemin, admitting that a unit of Serbian military intelligence had been given sanctuary in the embassy and that the Americans had presented evidence of Serbian communications from the building. The magazine enjoyed a record of high-level leaks from inside China and its report, in 2011, drew no denials.

It seems that both sides sought a face-saving exit. NATO officially called the bombing raid 'a tragic mistake' and Clinton apologised, blaming faulty target mapping by the CIA. In China, the propaganda was muted and the angry masses melted away. In September, Jiang met Clinton at an economic summit in New Zealand and agreed to restart the WTO talks.

The tempo quickened from then on. In mid-October the US president called Jiang again and sent a paper outlining concessions. Eventually Jiang responded, saying a deal could be done. On 10 November a US negotiating team led by Charlene Barshevsky, together with Clinton's hawkish economic adviser, Gene Sperling, landed in Beijing. The Americans set themselves a 48-hour deadline but two days of grinding talks with Trade Minister Shi Guangsheng went nowhere. It was time for brinkmanship.

On the night of Friday 12 November, the Americans packed their bags. A White House official went down to the marbled imperial-style lobby of the Palace Hotel to tell the desk clerk they were leaving the next morning. Oh no, the man responded, the Chinese government had booked the suites for six days, not two. That was how the Americans learned what the real Chinese deadline was.

American accounts of that weekend dwelt on its highs and lows. At 3 a.m. on Saturday, the Chinese called to say Premier Zhu Rongji would see them at Zhongnanhai, the leadership compound. Both sides tested their limits on fraught issues like telecommunications and the 'dumping' of products at low prices. There was optimism on Saturday night, but on Sunday the talks went badly. Once again the US delegation trekked back along Chang'an Avenue to the Palace Hotel to pack their bags. Once again the phone rang at 3 a.m. The two sides reconvened at the Trade Ministry, where harsh words were exchanged. Barshevsky and Sperling took a corridor break and bumped into Wu Yi, a state councillor, who said that Zhu himself had come back to the building. That was the moment, Barshevsky recalled, when she knew the Chinese side had reached their bottom line. With Zhu on hand, the deal was swiftly done.

We now know from the Chinese side that Barshevsky and Sperling's opponents were playing a well-planned game. According to the trade negotiator, Long Yongtu, while the Americans wondered what was going on that weekend, China's State Council, with Zhu in the chair, convened to take the difficult decisions it had postponed until the last minute. It was straight out of the handbook of Chinese negotiating tactics. 'Everything was decided at that high level meeting of the State Council,' Long recalled. 'The biggest thing for us was the anti-dumping clause. It was clearly discriminatory against China. So why did China agree?' His answer was that Zhu himself said Chinese businesses still indulged in dumping and price wars at home. Ministries had tried in vain to fix these problems but now they could be solved by the rules of the WTO. 'The premier said "I think we can accept this clause in order to put pressure on our own companies to stop them cutting each other's throats." In addition, he said, we could use it to extract more concessions from the Americans.'

There was much more to settle, but the Chinese leaders had made their political decision. Armed with the mandate from his comrades, Zhu was able to show up at the Trade Ministry in the early hours of Monday. The devil would be in the details but the Americans – sleepless and whipsawed – felt they had got the best deal they could.

Or so they thought. According to Barshevsky there was one last leaf from the Chinese negotiating playbook to endure. Just before the agreement was due to be signed she was visited in her hotel room by a group of officials from the Trade Ministry, who wanted to reopen some of the terms. 'Oh, please,' she said. 'Too complicated. Can't possibly deal with it. What time is the signing?' After the ceremony, Jiang Zemin himself donned an overcoat to give Barshevsky and her team a tour of the wintry lakes and pavilions of Zhongnanhai, making small talk in Chinese and English to display his pleasure.

The establishment consensus in favour of China's accession was summed up by Nicholas Lardy, then a senior fellow at the Brookings Institution, in testimony to the US-China Security Review Commission in 2001: 'The United States has a substantial stake in China's further domestic economic reforms and its deepening integration in the global economy. Most obviously it serves U.S. economic interests.

'China can continue to contribute to the dramatic growth of U.S. trade, which doubled to $2.5 trillion in the eight years ending in 2000.' The flow of cheap imports allowed the US to grow while experiencing an 'unusually low' rate of price inflation. Apart from the economic benefits, Lardy stated the widely held view that a richer China would make the world more stable, while prosperity could bring about political change in China itself, as it had in Taiwan: 'An economically failing China, by contrast, would impose substantial costs on the United States and the rest of the world.'

Thus the optimistic case was argued according to a theorem linking economic growth with political liberalisation; a proposition that was not self-evident to those who had seen what passed for grassroots elections in China.

Clinton's words raised even loftier expectations. In a keynote speech urging Congress to seal the deal by granting China permanent normal trading relations, he said: 'We'll be able to export products without exporting jobs. Meanwhile, we'll get valuable new safeguards against any surges of imports from China. By joining the WTO, China is not simply agreeing to import more of our products; it is agreeing to import one of democracy's most cherished values: economic freedom.'

Clinton had faith that when individuals had 'the power, not just to dream but to realize their dreams', they would demand a greater say. He conjured up a new world of democratisation driven by data. 'We know how much the Internet has changed America, and we are already an open society,' he said. 'Imagine how much it could change China.' The Communist Party, as it happened, was already well aware of that possibility, but Clinton appeared to believe that a digital Great Wall would fail to repel the barbarians: 'Now there's no question China has been trying to crack down on the Internet,' the president said.

There were chuckles in the audience. 'Good luck!' Clinton joked. 'That's sort of like trying to nail jello to the wall.' The audience laughed. 'But I would argue to you,' Clinton went on, 'that their effort to do that just proves how real these changes are and how much they threaten the status quo.' The president said this did not argue for slowing down the effort to bring China into the world but for accelerating it: 'In the knowledge economy, economic innovation and political empowerment, whether anyone likes it or not, will inevitably go hand in hand.'

Clinton dwelt in his peroration on the sunlit uplands that beckoned to his advisers and which persuaded America's governing elite that principle and profits could go together.

'Now of course, bringing China into the WTO doesn't guarantee that it will choose political reform,' he said. But speeding up economic change would 'force China to confront that choice sooner'. Americans naturally assumed there was only one right way for the rulers of China to go: 'These leaders are very intelligent people; they know exactly what they're doing – if they're willing to take this risk, how can we turn our backs on the chance to take them up on it?'

These convictions were well known in China, where the men at the top took an entirely different view of the future. President Jiang Zemin, who was head of both the state and the party, warned a group of governors and ministers that 'the contest will be long' and explained to them that the Americans meant to end his regime. Jiang, who was sometimes carica-tured as a crowd-pleaser, showed himself to be a politician of cold realism.

'After we join the World Trade Organisation the struggle will be even harder,' he said. 'Fifteen years at the negotiating table yet the real battle is yet to come, at home and abroad. The contest will be long.' It would not be easy for China to safeguard its interests because 'the other side hope to fix the rules in their favour.'

Jiang understood that the West saw his nation's integration into the global economy as an act with inevitable political results. He was having none of it. 'Why did America reach an agreement with us on the WTO deal?' he asked. It was not because of its 'sudden benevolence'. America, he said, had a covert strategy. 'We should not be naïve about it. Through economic liberalisation it means to promote so-called political liberalisa-tion in China. This is a key method for Western political forces to implement westernisation and sow divisive political plots in the socialist countries.'

The Chinese leader quoted Clinton's own words, saying the US thought joining the WTO would hand millions of people in China an information revolution which the Chinese government could not control, accelerating the collapse of state-owned enterprises, getting the state out of people's lives and creating social and political change. Jiang concluded: 'We must remain conscious of this and see the essence of it, be prepared and stay committed to achieving our strategic goals.'

As the American president said, Chinese leaders were very intelligent. It was just that they and he reached diametrically opposed conclusions.

The agreement between China and America had turned the key for Beijing to enter the WTO, but there was still a long way to go. The action shifted back to Geneva, where negotiators spent 2000 and the first ten months of 2001 working through a mass of agreements on tariffs, agriculture, legis-lation, intellectual property, subsidies and services.

The transfer of power in the United States from Bill Clinton to George W. Bush did not change the fundamental tenets of trade relations between America and China. The terrorist attacks on New York and Washington of

11 September 2001 reinforced them and, as an unintended consequence, created a temporary alliance between the rivals against 'terror'. Diplomats recalled the stunned silence when news of the attacks reached the conference chamber in Geneva and the immediate, spontaneous sympathy with the United States. In this atmosphere the accession of China was approved by the WTO ministerial conference in Qatar on 10 November 2001 and its membership became formal on 11 December. The agreement imposed harder conditions upon the People's Republic than on any other applicant. The text ran to 1,500 pages and weighed thirteen kilograms.

No history of this achievement for China would be complete without a verdict from its negotiator Long Yongtu, who spoke a decade later about his surprise at what happened next. 'The biggest change brought about by China's accession to the WTO was its rapid rise,' he said. Long had never dreamed that, ten years after China joined, its trade would exceed one trillion dollars. 'We were at $500 billion at that time,' he recalled, 'we didn't expect to become the world's biggest exporter just nine years after joining. Nor did I expect to become the country with the world's largest foreign exchange reserves just a few years later.'

For Hong Kong, the accession was a moment to celebrate. The opportunities seemed boundless, the goodwill infinite and the profits certain. Hong Kong's representative, Stuart Harbinson, recalled the spirit of the times among the trading nations gathered in Geneva: 'At the time everyone assumed that China was on a one-way journey.' Major economies like the US and the EU saw the opportunity at hand. 'There was huge investment in China. It was globalisation. Increasing integration of the world economy. It was win-win. That was the conventional wisdom.'

13

One Country, Two Cultures

'One country, two cultures' was not an official slogan. Perish the thought. Yet to cross from southern China to Hong Kong was to quit one realm of the mind for another. Cantonese culture flourished in both places, but in the People's Republic at the end of the twentieth century it found expression in stylised traditional arts such as opera, while in Hong Kong a raucous demotic genre of films and music held audiences in thrall. In China, the state and the party remained arbiters of taste. In Hong Kong the market ruled, the dominant theme in popular culture was crime and its characters, slang and action came straight from the streets.

During the late colonial period the underworld had been the enduring staple of Hong Kong cinema, television series, videos, comic novels and best-sellers. A running joke held that local movies were made by gangsters, with gangsters and about gangsters. It was no joke, however, when masked gunmen stole reels of film, thugs threatened actors and gangs extorted fees for location filming. Organised crime infiltrated the film business when it was a profit machine like any other racket. Revenues boomed because people in Hong Kong had limited entertainment choices. Millions lived in cramped apartments and a trip to the cinema provided cheap escapism. Hong Kong became the Hollywood of east Asia.

The movies attracted predators in the same way that Macau's casinos drew loan sharks. In 1992, Jim Choi, the manager of martial arts star Jet Li, was shot dead in his office in Kowloon by assassins dressed as security guards. That same year, Anita Mui, a Canto-pop singer and actress, was accosted in a karaoke club by a Triad movie producer, Wong Long-wai, who slapped her across the mouth. The next day, three men from a rival Triad attacked Wong as he left a restaurant, slashing his face. Taken to hospital, he was shot dead in his bed forty-eight hours later. The singer, who was known to have friends in the underworld, left Hong Kong until the hue and cry died down. She became a much-loved tabloid diva until her death from ovarian cancer in 2003.

The aura of crime lent a certain glamour to the business which some stars and producers were not shy of exploiting. John Woo's classic *A Better Tomorrow* (1986) romanticised the brooding bad guy, played by Chow Yun-fat. The director Wong Kar-wai made his debut with *As Tears Go By* (1988), whose Cantonese title was *Mongkok Carmen*, a tale of brotherhood, tragic love and macho violence. The 1996 film *Young and Dangerous*, starring Ekin Cheng, refreshed the formula and spawned sequels. The genre evolved from trash to cult as Hong Kong audiences grew more sophisticated, competition from Hollywood arrived and film-makers turned to riffs on crime from comedy to semi-documentaries, dealing with loyalty, corruption and generational conflict. The Triads offered them an irresistible palette, rich in characters, plots and vendettas. In that, the cinema held up a mirror to real life.

Triad secret societies traced their foundation myth to the resistance by warrior monks of the Shaolin monastery against the Manchu dynasty, the Qing, in seventeenth-century China. By the end of the imperial era they had become criminal syndicates clinging to symbols and rituals of the past. Interwoven with Republican China's political, military and commercial order, they counted Sun Yat-sen and Chiang Kai-shek among their allies. The Communist victory in 1949 exiled the Triads from their strongholds in China's coastal cities to Hong Kong, Taiwan and southeast Asia. Like the Sicilian mafia, Triads sought a balance of power with the ruling order, allowing them to run their rackets undisturbed while from time to time conceding an arrest or two and serving as muscle against troublemakers.

All but extinguished on the mainland by Mao's trials and executions, the Triads found a redoubt in the British colony. They co-operated down the decades with the British and the representatives of the Kuomintang. They were tolerated in part because of their ardent anti-communism. They helped democracy activists escape mainland China in 1989 by smuggling them out in boats and trucks, for a fee. But they also got along warily with the Communist Party in Hong Kong, which was itself an underground movement and liked to define the triads' chauvinist origins as 'patriotic'.

'The Communist Party is essentially a secret society,' wrote the Sinologist Simon Leys. In its methods and mentality, he said, it bore 'a troubling resemblance' to the underworld: 'It dreads daylight; to grow and develop it needs the shadows.' The party lived by 'intrigues and lies' and imposed its will by 'blackmail, conspiracy and terror'. Leys was citing the conclusion of a Hungarian Jesuit priest and scholar, Father László Ládányi, who wrote a history of the party based on its own internal documents from 1921 to 1985. He collected the material over four decades from his perch at Hong Kong University, all the while publishing a newsletter avidly read by those who followed Chinese affairs.

The parallels were not lost on Deng Xiaoping himself. As Deng told a delegation of Hong Kong business people in 1984: 'Hong Kong black societies are very powerful. They are even more powerful than their counterparts elsewhere. Of course, not all black societies are dark. There are many good guys among them.' A retired Chinese official, Wong Man-fong, told a forum at the city's Baptist University in 1997 that his job as deputy head of the New China News Agency included striking an unwritten pact with the Triad bosses that China would not come after them if they kept things 'stable' after the handover. For the Triads it was not a matter of ideology, just perpetual realignment in the quest for turf and revenue. They kept out of mainstream politics but emerged later on to pose as defenders of the little man and rented out their muscle to attack the pro-democracy movement. Like the Sicilians, they were at home in an old society where family and clan counted for more than a distrusted and distant state.

Organised crime in Hong Kong was the subject of wildly inaccurate rumour and reporting, which added to its mystique and thus suited the criminals. An academic study in 2014 found there were four big Triad consortiums in the Special Administrative Region. The 14K Triad had eight sub-groups, the Wo group numbered thirteen gangs, the influential Chiu Chau group, whose roots lay in coastal China, had four, including the powerful Sun Yee On Triad; and a 'Big Four' consortium numbered eleven, including a branch in Macau. All of these competed for territory in the ceaseless ebb and flow of underworld rackets in Hong Kong, while a second and third generation of mobster families graduated to polite society and ran legitimate businesses with the seed capital amassed from crime. They had in common a singular contribution to the unity of Hong Kong with China, the integration of cross-border criminal enterprises as the People's Republic opened up.

Rituals and spurious honour codes masked with folklore the squalor and banality of Triad crime. It was a potent heritage, echoing the bandit tradition celebrated in classical Chinese literature, with its sanguine rites of loyalty and punishment. In a 1987 court case, a witness, Anthony

Chung, described his own initiation by a man in monk's robes, holding a symbolic sword, who paraded the new recruits before a Taoist altar, where they drank from porcelain cups containing a mix of rice wine and drops of their own blood, mingled with that of a freshly decapitated chicken.

That prosecution of alleged members of the Sun Yee On triad ended with convictions by the jury and was hailed by the Royal Hong Kong Police as a breakthrough. The appeal was heard by the chief justice, Sir Ti-liang Yang, a rock of the colonial establishment, who freed all the appellants on technical grounds. The men walked out of court proclaiming their righteous innocence. The crown prosecutor in the case, Kevin Egan, a burly Australian with a ripe command of the English language, resigned. He went into private practice as a criminal barrister and did a profitable business representing members of the Sun Yee On, whom he cheerfully described as a bunch of rogues. Before his death in 2018, he enjoyed tilting at the 'respectable' Hong Kong elite, usually over drinks at his favourite club.

The reality was that the elite, the party and the Triads had intermingled for generations. A good example was the lineage of Rita Fan, who accepted an appointed seat in the colonial legislature, the title of Commander of the British Empire and a place on Governor David Wilson's executive council. Fan was born in Shanghai. Her father, the banking tycoon Hsu Ta-tung, was linked in street lore to Du Yuesheng, the boss of the city's most powerful Triad, the Green Gang, which ran the drug trade, worked with Chiang Kai-shek's Kuomintang and massacred Communists. Wisely, both men decamped to Hong Kong before the Communist 'liberation' of Shanghai. Nobody ever suggested that Fan conducted herself with less than the utmost probity despite this colourful background. She later denounced the British and cultivated the image of a suburban Madame Mao, embracing a new role chosen for her by Beijing as head of the Legislative Council after 1997.

From time to time, unspoken pacts were broken. In 1996 a mainland-born gangster, Cheung Tze-keung, nicknamed 'Big Spender', kidnapped Victor Li Tzar-kuoi, the eldest son of Hong Kong's richest tycoon, Li Ka-shing. Big Spender had the audacity to go in person to the Li dynasty's coastal villa to bargain over a ransom reported to exceed US$120 million. The tabloid press hung on every sensational, if unconfirmed, detail of this escapade.

A year later, Big Spender struck again with reckless ease. This time his target was Walter Kwok, the eldest of three fabulously wealthy brothers who owned Sun Hung Kai Properties, one of the cartel of real estate developers. Kwok epitomised the urbane cosmopolitans at the top of society. 'Why,' he sighed over dinner at the governor's residence, 'do these local politicians have to make so much fuss about democracy? Don't they realise that if they hold demonstrations that will just cause trouble and annoy the Chinese government? It will be bad for business.'

Less than a year after that conversation, Kwok's concerns for law and order took a personal turn. Big Spender's gang snatched the tycoon off the street, tied him up, beat him and kept him like an animal in cramped captivity. This time a ransom of more than US$60 million was paid. Kwok was set free but never recovered from his ordeal, suffering psychological trauma which led to a feud in the family business and a humiliating court case before his death from a stroke in 2018 at the age of sixty-eight.

Neither kidnapping was reported to the Hong Kong police, according to Regina Ip, the secretary for security. The public soon learned that the Chinese government had other methods of restoring law and order and protecting friendly tycoons.

Big Spender fled to Guangdong province, where he lived lavishly, protected by bribes, until the police arrested him and thirty-five members of his gang. Their trial was swift. Confessions had been extracted and the verdicts were meant to be salutary. Big Spender bowed out in vintage style. Television pictures showed the condemned men singing and laughing, drunk on bottles of spirits, as they were thrown into the back of an open truck to the execution ground where guards killed each one of them with a shot to the back of the neck.

That night in Macau, supposedly a Triad fiefdom, people cheered and danced on their balconies when the news was broadcast. Some had feared that Big Spender and his ilk commanded a genuine popular following. In the mass media he was sometimes compared to one of the bandit rebels who, time and again in Chinese history, had threatened the ruling class. That was an exaggeration. It turned out that few mourned his end: Triads and their host communities existed in a state of raw nature, and nobody likes a parasite. By killing Big Spender, the Communist Party restored the balance of power. Organised crime in Hong Kong, Macau and the cities of the Delta resumed its low-key, profitable rhythm, in league with compliant businesses and corrupt policemen. But the themes of defiance, scorn for authority and fierce local identity remained to trouble the party. In time they would cohere into a wholly different kind of challenge.

* * *

In the late 1990s, Jimmy Lai's *Apple Daily*, the best-selling newspaper in Hong Kong, published a regular column of consumer ratings of prostitutes in a red-light district of three hundred small brothels around Portland Street in Kowloon, all run by the local gangs. Its author, a self-admitted Triad member who went by the *nom de plume* of 'Fat Dragon', was clearly an habitué of their dim stairwells, lit by pink and yellow neon, and of the late-night food stalls where contented patrons wolfed down noodles and marked up the betting odds in their newspapers while the hot rain hissed on canvas awnings. 'Fresh new girls from northern China and Malaysia, plenty to choose from around midnight and a fair brothel keeper,' read a typical review of one establishment. 'This place has a new porn movie with a Japanese star taking her clothes off for the first time to show her pubes, plus tall Russian and Chinese girls fighting in bed,' enthused the writer, 'all the action is highly realistic and I give it seventy out of a hundred. You'll enjoy it.'

Prostitution was not illegal in Hong Kong, but pimping was. Hence the ingenious system of one-woman brothels in warrens of tiny rooms. The police vice squad and the Triads waged a cat-and-mouse game. Bribery was common. Nobody could imagine that women in this twilight world were free from violence and coercion. They existed in a Petri dish of criminality. Yet Fat Dragon's pithy musings, mixed with dark sarcasm against the Chinese government, found a popular niche in Hong Kong's most prominent pro-democracy newspaper with the approval of its staunch Roman Catholic proprietor.

Fat Dragon was so popular and so artful that his prose was recognised as a prime example of the evolving Cantonese language. In a 1997 study, the academic Chin Wan-kan defined his use of vulgar colloquial expressions as a model of separate linguistic development. In the People's Republic, citizens were supposed to speak a Mandarin common tongue, *Putonghua*, as a badge of unity within a nation of dialects. Chin argued that far from dying away, Cantonese had become a resurgent symbol of identity and resistance. In one column, Fat Dragon wrote: 'if I get no freedom after 1997, I'll fight as a guerrilla on Lantau Island. Ha! Ha!' Vulgar or not, it was profoundly political.

The British did not allow the use of Chinese as an official language until 1974, presumably on the assumption that it might foster unwelcome cohesion among their subjects. People in Hong Kong wrote in a form of standardised Chinese developed by intellectuals in the 1930s. But they traditionally spoke their own tongues, so the streets resounded to a babel of Cantonese, Hakka, Fukienese, Shanghainese and other dialects. Among these Cantonese predominated. At the time of the handover, government figures showed it was understood by 95.2 per cent of the population. Only a quarter could speak *Putonghua*.

In general, a literate speaker of any dialect can read a text in standard Chinese. The emergence of written Cantonese, which uses locally invented Chinese characters to convey its distinct grammar and vocabulary, began to change that. The earliest examples included a book of folk songs and a translation of the New Testament from the nineteenth century. Its popularity grew. By the 1990s, new written Cantonese had spread to opera, theatre, pop lyrics, comics, advertisements and popular newspapers. 'The economy and ideology of mainland China have failed to impose their cultural orthodoxy on Hong Kong people,' Chin wrote. 'On the other hand, Cantonese has gained status.'

Communist Party officials viewed Cantonese as a mere southern dialect. They ordered a campaign to erase it from billboards in Guangzhou and fined the Hong Kong advertising agencies who had put them up. But they could not stop its renaissance in Hong Kong itself. Linguistic subversion spread into highbrow newspapers read by the well-educated, into television subtitles and into government advertising slogans against drugs and drunk driving. The daily *Sing Tao* conceded by using quotes in Cantonese set in an orthodox text. The Hang Seng Bank, which targeted the growing middle class, had no hesitation in pitching its credit cards in Cantonese advertisements. The advent of computers allowed writers to coin new characters in beautiful graphic style and readers could download software to update their typescript. People even borrowed English words and put them into characters. They created a demotic, living language that was not standardised by an academy, regulated by the government or taught in schools.

As business with China expanded and the handover drew near, the colonial authorities promoted standard Chinese, but it was not until after 1997 that the policy hardened into a political imperative. According to Chin, the academic, the Chinese government worried early on that a separate language might lead to separate ideas. Intellectuals, publishers and writers in Hong Kong seemed to agree as they adopted a distinctive local style. Chin cited a proverb: 'written in bamboo and silk, the message will reach afar and last long.'

The division between Cantonese and Mandarin was an ancient one separating north and south China. From Beijing, it appeared that all linguistic dissonance was a path to betrayal. The Chinese media tore into Lee Teng-hui, the first democratically elected leader of Taiwan, when he gave his inaugural speech in 1996 in both Mandarin and his native Taiwanese. It reminded them of the unpalatable truth that imperial China had been a bilingual state employing Manchu and Mandarin until the fall of the Qing Dynasty in 1911. Nor did the Communists forget that Sun Yat-sen, the founder of the republic, delivered his speeches to its parliament at Nanjing in Cantonese.

Language, therefore, was a weapon in the hands of both unifiers and dissenters. In a peaceful and entirely unplanned way, Hong Kong's people had embarked on an experiment in diversity which created passive resistance to absolutism. 'Never in Chinese history have the people been allowed such a high degree of freedom to divert from the imperial form of the written language and have it spread in the mass media,' Chin wrote. In Chinese tradition, he noted, 'the word speaks to power'. Here lay one source of the identity politics which blossomed in the city under Chinese rule.

Across the Shenzhen River, the two cultures came face to face. In its early years Shenzhen was rough and ready, a fishing village mutating into a metropolis. A traveller crossing from the cleanliness and order of the Lo Wu railway station stepped out into a hubbub of vendors, labourers, migrants, hustlers and beggars, all watched by a few bored policemen. One day, visitors from Hong Kong saw a middle-aged man in green army uniform lying dead on a sidewalk with his wife and daughter tearing at their hair and wailing over him. A few paces away, patrons at a restaurant ignored the tableau, preferring to watch a waiter as he leisurely slit the throat of a snake and squeezed its blood into their lunchtime hotpot.

The traffic grew chaotic. Bars, saunas and karaoke clubs sprang up to serve the throngs of men from Hong Kong and new arrivals from all over China. The mingling of people made the city a polyglot enclave. Cantonese was not their lingua franca and most newcomers spoke Mandarin to each other, evolving their own slang and colloquialisms. Shenzhen sucked people in to a gigantic experiment and it was no surprise that there were 'negative effects' as young men and women found themselves free from the constraints of family, village or work unit.

Sex figured prominently in contemporary Chinese accounts of life in Shenzhen. In 1989 a youth magazine published an investigation of female prostitution, recounting in shocked tones how young factory workers sold sex as a sideline. 'Shenzhen has attracted the attention of the whole country after nine years of struggle and of course there is no doubt that the party's reform and opening up policy is correct,' it cautiously began, 'but open and indulgent Western ideas on sex are impacting the special economic zone, such as the ideological trends of "sexual freedom" and "sexual liberation". The writer pointed out that in the old society, women had often been 'forced into the fire of prostitution'. The revolution had abolished such evils but now the majority of young women who engaged in the trade did so 'in pursuit of enjoyment and the icing on the cake'. The Shenzhen police arrested 280 prostitutes in one twelve-month period, finding that only one was a local girl and most of the others came from the industrial rustbelt of northeast China 'in search of money that makes the world go round, to satisfy their vanity and their urge for consumption, dressing up to the nines, buying necklaces and enjoying delicacies'.

The author interviewed several girls in the trade. Jiang Mou, from Shanghai, 'a slender girl with curly black hair and a pretty white face', rented herself out to a man from Hong Kong and entertained others while he was away. When arrested, she was found with a bank passbook showing she had saved 20,000 yuan, a huge sum for the time, and she declared that 'the man paid me, I sell my body, we have a happy co-operation and nobody is hurt.'

A girl called Li saw herself as an entrepreneur, having abandoned journalism studies in Shanghai to make enough money in Shenzhen 'to realise my long-cherished wishes and travel far away'. Li had serviced more than two hundred men in the previous twelve months, including Hong Kong businessmen, local salesmen, drivers, contractors and waiters.

A third girl, Caifeng, testified at her trial to the harsh calculations that made some choose prostitution. Disgusted with poor pay and conditions in a factory, she opted to sell sex instead, telling the court 'unbuttoning your pants once is better than going to work for half a year'. But her clients included 'sailors, porters, rogues and local ruffians', some of whom, she knew, had venereal diseases.

Throughout the period, mainland Chinese media identified Hong Kong as a source of moral contamination. In the late 1990s, it estimated that 100,000 men from Hong Kong and Macau kept mistresses in the Pearl River Delta, claiming that 50,000 children had been born out of wedlock with no legal documents, denying them education or health care. Whole villages of 'second wives' grew up along the north bank of the Shenzhen River, inhabited by the concubines of container truck drivers, white-collar workers, factory managers and business executives. 'Most of them are middle aged, they have woken up to find that their youth is gone … but as Shenzhen and Hong Kong unite, they suddenly discovered that money can get them fresh things like youthful bodies and erotic stimuli,' said one account.

The boom in economic activity, cross-border trade and huge inflows of people created a unique laboratory in Shenzhen. Serious scholars and politicians believed that beyond coarseness, vulgarity and greed, it offered China something new.

'Hong Kong and Shenzhen are separated only by a bridge,' wrote scholar Guang Zhigang, 'the continuous influx of Western culture has triggered the collision, infiltration and integration of two totally different cultures here.' Naturally, the writer warned Chinese readers that 'serious, elegant literature and art' got scant support in Hong Kong, the humanities and social sciences were undervalued and there was little highbrow culture. On the other hand its films and magazines 'promoted sexual indulgence and stimulated the audience's senses with murder, fighting, obscenity, feudalism and low taste', damaging young people's mental health. 'These toxins in Hong Kong's culture have seriously spread to Shenzhen … the problem is likely to grow more serious after 1997,' he said. It was lamentable that people in Shenzhen were obsessed with foreign brands and gave their children 'Western' names, while students in Hong Kong spoke more English than Mandarin, knew little of Chinese history or geography and lacked 'a sense of identity and belonging to their motherland'.

But there was, intriguingly, more to Guang's analysis than the scripted denunciation. It was a classic case of a Chinese writer cloaking a thoughtful message in conformity. As he explained, it was 'a simple and one-sided understanding' to see only the 'yellow, vulgar things in Hong Kong's films, television serials and popular papers'. Light regulation made Hong Kong culture 'full of vitality and vigour' and while there was official censorship of film and television, the basic policy was to let competition regulate the market. 'Theorists and artists are generally free to write or create, they enjoy greater academic democracy and creative freedom, giving them greater scope for all their talents.' Freedom of the press, driven by commercial competition, was recognised as a fundamental principle of the mass media in Hong Kong.

Guang acknowledged that freedom was key to the 'modern enterprise culture' which had dynamised the economy of Shenzhen and was 'changing people's spiritual outlook' with a management system based on ethics, staff responsibility, integrity, efficiency and an emphasis on quality and information. 'This is perhaps the biggest and most beneficial influence of Hong Kong culture on Shenzhen,' he stated. There was also much to learn from the colony's rule of law: 'Over the years the sense of using the law to restrain oneself and relying on the law to protect oneself has been deeply rooted in the hearts of Hong Kong people and has become their way of life.'

Such was the liberal strain in Chinese thinking, all but invisible in today's authoritarian era. It not only recognised the values outlined by Guang but dared to argue that personal and economic liberty could develop into democratic politics in a testbed like Shenzhen. This was the view of Zhang Siping, the city's vice mayor from 2003 to 2010: 'Shenzhen was the first to contact ... the core values and lifestyle of Hong Kong, such as legal freedom, democracy, multiculturalism, clean government, integrity and transparency.' As the zone grew richer, its society 'will inevitably demand corresponding changes in social, political and cultural aspects'. Shenzhen was a pioneer of citizen political participation, grassroots democracy, better understanding of the law and civic consciousness, he said. While adding that 'this process is full of difficulties and twists and turns, and many efforts have been abandoned', Zhang none the less believed that Shenzhen's role in promoting China's social transformation and modernising its system of governance was 'immeasurable'.

The Portuguese colony of Macau lay across the Pearl River Delta, sunk in a reverie broken by the clatter of tumbling dice. The tides of history had washed past it. A neutral haven in the Second World War, escaping the destruction visited on Hong Kong, Macau had failed to capitalise on the post-war boom. It was a relic. Sombre churches stood within its fortifications; a few colonial residences, all airiness and stucco, adorned the seafront; and a bustling Chinese city enveloped the rest of the past. Macau had one asset. Gambling was legal. Crowds of punters came from China, where it was banned, while from Hong Kong, where the only bets allowed were on horse races run by the Jockey Club, ferries brought over the water those thirsty for chance. In Macau casinos resonated day and night to the din of slot machines, the calls of the croupiers and the murmurs exchanged whenever the Chinese clientele, otherwise grimly silent, found fortune's wheel too capricious even for them. A natural order of tycoons, the underworld and corrupt officialdom fed on the cash flow.

For the Portuguese dictatorship of António Salazar, Macau had been a forgotten outpost of its disintegrating empire. The regime was preoccupied by African wars until late in 1966, when a dispute broke out in Macau over education, which was segregated between Catholic and Communist schools. Local Maoists, inspired by the Red Guard movement inside China, launched a violent campaign, for once correctly labelling their targets as 'fascists'. The police were unequal to the challenge, the merchant classes quailed and the government gave in, accepting de facto Chinese authority in exchange for a military and naval blockade to stop a Red Guard invasion. After that the dictatorship in Lisbon exercised only nominal control until it was overthrown by a left-wing coup in the spring of 1974. The new Portuguese government recognised Chinese sovereignty, withdrew its last troops a year later and offered to hand over the colony in 1978. But it was hamstrung by the lack of an embassy in China while, with a suitable touch of operetta, diplomatic communications were sometimes lost in the post office sorting room in Beijing.

In 1979 a young diplomat, João de Deus Ramos, flew to Beijing to reopen the Portuguese mission. He exchanged courtesies in English with the foreign minister, Huang Hua; called on the Soviet ambassador, who gave him a long and lugubrious explanation of why he should expect nothing from the Chinese; and dined at the British embassy with Sir Percy Cradock, who recalled that their two countries enjoyed their oldest alliance and warned him not to fall into the trap of thinking he understood everything about China after a few months.

Ramos endured the familiar lot of diplomats in Beijing, being isolated from the people, confined to ritual contacts with officials and forced to decipher politics and policy through the pages of the official media. But it made him one of the few Portuguese diplomats with experience of China. When a visit by President Ramalho Eanes to Beijing in 1985 led to a breakthrough, he was appointed to the team negotiating the handover of Macau. The chief, an ambassador, handed his subordinates a handbook on Chinese negotiating behaviour written by Richard Solomon of the US National Security Council and published by the Rand Corporation. Given that Portugal had ruled Macau since 1557, some two centuries before American independence, this was proof that the Salazar years had bequeathed to its administrative class little but isolation.

Despite their disadvantages, the Portuguese played a weak hand well when talks opened in June 1986. Their trump card was that they had no deadline. Formally, Portugal held Macau in perpetuity; it did not face the guillotine of an expiring lease as Britain did in Hong Kong's New Territories. The pressure was on the Chinese side to achieve an agreement within the leadership's timetable. They wanted to take back Macau at the same time as Hong Kong in 1997. The Portuguese, recovering their pride, said no.

A familiar round-after-round endurance test followed. Almost five hundred hours of negotiation were presided over by the chain-smoking Zhou Nan, who was taken aback by the resistance, having assured his masters it would be plain sailing. The Chinese, perhaps underestimating their opponents, wanted to wrap up the talks before the thirteenth party congress in October 1987. On the Portuguese side, according to Ramos, some thought the negotiations were just a matter of handing over a better translated version of China's original proposals. 'What's the rush?' he thought.

Holding out proved to be a good strategy. Portugal yearned to hang on to the city until the new century; China had vowed to take it back before then. Faced with a self-imposed deadline, the Chinese reached a compromise on two key points. Macau would return to the motherland in 1999, two years after Hong Kong. And China recognised the Portuguese passports held by about a fifth of the population, in effect breaking its practice of refusing to acknowledge dual nationality. To the Portuguese this was a fundamental distinction between their agreement and the British settlement.

The Joint Declaration signed on 13 April 1987 guaranteed Macau rights and freedoms, allowed its capitalist economy to continue and set up a political system dominated by the pro-China elite. Over the next twelve years the Portuguese conducted their retreat with intermittent skill. They took advantage of China's political weakness after the Tiananmen Square massacre to win better terms for infrastructure projects. A new airport was built on reclaimed land, providing local exporters with a direct freight route to world markets when it opened in 1999.

The Portuguese left Macau's casino industry to its monopolistic tycoon, Stanley Ho, and tried to stay out of a turf war which broke out between the 14K and Shui Fong Triads over its gambling and prostitution rackets. An early priority for the incoming administration was to break Ho's monopoly and allow in foreign investors. By 2020 Macau had more than forty casinos and gambling contributed almost half of gross domestic product. It had a whiff of Casablanca with bags of cash, dodgy policemen, officials on the take and crooks on the prowl. Occasionally a dead body turned up when the thieves fell out. After the handover, the Chinese security forces stamped on the gangs and tried to staunch the flow of corrupt money,

arresting fugitive officials. Ho himself weathered the commercial challenge, fought dynastic battles and enjoyed four marriages, dying peacefully
in Hong Kong at the age of ninety-eight.

Macau's civic activists felt that the Portuguese had done little to build
up a democratic society in comparison with the steps taken by the British
in Hong Kong. The last governor, Lieutenant-General Vasco Rocha Viera,
went into quiet retirement in Lisbon. Edmund Ho Hau Wah, scion of a
prominent business dynasty, was appointed by China to take over as the
first local chief executive. Ho was re-elected by committee in 2004 with
almost ninety-nine per cent of the vote. He also served as president of the
Macau Golf Association.

There was an air of melancholy about the Portuguese withdrawal.
Despite the smooth handover, academics and officials debated in later
years whether Portugal's fractious coalitions and its poorly trained cadre
of diplomats had weakened its hand in negotiating with the Chinese
government. In truth, the pass had been sold when the Salazar dictatorship surrendered its authority to the Maoists in 1966, for there was no
regaining lost ground after such a retreat. Nations that were once great
powers deal with decline in different ways. For Portugal, the future lay in
a modernised Iberian peninsula that was part of Europe, keeping one eye
on the family of Lusophone countries, including Brazil and Angola, where
270 million people spoke its tongue. Its Chinese legacy yielded one diplomatic sweet when the former prime minister António Guterres, with
Beijing's support, took office in 2017 as the ninth secretary-general of the
United Nations.

In Hong Kong, these were the years that the locust ate, but the locust grew
very fat. Money flowed into the city from trade with China. The trains
north from Kowloon to Guangzhou were packed with business people.
There was always an air of excited anticipation for first-timers as the
air-conditioned rail carriages rolled past the barbed wire fence and through
a landscape where duck ponds and village temples remained amid
construction sites and factories that billowed smoke night and day. The
traveller overheard the tones of Finnish computer geeks, French supermar-
ket buyers or a Nigerian trader engaged in lively bargaining on his mobile
phone – which, miraculous though it seemed, worked on both sides of the
border. China had opened up in ways unimaginable to the old hands.

Visitors could get a business visa in Hong Kong without delay and be
trading in Shenzhen or Zhuhai the next day. Foreigners settled in the cities

of the Pearl River Delta on a scale unseen in living memory. China abolished layers of bureaucracy and streamlined procedures for anyone wanting to bring money in, ship goods out or profit from the legal, logistical and financial services associated with trade. Hong Kong turned itself into a machine that made it all work. When the new airport opened on a reclaimed site off Lantau Island in 1998, it established itself after a start marred by technical hitches as one of the world's leading aviation hubs. The city reaped fresh benefits from China's entry to the World Trade Organisation. Sea traffic grew as the Chinese export economy moved into high gear. Hotels, restaurants and shops all prospered thanks to the flow of people. Banking and finance boomed. These were heady years for anyone with an appetite for opportunity and risk.

Above all there reigned a sense of stability, mingled with relief that the dire predictions about Chinese rule had not come true. In Beijing, the regime of Jiang Zemin and Zhu Rongji held power into the new millennium. Its only challenge came from a spiritual group named Falun Gong, which was crushed by the security apparatus in 1999 and branded as 'an evil cult' after a silent, peaceful protest encircled the leadership compound at Zhongnanhai. Its banished adherents could be seen in the streets of Hong Kong, waving placards and pamphlets accusing Jiang of monstrous crimes. The police did not arrest them. Politics in Hong Kong fell into a lull. The legislature was controlled by appointees, while Tung Chee-hwa affected an air of avuncular serenity which suited the temper of the times. On one occasion he summoned the feisty opposition lawmaker Emily Lau. 'Emily, Emily,' he said, as if correcting an errant child, 'don't talk too much.'

In the media, pressure to conform came by stealth. Despite a daily circulation of only a little above 100,000, the *South China Morning Post* was one of the most profitable newspapers on earth thanks to its high advertising revenue, including dominance in classified pages. Its proprietor, the Malaysian-Chinese magnate Robert Kuok, while persuading the staff and the readers that the *Post* was a credible source of news, was keen at the same time not to antagonise Beijing. The editor, Jonathan Fenby, acted as the buffer between these contending aspirations. He recalled a regular 'Monday afternoon charade' when he would be summoned to the executive floor to be told that 'Mr Kuok's most unhappy again' about the weekly column by the outspoken Emily Lau, which he said must be dropped. Inevitably the management backed down when Fenby, who had edited *The Observer* in London, said that if the column went, he did too.

The editor was then informed that his proprietor thought that 'editorial needs more knowledge and guidance about how things work in China'. The need was fulfilled by the arrival in the office of an urbane, elderly former propaganda official from Beijing, whose duties were vague. Fenby, who had acquired a few scars in the newsroom wars of Fleet Street, was equal to the challenge. The interloper was placed with due deference in a new glass office, his computer was cut off from the editing system and he was neither invited to daily conferences nor given the news list. Eventually he vanished with as little fuss as he had arrived.

Such tactics could only delay the inevitable. Fenby left the newspaper in 1999. A year later its renowned China analyst, Willy Wo-lop Lam, resigned after Kuok said his coverage was marked by innuendo and distortion. Other staff also departed. A talented journalist from north China, Wang Xiangwei, who had worked for the BBC and was hired under Fenby, emerged as a power in the newsroom and became editor-in-chief in 2012. Wang, who also served as a delegate to the Chinese People's Political Consultative Conference, a body which existed to validate party decisions, was evidently more attuned to the politics of the day.

It was in China's interests for calm to prevail. The government's attention was consumed by its triumphant entry into the WTO, which required it to re-engineer the state and to mitigate the shock effects on workers and industries. Now the Communist Party had its eyes on a further prize. It wanted to host the 2008 Olympic Games, an event it saw as a prestigious way to mark China's return to the world stage.

The party was willing to curb its own people when it had to keep public opinion in Hong Kong on side. Its readiness to intervene was demonstrated in the resolution of one early problem: the right of children born on the mainland to permanent residents of Hong Kong to settle in the city. Mostly the offspring of Hong Kong men working across the border, their numbers raised fears of an influx of more than one and a half million people that would strain hospitals, housing and schools. In 1999, when the Court of Final Appeal handed down two judgments upholding their right of abode in Hong Kong, there was an outcry in the media, which reported tales of pregnant mainlanders occupying so many maternity beds that local mothers-to-be were unable to find a bed. Local workers began to feel uneasy: from 1997 to 2002 the economy grew by an average of only 1.6 per cent a year compared with the boom years of the eighties when it averaged 7.6 per cent. The fruits of reunifying with the motherland were unequally spread and not obvious to all.

Tung Chee-hwa raised his concerns with the leadership in Beijing. In response, the standing committee of the National People's Congress over-ruled the Court of Final Appeal. It did so using its powers to reinterpret the Basic Law – in this case, Articles 23 and 24 – restoring the rule that people from mainland China must have a permit from their own govern-ment to enter Hong Kong. With that, the crisis ebbed. The ruling set a precedent which vexed constitutional lawyers and democratic politicians, who argued that if the law was wrong it should be amended rather than be subject to arbitrary review. But, such was the widespread relief, the issue failed to gain traction among the Hong Kong public.

The governance of Hong Kong looked like a model of stability. In real-ity, Tung was beginning to make changes to the way it worked. Behind a cordial façade, disagreements were growing between Tung and his head of the civil service, Anson Chan. The chief secretary was a product of the colonial meritocracy. She believed that civil servants should be politically neutral, promoted by ability and loyal to core standards inherited from Western systems of administration. Tung was a Chinese patriarch who observed different values. He prized harmony over debate and favoured consensus, by which he meant obedience. Hong Kong was part of China and it had to accept a new set of rules.

The new order began when people sympathetic to Beijing were placed inside a web of advisory committees which influenced government poli-cies. The chief executive received a stream of phone calls from such worthies seeking a slot to showcase their patriotic credentials. He tended to take the line of least resistance, thereby annoying Chan, who felt pres-sure to admit these supplicants to the circle of government.

Chan and her colleagues who had served under the British had no illu-sions about what was happening. The Communist Party had already infiltrated the hard power sectors of government, the disciplined services such as the police and the immigration department, the Independent Commission against Corruption and the department of the secretary for security. Now it was the turn of the bureaucratic administration as a whole.

Tung installed advisers in his own office whose fidelity to the new line was assured. These were normal moves in any political system, but the chief executive decided to extend the test of reliability down the ranks of the public administration. His scheme enjoyed the bland title of the Principal Officials Accountability System. The top jobs, hitherto held by career civil servants, became ministerial-type posts held by political appointees reporting directly to Tung. Any bureaucrat appointed to such a post would leave the civil service to be employed on contract at his discretion. It was revolution at the stroke of a pen; the end of government by permanent officials and the introduction of rule by favour and preferment in the gift of the leader.

Anson Chan felt the move would cost the civil service its neutrality and accountability. It would lack checks and balances. Bright young officials would see their career prospects dimmed if they could not aspire to the well-paid top posts – some of which came with salaries of more than half a million US dollars a year. She was not against salting the ranks with talent picked from the private sector but she resisted the trend towards hiring people who were not up to the job, merely because of their readiness to comply with whatever Chinese officials in the Liaison Office or the Hong Kong and Macau Affairs Office ordained for the day.

She and Tung did not quarrel. The chief executive would listen; he was merely impervious to argument. A chasm of misunderstanding divided the two of them. Chan said that the system Tung wanted was fundamentally flawed because it would politicise the civil service. She either failed to appreciate or chose not to acknowledge that from his perspective this was entirely the point. It was not about excellence but conformity. That, in Tung's view, was the essence of the new Chinese-ness of Hong Kong.

Chan spent a year trying to talk Tung out of his plans for the civil service. When it was clear that she had failed, the long-serving chief secretary decided to retire, a year earlier than planned. At one point the most popular and respected public figure in Hong Kong, Chan did not play a role in government again. She was correct in anticipating the effects of the Tung plan, which took effect in 2002.

Tung's new government, which he called open, enlightened and progressive, was a mixed bag of ambition, cronyism and debatable levels of competence. It was packed with friends of the chief executive and place-holders obedient to his wishes. Some were hand-picked outsiders, such as the reliable academic Arthur Li, vice-chancellor of the Chinese University of Hong Kong, who would faithfully support the government line when the campuses erupted in later years. Others, like the financial secretary Donald Tsang, withdrew from the civil service and began to act like politicians. The industrialist Henry Tang, a lifelong friend of the Communist Party, was secretary for commerce. The lawyer Elsie Leung showed a talent for anticipating Tung's wishes in her role as secretary for justice. Regina Ip, in charge of the disciplined services, was to play the main role in bringing forward legislation on national security. Everything seemed set fair for the new order – until the calamitous year of 2003.

In the late autumn of 2002, rumours began to circulate about a mysterious illness in the crowded cities of southern China. They spoke of a frightening strain of pneumonia which was highly contagious. The first known case was seen in the city of Foshan on 16 November. The patient was a thirty-five-year-old man, Huang Xinchu, who was admitted to hospital suffering from fever and breathing difficulties. Before he died, he infected seven medical staff. Foshan was a typical industrial conurbation, barely known outside China, but home to more than two million people. It was a junction for rail and road networks. Before long, cases were reported in six cities across Guangdong province.

Not a word appeared in the Chinese media. That did not stop the spread of panic as families learned of the deadly sickness from relatives, friends and workmates. A foreign diplomat in Guangzhou, the regional capital, heard a whispered story from one of her staff, who said dozens of people were dying in the city hospitals but the outbreak was being kept secret. Her informant said the local government did not want to slow economic growth or put social stability at risk. Medical staff had been threatened with severe punishment for 'spreading rumours'.

Residents rushed to stock up on dried food and household staples. People exchanged recipes for traditional medicinal remedies, such as hot soups laced with vinegar. That prompted the first publication in the local papers on 3 January 2003 of a message from the health authorities, who were responsible for the wellbeing of the province's 80 million people. There was no epidemic, they said, merely the usual ills that came with the turn of the year. It was a time of mists, a damp and lowering season on the South China coast when colds and flu regularly blossomed as millions of people migrated across the land to reunite with their families in the weeks before the Chinese lunar new year. Although it was called the spring festival, the lunar calendar meant that the new year often fell in the depths of the chill. In 2003 the Year of the Goat began on 1 February, a Saturday.

Those five weeks of the official cover-up proved decisive. Migrant workers and business travellers left Guangdong for the four corners of China and beyond. In late January, a second message from the authorities appeared in the provincial press. There had been an outbreak of a virus over the last month, it conceded, but it was under control, there was an effective treatment and the masses should not panic.

On 10 February, the office of the World Health Organisation in Beijing received an email message describing a 'strange contagious disease' that had 'already left more than one hundred people dead' in Guangdong province in the space of one week. The writer described 'a "panic" attitude, currently, where people are emptying pharmaceutical stocks of any medicine they think may protect them'.

The news was out. The very next morning, local government officials convened a press conference in Guangzhou. They admitted there had been an outbreak of an illness dubbed severe acute respiratory syndrome, which was shortened to SARS. Once again they insisted it was under control and there was no cause for panic.

This did not satisfy the curiosity of local journalists. They were joined by television reporters sent up from Hong Kong, who were not scared of reprisals. Later that day they subjected the director of public health, Huang Qingtao, to a barrage of questions. Under pressure, Huang read out a list of cases in the six cities. There were more than two hundred in Guangzhou. Over a hundred medical workers had caught the virus. And it had spread to Shenzhen, where thousands commuted every day to and from Hong Kong. Why had this only been published now, a reporter asked? Huang replied lamely that atypical pneumonia was not on the list of infectious diseases subject to statutory reporting. None the less, the Chinese ministry of health formally informed the WHO on 14 February that the outbreak was consistent with atypical pneumonia, repeating that it was under control. The WHO, unconvinced, put its global influenza laboratory network on alert.

One man who knew the truth was a distinguished doctor, Professor Liu Jianlun, who was supervising the care of SARS patients at the Zhongshan Hospital in Guangzhou. At sixty-four, Liu ranked high in the medical hierarchy in southern China, a status which gave him privileged access to pathology reports that the government considered to be state secrets. For weeks he had observed how contagious this new strain of pneumonia was. The evidence lay before his eyes in Zhongshan Hospital, where his patients spread infections among the medical staff with frightening speed. The first, a seafood vendor, infected ninety-five other people within forty-eight hours. A child passed the virus on to five medical workers, including a doctor and an ambulance driver who both died. Professor Liu himself began to develop symptoms of cold and flu. Then he did something which, given his professional responsibility, remains inexplicable. On the morning of 21 February, Liu boarded a blue-and-white China Southern Airlines

Boeing 737 at Guangzhou for the flight to Hong Kong, arriving forty-five minutes later at one of the busiest international airports in the world.

The professor was about to become the city's 'patient zero'. He was already unwell with a high fever and a cough when he disembarked from his aircraft, caught a taxi to Kowloon and checked into room 911 at the Metropole Hotel. But Liu had a family wedding to attend and did not wish to cancel his trip. He was also aware that his superiors had emphasised the need to show that under the party's guidance everything was normal.

Liu was coughing as he waited for the lift to the ninth floor. The virus was carried by saliva and droplets in the air. It might remain on lift buttons and door handles, spreading to anyone who touched them. He shared the lift with half a dozen fellow guests. That afternoon he felt strong enough to go out shopping in the packed district of Mongkok with his brother-in-law, a man of fifty-three who lived in Hong Kong.

Liu awoke the next day feeling so ill that he went to the nearby Kwong Wah hospital. At first the staff thought they were dealing with a standard case of pneumonia. They knew little of what was happening inside China. Liu warned the staff that he was highly contagious, asked for a mask and was put in an isolation room behind a double-sealed door. On his death-bed, he told the doctors everything. Stunned, they hastily instituted isolation measures, too late for seventy-seven hospital staff who contracted the virus. Liu died on 4 March.

In his short stay at the Metropole Hotel, Liu had spread the SARS virus to between seven and twelve guests. A local man aged twenty-six, who had visited the ninth floor of the Metropole, was admitted to the Prince of Wales Hospital, spreading his illness among its staff. Worse was to come. Among the infected guests was a woman of seventy-eight from Toronto, who passed the virus on to her family before dying. A young woman carried it to Singapore and a Chinese-American businessman, Johnny Chen, brought it to Vietnam. The businessman infected staff treating him at the French Hospital in Hanoi, including Dr Carlo Urbani of the WHO. Taken aback by the unusual illness and concerned it might be a form of avian influenza, or bird flu, the doctor warned WHO headquarters, which raised its state of alert. Both Chen and Dr Urbani died. So did Professor Liu's brother-in-law, who had gone out shopping with him. The Chinese doctor earned the epitaph of a 'super-spreader', one of the most efficient carriers of disease in medical history.

The epidemic brought a strange hush to Hong Kong. The fabled Mandarin Hotel offered rooms at a pittance but attracted only a handful

The last governor: Christopher Patten, a Conservative politician, was sent to Hong Kong to make the colony more democratic before the end of British rule.

The Governor, flanked by the Chief Justice and the Commander of British Forces, speaks to the people of Hong Kong – 95 per cent of whom were Chinese.

The Handover, 30 June 1997. China's Foreign Minister Qian Qichen
said it 'washed away a century of humiliation'.

A group gathers in the rain outside Government House to bid Patten farewell.
Many in Hong Kong distrusted the Communist Party.

The SARS epidemic of 2003 brought a new world of face masks
and strict hygiene to even the youngest in Hong Kong.

Medical staff mourn the deaths of their colleagues in the epidemic,
which started in south China's Guangdong province.

Opposite: Occupy Central: mass protests in 2014 brought the city to a halt and took both the organisers and the government by surprise.

Joshua Wong, the rebel teenage orator, rouses supporters of the 'Umbrella Movement' on a hot harbourside night.

'Lennon Walls' blossomed as thousands of people posted poems, slogans and political demands on government buildings.

Hong Kong's second wave of protest in 2019 drew huge crowds to its rallies.

'Tameless and swift and proud,' the new young insurgents fought
riot squads and flowed 'like water' around the city.

Violence becomes routine: a protester dressed for battle is hauled away by the police.

The 2019 protests reach a climax: petrol bombs, tear gas and barricades on the streets of 'Asia's World City'.

Defiance punished: the barrister Martin Lee, founder of the Democratic Party, arrives
at West Kowloon Magistrates Court to receive a suspended sentence for organising an
illegal assembly, April 2021. Many other campaigners went to prison or into exile.

of guests. The nightclub districts fell silent, empty taxis cruised Central, schools closed and people stayed at home. The government commandeered a holiday camp to quarantine residents from Amoy Gardens, a housing estate where a cluster of cases turned out to have been caused by a faulty sewage pipe leaking human faeces, which carried the virus. A forlorn young man, Li Tai, waited outside the camp in the hope of seeing his girlfriend. 'Chinese people can be very superstitious and many of them will feel they are outcasts,' he said.

The outbreak infected 1,755 people in Hong Kong and killed 299. When it was over, a select committee of the Legislative Council criticised the authorities for their lack of readiness and poor communication with the public. The secretary for health, welfare and food, Dr Yeoh Eng-kiong, and the chairman of the Hospital Authority, Dr Leong Che-hung, both resigned.

The shortcomings were analysed in a paper by Professor Lee Shui Hung of the Chinese University of Hong Kong: 'Initially there was an acute shortage of masks and protective clothing for the medical and health personnel, who were hard hit by the disease.' There was a lack of information about how the virus spread, which made it hard to control. 'Because of inadequate communication, panic developed in the community and weakened cooperation and support from the public,' Lee reported. Hong Kong had no infectious-disease hospital as such. Since the wards of the general hospitals were not designed for patients with these diseases, the risk to healthcare staff became a serious issue. According to Lee, almost four hundred medical, nursing and ancillary staff developed SARS and eight of them died, including four doctors.

For more than a century, pandemics had sprung out of the crowded provinces of south China. The Asian flu of 1957 and the Hong Kong flu of 1968 were both traced to its paddyfields and chicken coops. Scientists still debate whether the flu pandemic of 1918, which killed seventy million people, more than the First World War, started there. In May 2003 researchers announced that they had found a SARS-like virus in the masked palm civet and the raccoon dog, two wild animals sold in live markets. Suspicions focused on the civet cat, a fierce, ragged-furred beast with a pink mucous membrane for a nose. Genetic tests proved that there was a 99.8 per cent correlation between virus samples taken from civets in markets and the human virus. In addition, the researchers found a direct link between a sick civet cat and two health workers infected in Guangdong. They did not know how the virus had jumped the 'species barrier' from animals to humans but there was a strong suspicion that it passed from wildlife via poultry, which had weak immune systems, to pigs and then to humans. Any layman could spot a probable chain of infection by visiting the markets of southern China. They were a virologist's nightmare.

When the epidemic broke out Guangzhou was a new hub of global trade. Manufacturers and buyers flocked to its trade fairs, traffic jams crawled past skyscraper hotels and nightclubs pulsated until dawn. Four hundred flights a day connected the metropolis to the world. China's entry to the WTO had propelled its headlong rush to modernity.

A few miles from the centre was the old China, yet to be sanitised by steel and fibre optics. The live animal market was a reeking shambles that belonged to another age. Teams of bare-handed slaughterers steamed and skinned the carcasses of dogs, pigs and cows. Blood, skin and offal were stamped into the mud, mixing with the droppings of ducks and chickens confined by the thousand in cages stacked one upon another. Cantonese customers expected their meat to be fresh and many came in person to buy the day's supply. The crowds tramped through filthy lanes between stalls, jostling and bargaining at the top of their voices. The Chinese authorities ran frequent public health campaigns against habits like spitting, coughing and sneezing without covering the face; to little avail, it seemed, as pools of human saliva congealed alongside heaps of rubbish and discarded animal parts in the market alleys. The government had legions of first-rate scientists who issued regular warnings about the need to clean up the markets, but somehow their message always got lost in the thickets of bribe-taking officialdom.

Once scientists proved there was a link between wild animals and the human SARS virus, the Communist Party apparatus swung into gear. A ban on the sale of wild animals, including civets, was imposed. Border checks between China and Hong Kong were intensified. Airports installed temperature checks. While cases continued to appear around the globe, the virus slowed, then ebbed, in its place of origin. The WHO finally declared the epidemic contained on 5 July.

Inside China, there was an unusual level of public retribution. The disease was an early test for Hu Jintao, who had just taken over as leader. He sacked the minister of health, Zhang Wenkang, and the mayor of Beijing, Meng Xuenong, both of whom had played down the severity of SARS. The new mayor, a rising star named Wang Qishan, shut schools and imposed strict quarantine rules in the capital to bring the virus under control. The Politburo warned provincial officials not to cover up outbreaks in future on pain of 'severe punishment'.

The Chinese government even apologised, after a fashion, for not keeping the WHO informed. Even so, its authoritarian reflexes were ingrained. The official WHO timeline records that its first team of experts arrived in February but were forbidden to work with anyone outside the central government. It was a month before China asked for technical and laboratory support. It did not provide a report on the Guangdong outbreak until 17 March, and that was only in brief. A second specialised WHO team were kept waiting in Beijing for almost a fortnight before getting permission to go to the south. The organisation's experts were barred from visiting military hospitals in Beijing, where the illness was rife. When they finally gained admittance they were not authorised to report their findings.

All of this came straight from the security state playbook. It was only due to political backing from the WHO director-general, Gro Harlem Brundtland of Norway, who was near the end of her term and thus immune to Chinese pressure, that the organisation's team in China were able to take a robust stance. If lessons were learned, they must have been buried in the WHO's archives in Geneva.

In hindsight, it was remarkable that so little changed. The ban on wildlife sales was quietly abandoned in August. The WHO ventured to call the move 'premature' and some of its experts urged that the markets should be shut down completely and for good. But the organisation was treading carefully to keep its relations with the government intact and to avoid conflict. Its team leader in China, Julie Hall, acknowledged that eating wildlife was 'heavily embedded culturally' and that closing down the markets would simply drive the trade underground. It was a fair point. By the end of the year, however, it was business as usual, and in December 2003 a visitor to the Xinyuan wholesale market in Guangzhou could witness the same bloody squalor that existed before the epidemic.

The virus was found in seven types of animal in the Xinyuan market – the civet cats, raccoon dogs, Chinese ferret badgers, macaques, fruit bats, snakes and wild pigs. These animals shed the virus in saliva, urine, tears and faeces, all of which mingled as the creatures were killed and gutted before the hungry eyes of waiting gourmets. The civets and other virus-carrying creatures were still stacked in cages. A cascade of excrement, fur, feathers and fluids coated the bars with a toxic crust. Large black and white cats clawed at the bars of their solitary cages, thrashing and spitting as they were hauled out to be bashed to death or stuffed into sacks. It was a profitable trade. A three-kilo cat cost about 180 yuan, or about twenty US dollars. 'Very good for winter hotpot,' its buyer explained.

Some families lived in simple homes next to their livestock. Children played in the morass, taking no notice as adults pulled out animals and cut their throats on the spot or bludgeoned them with a hammer. Some of the youngsters picked up body parts and played with them. 'We're all healthy, there's nothing wrong,' declared a cheery woman trader whose five-month-old son rolled happily in the mire. A few feet away his grandfather sat on a plastic stool, playing cards.

The researchers had seen all this and more as they investigated the link between wildlife and the disease, amassing evidence that made SARS explicable yet still enigmatic. About 40 per cent of wild animal traders and 20 per cent of slaughterers in Guangzhou tested positive for SARS antibodies, meaning that they had at some point contracted the virus. Yet none of them reported any of the flu-like symptoms observed in severely ill patients, suggesting that continuous exposure to the virus may have conferred a level of immunity. These were questions that would return to vex a later group of investigators.

SARS scythed across the world along international airline routes. Its eventual death toll was small – fewer than eight hundred people out of more than eight thousand cases – but that represented a fatality rate of about one in ten. Tourism and aviation were crippled for months, costing the Asian economies billions of dollars in lost revenues. The World Health Organisation continued to monitor cases in China. One outbreak was connected to the National Institute for Virology in Beijing, where specimens were stored and two researchers fell ill. But the organisation was confident enough to declare in 2004 that the chain of human-to-human transmission had been broken. SARS inflicted more psychological and economic damage than the number of its victims may have warranted. In terms of medicine and public policy, though, it was a precursor to a greater scourge that would one day come out of China.

It was Tung Chee-hwa's bad luck that the SARS epidemic coincided with his plan to introduce a law against subversion. Beaming and affable, the chief executive had kicked off his campaign at a series of stage-managed consultations in January 2003. Tung sat around a table with district council leaders and radiated reassurance. It was, he said, necessary to pass laws protecting national security so that Hong Kong could find its place in the motherland amid trust and respect from the rest of the nation.

Article 23 of the Basic Law ordained that the territory must pass legislation to outlaw 'treason, secession, sedition, subversion' and the 'theft of state secrets'. It required a ban on activity by foreign political groups or bodies in Hong Kong, a clause which was left vague, and a ban on local political groups establishing links with their foreign counterparts.

Some of Tung's ministers preferred not to sugar-coat the message. The secretary for security, Regina Ip, told a dinner at a five-star hotel that society was in danger: 'sometimes I see an unhealthy wind blowing across society. People mix up what is right and what is wrong, what is black and what is white. I even sense a Cultural Revolution-era mentality and language in some of the media.' Her listeners, a group of pro-Beijing trade unionists, applauded. There was less applause, however, when Ip addressed a hostile university audience in even blunter terms: 'Don't believe democracy will be a panacea. Adolf Hitler was returned by universal suffrage and he killed seven million Jews.'

Ip later said she regretted this statement, adding that she had been misunderstood when she said that people like taxi drivers and waiters would not be particularly interested in the details of the bill. The latter was the kind of ineffable remark heard over afternoon tea in luxury hotels which gave away how the elite really thought about their subjects.

While the epidemic took hold, Tung ploughed on with his draft legislation in the face of intense and detailed criticism. The formidable barrister Margaret Ng, who represented the legal constituency, singled out its vague definitions of crimes like subversion, arguing that 'people would not know whether they were breaking the law or not'. This was, of course, precisely the way the law worked in China. It was meant to intimidate as well as allowing infinite grounds for enforcement. That was not, Ng argued, the common law tradition of Hong Kong. Such representations made little headway.

Tung was on trickier legal ground against the argument that he did not need a new law because existing legislation from the colonial era meant Hong Kong already fulfilled its constitutional duty. There were, indeed, draconian powers on paper. But they were not enforced and had, in many cases, fallen away as the territory made new commitments under international conventions.

The Beijing government and its acolytes could have lived with and even revelled in criticism from lawyers, human rights groups and people like the Committee to Protect Journalists, which termed the legislation 'out of place in the modern world'. What Chinese leaders did not like was incompetence. The draft bill showed all the signs of a syndrome the last governor, Chris Patten, had dubbed 'the pre-emptive cringe'. Some of its proposals, such as those granting more powers to the police, went beyond anything required by the Basic Law. People feared for their liberties. Tung was out of touch with the public mood, his political misjudgement compounded by a billionaire's insulation from the collapse in property values and a slowing economy. Both dented the aspirations of hard-working Hong Kongers. The impact of SARS made people even angrier. It reminded them of the risks of living next door to southern China. That did not augur well for national unity.

Unease grew in official Chinese circles as Tung's team ploughed on through five rounds of amendments in the legislature which significantly weakened the powers in the bill but failed to satisfy the democratic camp. The final draft, in fact, was a more liberal document than the national security law imposed on Hong Kong in 2020. But the democrats could hardly read the future. Public resistance grew from a growl into a roar. On 1 July, more than half a million Hong Kongers marched in the streets, marking the sixth anniversary of their return to the motherland with a humiliating rebuke to the leader chosen for them by China. While the protest's headline cause rallied people against the subversion bill, it broadened into a general rejection of Tung's government for its economic policies and its mishandling of the SARS epidemic.

Tung never recovered his political footing. Within days, the leader of the pro-business Liberal Party, James Tien, withdrew his support for the bill and resigned from Tung's Executive Council, saying that Hong Kong risked becoming a joke in the eyes of the world. Allies of the chief executive sought out Chinese officials to confide that it was all a mess. The legislation was shelved, then dropped.

Regina Ip resigned as secretary for security and went to study in Canada. She would return in 2006 to contest a by-election in the Hong Kong island constituency, losing to Anson Chan, who came out of retirement to take the seat. Thanks to Ip's steadfast loyalty to the patriotic cause, she made a comeback and won the constituency two years later. She failed, however, in two bids to become chief executive; even the most faithful adherents to the Beijing line must have doubted her political skills.

China's leaders affected to believe that their compatriots in Hong Kong could be won over to love the motherland if only they could see its rewards. In June 2003 they authorised a free trade deal with the city, known as the Closer Economic Partnership Arrangement (CEPA). An individual visit scheme opened up Hong Kong to single Chinese travellers, no longer restricting them to group tours. It was meant to help the tourism industry recover from SARS and was a success by commercial criteria, attracting several million visitors. Neither initiative won many hearts and minds; the gains from CEPA were too abstract and Hong Kongers soon tired of jostling with crowds of Mandarin-speaking gawkers in the busy shopping streets. The psychological distance between Hong Kong and Beijing did not narrow with familiarity.

The fiasco of the anti-subversion law was a humiliation for Tung and his patrons. It was the start of a hapless spiral downwards through scandals, blunders and a public rebuke from Hu Jintao, the Chinese leader. Tung resigned as chief executive in March 2005, two years before his term was up, citing personal reasons. He was succeeded by Donald Tsang, the bow-tied chief secretary for administration, who was elected unopposed. Tsang was not China's first choice, but if the Communist Party knew one thing, it was how to bide its time.

In 2008, the morale and prestige of the Communist Party received a double boost from the Olympic Games and a financial crisis in the West, reviving its confidence and strengthening its resolve to defeat its opponents at home and abroad.

The Olympics showcased China's debut on the world stage as a reforming economic superpower. The party leadership welcomed more than ten thousand athletes and visitors from around the world, staging between 8 and 24 August a spectacle of precision and authority. Nothing was left to chance. A computer-generated fireworks show kicked off an opening ceremony with a martial tone; massed drummers beat out a thunderous tattoo, soldiers goose-stepped across the arena to snap the red flag up its pole, a little girl mimed a sugary song and a praetorian guard kept troublemakers out of sight. Hong Kong hosted the equestrian events. Its athletes marched in the opening parade under the Bauhinia banner. For many Chinese it was a moment of intense pride.

The party had not relied on fuzzy sentiments or goodwill. The former sports minister, Yuan Weimin, wrote in an unguarded memoir that Beijing won the Olympics thanks to a strategy of deception borrowed from ancient Chinese warfare. He revealed that the Politburo had approved a secret deal to back Jacques Rogge, a Belgian surgeon and former Olympian, for the top job at the International Olympic Committee (IOC) in return for Rogge delivering European support for Beijing's bid.

Yuan went with the mayor of Beijing, Liu Qi, to meet Rogge at a discreet apartment in a Geneva conference centre. They talked about the forthcoming vote at a meeting in Moscow, where Beijing was up against Paris, Toronto and Istanbul. 'Rogge told me he was very grateful to me for supporting him in his run for president and he would completely support China's bid,' Yuan wrote. Rogge asked the Chinese to understand that he could not publicly express his stand. He was, after all, chairman of the European Olympic Committee and both Paris and Istanbul were in Europe – 'but that none the less he would work for Beijing'. The Politburo's plan nearly went wrong when China's own chief delegate, He Zhenliang, showed signs of voting for a fellow Asian, Kim Un-yong of South Korea, evidently unaware that talk of Asian solidarity was meant solely to deceive. He was briskly whipped into line. China was awarded the 2008 Olympics on 13 May 2001, and Rogge was elected IOC president three days later. His spokesman noted that he had been voted in by a large majority and said: 'any suggestion that deals would have been made is absolutely false.'

Even by the contaminated standards of the International Olympic Committee, giving the games to an authoritarian state with hundreds of millions of poor rural inhabitants was a terrible idea. Hong Kong-based magazine *Kaifang* (Open) calculated that China spent over US$40 billion on the event, more than its annual education budget.

The iron-fisted and corrupt chief of security, Zhou Yongkang, made the Olympics a test for his pioneering methods of high-tech mass surveillance and repression. Chinese rights groups complained that the regime had broken its promises to the IOC to allow peaceful demonstrations and free access to the internet. A handful of pro-Tibetan protests were suppressed. Before the games, the security forces evicted thousands of migrant workers from Beijing and arrested dissidents in their hundreds. Many of the events played in half-empty stadiums because the authorities feared unrest. Tickets were allocated to trusted party, government and business groups, which often did not include many sports fans.

The highest price was paid by farmers in the parched plains around the town of Baoding, south of the capital. Engineers cut off their water supply to make sure the fountains of Beijing never ran dry and police sealed off the city with roadblocks to stop them protesting. Thousands fell destitute and several committed suicide.

The games were a watershed, but not in the way imagined by foreign diplomats, who argued that they would engage China with the world and promote reform. In fact, the Olympics achieved the opposite. They were a gift to the party's authoritarians, who rebuilt the national security state on the pretext of guarding the games against terrorism and then turned the people's zeal to their own ends. According to official propaganda, 'hostile foreign forces' were behind worldwide protests against China's human rights record and demonstrations along the route of the Olympic torch. The media claimed that jealous rivals were bent on keeping China down. From then on Chinese politics and attitudes to the outside world would take on a harder tone.

China's leaders stepped down in triumph from the Olympic podium to deal with a financial crisis which started in the American credit markets, led to recessions around the world, crippled trade and shook up economic theory as governments and central banks intervened to save the liberal capitalist system. China was not immune to the crisis, for it was part of the global economy. But the Chinese response was overwhelming in scale and decisive in result. Its success persuaded many in Beijing that the West was in decline.

In Hong Kong, Donald Tsang was running a sideshow. Reaching for his textbook from the currency war of 1998, he moved early, announcing HK$87 billion (US$1.1 billion) in loan guarantees, handouts and relief for employers. The Hong Kong Monetary Authority brought in a deposit protection scheme to avert a run on the banks. The SAR had a war chest amassed during years of prudence and could afford all this. It still paid a heavy price. Over the year, growth in gross domestic product slowed from 6.7 per cent to 2.5 per cent, unemployment rose to 6.4 per cent, property prices declined by 19 per cent and the Hang Seng Index, the benchmark for stock prices, lost nearly half its value amid 'heightened risk aversion and shattered investor confidence'. The public mood darkened again.

In China, the leadership moved more ponderously but on a gigantic scale. Its vital interests were at stake. After joining the WTO, the Chinese trade surplus with the United States had soared from US$83 billion in 2001 to US$268 billion in 2008. In theory this should have pushed up the value of the Chinese currency. But the central bank had fixed the exchange rate to spur exports: it bought up dollars from exporters and made them accept freshly printed yuan in return. To stop inflation, it ordered banks to hold big capital reserves, in effect taking the money out of circulation. As a result China had world's largest foreign currency reserves, more than US$1.5 trillion, at the end of 2007.

This made China mighty but vulnerable. Only an authoritarian state could force economic actors to submit to its currency regime, but all the yuan it issued in exchange for dollars were, in theory, contingent liabilities on the state and had to be backed by foreign currency reserves. China had little option but to invest these dollars back in the United States. A collapse in the US dollar's value or the confiscation of China's Treasury holdings, though extremely remote possibilities, exercised the minds of its leaders. While Americans fretted about China's hold over their national debt, the Chinese distrusted American policy-makers.

So the last remaining major Communist power became the second largest holder of American securities after Japan. It owned US$922 billion in US government debt, corporate debt, equities and short-term credit notes. Its single biggest holding was US$491 billion in Treasury certificates issued by the US government, deemed to be the safest assets in the world. From time to time analysts in China, safely distanced from officialdom, uttered vague threats to sell off its US debt and sink the dollar, oblivious to the logic that in that case demand for Chinese exports would collapse. In truth, the rivals were coupled so closely that they ran the risk of mutually assured economic destruction.

In the panicky early autumn of 2008, the Chinese government kept its head. Its direct exposure was modest. Chinese entities owned US$28 billion in American corporate asset-backed securities, while the Bank of China (a state-owned commercial institution separate from the People's Bank of China) held US$7.5 billion in the riskiest financial instruments, sub-prime asset-backed securities; annoying but not lethal sums.

None the less, the bankruptcy of the American investment bank Lehman Brothers on 15 September concentrated the minds of governments everywhere. In November, President Hu Jintao and his premier, Wen Jiabao, announced a spending programme worth more than US$580 billion, the earliest big fiscal response to the crisis.* China's leaders opted for fiscal intervention led by state and party officials, leaving market-minded technocrats on the sidelines. This was a flight to safety, reflecting the fact that the Hu–Wen regime was left-leaning in a Chinese context. Neither man was a red aristocrat. Hu was born to a family of tea merchants and Wen worked his way up from provincial origins in Tianjin; both were diligent cadres who had risen through party networks without inherited

---

* Fiscal policy means government decisions on tax and spending, monetary policy means central bank actions to control the amount of money and credit.

privilege. They were preoccupied by inequality, distrustful of private capital and in favour of 'popular' economics.

Hu and Wen poured the money into infrastructure, housing and a
high-speed rail network. They used the opportunity to expand health
insurance to reach nine-tenths of the population and to create jobs as
millions of factory workers trekked home from the idling coastal export
zones. In the process they discovered that China's economy was not, as
many assumed, dependent on exports. Its home market was so big that,
with investment, its momentum was unstoppable. 'In 2009, for the first
time in the modern era, it was the movement of the Chinese economy that
carried the entire world economy,' wrote the economic historian Adam
Tooze.

Triumphant from the Olympic Games, China's leaders watched liberal
capitalism fall into disarray. They contemplated the superiority of their
own system and began to think about the future with new confidence.

The changes coming to China and their impact on Hong Kong would have
challenged the most far-sighted leader. Donald Tsang, the chief executive,
was an astute administrator but no statesman. Tsang's slogan was 'I will get
the job done', but it was not clear to many what the job was. He thought it
was to modernise the city's politics and to spur its economy back to higher
growth. His record on both in seven years of office was mixed.

China had already intervened to stop fully democratic elections for the
leader of Hong Kong. Tsang had tried to find a way around this in 2005 by
attempting to raise the number of electors who chose the chief executive.
He also proposed to have more elected seats on the Legislative Council.
Both measures needed a two-thirds majority in the council. At first the
chief executive enjoyed a honeymoon with the Democrats, allowing him
to hope for a compromise. He even persuaded the Guangdong provincial
government to invite all members of the council on an official visit, the
first time that figures like Martin Lee had set foot in China since 1989. His
aim was to persuade them that this was the best deal they could get; Hong
Kong should pocket it and move forward.

Predictably, the proposals were not enough for the radical wing of the
democracy movement. Buoyed by a rally of 100,000 people in Central, it
held fast to its demand for a roadmap to universal suffrage. For the first
time religious figures entered the fray. The Roman Catholic bishop of
Hong Kong, Joseph Zen, and the Reverend Chu Yiu-ming, a Baptist
minister devoted to human rights, opposed the plan. Tsang went on tele-

vision and radio to make his case. When he failed to win the required number of votes, the plan was shelved. But its legacy was a broad-based opposition – one that united political, religious and academic figures with students and the middle class.

Despite this loss of face, Tsang persuaded the leaders in Beijing that Hong Kong should move towards democracy. He went to the capital two or three times a year, and as a lifetime bureaucrat, was awed by the thoroughness of the Chinese administrative machine. 'They know what is going on,' he said, 'They do. They know. They have reports from many sources. One thing I find about the Chinese bureaucracy is they're very good at written work. People coming in with all sorts of papers and reports of all kinds.' He was also impressed by the leaders he encountered, men who had climbed to the top of a hard political system alien to everything Tsang had known in Hong Kong. They were 'big figures', he felt, some of them larger than life, but always 'sincere and affable', He struck up a relationship with Hu Jintao, finding the Chinese leader 'exceedingly warm and friendly' in private, a contrast to his wooden public image.

In 2007, on Hu Jintao's orders, the standing committee of the National People's Congress issued a ruling that the leader of Hong Kong could be chosen by universal suffrage in 2017 and that all members of the legislative council could be elected in the same way in 2020. These commitments were buried in legalistic prose. They gave no ground on who could stand for election: on this China held the whip hand. But they were concessions which, if faithfully implemented, might have created a better political climate.

There were good reasons for the gesture. It was not a good time for China to offend world opinion: the economy was growing thanks to foreign investment and its leaders wanted to present a benign face as they prepared to stage the Olympic Games. Back then, universal suffrage in Hong Kong seemed as far-off to ardent democrats as it did, no doubt, to Hu and his colleagues. It was another interlude of flexibility in Chinese politics whose limited opportunities were to be lost.

Donald Tsang won his own election as chief executive under the old system in 2007 and served a five-year term. Towards the end of his time in office, he revived his plan for electoral 'reform'. Tsang felt confident that China's leaders would learn that they could trust Hong Kong. He had cultivated a rising figure called Xi Jinping, who had become vice president and handled Hong Kong and Macau affairs. The two men chatted affably as they drove around Hong Kong to meetings and events. Xi gave his host the impression that he knew the local personalities as well as the issues. The vice president had served as party leader in Shanghai and governor of Fujian, places where Hong Kong investors were streaming in to open businesses. He had forged personal connections with many of them.

Fortified by his talks with Hu Jintao and Xi Jinping, the chief executive put a new reform plan before the Legislative Council to govern the elections of 2012. Once again it fell short of full democracy, but this time the promise of universal suffrage five years on was seductive. It widened the election committee which would pick the next chief executive to 1,200 people and raised the number of seats in the legislature from sixty to seventy. There were other innumerable and complex sub-clauses, as was now habitual in Hong Kong politics, but that was the essence of it.

In practice, China would retain a veto over who could stand for office. Under its system there was no need to fix the vote, just the candidates. The rest would look after itself; Anson Chan told the American consul-general privately that Tsang had lost the will to lead and that he meant to create a 'managed democracy' with the 'connivance' of Beijing. The genius of the plan lay in its potential to split the democracy movement between 'moderates' who wanted to take the gains on offer, and 'radicals' who held out for complete democracy. Tsang and the Chinese leadership worked hard to exploit the opportunity. Communist officials in Hong Kong issued an unprecedented invitation to democrats like Emily Lau and Albert Ho for dialogue. The government agreed to sweeten the package with a few more popularly elected seats. Officials let it be known that Tsang had written a letter to his friend Xi Jinping urging Chinese leaders to endorse the compromise, because if it failed 'his ability to govern Hong Kong effectively would be in doubt.'

Hu Jintao gave his approval. With that, the Hong Kong government put it to a vote and won. Defying appeals from their party's veterans – and ignoring warnings that no genuine free elections could result from a system designed to be rigged – all the Democratic Party members of the council voted for the bill. Tsang's signature political accomplishment, it left the pan-democratic movement splintered and destroyed the credibility of the Democratic Party as its standard-bearer. But instead of assuring the ascendancy of a pro-Beijing order it paved the way for the emergence of an opposition that was entirely new; one that would be young, utopian, innovative, cheeky, radical and dauntless. This was, therefore, a hollow victory. It had driven politics out of the legislature, channelling it into social media and onto the streets.

The pro-Beijing politicians in Hong Kong had never liked Donald Tsang. They saw him as an arrogant colonial bureaucrat with a sharp tongue who was out of touch with the masses. His economic policies were also out of step with the times. While China under the Hu–Wen regime was raising incomes and improving people's material lot, his administration had failed to make Hong Kong people feel better off.

Tsang talked a textbook managerial game. He singled out new industries, including education and medical services, testing and certification, environmental science and biomedical technology, in which he felt Hong Kong had a competitive edge. But Hong Kong had no history of successful state involvement in business; its whole story was one of letting the market operate. Watching China's success, the pro-China parties claimed that 'positive non-intervention' was an idea whose time had gone. The Special Administrative Region should intervene and control more business activity. This went against Tsang's 'Chicago School' instincts. Hampered by politics, the government opted to drift. The result of their inertia was that Hong Kong failed either to grow innovative industries or to turn itself into a digital power, relying instead on the old props of high real estate prices and infrastructure spending. While China began – within limits – to unleash the animal instincts of its smaller entrepreneurs, Hong Kong remained in the grip of a clique of property developers and conglomerates who squeezed out competition in every sector they entered.

Travelling in south China during these years, travellers often heard people say that for all its harshness, life had improved during three decades of reform. 'We are confident that tomorrow will be even better,' was a constant refrain, 'why even think about politics?' By contrast, in Hong Kong a few people got very rich but the quality of life declined for many others. Prosperity – or the lack of it – became political. In September 2010 researchers for Hong Kong University found only 23 per cent of respondents were satisfied with their livelihood. The incomes of the lowest fifth of society had not improved in five years. According to the local branch of the charity Oxfam, the number of 'working poor' families rose 12 per cent in the same period, from 172,600 in 2005 to 192,500 in 2010. A survey found that 20 per cent of 'fourth generation' Hong Kongers born between 1976 and 1990 had experienced downward social mobility. In October 2010 the Hong Kong Council of Social Sciences calculated that 1.26 million people, about 18 per cent of the population, belonged to poor families.

University graduates worked their way up through a gruelling exam system to find that the median monthly starting salary on offer was a mere

HK$11,000 (US$1,413). A major grievance was that pay barely increased after ten years of work. Combined with sky-high residential property prices, this made it impossible for most young professionals to own their own home. Tsang, who was paid HK$4.2 million (US$540,000) a year, displayed his tin ear for the public mood on a radio phone-in when a young couple called to complain that they could not afford to buy a flat or to start a family. The chief executive told them to consider moving to the northwest districts of the New Territories, where soulless ranks of apartment blocks were rising in the fields; practical but insensitive advice. 'Seven years of inaction in housing, pensions systems, and long term finance of medical services have exacerbated the territory's socio-economic problems and widened the gap between rich and poor,' concluded Joseph Cheng, professor of political science at the City University of Hong Kong.

To be fair to the chief executive, Cheng did not downplay the contradictions Tsang had to face. Most Hong Kong people wanted a better social security system, but few would accept the Singaporean model of handing over a substantial part of their incomes to fund a solid pension scheme and universal medical insurance. In a democracy, hard choices may be settled by a majority vote. But Hong Kong people saw democracy as an ideal beyond their grasp, Cheng concluded, and so 'the most they can do is take part in protest rallies'.

The shadows were lengthening around Donald Tsang as he drew to the end of his term in 2012. Allegations appeared in the Chinese-language press that he had accepted favours from tycoons, including yacht trips and flights in private jets. It emerged that the Tsangs had been negotiating to rent a luxury retirement penthouse in Shenzhen from a mainland Chinese property developer who was seeking a broadcasting licence from the Hong Kong government. Tsang had participated in the Executive Council meetings which approved the licence without declaring his interest. The chief executive offered 'sincere apologies' to the public before he stepped down on 30 June.

Tsang's ordeal did not end there. The Independent Commission against Corruption pursued a case against him. Three years after leaving office he was charged with two counts of misconduct in public office and one of accepting an advantage under the Prevention of Bribery Ordinance. In 2017 a jury convicted him of one offence of misconduct in public office for failing to declare his interest in the Shenzhen property, although it acquitted him of the other count of misconduct and failed to agree on the bribery charge. The judge, Andrew Chan Wing-hai, sentencing him to twenty months' imprisonment, said that 'never in my career have I seen a man fallen from so high.'

Tsang became so ill in the maximum security prison at Stanley that, in his own words, 'I nearly died of despair.' He fell back on his Roman Catholic faith, without which he believed he would not have survived. He prayed every day. An old foe, Cardinal Joseph Zen, came to his cell to say mass. His wife and family stood by him. His lawyers continued the fight while their client was in and out of hospital. His jail term was cut to twelve months. The fallen chief executive completed the sentence in a hospital bed before emerging, gaunt and white-haired, yet defiantly sporting a chequered bow tie, on 15 January 2019.

In June 2019, the Court of Final Appeal unanimously quashed Tsang's original conviction and sentence on the grounds that the jurors had not been given proper guidance on whether his failure to disclose an interest in the Shenzhen property was 'wilful' and serious enough to constitute a crime. 'The trial judge's directions ... were inadequate,' it ruled. There could be no retrial because Tsang 'had suffered a just punishment for the offence in respect of which he would be re-tried' and thus the interests of justice did not require it.

It was a bitter vindication which Tsang turned into a Christian parable of persecution and endurance, refusing to speak with malice about his prosecutors. In an interview nine months after his release he appeared a weakened man, his voice soft, his ebullience dashed. Sir Donald Tsang, the brilliant high-flyer knighted by Queen Elizabeth II, may have fallen into the shifting sands of elite Chinese politics. Whatever the legal merits of his case, it served as a salutary example that the Communist Party's protection, once extended, could be withdrawn. Despite Tsang's professed warmth towards both Hu Jintao and the man who succeeded him, Xi, he received no mark of favour from Beijing after stepping down. Instead he was pursued through the courts, his reputation destroyed and his health ruined. Some saw in his downfall a warning to all later leaders of Hong Kong, one which replicated a cycle of purge and renewal unfolding in China.

A great ferment of rumour and scandal had always bubbled out of the People's Republic and onto the booksellers' shelves in Hong Kong, piled high with magazines promising scoops about the plots and private lives of China's cloistered leaders. From time to time the stories turned out to be true.

Being free from censorship, the Hong Kong media was a playground for factions in China to leak stories about their rivals. Purported memoirs, diaries and secret documents were the stock-in-trade of people inside the Chinese labyrinth who chose to bring selected titbits into the daylight. There were tales for all tastes, from the arcane financial dealings of the party's leading families to adulteries at the top and a biography of Zhou Enlai which maintained that Mao's deputy was gay. Authentication was always tricky and readers were wise to be sceptical. But when a power struggle broke out in China, events outpaced the most imaginative writer.

In November 2011, a British businessman, Neil Heywood, died in Chongqing in western China. His body was found in a room at the Lucky Holiday Hotel, a faded resort set amid gardens on the far side of the Yangtze River from the city. Heywood was cremated on 18 November. His Chinese widow, Wang Lulu, attended the ceremony. Officials told the British consulate that the cause of death was 'overconsumption of alcohol'. By an odd coincidence, a British foreign office minister, Jeremy Browne, had been in Chongqing that day to meet its party boss, Bo Xilai.

From that day on the saga required a suspension of disbelief. It was chronicled in books and documentaries, all on the basis of very few ascertainable facts. The British government, for example, never had any independent forensic or witness evidence as to how Heywood died. The narrative was a farrago of tainted testimony from Chinese show trials, unreliable and selective leaks by foreign intelligence services, constipated official statements and a collection of thinly sourced stories published by Hong Kong magazines and overseas Chinese websites. There were, however, a few undisputed elements to it.

Bo Xilai was the charismatic, unprincipled and corrupt heir to one of the 'Eight Immortals' of the revolution, Marshal Bo Yibo. He belonged to a select group, the children of modern China's founding fathers, whose name in Chinese was 'the party of Crown Princes', commonly shortened to 'princelings'. Its clan networks competed in perpetual dynastic rivalry, their privileges tempered by the ever-present risk of downfall, all aware from one generation to the next that life at the top in China meant living on a precipice. Among the ever-shifting relationships within this elite was a troubled one between the family of Bo Xilai and the family of Xi.

Bo rose to prominence as mayor of the port of Dalian on the northeast coast, then became governor of Liaoning province, minister of commerce and a member of the Politburo. He arrived in Chongqing breathing fire against organised crime, which he crushed with show trials and executions. For these he relied on his police chief, Wang Lijun, an ethnic Mongolian adept in torture, whose self-proclaimed skills ran to performing amateur autopsies and harvesting the organs of executed prisoners while they were still in their death throes.

Bo and Wang reaped fortunes through extortion and the confiscation of wealth from their victims, while bribes flowed from businessmen via a law firm controlled by Bo's second wife, Gu Kailai, and called by those in the know 'the gateway to Chongqing'. A façade for these operations was provided by Bo's neo-Maoist campaign of stridently proclaimed Communist values and nostalgic 'red songs' performed en masse, which drew admiring visitors including his fellow 'princeling' Xi Jinping and China's security chief, Zhou Yongkang. Bo was running what looked like a campaign for higher office.

As China neared the end of the Hu–Wen years, its politics became intensely competitive. The long calm since 1989 – which had seen the party's factions reach a balance of power, with a more collective leadership, no strongman, term limits and bloodless handovers of office – was drawing to a close. The future would reward big personalities. Bo's ambitions were limitless. The discovery of Neil Heywood's corpse put an end to them.

Heywood was a smooth-talking expatriate in his early forties. Educated at Harrow, one of Britain's top schools, and proficient in Chinese, he had charmed his way into the Bo family as a fixer and companion. He helped Gu Kailai with her overseas investments and mentored the couple's son, Guagua ('Watermelon'), on the youth's gregarious progress from Harrow to Oxford University. Bo Xilai, busy pursuing his own extramarital adventures, paid little attention to his wife's relationship with the Briton.

The story which unfolded at Gu's trial was that she fell out with Heywood over money. Fearing blackmail, she lured him to Chongqing on the pretext of a reconciliation and poisoned him with the aid of a retainer, Zhang Xiaojun, after a drinking session. If the official account was to be believed, it was a sordid murder: 'Heywood got drunk and fell in the hotel bathroom ... he vomited and asked for water. They put him on the bed. Gu Kailai poured cyanide compound into a small soy sauce container she had prepared beforehand, mixed it with water and walked to the left side of the bed. She dripped the toxic mixture into Heywood's mouth as she was talking to him. Then she scattered capsules of drugs on the floor, making it seem as though Heywood had taken the drugs.'

Whether or not any of this was true, the alliance between Bo Xilai and Wang Lijun was broken by Heywood's sudden death. In February 2012, the police chief fled to the American consulate in the city of Chengdu, seeking to defect in exchange for his revelations, which he unfolded to stunned diplomats. A transcript was shared with America's 'Five Eyes' intelligence partners, the UK, Australia, New Zealand and Canada, and with Japan. But Wang Lijun's own crimes made it an impossible bargain. He gave himself up to an emissary from the Ministry of State Security and vanished.

Bo could not survive the scandal. He clung on for a month, boldly defending himself at the National People's Congress. In due course he was stripped of his offices and put through a lurid show trial, at which he kept his dignity. Sentenced to life for corruption and abuse of power, he was dispatched to Qincheng prison, a facility for prisoners of high rank at the foot of the Yan mountains north of Beijing. His wife received a death sentence, later commuted to life imprisonment. Her accomplice, Zhang Xiaojin, got nine years but was freed early. In 2018 he was spotted in a group paying a memorial tribute to the clan patriarch, Bo Yibo, at the Babaoshan cemetery in the capital.

As for Wang, he resurfaced to testify against his old patron before receiving a fifteen-year jail term for abuse of power, bribetaking, defection and 'bending the law' to his own ends. It was notable that the charges did not include treason and the court said Wang had performed 'major meritorious service' by exposing the crimes of others.

Hong Kong was more than a spectator to these events; it was an echo chamber where the rivals spread innuendo and disinformation, mingled with the occasional fact. One magazine, *Qianshao*, published a detailed account of the supposed affair between Heywood and Bo's wife, claiming that the British Secret Intelligence Service, MI6, had used him in a bid to secure secrets from within the Chinese elite. The magazine's editor said his source was 'the relevant department of the central committee'. The British foreign secretary, William Hague, who supervised the security services, told Members of Parliament that Heywood 'was not an employee of the British government in any capacity'. That was true, as far as it went.

Heywood gave the impression of being an uncomplicated patriot who enjoyed sharing his insights on a world from which most foreigners were shut out. He openly chatted about his contacts with the British embassy. He had carried out due diligence investigations into Chinese companies on behalf of Hakluyt, a strategic advisory firm founded by former officers of MI6. In a paranoid environment, this was living dangerously. 'Just another businessman down on his luck and out of his depth' was the verdict of a veteran intelligence officer in Asia.

For the Chinese security services, one useful by-product of the trials was that they served as a warning not to trust in foreigners. Heywood's widow, Wang Lulu, was a loyal Chinese citizen who gave her full co-operation to the Ministry of State Security and never spoke publicly about the case. Her conduct was deemed to be exemplary.

For a while, indiscretion continued to suit the new power-holders in Beijing. The Hong Kong media and overseas Chinese websites recycled every bone of gossip thrown to them. The next target was Bo's ally Zhou Yongkang, once the most sinister figure in China, who controlled the security apparatus, made the oil industry a personal fiefdom and ran his own foreign policy in rough neighbourhoods like North Korea and Sudan. The public now learned of rumours in high society that Zhou was a priapic pest, mired in corruption, who had set up the death of his first wife in a car crash in order to marry his second, a television personality twenty-eight years his junior. *Qianshao* printed a detailed account of a drama in central Beijing on the night of 12 March 2012, when, it said, shots had been fired in the air during a confrontation between Zhou's guards and regular troops; the incident sparked rumours of an attempted coup. Infuriated, Zhou sent his minions to Hong Kong to find and punish the leakers, but his power was ebbing away. It was none other than the pro-democracy tabloid *Apple Daily* which broke the news that he faced investigation and disgrace. He, too, went to Qincheng prison to serve a life sentence.

The fall of Bo sealed the ascent of Xi Jinping, who took power as head of state, leader of the party and chief of the military. After much strife, the elite rebalanced its power equation to place Xi, another 'princeling', at the top with Li Keqiang, a protégé of the Hu Jintao group, as prime minister. The new leader promised to fight corruption and lead a great rejuvenation of the Chinese nation, vows which most of his listeners took to be mere slogans. Foreign diplomats breathed a sigh of relief that China was in the safe hands of a member of the establishment. Finance and business rejoiced at the end of uncertainty. The Hong Kong publishing industry celebrated a vintage year. The city's democrats, emboldened by the scandals, prepared to take their fight to the streets. Little did any of them know what Xi Jinping had in store.

14

Chaos under Heaven

One dreary day in term time, a schoolboy named Joshua Wong Chi-fung read about government plans to change his education syllabus. This was not the sort of thing to quicken the pulse of the average fifteen-year-old in Hong Kong, or anywhere else, but Wong was a prodigy. A scrawny, crop-headed youth in T-shirt and jeans who scrutinised the world through wiry spectacles and fiddled constantly with his mobile phone, he would have passed unnoticed in any crowd on the Mass Transit Railway. He had been born in the last months of British rule, on 13 October 1996; his parents, Roger Wong and Grace Li, christened him Joshua after the biblical figure who spied out the promised land and led the Israelites to conquer it. His Chinese name, Chi-fung, meant 'something sharp'.

Wong lived in a modest apartment with his mother, father and younger brother. The boys bunked in a cramped room, its shelves lined with neatly stacked books and study folders. Diagnosed with dyslexia at seven years old, Wong had an offbeat mind that could absorb huge quantities of information and turn them into clear, rapid-fire sentences that rolled off his tongue in his native Cantonese. He could not shut up. His father recalled that even as a small child he tried to talk with a bottle in his mouth.

Roger Wong, who was in his early fifties, had worked for a firm in information technology before running his own business. Grace Li cared for her boys and worked in a community centre. The couple were ordinary members of Hong Kong's 'sandwich class', so called because it inhabited the 'squeezed middle' between welfare and riches. Their flat was located in a cluster of white tower blocks named South Horizons at Ap Lei Chau, a promontory jutting out to sea on the south side of Hong Kong island. Inside were Bibles, religious books and holy images. The Wongs were a devout Christian family. It was their evangelical faith, combined with their elder son's quirky eloquence, that created the Joshua Wong phenomenon.

The boy made his way every school day to Kowloon, where he attended the United Christian College, a private secondary school for boys and girls. Its stated values included the cultivation of virtue and living life according to God's will. A Protestant community church attached to the school played a dominant role in its spiritual and social life. The pupils learned traditional written Chinese and were also taught in English. They played basketball on a green tarmac court. It was the kind of education that aspirational families in Hong Kong made sacrifices to pay for. In return they got the kind of school that many parents in Western countries would envy.

The United Christian College was not set up to be an incubator for rebellion, but in Joshua Wong it had a natural rebel on its hands. Wong struggled with the academics. More to the point, he disliked the food, which was institutional. At thirteen, he organised a petition on a Facebook page to complain about it. His mortified parents were summoned to see the headmaster. It was the start of a career as an agitator, and Wong never looked back.

Together with a schoolmate, Ivan Lam Long-yin, Wong began a group for teenagers with the general aim of making adults aware of their grievances. They did so with tactical guile which the young Mao, who had also been a rebellious pupil, would have admired. They called it a club, which to parents suggested innocent pursuits like chess or homework. Wong was its convenor, not its boss. Its name could not have been more reassuring: Scholarism. The 'ism' was added, Wong later admitted, to lend it an air of gravitas.

The duo were joined by Agnes Chow, a pupil at the Holy Family Canossian College, whose Roman Catholic upbringing inspired her social commitment. Scholarism attracted bright, idealistic youngsters who knew that something was wrong in Hong Kong. They joined the opposition's rituals; a vigil every June Fourth for the souls of Tiananmen and a march on 1 July to mourn the loss of democracy after the handover. Wong was an enthusiast for such protests and could orate from a soapbox outside any 7-Eleven store at the sight of a microphone. But Scholarism's young agitators lacked a campaign focus. They were rebels in search of a cause. Then a dour adult named Leung Chun-ying handed them one.

C.Y. Leung, as he was usually known, took over from Donald Tsang in 2012 as chief executive. He won 603 votes from an election committee numbering 1,193 members, which put him in charge of seven million people. It was, his backers claimed, a real contest. Leung defeated Henry

Tang, the chief secretary for administration, who was felled by scandals verging on the absurd about infidelity, dodgy home improvements and a phantom wine cellar. Tang had been favoured by China but his idle airs of entitlement made him a liability. His rival moved in for the kill and easily beat off a token third candidate, Albert Ho, a Democrat.

The C.Y. Leung administration was the point at which the gloves came off. At fifty-seven, the new chief executive had form. Like his predecessor, he was the son of a policeman. His family origins lay in northeast China. Leung had benefited from a meritocratic colonial education and went on to excel in postgraduate studies in Britain. He came home to make a lucrative career as a property surveyor for Jones Lang Wootton, then struck out on his own. His business was so successful that he caught the eye of Zhu Rongji, then the mayor of Shanghai, and moved effortlessly into the ranks of executives serving the patriotic cause. British security officials believed Leung was a secret member of the Communist Party. He denied it, but that did not convince his foes: the party operated underground in Hong Kong, thus its code of discipline imposed silence and, if necessary, dissimulation. Leung undeniably enjoyed the party's trust and the privileges that came with it. Untainted by ties to the colonial system, he served on groups chosen by the party to draft the Basic Law, and he joined the Tung administration after the handover. In mentality and management style he was the right man for China.

One of Leung's early initiatives aimed to please the patriots who had long complained that education in Hong Kong was too westernised, too Christian and too liberal. Under Donald Tsang officials had drafted a new school curriculum to improve 'moral and national education'. Anodyne in form, it called for pupils to be instructed in the merits of Chinese culture and governance, set a timetable for consultations and proposed a three-stage conversion to the new system so that all Hong Kong schoolchildren would be on the correct path within seven years. In July 2012, the new chief executive launched the plan with a presentational mixture of paternalism and blandness. Joshua Wong saw straight through it. At last Scholarism had found its cause.

Perhaps Leung had lived in the rarefied circle of red capitalists for so long that he had forgotten that ordinary people in Hong Kong, even schoolchildren, were a street-smart lot. His promotion of the curriculum with a message that the Communist government of China was an advanced and selfless regime, its rule contrasting with the toxic politics of Western democracy, which all wise observers knew to be a failure, was not the way to win hearts and minds. And there was more in the same vein. It was a gift to the youth movement, which graduated in a flash from Facebook indignation to street protests.

Exhilarated, Wong and his comrades called their supporters to a rally on 29 July which drew 100,000 people. They collected petitions, staged pickets at schools, argued with their parents and won teachers over to the resistance. At the end of August, they appealed to students to occupy the space outside the government headquarters in Admiralty, a district of dull skyscrapers on the north shore of Hong Kong island. They baptised it 'Civic Square'. Ivan Lam and two others went on a hunger strike for three days.

The media fell upon these clean-cut, articulate and serious young troublemakers. Wong slept in a tent and lurched bleary-eyed from one interview to the next. An avid Hong Kong public watched television footage of neatly uniformed pupils doing their homework at the sit-in. On Friday 7 September, more than 120,000 people joined them. Wong gave the speech of his life. The curriculum was 'brainwashing propaganda', he said, and C.Y. Leung must withdraw it. The next day, to the delirium and disbelief of the protesters, the chief executive did just that.

The Communist Party saw the fight against opponents like Scholarism as a clash of values. They were right. The political conflict was about the right of Hong Kong people to decide their future. But it came from a more profound schism between two visions of what it meant to be Chinese.

The David-and-Goliath image of a teenage Joshua Wong versus a mighty Xi Jinping was eagerly taken up by the world's press, to the discomfort of the young man himself. In the Chinese media, he was a puppet of Westerners, most likely paid by the Americans to betray the motherland. Both portraits had elements of caricature, ignoring the reality that Hong Kong's political revolution was leaderless and grew out of the city's unique way of life.

While Hong Kong lived in a ferment of ideas and contending schools of political thought, the new China under Xi Jinping was developing its own ideology. It was innovative and constantly evolving, but – based on evidence – three things could be said about it. It was 'civilisational', being proudly Chinese; it restated Marxism as its founding belief; and, less publicly, it borrowed the theory and practice of dictatorship from the late Joseph Stalin.

Foreigners who said with glib assurance that the Communist Party had no principles any more were wrong. It stood for socialism with 'Chinese characteristics', which restored the state to a paramount role and put the party back in command 'north, south, east and west' with Xi as 'the people's leader', a title accorded to no Chinese politician since Mao.

There were inconsistencies, of course. One paradox was the contrast between the new regime's brittle nationalism and its own reliance on doctrines borrowed from abroad. It was all very well to denounce people like Joshua Wong, who worshipped as his Lord and Saviour Jesus Christ, a preacher active in first-century Palestine. But Xi himself upheld the doctrines of a philosopher born in Germany, Karl Marx, whose theories owed much to revolutionary Paris and whose later works were composed in Victorian England. All such contradictions were blotted out by shrill slogans. There was often scant logic to the propaganda, which did not prevent its wearisome repetition.

Xi Jinping himself did not pretend to be an intellectual; that claim was made later on by the burnishers of his personality cult. His education had suffered during the Cultural Revolution, when he was banished to the countryside. He earned a chemistry degree as a 'worker-peasant-soldier', a category which rewarded political fidelity but carried low prestige. On his path to power he was awarded a postgraduate doctorate in law by Beijing's Tsinghua University in 2002. Sceptics questioned how much of his 116-page dissertation, which cited ninety-seven books in Chinese and twenty-six in English, was his own work. They noted that an influential member of the law faculty, Chen Xi, afterwards received rapid promotion to high state and party ranks.

The Chinese leader spoke of Marx as a guide. He took the party line that Marx had illuminated an entirely new way of looking at history as a dynamic, progressive and scientific force which set humanity on the path to a better future. This broke with the fatalistic ancient Chinese concept that man was trapped in a cosmic cycle which doomed society forever to rise and fall from splendour to decay. Every educated Chinese person knew the opening lines of the fifteenth-century epic *The Romance of the Three Kingdoms*, that the empire once united, must divide and once divided, must unite.

The task for Communists was to reconcile nation and ideology, and for that Xi turned to a political theorist, Wang Huning. This shadowy academic, born in Shanghai, advised three leaders on perfecting the theories that are officially attached to their names. He devised the cumbersome 'Three Represents' to codify Jiang Zemin's idea that the party unified the economic, cultural and political interests of the majority. Hu Jintao's 'scientific development' spoke for itself. As for 'Xi Jinping Thought', it evolved in Wang's hands from a slogan, 'the Chinese dream', to a corpus of wisdom that was miraculously applicable to anything from diplomacy to medicine.

Wang Huning was hardly known in the West. But he was like an old friend to scholars who pondered the workings of the People's Republic from afar. As far back as 1994, Wang, an academic at Fudan University in Shanghai, had been a pioneer of 'cultural sovereignty' – the belief that in Chinese civilisation the security and sovereignty of the state ranked above human rights. Wang was familiar with the American political scientist Samuel Huntington's thesis that a clash of civilisations, not nation states, would shape future conflicts. The theory had been published as an article in *Foreign Affairs*, a specialist journal, causing widespread debate. It did not appear in book form until 1996 but it had already drawn officially sponsored criticism in China, where it was held to be prejudiced, even hostile. In Chinese ruling circles there was particular alarm at Huntington's view that no evidence existed for the liberal internationalist assumption that commerce promoted peace. Nor did they appreciate his warning that it was an illusion to talk of the harmonious convergence of civilisations in a global economy. Both propositions were at the core of China's engagement with the rest of the world.

Wang Huning thought Huntington was spot-on. He too believed that culture would play a determining role in world affairs. Resistance to 'cultural hegemony' was vital. He quoted Deng Xiaoping, who said sovereignty and security were supreme and that the former was 'much more important than human rights'. China had to conduct an independent diplomacy to keep its status among nations, Wang said, so the alien Western concept of human rights offered a convenient focus for international struggle. For China to stand against it was a test of national sovereignty.

Wang's writings were spotted by the editors of *China News Analysis*, a newsletter founded in Hong Kong by the Jesuit Father László Ládányi. They published extracts in a survey of work by intellectuals seeking to formulate a Chinese definition of human rights. Its author commented: 'For many writers it seems implicit that "Asians" tend to give primacy to collective rights while "Westerners" favour those of the individual.' The problem for such writers was that the people of Hong Kong confounded their thesis. They were indisputably Chinese yet held to a fierce independence of mind, free speech and the idea that the state should serve its citizens, not vice versa.

By the time Xi Jinping took power, Communist Party theorists had come to see Hong Kong as a corner of China that could not easily be reconciled to his project of the 'great rejuvenation'. In their vanguard was Wang Huning, who rose to join the Politburo and was picked by Xi five years later to become one of just seven men on its standing committee, the supreme ruling body in China. The third part of Xi's new order after ideology and culture was dictatorship. This was its most menacing aspect for Hong Kong and for fragile democracies everywhere.

In December 2012, Xi made his first tour as party leader to south China, where he laid a wreath at a statue of Deng Xiaoping in Shenzhen, the foundry of reform, and declared that the Soviet Union had collapsed because nobody was 'man enough' to fight for it. To dismiss Lenin and Stalin, he said, was 'to engage in historical nihilism'. For Chinese Communists, Stalin was the great intermediary, the man who transmitted Marxism-Leninism to their founding comrades. Stalin's work *A Short Course on the History of the Bolsheviks* was a source of inspiration to the new Chinese leader, according to John Garnaut, an Australian government adviser who served as a correspondent in Beijing and knew its elite well. 'The practical utility of the book is that it prescribes an antidote to the calcification and putrefaction that inevitably corrodes and degrades every dictatorship,' Garnaut told an internal government seminar. Xi grasped its insights: the party became strong by purging itself, class war meant perpetual struggle and the revolution always needed enemies; thus, for a trainee dictator, foreign plots were abundant and useful.

The Stalinist references scattered through Xi's early speeches served notice that he aimed to restore total ideological control. Stalin had acknowledged that the Chinese revolution was different from Russia's because it was a struggle against foreign imperialism as well as a fight against feudalism and class oppression. This, too, was appealing to Xi Jinping. As a result, according to state media journalists in Beijing, Chinese officials were instructed to study the Soviet dictator's advice on how to defeat interference in their internal affairs. 'Intervention is by no means confined to the incursion of troops ... [it] assumes more flexible and more camouflaged forms,' Stalin had said, 'imperialism prefers to intervene in a dependent country by organising civil war there, by financing counter-revolutionary forces ... by giving moral and financial support to its Chinese agents.'

These were the lessons absorbed by Xi and his lieutenants. They provided a theme to which Chinese officials would return: the trouble in

Hong Kong was stirred up by colonial lackeys, agents of American imperialism and enemies of the nation such as the rulers of Taiwan. At home,
Xi began a mass campaign against corruption which felled about one
million officials. Conveniently, it tended to target his rivals. The opposition in Hong Kong was so intoxicated by its victory over the school
curriculum that it seemed not to heed the warning signs that a stronger
dictatorship had come to power in China. As for C.Y. Leung and his
administration, they either failed to notice it or decided to pretend that all
was well. Perhaps, in the early twenty-first century, even they did not
imagine that the spectre of Stalin was stalking the halls of the people's
government.

It was, in any case, too late to halt the momentum of protest. In early 2013,
a mild-mannered professor of law, Benny Tai Yiu-ting, published an article in the *Hong Kong Economic Journal* outlining a plan to 'Occupy Central
with Love and Peace'. It borrowed a non-violent strategy from protests in
America against Wall Street. Tai proposed to bring the downtown business
district on Hong Kong island to a halt, putting pressure on the establishment and China to allow free elections. His article was headlined 'The
deadliest weapon of civil disobedience'. It was pure millennial politics,
appealing to the young, the digitally literate and the idealistic.

Tai was joined by Chan Kin-man, a professor at the Chinese University
of Hong Kong, and the influential Baptist minister the Reverend Chu
Yiu-ming. They chose a church in Kowloon as the venue of a news conference to announce their campaign. It was to unfold through dialogue,
popular deliberation, a referendum and, as a last resort, a peaceful mass
sit-in. The commissioner of police, Andy Tsang Wai-hung, was quick to
respond that the authorities would not tolerate protests blocking main
roads in Central. He warned people against joining the demonstrations, if
they happened.

In late 2013, Leung announced yet another 'consultation' on democracy. He set up an electoral reform taskforce under Carrie Lam, a bustling
administrator who had risen to be chief secretary. It collected thousands
of views from politicians, chambers of commerce, academics, civic groups
and ordinary members of the public. Few if any dissonant opinions were
put into the report eventually submitted to Beijing as the 'mainstream
consensus', and none of the democrats were fooled.

Carrie Lam's labours were still in progress in the early summer of 2014
when the State Council in Beijing dealt a blow to their credibility. It issued

an unbending White Paper to remind Hong Kongers that 'the Central Leadership directly exercises jurisdiction' over them. 'The fact that Hong Kong must be governed by patriots is well grounded in laws,' it said, progressing through slabs of bureaucratese to reach its main point: 'it is necessary to stay alert to the attempt of outside forces to use Hong Kong to interfere in China's domestic affairs.' China would prevent and repel such attempts by 'a very small number of people' who acted 'in collusion with outside forces'.

In short, no compromise. The people of Hong Kong might choose their leader by universal suffrage in 2017 but the Chinese government would decide who could stand for the job. The candidate would be anointed by the inevitable committees picked by Beijing.

Long subdued, the democracy movement rose up. After years of economic and social disruption, ordinary citizens felt pushed into its ranks. From the influx of mainlanders to sky-high home prices, the 'sandwich class', people like Joshua Wong's parents, saw their gains eroding. Some felt they had little to lose. Plenty of Hong Kongers dusted off their foreign passports or applied for green cards, which gave the right of residence in the USA. Those who had emigrated to Britain, Canada and Australia no longer looked like fools. Some of the émigrés who had come back in the years of calm started to think about leaving again.

But as Wong put it eloquently and often, most people did not have a choice. In any case, Hong Kongers were tougher than they were sometimes given credit for. The oldest generation had endured hardship and war, the middle-aged had kept steady heads through decades of uncertainty and the youngsters wanted a decent future. The other truth was that most people really loved their home; its islands and seas, its sunsets and summer downpours, the sizzle of fresh food at the roadside and the din of family banquets, loyalties to school, clan, church and temple, the chance to hustle and the lightly taxed rewards of work, all conducted to a soundtrack of quick-witted chatter on the airwaves and a cacophony of entertainment from all over Asia. It was worth a fight.

Undaunted, the Occupy movement conducted a pioneering exercise in consultative democracy. In June it organised a 'civic referendum' with the help of Hong Kong University. People could vote via a smartphone app, online or in person at unofficial polling stations. Almost 800,000 people, around a fifth of the electorate, participated. A majority wanted citizens to nominate candidates for chief executive candidates directly. This was anathema to Beijing. Its acolytes duly heaped abuse on the organisers. None other than Zhang Junsheng, the handover diarist from the New China News Agency, was resurrected to denounce it. The *Global Times*, a tabloid offshoot of the *People's Daily* which was finding its own strident key, called it an illegal farce. The Chinese government also unleashed a more sophisticated weapon in its battle for Hong Kong: cyberwarfare.

The referendum system was dubbed PopVote. Its inventors built in a series of then-innovative data security measures, including a firewall, which was meant to shield it from hackers, and a second layer of protection, a Secure Sockets Layer (SSL), as well as a system to 'hash' personal data. The ballots were encrypted and the keys kept within a limited circle. PopVote only accepted Hong Kong IP addresses, because only locals could vote. They had to present a valid ID card, which all citizens carried, and a cellphone number. The Domain Name System (DNS) connecting PopVote to the 'phonebook of the internet' was managed by CloudFlare, a US-based online security firm.

Even before PopVote went live it came under attack. On the second day of its test period it was hit with a massive Distributed Denial of Service (DDS) offensive, a tactic used to flood a target and shut it down. On 15–16 June, 100 billion DNS queries swamped PopVote and paralysed the voting system. Specialists at Amazon, Google and UDomain, a specialist firm, initially helped to mitigate the attacks. The volume was so great that they gave up.

Cloudflare deployed a counter-measure codenamed Project Galileo when real voting began on 20 June. It deflected a fresh attack by using buffers and filters and expanding the available bandwidth to channel traffic through multiple sites, blunting its impact. The firm traced five networks of the 'zombie computers' called botnets. It blocked them one by one. These cyber defences held for the nine days of online voting.

The hackers did not stop there. They created fake apps, resembling the official PopVote voting application. They broke into the campaign's app store account, prompting the organisers to contact Apple to seal the breach. They set up fake websites to lure internet users away from the real one. Finally, they flooded phone, fax and email contacts with calls. Cybersleuths concluded afterwards that the aim of their opponents had been to disrupt the poll, to falsify votes or discredit the exercise.

None of it worked. But it was just an opening skirmish on the new electronic battleground. In the lull that followed, both sides went back to old-fashioned means.

The Chinese government felt that Hong Kong had not got the message. So on 31 August, the Standing Committee of the National People's Congress spelt it out. It considered C.Y. Leung's public consultation 'extensive and in-depth' and noted that the next leader must be 'a person who loves the country and loves Hong Kong'. It ruled that candidates in 2017 must be chosen by a 'broadly representative nominating committee' which would pick two or three suitably patriotic individuals. Then all the electors of Hong Kong could vote on the choice. It was the old formula: a committee of 1,200 worthies appointed by the Communist Party, a list of vetted candidates and an election by 'universal suffrage' that would resemble the rituals carried out in the People's Republic. For good measure, the NPC forbade any reform of the 2016 elections to the Legislative Council, where the dead hand of functional constituencies would remain on the tiller. It was, said the NPC, 'gradual and orderly progress in developing a democratic system that suits the actual situation in Hong Kong'.

In a public statement, flanked by members of his administration who all wore the expressions of mourners at a funeral, C.Y. Leung hailed the verdict as 'a major step forward'. Carrie Lam, who had delivered what the NPC called a 'broad consensus' of views, told Hong Kongers that they had been called to order. It was an early step in her transformation from a dutiful civil servant who attended Roman Catholic mass to an ardent spokesperson for the authoritarian atheists who governed China.

Benny Tai, the co-founder of the Occupy Central movement, called a news conference at which he joined an array of democratic politicians and activists to label 31 August the darkest day in the city's recent politics. 'This is the end of the road for dialogue,' he said. It was, however, the irrepressible young people who kicked off the next step. There were scattered protests immediately after the NPC decision. Then on 13 September, Joshua Wong led Scholarism to a mass demonstration at the harbourside government headquarters.

It was a model of decorum. Hundreds of pupils, neatly turned out in their school summer uniforms, sat in obedient rows while their teachers read out lectures on maths and Chinese literature so that they would not fall behind in their work. Most of the protesters were in their mid-teens. They adopted yellow ribbons as their symbol.

University students were next to join the movement after months of debate and internal wrangling on campus. In late September the Hong Kong Federation of Students (HKFS) staged a five-day boycott of classes at the city's universities and called student assemblies to discuss the fight for democracy. At the Chinese University of Hong Kong, which had a tradition of political engagement, more than ten thousand students massed on campus to hear speeches by student union leaders, professors and political commentators. The leaders of the federation, secretary-general Alex Chow and his deputy, Lester Shum, emerged as a telegenic duo who shared a gift for public oratory. It made them instant stars. Chow was the child of wealthy, conformist parents who despaired of his activism. They hoped he would go to the University of California, Berkeley, to do a doctorate. Shum was born in the United States, came to Hong Kong as a small child and grew up in a middle-class household. Both quickly forged a bond with Joshua Wong, uniting their movements.

The die was cast on the hot, sticky evening of 26 September. The students had moved to the government quarter. Thousands collected at Civic Square, the area claimed by Scholarism as a free space during its earlier protest, but now fenced off. During the afternoon, Wong sat down with the student leaders to work out their next step. One of them, Nathan Law, who represented Lingnan University, argued that they had to escalate the protest. Wong lit on a bold idea. That night they would reclaim Civic Square.

Just after 10.30 p.m., after hours of tireless student rhetoric, Wong took the microphone. He called on everyone to storm the fence. He, Chow and Shum led the crowd as they clambered over the fence in a chaotic scramble. The police rushed in, doused the protesters with pepper spray and grabbed Wong, who lost his glasses and one of his trainers in the fray. The next day officers arrested Chow and Shum.

The news ignited the protest movement as nothing before it. The crowds at Civic Square multiplied by tens of thousands while Wong, who was seventeen, endured forty-six hours in custody, during which he was interrogated by sneering policemen who asked how much money the Americans had paid him. The spark had lit the prairie fire.

The rise of a democratic street movement coincided with the collapse of public trust in Hong Kong's police, a force known, at least in its own handouts, as 'Asia's Finest'. The reality was that, like so many aspects of Hong Kong's slow-motion decline, the rot had set in over many years.

Policing Hong Kong had a chequered history ever since Sir Henry Pottinger established the force by an ordinance of 1844. The first superintendent, Charles May, recruited Chinese and Indian officers to serve under British command. In the late nineteenth century recruits from Britain, who had to be 'men of good character' under thirty-two years of age, were given free passage to the colony, clothing and quarters when they got there, and a salary equal to nine pounds sterling a month.

Throughout the colonial period the police were led by expatriates until the appointment of the first ethnic Chinese commissioner, Li Kwan-ha, in 1989. The authorities modernised the force after the Second World War, recruiting officers from the defunct Shanghai Municipal Police, doubling the size of the force and bringing more Chinese men into its ranks. Detection methods improved and the force won credit for its handling of riots in 1956 and 1967 with minimal loss of life, as well as its humane management of illegal immigration from China. Along the way, however, it became fantastically corrupt.

In the early post-war years, rogue cops had dabbled in gun running and smuggling. Their successors colluded with drug traffickers, while the men on the beat accepted a routine and insidious co-existence with the Triads. Expatriate officers shared the spoils with a mafia of staff sergeants, whom locals called 'the tigers'. When the government set up the Independent Commission against Corruption in the 1970s to root out graft, it was so effective that the police themselves took to the streets in protest, forcing the governor, Murray MacLehose, to back off.

Yet by the time of the handover, a lot had changed for the better. The worst rogues had been pensioned off or prosecuted. Training included instruction on the Bill of Rights, racial discrimination and legislation against torture. It was generally accepted that the British had not used the police as a tool of repression. The Special Branch, which had kept an eye on Communist activity, was merged with the Crime (A1) division in 1995 into a combined Crime and Security Department. The city had a modern, professionalised force enjoying a high reputation among international law enforcement agencies. Its top officers were Chinese, and progressive local-isation meant that the force more truly reflected the community it served. The crime rate was low. The streets of Hong Kong were among the safest in the world's big cities. In 1997, a poll for Hong Kong University found that 76.2 per cent of the public had a 'quite positive' view of the police.

Soon all that began to erode. Behind the façade of modernity, officers chafed at curbs on their old tradecraft and resented the new managerial class at the top. The men at street level felt they were losing ground. Their traditional ways of turning a blind eye to keep informants sweet were deemed corrupt. They felt the senior ranks played corporate-style politics and would not back up their staff. Some even preferred the old master–

servant roles of the colonial force. Many felt they had lost authority. One admitted that 'the bad guys' were not afraid of them any more.

The decline was measured in polls taken after scandals, corruption cases and instances of misconduct. At first these were rare. In 2001 there was a hue and cry after police and unruly teenagers exchanged slaps and shoves late on New Year's Eve. Amid mutual accusations of bad behaviour, lower ranks felt the top brass had failed to back up its men. The incident was trivial but it became emblematic of the broken bond between the police and the public. By the time of the Occupy movement, Hong Kong had a politically obedient police force wedded to management jargon and a radicalised young population who, in the words of one study, were 'no longer a docile bunch' but were emboldened to take on the forces of law and order over every issue. There was another, undocumented fact. After the handover more than a million people had left mainland China to live in Hong Kong. An unknown number of them joined the police. The city's tradition of peaceful mass protests was more fragile than people imagined.

In 2011, pollsters for Hong Kong University found that fewer than half of those surveyed now held a 'quite positive' attitude towards the police. Compared to the force's high prestige at the handover that augured badly, but few realised it would tear society apart.

Benny Tai took the stage at the protest site shortly before two o'clock in the morning on Sunday 28 September. To huge cheers he announced that 'Occupy Central' was on. The young rebels had set the pace. The original plan had been to start on 1 October, China's National Day. But Tai and his peers were giddy with the momentum of events and were now being propelled by forces they did not control.

After dawn, hundreds of thousands of Hong Kongers of all ages converged on the area, many wearing yellow ribbons. Throughout the day they came in great numbers. The area became a giant camp site as people settled in for a long stay. Riot police deployed to cut off and contain the demonstration were swamped by late afternoon. Traffic came to a halt on the arterial highways spanning the north shore of Hong Kong island.

Just before six o'clock in the evening, a group of riot police advanced. Having unfurled banners in Chinese and English warning people to disperse or face tear gas, they proceeded to fire tear-gas grenades into the crowd, charging with riot shields and batons. Officers also used pepper spray at close quarters. In the melee, more than thirty people were injured. Police said later that eighty-seven rounds of tear gas were fired. They defended its use as proportionate and restrained response to violent provocation.

For many law-abiding middle-class Hong Kongers the violence on 28 September was a psychological breaking point. It was the first time police had fired tear gas since 2005, when a group of South Korean farmers tried to storm a World Trade Organisation meeting. Even the government recoiled in shock, partly because it realised that scenes of chaos televised around the world did it no good. The police were ordered to step back. They took a softer line and sent negotiators to talk to the protest leaders, but it was too late to stop the blossoming campaign of disobedience. New protest encampments appeared in the shopping district of Causeway Bay and on a block of streets in Mongkok, the Triad heartland over in Kowloon.

What happened next reminded Hong Kong people of how their city was still different from China. The High Court sat on Sunday night to hear the case of Joshua Wong and his fellow protesters. Visibly annoyed with the police, the judge, Mr Justice Patrick Li Hon-leung, ordered their release, granting a writ of habeas corpus and saying their continued detention was illegal. They were freed without charge.

Even as the court was sitting, the fighting nearby between protesters and the police took on a newly vicious character. Time and again the riot squads fired tear gas, used pepper spray and struck young people with their batons. When the protesters unfurled brightly coloured umbrellas to defend themselves, the uprising gained a symbol, a hashtag and a name: the umbrella revolution.

Two days later, the young people gathered at sunrise on the waterfront. It was China's National Day, 1 October. Helicopters and planes of the People's Liberation Army staged a flypast over a flotilla of boats in Victoria harbour, while officers from its 1,200-strong garrison flanked C.Y. Leung and the ranks of the establishment inside Golden Bauhinia Square, where an uninspiring statue of the city's floral emblem overlooked the water. All stood to attention as the banner of Hong Kong and the starry red flag of the People's Republic were raised. Outside a ring of guards, Wong and his group turned their backs and raised their arms in a mock salute borrowed from cult teenage film *The Hunger Games*. A few radicals broke the silence with jeers. The grandees had to leave by boat.

In the weeks that followed a hallucinatory calm settled over Occupy Central. Thousands of young protesters, dazed at their own audacity, created a street festival of politics and culture that was part sleepover, part sit-in and part Woodstock. They were the world's politest demonstrators.

Philip Yueng, who was seventeen, said his parents supported him but were worried for his safety. 'This is my idea alone,' he said. The older generation was represented by Albert Ho, the veteran democrat, who looked around in wonder as he declared it was 'a precious opportunity'. But the hour did not belong to the traditional politicians, who were left in the slipstream of a new generation of activists. Martin Lee was listened to respectfully when he told the crowds 'this is the last stand in defence of Hong Kong's core values', but they knew that anyway.

The youngsters lit on the idea of scribbling messages on multi-coloured Post-it notes, which festooned a 'John Lennon Wall' on the grey concrete around them. A big yellow sign identified the office blocks as 'Government and Triad Headquarters'. Placards and Post-its could be ironic, witty or bitter: one bore the words 'I'm so angry, I made a sign'; another read: 'We do not want to live like robots'; a third asked: 'Where has my dream city gone?' A few quoted tags from classical poetry. Somebody found a photo of Xi Jinping holding an umbrella, copied it and turned it into a poster. There were help points, food stalls, counsellors, medical assistance, water supplies and, inevitably, a cluster of desks where young heads bent over their homework. Romances flowered amid the tents. One evening, when a warm, soft rain was falling, everyone swayed, clapped and cheered to music and singing from the stage in a break from political speeches.

The soundtrack to the umbrella revolution was short on angry rap, long on heartstrings. Its staples were John Lennon's 'Imagine' and the hymn 'Can You Hear The People Sing?' from *Les Miserables*, but the hometown favourite was a Cantonese ballad, 'Seas Wide, Boundless Skies' by local rock band Beyond. The movement gained its own anthem when twenty-five-year-old Lo Hiu-pan scribbled down the music and lyrics of 'Raise the Umbrella' in a blaze of indignation after the police first used tear gas. His song was recorded by two Canto-pop stars, Anthony Wong and Denise Ho, whose video was a hit on YouTube and put them on a Chinese government blacklist. Throughout its short life, Occupy Central always had better tunes.

The air of dreamy innocence meant that few heeded a warning from pro-regime lawmaker Regina Ip, who said: 'People have to understand how Beijing sees this … it's a frontal challenge to their authority. China feels threatened.' According to the *People's Daily*, a 'Pandora's Box' was being opened to release 'devils'.

The authorities had already decided on a patient, methodical policy. They would not give in but they would wait out the protesters and wear them down. The first gambit was an offer of dialogue with the Federation of Students. It was entrusted to Carrie Lam, who was emerging as a more acceptable public face than the chief executive. After weeks of on-off bargaining, the talks took place in front of television cameras, moderated by Leonard Cheng, the president of Lingnan University. It was one of the most watched broadcasts in Hong Kong's television history.

On one side sat Lam and four men in suits, on the other four youths in black T-shirts and a girl, Yvonne Leung. They were respectful, articulate and calm. It was hard to see them as traitors or the naïve dupes of foreign powers. They looked and sounded like the sort of children most local families would have been proud to call their own. The officials, for their part, played the role of concerned parents, calling the students by their first names, 'Alex', 'Lester' and so on, although the mask slipped occasionally when Carrie Lam came over as the chiding auntie of a myriad Cantonese soap operas. 'You cannot only be idealistic. You must be pragmatic,' she said, in tones suggesting she had long forgotten what it was like to be a student. There were some things that could not be changed.

It was Yvonne Leung, a third-year student of government and law at Lam's alma mater, Hong Kong University, who skewered the chief secretary's arguments. Of course things could be changed, she said. She mentioned the Chinese constitution; everyone knew its clauses on free speech and assembly bore no relation to reality. But one could always pretend that they did, right? Lam remained po-faced at this remark.

The other students, Alex Chow, Lester Shum, Nathan Law and Eason Chung, weighed in to say that the Basic Law could be amended. It was not a sacred text. The committee to select leadership candidates could be more democratic. They suggested that Lam's report to Beijing on public opinion had not exactly been truthful and proposed that she send another one. To general surprise, she agreed. It was, however, the only signal of conciliation in a dialogue of the deaf. The new report was not sent until the following spring, when it had already been forgotten.

The television show changed no political realities but it shifted the psychology of Hong Kong. The *South China Morning Post* pointed out that it was the first face-to-face dialogue between activists and top officials in the city's history. It made stars out of the young participants; a price that the government must have thought worth paying for a show of soft power. Inside the velvet glove, it retained an iron fist.

The government's counter-revolution was efficient, broad-spectrum and straight from the Communist Party's United Front textbook. A group of pro-Beijing politicians launched a 'blue ribbon' campaign to back law and order. Several hundred blue ribbon-wearers assembled outside a mall at the protest site but were peacefully engulfed in a sea of yellow. Later on, they besieged the offices of Jimmy Lai's *Apple Daily* and tried to stop its deliveries. A deputation trooped to the university authorities to complain that Benny Tai and Chan Kin-man had 'incited' their students to rebel. Over in Kowloon, where there were fewer cameras, the methods got rough. A gang of burly, tattooed men attacked the protest camp in Mongkok, throwing wood blocks and metal piping. When they tore down a barricade of wooden crates and railings, shouting 'scum', the protesters howled with rage and fought back. Local journalists chased one bald, stocky man down a sidestreet. 'Where are you from? Where are you from?' they shouted. He turned and spat. 'Go fuck your mothers,' he said, in a mainland Chinese accent.

The police arrested eighteen people and found, according to the secretary for security, Lai Tung-kwok, that eight of them had links to Triads. While Lai denied the opposition's claim that the gangs were working hand in glove with the authorities, the protesters believed that the Triads had discovered their 'patriotism' and were providing muscle for Beijing.

As the weeks went by, the scuffles in Kowloon turned into regular battles with police, Triads and bailiffs. The protest camps waxed and waned in number, while the movement divided and lost its focus. Its leading lights welcomed the annual Pride Parade to the Admiralty site but Joshua Wong did not join them out of respect for his father, who opposed same-sex marriage. Fresh causes grew from the fertilised soil of protest, the most significant being an 'indigenous' subcurrent of radicals, who argued for a 'localist' Hong Kong identity and agitated against mainland Chinese influence, investment and immigration. A handful called for independence from China, a cause that never attracted much support. Wong noted that with so many stakeholders it was becoming difficult, if not impossible, to forge a consensus. At the end of October, Benny Tai and Chan Kin-man said they would quit the camp and go back to their lecture rooms. The protesters realised they had reached a stalemate.

They were also under siege in cyberspace. There was a false assumption that smart, tech-savvy Hong Kong kids would own a monopoly on data skills. In fact they were up against a high-grade opponent, one honed in the cyberschools of the PLA, most likely wearing a young and intelligent visage like their own. The electronic assault was relentless in its aims to disrupt, to demoralise and to discover. Resistance to it, while clever, was sporadic and often ineffective. A flood of WhatsApp messages deluged protesters' smartphones, planting spyware and freezing the devices at critical moments. At the time WhatsApp was an open system, so users turned to Telegram, an encrypted service based in Germany, as an alternative. They adopted FireChat, an app that let smartphones communicate at short range without using the mobile network.

In the laptop world, meanwhile, hackers infected email accounts with links that stole contacts and read messages. They targeted Chinese-language media organisations with 'phishing' mails inviting the recipient to a press conference or purporting to come from a campaign group, forcing the staff at *Apple Daily* to go back to pen-and-ink, faxes and couriers. Private messages about funding in Benny Tai's college account were leaked to the pro-Beijing newspapers.

There was a quixotic counterstrike by Anonymous, a hackers' collective, which launched an online insurgency against websites of the Hong Kong government, the pro-Beijing parties, the Chinese government's Liaison Office and, eventually, databases inside the People's Republic. Some democrats feared this merely sowed confusion by allowing the Chinese government to play the victim. Their adversaries were also learning to turn the internet's rules into a weapon against free speech: Facebook took down Tai's page after a stream of complaints that it was counterfeit. It was a campaign so overwhelming and sophisticated that most experts believed it could only be the work of a powerful state actor.

The democracy movement was strongest when exploiting its freedom to communicate. When on 15 October a group of plainclothes police were caught on video by a local news cameraman as they handcuffed a man named Ken Tsang, a social worker and member of the Civic Party, dragged him into an alley and beat him up, internet users made sure the footage went viral and was seen worldwide. The social media war never stopped. By nature fleeting, it hit a few high points. One came when C.Y. Leung's daughter, Chai-yan, a student at the London School of Economics, posted a picture on her Facebook page showing herself wearing a jewelled necklace and thanking 'silly taxpayers' for funding it. The page was hastily taken down, while Leung himself shrugged off a revelation that Australian engineering company UGL had been paying him millions of dollars in fees under a pre-existing contract while he was in office. His foes pointed out that UGL had a train maintenance contract with the MTR Corporation, which was majority-owned by Leung's government. Although all sides denied any wrongdoing, it was little wonder that the chief executive's face grew longer and longer as the protesters made his resignation a core demand.

Leung's foreign connections were natural for a businessman in a place that called itself 'Asia's World City'. But moneymaking was one thing, politics another. The party's United Front had an app for that. Faithful to Stalin's precepts, it hammered away at the themes of foreign spies, paid agents and interference in China's affairs. It was a line from which the party never deviated, presumably in the belief that ceaseless repetition would grind the enemy down, and over the long term it was proved right. Chinese public opinion rallied behind the flag, while the security and theoretical panjandrums realised that they had found a counter to the 'colour revolutions' against authoritarian rule and the youth revolts of the 'Arab Spring' in 2011.

It began with time-tested disinformation techniques. The newspaper *Wen Wei Po* ran an 'exposé' of Joshua Wong. It claimed that the CIA had talent-spotted Wong at the age of fourteen while he was on a visit with his parents to a casino in Macau. Leaving aside the improbable idea that the devout Christians might take their children to a gambling den, the story credited the CIA with a foresight bordering on genius that few had suspected. It doubled down with a line that the Americans had paid Wong hundreds of thousands of dollars and arranged for the slight, skinny teen-ager to get combat training from a US Navy Seal. Wong called the story 'science fiction' and said it was 'false in every detail'. He added in a sarcastic Facebook post: 'My links to foreign countries are limited to my Korean cellphone, my American computer and my Japanese Gundam [an animated game]. And of course all these are "Made in China".'

The *China Daily*, an English-language state newspaper, targeted a wider audience with a column saying that American diplomats and spies were behind the protests, grooming student leaders and infiltrating schools while handing out passports and visas with promises of asylum if it all went wrong. 'Dirty politics' lay beneath the veil of democracy, concluded the writer, who was identified as Hong Chen, a 'current affairs commentator'. Enquirers were told that Hong Chen was not available to elaborate on his scoop. He was said to be a professional journalist from Hong Kong who lived across the border in Shenzhen. The source of his information, an editor conceded, was *Wen Wei Po*.

People who laughed this off were making a mistake. The Chinese government treated Hong Kong in 2014 as a testbed for methods of disinformation and propaganda which turned out to be effective and adaptable.

Its first smart move was to stop censorship inside China of news about the demonstrations, reasoning that word would spread anyway. Instead it opted to create its own narrative, learning from Vladimir Putin's Russia.

One evening, viewers of China Central Television's soporific nightly newscast sat up and took notice. The anchor explained to viewers that 'an illegal gathering is currently taking place in our country's Hong Kong Special Administrative Region.' A lively infographic then unfolded a web of conspiracy linking American neo-conservatives, the CIA and Occupy Central. It labelled an American called Dan Garrett as 'a flagrant spy' based at the US Consulate, whose mission was to sow subversion.

The US Consulate was swift to deny the story, but it contained a strand of fact. There was an American in Hong Kong called Dan Garrett, a free-lance author, photographer and political scientist who had devoted much time to covering Occupy Central. Garrett had served in the US Air Force, the Defence Intelligence Agency and the National Security Agency. He later published analytical work on protest culture, 'counter-hegemonic resistance' in Hong Kong and China's 'securitisation' of the city. He testified to the US Congressional-Executive Commission on China in 2019 – alongside Joshua Wong and Denise Ho – and was subsequently barred from returning to Hong Kong.

Communist propaganda emphasised that all foreign connections were suspicious. It mattered little that the early revolutionaries had absorbed their political theories in Japan, nor that many children of the regime went to college in America. (Xi Jinping's daughter, Mingze, was studying at Harvard University in 2014, where she was taught by the historian of Maoism, Roderick MacFarquhar.) It did not bother the writers that few people in Hong Kong believed them, or that anyone could see that the protests were spontaneous and local in character. What counted was the relentless insistence to the ordinary citizen of the People's Republic that hostile powers were once again plotting against China. The *People's Daily* set the bar with a flagship editorial warning against 'foreign interference' in Hong Kong. 'The US purports to be promoting the "universal values" of "democracy," "freedom" and "human rights" but in reality the US is only defending its own strategic interests,' it declared. It was a message that did not change in years to come.

As it turned out, the democracy movement's weaknesses were home-grown. It retained a talent for stunts: the 'Spider Kids' scaled Lion Rock to hang a banner demanding universal suffrage; young people staged slow walks en masse to paralyse shopping streets; a statue of Xi Jinping holding a yellow umbrella greeted passers-by in Admiralty. But daring and wit got nowhere without political traction. The government's patient strategy began to work. When the Federation of Students staged an ill-judged bid to besiege the government offices at the end of November, it was easily repulsed with tear gas and water cannon. Carrie Lam gratefully received a petition from the 'Anti-Occupy Alliance' bearing almost two million signatures, which the blue-ribbon group said it had collected from fed-up citizens. The end game was drawing near.

Without fanfare, the Hong Kong government turned to a mundane tool to end Occupy Central. It encouraged businesses and transport operators to go to court for injunctions against the protesters. Armed with court orders, bailiffs and police began to clear the encampments. Already adrift, the movement did not unite to resist effectively. Violence broke out in Mongkok and Joshua Wong went on hunger strike, but everyone knew the cause was lost. On 15 December the last barricades were torn down. Occupy Central had lasted seventy-nine days. More than a million people took part, of whom about a thousand were arrested. But nobody was killed, or even seriously hurt. On that level alone it was a tribute to Hong Kong.

In the aftermath, all sides drew their own conclusions. The administration of C.Y. Leung realised that henceforth it could use the law to enforce its will. In Beijing, the Politburo accepted Leung's submission that his prosecutors and police could be trusted to do the job. It was far from a triumph: in 2015, Leung lost a vote in the Legislative Council on his electoral 'reform' bill by twenty-eight votes to eight, leaving politics in limbo and the election of a leader by universal suffrage as far off as ever. Across Hong Kong, angry and disillusioned young people argued over what had gone wrong and debated their tactics for the inevitable reprise. Next time they would not repeat the mistake of collecting in one easily targeted mass, instead they would flow 'like water' around their opponents. In secret, radicals planned for a violent confrontation, arguing that the time for moderate means had passed. Meanwhile, the movement's reasonable public faces prepared for years of court cases, harassment and intimidation. Some lost their careers, several went to prison.

Among those jailed were Joshua Wong, Alex Chow and Nathan Law, who were sentenced to six to eight months for unlawful assembly. Wong was also convicted of contempt of court in a separate case. He later served a second short sentence for his actions at a protest site in Mongkok. Prosecutors were still pursuing him in 2020, when he was briefly held on a new charge of unlawful assembly. Nathan Law became the youngest elected Hong Kong lawmaker when he stood for the new party Demosistō in 2016, but lost his seat for speaking the words of his oath of office in a way that the government held to be incorrect.

Almost five years after the Occupy protests, Benny Tai and Chan Kin-man were sentenced to prison terms of eighteen months for conspiracy to commit a public nuisance. The third original leader, pastor Chu Yiu-ming, who was seventy-five years old, received a suspended sentence.

As for the fabled foreign forces, they melted away. The United States expressed support for freedom in Hong Kong and regretted the persecution of its democrats, but did nothing to sanction or deter the individuals responsible. The administration of Barack Obama had no illusions. It had started a 'Pivot to Asia' after the president's cold treatment on his first visit to China, but it sought to engage Beijing across a spectrum of big issues and did not want a confrontation over a small one. In Europe, Chancellor Angela Merkel welcomed the Chinese premier, Li Keqiang, for cordial talks about the boom in German exports to his country.

The British government had embarked on what it called a 'golden era' of relations with China and did not want to rock the boat. The Foreign Office concluded in its six-monthly reports to Parliament that 'one country, two systems' was 'working well' in Hong Kong. The Foreign Affairs Committee of Parliament called the reports 'comprehensive if somewhat bland'. It was left to the former governor, Chris Patten, to find the last word on this insouciance, which he did with aplomb: 'On the day that the sans-culottes stormed the Bastille, Louis XVI wrote in his diary, "Rien".'

15

Hunger Games

Months of turmoil had exhausted the people of Hong Kong, but the Chinese security services were indefatigable. As mass political action ebbed away from the streets they began a twilight struggle against dissent. The Ministry of State Security had been expanding its footprint in Hong Kong ever since the handover, seeding the police, customs and immigration departments with 'patriotic' local staff and settlers from the mainland. This assiduous, patient work had begun well before the Occupy Central protests.

In the summer of 2014, a Democratic Party legislator, James To, alerted police after two silver Mercedes cars began following him on his daily commute to the Legislative Council. On one occasion a man tailed To, who was with his three-year-old son, to a café near their home. Plainclothes officers kept watch, then arrested two Hong Kong men aged fifty-six and fifty-four, impounding the two Mercedes. According to an investigative report by Reuters news agency, they had stumbled on a covert Chinese surveillance operation targeting pro-democracy figures.

A state security team had been put on To's tail in early August, the story said. The politician believed its task was to monitor him for compromising information. To was no extremist and did not even campaign for popular votes; he was a moderate lawyer who represented the legal profession in a functional constituency. Yet he was deemed a suitable target. The facts were never tested in court because the two arrested men, who were not named, walked free after police quickly dropped their investigation. The Reuters report said Chinese security agencies had recruited about twenty former Hong Kong police officers to work alongside mainland agents on political surveillance operations, selecting men trained in undercover work who were sympathetic to Beijing.

Other figures who came under round-the-clock watch were Chan Kin-man, the co-founder of Occupy Central, and Robert Chung, an academic pollster, who found photos of his car plastered all over the pro-Beijing daily *Ta Kung Pao* in a story accusing him of driving dangerously like a spy trained to throw off pursuit.

The Ministry of State Security had authority to call on the whole spectrum of China's information-gathering apparatus, from banks, churches and cultural institutions to the local branch of the United Front Work Department. Its reach was long. Joshua Wong put his own experience on his Facebook page after he went with friends to Taiwan. Calls were made to their hotel room and the boys were followed by at least two men. One photographed them in the street with his mobile phone. Confronted by one of the students, he said he had been told to trail them in the hope of catching them with women. The purpose of these costly and time-consuming surveillance operations mystified many observers. Then people began to disappear.

The publishing house Mighty Current Media specialised in scandalous exposés of intrigue, adultery and crime at the top of the Communist Party; it was one of the biggest and most profitable publishers trading in books banned in China but snapped up in their thousands by Chinese visitors to Hong Kong. The titles were sold all over the city and piled high at bookstalls at the city's airport, alongside muckraking political magazines. In late 2015, five of the firm's staff went missing.

Mighty Current operated at the raw end of the long-established industry which sometimes published genuine memoirs and documents of serious political import from inside China. Its customers, however, preferred salacious gossip to debates on Marxism; its titles included a book predicting the fall of Xi Jinping, while a supposed autobiography of Wang Guangmei, the wife of China's late president Liu Shaoqi and a hallowed figure until her death in 2006, drew condemnation from her family as 'fabrications, malicious slander, excessively vulgar and fake'. More ominously, the book prompted the pro-Beijing daily *Wen Wei Po* to warn of dire consequences for those who 'slandered' state leaders. This admonition had not deterred the publisher, Gui Minhai, from pressing ahead with a book on the love life of Xi himself, a topic which may not have exercised a wide appeal but undoubtedly had a niche somewhere in the market.

Gui had last been seen leaving his holiday beach apartment in Thailand on 17 October 2015 with an unidentified Chinese man in a white car. Three weeks later four Chinese men gained access to the apartment after a call to the manager, apparently from Gui. Once inside, they worked on his computer for two hours, then tried to take it away. Suspicious, the staff threatened to summon the police. A few days afterwards, Gui called his wife, said he would return home later than expected and told her not to worry. He was already in the northeast Chinese city of Ningbo, having been spirited by security agents across the Thai border to Cambodia, which had become a virtual client state of China, and onwards to the motherland.

Soon afterwards, two of Gui's employees, Lui Bo and Cheung Jiping, who had been unwise enough to visit their families in southern China, were taken into custody. The company's retail bookseller, Lam Wing-kee, was arrested on 24 October when he crossed the border to Shenzhen carrying a stack of banned books for sale. On 30 December, Lee Bo, who delivered books and managed stock for Mighty Current Media, and whose wife, Sophie Choi, was a shareholder in the firm, failed to come home at the end of a working day. He had talked to the press about his missing colleagues, perhaps thinking that he was protected by a British passport. That was a mistake. Britain's foreign secretary later told Parliament Lee had been 'involuntarily removed to the mainland without any due process'.

After Chinese state television broadcast a 'confession' by Gui Minhai in which he told viewers he had 'voluntarily' gone back to China to face justice over a fatal traffic accident, the case of the booksellers became an international cause célèbre. The abductions set off protests and demonstrations; even the chief executive, C.Y. Leung, said it was 'unacceptable' if mainland agencies were operating in Hong Kong. Unfazed, the Chinese security services played their game well. A bewildering drama ensued of disappearance, reappearance, betrayal and mystery. It was designed to confuse, to punish and to deter. Four of the missing men resurfaced in Hong Kong but only one, Lam Wing-kee, defied the Chinese state to speak out. He eventually moved to Taiwan, where he opened a bookstore selling political works.

Gui Minhai was to endure a cruel period of release and re-incarceration until he was handed a ten-year jail sentence in 2020 for 'illegally providing intelligence to foreign powers'. Although his disappearance had not gone unnoticed – he was a naturalised Swedish citizen – the government in Stockholm was consigned to years of troubled and fruitless diplomacy on his behalf. Indeed, his kidnapping entangled Sweden in a scandal when its former ambassador to Beijing, Anna Lindstedt, was put on trial in Stockholm for exceeding her authority in dealing with a foreign power, having brokered a private meeting between Gui's daughter and a pair of

Chinese 'businessmen' who offered to help. She was acquitted, but the episode was a warning to diplomats about the risks inherent in dealing with a police state that was also a big trading partner. To the controllers of state security in Beijing, that was a useful by-product of the case.

Although the plight of the five booksellers commanded world attention it was just one action among many. Two Hong Kong magazine publishers, Wang Jianmin and Guo Zhongxiao, were jailed for five years by a court in Shenzhen in 2016 for 'running an illegal business' and bribery. A third Hong Kong publisher, Yiu Man-tin, got ten years in jail in 2014 after prosecutors accused him of smuggling industrial paint into Shenzhen; his real offence was to commission a dissident writer's book called *Godfather Xi Jinping*.

The blueprint for these operations was an internal party document titled the 'Guangdong Action Plan'. Based on a central government directive of 25 April 2015, it authorised a 'counter-attack' to 'exterminate' banned books and magazines at their source, identifying as targets fourteen publishers and twenty-one publications in Hong Kong. Extracts from the plan fell into the hands of Hong Kong legislators, who shared them with activists and local reporters.

Emboldened, the Chinese security services expanded their cross-border operations to carry out a well-documented programme of abductions and disappearances of dissidents from Thailand, Laos, Cambodia and Burma. These were the forgotten victims of the new national security state. One of them was a young journalist and human rights activist, Li Xin, who worked for the *Southern Metropolis Daily*, a popular newspaper in Guangdong. Li fled China after pressure from state security operatives but failed to win asylum from the US or India. He was last seen boarding a train in Bangkok bound for the Thai border with Laos. His wife and child were forbidden to leave Guangdong. He later called her to say he was in the hands of the police back in China.

International law was not much help in such cases. The Thai military government sent two veteran dissidents, Jiang Yefei and Dong Guanping, back to China even though the pair had been granted refugee status by the United Nations, which summoned up all its reserves of indignation to call the rendition 'a serious disappointment'. The American law scholar Jerome Cohen, who had devoted decades to constructive engagement with legal reform in China, declared that it showed 'not only the extending reach of Chinese law but the extending reach of Chinese lawlessness'.

* * *

The ascent of Xi Jinping had introduced an age of uncertainty for Hong Kong, which although different from the existential doubts of the 1980s, brought a new sense of unease. The return to a hard dictatorship ended dreams of a more liberal, internationalist outlook in China under the benign influence of trade. Now, as economic shocks set loose forces which its prophets had not foreseen, globalisation no longer seemed inevitable. Caught up in this whirlwind, Hong Kong was just a small enclave on the South China Sea, although it was home to some of the most connected, cosmopolitan young people on earth. It became a mirror to the times.

Hong Kong depended on free trade to flourish. The integration of China into world commerce and the growth of the digital economy in the early twenty-first century had seemed to offer limitless opportunities. Hong Kong had profited as millions of Chinese workers left poverty to toil in the factories on the coast, cheap goods flowed to the West and money flowed back to the East. That had kept inflation and interest rates low worldwide. It also destroyed manufacturing jobs in rich nations, most of which were not replaced by the new service industries. Instead blue-collar workers faced lower pay and insecurity. President Clinton's boast that America would export goods but not jobs rang increasingly hollow. Perhaps a million Americans were put out of work by Chinese competition.

When China joined the World Trade Organisation, its share of world exports had surged as the volume of trade went up. Global supply chains had embedded the People's Republic into multinational production and woven emerging markets in Asia into one interconnected economy. Chinese products went to car makers in Germany, electronics giants in Japan and new technology giants like Apple, the maker of computers and smartphones. It was a seamless operation, made possible by computerised management. Huge capital flows across the Pacific and Atlantic were going into ever more intricate financial transactions. The US Federal Reserve said there was a global savings glut. With all the certainty of Lenin heading for the Finland Station, executives shared their visions of a borderless future at portentous corporate 'summits'. Only a handful of financial analysts had studied complexity theory, a discipline founded in natural sciences which taught that complex systems bred uncertainty, process was not linear and order was no more inevitable than chaos.

This was shown to be the case when the financial crisis of 2008 led to a collapse in demand around the world. Globalisation stalled and interest rates fell to near zero as central banks tried to keep markets functioning.

The rise of technology led to reduced competition, concentrating profits in the hands of a few giant tech firms. Workers in the industrialised democracies did not share equally in the gains and the middle classes felt squeezed. Chinese leaders saw this as proof of the decline of liberal capitalism and the superiority of their own system. They would soon find out that economic disruption was not as simple as that.

Inside China, trade ceased to grow as a share of gross national product. As foreign direct investment fell, the economy turned inward. A new middle class had money to spend, consuming more of what they produced. Around 2015 the Chinese share of world exports stopped rising, although the share of imports grew. Automation and technologies like 3D printing cut into the huge cost savings that firms had reaped by moving production to exploit cheap Chinese labour. The explosion of social media and 'fast fashion' ignited consumer demand for fast, cheap goods made nearer home. The long supply chains linking firms to 'just-in-time' delivery could snap under unexpected stresses, like an earthquake and tsunami that paralysed car makers in Japan, and floods which shut down computer factories in Thailand. Companies began to think supply chains might also be shackles. Some tired of the bureaucracy, corruption and arbitrary use of law in China.

Then there was political risk. In November 2016, Republican Donald Trump won the US presidential election, having said during his candidature that he spoke for Americans left behind by globalisation in dying coal towns and shuttered factories. Blaming China for what he called 'unfair' practices, he proceeded to launch a trade war.

Even Charlene Barshefsky, who had unlocked the WTO accession deal for Bill Clinton, admitted that China had defied expectations. In her view, it had turned away from market economics under Hu Jintao, handing privileges back to the state sector, discriminating against foreign firms, forcing them to transfer technology and stealing their intellectual property. These trends had accelerated when Xi Jinping took power with a view to using economic power in his national transformation, said Barshefsky. She blamed both Republican and Democratic presidents for failing to act: 'The shame of it … is that the United States missed many opportunities to enforce the WTO agreement against China.' It had not used the mechanisms available to hit back, she said, and its much-touted economic dialogues were just 'talkfests'.

The former trade negotiator said America should work with its allies and use the multilateral system, but the Trump administration was impervious to such advice from people it considered elite insiders. The WTO was meant to adjudicate disputes, but according to the president it was ineffective and biased. His representative in Geneva paralysed it by a clever expedient, blocking the appointment of judges its appeals panel. Average American tariffs on Chinese imports were increased from 12 per cent to 21 per cent. When in response Beijing hiked tariffs from 17 per cent to the same level, the US launched campaigns against the telecoms firms Huawei and ZTE, flagships of the new Chinese economy.

For the first time since the 1970s, America was playing rough. It was economic nationalism, a rejection of the orthodoxy of previous decades practised by Barshefsky and her peers. The immediate result was not, perhaps, what Trump's team had calculated. In 2017 President Xi Jinping went to the World Economic Forum in Davos, where he was hailed as an apostle of globalisation, development and good governance. He said China had taken a brave step to embrace the global market and cited an ancient verse: 'Honey melons hang on bitter vines; sweet dates grow on thistles and thorns.' The audience gave him an ovation.

As his regime grew more assertive abroad, it grew harsher at home. Inside China, Xi put in place the legal and bureaucratic furniture typical of efficient dictatorships. He had inaugurated a National Security Commission in 2014 to act as a 'nerve centre' for the police state appara-tus. Its activities were secret but Xi applauded it for 'solving tough problems'. The next year a new National Security Law was passed with an expansive definition of offences against the state. There followed a National Intelligence Law, a Counter-Espionage Law, a Counter-Terrorism Law, a Cybersecurity Law and a Foreign Non-Governmental Organisations Management Law. Analysing the legislative edifice, the scholar Tai Ming Cheung of the University of California, San Diego, commented that 'the Chinese national security state has unassailable legal authority to do anything it wants within its own borders and increas-ingly beyond.'

All this bore the stamp of one-man rule. Xi abolished term limits, allowing himself to stay in office as president for life. His personality cult grew extravagant. Deng Xiaoping had pushed the Communist Party towards collective leadership to stop another strongman like Mao coming to power. Now Xi tore up the rulebook. Supreme at home, he turned his attention abroad.

Xi made much of his good relations with Vladimir Putin of Russia and sundry authoritarians of clerical or mafia stamp. China began expanding its diplomatic and commercial footprint by an ambitious 'Belt and Road' initiative, ploughing investment into ports, roads and railways in Asia, the Middle East and Africa. Beijing called these projects 'win-win', which for China they often were. Its development loans flowed straight back to the state-owned Chinese firms awarded the contracts.

China's military presence was growing in the South China Sea, most of which it claimed. It built a blue-water navy, modernised its air force and raced forward in missile and stealth technology and electronic warfare. It tested the United States and its allies with naval and air patrols in the Pacific theatre. It propped up the nuclear-armed regime in North Korea, subsidised Pakistan and duelled with India in the Himalayas. In southeast Asia only Vietnam pushed back hard, while Thailand, the Philippines, Cambodia and Laos became compliant or tributary states.

The rise of China amounted to the greatest strategic challenge to the United States since the end of the Second World War. This was no brush-fire insurgency but a drive to expel the Americans from Asia. The Obama administration took a low-key, patient response, crafting a Trans Pacific Partnership in trade, working up alliances and persuading its partners to join naval operations in the sea lanes vital for world commerce. President Trump took a louder tone; his second Secretary of State, Mike Pompeo, spoke directly about confronting Chinese power, although their with-drawal from the Pacific trade pact and their diplomatic disarray did not help the cause. American policy was broadly bipartisan, however, for there was a consensus among Republicans and Democrats that 'engagement' had not worked. The Pentagon, the intelligence community and even many in American business felt a tough line was long overdue. Soon Trump, his cabinet officers and senior members of Congress were all singling out Hong Kong as a test of the future relations between America and China.

The Xi dictatorship and the cold war between China and America meant that Hong Kong was no longer a sideshow. It captured the key political questions of the era: freedom versus order, the individual versus the state, tolerance versus identity, obedience versus dissent, the rule of law versus the strongman. The city's local conflicts drew worldwide attention. And events began to move fast.

In January 2017, mainland security agents entered the service apart-ments at the Four Seasons Hotel, which had become a luxurious refuge for wealthy business figures out of favour with the Chinese government. They took away a billionaire, the vanished tycoon Xiao Jianhua, covering his head with a hood as he was pushed in a wheelchair to a waiting car, which drove him across the border into China. Nothing was seen of Xiao for the next few years. The government took over his companies. His fall was part of Xi's campaign against corruption, which scythed through the mainland's commercial elite. The manner of his exit from Hong Kong made it clear there were no boundaries any more.

Two months later, Carrie Lam took over as chief executive from the unpopular C.Y. Leung, who did not stand for a second term. She won with 777 votes from an election committee of 1,194 members, defeating the former finance secretary, John Tsang, and a retired judge, Woo Kwok-hing. The 7.7 million people of Hong Kong had no further say in the matter. A more sophisticated choice might have been Jasper Tsang Yok-sing, an astute politician on the left who led the biggest pro-Beijing party and chaired the Legislative Council. Tsang was a Marxist teacher, born in Guangzhou, but he grew up in Hong Kong and knew its society better than the elite civil servants and businessmen who dwelt at its summit. Opinion polls regularly ranked him as one of the city's most popular legislators. That opportunity lost, the Chinese government was stuck with Lam, a distant and icy bureaucrat whose political instincts were weak. It did not take long for the former chief secretary to take her first step to disaster. It was due, she said, to the best of intentions.

Like many Hong Kongers, Lam was horrified by the murder of a young pregnant woman, Poon Hiu-Wing, killed by her jealous boyfriend, Chan Tong-kai, on a holiday in Taiwan. He fled to Hong Kong, where he could neither be tried for the murder nor sent back to face justice in Taiwan because no extradition treaty existed between them. Chan served a short sentence for other crimes but his immunity infuriated the victim's family. Lam said the case had persuaded her to examine Hong Kong's limited extradition arrangements – it had treaties with just twenty countries – and convinced her that it needed a new law. There was, she maintained, no other motive.

Lam took advice from John Lee Ka-chiu, the first security secretary to be promoted from the ranks of the police, who took a plain law-and-order line. Her top civil servant, Matthew Cheung Kin-chung, joined the consultations. Between them, the bureaucrats came up with a bill allowing extradition to and from jurisdictions outside Hong Kong. It meant that suspects could be sent to mainland China, where the courts served the Communist Party.

The bill was unveiled in February 2019 and promoted as a crime-fighting measure. Its provisions set off a storm. Perhaps the government thought it was secure because the Legislative Council elected in 2016 had a pro-establishment majority among its seventy members. That, too, was a miscalculation. There were scuffles in the council chambers as democrats tried to block the bill in committee hearings. But even members sponsored by the business community were uneasy. It had dawned on the tycoons of Hong Kong that if the bill became law any of them who got into a dispute in mainland China could share the fate of Xiao Jianhua, exchanging a boardroom for a cell. They were not reassured when the head of the Hong Kong and Macau Affairs Office, Zhang Xiaoming, called the legislation 'necessary'.

The Liberal Party, which spoke for corporate interests, lined up with the Business and Professional Alliance in the council to seek amendments. The American Chamber of Commerce, a business group that was normally a reliable cheerleader for the establishment, expressed dismay. The Bar Association condemned the bill. So did the more conservative Law Society.

When opposition turned into a cascade, Lam seemed paralysed. It started quietly when Joshua Wong's new political party, Demosistō, staged a sit-in. The first march against the bill drew 12,000 people, the second got 130,000 onto the streets. Sensing a cause, the democratic movement awoke. Petitions circulated at schools and colleges. The internet ignited. Activists mustered around an online forum called LIHKG, which became a bulletin board to rally protests, organise supplies and select targets. Its threads used classical Chinese, demotic Cantonese characters and the occasional ill-chosen obscenity in English. It was a living thing. On 9 June, the organisers said a million people marched.

To be in Hong Kong that spring was to sense a change in the air. Gone were the dreamy pacifists of Occupy Central, serenading their cause with Canto-rock and cuddling in tents as academics orated. Now bitterness, anger and covert planning marked the first mass protests in five years. The chanting was harsher, the music plangent. '*Faan sung zung!*' they chorused, 'oppose being sent to China!' It was a pun on words that meant sending someone to their death. The Occupy crowd had liked cartoons of Xi Jinping as Winnie-the-Pooh, a hapless bear. This generation drew Carrie Lam and other enemies in their death throes, dripping blood. A new breed of street fighter appeared, black-clad, in helmets, goggles and cling-film masks, boots laced and smartphone in a rugged case, ready for trouble.

On 12 June, the dam broke. Hundreds of businesses shut as staff joined a general strike. A huge demonstration headed for the Legislative Council building to stop a second reading of the bill. Police used tear gas for the first time since Occupy Central, also firing rubber bullets and 'bean bag' sponge rounds. The whirlwind of violence spared neither old nor young. This was a different police force, one that was hostile, aggressive and cold, whose officers tore their serial numbers off their uniforms so they could not be brought to book. Their opponents fought with unexpected fury. A marcher showed his smartphone messages rallying the *jung mou*, 'the brave and fierce', who were in the front lines. They were *san zuk*, brothers and sisters in arms.

Lam was shaken. On 15 June she suspended the extradition bill. It was too late; the uprising had taken off. It became a whirling, chaotic urban insurgency. In July Lam declared the bill dead, in September it was withdrawn and in October it was formally removed from the order papers. By then its fate no longer mattered. The city had fallen into an abyss.

In early summer the protest movement rapidly expanded its demands. It wanted a formal apology from Lam, a commission of inquiry into alleged police brutality, a declaration that the clash on 12 June was not 'a riot', an amnesty for those arrested and – almost as an afterthought – universal suffrage. On 16 June so many demonstrators came out that the marches took seven hours to wind across Hong Kong island. The organisers said there may have been two million in the streets. The police put it at less than a quarter of that but it still looked like the biggest protest in the history of Hong Kong. Lam apologised but would retreat no further. Even if she had been tempted to concede, the Chinese government would not have let her do so. There was endless debate about whether the spasms of violence served the Communist Party's interests. Older heads recalled the catchphrase cited by Lenin: 'the worse, the better.'

The young did not care for theoretical puzzles. Exhilarated, they were inventing their own lexicon of street fighting. Its mantras were swapped on Telegram and other apps. The protesters must be strong like rice, which meant grains cohering in a mass. They would flow like water. They would gather like dew and fade away as mist. They loved these granular and organic themes, which endowed street violence with a cool philosophical aura. There were hashtags for the bold and for the hesitant.

Tactics were co-ordinated on LIHKG, masked by an online game played out in a fictional city called Heung Shing. The movement developed its own ecostructure, exchanging ideas with activists overseas like climate campaign group Extinction Rebellion. It used texts and Telegram messages to direct flash mobs, organise supplies and call on first aid. It even had a volunteer fleet of 'Uber ambulances' to ferry casualties to hospital. Like the Umbrella Movement, it found an anthem in 'Glory to Hong Kong', composed by the anonymous 'Thomas dgx yhl'. A performance by an orchestra all clad in black, wearing masks and goggles, was viewed more than four million times on YouTube. It was impossible to overestimate the power of social media in a city where 4.4 million people out of 7.7 million were registered on Facebook. Not surprisingly, the protesters grew in boldness. A favourite threat came from the movie *The Hunger Games*: 'if we burn, you burn with us'. Many who uttered it were too young to have joined Joshua Wong's peaceful *Hunger Games* salute protest in 2016.

One by one, boundaries collapsed. Protesters besieged police headquarters and marched to foreign consulates begging for help. The annual march on 1 July marking the twenty-second anniversary of the handover descended into wild scenes when a small group of militants smashed their way into the Legislative Council building. They stormed into the chamber, broke up furniture, smeared the ceremonial insignia with paint, paraded with portraits of their enemies and hung black banners on the dais. Most insulting of all, they draped the British colonial flag of Hong Kong across the benches. One young man, Brian Leung Kai-ping, ripped off his mask to read a manifesto demanding democratic elections (he later fled to the United States). The vandalism cost more than US$5.1 million to put right. The true cost was captured in a spray-painted slogan: 'You have taught me that peaceful protest is useless.'

The summer turned into a carnival of disorder. Hong Kong had seen nothing like it since the riots of 1967. On 21 July, the threat of civil conflict raised its head when a mob of white-shirted men charged into the Yuen Long mass transit station with staves and Chinese flags, attacking anyone who looked like a protester. Innocent passengers, including a pregnant woman, were clubbed as they screamed for help, but the police were nowhere to be seen. The men were local Triad gangsters. Afterwards they were complimented by a pro-Beijing local legislator, Junius Ho, who said they were defending their homes and families.

On the same evening, demonstrators attacked the Chinese government's Liaison Office in the old western district of Sai Ying Pun. This fortified symbol of central authority soared forty-one floors above the markets and flats around it, offering its cadres plush conference rooms, a gym, a subsidised canteen and a library of 13,000 books, including both tracts on Marxism and essays on democracy. It was impregnable, but a group of militants broke away from clashes spiralling across the western districts to hurl eggs and paint at it, defacing the national emblem outside.

In late July and August, demonstrators occupied concourses at Hong Kong airport, employing tactics that veered from politely picketing passengers to blocking them altogether. A baying crowd beat up two mainland Chinese men who aroused their suspicions. One of them was Fu Guohao, a journalist for the nationalistic *Global Times*, whose editors made the most of their man's ordeal with a flair worthy of any Fleet Street tabloid. The story spread like wildfire on Chinese social media. The incident marked the point when the state propagandists stopped ignoring the Hong Kong protests and took the offensive against them.

The Chinese media began to accuse protesters of agitating for independence. In fact the authorities had already crushed a small political movement dedicated to it, a party called Hong Kong Indigenous whose sympathisers had organised rallies against mainland Chinese 'parallel traders' who crowded into the towns of the New Territories to buy up goods for resale across the border. In 2016, they had joined a protest by street hawkers in Mongkok that turned into a violent clash with the police.

When the group's spokesman, an intelligent and articulate young politician named Edward Leung Tin-kei, stood in a by-election he won only 15 per cent of the vote. None the less, the government had him in their sights. In 2018 he was convicted of rioting and assault at the Mongkok protests and sent to prison for six years. Independence was still a minority cause, but Leung bequeathed the protesters a slogan which had mass appeal: 'Liberate Hong Kong; revolution of our times'.

It was easy to find proof of hostility to the People's Republic. Demonstrators trashed mainland Chinese banks, shops, offices and restaurants, boycotting or vandalising outlets that offended them. One of their targets was the Maxims chain of restaurants. Its founder's elder daughter, Annie Wu Suk-ching, was a faithful member of the pro-Beijing business elite who called the protesters 'brainwashed zombies'. With its unerring grasp of public relations, the Hong Kong government sent her to represent the views of average women at the United Nations Human Rights Council in Geneva, along with Pansy Ho, daughter of the casino billionaire Stanley Ho. Some of the estimated 77,000 young mainland professionals, dubbed *gangpiao*, or drifters, who had settled in Hong Kong packed their bags for home. If the protesters had set out to bring down the wrath of the Xi Jinping regime on their heads they had succeeded.

Hong Kong's society began to fracture. Vicious, personalised attacks, unusual in the past, became the norm. Police morale frayed as digital insurgents found officers' personal data, including their home addresses and the names of their children, and posted it online, a practice known as 'doxing'. A crowd besieged police family quarters on a street that bore the name of 'harmonious neighbourhood' in the district of Wong Tai Sin, hurling bricks and bottles, while the residents threw back glass and bags of faeces. Families and generations divided over the violence. Public opinion polls showed that a remarkable number of hitherto peaceable Hong Kongers were ready to justify it.

'Lennon Walls' now sprouted all over the city in a flowering of wit and bile. But as violence became common, the language of public life coarsened. The mildly spoken leader of the Democratic Party, Wu Chi-wai, shouted at Lam: 'You are useless, dead or alive, bitch!' as he was ejected from the Legislative Council. On the streets, policemen sneeringly called protesters 'cockroaches'. They hit back with taunts of *hak ging* – 'black cops'. Some restaurants began to bar partisans of one side or another from their tables. In midsummer the ageing billionaire Li Ka-shing made an enigmatic intervention the old-fashioned way by taking out newspaper advertisements. He quoted a line from a Tang dynasty poem, 'the melon of Huangtai cannot bear being picked again', by the seventh-century prince Li Xian, a son of the formidable Empress Wu. Li Ka-shing seemed to be saying that Hong Kong was too delicate a fruit to be bruised and survive.

As the autumn of 2019 drew on, politicians and commentators feared events were moving towards a climax even though the extradition bill had been dropped. Week by week trust corroded, tear gas filled the air, shops and metro stations burned, bloodied protesters and policemen filled the emergency rooms. The mayhem became routine. A survey for the Chinese University of Hong Kong found that only 58.8 per cent of respondents still felt that protests must be peaceful, down from almost 75 per cent when Carrie Lam took office. A quarter felt that 'radical' methods were justified, while many more people declined to condemn them.

A psychological chasm had developed between Hong Kong and Beijing. Wang Xiangwei, a former editor of the *South China Morning Post* who was close to the Communist Party, predicted that Xi Jinping would get tough. He pointed to a speech at the party's school for cadres in which Xi used the word 'struggle' almost sixty times in nine minutes, evoking Mao Zedong. It was a smart analysis. But few in Hong Kong were disposed to take notice.

The crisis came to a head on China's National Day, 1 October. The chief executive led a delegation of 240 worthies to Beijing, where Xi reviewed a huge military parade from his perch atop Tiananmen Gate and declared that 'no force can stop the Chinese people and nation'. Back in Hong Kong, violent protests spread across the city by mid-afternoon. Commerce and transport shut down in the worst-hit areas. Masked street fighters in black burned the red flag and set fire to portraits of Xi and Lam. They hurled bricks, petrol bombs and acid bombs, spray-painting insults on the premises of mainland banks and businesses. The mood was summed up in a hashtag, #notmynationalday.

Disorder broke out in Kowloon and the New Territories, where police charged the crowds with batons and fired round after round of tear gas. Smartphones recorded policemen beating people and protesters fighting police. One group armed with staves surrounded a fallen policeman, prompting a fellow officer to shout a warning before he shot a teenage protester, Tsang Chi-kin, in the chest. Doctors saved the youth's life and he was charged with rioting. Police squads in Mongkok fired live rounds in the air. In all the force used 1,400 tear gas canisters, 900 rubber bullets and 420 non-lethal rounds – statistics comparable to days of violence in the Israeli-occupied territories or the Troubles in Northern Ireland. Carrie Lam and her delegates flew home to a city of shocked inhabitants, their surroundings pitted here and there with smoking debris.

'There was a feeling that this simply could not go on,' said one of Hong Kong's best-known figures, who, having decided like many that anonymity was now the better part of valour, spoke to put the record straight that November. 'We felt that if nothing was done Hong Kong would see a tragedy like Tiananmen Square, whatever our differences none of us here in Hong Kong wanted to see that.' Many of the elite believed that infiltrators had spurred the protest movement on to a violent intensity hitherto unknown among young Hong Kongers. Some blamed the Taiwanese intelligence services, others thought rival factions in China sought to stir chaos either to discredit Xi or to goad him into military intervention. One theory held that partisans of Bo Xilai and sundry fallen rivals of the leader were spending money to undermine him. There was no proof for any of these beliefs, but the fact that they were profoundly held spoke to the insecurity and doubts of those at the top in Hong Kong. The phone lines ran hot between politicians, billionaires and administrators. All despaired at Lam's mismanagement and lack of leadership, even if they disagreed among themselves on politics. None of them was able to exercise decisive influence. Tung Chee-hwa, who was in virtual seclusion, none the less urged Chinese officials to be patient and to exercise restraint.

Things could of course get worse, and they did. On Sunday 4 November a young student, Chow Tsz-lok, fell from a car park in unexplained circumstances while clashes raged nearby. He lingered in a coma and died less than a week later. The president of the Hong Kong University of Science and Technology, Wei Shyy, announced his death at a graduation ceremony where many, including Wei himself, shed tears. But the students then went on an infuriated rampage across their own campus, wrecking a branch of Starbucks, the cafeteria, a branch of the Bank of China and the president's own residence. As word spread, clashes broke out around the city and some policemen taunted the 'cockroaches' over the young man's death. That day, the mood in the old establishment turned darker than ever before. A writer for the *South China Morning Post*, Chow Chung-yan, compared his city to the frozen ninth circle of hell in Dante Alighieri's *Divine Comedy*, which he had studied in his youth; the poet's fallen angel Lucifer, he recalled, was a thrashing giant, blinded to the views of others, full of hatred and trapped forever in ice.

The next week plumbed new depths. On Monday 11 November, activists called a general strike, blocked trains and buses, then popped up in 'flash mob' rallies against the police. One group poured fuel over a fifty-seven-year-old man, Lee Chi-cheung, who confronted them at a station, and set him ablaze. Lee survived, but an elderly man knocked to the ground in a separate clash between rival protesters did not.

At lunchtime, shoppers and office workers in Central's smartest street got a taste of what rougher districts had endured for weeks. Hundreds stood watching as riot police confronted a small group of peaceful protesters who had blocked a crossroads. Most of the onlookers were young office workers in business attire, wearing their corporate ID tags, munching sandwiches and chattering into their smartphones. None showed the least inclination to violence. At a sudden command, masked policemen whirled and fired tear gas canisters spinning directly into the crowd, who scattered and ran past Tiffany and Gucci with a collective howl of rage and contempt. It was a scene that crystallised the estrangement between the Hong Kong police and the aspirational middle class.

Amid the chaos the protesters changed their tactics. No longer flowing 'like water', they retreated to occupy university campuses, fortifying them with barricades and burning tyres. It was a blunder. At last the police had an opportunity to do what they had trained for. Commanders rushed reinforcements to seal off the campuses and place them under siege. In the days that followed, the militants lost momentum on the streets and public sympathies began to waver.

The first defeat for the radicals came at the Chinese University of Hong Kong, whose 20,000 students worked on a verdant campus in the New Territories. Over-confident and under-planned, they held off the police at each entrance, seized the canteen and set up a makeshift armoury at the sports centre, taking bows and arrows, chainsaws and javelins. Volunteers staffed a petrol bomb production line. One softly spoken militant confided from behind his black mask that he and his friends had 'learned how to make Molotov cocktails from the internet'. He said they were studying home-made explosive devices but had not yet succeeded in making one that worked. If there were indeed spectral infiltrators from China and Taiwan in the protest ranks, they did not seem to include any munitions experts.

Undeterred, the police brought in water cannon and fired hundreds of rounds of tear gas. The protesters shot arrows at them, threw dozens of petrol bombs and hurled bricks onto a main road. College administrators tried to broker an exit deal but neither the leaderless radicals nor the increasingly confident police commanders were interested. In a whirl of conflicting, angry accounts it was impossible to establish the truth, but it was clear that most of the people occupying the campus were not students. Over five days, a well-regarded seat of learning was trashed as its academics appealed to reason. Some students from mainland China were escorted to a boat for evacuation by sea. Eventually, most of the occupiers melted away. The police swept the campus and said they found 3,900 petrol bombs. The action had moved on.

The place chosen for a showdown was located for maximum effect. The Polytechnic University stood in a busy district of Kowloon near the cross-harbour tunnel and a big rail station at Hung Hom, which served southern China. Masked protesters appeared on campus on 11 November. They began to close it off, checking people coming in and out, and set to building stockpiles of petrol bombs and missiles. Two days later they smashed and burned the toll booths at the tunnel, forcing it to shut. That night the scent of petrol bombs replaced the reek of car exhausts and the empty road lanes presented an eerie scene. Traffic was diverted through two other tunnels, but the psychological impact of severing Hong Kong from Kowloon was important: nobody could claim that it was business as usual.

For thirteen days, the police ringed the campus and fought duels with militants holed up inside. They sealed off every exit and issued an ultimatum to protesters to come out and submit to having their identities checked as a prelude to criminal charges. Those under eighteen would be taken home; anyone else was to be held in custody. Conditions became dire. Hundreds slept in the gymnasium and corridors. Instant foods ran short. Rubbish littered the site. Unwashed, sleepless and scared, young people tried to escape any way they could find. Some splashed through sewers, others slid down ropes suspended from a bridge and raced off on waiting motorbikes. Few got away.

As the siege of Polytechnic University dragged on, the elite network began to buzz once again. 'There was a great fear of bloodshed if the police tactical units went in,' said the same person who had evoked the spectre of Tiananmen, 'and some hardline elements in government would have been happy to see that but it would have been a catastrophe for Hong Kong and thus very bad for investment.'

The Chinese leadership was persuaded by such arguments and did not press Lam's administration to use maximum force. Once again, they opted for time and patience to wear down their opponents. It became an exercise in saving face. The police held back while the Polytechnic authorities inspected their wrecked campus. As protesters filed out, their names were taken, but not all were arrested. Some 300 people later faced charges of rioting. When the police moved onto a silent, haze-shrouded campus on Friday 29 November, the siege was over. The protest movement had reinvented itself with new ideas and technology, its urban warriors tameless and swift and proud. Once again, it had failed.

The collapse of resistance at Polytechnic University effectively ended the insurrection of 2019. Protesters went on the march again but faced rapid, determined intervention by the police. They reverted to small flash mob demonstrations and social media campaigns.

The government had not won – far from it. On 24 November Hong Kong voters delivered a rebuff to their rulers by going peacefully to the ballot boxes in district council elections. They handed a landslide victory to democratic candidates, who took control of seventeen out of eighteen councils. More than three million people, 71 per cent of registered voters, made it a record turnout. There was no way to sugar-coat the result for Beijing. It was time for a change of strategy. Then events took an unexpected turn.

On 23 January 2020, the first case of a new coronavirus was confirmed in Hong Kong. The victim was a man from Wuhan, where the outbreak had begun the previous autumn. After initially bungling their response, the Chinese authorities instituted draconian rules confining the population and sealing off Wuhan, although many travellers left the city before they intervened. The world was slow to recognise that it faced a pandemic, but Hong Kong was well prepared after its experience of SARS in 2003. Patients were treated at an isolation hospital and medical staff had adequate supplies of protective gear. Most people wore masks and followed public health messages to wash their hands and keep their distance from others. These were time-tested habits that stood the city in good stead.

Once more the Hong Kong government faced a politically sensitive decision. The city's second confirmed case was a local man who had visited Wuhan. When medical workers went on strike to demand that the border with China be closed, the authorities conceded by shutting all but three entry points. Mass travel from the mainland ceased for the first time since the 1970s. Inside Hong Kong, life went on under restrictions, which were less onerous than in many Western democracies. However, the government banned gatherings of more than four people, later raising the limit to eight. It shut bars, pubs, karaoke lounges and massage parlours, and imposed rules on social behaviour. Non-residents could no longer fly in to the airport. Testing and quarantine systems were put in place for returning citizens. The toll in Hong Kong remained low when compared to many other societies. While they lived in strange isolation, with the world's attention consumed by the pandemic, the people of Hong Kong found themselves confronting the profoundest change to their way of life since the end of the Second World War.

It began with a Communist Party reshuffle. In January 2020, Xi removed the head of the Liaison Office in Hong Kong, Wang Zhimin, who had failed to communicate political reality to his masters before the local elections. Into his place stepped Luo Huining, the party chief in Shanxi province, the coal-mining core of China, where he was fighting graft so corrosive that it was compared to a cancer. Xi's next move was to demote the chief of the Hong Kong and Macau Affairs office, Zhang Xiaoming, who was also blamed for misinforming the leadership. He was replaced at the top by Xia Baolong, a trusted hardliner past retirement age, who had earned his credentials by persecuting Christian churches while serving as party leader in Zhejiang province.

In short order, China had put two tough operators in charge of Hong Kong affairs. It was soon declared that their offices were not bound by restrictions in the Basic Law on the activities of Chinese government bodies in Hong Kong. This was the moment when Beijing imposed clarity on the status quo, ending decades of useful ambiguity.

The results were swiftly apparent. Having vanquished its foes on the street, Beijing would now turn to the police, the courts and the jails, wielding the law as it did in mainland China. Even though protests had dwindled in the early months of the pandemic, democrats warned that the authorities would use the public health crisis as cover for more repression. The campaign illustrated how faithfully Communist Party methods were now being replicated in Hong Kong. It began with a National Security Education day, featuring a website which offered texts, video speeches, a question-and-answer game and an essay competition.

Luo Huining, the new boss of the Liaison Office, issued a video message telling Hong Kongers that 'we must fight the pandemic together and oppose the slogan "if we burn, you burn with us"', which at least indicated that Luo might have watched *The Hunger Games*. He talked of 'struggle' and of 'taking the defence line forward', words from Maoist vocabulary. The *People's Daily*, for its part, said everyone must 'build a great steel wall of national security', while the minister of state security, Chen Wenqing, contributed his thoughts to the party journal *Qiushi* ('Seeking Truth'), saying China could not achieve national rejuvenation 'by beating drums and gongs' but must fight. 'We must stand up for ourselves and not be afraid of a showdown,' he said. That meant passing a National Security Law for Hong Kong so that the city was finally brought into line with the rest of China. For twenty-three years after the handover its people had successfully resisted such legislation. It was required under Article 23 of the Basic Law, but no Hong Kong government had managed to win public opinion or rally the required majority in the Legislative Council to do it. The time for such excuses had passed, in the eyes of Xi Jinping. If Hong Kong could not comply, China would do the job.

The local campaign was well-organised. Junius Ho, a pro-Beijing politician, said he had collected 1.86 million signatures in an online petition from anxious citizens who desired such a law. Luo's Liaison Office called protesters 'a political virus'. Chinese officials tore into a critical report by the National Democratic Institute for International Affairs, a body funded by the US Congress, calling it 'gross interference' and saying it 'glorified inhuman, terrifying, criminal acts of extremists'. The representative of China's foreign ministry, Xie Feng, said that a national security law was coming and warned foreign powers that opposing it would cross a red line for Beijing, adding: 'no attempt to endanger national sovereignty will be tolerated.'

That was made clear on 18 April, when police arrested the veteran democracy campaigner Martin Lee, now aged eighty-one, and fourteen other prominent figures in the movement, including Jimmy Lai, the owner of *Apple Daily*, the lawyer Albert Ho, trade unionist Lee Cheuk-yan and lawyer Margaret Ng. They faced charges in connection with the anti-extradition protests and were granted bail. Lee said that China had abandoned Deng Xiaoping's promise of 'one country, two systems', and that the international community had a 'moral responsibility' to support Hong Kong people.

At the end of April, Carrie Lam was summoned to a meeting in Shenzhen, where she was warned by Xia Baolong, the new head of the Hong Kong and Macau Affairs Office, that time was running out. Her city, he said, was becoming a loophole in national security and must not become a weak link. In Beijing, officials began to hint that the National People's Congress would act at its spring session.

A broad-spectrum campaign to bring Hong Kong into line unfolded to textbook perfection. Local legislators moved to ban insults to China's national anthem, 'The March of the Volunteers', whose stirring tones had attracted jeers at sports events. To general scorn, the city's Independent Police Complaints Council issued a report clearing the police of misconduct during the protests, although it conceded that the force 'had lost its lustre'. The *People's Daily* said that Hong Kong's education system had become 'a poison factory'. The former chief executive, C.Y. Leung, encouraged people to report any teachers 'spreading dangerous ideas' to a website for government tip-offs. Chinese state television accused Martin Lee, Anson Chan, Jimmy Lai and Albert Ho of collusion with 'hostile foreign forces', calling them the Hong Kong 'Gang of Four'.

Such language foreshadowed decisive measures. In due course a spokesman announced that the proposed security legislation was on the Congress agenda, although the details were kept secret. China dismissed a remark by President Trump that the US would react 'very strongly' to the law. But there was dismay – unvoiced, of course – among Hong Kong business leaders when the US Secretary of State, Michael Pompeo, told the US Congress that the city no longer warranted special treatment under US law. 'No reasonable person can assert today that Hong Kong maintains a high degree of autonomy from China, given facts on the ground,' he said. 'While the United States had once hoped that Hong Kong would provide a model for authoritarian China, it is now clear that China is modelling Hong Kong after itself.' The US was joined by Britain, Australia and Canada in a statement saying that China's decision 'lies in direct conflict with its international obligations under the principles of the legally-binding, UN-registered Sino-British Joint Declaration' the document by which Deng Xiaoping and Margaret Thatcher had forged an agreement for half a century ahead.

The Chinese leadership was not intimidated by such criticism. It responded in an astute and well-thought-out manner with diplomatic, political and economic counter-measures. The West, disunited and in disarray as it struggled with the pandemic, could not catch up. The Joint Declaration was 'not relevant', the Chinese foreign ministry said. The Russian foreign minister, Sergei Lavrov, swiftly expressed his approval and Chinese diplomats were eventually to rally fifty-three countries, led by Cuba, who welcomed the law at a session of the United Nations Human Rights Council in Geneva. Only twenty-seven nations lined up with the West. To reassure investors, the head of the Hong Kong Monetary Authority, Eddie Yue, said there would be no change to the fundamentals of its financial system, adding that the free flow of capital and free convertibility of the local dollar were guaranteed. The tycoon Li Ka-shing expressed the hope that the law would allay the worries the Chinese government felt about Hong Kong.

In Beijing, officials prepared to unveil new measures liberalising foreign investment in the financial sector, promising huge benefits to Wall Street firms in search of new markets. Chinese companies, increasingly shut out of the United States, planned to list initial public offerings on the Hong Kong stock exchange, which would generate lucrative fees. As Western markets reeled, the Chinese alternatives looked solid. In Communist Party style, however, the blandishments came accompanied by menace.

The banking giant HSBC was a prime example. It faced criticism for its compliance with US prosecutors investigating alleged crimes by a senior executive of the Chinese telecoms firm Huawei, Meng Wanzhou. The *People's Daily* called it 'two-faced' and a storm of social media abuse ensued. The ever-vigilant C.Y. Leung told locals to consider closing their accounts, noted that HSBC made most of its profits in Asia and observed that most of its top management was still British. It was to little avail that executives belatedly expressed their support for the new security law. The bank's share price, already under pressure from adverse market conditions, went into a steady decline. The state-owned Chinese insurance behemoth, Ping An, took advantage of the fall to raise its stake in HSBC to 8 per cent. It would, said some, be a fitting end if China took over the greatest colonial money box of all.

The multiple crises of 2020 had made such ambitions realistic. A phrase of Lenin much quoted at the time held that there were decades where nothing happened and weeks when decades happened. The pandemic, the trade war, a global slump and political turmoil in the democracies emboldened the Xi regime to accelerate its plans.

Xi directed the party to prepare to turn inwards once more, no longer talking of globalisation but 'global co-operation'. Meanwhile China focused on its giant internal market, building domestic supply chains and insulating itself against foreign pressure by innovating core technologies at home. At the same time it would tighten the dependence of the international industrial chain on China and ensure alternative sources of commodities to deter outsiders from cutting off supply. The platitudes of Davos lay in the past.

The southern powerhouse was crucial to this semi-autarchic vision. China already planned to absorb Hong Kong into a Greater Bay Area encompassing the cities of Shenzhen, Zhuhai and Macau in a common economic zone where finance and trade would be dominated by mainland institutions. The world's longest sea bridge and tunnel, connecting Hong Kong to its neighbours, opened in 2018. Now Xi stated that industrial security and national security were one and the same. There would be no undefended fortress in his strategy.

The National Security Law came into effect on 30 June 2020. Fittingly in Chinese eyes, its six chapters and sixty-six articles were made public as Hong Kong marked twenty-three years since the handover. The text was passed by the National People's Congress and adopted by the Hong Kong government at 11 p.m. that night. It was 'a birthday present', said a senior official, Zhang Xiaoming.

The details had been kept secret until the law was unveiled to the people of Hong Kong. They woke up to find that they were living in a new society. Even the city's leading political and business figures had been left in ignorance of the exact provisions. These were more sweeping and draconian than many had expected: in effect the law brought Hong Kong under the vague but absolutist powers which reigned over the rest of China. It banned secession, subversion and terrorist activities, fixing a maximum sentence of life imprisonment. It made 'collusion with a foreign country or external elements' a crime. People could be prosecuted for disclosing state secrets, a practically limitless category in China. Article 38 extended the law's reach worldwide to anyone committing an offence, even if they were neither in Hong Kong nor a citizen or permanent resident of the city. The law emphasised the necessity of foiling foreign plots, which, as Stalin had taught, were both multifarious and useful. It commanded all the organs of state to take 'necessary measures' to 'strengthen the management' of foreign representatives, international organisations, the global media and non-governmental groups.

This new order required a new bureaucratic machine, a task to which the party was more than equal. The chief executive was to head a Committee for Safeguarding National Security, whose main adviser was Luo Huining of the Liaison Office. For the first time, the central government set up its own agency with extraordinary powers in Hong Kong, styling it the Office for Safeguarding National Security. It was headed by Zheng Yanxiong, who had won his spurs by stifling a minor rebellion in Wukan, a southern Chinese village. He was to liaise with the garrison of the People's Liberation Army and direct his own team of mainland security agents, who enjoyed legal immunity. They and their vehicles were not subject to inspection, search or detention by the Hong Kong police.

The police were, however, handed new powers to conduct searches without a warrant, to freeze assets, intercept communications and demand data from internet companies. A special police unit was dedicated to national security cases. Informers were encouraged to denounce offenders to a hotline or website. A special team of prosecutors was established. The chief executive would choose suitable judges to sit in national security cases. This prerogative astonished the judiciary yet it, too, was limited. The Chinese government reserved the right to take over cases and to prosecute them in its own courts if it saw fit.

'The first of July is a watershed,' commented Hu Xijin, editor of the *Global Times* in Beijing. For once it was an incontestable statement. Hu said that people 'will be safe if they act wisely and change their ways'. The pro-Communist newspapers in Hong Kong rejoiced.

Carrie Lam, the chief executive, assured the United Nations in a video message that the law was not retroactive and would be used only in a handful of extreme cases. 'No central government could turn a blind eye to such threats to sovereignty and national security as well as risks of subversion of state power,' she said.

The first day of the new order did not prove her point. The police arrested 370 people as demonstrations broke out in the city, using water cannon and pepper spray against protesters and onlookers alike. They displayed purple flags warning people against displaying flags or banners, chanting slogans or conducting themselves with an intent to commit secession or subversion. Police said seven officers were injured, one 'stabbed by a rioter with a dagger' and three 'hit by a rioter riding a motorcycle'.

Six men and four women became the first to face charges under the national security law. The police Twitter feed proudly displayed the spoils of a swoop on three girls 'showing materials with Hong Kong independence slogans' in the Causeway Bay shopping district. These amounted to a pathetic handful of leaflets including a cartoon of Xi Jinping clad in a Soviet-style marshal's uniform with a coronavirus-shaped head, stickers saying 'liberate Hong Kong', a smiley cartoon with a 'me too' tag and a black leaflet bearing a biblical quotation, 'let judgement run down as waters and righteousness as a mighty stream'.

These words of chapter five, verse twenty-four of the book of Amos were not patently criminal in nature. Perhaps the fact that an accompanying English translation came from the King James Bible was sufficient to certify the leaflet's inclusion as the work of foreign forces.

Lest anyone doubt that China was serious, state television broadcast video of the PLA garrison staging drills to track down fugitives on land and sea in Hong Kong with the aid of special forces, warships and aircraft. A group who tried to escape to Taiwan by speedboat were tracked by the authorities, intercepted and taken to Shenzhen, where they were later put on trial and given jail terms for illegally crossing a border. The episode struck a chord with many families in Hong Kong whose forebears had fled Maoist China in small boats. Michael Tien, a long-serving legislator, went on Bloomberg television to tell multinational companies they could go on trading, dancing and going to the horse races as long as they avoided even speaking about the Communist Party. The heads of Hong Kong's eight publicly funded universities all expressed their support for the law.

Hong Kong's best-known student did not agree. 'From now on, #Hongkong enters a new era of reign of terror,' Joshua Wong wrote on Twitter. He and his comrades disbanded their short-lived political party, Demosistō. 'I will continue to hold fast to my home – Hong Kong, until they silence and obliterate me from this land,' he said in a Facebook posting. The pro-Beijing daily *Wen Wei Po* celebrated with an exclusive story purporting to reveal that Wong, Agnes Chow and Nathan Law had taken millions of dollars from the Demosistō funds and planned to seek asylum in the American consulate. None of them showed any signs of ostentatious wealth and when Nathan Law eventually sought asylum he chose Britain.

Wong did not flee. He was arrested, convicted of incitement and unauthorised assembly, and sent to prison for thirteen and a half months. While in jail, he pleaded guilty to further charges of unlawful assembly and defying a pre-pandemic ban on masks. Then prosecutors charged him with subversion under the National Security Law, a crime that could draw a life sentence. Fifty-two others were charged the same day. Wong's parents sold their flat and quietly moved to Australia with his younger brother.

The Hong Kong courts began to echo those in mainland China. Jimmy Lai, the owner of *Apple Daily*, was convicted of unlawful assembly and jailed for fourteen months. He was then accused of 'collusion with foreign forces' and breaking the National Security Law. Police later raided the newspaper, arrested its editors, seized documents and froze its bank accounts. It was forced to close after twenty-six years. Martin Lee and Margaret Ng got suspended sentences of eleven and twelve months respectively for unlawful assembly. Both faced an inquiry by the Bar Association.

Magistrates denied bail to many defendants. A judge, Madame Justice Esther Toh Lye-ping, ruled that one of them, Jeremy Tam of the Civic Party, was 'a person of interest' to foreign powers because the American consul had invited him for coffee. According to her own official biography, Judge Toh was born in Singapore and educated in Britain, where she was called to the English Bar in 1974. She was the kind of figure that Hong Kong showcased in publicity branding itself 'Asia's World City'.

The Chinese audience was invited to contemplate the penalties for dissent. An anchor on state television waxed approving at the news that schools and libraries in Hong Kong were already removing suspect books from their shelves, telling viewers that the 'poison' was at last being purged. Legality was not enough, however, for 'the red line must be inscribed in the hearts'. There was much more in this vein.

Pro-democracy candidates were set to win elections to the legislature in September, so at the end of July Lam deferred that problem by postponing the polls for a year, claiming that they posed a risk to public health. 'There were no political considerations,' she said. (Elections were held safely during the pandemic in Taiwan, South Korea, Nepal, Singapore, Mongolia and India.) As a precaution the government had already disqualified a dozen democrats, including Wong and Lester Shum, from standing on the grounds that they were 'not fit for office'.

The United States insisted it 'would not stand idly by while China swallows Hong Kong into its authoritarian maw'. The State Department claimed China's international commitments were empty words: 'The CCP promised fifty years of freedom to the people of Hong Kong and gave them only twenty-three.' This had become a pattern of behaviour, according to the US, because China had also broken agreements with the World Health Organisation, the World Trade Organisation and the United Nations. The Trump administration moved quickly to impose sanctions on Carrie Lam and other officials, to end exports of defence and dual use technology to Hong Kong, and to eliminate trade privileges the Special Administrative Region had enjoyed by virtue of its status.

Matthew Pottinger, Trump's deputy national security adviser, was a key advocate of blunt measures. He combined expertise with a bleak realism peculiar to those who had experienced the People's Republic at first hand. Pottinger was fluent in Chinese, had spent years as a journalist in Beijing, knew Taiwan and had served as an intelligence officer in the US Marine Corps. His tactics broke with American practice since the beginning of 'engagement' in the 1970s. Quiet diplomacy was consigned to the past. In its place came high-profile legal cases, reciprocal expulsions of journalists and sanctions against Chinese officials. Loss of face, it seemed, was part of the new policy. Pottinger was that most dangerous of foes, a man who knew how to hurt his adversary.

He was not alone. Joe Biden, the Democrat running for president, said the national security law dealt 'a death blow to the freedoms and autonomy that set Hong Kong apart from the rest of China'. He pledged to prohibit US companies from 'abetting repression and supporting the Chinese Communist Party's surveillance state' With an eye on the law's sweeping provisions, he threatened to impose swift economic sanctions if China tried 'to silence U.S. citizens, companies, and institutions for exercising their First Amendment rights'.

This was an instance in history when the destiny of a single city – like Calais, Danzig or Berlin – exercised an outsize influence on international affairs. The fate of Hong Kong helped to cement the conviction among both Republicans and Democrats in the United States that it was time to get tough on China, a remarkable consensus in a polarised political system. There was bipartisan support for a swiftly passed bill to sanction Chinese officials who eroded Hong Kong's autonomy as well as banks and firms that did business with them. A second piece of legislation, the Hong

Kong Safe Harbor Act, gave refugee status to Hong Kongers fearing political persecution. It also had backing across the aisle.

When Biden won the US election in November 2020, he came into
office pledging to work with America's allies in a concerted policy towards
China, and he assembled a team of seasoned Asia hands to turn Trump's
rhetoric into effective measures. America had found a rare political unity
that foreshadowed a patient, sustained push back against Beijing. Europe
found a less coherent and direct response while its governments were
submerged by the coronavirus pandemic; some feared the loss of trade
with China as they sought to rebuild their crippled economies. But Hong
Kong was added to the list of reasons to think again about how the West
should deal with the People's Republic. For the first time in half a century
its politicians began to reverse their dependence on a giant authoritarian
state.

The greatest change of heart came in the former colonial power. 'There
is nothing to be done for those of Chinese race', a British official had
written on a memo for Margaret Thatcher as Britain and China closed
their deal in 1984. Her heavy underlining of the words in blue ink spoke
for itself. The Iron Lady distrusted Communists, felt a genuine moral
pang for people in Hong Kong and comforted herself with the thought
that Britain had done its best for them. Yet her own immigration policies
had shut the door on the millions entitled to British passports. They were
called British National (Overseas) Citizens and denied the right to settle
in the United Kingdom, while China considered them Chinese and did
not recognise dual nationality. At the handover in 1997 Mrs Thatcher had
said that she wished Hong Kong had won independence and voiced her
regret that it had not been possible; she nourished to the end of her days
a sense of unease about the people she consigned to Chinese rule. But
there the matter rested, to the relief of the diplomats and the China
traders.

The Xi Jinping government had succeeded, however, in changing
British minds where more than three decades of lobbying had failed. On
1 July 2020 the Conservative Foreign Secretary, Dominic Raab, rose in the
House of Commons to announce the 'sobering conclusion' that the
National Security Law was 'a clear and serious breach of the Joint
Declaration'. It violated the high degree of autonomy and judicial inde-
pendence promised to Hong Kong, Raab continued, saying that even
under Chinese law there was no justification for it. Echoing the US State
Department, he said that China had broken its commitment to apply the

UN International Covenant on Civil and Political Rights to the city, a move 'which cannot be reconciled with … its responsibility as a leading member of the international community'. If there ever was a golden era of relations between London and Beijing, it surely came to an end at that sitting of Parliament. 'China has broken its promise to the people of Hong Kong under its own laws. China has breached its international obligations to the United Kingdom under the Joint Declaration,' the foreign secretary said.

In a hush broken only by murmurs of approval, Raab told the house that Britain would now honour its commitment to those who held British National (Overseas) status. They could apply to come to Britain for five years, gain settled status and progress to citizenship. That meant that up to three million people living in Hong Kong, China, could move to the United Kingdom in the years ahead. Only some of them would go, but at last all of them had an insurance policy.

The Home Office, which handled immigration, made an even more stunning concession. It extended the privilege to whole families and to anyone born after the handover on 1 July 1997. Not only that, but applicants need not even produce a British passport, only proof of identity – a move designed to forestall restrictions and reprisals by China.

The decision drew a sharp reaction from Beijing, which condemned it as a breach of agreements and said it threatened good relations between the two countries. It was, however, the cause for which David Wilson had gallantly lobbied Mrs Thatcher after Tiananmen Square and which so many Britons connected to Hong Kong by family, business or service felt was just. Even critics of the British government, which was in dire straits over the pandemic and its European policy, felt that its decision was decent, pragmatic and overdue. It turned out, after all, that something could be done.

Afterword

Early in the 1980s a youth named Bao Pu found a man waiting to see his father, the high party official Bao Tong, in the library of their home in Beijing. The caller explained that he was an anthropologist. He studied street names in Hong Kong, which often commemorated long-deceased proconsuls and soldiers. In China, the revolution had erased all such relics of foreign power. It was the caller's task to prepare a list of streets to be renamed when China took over the colony.

Bao Pu ended up in Hong Kong, where he ran a publishing company that scored notable success with memoirs and documents from inside China, while his father passed into old age under house arrest in the capital for his part in the lost cause of political reform. This was how 'one country, two systems' worked in practice for one family.

The street names did not change. Perhaps officials from the north discovered that local people had long ignored the English signs and got around town just fine. It is unlikely that they simply forgot. There was symbolism in it, for Confucius had declared that without the rectification of names there could be no righteous governance. Yet in their wisdom the men who ruled China decided to leave well alone. For a long time it seemed that Hong Kong could be free while the rest of the country was not. The guarantee of a high degree of autonomy led people to accept central rule. The promise that the capitalist system would continue for fifty years assured their compliance if not their enthusiasm.

That was the bargain offered by Deng Xiaoping. It was secured in the hope that China would be more liberal by the time half a century passed. Some people persuaded themselves that Hong Kong might even light the way. We now know that was not how the story ended.

Hong Kong lived with a contradiction: it had freedom but not democracy. It could not make the course corrections through which societies governed by the people adjust to change and adversity. Politics fled from the legislature to the street, starting a cycle of conflict which could have only one outcome. Eventually China took control, as it had always warned that it could. Striving to gain freedom and democracy, Hong Kong ended up with neither. The question for the historian is what could have been different.

By drawing on memoirs and documents publicly available in China, this account has sought, imperfectly, to give full scope to the Chinese point of view. The 'what ifs' so tempting in a counterfactual history of elite politics are beyond its scope. It is, however, a fact that the Communist Party did have a liberal faction. It was vanquished, yet achieved much and might have done more. What can be said for certain is that Hong Kong lost out when the wily and sophisticated Liao Chengzhi died in 1983. None of his successors in the Communist apparatus matched him in stature, as their self-serving recollections make clear. It is only when the archives, diaries and papers of the period become available to Chinese historians that the internal debates may emerge into daylight. Until then, as a gifted Sinologist once wrote, the confession of ignorance is the beginning of wisdom.

Among the Westerners, blame and credit are easier to apportion. From the end of the Opium Wars until the late twentieth century, colonial powers adhered to Queen Victoria's dictum that it was good to keep what one possessed, and in the high and palmy days of empire Britain had no incentive to grant democracy to its Chinese subjects. After the Second World War Sir Mark Young produced a plan to strengthen the legitimacy of British rule by giving people the vote. This was the best chance to establish a robust and modern political system, but it was interred by Whitehall. Later British governments of all stripes deferred to governors who assured them that things in the Far East were different and most Chinese people did not want the burden of a vote. The Cold War made risk-taking unthinkable, for what if the Communist underground stepped forth and won an election? It was a convenient, if cynical, excuse. And by the time Deng Xiaoping summoned the governor to his presence in 1979, officials could maintain it was too late. They argued that out of discord sprang chaos, political strife would wreck confidence and spell the end of Hong Kong's riches. China might march in.

Britain was a liberal custodian of its last Chinese possession but its refusal to give its subjects a voice in their own future, apart from canvassing a few privileged worthies, was a stain on its record. That was the moral dilemma which confronted Margaret Thatcher and with which she wrestled, almost single-handed, until she was forced to accept a solution she did not like. The documents show that Britain and China negotiated in the void of misunderstanding which had characterised their encounters since 1840. The British tried to win an exit with honour from Hong Kong which would insure their assets and put them on the right side of China. The Chinese side never deviated from their sole purpose, the resumption of sovereignty and control over all their land. To them, all the rest was detail. Fortified by this certainty, Deng was content to discard treaties, issue threats and take negotiations to the brink. He left the management of retreat to his British opponents. It was a shrewd approach and in Sir Percy Cradock, Deng found a gifted pessimist who quailed before his militant realism.

Despite that, Cradock masterminded a settlement that gave Hong Kong more than two decades when millions prospered and the Joshua Wong generation freely came of age. He also won a greater prize. The Joint Declaration bound China to the principle that nations do not break pacts but negotiate to change them. Without that the nuclear-armed world might have returned to the inter-war decades when rising powers cared nothing for scraps of paper. This was an unsung victory for the international order. Cradock did not live to see most of his predictions come to pass. Perhaps this book will put his achievements as well as his mistakes in a proper perspective.

The next test is what could have been done to make Hong Kong freer and stronger at the handover to Chinese rule. As governor, David Wilson steps out of the shadows in this book. His steps to expand higher education, to extend political representation and to modernise infrastructure stood the colony in good stead. It was on his watch that Hong Kong incorporated the key international human rights statutes into its own law. Wilson was present at the creation; he was in the room with Deng Xiaoping in 1979, he negotiated the text of the Joint Declaration and, with quiet courage, he flew to London to tell Mrs Thatcher that there was a moral duty to give the people of Hong Kong passports after the massacre at Tiananmen Square, an obligation fulfilled only thirty-one years later.

The Last Governor, Chris Patten, outshone his predecessors in the public eye. He brought controversy where elite consensus had reigned, upset apple-carts and defied the wrath of China to bring in more democracy, for which he basked in liberal approval. Afterwards he had no regrets. He said that Britain had no choice but to strengthen democracy and the rule of law before it left in 1997. He refused to accept that for fear of reprisal it should have avoided arguments and retreated from the promises made to Parliament when it agreed to hand back Hong Kong to China. His political reforms did not survive.

Patten defended his record by saying it was correct to push rights and freedoms as far as possible on the principle that one did not concede defeat in advance. In an interview for this book in 2019 he said Hong Kong had done pretty well for ten to twelve years after 1997 and that by and large the Chinese stuck to what they promised until Xi Jinping took power. From time to time he returned to the former colony, where he was greeted by audiences of young people eager to engage him in debate and not afraid to disagree with his counsel of moderation or his refusal to support independence. Many who were not born or were at primary school when Britain left Hong Kong had none the less an extraordinary sense of the relationship between economic and political freedom. The Last Governor could be proud of that legacy.

The history of Hong Kong within China is a lesson still in progress. It poses the problems of our time: how free societies deal with authoritarian states; how trade may liberate or enslave; and how politicians and diplomats must endlessly learn the arts of bargaining, concession and resistance if nations are to manage profound conflicts without war. Much that is said about modern China is overdone and comparisons with the past are treacherous. Yet some tentative conclusions can be drawn.

The great historian Jonathan Spence wrote that Deng, the elders, and their younger clique threatened jointly by their actions in 1989 to commit the government again 'to the nineteenth-century fallacy', that China could join the modern world entirely on its own terms. There could be no better description of Xi Jinping's project thirty years later.

One Western fallacy is that the Chinese Communist Party deceived its interlocutors, persuading leaders and businessmen that it was something it was not. This is untrue. If this story shows anything, it is that the foreigners deceived themselves. Envoys, executives, investors and scholars; all were prone to selective blindness. Yet to anyone with eyes to see, the facts were in plain sight. China was a dictatorship; it would remain one. Deng said so himself. The patriarch ruled that China must hide its strength and bide its time. The party did exactly what it had said it would do. It was laid out in windy speeches and written down in countless columns. It never conceded, for that would be the end of authority.

From a global perspective – for it is not just 'the West' but the rest, in Asia, Africa and Latin America who watch the rise of China – Lenin's famous question of 1901 is the right one: What is to be done?

Even hawks like Patten conceded that the best that could be done for Hong Kong was to raise the cost to China of its dictatorial policies. The democracies had developed a toolkit of sanctions, visa bans and individual asset freezes. The United States, still their leading power, sought a balance between getting the politics right over the long term and meeting the strategic demands of the present: to keep the peace and to co-operate with China on big things like climate change, trade and public health. The past suggests it will not be an easy task.

Much of this book was written in Geneva, where, a short walk from the World Trade Organisation, the halls of the League of Nations stand as a reminder of what can go wrong. Here in the 1930s a young British statesman, Anthony Eden, negotiated with the rising powers of the day on lost causes like Abyssinia and Spain, in one case striving to spare China the cruelties of invasion by Japan. Eden wrote that if a leading power does not lead it is not likely to see its policies succeed. Appeasement fed by wishful thinking is more likely to breed doubting friends than daunt would-be enemies. To the new powers, the old order is in decay: 'Obligations are ignored, engagements cynically torn up, confidence … shaken, methods of making war without declaring war are being adopted, while all the time each nation declares that its one desire is for peace.'

In a world like this symbols matter, even ones as minor as street signs, because the fate of small places has often sent a warning about the future. Hong Kong was still a city where capitalists traded and Communists invested, where people enjoyed free personal lives and students could debate the flaws of Athenian democracy, where the ancient arts of China flourished, the incense rose in temples undisturbed and churches resounded to hymns on a Sunday. None of this would vanish in a day or a year. Equally, none of it was imperishable.

Notes

ABBREVIATIONS

CNA China News Analysis
PREM Prime Minister's Office, The National Archives, Kew
THCR The Papers of Baroness Thatcher, Churchill Archives Centre,
Churchill College, Cambridge

INTRODUCTION: HONG KONG, CHINA

3 **cost its shareholders** Richard Roberts and David Kynaston, *The
Lion Wakes: A Modern History of HSBC* (London: Profile Books,
2018), p160
6 **the gate through which** A phrase coined by John Pomfret, 'A Long
Wait at the Gate to Greatness', *Washington Post*, 27 July 2008
9 **That isolation having come** Karl Marx, 'Revolution in China and
Europe', *New York Daily Tribune*, 14 June 1853
9 **Only by knowing** Xinhua, report from Macau, Dec 2019

1 MERCHANTS AND MANDARINS

11 **In the ninth century** Abu Zayd al-Sirafi, *Accounts of China and
India* and Ahmed Ibn Fadlan, *Mission to the Volga*, in *Two Arabic
Travel Books* (New York/London: New York University Press,
2014)
12 **One account spoke** Edward H. Schafer, *The Golden Peaches of
Samarkand* (Berkeley and Los Angeles: University of California
Press, 1963)
12 **the babble** ibid.
13 **an age of suspicion** ibid.

13 **was never free** ibid.

14 **for all the ships** *The Travels of Marco Polo*, tr. Ronald Latham (London: Penguin, 1958), p237

15 **Here was a country** J.H. Elliott, *Imperial Spain 1469–1716* (London: Edward Arnold, 1963)

16 **like fabrics of enchantment** Percy Bysshe Shelley, *Julian and Maddalo* (1818), l. 92

21 **The Empire of China** Lord Macartney, *An Embassy to China, Being the Journal Kept by Lord Macartney during his Embassy to the Emperor Ch'ien-lung 1793–1794*, ed. J.L. Cranmer-Byng (London: Longmans, 1962), p212

21 **The first American vessel** Carl L. Crossman, *The Decorative Arts of the China Trade* (Woodbridge, Suffolk: Antique Collectors Club, 1991), p16

22 **The value of Chinese exports** John K. Fairbank (ed.), *The Cambridge History of China*, Vol 10 (Cambridge University Press, 1978; Caves Books, Taipei, 1986), p 164

25 **the world's most valuable** ibid., p173

25 **By 1838** ibid., p178

25 **A study by** Jonathan Spence, 'Opium Smoking in Ch'ing China' in Frederic Wakeman and Carolyn Grant (eds), *Conflict and Control in Late Imperial China* (Berkeley and Los Angeles: University of California Press, 1975), pp143–73

26 **Within the empire** *The Cambridge History of China*, Vol 10, p179

26 **A final complication** Steve Tsang, *A Modern History of Hong Kong* (London: Bloomsbury, 2003), p6

27 **the aspirin and benzodiazepine** Wayne Hall, 'Opium in Britain', *The Lancet*, 24 Apr 1999

28 **protocol was the essence** *The Cambridge History of China*, Vol 10, p177

29 **belonged to a country … A war more unjust** Hansard, House of Commons debate, War With China, 7 and 8 April 1840

31 **unaccountably strange … completely disobeyed** Queen Victoria, Letter to the King of the Belgians, 13 April 1841

31 **remove, carry away** George Pottinger, *Sir Henry Pottinger, First Governor of Hong Kong* (Stroud, Glos: Sutton Publishing, 1997), p79

32 **great proof of their ferocity** ibid., p92

32 **realised that he was dealing** ibid., p93

32 **During the retreat** ibid., p89

33 **It is almost impossible** Cecil Woodham-Smith, *The Reason Why* (London: Penguin, 1968), p16

33 **the army was not** ibid., p88

33 **a typical example** Philip Bowring, *Free Trade's First Missionary, Sir John Bowring in Europe and Asia* (Hong Kong: Hong Kong University Press, 2014), p131

34 **It has been called** Jonathan Spence, *The Search for Modern China* (New York: W.W. Norton & Co, 1991), p158

37 **the most long-continued** *The Cambridge History of China*, Vol 10, p213

37 **The Qing dynasty** Roberto Peruzzi, *Diplomatici, banchieri e mandarini, Le origini finanziarie e diplomatiche della fine dell'impero Celeste* (Milan: Mondadori, 2015), pp89–103

37 **The City of London** ibid., p147

38 **The indemnity amounted** Shinkichi Nagaoka, 'Indemnity Considerations in Japanese Financial Policy after the Sino-Japanese War', *Hokudai Economic Papers* 11 (1981), 1–29

2 REFORM AND OPENING UP

41 **He sat impatiently** *Guangdong Provincial Archives: Important Archive Documents on 30 Years of Reform and Opening Up in Guangdong, a collection of 226 documents, Dec 1978–Jul 2008* (China Archives Publishing House, 2008)

42 **The huge contrast** Report by Wu Nansheng of February 21, 1979, *Guangdong Provincial Archives: Archive Documents on 30 Years of Reform and Opening Up*

43 **Zhou Ziyang began** *Prisoner of the State, The Secret Journal of Zhou Ziyang*, tr. Bao Pu, Renee Chiang, Adi Ignatius (New York: Simon & Schuster, 2009)

44 **According to a memoir** Hu Bangding, 'Recalling comrade Duan Yun', in *Price Theory and Practice*, Beijing, Feb 1997

44 **The formation of** Official history of the People's Republic of China, http://www.hprc.org.cn

45 **the official history** ibid.

47 **Shenzhen and Zhuhai** Report of comrade Duan Yun on the economic investigation group and research in Hong Kong and Macao, 1978, http://www.hprc.org.cn

48 **The journey is recounted** Jia Juchuan et al, *Xi Zhongxun (1913–2002), A Chinese revolutionary and political leader of the CCP*, 2 vols (Beijing: Central Literature Publishing House; vol 1 2008, vol 2 2013)

50 **I looked up** Interview with Zhang Weihang, Guangzhou, 1998

51 **It looked like hundreds** Interview with Wei Han, Guangzhou, 2001

51 **The trip came** Jia et al, *Xi Zhongxun (1913–2002)*

54 **Li became an expert** *The Biography of Li Qiang: 90 Years of Experience* (Beijing: People's Publishing House, 2004)

58 **MacLehose did a lot** *News and History of the Communist Party of China*, http://cpc.people.com.cn

59 **From the 18th** Third Plenum of the 11th CPC Central Committee, 1978; the official accounts are at http://www.hprc.org.cn, the 'Chronology of Deng Xiaoping 1975–1997', ed. literature research office of the CPC Central Committee (Beijing: Central Literature Publishing House, 2004)

60 **Deng Xiaoping has come** *News and History of the Communist Party of China*

61 **It ended two years** ibid.

63 **He went carrying** *Guangdong Provincial Archives: Important Archive Documents on 30 Years of Reform and Opening Up*

63 **Let Guangdong go first** 'Dare to be First – One Thousand Pioneers of Reform and Opening Up in Guangdong', compiled by Zhang Hanqing and others for the Chinese People's Political Consultative Conference, *Nanfang Daily*, 12 Oct 2015

63 **Though the sparrow** Guangdong Provincial Archives: Speech of Comrade Xi Zhongxun to the Central Committee Work Conference, 8 Apr 1979

65 **The whole province's** Guangdong Provincial Archives: Speech of Comrade Xi Zhongxun to the Fifth People's Congress of Guangdong Province, 17 Dec 1979

66 **Guangdong has been** *The Chronicle of Guangdong Province since Reform and Opening Up* (Nanfang Daily Publishing House, 1998)

68 **If the names are not** *The Analects of Confucius*, tr. Simon Leys (New York: W.W. Norton & Co, 1997)

3 A LONG FAREWELL

70 **For a century** 'Mao Zedong: Reply to Liu Yazi', in *Poems of Mao Zedong*, tr. Gu Zhengkun (Beijing: Peking University Press, 1993)

70 **The forces of** 'Is it right to "Lean to One Side"?', talk by Mao Zedong, 8 Dec 1956, in *Mao Zedong on Diplomacy* (Beijing: Foreign Languages Press, 1998)

70 **The Western world is** 'Imperialism is nothing to Fear', talk with activists by Mao Zedong, 7 May 1960, ibid.

71 **In his memoir** Li Zhisui, *The Private Life of Chairman Mao* (New York: Random House, 1994)

72 **If he had asked** 'Talk With Edward Heath', 25 May 1974, in *Mao Zedong on Diplomacy*

72 **twenty-five times** Embassy of the People's Republic of China in the UK, news release, 14 Jul 2014)

73 **As for doing business** 'Systematically and completely destroy imperialist domination in China', report by Mao Zedong to the Second Plenary of the 7th central committee, 5 Mar 1949, in *Mao Zedong on Diplomacy*

74 **Why did the People's** Xu Bing, *The Wind and the Cloud of the Return of Hong Kong to China* (Jilin Provincial Publishing House, 1996), pp54–7

74 **it would be a historic** ibid.

74 **it could not be** ibid.

75 **Hong Kong is of great benefit** ibid.

76 **Entranced by Hong Kong** Douglas Hurd, *Memoirs* (London: Little, Brown, 2003), p100

77 **a place where bare feet** *Hong Kong 1991* (Hong Kong: Government Information Services)

77 **Only one copy** Austin Coates, *Myself a Mandarin: Memoirs of a Special Magistrate* (London: Frederick Muller, 1968)

77 **A stroll through the streets** *Hong Kong 1993* (Hong Kong: Government Information Services)

78 **To the Chinese experts** Interview with Shen Guofang, Bejing, 1996

78 **For more than two thousand** *The Analects of Confucius*, tr. Leys

79 **We ate roast beef** Hurd, *Memoirs*, p101

79 **On receiving his letter** Coates, *Myself a Mandarin*

81 **were intrigued and appreciative** *Hong Kong 1992 Annual Report* (Hong Kong: Government Information Services)

81 **We had a myth** Interview, London 2019, identity withheld at the
    interviewee's request

81 **numbered 6.3 million** Hong Kong 1996 annual report, (Hong
    Kong: Government Information Services)

81 **generally followed** ibid.

84 **According to official obituaries** *China Daily*, 18 Jun 1983

84 **foreign ministry website** https://www.fmprc.gov.cn/mfa_eng/
    ziliao_665539/wjrw_665549/lrfbzjbzzl_665553/t222815.shtml

84 **The Chinese exiles** Mayami Itoh, *Pioneers of Sino-Japanese
    Relations* (New York: Palgrave Macmillan US, 2012)

85 **He was seen** Jay Taylor, *The Generalissimo* (Cambridge, MA: The
    Belknap Press, 2009), pp50–2

85 **totally unlikely** Interview with Lord Wilson of Tillyorn, London,
    2019

85 **devoted to the cause** National People's Congress of the People's
    Republic of China, http://www.npc.gov.cn/

87 **One author specialising** Roger Faligot, *Chinese Spies* (London:
    Hurst & Co, 2019), p128

87 **extremely well informed** interview with Lord Wilson of Tillyorn,
    2019

88 **The party's own** Fang Kanshi, '1978–1982: The process of China's
    decision to take back Hong Kong', in *Contemporary Chinese History
    Studies* (Chinese Academy of Social Sciences, Sep 2017)

88 **all our work** ibid.

89 **specialised in cultural** ibid.

89 **One thinks back** Interview with Lord Wilson of Tillyorn, 2019

89 **There will be no** ibid.

90 **The normal way** ibid.

91 **My impression** ibid.

91 **The idea had been** David Owen, *Time to Declare* (London:
    Penguin, 1991), p405

92 **told his political secretary** Interview with Bao Pu, Hong Kong, 2019

94 **Hong Kong is Chinese** Fang, '1978–1982: The process of China's
    decision to take back Hong Kong'

95 **would not pursue** Confidential: Record of a discussion between
    the prime minister and Premier Hua Guofeng, 1 Nov 1979, PREM
    19/3

95 **One country, two systems** Fang, '1978–1982: The process of
    China's decision to take back Hong Kong'

95 **The fact is** Zong Daoyi, Zhou Nan, *Oral History: Recalling Those Days* (Beijing: Qilu Press, 2007)

96 **China was ready** Fang, '1978–1982: The process of China's decision to take back Hong Kong'

4 THE IRON LADY VERSUS THE STEEL FACTORY

98 **This so-called iron lady** Zhou, *Oral History*

98 **ready to resort** Lu Ping, interview with Dragon TV, 2007

98 **non-peaceful means** Zhou, *Oral History*

99 **There is therefore** Letter from Lord Shepherd, 10 Aug 1982, PREM 1/10/30

99 **Like you, I doubt** Margaret Thatcher, letter to Lord Shepherd 25 Aug1982, THCR 3/2/99 f44

99 **they took the view** Letter, 31 Aug 1982, THCR 1/10/37

100 **research group report** CPS Report on Hong Kong, THCR 1/10/37, f58

101 **we must not allow** PREM 19/1054

101 **The diplomats reminded** Letter from Anthony Acland to Robert Armstrong, THCR 1/10/39

103 **with the largest number** THCR 1/10/37A

103 **promised to keep up** Cradock telegram, THCR 1/10/37A

103 **The 50 yuan per head** meal ibid.

104 **no – far too expensive** THCR 1/10/37A

104 **one of those glorious** Cradock dispatch, 'visit of the PM to China', 7 Oct 1982, PREM 19/962

104 **that the Chinese government** Secret: record of a conversation between the prime minister and premier Zhao Ziyang, PREM 19/962

106 **she could not recommend its handover** Secret: record of a conversation between the prime minister and Vice Chairman Deng Xiaoping at the Great Hall of the People, 24 Sept 1982, PREM 19/790

109 **did not recall hearing words** Email from Bob Peirce, 25 May 2021

109 **I had very high heels** Hong Kong television interview, Jun 1997

110 **The prime minister wished** Secret: telegram 596/24, Sep 1982, PREM 962

110 **The Chinese had already** Secret: note on Sir Y.K. Pao, private secretary John Holmes, 10 Downing Street, 28 Sep 1982, THCR 1/9/18A

111 **I … wish to goodness** Hong Kong television interview, Jun 1997

112 **had a very limited** No 10 record of conversation, PREM 19/790

113 **not all the cards** PREM 19/790

114 **the military effort** PREM19/1053, f29

114 **The crucial meeting** PREM 19/1054

116 **Apart from iciness** *Daily Telegraph*, 27 Jul 1993

117 **China's negotiating style** Note of a meeting at the State
     Department, 4 Nov 1982, PREM 19/1053

5 A JOINT DECLARATION

122 **It was called** 'Our basic position on the question of Hong Kong', in
     Documents on 30 years of Reform and Opening Up (Beijing: Central
     Literature Publishing House, 2008)

123 **no link of authority** Cradock to FCO, 8 Nov 1983, PREM 19/1059

124 **Hong Kong apart** THCR 1/10/74

126 **Deng Xiaoping was afraid** Zhou Nan, *Oral History*

126 **deep mistrust** PREM 19/1264

128 **told [the British]** Zhou Nan, *Oral History*

128 **The senior level negotiations** Interview with Lord Wilson of
     Tillyorn, 2019

130 **I think we should** Secret: Note to Charles Powell, 13 Jul 1984,
     THCR 1/10/74

131 **I spoke out** Zhou Nan, *Oral History*

132 **we are therefore** THCR 1/10/75

133 **Zhou Nan has remained** PREM 19/1267

134 **the answer is** Secret: FCO note to Downing Street, 21 Sep 1984,
     PREM 19/1267

134 **The second day** *South China Morning Post*, 21 Sep 1984

134 **There is nothing** Hansard, 5 Dec 1984

134 **She would have loved** Interview with Lord Wilson of Tillyorn,
     2019

135 **In his memoir** Percy Cradock, *Experiences of China* (London: John
     Murray, 1994)

6 THE EIGHTIES

136 **Fly-by-night companies** David Bonavia, *Hong Kong 1997: The
     Final Settlement* (Hong Kong: Columbus Books, 1985), p58

139 **Campbell's article** Duncan Campbell, 'Colonialism: A Secret Plan for Dictatorship', *New Statesman*, 12 Dec 1980

140 **Special Branch confirmed** https://www.legco.gov.hk/yr94-95/english/lc_sitg/hansard/h950510.pdf

141 **For the first half of 1982** Bank of England historic data

142 **uncontrollable tailspin** John Greenwood, *Hong Kong's Link to the US Dollar: Origins and Evolution* (Hong Kong: Hong Kong University Press, 2007), p140

142 **the classic error** ibid., p142

143 **But according to** https://www.hkma.gov.hk/eng/news-and-media/insight/1999/11/19991104/

145 **It cost the bank** Roberts and Kynaston, *The Lion Wakes*, p155

145 **sounded a bit artificial** ibid.

146 **It was announced** Interview with Sir William Purves, London, 2019

147 **In 1982 the population** Spence, *The Search for Modern China*, p683

148 **In China, citizens** ibid.

150 **No one had foreseen** Zhao Ziyang, *Prisoner of the State* (New York: Simon & Schuster, 2009), p139

150 **In Guangzhou, the modern** Notes on an eyewitness trip, 1985

153 **the danger of** Resolution of the 16th meeting of the standing committee of the Fifth Guangdong Provincial People's Congress, 13 Mar 1982, in *Guangdong Provincial Archives: Important Archive Documents of 30 Years of Reform and Opening Up*, pp147–8

154 **strike hard against** Zhao, *Prisoner of the State*, p103

155 **The workers started** *Following the Dictates of Reform*, documents ed. Guangdong Provincial Archives, 2008, pp15–19

155 **equal at the time** World Bank historical exchange rates

156 **When we got there** *South China Morning Post*, 17 Nov 2018

156 **a sense of contributing** Michael Enright, *Developing China* (London: Routledge, 2017), p156

156 **Between 1985 and 2014** ibid.

157 **In 1981 local manufacturers** ibid., p160

158 **Chen Yun believed** Zhao, *Prisoner of the State*, pp102–4

159 **In the early stage** Cai Chimeng, 'The Evolution of Hong Hong in Opening Up from 1978–2007', in *Research on China's Economic History* 2, HKMAO Institute, 2018

160 **Never before have** Martin Wolf, *Why Globalisation Works* (New Haven: Yale University Press, 2004), p142

160 **In the decade** ibid., p144

161 **The seating plan** Thatcher papers, Churchill College, Cambridge

165 **It pumped more** Roberts and Kynaston, *The Lion Wakes*, p98

165 **The bank runs and hoarding** Zhao, *Prisoner of the State*, p223

167 **Freedom and democracy** Andrew Nathan and Perry Link (eds),
     The Tiananmen Papers, compiled by Zhang Liang (Perseus Books,
     2001), p34

168 **A secret report** ibid., p338, 'On ideological and political infiltration
     into our country from the United States and other international
     political forces', 1 Jun 1989

169 **Look at Hong Kong** ibid., p326

170 **Many facts demonstrate** ibid., p348

170 **We had several** Private interview, London, 2019

171 **Hong Kong was the single** Richard J. Aldrich, *GCHQ* (London:
     HarperPress, 2010), p475

7 THE CHANGE

172 **We knew about** Interview with Martin Lee, 8 May 1997

172 **There was a growing** Interview with Lord Wilson of Tillyorn, 2019

174 **The market was berserk** Contemporary reporting notes, 5 Jun
     1989

176 **Bribery worked as well** Interview with western intelligence official,
     1997

177 **could not imagine** Interview with Chris Patten, London, 2019

177 **We didn't have any** Interview with Lord Wilson of Tillyorn, 2019

180 **The party leadership** Kam C. Wong, *Policing in Hong Kong*
     (Farnham: Ashgate Publishing, 2012) p286

181 **We are all well aware** https://api.parliament.uk/historic-hansard/
     lords/1989/jun/21/hong-kong

185 **lay a profound suspicion** Cradock, *Experiences of China*, pp229–32

185 **a faithful emissary** Qian Qichen, *Ten Important Events in Foreign
     Affairs* (Beijing: World Knowledge Press, 2004)

186 **fresh disagreements** ibid.

186 **we had clear understandings** Cradock, *Experiences of China*

187 **When Bush tried** Patrick Tyler, *A Great Wall: Six Presidents and
     China* (New York: Century Foundation Books, 1999), p 364

188 **To be frank** https://www.chinafile.com/library/reports/
     us-china-diplomacy-after-tiananmen-documents-george-hw-bush-
     presidential-library

188 **America had to deal** Tyler, *A Great Wall*, p364

189 **a more directly** *Hong Kong 1990* (Hong Kong: Government Information Services, 1991)

189 **There was during my time** Interview with Lord Wilson of Tillyorn, 2019

190 **We were ushered** Interview with Sir William Purves, London 2019

192 **In 1963 the Soviet Union** https://nsarchive2.gwu.edu/NSAEBB/NSAEBB38/

192 **An official Chinese history** https://www.scmp.com/article/714064/nixon-intervention-saved-china-soviet-nuclear-attack

192 **front page** *People's Daily*, 26 and 27 Dec 1989

193 **He offered Martin Lee** https://www.nytimes.com/2016/07/28/world/asia/china-communist-party-xu-jiatun-exile.html

194 **The party appointed** Zhou, *Oral History*

194 **special mission** ibid.

195 **Kam later told** https://www.nytimes.com/2016/07/28/world/asia/china-communist-party-xu-jiatun-exile.html

195 **succumbed to the worship** Zhou, *Oral History*

196 **arbitrary personal decisions** ibid.

196 **In his own eyes** Xu Jiatun, *Memoirs of Hong Kong* (Taipei: Lian Jing Publishing House, 1993)

196 **The harbour is** *Hong Kong 1991* (Hong Kong: Government Information Services, 1992)

198 **a man who knew** Qian, *Ten Important Events in Foreign Affairs*

198 **the governor wrote** Letter from Sir David Wilson of 6 July 1991, Cradock papers, St John's College, Cambridge

199 **All this would come** *Hong Kong 1991* (Hong Kong: Government Information Services, 1992)

200 **It had a population** ibid.

201 **Between 1988 and 1990** *Statistical Yearbook of Guangdong Province, 1996*

201 **By 1990** *Hong Kong 1991* (Hong Kong: Government Information Services, 1992)

202 **A dedicated** Hurd, *Memoirs*, p478

203 **In every negotiation** Liu Zhenwu, *Living History, the return of Hong Kong to the motherland*, interviews with Zhang Junsheng (Beijing: Liberation Press, 2010)

8 TWO JOURNEYS

205 **The paper reported** *Ta Kung Pao*, 22 and 27 Jan 1992, cited in CNA 1453, 1 Feb 1992

205 **The southern tour** Yang Jisheng, *China Business News*, 31 Jan 2012

207 **privatisation … which is incompatible** *Seeking Truth*, 2 Sep 1991, cited in CNA 1460, 15 May 1992

207 **the sound of** *China Youth Daily*, 15 Apr 1992, ibid.

208 **reported rumours** *Chengming*, Hong Kong, Mar 1992

208 **Reform and opening up** Deng Xiaoping, Speech in Shenzhen (full text), *People's Daily*, 17 Nov 1994

212 **I've thought that** Interview with Chris Patten, 2019

215 **We were asked to go** ibid.

217 **Patten was a typical** Liu, *Living History*

217 **Patten has got them** Chris Patten, *East and West* (London: Macmillan, 1998), p70

218 **Whoever had devised them** ibid., p58

218 **We straight away agreed** Interview with Chris Patten, 2019

221 **The damage has been done** Interview with Martin Lee, 1997

222 **The plane was late** Liu, *Living History*

222 **Always a cautious** Hurd, *Memoirs*, p484

223 **I made a statement** Qian, *Ten Important Events in Foreign Affairs*

224 **The British side** ibid.

224 **councillors elected** Lu Ping, *Oral History of The Return of Hong Kong*, excerpted in *Wen Wei Po*, 24 July 2009

225 **The idea that** Interview with Chris Patten, 2019

227 **I said, Mr Patten** Lu, *Oral History of The Return of Hong Kong*

227 **locked in fruitless exchanges** Patten, *East and West*, p67

228 **If things were** Interview with Sir William Purves, 2019

228 **when the black dog** Patten, *East and West*, p70

229 **talking like a Buddha** *Ta Kung Pao*, 18 Mar 1993, cited CNA 1494

230 **An article** *Liberation Daily*, 23 Mar 1993, cited CNA 1482

230 **The route had been** Lu, *Oral History of The Return of Hong Kong*

230 **At the time many things** ibid.

231 **old-time Communist coelacanths** Patten, *East and West*, p81

231 **The talks fell apart** Qian, *Ten Important Events in Foreign Affairs*

231 **I never knew really** Interview with Chris Patten, 2019

9 A MANDARIN FOR ALL SEASONS

233 **You have served** Handwritten card from Robert Gates, 27 May 1992, Cradock papers

234 **so disturbing and inaccurate** Sir Percy Cradock, letter to Sir John Coles, 28 Sep 1993

235 **I take a bleak view** THCR 1/10/74

236 **a demented environment** Cradock, *Experiences of China*, p90

236 *forsan et haec* Virgil, *Aeneid*, 1.203

237 **will be ever green** Note from Wang Guangmei, 19 Dec 1983, Cradock papers

239 **personal and confidential** letter to the prime minister, 17 Nov 1992, Cradock papers

241 **They feel they have** Testimony to Foreign Affairs Committee, 8 Dec 1993

242 **From one side** Letter from Lord MacLehose, 12 Apr 1994

242 **her autobiography** Letter to Lee Kuan Yew, 2001, Cradock papers

242 **I entirely support** Letter from Lord Callaghan, 25 Apr 1994, Cradock papers

243 **a tour de force** Letter from Lee Kuan Yew, undated, Cradock papers

243 **I cannot help thinking** Personal letter from Margaret Thatcher, 10 Jul 2001, Cradock papers

243 **We are clearly** Letter from Len Appleyard, undated, Cradock papers

244 **I recall myself travelling** Lord Thomas of Swynnerton, email of 5 Feb 2010, Cradock papers

10 TRANSITIONS

245 **It showed that** Interview with Martin Lee, 1997

246 **great shagger** Interview with former intelligence official, 2019

247 **He showed me** Lu Ping, *Oral History*, Wenhui Reading Weekly, 24 Jul 2009

247 **We have a clear** Hong Kong Government Report for 1995 (Government Information Services, 1996)

249 **They had already** Interview with Martin Lee, 1997

250 **He says to me** Interview with Chris Patten, 2019

253 **a tough Fujianese** Hugh Davies, *Hong Kong 1997: Handling the Handover* (privately published, 2016), p74

253 **Chen later described** Zhang Yawen, *The Summons of Centuries Past*, tr. Matt Schrader (Xia'an: Shaanxi People's Education Press, 2013)

253 **They are all very much** Interview with Brian Dutton, Hong Kong, 26 May 1997

256 **The child stolen** Zhang, *The Summons of Centuries Past*

257 **Vickers explained** Interview with Simon Vickers, Hong Kong, 1997

258 **received a tipoff** Interview with Jonathan Mirsky, London, 23 Oct 2019

261 **Its director, Xie Jin** *Wenhui Daily News*, Shanghai, 7 Jun 1997, cited CNA 1593

262 **the mountain is high** *People's Daily*, 13 Feb 1997, cited CNA 1580

262 **Maybe the foam** Xinhua, 3 Mar 1997, cited CNA 1581

262 **a moment which the Chinese** *People's Daily*, 1 Jul 1997

263 **to put an end** Interview with Lu Ping, Dragon TV, 2007

264 **According to intelligence** Interviews with intelligence officials, 1997, 2018, 1019

267 **I remember the emotion** Interview with Chris Patten, 2019

269 **a hope that things** Interview with Anson Chan, Hong Kong, 2019

270 **Watching the five starred red flag** Qian, *Ten Important Events in Foreign Affairs*

270 **Now I knew** Chris Emmett, *Hong Kong Policeman* (Hong Kong: Earnshaw Books, 2014)

272 **more like a philosophical debate** Interview with Tung Chee-hwa, Hong Kong, 1997

273 **later published an article** *Far Eastern Economic Review*, 13 Mar 1997

274 **Chiang Kai-shek wanted** Interview with Anson Chan, 2019

11 TO SEEK A WIDER WORLD

279 **In 1996, the World Health Organisation** https://www.who.int/influenza/human_animal_interface/avian_influenza/H5N1_avian_influenza_update.pdf

281 **Frightened Chinese families** Eyewitness notes, 1998

281 **I explained to him** Interview with General Wiranto, Jakarta, April 2004

282 **The Bank of Korea** Joo Yun Hong and Franklin Allen, 'Why are there large foreign exchange reserves? The Case of South Korea', *Korean Social Science Journal*, Dec 2011

283 **This is the sort** Interview with Donald Tsang, Hong Kong, 2019

283 **Exchange controls are out** Joseph Yam, Inside Asia Lecture, Sydney, 1998, https://www.info.gov.hk/gia/general/199811/23/1123153.htm

284 **We are conservative** Interview with Donald Tsang, 2019

285 **They then sought** Yam, Inside Asia Lecture, 1998

286 **That's why I had** Interview with Donald Tsang, 2019

286 **the authorities held enough** Yam, Inside Asia Lecture, 1998

288 **By directly intervening** David Webb, letter to *South China Morning Post*, 20 August 1998

288 **Our actions in August** Yam, Inside Asia Lecture, 1998

12 THE RIVALS

291 **World War Two was caused** Interview with Lee Kuan Yew, Singapore, 24 Sep 1996

292 **It was almost** Fung, Yeh, Zhou, Chan (eds), *Developing a Competitive Pearl River Delta in South China under One Country Two Systems* (Hong Kong: Hong Kong University Press, 2006)

292 **According to the** *People's Daily*, 30 Dec 1992, cited CNA 1477

292 **With only 0.25 per cent** *Shenzhen Special Zone Daily*, 31 Mar 1994, cited CNA 1508

293 **In the five years** *Statistical Yearbook of Guangdong* (People's Publishing House, 1996)

293 **When it comes to cleverness** *Zhu Rongji: On the Record* (Beijing: Foreign Languages Press, 2018), Ch 88

293 **lightbulb moment** Interview with Sir John Bond, Hong Kong, 2019

294 **Speaking in a 2003 interview** Roberts and Kynaston, *The Lion Wakes*, p474

294 **photographs of the dormitories** *People's Daily*, 20 May 1993, cited CNA 1502

294 **On 19 November 1993** ibid.

295 **The local press** *Nanfang Daily*, 27 Jun 1993, cited CNA 1502

295 **extremely hot, noisy** *Workers Daily*, 22 Jun 1993, cited CNA 1502

296 **in 1978 foreign trade** *People's Daily*, 9 Jan 1994, cited CNA 1510

296 **reciprocal and mutually advantageous** https://www.wto.org/
     english/docs_e/legal_e/gatt47.pdf

297 **admission to GATT** *People's Daily*, 3 Aug 1993, cited CNA 1510

297 **more than US$12 billion** https://wits.worldbank.org/
     CountryProfile/en/Country/CHN/Year/1993/SummaryText

297 **The GATT was a bit** Interview with Stuart Harbinson, Geneva,
     2019

298 **the offshore rate** *The Economist*, 11 Dec 1997

298 **The real devaluation** *China Daily*, 11 Oct 2004

298 **This was by far** Interview with Sir John Bond, 2019

299 **if a pretty young lady** Song, Zhang and Qiao, *China Can Say No*
     (Beijing: China Industrial and Commercial United Publishing
     House, 1996)

299 **'restricted' report** WTO Report of the working party on the
     accession of China/WT/ACC/CHN/40, 1 Oct 2001

300 **and therefore should have** ibid.

301 **The representative of China** WTO: /WT/ACC/CHN/40

302 **a private memoir** *Qianshao*, Hong Kong, Feb 2011

303 **On the night of Friday** 'Anatomy of a WTO Deal', *Time*, 29 Nov
     1999

304 **Everything was decided** Long Yongtu, 'Zhu Rongji and WTO
     talks', *China Business News*, 12 July 2011

304 **According to Barshevsky** *Time*, 29 Nov 1999

304 **The United States has** https://www.brookings.edu/testimonies/
     issues-in-chinas-wto-accession/

305 **We'll be able to export** Speech by President Bill Clinton at the Paul
     H. Nitze School of Advanced International Studies of the Johns
     Hopkins University, 8 Mar 2000

306 **After we join** Speech by President Jiang Zemin, 25 Feb 2002, in
     Selected Documents of Thirty Years Reform and Opening Up
     (Beijing: Central Literature Publishing House, 2008)

307 **The text ran** https://www.wto.org/english/thewto_e/minist_e/
     min01_e/min01_11nov_e.htm

307 **The biggest change** Long Yongtu, *China Business News*, 12 Jul
     2011

13 ONE COUNTRY, TWO CULTURES

308 **The movies attracted** Fredric Dannen, 'Hong Kong Babylon', *New Yorker*, 7 Aug 1995

309 **But they also** Christine Loh, *Underground Front, The CCP in Hong Kong* (Hong Kong: Hong Kong University Press, 2010)

309 **The Communist Party is** Simon Leys, *Essais sur la Chine* (Paris: Editions Robert Laffont, 1998), p789

310 **Hong Kong black societies** *South China Morning Post*, 4 May 1997

310 **An academic study** T.W. Lo and S. I. Kwok, 'Chinese Triads and Tongs', in G. Bruinsma and D. Weisburd (eds), *Encyclopedia of Criminology and Criminal Justice* (New York: Springer, 2014), pp5332–43

310 **In a 1987 court case** Crown vs Heung Wah-yin and others, 1987

312 **'Why,' he sighed** Conversation with Walter Kwok, Hong Kong, 1996

313 **Fresh new girls** *Apple Daily*, 23 May 1997

313 **In a 1997 study** Chin Wan-kan, 'From Dialect to Grapholect', *Hong Kong Journal of Applied Linguistics*, 1997

314 **The economy and ideology** ibid

314 **written in bamboo and silk** ibid.

315 **Never in Chinese history** ibid.

315 **Shenzhen has attracted** *Youth Research Journal* 8 (1989)

316 **Most of them are middle aged** *Sixty days of Bitter Marriage* (Shenzhen, 1996)

317 **Hong Kong and Shenzhen** Guang Zhigang, 'Characteristics of Hong Kong culture and its influence on Shenzhen', *Theoretical and Practical Journal of Shenzhen SEZ*, June 1996

318 **Shenzhen was the first** *Special Economic Zone Journal* 6 (2018)

319 **In 1979 a young diplomat** João de Deus Ramos, *Em Torno da China, Memórias Diplomáticas* (Lisbon: Caleidoscopio-Ediçao, 2016), pp50–3

319 **The chief, an ambassador** ibid., pp80–4

322 **Emily, Emily** Interview with Emily Lau, Hong Kong, 2019

322 **Monday afternoon charade** Interview with Jonathan Fenby, London, 2019

323 **from 1997 to 2002** https://www.censtatd.gov.hk/FileManager/EN/Content_1064/A2_E.pdf

326 **The first known case** World Health Organisation: https://www.who.int/csr/don/2003_07_04/en/

327 **strange contagious disease** ibid.

329 **Chinese people can be** Contemporary reporting notes, Hong Kong, March 2003

329 **When it was over** https://www.news.gov.hk/isd/ebulletin/en/category/issues/040705/html/040705en05004.htm

329 **Initially there was** Lee Shui Hung, 'The SARS epidemic in Hong Kong: what lessons have we learned?', *Journal of the Royal Society of Medicine*, Aug 2003

331 **The official WHO timeline** World Health Organisation: https://www.who.int/csr/don/2003_07_04/en/

332 **We're all healthy** Contemporary reporting notes, Guangzhou, Dec 2003

333 **sometimes I see** *South China Morning Post*, 12 Mar 2003

333 **out of place** https://cpj.org/2002/12/hong-kong-proposed-antisubversion-legislation-thre/

336 **Rogge told me** Yuan Weimin, *Yuan Weimin and the Winds and Clouds of the World of Sports* (Beijing: Fonghong Media Company, 2009)

336 **any suggestion** Contemporary notes, 16 Oct 2009

337 **heightened risk aversion** HKMA, Annual report 2008

337 **soared from US$83 billion** https://www.census.gov/foreign-trade/balance/c5700.html#2001

338 **Its single biggest holding** Congressional Research Service, 'China's Holdings of U.S. Securities: Implications for the U.S. Economy', May 2008

338 **Chinese entities owned** ibid.

339 **In 2009, for the first time** Adam Tooze, *Crashed: How a Decade of Financial Crises Changed the World* (London: Allen Lane, 2018), p251

340 **They know what** Interview with Sir Donald Tsang, 2019

341 **managed democracy** https://search.wikileaks.org/plusd/cables/09HONGKONG165_a.html

341 **his ability to govern** *South China Morning Post*, 19 Jun 2009

342 **We are confident** Interview with electrical salesman, Guangzhou, 2008

342 **In September 2010** *Ming Pao*, 29 Sep 2010

343 **Seven years of inaction** Joseph Y.S. Cheng (ed.), *Evaluating the Tsang Years* (Hong Kong: City University of Hong Kong Press, 2013)

344 **had suffered a just punishment** https://www.doj.gov.hk/eng/
public/pdf/2019/FACC_29_2018e.pdf

345 **overconsumption of alcohol** Statement by foreign secretary
William Hague, 17 Apr 2012

345 **He belonged to** John Garnaut, *The Rise and Fall of the House of Bo*
(London: Penguin Books, 2012)

346 **Heywood got drunk** Xinhua, 8 Nov 2012

347 **In 2018 he was spotted** *South China Morning Post*, 20 Jan 2018

347 **bending the law** Xinhua, 24 Sep 2012

348 **Just another businessman** Confidential interview, London 2019

14 CHAOS UNDER HEAVEN

349 **His father recalled** Agence France-Presse, 13 Oct 2017

350 **The 'ism' was added** Joshua Wong and Jason Y. Ng, *Unfree Speech*
(London: Allen Lane, 2020)

353 **Sceptics questioned** Information from Chinese academic sources,
Hong Kong, Aug 2013

353 **This broke with** Kerry Brown, 'What Has Karl Marx Ever Done for
China?', *The Diplomat*, 14 May 2018

354 **cultural sovereignty** Wang Huning, 'Cultural Expansionism and
Cultural Sovereignty: Challenges to the concept of Sovereignty',
Fudan Journal 3 (1994), cited in CNA 1518

354 **For many writers** Pierre Robert, 'Questions of Method', CNA 1518,
15 Sep 1994

355 **man enough** https://chinadigitaltimes.net/2013/01/
leaked-speech-shows-xi-jinpings-opposition-to-reform/

355 **The practical utility** John Garnaut, 'Engineers of the Soul: What
Australia needs to know about ideology in Xi Jinping's China',
lecture in Asian Strategic and Economic Series, Aug 2017

355 **Intervention is by no means** 'Prospects of the Revolution in China',
30 Nov 1926, in J.V. Stalin, *On The Opposition*, tr (Beijing: Foreign
Languages Press, 1974), p502

357 **the Central Leadership** http://english.www.gov.cn/archive/white_
paper/2014/08/23/content_281474982986578.htm

358 **Its inventors built in** Ian Williams, 'The use of cyberweapons
against the Hong Kong democracy movement', MSc dissertation,
Royal Holloway, University of London, 2018

358 **Cyber-sleuths concluded** ibid.

359 **extensive and in-depth** Full text of NPC decision on universal
     suffrage for HK Chief Executive selection, Xinhua, 31 August 2014
361 **quite positive** Wong, *Policing in Hong Kong*, p326
362 **the bad guys** ibid., p329
362 **no longer a docile bunch** ibid., p337
364 **This is my idea alone** Contemporary reporting notes, Oct 2014
366 **scum** Contemporary reporting notes, 2014
367 **There was a quixotic** Williams, 'The use of cyberweapons'
369 **There was an American** *Hong Kong Free Press*, 28 Sep 2019
371 **comprehensive if somewhat bland** https://publications.parliament.
     uk/pa/cm201415/cmselect/cmfaff/649/64908.htm

15 HUNGER GAMES

372 **they had stumbled** https://www.reuters.com/article/
     us-hong-kong-surveillance-special-report-
     idUSKBN0JT00120141215
375 **Guangdong Action Plan** Contemporary notes, confidential
     briefings with legislators, January 2016
375 **not only the extending** https://www.nytimes.com/2016/01/08/
     world/asia/hong-kong-lee-bo-bookseller-china.html
376 **Perhaps a million** *The Economist*, 10 Oct 2020
377 **The shame of it** https://www.brookings.edu/podcast-episode/
     former-ustr-charlene-barshefsky-on-the-obstacles-to-a-us-china-
     trade-deal/
378 **Honey melons** Speech by President Xi Jinping of China, World
     Economic Forum, 17 Jan 2017
378 **the Chinese national security state** https://www.prcleader.org/
     cheung
382 **the brave and fierce** Contemporary reporting notes, 2019
382 **the worse, the better** https://www.marxists.org/archive/lenin/
     works/1917/jul/19.htm
385 **You are useless** https://hongkongfp.com/2019/05/18/
     political-civility-early-casualty-hong-kongs-extradition-law-row/
385 **A survey for the Chinese University** https://www.cpr.cuhk.edu.hk/
     en/press_detail.
     php?id=3107&t=survey-findings-on-views-on-social-conflict-in-
     hong-kong-released-by-hong-kong-institute-of-asia-pacific-
     studies-at-cuhk

385 **He pointed to** *South China Morning Post*, 7 Sep 2019

386 **There was a feeling** Confidential interviews, Hong Kong, Nov 2019

387 **A writer for** *South China Morning Post* Chow Chung-yan, *South China Morning Post*, 2 Nov 2019

387 **At lunchtime** Contemporary reporting notes, Nov 2019

388 **That night the scent** Contemporary reporting notes, Nov 2019

390 **It shut bars** https://www.news.gov.hk/eng/2020/04/20200402/2020 0402_195740_071.html

390 **It was soon declared** *China Daily*, 24 Apr 2020

391 **build a great steel wall** *People's Daily*, 15 Apr 2020

391 **by beating drums** *Quishi*, Apr 2020

392 **she was warned** *South China Morning Post*, 18 May 2020

394 **global co-operation** Xi Jinping, 'Major Issues for China's Economic Growth and Development', *Qiushi*, 1 Nov 2020

AFTERWORD

404 **Deng, the elders** Spence, *The Search for Modern China*, p746

405 **Obligations are ignored** Anthony Eden, *Facing the Dictators* (London: Cassell, 1962), p473

Bibliography

WORKS IN ENGLISH AND OTHER LANGUAGES

Agence France-Presse, *Hong Kong 1997: City on the Edge*, AFP
  Publications 1997

Aldrich, Richard J, *GCHQ: The Uncensored Story of Britain's Most Secret
  Intelligence Agency*, London: HarperPress, 2010

Auden, W.H. and Isherwood, Christopher, *Journey to a War*, London:
  Faber & Faber, 1939

Backhouse, E. and Bland, J.O.P., *Annals and Memoirs of the Court of
  Peking*, William Heinemann & Co, 1914

Barr, Pat, *The Deer Cry Pavilion*, London: Macmillan & Co, 1968

Bergamini, David, *Japan's Imperial Conspiracy*, New York: William
  Morrow & Co, 1971

Berger, John, *Ways of Seeing*, London: Penguin Books, 1972

Bernstein, Richard and Munro, Ross H., *The Coming Conflict with
  China*, New York: Alfred A. Knopf, 1997

Bonavia, David, *Hong Kong 1997, The Final Settlement*, Hong Kong:
  Columbus Books, 1985

Bowring, Philip, *Free Trade's First Missionary: Sir John Bowring in Europe
  and Asia*, Hong Kong: Hong Kong University Press, 2014

Brook, Timothy, *The Troubled Empire: China in the Yuan and Ming
  Dynasties*, Cambridge, MA: The Belknap Press, 2010

Brown, Jules, and Fisher, Sophy, *The Rough Guide to Hong Kong and
  Macau*, London: Rough Guides, 1999

Coates, Austin, *Myself a Mandarin*, London: Frederick Muller, 1968

Cottrell, Robert, *The End of Hong Kong: The Secret Diplomacy of Imperial
  Retreat*, London: John Murray, 1993

Cradock, Percy, *Experiences of China*, London: John Murray,
  1994

Crossman, Carl L., *The Decorative Arts of the China Trade*, Woodbridge: Antique Collectors Club, 1991

Dapiran, Anthony, *City of Protest: A Recent History of Dissent in Hong Kong*, London: Penguin Books, 2017

Davies, Hugh Llewellyn, *Hong Kong 1997: Handling the Handover*, privately published, 2016

De Bary, Wm. Theodore, and Lufrano, Richard, *Sources of Chinese Tradition, Vol II*, New York: Columbia University Press, 2000

Deng, Yong, *China's Struggle for Status*, Cambridge: Cambridge University Press, 2008

Dikötter, Frank, *The Cultural Revolution: A People's History 1962–1976*, London: Bloomsbury, 2016

Dimbleby, Jonathan, *The Last Governor*, London: Little, Brown & Co, 1997

Eden, Anthony, *The Eden Memoirs: Facing the Dictators*, London: Cassell, 1962

Enright, Michael, *Developing China*, London: Routledge, 2017

Faber, Marc, *The Rise and Fall of Great Cities*, Hong Kong: Marc Faber Ltd, 1997

Fairbank, John K. (ed.), *The Cambridge History of China, Vols 10 and 11*, Cambridge: Cambridge University Press, 1978 and 1980; special edition published by Caves Books, Taipei, 1986 and 1989

Faligot, Roger, *Chinese Spies*, London: Hurst & Co, 2019

Fenby, Jonathan, *Dealing with the Dragon: A Year in the New Hong Kong*, London: Little, Brown, 2000

Fleming, Peter, *The Siege at Peking*, London: Rupert Hart-Davis, 1959

French, Paul, *Through the Looking Glass: China's Foreign Journalists from Opium Wars to Mao*, Hong Kong: Hong Kong University Press, 2009

Fukuyama, Francis, *The Origins of Political Order*, London: Profile Books, 2001

Gao Wenqian, *Zhou Enlai, The Last Perfect Revolutionary*, New York: Public Affairs, 2007

Garnaut, John, *The Rise and Fall of the House of Bo*, London: Penguin Books, 2012

Gittings, John, *China Through the Sliding Door*, London: Touchstone, 1999

Goldblatt, Howard (ed.), *Chairman Mao Would Not Be Amused: Fiction from Today's China*, New York: Grove Press, 1995

Greenwood, John, *Hong Kong's Link to the US Dollar*, Hong Kong: Hong Kong University Press, 2007

Han Han, *This Generation*, London: Simon & Schuster, 2012

Harney, Alexandra, *The China Price*, London: Penguin Books, 2008

Hibbert, Christopher, *The Dragon Wakes, China and the West, 1793–1911*, Longman, 1970

Hinton, William, *Fanshen: A Documentary of Life in a Chinese Village*, London: Pelican Books, 1972

Huntington, Samuel P., *The Clash of Civilisations and the Remaking of World Order*, New York: Simon & Schuster, 1996

Hurd, Douglas, *Memoirs*, London: Little, Brown, 2003

Ibrahim, Zuraidah, and Lam, Jeffie (eds), *Rebel City: Hong Kong's Year of Water and Fire*, Hong Kong: South China Morning Post Books, 2020

Ko Tim Keung, and Wordie, Jason, *Ruins of War: A Guide to Hong Kong's Battlefields and Wartime Sites*, Hong Kong: Joint Publishing (HK) Co, 1996

Lam, Willy Wo-lap, *China After Deng Xiaoping*, Hong Kong: PA Professional Consultants, Hong Kong, 1995

Leys, Simon, *Essais sur la Chine*, Paris: Éditions Robert Laffont, 1998

Leys, Simon (tr.), *The Analects of Confucius*, New York: W.W. Norton & Co, 1997

Li Qi and Guo Chaoren (eds), *In Memory of Mao Zedong*, Beijing: Central Party Literature Publishing House, 1992

Li Zhisui, *The Private Life of Chairman Mao*, London: Chatto & Windus, 1994

Lilley, James, with Lilley, Jeffrey, *China Hands: Nine Decades of Adventure, Espionage and Diplomacy in Asia*, New York: Public Affairs, 2004

Link, Perry, *Evening Chats in Beijing*, New York: W.W. Norton & Co, 1992

Liu Kin-ming (ed), *My First Trip to China*, Hong Kong: East Slope Publishing, 2012

Liu Xiaobo, *June Fourth Elegies*, London: Jonathan Cape, 2012

Loh, Christine, *Underground Front: The Chinese Communist Party in Hong Kong*, Hong Kong: Hong Kong University Press, 2010

Macartney, Lord, *An Embassy to China, Being the Journal Kept by Lord Macartney during his Embassy to the Emperor Ch'ien-lung 1793–1794*, ed. J.L. Cranmer-Byng, London: Longmans, 1962

McGregor, Richard, *The Party*, London: Allen Lane, 2010

McNeil, William H., and Sedlar, Jean W. (eds), *Classical China*, Oxford: Oxford University Press, 1970

MacFarquhar, Roderick, and Schoenhals, Michael, *Mao's Last Revolution*, Cambridge, MA The Belknap Press of Harvard University Press, 2006

Mahbubani, Kishore, *Can Asians Think?*, Singapore: Times Books International, 1998

Mao Zedong, *On Diplomacy*, Beijing: Foreign Languages Press, 1998

Mao Zedong, *Poems* (tr. Gu Zengkun), Beijing: Beijing University Press, 1993

Martin, Claude, *La diplomatie n'est pas un diner de gala*, Paris: Éditions de l'Aube, 2018

Mo, Timothy, *The Monkey King*, London: André Deutsch, 1978

Mo, Timothy, *An Insular Possession*, London: Chatto & Windus, 1986

Moore, Charles, *Margaret Thatcher, The Authorised Biography, Vol 2, Everything She Wants*, London: Allen Lane, 2015

Morris, Jan, *Hong Kong*, London: Viking, 1988

Nathan, Andrew, and Link, Perry (eds), *The Tiananmen Papers* (comp. Zhang Liang), London: Little, Brown, 2001

Nathan, Andrew, and Gilley, Bruce (eds), *China's New Rulers: The Secret Files*, London: Granta Books, 2002

Needham, Joseph, *Science and Civilisation in China, vol II, History of Scientific Thought*, Cambridge: Cambridge University Press; special edition published by Caves Books, Taipei, 1985

Ng, Jason Y., *Umbrellas in Bloom*, Hong Kong: Blacksmith Books, 2016

Pantsov, Alexander V, and Levine, Steven I., *Deng Xiaoping, A Revolutionary Life*, Oxford: Oxford University Press, 2015

Patten, Chris, *East and West*, London: Macmillan, 1998

Peruzzi, Roberto, *Diplomatici, banchieri e mandarini, Le origini finanziarie e diplomatiche della fine dell'Impero Celeste*, Milan: Mondadori Università, 2015

Pillsbury, Michael, *The Hundred-Year Marathon: China's Secret Strategy to Replace America as the Global Superpower*, New York: St Martin's Griffin, 2015

Polo, Marco, *The Travels* (tr. Ronald Latham), London: Penguin Books, 1958

Pottinger, George, *Sir Henry Pottinger, First Governor of Hong Kong*, Stroud, Glos: Sutton Publishing, 1997

Ramos, João de Deus, *Em Torno Da China, Memórias Diplomáticas*, Lisbon: Edição Caleidoscopo, Lisbon, 2016

Ricci, Matteo, *Lettere (1580–1609)*, Macerata: Quodlibet, 2001

Roberts, Richard, and Kynaston, David, *The Lion Wakes: A Modern History of HSBC*, London: Profile Books, 2015

Schafer, Edward H., *The Golden Peaches of Samarkand, A Study of Tang Exotics*, Berkeley and Los Angeles: University of California Press, 1963

Schell, Orville, *Mandate of Heaven*, London: Little, Brown, 1995

Schram, Stuart, *Mao Tse-tung*, London; Penguin Books, 1966

Snow, Edgar, *Red Star Over China* (revised edition), New York: Grove Press, 1968

Spence, Jonathan D., *The Search for Modern China*, New York: W.W. Norton, 1990

Stalin, J.V., *On the Opposition (1921–1927)*, Beijing: Foreign Languages Press, 1974

Studwell, Joe, *The China Dream*, London: Profile Books, 2002

Taylor, Jay, *The Generalissimo: Chiang Kai-shek and the Struggle for Modern China*, Cambridge, MA: The Belknap Press, 2009

Tooze, Adam, *Crashed, How a Decade of Financial Crises Changed the World*, London: Allen Lane, 2018

Tsang, Steve, *A Modern History of Hong Kong*, Hong Kong: Hong Kong University Press, 2004

Tuchman, Barbara W., *Stilwell and the American Experience in China, 1911–45*, New York: Macmillan, 1971

Tyler, Patrick, *A Great Wall: Six Presidents and China*, New York: Public Affairs, 1999

Vines, Stephen, *Hong Kong, China's New Colony*, London: Aurum Press, 1998

Vogel, Ezra F., *Deng Xiaoping and the Transformation of China*, Cambridge, MA: Harvard University Press, 2011

Wang, David Der-wei and Shang Wei (eds), *Dynastic Crisis and Cultural Innovation: From the Late Ming to the Late Qing and Beyond*, Cambridge, MA: Harvard University Press, 2005

Welsh, Frank, *A History of Hong Kong*, London: HarperCollinsPublishers, 1993

Wolf, Martin, *Why Globalisation Works*, New Haven: Yale University Press, 2004

Woodham-Smith, Cecil, *The Reason Why*, London: Constable, 1953

Wong, Joshua, with Ng, Jason N. and Ai Weiwei, *Unfree Speech*, London: Penguin Books, 2020

Xi Jinping *The Governance of China*, Beijing: Foreign Languages Press, 2014

Xinhua News Agency, *China's Foreign Relations; A Chronology of Events 1949–1988*, Beijing: Foreign Languages Press, 1989

Zhang Xinxin and Sang Ye, *Chinese Lives: An Oral History of Contemporary China*, London: Macmillan, 1987

Zhao Ziyang, *Prisoner of the State* (tr. Bao Pu and Renee Chiang, with Adi Ignatius), New York: Simon & Schuster, 2009

Zhou Enlai, *In Quest: Poems*, tr. Nancy T. Lin, Hong Kong: Joint Publishing Co, 1979

The English text of the Basic Law of the Hong Kong Special Administrative Region is that published by the People's Publishing House, Beijing, 1990.

BOOKS PUBLISHED IN THE CHINESE LANGUAGE

Guangdong Provincial Archives: Important Archive Documents on 30 Years of Reform and Opening Up in Guangdong, a collection of 226 documents, Dec 1978–Jul 2008, China Archives Publishing House, 2008

The Chronicle of Guangdong Province since Reform and Opening Up, Nanfang Daily Publishing House, 1998

Following the Dictates of Reform, documents ed. Guangdong Provincial Archives, 2008

'*Chronology of Deng Xiaoping 1975–1997*', ed. literature research office of the CPC Central Committee, Central Literature Publishing House, 2004

The Biography of Li Qiang: 90 Years of Experience, Beijing: People's Publishing House, 2004

Jia Juchuan et al, *Xi Zhongxun (1913–2002), A Chinese revolutionary and political leader of the CCP*, 2 vols, Beijing: Central Literature Publishing House, vol 1 2008, vol 2 2013

Liu Zhenwu, *Living History: the return of Hong Kong to the motherland*, interviews with Zhang Junsheng, Beijing: Liberation Press, 2010

Lu Ping, *Oral History of The Return of Hong Kong*, Beijing: China Welfare Society Press, 2009

Qian Qichen, *Ten Important Events in Foreign Affairs*, Beijing: World Knowledge Press, 2004

Song, Zhang and Qiao, *China Can Say No*, Beijing: China Industrial and Commercial United Publishing House, 1996

Xu Bing, *The Wind and the Cloud of the Return of Hong Kong to China*, Jilin Provincial Publishing House, 1996

Xu Jiatun, *Memoirs of Hong Kong*, Taipei: Lian Jing Publishing House, Taipei, 1993

Yuan Weimin, *Yuan Weimin and the Winds and Clouds of the World of Sports*, Beijing: Fonghong Media Company, 2009

Zong Daoyi, *Zhou Nan, Oral History: Recalling Those Days*, Beijing: Qilu Press, 2007

Index

Abu Zayd al-Sirafi, 11–12
Afghanistan, 32
Ai Qing, 162
Aldrich, Richard J., 171
Amherst, Lord, 21
animal markets, live, 278, 329, 330, 331–2
Anonymous (hackers' collective), 367
Anson Chan, 341
Apple Daily (tabloid), 261, 313, 348, 366, 367, 392, 397
Appleyard, Len, 243
Arab Spring (2011), 368
art, political messages in, 68–9
Ashdown, Paddy, 134
Asian Development Bank, 214
Asian flu (1957), 329
Asian Monetary Monitor, 142
Asian Wall Street Journal, 137
Atkins, Humphrey, 97
Attlee, Clement, 74, 75
Auden, W.H., 244
Australia, 117, 179, 254, 260, 393

Balliol College, Oxford, 57, 162, 212
Bank for International Settlements, 248
Bank of China, 3, 229, 338
Bao Pu, 401
Bao Tong, 92, 161, 401
Bao'an country, 41
Baoding, 336
Barber, Anthony, 99–100
Barshefsky, Charlene, 299, 303, 377–8
Beidahe (seaside resort), 131, 133
Beijing: Anglo-French expedition, 8–9; in late Ming period, 16; Forbidden City, 17; English envoys at (1792), 19; Anglo-French forces destroy summer palace, 36, 70; youth football match (30 July 1977), 59–60; national art museum, 68–9; Great Hall of the People, 90, 103–4, 106–9, 134, 166, 167, 190, 262; Coca-Cola bottling plant, 156; Monument to the People's

Heroes, 167; handover celebrations in, 270; National Institute for Virology, 332
see also Tiananmen Square, Beijing
Beijing, Convention of (1860), 36
Beijing, Second Convention of (1898), 38, 81
'Belt and Road' initiative, 378–9
A Better Tomorrow (John Woo film, 1986), 309
Biden, Joe, 398–9
bird flu, 278–9
Blair, Tony, 255, 265, 268
Blye, Douglas, 143, 144, 146
Bo Xilai, 345–7, 348
Bo Yibo, 161, 345, 347
Bombay, 23
Bond, John, 293–4, 298
Bowring, John, 33, 35
Bowring, Philip, 137
Boxer Rebellion (1901), 38
BP, 156–7
Bray, Denis, 77
Bremridge, John, 100, 144, 145–6
Britain: seizure of Hong Kong (1840s), 8, 30–1, 32, 34; and maritime trade, 16; envoys to Qing China, 18–21, 22; rise to global power status, 22–3; military forces in nineteenth-century, 22, 28, 29–32, 33, 35–6; ends East India Company monopoly, 23; growth of City of London, 23; and opium trade, 24–5, 26, 27–8, 35, 36–7, 268; Napier incident (1834), 26–7; 'extraterritoriality' principle, 28, 29; Palmerston's gunboat diplomacy, 29–30; domestic politics of 1840s, 32–3; as 'most favoured nation,' 34; Convention of Beijing (1860), 36; loans to Qing, 37–8; placating of Japan in 1939–41 period, 86; east of Suez withdrawal (1967), 116; Foreign Office's corps of Sinologists, 116, 212, 237; US advises on China, 117–19; cultivating of Zhao and Hu, 161–2; Major

Britain (*cont ...*)
visits Beijing (1991), 199, 202; ends talks
with China (November 1993), 231;
Chinese embassy in Portland Place,
233–5; criticism of National Security Law,
393
Britannia (royal yacht), 265–6, 271
British Aerospace, 103
British Empire, 16, 22, 23, 24, 25, 74, 75,
179, 402
British Nationality Act (1948), 179
British Nationality Act (1981), 103, 126,
134, 179, 180–1
Brown, George, 57
Browne, Jeremy, 345
Brundtland, Gro Harlem, 331
Buccleuch and Queensberry, Duke of, 161
Buddhism, 4, 12, 280
bureaucracy and administration, Chinese:
officials chosen through rigorous
examinations, 13, 16, 33, 78; Qing
philosopher-officials, 18; corruption in
Qing era, 23; false reports from distant
provinces, 25–6; and reform in
Communist Party, 62–3; Communist
committees, 65; resilience built in layers,
65; corps of officials dealing with Hong
Kong, 76, 106; policy-making on post-
1997 future, 87–9, 91–2, 94, 95–6; script
on post-1997 future, 98, 106–10;
Communist style of diplomacy, 116,
117–19; Communist governing structure,
148–9; Communist *nomenklatura*, 149;
factions and competing agencies, 149;
unchanging mind of Chinese scholar-
official, 154; handover as end of national
humiliation, 255–6, 268–9; thoroughness
of Chinese machine, 340; and National
Security Law (2020), 395
Burma, 375
Bush, George, 169, 187–8, 190
Bush, George W., 306–7
Business and Professional Alliance, 381

Cai Chimeng, 159–60
Calcutta, 23, 25
Callaghan, James, 89, 95, 161, 242
calligraphy, 5
Cambodia, 375, 379; Khmer Rouge, 102,
238–9
Campbell, Duncan, 139
Canada, 179, 393
Cantonese language, 2, 5, 156, 313–15
capital punishment, 82
Carrian Group, 145
Carrington, Lord, 94, 95, 101

Cathay Pacific Airways, 144
Ceauşescu, Nicolae, 192–3
Chai-yan, 367
Chan, Anson, 230, 248, 251, 252, 269–70,
271, 274–6, 392; and politicisation of civil
service, 324–5; retirement of, 325; wins
Hong Kong island by-election (2006), 334
Chan, Norman, 285–6
Chan Kin-man, 356, 366, 371, 372
Chan Tong-kai, 380
Chan Wing-hai, Andrew, 343–4
Chang Chi (poet), 12
Changsha, 206
Charles, Prince, 266, 267, 269, 271
Chen, Johnny, 328
Chen Wenqing, 391
Chen Xi, 353
Chen Yun, 48, 152, 154, 157–8, 207, 208
Chen Zuo'er, 248–50, 253
Cheng, Ekin, 309
Cheng, Joseph, 343
Cheng, Leonard, 365
Chengde (Jehol), 19–20
Chengdu, city of, 347
Chengming (Hong Kong magazine), 208
Cheung Chau island, 221
Cheung Jiping, 374
Cheung Kin-chung, Matthew, 380
Cheung Kong (Holdings), 3
Cheung Tze-keung ('Big Spender'), 311–12
Chiang Ching-kuo, 86
Chiang Kai-shek, 79, 85, 272, 274, 309, 311
Chin Wan-kan, 313, 314, 315
China (1912–49), 38–9; civil war, 5–6,
38–9, 54–5, 178; Japan's invasion of
(1930s), 6, 39 *see also* Kuomintang
China, Imperial: abdication of last emperor
(1912), 5; Qing dynasty, 5, 8, 9, 17–23,
24–34, 309; exposure to capitalism and
liberty, 9; Tang dynasty, 11–14, 15, 24;
trade in Tang dynasty, 11, 12, 13–14, 15;
traders from West in late antiquity, 11;
eunuchs in Tang politics, 12; currency
and coinage, 13–14, 23, 25, 26; state as
active in ninth-century economy, 13–14;
social class in, 13, 17; early travellers' tales
about, 14; exalted/aloof attitude of rulers,
14, 18, 19; Han dynasty, 14; Han dynasty
trading ships, 14; overland trade with
Venice, 15; Venetian trade, 15; late Ming
period, 16–17; military forces, 16, 17, 23,
26–7, 29–32, 35–6, 37; Treaty of
Nerchinsk with Russia (1689), 17–18;
Ming dynasty collapses (1644), 17; Ming
scholar-priests, 17; British trade envoys to
Qing, 18–21, 22; foreign merchants in

late-eighteenth-century, 18; diplomatic encounters with the West, 19–21; Jiaqing's retreat into empty absolutism, 21; Qing balance of trade, 22–3, 24–5; rebellions and disorder in Qing era, 23, 25; import of opium banned (1729), 24; Napier incident (1834), 26–7; punitive indemnities on Qing, 30, 34, 37–8; first Opium War as beginning of the end, 32; Han Chinese subjects, 32; extraterritorial powers granted by, 34–6; Britain as 'most favoured nation,' 34; Taiping rebellion (1850s), 35; Qing dynasty sinks into decay, 36–8; equal basis diplomacy forced on, 36; defeated by Japan over Korea (1895), 37–8; Boxer Rebellion (1901), 38; fall of Qing (1912), 38; as bilingual state, 315

China Can Say No (Song, Zhang, Qiao), 298–9

China Investment Fund, 234

China Quarterly (academic journal), 176

Chinese Communist Party: crusade against the 'Four Olds,' 5; Maoist Red Guards, 5, 40, 51, 83, 236, 275, 319; victory in civil war (1949), 6, 39; condition of at death of Mao, 40, 42–3; elite transition after Mao, 40, 42–3, 56, 72; Politburo standing committee, 40, 48, 62, 166, 355; breaking up of Mao's communes, 43, 67, 148, 150, 153; socialism with Chinese characteristics, 44–8, 164, 207, 209–10, 352–3; 'rectification campaigns' (purges), 49; Yan'an pantheon, 49; May 30th Movement (1925), 54; in 1927 Shanghai, 55; sets up arms industry, 55; Central Commission for Discipline Inspection, 62; 'democratic centralism' principle, 62; United Front Work Department, 86, 218, 246, 266, 373; alliance with Hong Kong tycoons, 120–1, 193, 194; Xu's role in Hong Kong, 120–1, 169, 193–5; and system of governance, 148–9; opposition to Deng's reforms from, 152, 153–5, 157–8; as underground in Colonial Hong Kong, 193–6, 246, 266, 351; battle over policy (1992), 205–10; Lu Ping-Zhou Nan contrast, 246–7; Simon Leys on, 309–10; Laszlo Ladanyi's history of, 310; 'princelings' (children of founding fathers), 345, 348; long calm (1989–2012), 346; Xi's new order, 352–5

Chinese People's Political Consultative Conference, 113

Chinese University of Hong Kong, 83, 325, 329, 356, 360, 385, 388

Choi, Jim, 308

Choi, Sophie, 374

Chongqing, 345–6

Chongzhen (last Ming emperor), 17

Chow, Agnes, 350, 396–7

Chow, Alex, 360, 365, 370

Chow Chung-yan, 387

Chow Tsz-lok, 387

Chow Yun-fat, 309

Christianity, 120, 261, 390, 396; and democracy movement in Hong Kong, 4, 339–40, 356; missionaries, 34, 36; St John's Anglican cathedral, 80; and Joshua Wong phenomenon, 349–50, 353

Chu Yiu-ming, 339, 356, 371

Chuanbi, Convention of (1841), 30–1

Chung, Anthony, 310–11

Chung, Eason, 365

Chung, Robert, 372–3

Chung, Sir S.Y., 125, 127–8, 161

Citroën, 157

civet cats, 329–30, 331

Civic Party, 367, 397

Clinton, Bill, 248, 296, 299, 302–3, 305, 306, 376

CloudFlare (online security firm), 358

Coates, Austin, 77, 79, 81–2

Coca-Cola, 56, 156

Cohen, Jerome, 375

Coleridge, Samuel Taylor, 27

Coles, John, 104, 234

colour revolutions, 368

Committee to Protect Journalists, 332

Commonwealth Immigration Act (1962), 179

complexity theory, 376

Confucius, 4, 17, 83, 164, 401; 'rectify the names' comment, 68, 401

Cook, Robin, 255, 265

copper mines, Yunnan province, 26

coronavirus pandemic, 389–90, 391, 397

Cradock, Percy: as ambassador in Beijing, 89–91, 94, 99, 103–4, 109, 111, 112, 113, 114, 115, 123–4, 237; at Deng's meeting with MacLehose (May 1979), 89, 90, 91, 176; as ultra-realist, 99, 126, 235, 403; at Downing Street meeting (March 1983), 114, 115; experience of Cultural Revolution, 116, 236; disputes with Youde, 123–4, 132; as Thatcher's foreign policy adviser, 124, 125, 127, 128, 130, 131–2, 161, 184–7, 235; and Joint Liaison Group issue, 131–2; and endgame of negotiations, 133–4; and formal signing of agreement (19 December 1984), 135; and 'through train' proposal, 184–7; and

Cradock, Percy (*cont ...*)
  Hurd-Qian secret letters (1990), 186;
  Chris Patten's view of, 189, 214; mission
  over new airport, 198–9; and Major's visit
  to Beijing, 199, 202; chairs Joint
  Intelligence Committee, 214, 233, 243;
  Martin Lee on, 221; retires to
  Twickenham, 226; at Chinese embassy in
  Portland Place, 233–5; and Ambassador
  Ma's telegram, 234–5; influence and
  legacy of, 235, 237, 403; background of,
  236–7; intellectual background of, 237–8;
  and China's backing of Khmer Rouge,
  238–9; accurate forecast of the future
  (1992), 239–41, 403; opposes Patten's
  proposals, 239–41; becomes sharp critic
  of Patten, 241–2; and Lee Kuan Yew,
  242–3; views on Thatcher, 242; cruel last
  years of, 243–4; obituaries of, 244; and
  Portugal, 319
Craigie, Robert, 86
crime and disorder: in Tang dynasty
  China, 12; gangsters and opium trade, 24,
  32; and impact of Deng's reforms, 153–4;
  Triad activity in Hong Kong, 174, 257,
  308, 309, 310–12, 313; as low in Hong
  Kong at handover, 261; in late-Colonial
  Hong Kong, 308–9, 361; cross-border
  criminal enterprises, 310–11; mystique of
  organised crime in Hong Kong, 310–11;
  prostitution in Hong Kong, 313
Crowe, Eyre, 238
Cuba, 393
Culshaw, Robert, 162
Cultural Revolution, 6, 40, 44, 50–1, 83, 87,
  152, 164, 206, 237, 275; Xi Jinping
  banished during, 50, 353; PLA during, 51,
  75, 263–4; Cradock's experience of, 116,
  236
Cushing, Caleb, 34
cyberwarfare, 358, 366–7

Da Gama, Vasco, 15–16
Dalai Lama, 50
Dalian, port of, 345
Daoguang (Qing emperor), 25–7, 30, 32,
  270
Davies, Hugh, 252–3, 255
democracy movement: and Christianity, 4,
  339, 356; and colonial laws on human
  rights, 82; and 'election' sentence in 1984
  agreement, 130; model of forged after
  Tiananmen Square massacre, 173–4; and
  David Wilson's education reforms, 178;
  founding fathers of, 193; Triad attacks on,
  310, 366, 383; opposes Tsang's reforms

(2005), 339–40; 'moderate'–'radical' split,
  341; and accession of Xi (2012), 348;
  ultimate failure of, 401–2 *see also* protests
  and demonstrations (2019); umbrella
  revolution (2014)
Democratic Party, 245, 252, 341, 372, 385
Demosistō (political party), 370, 381, 396
Deng Pufang, 40, 275
Deng Xiaoping, 8; evokes 1898 Chinese
  shame, 38, 107; visits Guangdong
  province (1977), 40, 41, 42; accepts need
  for change, 42, 43; looks to learn from
  Hong Kong/Macau, 44–8, 53; socialism
  with Chinese characteristics, 44–8, 164,
  207, 209–10, 352–3; Third Plenum
  (December 1978), 58–9, 60–3, 164; policy
  on Hong Kong, 58, 88, 91–5, 98, 99,
  106–11, 402, 403; at youth football match
  (30 July 1977), 59–60; climbs Huang Shan
  mountain (1979), 63; in *Early Spring*, 69;
  chooses Liao for Hong Kong, 84, 87–8;
  meeting with MacLehose (May 1979),
  89–93, 403; 'one country, two systems'
  theory, 91, 95–6, 97, 104–5, 108, 113, 115,
  122, 133, 182, 270, 276; agrees policy plan
  for Hong Kong (1982), 96, 97; Thatcher
  meets in Beijing (September 1982),
  103–4, 106–10, 111, 141, 229, 264; and
  Thatcher's warnings of economic disaster,
  105, 106, 107–8, 110–11, 125; statement
  to Thatcher on sovereignty, 107; appoints
  negotiating team, 119–21; suspicion of
  UK during negotiations, 122–3, 128–9,
  141; call with Gaston Thorn, 123;
  proposes Joint Liaison Group, 125–6, 130,
  131–3; meets Chung and the 'unofficials,'
  127–8; and formal signing of agreement
  (19 December 1984), 134–5; anxieties
  over reform, 152; party opposition to
  reforms of, 152, 153–5, 157–8; reforms
  lauded in *River Elegy*, 163–5; and
  Tiananmen Square protests, 168, 170,
  171; on usefulness of Hong Kong, 169;
  and the new airport, 178, 190, 197–200,
  212; meeting with Scowcroft, 188;
  'southern tour' (1992), 205–9, 210; desire
  for *Xiaokang* (small prosperity), 207, 292;
  and Marxist theory, 209, 210–11; and
  traditional reverence for age, 211; and
  handling of Patten, 224, 230; death of
  (February 1997), 262; disdain for
  personality cults, 262, 378; on the Triads,
  310; statue of in Shenzhen, 355; tells party
  to hide strength/bide its time, 404
Dent, Lancelot, 27–8
Dickie, John, 127

digital technology: Clinton links to political liberalisation, 305, 306; and Cantonese language, 314; Chinese cyberwarfare, 358, 366–7; PopVote referendum system, 358; growth of digital economy, 376, 377; doxing tactics against police, 385

Dikotter, Frank, 50

Dinham, Martin, 218

Disraeli, Benjamin, 238

Donald, Alan, 114, 185, 215

Dong Guanping, 375

Du Yuesheng, 311

Duan Yun, 44, 45–7, 48, 53

Dunn, Lydia, 112, 180, 213

Dutton, Brian, 253–4

Eanes, Ramalho, 319

East India Company, 16, 18, 21, 23, 24, 25

Economic Daily, 169

economy, Chinese (communist era): Deng's opening up of, 6, 8, 44–8, 60–9, 152, 154–60, 200–2, 291–6, 321–2; 'supply chain' management, 6, 157, 276–7, 292, 376; vast expansion in recent decades, 9, 150, 201, 210, 291–6; at death of Mao, 40–1; Deng's domestic reforms, 43, 45–8, 62–9, 149–55; Zhao's reforms in 1970s/80s, 43, 165–6; Hong Kong and Macau economic and trade investigation team, 44–7, 53; Duan's report (1978), 46–7, 48; move to use of foreign capital, 46; foreign exchange operations, 56; 1978 as key year for globalisation, 62; foreign direct investment into, 65, 152, 156–8, 159–60, 200–2, 209, 261, 276, 291–3, 295; joint ventures with foreign firms, 66, 156–7, 158, 200–1, 291–3, 295; 'out-processing' transformation, 66, 154, 291–3; Deng's use of language, 67, 68; and free markets of 1980s, 147; impact of Deng's reforms, 150–8, 160, 200–2, 291–5; huge surge in production in 1980s, 150, 210; multinationals arrive in, 156–7; Hong Kong firms move production to China, 157, 160, 200–1, 291–3; trade deficits in 1980s, 157, 165; export development model, 158–60, 201–2, 291–2, 293–4, 337–8; questioning of reforms inside China, 160–1; developing country status, 160, 210, 278, 297, 300; reformers run into trouble (1989), 165–6; rising inflation in late 1980s, 165, 210; Deng prevents reversal of reforms, 205–10; Deng's roadmap for (1992), 210; and world trading system, 276–7, 290, 293–4, 296–302, 303–7, 322, 323, 330, 337, 376; research and development, 293; transformation from primary to advanced manufacturing, 293; internal migration to coastal zones, 294; floating exchange rate system (1994), 297–8; trade deficits in early 1990s, 297; reform package (1994), 300; early-twenty-first-century expansion, 307; Closer Economic Partnership Arrangement (CEPA, 2003), 334–5; fixed exchange rate, 337–8; foreign currency reserves (2007), 337–8; response to 2008 financial crisis, 337, 338–9; trade surplus with USA, 337; hold over US national debt, 338; Trump's trade war, 377–8; slow down of in 2015 period, 377; domestic supply chains, 394; giant internal market, 394; Xi's semi-autarchic vision, 394 *see also* Special Economic Zones

economy, Chinese (imperial era): in Tang dynasty, 11, 12, 13, 15; state controls in ninth-century, 13–14; as biggest in world during Tang dynasty, 15; growth of trade in Qing era, 23; deficits from 1820s, 24–5; silver inflation from 1820s, 25–6; foreign loans to cover indemnity, 37–8; Qing finance collapse (1890s), 37–8

economy, global: sixteenth-century silver crisis, 16–17; growth of London as centre of, 23, 26; silver shortage in early nineteenth-century, 26; loans to Qing, 37–8; Nixon cuts dollar-gold link (1971), 56; linking of economic with political liberalism, 61–2, 66, 210–11, 304–6, 404; recession of early 1980s, 140–7; falling inequality between countries, 160; stock market crash (October 1987), 165; 'triumph' of liberalism in early 1990s, 200; Asian financial crisis (1997–8), 278, 279–88, 299; Fukuyama's 'end of history', 296; Chinese foreign currency reserves (2007), 337–8; Chinese fiscal response to 2008 crisis, 338–9; problems with long supply chains, 377; technology reduces competition, 377

economy, Hong Kong: Victorian banks/ trading houses, 2, 3, 23, 26; 'supply chain' management, 6, 157, 276–7, 292, 376; Deng looks to learn from, 44–8, 53; reliance on foreign capital, 46; and Special Economic Zones, 47–8, 62, 65, 66, 200–1, 291–4, 295, 321–2; city's casino capitalism, 80–1, 136, 144–5, 311–12, 342; land auctions/property leases, 80–1, 92–3, 94, 136; land owned

economy, Hong Kong (cont ...)
  by the Crown, 80–1; colonial era
  business world, 83–4; uncertainty over
  post-1997 future, 93, 94–5, 106; Jardine
  Matheson moves to Bermuda, 125;
  'roaring eighties' boom in, 136–8;
  recession of early 1980s, 140–7; 'Black
  Saturday' (24 September 1983), 141–2;
  currency crisis (1982–3), 141–7; lack of
  central bank, 142; Greenwood's currency
  scheme, 143–4, 145–6; history of fixed
  exchange rates, 143; currency pegged to
  US dollar, 145–7, 201, 282, 283–6, 288;
  foreign direct investment into China,
  156, 200–2, 261, 276, 291–3, 295; firms
  move production to China, 157, 160,
  291–3; stock market crash (June 1989),
  173, 174; HSBC's plan to leave, 190–1;
  infrastructure bonds, 191; Chinese
  Chamber of Commerce, 218, 273;
  financial progress in 1990s, 229; Hong
  Kong Monetary Authority (HKMA), 229,
  248, 282–5, 337, 393; and world trading
  system, 247–8, 307; mandatory provident
  fund, 247; named world's freest economy
  (1995), 247; at handover, 261; Asian
  financial crisis (1997–8), 278, 279–88,
  299; currency board, 283–4; monetary
  base, 284*; Asian reserve currency idea,
  288; Hong Kong Exchanges and Clearing
  Limited, 288; delegation at WTO talks in
  Geneva, 300–2; response to 2008
  financial crisis, 337, 339; inertia under
  Tsang, 342–3; American Chamber of
  Commerce, 381; measures to liberalise
  foreign investment (2020), 393 see also
  Hongkong and Shanghai Banking
  Corporation (HSBC)
Eden, Anthony, 405
education, 83, 84, 160, 272–3, 392;
  universities in, 83, 177–8, 325, 359–60,
  365, 396; David Wilson's reforms, 177–8,
  403; Leung's reform proposals, 349,
  351–2, 356
Egan, Kevin, 311
Elgin, Lord, 33, 36
Elliott, Charles, 28–9, 30–1
Elliott, George, 29
Emmett, Chris, 270
Engels, Friedrich, 163
European Union, 296
Evans, Richard, 124, 126, 127, 128, 133,
  134, 161
Extinction Rebellion, 382–3
'extraterritoriality' principle, 28, 29, 34–5,
  54

Falklands War (1982), 97–8, 110
Falun Gong (spiritual group), 322
Fan, Rita, 311
Fang, Harry, 275
Fang Bao, 52
Fang Sheng, 207
Fang Zhenwu, 274
Far Eastern Economic Review, 137
farming economy: in Guangzhou
  (Canton), 11; at death of Mao, 40; Mao's
  people's communes, 43, 67, 150, 153;
  Zhao's reforms in 1970s/80s, 43; and Four
  Modernisations, 46; Deng's reforms, 62,
  67, 150–1, 206; impact of Deng's reforms,
  150–1, 153; huge surge in production in
  1980s, 150; impact of Olympics on, 336
Fatchett, Derek, 255
Federal Reserve Bank of New York, 287
Federation of Students, 365, 370
Fenby, Jonathan, 322–3
feng shui, 3
Fiat, 157
film industry, Hong Kong, 308–9, 317
financial crisis, global (2008), 337, 338–9,
  376–7
FireChat (app), 367
flu pandemic (1918), 329
Fok, Henry, 251, 252, 273, 274
Fok, Timothy, 252
Fokkema, Douwe, 236
Ford, David, 77, 78, 174, 189, 190
Foshan, 296, 326
Foster, Norman, 3
France, 16, 22, 34, 36, 37
French Revolution, 20
Friedman, Milton, 166
Fu Guohao, 384
Fudan University, Shanghai, 354
Fujian province, 64
Fukuyama, Francis, 296
Fung, Victor, 112, 292, 293
Fung, William, 292, 293
Fung Pak-liu, 291–2

Gang of Four, 40, 56, 61, 65, 72
Garnaut, John, 355
Garrett, Dan, 369
Gates, Robert, 233
General Agreement on Tariffs and Trade
  (GATT), 277, 296–7, 298, 300–2
General Motors, 156
George III, King of England, 17, 18–21
Germany, 37–8
Gilmore, David, 213
Gladstone, William, 29
Glenarthur, Lord, 181

Global Times, 384, 395
globalisation, 200–2, 204, 211, 248, 276–7, 288–9, 291–2, 307, 376–7; 1978 as key year for, 62; begins in coastal China, 160, 200
Goodhart, Charles, 145
Gorbachev, Mikhail, 168, 192
Graham, Peter, 99–100
Grantham, Alexander, 41, 74, 79, 175, 217, 220
Gray, John, 146–7
Greenwood, John, 142–3, 145
Gresham's law, 26
Gu Kailai, 346–7
Gu Mu, 64, 69, 155
Gu Yongliang, 298
Guang Zhigang, 317–18
Guangdong province: Xi Zhongxun as party secretary, 8, 48–9, 50, 51–4, 63–4, 65–7; Deng visits (1977), 40, 41, 42; border with Hong Kong, 41–2, 48–9, 51–3; access to Hong Kong for natives of, 41; Special Economic Zone status, 47–8, 63–4, 65–7, 69, 160, 200–1, 291–4, 296; impact of Deng's reforms, 150–1, 153–4, 200–1, 291–2, 293; Zhao's plans for, 166; Hong Kongers escaping from China (June 1989), 175–6, 177; investment from Hong Kong, 200–1, 261, 276, 291–3, 295; electronics industry, 201, 293; growth takes off in (late 1980s), 201, 210; and Deng's 'southern tour,' 206–8, 210; bird flu outbreak in, 279; SARS outbreak in (2003), 326–8, 329–30, 331
Guangxi province, 35
Guangzhou (Canton), 66–7, 156, 292; in Tang dynasty, 11–14, 15; Commissioner for Commercial Argosies, 13; the Cohong (guild), 18, 23, 34; US traders in Qing period, 21–2; in Qing dynasty, 22–3, 24, 27–9, 30, 34, 35; and opium trade, 24, 26, 27–9; Lin expels British from, 28–9; British bombardments of, 30, 35–6; fall of in second opium war, 35–6; Ye Mingchen as governor, 35–6; during Cultural Revolution, 50–1; Duan Yun in (1978), 53; PLA's occupation of, 74; Liao Zhongkai assassinated in, 85; train link to Kowloon, 93; population of, 149; impact of Deng's reforms, 150–1; and Cantonese language, 314; SARS outbreak in (2003), 326–8, 330; live animal market, 330, 331–2
Gui Minhai, 373–5
Gulf War (1991), 197, 200, 296
Guo Zhongxiao, 375
Guterres, Antonio, 321

Hague, William, 347
Hainan island, 166
Hakluyt (strategic advisory firm), 347–8
Hall, Julie, 331
Hammond, Peter, 147
Han Kehua, 237
Han Suyin, 74
Hang Lung Bank, 144
Hang Seng Bank, 314
Harbinson, Stuart, 297, 301–2, 307
He Xiangning, 84–5
He Zhenliang, 336
Heath, Edward, 70–2, 74, 97, 105, 122, 221, 265
Heilongjiang province, 153
Henan province, 149
Heritage Foundation (conservative think tank), 247
Heseltine, Michael, 114, 115, 249, 250
Heshen (Qianlong's favourite), 20, 21, 223
Heywood, Neil, 345, 346–8
Hinduism, 4, 261
Ho, Albert, 341, 351, 364, 369, 392
Ho, Denise, 364
Ho, Junius, 383, 391
Ho, Pansy, 384
Ho, Stanley, 7, 320–1
Ho Hau Wah, Edmund, 321
Holdridge, John, 117
homosexuality, 83
Hong Kong: distinctive geography of, 1, 2–3, 136; harbour and port, 2, 196–7; Kai Tak airport, 3, 87, 197; new international airport, 3, 137–8, 177, 178, 190, 197–200, 212, 322; tolerance and plurality in heritage of, 4–5; St John's Anglican cathedral, 4, 80; freedom but not democracy contradiction, 5, 8, 401–2, 404; British seizure of (1840s), 8, 30–1, 32, 34; Mass Transit Railway, 57, 138; Government House, 58, 79, 213; Communist Party newspapers, 74, 88, 133, 175, 203, 205, 261, 368, 373, 396–7; universities in, 83, 177–8, 325, 359–60, 365, 396; Mid-Levels redeveloped (1980s), 138; Prince of Wales Building, 230, 254, 255, 263; underground railway system, 246; naval base at Stonecutter's Island, 254; free media in, 260–1, 344–5, 347, 348; culture at end of twentieth century, 308–9, 317–18; and politics of language, 314–15; independence as minority cause, 366, 384; sea bridge and tunnel open (2018), 394; street names, 401, 405

Hong Kong, COLONIAL ERA:
architecture, 2–3, 136; Victorian banks/
trading houses, 2, 3, 23, 26; cosmopolitan
heritage, 4–5; foreign population, 4, 260;
and Chinese culture, 5, 39; lack of
democracy in, 5, 6, 57–8, 80, 83, 111–12,
114, 139, 214, 402; as place of refuge, 5, 6,
41, 49, 52–3, 73–4, 79, 141, 178, 200, 271,
272, 292; western culture in, 5, 308–9,
317–18; anti-British riots (1967), 6, 75,
88, 263; fall of to Japan (1941), 6, 39, 263;
and Tiananmen Square protests, 6, 168–9,
196; 'in perpetuity' phrase in Treaty of
Nanjing, 34, 99, 102, 107; expansion in
first half of twentieth century, 38, 39;
Second Convention of Beijing (1898), 38;
Britain reclaims after Second World War,
39; Cantonese culture of, 39; free
movement into abandoned (1950), 41;
Duan's group visits (1978), 45; Xinhua
news agency, 45, 74–5; Li Qiang-
MacLehose meeting (1978), 54, 58, 89;
MacLehose's reforms, 57, 81; Mao/Zhou
policy on, 70, 72, 74–6; prospers after
Second World War, 76–8; British
administration of, 78–84; constitution of,
79–80; Executive Council, 79–80, 111–13,
114, 123, 125, 126, 131, 180, 219, 228,
251, 271–2; governor's authority, 79–80;
flag of, 79; Legislative Council, 80,
111–13, 126, 139–40, 144, 145, 184–5,
189–90, 191, 217–19, 220, 225, 229, 231,
245–6; local government, 81; Bill of
Rights (1990), 82–3, 189, 191, 203, 361,
403; capital punishment abolished (1993),
82; Communist activity in 1939–41
period, 86; transport connections to
mainland, 89, 93, 321–2; UMELCO,
111–13; serious riots (January 1984),
124–5; Chinese-language newspapers,
136–7, 160, 172, 245, 261, 314; as
entrepot of knowledge/information
(1980s), 136–7; international business
media in, 137; public opinion in 1980s,
138–9; British surveillance of pressure
groups, 139–40; English-language
newspapers, 142, 143, 169, 261; British
listening station at Chum Hom Kok,
170–1; and Tiananmen Square massacre,
172–6, 177, 178, 188–9, 194; democratic
politicians in, 172, 182, 189, 202, 219,
220, 221, 245–6; Operation Yellow Bird,
176; surveillance of underground
communists, 179–80; British National
(Overseas) citizen status, 179, 399, 400;
British nationality scheme, 181–2, 189,

191; elections in 1990s, 191, 217–19;
electoral turnout in 1990s, 191, 245;
modern public transportation system,
191; underground Communist Party in,
193–6, 246, 266, 351; and split in Chinese
Communist Party, 193, 194–6; Wilson's
plan to shift industry to west of colony,
199; firms move production to China,
200–1; Vietnamese boat people, 214;
Patten's democratic reform proposals,
217, 218–20, 221–7, 228–9, 403–4;
reforms shelved (1952), 220–1, 402;
'Young Plan' (1946–7), 220, 402; deaths
on building site at North Point (1993),
229; fatal stampede in Lan Kwai Fong
district (1993), 229; civil service localised
under Patten, 230, 248, 275; Lu's shadow
government, 231; Legislative Council
elections (1995), 245–6; land owned by
the Crown, 254; quiet exodus of security
service personnel, 256–7; Chinese
invasion averted (1967), 263–4; Triads
exiled to, 309; elite intermingling with
Triads, 311–12; renaissance of Cantonese
language in, 314; as source of 'moral
contamination,' 316–17; horse races run
by Jockey Club, 318
Hong Kong Express News, 169
Hong Kong flu (1968), 329
Hong Kong Indigenous, 384
Hong Kong Observers (pressure group),
138–9
Hong Kong Polytechnic, 83
Hong Kong, POST-1997 FUTURE:
negotiations over post-1997 future, 60,
89–94, 402–3; Mao's meeting with Heath
(1974), 72; Mao/Zhou strategy on, 72, 74;
Zhou's 'red lines,' 74, 76; UN resolution
on Chinese sovereignty, 75–6; consistency
of Chinese position, 76, 97, 104–5; Liao
Chengzhi's role in diplomacy, 84, 87–8,
93, 95–6, 113, 115, 256, 402; Chinese
policy-making, 87–9, 91–2, 94, 95–6; role
of Xinhua (NCNA), 88–9; Deng's meeting
with MacLehose (May 1979), 89–93, 176,
403; continued British administration
idea, 91–2, 95; Chinese assurances to UK,
91, 93, 95; Deng's 'one country, two
systems' theory, 91, 95–6, 97, 104–5, 108,
113, 122, 133, 182, 270, 276; economic
uncertainty over leases, 92, 93, 94;
investment boom after 1979 talks, 93;
Hua meets Thatcher (November 1979),
94–5; Thatcher and negotiations, 94–5,
98–101, 102–11, 402–3; Taiwan policy
borrowed from, 95–6; democracy as not

on the table, 95, 96, 100, 114, 185–7; Deng agrees policy plan for (1982), 96, 97; Liao's twelve articles, 96, 122; Britain informed of Chinese policy decision, 97–8, 104–9; Chinese willingness to use force, 98–9, 108–9, 264; views of colonial elite, 99–100, 112–13; and Cold War politics of 1980s, 99, 101–2, 124, 238–9; international law arguments, 99, 105, 107–8; Thatcher-Deng meet in Beijing (September 1982), 103–4, 106–10, 111, 141, 229, 264; Thatcher's domestic economic concerns, 103; Thatcher's immigration policy, 103, 134, 179, 180–2, 240, 399, 400, 403; Thatcher's warnings of economic disaster, 105, 106, 107–8, 110–11, 125; Chinese sovereignty as 'pre-condition' for talks, 106–9, 110, 113, 115; disagreements on the British side, 113–14; Chinese delay start of talks, 113; crucial Downing Street meeting (March 1983), 114–15; letter to Zhao (March 1983), 115; Thatcher's crucial concession (March 1983), 115; Thatcher's letter to Zhao (March 1983), 115; Deng's negotiating team, 119–21; tactics to win over local opinion, 119–21; death of Liao Chengzhi, 119, 402; China's suspicion of UK during negotiations, 122–3, 128–9, 141; financial volatility during negotiations, 122–3, 125, 140–7; 'September storm' in negotiations, 122–3, 141; Sino-British negotiations begin (12 July 1983), 122–3; Deng's deadline for agreement, 122, 128; second UK concession, 123–4; negotiations resume (January 1984), 124–5; serious riots (January 1984), 124–5; Joint Liaison Group, 125–6, 130, 131–2, 252–3; Deng's Basic Law, 126, 128, 132, 182–4, 187, 189, 223, 231, 240, 248–9, 324, 333, 391; Deng's decision to deploy PLA, 126; Wilson leads British negotiating team, 128–31, 176, 403; Chinese and English texts of agreement, 129–30; Britain presses for elections, 130; Thatcher allows Howe to settle with Deng, 132–3; agreement reached (July 1984), 132–4; endgame of negotiations, 133–4; formal signing of agreement (19 December 1984), 134–5; Joint Declaration (1984), 134–5, 172, 176, 177, 181, 186, 223, 237, 240–1, 243, 393, 399–400, 403; secret Anglo-Chinese talks (1989–90), 184–7; 'through train' proposal, 184–7, 230; Hurd-Qian secret letters (1990), 186, 226,

227; Deng's 'start again' instruction, 224, 230, 240; China's Preparatory Committee, 230, 251–2; Provisional Legislative Council, 230, 251–2; Chinese plans for political transformation, 247; and justice system, 248–50; series of late-in-the-day agreements, 250–1; Selection Committee, 251, 252; and WTO accession, 300–1

Hong Kong, SPECIAL ADMINISTRATIVE REGION: Liaison Office, 2–3, 325, 383–4, 390, 391, 395; unique gains in early years, 6–7; National Security Law (June 2020), 7, 391–3, 394–8; 'fifty years' commitment, 126, 130, 182, 183, 397–8, 401; political system outlined in the Basic Law, 183–4, 223; chief executive role, 184, 245–6, 251, 270–2, 324–5, 339, 340–1, 350–1, 380, 395; Election Committee, 184, 217, 218, 219; functional constituencies model, 187, 217–18, 219, 245; passport holders given visa-free access to UK, 250; Tung and Chan head administration (1997), 275–6; avian influenza outbreak, 278–9; Asian financial crisis (1997–8), 278, 279–88, 299; Legislative Council, 311, 329, 339, 340, 341, 370, 380, 381, 382, 383, 385; identity politics under, 315; political lull in post-1997 period, 322–4; settlement rights of children born on the mainland, 323–4; governance moves in direction of Communists, 324–5; politicisation of civil service, 324–5; Principal Officials Accountability System, 324–5; Tung-Anson tensions, 324–5; Tung's new government (2002), 325–6; SARS outbreak in (2003), 328–30, 334; Tung's law against subversion, 332–4, 335; Closer Economic Partnership Arrangement (CEPA, 2003), 334–5; Executive Council, 334; public protests against Tung (July 2003), 334; Tsang replaces Tung (2005), 335; Tsang's democratic reform attempts, 339–40; Tsang revives electoral reform proposals, 340–1; universal suffrage for 2017/2020 elections announced (2007), 340; lack of prosperity becomes political, 342–3; 'sandwich class,' 349, 357; C.Y. Leung administration, 350–2, 356–9, 363, 367–8, 370; and Xi's new order, 355, 356, 391–400; 'consultation' on democracy (2013–4), 356–7, 359, 370; centre-stage in US-China cold war, 379; society fractures during 2019 unrest, 385–8; victory for democrats in council elections

(November 2019), 389, 390; coronavirus pandemic, 390, 391; Committee for Safeguarding National Security, 395 *see also* democracy movement; protests and demonstrations (2019); umbrella revolution (2014)

Hong Kong Standard, 169, 261

Hong Kong, TRANSFER OF POWER (30 June/1 July 1997): farewell/handover ceremonies, 37, 265–71; last day (30 June 1997), 37, 262–3, 264–9; British withdrawal preparations, 229–30; orchestrated transfer of power, 251–4, 262–3, 265–71; pro-democracy protesters, 251; entry of PLA as point of dispute, 252, 254–5; military handover, 254–5, 262–3; handover of land, 254; as end of national humiliation, 255–6; those needing to escape the Communists, 256–7, 258–9; Vickers' revelations of security breaches, 257–8; British destruction of sensitive information, 257; state of the city at handover, 259–61; fear of last-minute crisis, 264–5

Hong Kong University (HKU), 83, 365

Hong Kong University of Science and Technology, 83, 178, 357, 387

Hong Xiuquan, 35

Hongkong and Shanghai Banking Corporation (HSBC), 3, 37, 38, 84, 100, 109, 125, 133, 228, 229, 246; as de facto central banker, 140, 142, 146–7; and currency crisis (1982–3), 142, 143, 145, 146–7; Wardley (merchant bank), 145; and stock market crash (October 1987), 165; takeover of Britain's Midland Bank, 190–1; and Asian financial crisis, 286; and China's opening up, 293–4; trade finance as core business, 294; Chinese pressure on, 393–4

Hongkong Land (property developer), 136

Howe, Geoffrey, 102, 124, 125, 131, 221, 241; meets Deng in Beijing (1984), 125–7; meets Zhou Nan in Beijing, 131–2; final meeting with Deng, 132–3; and endgame of negotiations, 133–4

Hsu Ta-tung, 311

Hu Bangding, 44

Hu Jintao, 209, 330, 335, 338–9, 340, 341, 342, 344, 346, 348, 377; 'scientific development' theory, 353–4

Hu Xijin, 395

Hu Yaobang, 62, 69, 119, 155, 161–2; death of (April 1989), 166–7

Hua Guofeng, 48, 63, 64, 65, 69, 94–5, 116, 148

Huang Hua, 75–6, 319

Huang Jingbo, 53

Huang Qingtao, 327

Huang Xinchu, 326

Huang Yongsheng, 75, 263–4

Huang Zuomei, 74

Huawe, 393

Huawei, 378

Hui, Raphael, 285

Huizhou, 292

human rights, 82–3, 113, 189, 199, 203, 242, 299, 354, 399, 403

Hunan province, 206

The Hunger Games (film series), 363, 383, 391

Huntington, Samuel, 354

Hurd, Douglas, 76–7, 79, 186–7, 198, 202–3, 222–3, 225, 228, 229, 231, 236; secret letters exchanged with Qian (1990), 186, 226, 227

Ibrahim, Anwar, 281–2

Immigration Act (1971), 179

immigration policy, British, 103, 126, 134, 179–82, 240, 399, 400, 403

imperialism, Western: Portuguese at Macau, 8, 16, 17, 18, 22, 24, 29; opening of sea routes to East, 15–16; and sixteenth-century silver crisis, 16–17; British Empire, 16, 22, 23, 24, 25, 74, 75, 179, 402; East India Company, 16, 18, 21, 23, 24, 25; British rise to dominance, 22–3; and opium trade, 23, 24–5, 26, 27–9, 35, 36–7, 268; May 30th Movement (1925), 54; Mao Zedong on, 70

India: British Empire, 16, 22, 23, 24, 25; Mughal rule, 16; and China's opium supply, 24, 25; PRC's war with (1962), 101–2; and nuclear weapons, 102; and the 'Needham Question,' 161; Indian population in Hong Kong, 260; tension with China in Himalayas, 379

Indonesia, 82, 260, 280–1

industry, Chinese: migration from Shanghai to Hong Kong (1949–51), 6, 141, 178, 200, 271, 272, 274, 292, 311; copper mines in Yunnan province, 26; at death of Mao, 40; and Four Modernisations, 46; Mao's Great Leap Forward, 50; Deng's reforms, 67, 151–2; in 1980s Hong Kong, 138–9; huge surge in production in 1980s, 150, 210; impact of Deng's reforms, 151–2, 154–60, 210; advantage in labour-intensive industries, 159; Pearl River Delta as world's largest processing zone, 291–3; labour conditions in Special Economic Zones, 295–6; as unbeatable on price, 296, 297–8; migration from Shanghai to Hong Kong (1949–51)

intellectual property rights, 297, 302, 306, 377

intelligence services, British, 102–3, 117, 231–2, 246, 264–5; Second World War, 57; MI6 (Secret Intelligence Service), 134, 228, 347; listening station at Chum Hom Kok, 170–1; Cradock chairs Joint Intelligence Committee, 214, 233, 243; Thatcher's view of, 243; equipment removed from Hong Kong, 254

International Herald Tribune, 137

International Monetary Fund, 152, 280, 282

International Olympic Committee, 335–6

Ip, Regina, 312, 325–6, 333, 334, 364

Islam, 4, 12, 13, 34, 261

Japan, 8, 15, 36, 199, 260, 338, 377; invasion of China (1930s), 6, 39; Tokugawa clan, 16; defeats Qing China over Korea (1895), 37–8; birth of modern capitalist system, 38; Deng's economic missions to, 43–4; death penalty in, 82; elite Chinese diaspora in, 84–5; late Meiji period, 84; post-war relations with PRC, 86; Shanghai falls to (1937), 86; and Cold War politics of 1980s, 102; rise from from late nineteenth century, 290–1; accession to GATT/WTO, 302

Jardine Matheson, 125, 228; roots as opium merchants, 28, 29, 35, 125

Jesuits, 17–18

Jet Li, 308

Jewish community, 4, 261, 272

Ji Chaozhu, 172–3

Ji Pengfei, 119–20, 182

Jia Juchuan, 53–4

Jiang Enzhu, 229

Jiang Qing, 40, 259

Jiang Yefei, 375

Jiang Zemin, 185, 205, 207, 208, 209, 251, 254, 255, 262, 264, 265, 273–4, 322; at handover ceremony, 266, 268, 269, 270; and Clinton, 299, 302–3; and WTO accession, 299, 302–3, 304, 306; rejects linking of economic with political liberalism, 306; 'Three Represents' theory, 353–4

Jiangsu province, 119–21, 149

Jiaqing (Qing emperor), 21

Jin Zhong, 258

John Swire and Sons, 144

justice system, 2; enshrined xenophobia in Tang dynasty, 14; in Colonial Hong Kong, 77, 81–2, 156, 248, 259–60; in post-1997 Hong Kong, 127; and Deng's reforms, 156; law schools reopen after Mao, 156; court agreement revealed (1991), 248–9; Court of Final Appeal in Hong Kong, 248–50, 323–4, 344; dispute over post-1997 system, 248–50; Triad prosecutions, 311; mainland trials of Triads, 312; Independent Commission against Corruption, 324, 343, 361; Tung's law against subversion, 332–4, 335; and pro-democracy protesters, 363; Bar Association, 381, 397; Law Society, 381; under National Security Act, 395–6, 397

Kaifang (political magazine), 258, 336

Kaifu, Toshiki, 199

Kam Kin-yat, 195

Kangxi (Qing emperor), 17–18

Keswick, Simon, 125

Kim Il-Sung, 97, 111

Kim Un-yong, 336

King, Lord, 161

Kissinger, Henry, 71, 117, 119, 188, 290

Kokand, Khan of, 34

Korea, 15, 37

Korean War, 6, 75, 200, 220–1, 273

Kosovo war (1999), 299, 302–3

Kowloon peninsula, 3, 4–5; Britain awarded (1860), 36; 'in perpetuity' phrase in Convention of Beijing, 36, 99, 102, 107; Li's underground radio station in, 55; Triad activity in, 174, 308, 313; demolition of Walled City, 191; population density, 260; Harbour Plaza Hotel, 266; violence during umbrella revolution, 366; disorder during 2019 insurgency, 386

the kowtow, 19, 21

Kuok, Robert, 322–3

Kuomintang, 5–6, 38–9, 73–4, 258, 272; administration in Nanjing, 39, 315; and China's seat at UN, 75; Liao Chengzhi's connections with, 84, 85; massacre of Communists (1927), 85; rule in Taiwan, 95; financial chaos in last days of rule, 147; and the Triads, 309, 311

Kwok, Philip, 112

Kwok, Walter, 311–12

Ladanyi, Laszlo, 310, 354

Lady Maurine (governor's motor vessel), 213, 216, 221

Lai, Jimmy, 261, 313, 366, 392

Lai, Peter, 139
Lai Tung-kwok, 366
Lam, Carrie, 356, 358, 365, 370; extradition bill (2019), 380–2; becomes chief executive (2017), 380; and 2019 insurgency, 382, 385; in Beijing (October 2019), 385; mismanagement and lack of leadership, 386; warned by Xia Baolong (April 2020), 392; assures UN over National Security Act, 395; postpones 2020 elections, 397; Trump's sanctions on, 398
Lam Long-yin, Ivan, 350, 352
Lam Wing-kee, 374
Lamy, Pascal, 297
language: Chinese in official Hong Kong, 248, 260; dialects in modern Hong Kong, 260; *Putonghua* (Mandarin common tongue), 260, 313, 314–15; street language in Hong Kong, 313–14; Cantonese-Mandarin division as ancient, 314–15; politics of in Communist China, 314–15; Communist campaigns against Cantonese, 314; emergence of written Cantonese, 314; Manchu, 315; Shenzhen as polyglot enclave, 315
Lantau Island, 3, 137–8, 177, 199, 322
Laos, 102, 375, 379
Lardy, Nicholas, 304–5
Latter, Tony, 143
Lau, Emily, 251, 322, 341
Lavrov, Sergei, 393
Law, Nathan, 360, 365, 370, 396–7
Lee, Martin, 7, 172, 182, 193, 219, 221, 245, 249, 250, 271, 339, 364; arrest of (April 2020), 392, 397
Lee Bo, 374
Lee Cheuk-yan, 251, 392
Lee Chi-cheung, 387
Lee Ka-chiu, John, 380
Lee Kuan Yew, 216, 242–3, 290–1
Lee Shui Hung, 329
Lee Teng-hui, 315
Lehman Brothers collapse (2008), 338
Lenin, 157–8, 355, 404
Lennon, John, 364
Leong Che-hung, 329
Lepanto, sea battle of (1571), 15
Leung, Elsie, 325
Leung, Laurence, 257–8
Leung, Yvonne, 365
Leung Chun-ying, 138, 251, 350–2, 356–7, 363, 367–8, 370, 374, 392, 393
Leung Kai-ping, Brian, 383
Leung Tin-kei, Edward, 384
Leys, Simon, 68, 309–10

Li, Arthur, 325
Li, Grace, 349
Li, Simon, 251
Li & Fung, 112, 291–2, 293
Li Bai, 162
Li Chuwen, 120, 273–4
Li Hongzhang, 37, 38
Li Hon-leung, Patrick, 363
Li Hou, 196
Li Jusheng, 89
Li Ka-shing, 3, 7, 191, 266, 274, 311, 385, 393
Li Keqiang, 348, 371
Li Kwan-ha, 361
Li Peng, 166, 188, 189, 190–1, 198, 199, 202, 229, 251, 266
Li Qiang, 8, 54–6, 58, 89, 156
Li Shangyin, 207
Li To-ming, 291–2
Li Tzar-kuoi, Victor, 311
Li Xian, 385
Li Xianian, 64
Li Xiannian, 119, 121
Li Xin, 375
Li Zhao, 166
Li Zhisui, 71, 259
Liao Chengzhi, 8, 84–8, 93, 95–6, 113, 115, 119, 256, 402
Liao Zhongkai, 84, 85
Liaoning province, 345
Liberal Party, 334, 381
Liberation Daily (Shanghai newspaper), 230
Lilley, James, 188
Lin Piao, 65, 264
Lin Zexu, 27–9, 30
Lindsay, John, 212
Lindstedt, Anna, 374–5
Lingnan University, 360, 365
Lintin Island, 24
Liu Qi, 336
Liu Shaoqi, 237
Liu Xiaoming, 72
Liu Zhenwu, 252
Liverpool Football Club, 273
Llewellyn, Edward, 218, 226
Lo Hiu-pan, 364
Loh, Christine, 138
Long Term Capital Management, 287
Long Yongtu, 299–300, 302, 303–4, 307
Lu Chun (governor of Guangzhou), 12–13
Lu Ping, 98, 190, 191, 223, 224, 227, 230–1, 252, 256, 263, 264, 275; contrast with Zhou Nan, 246–7; and Preparatory Committee, 251

Lui Bo, 374
Luo Huining, 390, 391, 395
Luo Keming, 89

Ma Yuzhen, 221, 233–5
Macartney, Lord, 18–21, 22, 36, 223
Macau, 8, 16, 17, 18, 22, 24, 29, 42, 60, 95, 158; Deng looks to learn from, 44–8, 53; Duan's group visits (1978), 45; and Special Economic Zones, 47–8, 65, 66; harbour at, 196; and the Triads, 312, 320–1; as forgotten outpost for Salazar, 318–19; gambling industry, 318, 320–1; Second World War neutrality, 318; handover negotiations (1986), 319–20; Portugal recognises Chinese sovereignty, 319; Red Guard activity in 1960s, 319, 321; segregated education in, 319; Joint Declaration (13 April 1987), 320; Portuguese withdrawal, 321; in Greater Bay Area, 394
Macaulay, Thomas Babington, 29
MacDonald, Claude, 38
MacFarquhar, Roderick, 369
MacLehose, Murray, 54, 56–9, 81, 83, 86, 87–8, 89–93, 94, 176, 221–2, 361; and immigration status of Hong Kong residents, 180–1; deals with Patten and Rowlands, 214; views on Patten's proposals, 241–2
Macleod, Hamish, 229, 247
Major, John, 197–8, 199, 202, 211–12, 214, 239–41, 250
Malaysia, 82, 137, 260, 281–2
Manchuria, 37, 38
Mao Anying, 75
Mao Zedong, 8, 32, 39, 68; death of (1976), 39, 72; Yan'an Soviet, 49, 55; Great Leap Forward, 50; meeting with Heath (May 1974), 70–2; policy on Hong Kong, 70, 72, 74–5; extreme ill health in final years, 71; casting of long shadow by, 73; principles for dealing with foreign imperialists, 73; legal tradition destroyed by, 156; swim in the Yangtze (July 1966), 206; revolution as rural Third World phenomenon, 209; mistresses of, 258–9
Marco Polo, 14, 16
Marconi, 103
Marx, Karl, 9, 26, 84, 163, 164, 211, 353
Maxims chain of restaurants, 384
May, Charles, 360
McGregor, James, 100
McLaren, Robert, 184, 198, 229
medicine, 24
Meng Wanzhou, 393

Meng Xuenong, 330
Merkel, Angela, 371
Mexico, 297
MI6 (Secret Intelligence Service), 134, 228, 347
Mighty Current Media (publishing house), 373–5
The Mikado (Gilbert and Sullivan), 81
Ming Pao (daily newspaper), 133, 261
Mirsky, Jonathan, 215, 244, 258
Les Miserables (musical), 364
Mohamad, Mahathir, 281–2
Montesquieu, 16
Moore, Raymond, 125
MTR Corporation, 367
Mugabe, Robert, 123
Mui, Anita, 308–9

Nanjing, 39, 315
Nanjing, Treaty of (1842), 33–4
Napier, Lord, 26–7
Nathan, Matthew, 5
National Democratic Institute for International Aff airs, 391
national security state, PRC: National Security Law (June 2020), 7, 391–3, 394–8; Beijing Olympics as test-ground for, 336–7; and Zhou Yongkang, 348; targeting pro-democracy figures, 372–3; Mighty Current disappearances, 373–5; jailing of magazine publishers, 374–5; abductions and disappearances of dissidents abroad, 375; 'Guangdong Action Plan,' 375; legislative edifice of, 378; National Security Commission (2014), 378; abduction of Xiao Jianhua, 379–80, 381; fully imposed on Hong Kong (2020), 390–2; Office for Safeguarding National Security, 395
Needham, Joseph, Science and Civilisation in China, 161, 164
Netherlands, 16, 18, 22, 24
New Territories, 42, 81, 104, 105; extent of, 38; ninety-nine year lease on, 38, 99, 107; justice system in, 81–2; redevelopment of (1980s), 138; governor's rural retreat at Fanling, 213; air base at Sekhong, 254; population of at handover, 260; disorder during 2019 insurgency, 386
Ng, Margaret, 249, 333, 392, 397
Ningbo, port of, 30, 31
Nissan, 157
Niu Jian (Nanjing treaty signatory), 33–4
Nixon, Richard, 56, 72, 117, 188, 192
North Korea, 348, 379
nuclear weapons, 40, 101–2

Obama, Barack, 371, 379
Occupy Central movement, 356, 357–8, 362–4, 369–70
Olympic Games (2008), 277, 323, 335–7, 340
opium: opium trade, 23, 24–5, 26, 27–9, 35, 36–7, 268; 'legalisers' and 'moralists' debate, 25–6; and critics of imperialism, 26; Lin Zexu's crackdown on, 27–9; use of in Victorian England, 27; and Jardine Matheson, 28, 29, 35; British behaviour as 'international crime', 36–7; domestic Chinese production, 36; and Treaty of Tianjin, 36
Opium Wars, 8, 9, 23, 29–32, 35–6, 79, 268
Orient Overseas Line, 272–3
Ottoman Turks, 15, 16
Owen, David, 89–90, 91, 213

Palmerston, Lord, 28, 29–30, 35, 238
Panichpakdi, Supachai, 297
Pao, Sir Y.K., 110–11
Parkes, Harry, 33, 35
patent and trademark laws, 156, 297, 302
Patten, Chris, 7; at farewell/handover ceremonies, 37, 266–8; view of David Wilson, 177; background/political career, 211–12; Major offers governorship to, 212–13; preparations for governorship, 213–14; in Beijing (May 1989), 214–15; Chinese reaction to, 216–17; arrives in Hong Kong (July 1992), 216; Lee Kuan Yew's advice to, 216; democratic reform proposals, 217, 218–20, 221–7, 228–9, 403–4; wins cabinet approval for proposals, 221–2; dinner with Zhou Nan, 222; speech unveiling proposals (October 1992), 225; Chinese campaign of vitriol against, 226, 227–8; talks in Beijing (November 1992), 227, 228, 239; Chinese barrage stops, 228–9; dissent within Executive Council, 228; support from Charles Powell, 228; formal talks on proposals of (1993), 229, 231, 233–5; has angioplasty for heart problem, 229; civil service localised under, 230, 248, 274; on Lu's Preliminary Working Committee, 231; reform bill passes by one vote (February 1994), 231; Cradock opposes reform proposals, 239–41; Cradock becomes sharp critic of, 241–2; and China's Most Favoured Nation status in US, 248; and post-1997 justice system, 249–50; criticises China's election process, 252; dispute over entry of PLA, 255; departs on Britannia, 271; on

Occupy Central, 371; accepts limit to British power on Hong Kong, 405
Paul, Alan, 253
Pei, I.M., 3
Peirce, Bob, 109
Pelli, Cesar, 3
People's Bank of China, 338
People's Liberation Army (PLA): at death of Mao, 40; and Hong Kong frontier area, 42, 52; during Cultural Revolution, 51, 75, 263–4; occupation of Canton, 74; Deng's decision to deploy in Hong Kong, 126; and system of governance, 148–9; and Tiananmen Square protests, 170, 171; and Deng's 'southern tour', 205; headquarters in Hong Kong, 230; border war against Vietnam (1979), 252; dispute over entry to Hong Kong, 252, 254–5; preparations for entry into Hong Kong (1997), 252, 253–4, 264–5; units enter Hong Kong (April 1997), 254; entry into Hong Kong (30 June 1997), 262–3, 264; invasion of Hong Kong averted (1967), 263–4; and National Security Act, 395, 396
People's Republic of China (PRC): decades of righteous seclusion, 1, 8, 9, 39, 40, 66, 89, 158, 272; antiques from, 5; foreign plot narrative, 5, 168, 178, 188, 306, 355, 369, 395; and memory of past humiliation, 9, 38, 45–6, 171, 208, 255–6, 268–9; death of Mao, 39, 56, 72; establishment of (1949), 39, 220–1; condition of at death of Mao, 40–1, 42–3; reconciliation with USA in 1970s, 40, 102, 116–17; poverty in 1970s, 41, 42, 52–3; restrictions on travel from, 41; bamboo curtain at Hong Kong frontier, 42; Deng's economic missions, 43–4; Zhao's memoir, 43, 48, 61; Four Modernisations, 46, 65; Sino-Soviet split (1950s/60s), 55, 101, 192; internal security apparatus in 1970s, 59; Hong Kong and Macau Affairs Office (HKMAO), 60, 88, 175, 191, 196, 223, 224, 252, 263, 275, 325, 381, 390, 392; West links economic reform with political liberalism, 61–2, 66, 210–11, 304–6, 404; Deng's use of language, 67, 68; and foreign news bureaux, 73; as world's top executioner, 82; and Soviet Union in 1980s, 101–2, 124; strategic encirclement in 1980s, 101–2; war with India (1962), 101–2; short war with Vietnam (1979), 102; population control policies, 147–8; population reaches one

billion (1982), 147–8; top-down system of governance, 148–9; social structure, 148; Central Military Commission, 149, 208, 252, 253; vast scale of, 149; political risks of Deng's reforms, 152–5, 157–8; political reform question in 1980s/1990s, 161, 163–5, 210–11, 317–18, 402; Ministry of State Security, 162, 168–70, 347, 348, 372, 373, 391; martial law declared (20 May 1989), 168, 175; and the new airport, 178, 190, 197–200, 212; and collapse of Soviet Union, 192–3; Deng prevents reversal of economic reform, 205–10; Deng's political roadmap for (1992), 210–11; initial reaction to Patten, 216–17; rejection of Patten's proposals, 223–5; campaign of vitriol against Patten, 226, 227–8; Britain ends talks with (November 1993), 231; Red Guards storm British embassy (1967), 236; and post-1997 justice system, 248–50; navy of, 254; and WTO accession, 277, 297–302, 303–7, 322, 323, 330, 337, 376; killing of 'Big Spender,' 312; liberal strain in Chinese thinking, 317–18, 402; foreign settlers in Pearl River Delta, 321–2; response to 2003 SARS pandemic, 326–8, 330–1; ban on the sale of wild animals (2003), 330, 331; Olympics as gift to party's authoritarians, 336–7; use of Hong Kong media by factions, 344–5, 347; Wang's 'cultural sovereignty' theory, 354; Stalin's influence on Xi, 355, 395; State Council White Paper to Hong Kong (2014), 356–7; NPC warning to people of Hong Kong, 359; Hong Kong as testbed for disinformation/propaganda, 368–9; drive to expel USA from Asia, 379; presence in South China Sea, 379; move to full repression in Hong Kong (2020), 390–2 *see also* Chinese Communist Party; national security state, PRC
Peretz, David, 145
Peugeot, 157
Philippines, 41, 260, 282, 379
Ping An (insurance behemoth), 393–4
policing in Hong Kong: corruption in, 81, 361, 362; Royal Hong Kong Police, 81, 86, 174, 178, 179–80, 251, 256–7, 263, 266, 270, 311, 360–1; Special Branch, 86, 139–40, 179–80, 356–7, 361; and protests against Tiananmen massacre, 174; and fears over handover, 178, 179–80, 256–7; Crime (A1) Department, 179–80, 361; and pro-democracy protesters, 251, 360, 362–3, 367, 382, 385, 386, 387–9; vice

squad, 313; history of, 360–1; decline in public confidence in, 360, 361–2; first ethnic Chinese commissioner (1989), 361; modernised after Second World War, 361; doxing tactics against police, 385; Independent Police Complaints Council, 392; new powers under National Security Act, 395–6
Polytechnic University, 388–9
Pompeo, Mike, 379, 392–3
Poon Hiu-Wing, 380
Portugal, 18, 22, 24, 29; and maritime trade, 16; Salazar dictatorship, 318–19, 321; Macau handover negotiations (1986), 319–20; left-wing coup (1974), 319; withdrawal from Macau, 321
Pottinger, Henry, 31–2, 33–4, 360
Pottinger, Matthew, 398
Powell, Charles, 228
Power, Noel, 248
prostitution, 313, 315–16
protests and demonstrations (2019): change in tone from umbrella revolution, 7, 381–9; huge demonstrations of 16 June, 7, 382; outbreak of, 381–2; LIHKG (online forum), 381, 382–3; general strike (12 June), 382; Liaison Office attacked (21 July), 383–4; Legislative Council stormed (1 July), 383; Triad attacks on, 383; activities at Hong Kong airport (July/ August), 384; Chinese propaganda offensive, 384; society fractures during, 385–8; doxing tactics against police, 385; retreat to occupy university campuses, 387–9; siege at Polytechnic University (November), 388–9
public health: wild animals and disease, 278, 329–30, 331–2; and cigarette imports, 302; SARS outbreak (2003), 326–33, 334, 390; National Institute for Virology, Beijing, 332; coronavirus pandemic, 389–90, 397
Purves, William, 7, 146, 190–1, 228, 246
Putin, Vladimir, 378
Pym, Francis, 101, 113–14

Qian Qichen, 185–6, 198, 222–4, 226, 227, 228–9, 231, 275; and Preparatory Committee, 251, 252
Qiang Xiaochu, 262
Qianlong (Qing emperor), 17, 18–21
Qianshao (Hong Kong magazine), 302–3, 347, 348
Qiao Bian, 298–9
Qiao Shi, 208, 265
Qinghai, province of, 49

Qishan (Manchu governor), 30
Qiying (Nanjing treaty signatory), 33–5
Queen Elizabeth (ocean liner), 272
Queen's College, Hong Kong, 84

Raab, Dominic, 399–400
Radio Television Hong Kong (RTHK), 260
Ramos, Joao de Deus, 319, 320
Reagan, Ronald, 102
Ricci, Matteo, 17
Richelieu, Cardinal, 238
Ricketts, Peter, 213
Ridley, Nicholas, 161
River Elegy (Chinese Television series),
   163–5
Rogge, Jacques, 335–6
Rolls-Royce, 103
The Romance of the Three Kingdoms, 353
Romania, 192–3
Rowlands, Ted, 214
Ruan Xiangfa, 154–5
Russian Empire, 8, 17–18, 34, 36, 37–8
Russian Federation, 393

Salazar, Antonio, 318–19, 321
Salem, Massachusetts, 22
Sandberg, Michael, 100, 125, 145
SARS (severe acute respiratory syndrome)
   pandemic, 326–33, 334, 390
Schork, Kurt, 265–6
science and technology, 208, 210, 279, 330;
   and Four Modernisations, 46; and Li
   Qiang, 54, 55; and the 'Needham
   Question', 161, 164
Scott, Alan, 124
Scowcroft, Brent, 187–8
Second World War, 39, 86–7, 263, 291
Seeking Truth (Communist Party journal),
   207
September 11 terrorist attacks (2001),
   306–7
sexual behaviour: in Tang dynasty, 11–12;
   prostitution in Hong Kong, 313; in
   Shenzhen, 315–17; Communist China's
   moral concerns, 316–17
Seymour, Michael, 35
Shandong province, 149
Shanghai, 120, 210, 247, 273–4, 293–4, 341,
   351; capitalists in Hong Kong from, 6,
   141, 178, 200, 271, 272, 274, 292, 311; Li's
   underground radio station in, 54–5; May
   30th Movement, 54; Municipal Police, 54,
   361; Communist Party decimated in
   (1927), 55; falls to Japanese (1937), 86;
   crabs from, 89; stock exchange reopened,
   165

Shanghai Automotive Industry
   Corporation, 156, 158
Shantou, 64
Shanxi province, 390
Shaolin monastery, 309
Shaw, Sir Run Run, 193
Sheinwald, Nigel, 265
Shekou, port at, 154–5, 158, 292
Shelley, Mary, 27
Shelley, Percy, 16
Shenzhen, 41, 47, 52–3, 164–5, 194–5, 205,
   206, 207–8, 209; as Special Economic
   Zone, 292, 294–5, 315–18, 321–2; rapid
   expansion of, 315–18; as unique
   laboratory, 317–18; SARS outbreak in
   (2003), 327; statue of Deng Xiaoping,
   355; in Greater Bay Area, 394
Shepherd, Lord, 99
Sherman, Alfred, 100
Shi Guangsheng, 303–4
Shimonoseki, Treaty of (1895), 37
Shultz, George, 226, 227
Shum, Lester, 360, 365, 397
Shunde, 205
Sichuan province, 43, 149, 162
Silk Road, 14
silk trade, 17, 22
silver currency, 17, 23, 25, 26, 37
Sing Tao (daily newspaper), 314
Singapore, 22, 64, 82, 137, 216, 247, 290–1,
   328, 343
Solomon, Richard, 188, 319
Song Qiang, 298–9
Song Zhiguang, 94
Soros, George, 282, 285
South China Morning Post, 142, 143, 169,
   261, 322–3, 365, 385, 387
South Korea, 41, 282, 284
Southern Metropolis Daily, 375
Soviet Union, 40, 55, 94, 101, 124;
   invasion of Afghanistan (1979), 101–2;
   collapse of (1991), 192–3, 200, 204, 239,
   355; Warsaw Pact disintegrates, 192–3,
   204
Spain, 15, 16, 17, 24
Special Economic Zones: proposals for
   (1978), 46–8; Guangdong province, 47–8,
   63–4, 65–7, 69, 160, 200–1, 291–4, 296;
   and Hong Kong, 47–8, 62, 65, 66, 200–1,
   291–4, 295, 321–2; as export zones, 47,
   154–5, 158; Chen Yun opposes, 48;
   Xiamen added to list, 48; and Third
   Plenum (December 1978), 58–9, 60–3; Xi
   Zhongxun's role in reforms, 63–4, 65–7,
   69; experiments agreed (July 1979), 64;
   National People's Congress approval (late

1982), 113; 'development triangles', 152; fourteen authorized (1984), 152; Maoist opposition to, 158; and *River Elegy*, 164–5; Deng's 'southern tour' of (1992), 205–9, 210; Chinese term for, 209; of Shenzhen, 292, 294–5, 315–18, 321–2; and export development model, 293–4, 297–8; harsh conditions in, 294–6; Dickensian workplace conditions, 295–6; labour disputes in, 295–6; cross-border traffic, 321–2; foreign settlers in Pearl River Delta, 321–2

Spence, Jonathan, 25, 404

Sperling, Gene, 303

St John-Stevas, Norman, 236

Stalin, Joseph, 355–6, 395

Standard Chartered Bank, 99–100, 142, 143, 144, 229

Staunton, George, 30

Su Xiaokang, 165

Sudan, 348

Suharto, 280, 281

Suleiman the Magnificent, 15

Sun Hung Kai Properties, 311–12

Sun Tzu, 7–8

Sun Yat-sen, 85, 309, 315

Sweden, 374–5

Sze, Michael, 218–19

Ta Kung Pao (Communist Party newspaper), 205, 261, 373

Tai Yiu-ting, Benny, 356, 358, 362, 366, 367, 371

Taiping rebellion (1850s), 35

Taiwan, 5, 24, 70, 82, 86, 152, 169, 258, 272–3, 315; loss of to Japan (1895), 37; 'nine articles' for reunification, 95–6; 'one country, two systems' theory, 95–6; and Cold War politics of 1980s, 102; and Reagan, 102; computer manufacturing relocated to mainland, 293; Triads exiled to, 309; murder of Poon Hiu-Wing in, 380

Tam, Jeremy, 397

Tan, George, 145

Tang, David, 7

Tang, Harry, 350–1

Tang, Henry, 325

Tang Xianzu (dramatist), 16

Taoism, 4

taxation: in Tang era, 11, 13; in Ming era, 16; in Qing era, 25–6; and silver inflation from 1820s, 25–6; and Deng's reforms, 156

tea trade, 22, 23, 24, 26

Tennyson, Alfred Lord, *Ulysses*, 135

Thailand, 41, 82, 260, 278, 279–80, 286, 375, 377, 379

Thatcher, Margaret, 7, 93–4, 141, 202, 402–3; and Hong Kong negotiations, 94–5, 98–101, 102–11, 402–3; and arms sales, 94, 103; Chinese perspective on, 98, 109–10; political strength in 1982 period, 98; anger at realism/defeatism on Hong Kong, 101, 113–14; meets Deng in Beijing (September 1982), 103–4, 106–10, 111, 141, 229, 264; immigration policy, 103, 126, 134, 179, 180–2, 240, 399, 400, 403; and immigration status of Hong Kong residents, 103, 126, 134, 179, 180–2, 240, 399, 400, 403; meeting with Zhao (September 1982), 104–6; warnings of post-1997 economic disaster, 105, 106, 107–8, 110–11, 125; in Hong Kong (September 1902), 111–13; crucial Downing Street meeting (March 1983), 114–15; sees Exco members in London (April 1984), 125; vigilance over negotiations on Hong Kong, 128; and Joint Liaison Group issue, 131, 132–3; allows Howe to settle with Deng, 132–3; formal signing of agreement (19 December 1984), 134–5; 'unofficials' last plea to, 134; cultivating of Zhao and Hu, 161–2; and 'through train' proposal, 184–7; fall from power (1990), 197; Patten briefs (1992), 221; visits Hong Kong (May 1993), 230; supports Patten's proposals, 242; view of intelligence services, 243; pays tribute to Cradock, 244

Thomas, Hugh, 244

Thorn, Gaston, 123

Tiananmen Square, Beijing, 104; massacre (3–4 June 1989), 6, 83, 171, 172–6, 177, 178, 188–9, 194, 208, 215–16; student protest camp at (April–June 1989), 167–9, 170–1, 192, 214–15; Monument to the People's Heroes, 167

Tianjin (Tientsin), 86

Tianjin, Treaty of (1858), 36

Tien, James, 334

Tien, Michael, 396

Tin Hau (goddess of the sea), 2

To, James, 372

Toh Lye-ping, Esther, 397

Tooze, Adam, 339

tourism, 150–1; to Hong Kong from mainland, 334–5

Toyota, 157

trade union movement, 83, 201; Hong Kong Federation of Trade Unions, 100

treaty ports, 1, 34, 46, 48
Triad secret societies, 24, 174, 257, 308,
    309, 310–13, 320–1; and attacks on
    democracy movement, 366, 383
tribute system, 11, 13, 14, 18, 19, 20–1, 28;
    and Treaty of Tianjin, 36
Trump, Donald, 377–8, 379, 392–3,
    397–8
Tsang, Donald, 248, 282–3, 284, 285–7,
    288, 325, 335, 337, 339–43, 351;
    imprisoned for corruption, 343–4
Tsang, John, 380
Tsang, Ken, 367
Tsang Chi-kin, 386
Tsang Wai-hung, Andy, 356
Tsang Yok-sing, Jasper, 380
Tsinghua University, Beijing, 353
Tung Chee-hwa, 251, 252, 270, 271–4,
    275–6, 278, 279, 283, 286, 322, 387;
    politicisation of civil service, 324–5; new
    government of (2002), 325–6; law against
    subversion, 332–4, 335; public protests
    against (July 2003), 334; resigns as chief
    executive (2005), 335
Tyler, John (US President), 34

UGL (engineering company), 367
Uighur Muslims, Turkic, 13
umbrella revolution (2014): as broadly
    peaceful, 7; emergence of, 341, 349–52;
    Joshua Wong 's Scholarism, 349–50,
    351–2, 353, 359, 360; and Leung's
    reforms, 351–2, 356; victory over the
    school curriculum, 352, 356; Chinese
    government warnings to, 356–7, 359;
    Occupy Central movement, 356, 357–8,
    362–4, 369–70; Tai advocates civil
    obedience, 356; 'civic referendum' (2014),
    357–8; and State Council White Paper
    (2014), 357; Chinese cyberwarfare
    against, 358, 366–7; university students
    join, 359–60; mass demonstration at the
    harbourside (September), 359; Civic
    Square protests (26 September), 360;
    police violence of 28 September, 362–3;
    acquires 'umbrella revolution' name, 363;
    protest encampments appear, 363;
    authorities' policy towards, 364–6;
    television debate between students and
    officials, 365; attacks on protest camps,
    366; and 'localist' Hong Kong identity,
    366; Pride Parade, 366; Triad attacks on,
    366; Communist propaganda war against,
    368–70; imprisonment of main figures,
    370, 371; Occupy Central ends (15
    December), 370

United Nations, 75–6, 297, 321, 393,
    395
United States: early trade voyages to China,
    18, 21–2; and opium trade, 29;
    extraterritorial powers granted to, 34;
    trading privileges agreed (1840s), 34;
    reconciliation with China in 1970s, 40,
    102, 116–17; Mao/Zhou policy on, 74, 75;
    Carter administration recognizes PRC
    (1979), 102; advises UK on China,
    117–19; 'China's negotiating style' (secret
    document), 117–19; and Chum Hom Kok
    intelligence, 171; Cantonese-speaking
    communities, 179; Scowcroft' meeting
    with Deng, 188; and China's Most
    Favoured Nation status, 190, 248, 299;
    and Sino-Soviet split, 192; Xu Jiatun's
    escape to, 195–6; bombing of Chinese
    embassy in Belgrade, 299, 302–3; and
    China's WTO accession, 299, 302, 303–6;
    Chinese hold over national debt of, 338;
    jobs lost to Chinese competition, 376;
    Trump's economic nationalism, 377, 378;
    China's drive to expel from Asia, 379;
    Obama's Trans Pacific Partnership, 379;
    criticism of National Security Law, 392–3,
    397–400; unity in over fate of Hong
    Kong, 398–9; Hong Kong Safe Harbor
    Act (2020), 398
Urban VIII, Pope, 238
Urbani, Carlo, 328

Venetian republic, 15–16
Vickers, Simon, 257–8
Victoria, Queen, 27, 30–1
Viera, Vasco Rocha, 321
Vietnam, 379; Vietnam War, 6, 8, 56, 57,
    102; invasion of Cambodia (1978), 239;
    border war against China (1979), 252;
    SARS outbreak in (2003), 328
Volkswagen, 156, 158
Vosper Thorneycroft, 103

Wah, Szeto, 182, 193
Wakeman, Frederic, 25
Walden, George, 116
Wan Li, 62
Wang Guangmei, 237, 373
Wang Hairong, 71
Wang Hongwen, 40
Wang Huning (political theorist), 353–4,
    355
Wang Jianmin, 375
Wang Jin, 253
Wang Kuang, 88–9
Wang Lijun, 346, 347

Wang Lulu, 345, 348
Wang Luxiang, 165
Wang Nanguo, 51–2
Wang Qishan, 330–1
Wang Xiangwei, 323, 385
Wang Zhen, 171
Wang Zhimin, 390
Webb, David, 287–8
Wei Han, 51
Wei Jingsheng, 47, 217
Wei Shyy, 387
Wellington, Duke of, 33
Wen Jiabao, 338–9, 342, 346
Wen Wei Po (Communist Party newspaper), 74, 175, 203, 205, 261, 368, 373, 396–7
Western powers: Age of Discovery, 15–16; rise of in sixteenth century, 15; maritime nations, 16; and suppression of Taiping rebellion, 35; Anglo-French forces destroy summer palace, 36, 70; Deng's economic missions to, 43–4; linking of economic with political liberalism, 61–2, 66, 210–11, 304–6, 404; lack of support for Thatcher over Hong Kong, 102–3; and Tiananmen Square protests, 170–1; offer no support for Occupy Central, 371; Xie Feng warns, 391–2; criticism of National Security Law, 392–3, 397–400; future task for over China, 404–5 *see also* entries for individual countries
Wilson, David, 80, 87, 99, 119, 134, 189–90, 216, 221; and Bill of Rights (1990), 82–3, 189, 191, 203, 403; at Deng's meeting with MacLehose (May 1979), 89–93, 176, 403; meets Liao Chengzhi, 93; leads British negotiating team, 128–31, 176, 403; appointed governor of Hong Kong (1986), 161, 176–7; and Tiananmen Square massacre, 172–3, 174–5, 176, 177; and education reform in Hong Kong, 177–8, 403; and immigration status of Hong Kong residents, 180, 181–2, 400, 403; modernising of infrastructure, 198–9, 403; decision to replace as governor, 202–4, 212; Chinese perspective on, 203; invited to China after June Fourth massacre, 203
Wilson, Harold, 57, 71
Wing On (chain of department stores), 112
Wiranto, General, 281
Witte, Count, 38
Wolf, Martin, 160
Wolfowitz, Paul, 117

Wo-lop Lam, Willy, 323
Wong, Anthony, 364
Wong, Joshua, 7, 349–50, 351–2, 353, 357, 359, 366, 369; arrested at Civic Square, 360; High Court orders release of, 363; disinformation campaign against, 368; imprisonment of, 370–1, 397; Demosistō (political party), 370, 381, 396; surveillance operation on, 373; criticism of National Security Act, 396; declared 'not fit for office,' 397
Wong, Kam C., 180
Wong, Roger, 349
Wong Kar-wai (film director), 309
Wong Long-wai, 308
Wong Man-fong, 310
Woo, Peter, 251
Woo Kwokhing, 380
World Bank, 152
World Health Organisation (WHO), 279, 327, 328, 330, 331, 332
World Trade Organisation (WTO), 117, 119, 248, 277, 297–302, 303–7, 322, 323, 330, 337, 376, 377, 378
Wu, Anna, 139–40
Wu, Gordon, 112
Wu Chi-wai, 385
Wu Jiangguo, 207
Wu Jianmin, 301
Wu Nansheng, 42
Wu Suk-ching, Annie, 384
Wu Xueqian, 131, 241
Wuhan, 205–6, 389–90
Wu-Tai Chin, Larry, 87
Wuxi area, 292

Xi Jinping: as son of Xi Zhongxun, 8, 49; on nation's history of humiliation, 9; banished during Cultural Revolution, 50, 353; succession to power (2012), 53; 'anti-corruption' campaign of, 62, 356, 380; combines three top offices, 149; and Donald Tsang, 340–1, 344; and Bo Xilai, 346; fall of Bo seals the ascent of, 348; takes power as head of state (2012), 348, 404; ideology under, 352–4, 355; personality cult, 353, 378; culture under, 354; dictatorship under, 355–6, 376, 378; 'great rejuvenation' project, 355; Stalinist references in early speeches, 355; tour to south China (2012), 355; 'Belt and Road' initiative, 378–9; applauded at Davos (2017), 378; friendships with foreign authoritarians, 378, 379; speeches during 2019 insurgency, 385, 386; accelerates plans due to 2020 turmoil, 394

Xi Zhongxun, 8, 48–50, 51–4, 63–4, 65–7, 69, 93, 201
Xia Baolong, 390, 392
Xiamen, 31, 48
Xianfeng (Qing emperor), 35, 36
Xiang Huaicheng, 287
Xiao Jianhua, 379–80, 381
Xie Feng, 391–2
Xie Jin, 261
Xinhua (New China News Agency, NCNA), 45, 74–5, 85–6, 87, 88–9, 92, 120, 124–5, 155, 203; and Tiananmen Square protests, 168, 169, 196; Xu as director of, 169, 193–6; and Tiananmen Square massacre, 175, 194; Zhou Nan at, 194, 224, 252; and Patten's proposals, 224, 225; Li Chuwen at, 273–4; and the Triad bosses, 310; and 'civic referendum' (2014), 358
Xinjiang, 49
Xiong Ziren, 252
Xu Bing, 74
Xu Jiatun, 119–21, 169, 193–6
Xu Qinxian, 170

Yam, Joseph, 143, 144, 282–5, 286, 288
Yang, Sir Ti-liang, 216, 248, 251, 311
Yang Baibing, 208
Yang Jisheng, 50, 206, 208–9
Yang Shangkun, 69, 170, 188, 193, 208
Yantian, 292
Yao Guang, 115, 124, 126
Yao Wenyuan, 40
Yao Yilin, 166
Ye Jianying, 95–6
Ye Mingchen (Qing governor), 35–6
Yellow River, 163–5
Yeoh Eng-kiong, 329
Yeung, Charles, 113
Yilibu (Nanjing treaty signatory), 33–4
Yip Kwok-wah, 155–6
Yiu Man-tin, 375
Yongchaiyudh, Chavalit, 280
Youde, Edward, 104, 109, 112, 113, 114, 123–4, 131, 132, 145, 176
Young, Mark, 220, 402
Yu, Denise, 248
Yuan Weimin, 335–6
Yuanming Yuan (Gardens of Perfect Brightness), 19, 20, 36, 70
Yue, Eddie, 393
Yueng, Philip, 364

Zen, Joseph, 339, 344
Zeng Decheng, 203
Zhang Chunqiao, 40

Zhang Hanqing, 51–3
Zhang Junsheng, 203–4, 217, 222, 224, 225, 358
Zhang Siping, 318
Zhang Weihang, 50–1
Zhang Wenkang, 330
Zhang Xiaojin, 346, 347
Zhang Xiaoming, 381, 390, 394
Zhang Zangzang, 298–9
Zhao Jihua, 255
Zhao Ziyang, 43, 48, 61, 62, 92, 97, 99, 111; meeting with Thatcher (September 1982), 104–6; Thatcher's letter to (March 1983), 115; given control of Hong Kong affairs, 119, 131, 132; and formal signing of agreement (19 December 1984), 134; anxieties over reform, 152; on Chen Yun's views, 158; dines at 10 Downing Street with Thatcher (1985), 161, 176; and the 'Needham Question,' 161, 164; and reform of political system, 161, 163; replaces Hu, 162–3; on price reforms, 165; power slips from, 166; state visit to North Korea, 167–8; dismissed from all positions (May 1989), 168; and the Basic Law, 182; and Xu Jiatun, 193, 195; Patten encounters (May 1989), 215
Zhejiang province, 390
Zheng Yanxiong, 395
Zhenjiang, 32
Zhongnanhai leadership compound, 303, 304, 322
Zhongshan, 205
Zhou Borong, 252, 253
Zhou Enlai, 8, 50, 54–5, 56, 71, 345; policy on Hong Kong, 70, 74–6; three 'red lines' on Hong Kong, 74, 76; stops PLA invasion (1967), 75, 263; death of (April 1976), 167
Zhou Nan, 95, 98, 109, 126, 128, 129, 130, 131–2, 133, 134, 161, 162, 264; and Xu Jiatun, 194–6; at NCNA, 194, 224, 252; amorous exploits, 196, 246; dinner with Patten, 222; contrast with Lu Ping, 246–7; and Preparatory Committee, 251; Hugh Davies on, 252–3; delays cancer treatment, 256; Macau handover negotiations (1986), 320
Zhou Yongkang, 336, 346, 348
Zhoushan, 30, 31
Zhu Rongji, 233, 265, 287, 293–4, 299, 302, 303–4, 322, 351
Zhuhai, 47, 64, 205, 208, 292, 295, 321–2, 394
ZTE, 378